PREFACE

To the Instructor

Teaching Strategies

There are three popular strategies in teaching Java. The first, known as *GUI-first*, is to mix Java applets and GUI programming with object-oriented programming concepts. The second, known as *object-first*, is to introduce object-oriented programming from the start. The third strategy, known as *fundamentals-first*, is a step-by-step approach, first laying a sound foundation on programming concepts, control statements, methods, and arrays, then introducing object-oriented programming, and then moving on to graphical user interface (GUI), applets, and finally to exception handling, I/O, data structures, multithreading, and multimedia.

The GUI-first strategy, starting with GUI and applets, seems attractive, but requires substantial knowledge of object-oriented programming and a good understanding of the Java event-handling model; thus, students may never fully understand what they are doing.

The object-first strategy is based on the notion that objects should be introduced first because Java is an object-oriented programming language. This notion, however, overlooks the importance of the fundamental techniques required for writing programs in any programming language. Furthermore, this approach inevitably mixes static and instance variables and methods before students can fully understand classes and objects and use them to develop useful programs. Students are overwhelmed by object-oriented programming and basic rules of programming simultaneously in the early stage of learning Java. This is a common source of frustration for first year students learning object-oriented programming.

From my own experience, confirmed by the experiences of many colleagues, I have found that learning basic logic and fundamental programming techniques like loops is a struggle for most first year students. *Students who cannot write code in procedural programming are not able to learn object-oriented programming.* A good introduction on primitive data types, control statements, methods, and arrays prepares students to learn object-oriented programming. Therefore, this text adopts the fundamentals-first strategy, proceeding at a steady pace through all the necessary and important basic concepts, then moving to object-oriented programming, and then to using the object-oriented approach to build interesting GUI applications and applets with exception handling, I/O, data structures, multithreading, and multimedia as shown in the following diagram. The fundamentals-first approach can reinforce object-oriented programming by demonstrating how procedural solutions can be improved using the object-oriented approach. Students can learn when and how to apply OOP effectively.

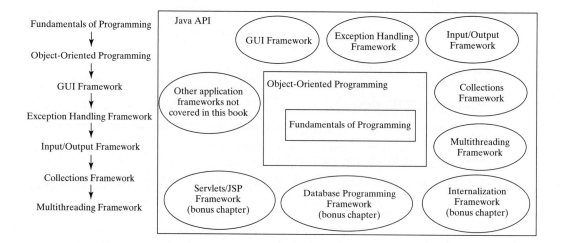

This book is not simply about how to program, for it teaches, as well, how to solve problems using programs. Applying the concept of abstraction in the design and implementation of software projects is the key to developing software. The overriding objective of the book, therefore, is to teach students to use many levels of abstraction in solving problems and to see problems in small and in large. *The examples and exercises throughout the book foster the concept of developing reusable components and using them to create practical projects.*

Instructor Resources

The Instructor's Manual on CD-ROM is available for instructors using this book. It contains the following resources:

- Microsoft PowerPoint slides for lectures, with interactive buttons to view syntax-highlighted source code and to run programs without leaving the slides.

- Ten sample exams. In general, each exam has four parts: (1) multiple-choice questions or short answers (most of these are different from the ones in the Self-Test on the Web site); (2) correct programming errors; (3) trace programs; (4) write programs.

- Solutions to all the exercises. Students will have access to the solutions of even-numbered exercises in the book's companion CD-ROM.

- More than forty supplemental exercises and their solutions.

- Suggested syllabi for teaching Java to beginning students, for teaching Java as a second language, and for teaching Java to corporate employees.

To obtain the Instructor's Manual, contact your Prentice-Hall sales representative. Some students have requested the solutions to the odd-numbered programming exercises. Please understand that these are for instructors only. Such requests will not be answered.

Introduction to

Java™

Programming with JBuilder

Third Edition

Y. Daniel Liang
School of Computing
Armstrong Atlantic State University

PEARSON

Prentice
Hall

Upper Saddle River, New Jersey 07458
http://www.prenhall.com

Library of Congress Cataloging-in-Publication Data

Liang, Y. Daniel.
    Introduction to Java programming with JBuilder/Y. Daniel Liang.--3 rd ed.
        p.   cm.
    Includes index.
    ISBN 0-13-143049-1
    QA76.73.J38L523 2004
    005.2'762—dc22

                                                    2003065629

Vice President and Editorial Director,
    ECS: Marcia J. Horton
Publisher: Alan R. Apt
Associate Editor: Toni Dianne Holm
 Editorial Assistant: Patrick Lindner
Vice President and Director of Production
    and Manufacturing, ESM: David W. Riccardi
Executive Managing Editor: Vince O'Brien
Managing Editor: Camille Trentacoste
Production Editor: John Keegan
Director of Creative Services: Paul Belfanti
Creative Director: Carole Anson
Art Director: Kenny Beck

Cover Designer: Suzanne Behnke
Managing Editor, AV Management
    and Production: Patricia Burns
Art Editor: Xiaohong Zhu
Front cover photo: Mexico, Uxmal, Mayan
    Pyramid of the Magician. © James Hackett/
    Estock Photo
Back cover photo: Mexico, Ruins of Uxmal,
    Cuadrangulo de Monjas. © Ben Nakayama/
    Estock Photo
Manufacturing Manager: Trudy Pisciotti
Manufacturing Buyer: Lisa McDowell
Marketing Manager: Pamela Hersperger

© 2004, 2002, 2001 Pearson Education, Inc.
Pearson Prentice Hall
Pearson Education, Inc.
Upper Saddle River, NJ 07458

The author and publisher of this book have used their best efforts in preparing this book. These efforts include the development, research, and testing of the theories and programs to determine their effectiveness. The author and publisher make no warranty of any kind, expressed or implied, with regard to these programs or the documentation contained in this book. The author and publisher shall not be liable in any event for incidental or consequential damages in connection with, or arising out of, the furnishing, performance, or use of these programs.

Printed in the United States of America

10 9 8 7 6 5 4 3 2 1

ISBN: 0-13-143049-1

Pearson Education Ltd., *London*
Pearson Education Australia Pty. Ltd., *Sydney*
Pearson Education Singapore, Pte. Ltd.
Pearson Education North Asia Ltd., *Hong Kong*
Pearson Education Canada, Inc., *Toronto*
Pearson Educación de Mexico, S.A. de C.V.
Pearson Education—Japan, *Tokyo*
Pearson Education Malaysia, Pte. Ltd.
Pearson Education, Inc., *Upper Saddle River, New Jersey*

To Samantha, Michael, and Michelle

Microsoft PowerPoint slides are also available at the book's companion Web site at **http://www.prenhall.com/liang/introjb3e.html**. The Web site also contains interactive online self-tests and other supplemental materials.

Lab Manual

The lab manual for the book was developed by Pete Dobbins of the University of Florida. To bundle it with the book, contact your Prentice-Hall sales representative.

Pedagogical Features of the Book

The philosophy of the Liang Java Series is *teaching by example and learning by doing*. Basic features are explained by example so that you can learn by doing. The book uses the following elements to get the most from the material:

- **Objectives** list what students should have learned from the chapter. This will help them to determine whether they have met the objectives after completing the chapter.

- **Introduction** opens the discussion with a brief overview of what to expect from the chapter.

- Programming concepts are taught by representative **Examples**, carefully chosen and presented in an easy-to-follow style. Each example has the problem statement, solution steps, complete source code, sample run, and review. The source code of the examples is contained in the companion CD-ROM.

- **Chapter Summary** reviews the important subjects that students should understand and remember. It helps them to reinforce the key concepts they have learned in the chapter.

- **Review Questions** help students to track their progress and evaluate their learning.

- **Programming Exercises** at the end of each chapter provide students with opportunities to apply the skills on their own. The trick of learning programming is practice, practice, and practice. To that end, the book provides a large number of exercises.

- **Interactive Self-Test** helps students to test their knowledge interactively online. The Self-Test is accessible from the book's companion Web site at **www.prenhall.com/liang/introjb3e.html**. It provides more than six hundred multiple-choice and true/false questions organized by chapters.

- **Notes, Tips**, and **Cautions** are inserted throughout the text to offer valuable advice and insight on important aspects of program development.

 NOTE
Provides additional information on the subject and reinforces important concepts.

TIP

Teaches good programming style and practice.

CAUTION

Helps students steer away from the pitfalls of programming errors.

What's New in This Edition

This book improves upon *Introduction to Java Programming with JBuilder 4/5/6/7, Second Edition*. The major changes are as follows:

- The book is updated to JDK 1.4 and JBuilder 8/9. JBuilder 8/9 uses JDK 1.4.

- The new edition tightly integrates JBuilder with Java to exploit many advantages of learning Java with JBuilder. JBuilder is not only an excellent tool for developing Java programs but also helps in learning Java effectively.

- Debugging is introduced early in Chapter 2 and integrated in several chapters so that students can trace the execution of their programs to find logic errors.

- The proprietary MyInput class for getting input from the console is replaced by the standard JOptionPane class. Students don't have to learn the proprietary MyInput class that is not used in the workplace.

- Every chapter is thoroughly revised and improved in terms of content, presentation, examples, and exercises. Twenty percent of the examples and exercises were replaced by new practical applications, such as computing loan payments, taxes, and printing payroll statements.

- Chapter 8, "Class Inheritance and Interfaces," in the second edition has been reorganized into two chapters in this third edition: Chapter 8, "Inheritance and Polymorphism," and Chapter 9, "Abstract Classes and Inheritance." New organization improves the presentation of object-oriented programming.

- Chapter 10 in the second edition has been split into two chapters in this edition: Chapter 11, "Getting Started with GUI Programming," and Chapter 12, "Event-Driven Programming." This change enables Chapter 11 to be covered earlier.

- The new Part V for bonus chapters covers the advanced Java features used in upper-level courses. This part is on CD-ROM only so that the main text is focused on the core subjects. Internationalization and networking have been moved to this part. Three new chapters on database programming, servlets, and JSP were also included in this part.

- Optional materials, such as overview of computer systems, number systems, coding style guidelines, packages, HTML, event adapters, and rapid Java application development, are moved to the supplements. The supplements are contained in the CD-ROM only, so that the book is focused on the core subjects.

To the Student

There is nothing more important to the future of computing than the Internet. There is nothing more exciting on the Internet than Java. A revolutionary programming language developed by Sun Microsystems, Java has become the de facto standard for cross-platform applications and programming on the World Wide Web.

Java is a full-featured, general-purpose programming language that is capable of developing robust mission-critical applications. In recent years, Java has gained enormous popularity and has quickly become the most popular and successful programming language. Today, it is used not only for Web programming, but also for developing stand-alone applications across platforms on servers, desktops, and mobile devices. Many companies that once considered Java to be more hype than substance are now using it to create distributed applications accessed by customers and partners across the Internet. For every new project being developed today, companies are asking how they can use Java to make their work easier.

Java is now taught in every university. This book teaches you how to write Java programs from the beginning.

Java's Design and Advantages

- **Java is an object-oriented programming language.** Object-oriented programming is a favored programming approach that has replaced traditional procedure-based programming techniques. An object-oriented language uses abstraction, encapsulation, inheritance, and polymorphism to provide great flexibility, modularity, and reusability for developing software.

- **Java is platform-independent.** Its programs can run on any platform with a Java Virtual Machine, a software component that interprets Java instructions and carries out associated actions.

- **Java is distributed.** Networking is inherently built-in. Simultaneous processing can occur on multiple computers on the Internet. Writing network programs is treated as simple data input and output.

- **Java is multithreaded.** Multithreading is the capability of a program to perform several tasks simultaneously, such as downloading a video file while playing the video at the same time. Multithreading is particularly useful in graphical user interfaces (GUI) and network programming. Multithread programming is smoothly integrated in Java. In other languages, you can only enable multithreading by calling procedures that are specific to the operating system.

■ **Java is secure.** Computers become vulnerable when they are connected to other computers. Viruses and malicious programs can damage your computer. Java is designed with multiple layers of security that ensure proper access to private data and restrict access to disk files.

Java's Versatility

Stimulated by the promise of writing programs once and running them anywhere, Java has become the most ubiquitous programming language. Java programs run on full-featured computers, and also on consumer electronics and appliances, such as personal digital assistants and mobile phones.

Because of its great potential to unite existing legacy applications written on different platforms so that they can run together, Java is perceived as a universal front-end for the enterprise database. The leading database companies, IBM, Oracle, and Sybase, have extended their commitment to Java by integrating it into their products. Oracle, for example, enables Java applications to run on its server and to deliver a complete set of Java-based development tools supporting the integration of current applications with the Web.

Learning Java

To first-time programmers, learning Java is like learning any high-level programming language. The fundamental point in learning programming is to develop the critical skills of formulating programmatic solutions for real problems and translating the solutions into programs using selection statements, loops, and methods.

Once you acquire the basic skills of writing programs using loops, methods, and arrays, you can start to learn object-oriented programming. You will learn how to develop object-oriented software using class encapsulation and class inheritance.

Once you understand the concept of object-oriented programming, learning Java becomes a matter of learning the Java API. The Java API establishes a framework for programmers to develop applications using Java. You have to use these classes and interfaces in the API and follow their conventions and rules to create applications. The best way to learn Java API is to imitate examples and do exercises.

Learning Java with JBuilder

You can use Java 2 SDK to write Java programs. Java 2 SDK (formerly known as JDK) consists of a set of separate programs, such as compiler and interpreter, each of which is invoked from a command line. Besides Java 2 SDK, there are more than a dozen Java development tools on the market today, including Borland JBuilder, Sun ONE Studio, IBM Visual Age for Java, and WebGain Visual Café. These tools support an *integrated development environment* (IDE) for rapidly developing Java programs. Editing, compiling, building, debugging, and online help are integrated in one graphical user interface. Using these tools effectively will greatly increase your programming productivity.

The overriding objective of this book is to introduce the concepts and practice of Java programming. To facilitate developing and managing Java programs, the book is aided by JBuilder. With a tool like JBuilder, students can not only develop Java programs more productively, but can also learn Java programming more effectively.

JBuilder is a premier Java development tool for developing Java programs produced by Borland. Borland products are known to be "best of breed" in the IDE tool market. Over the years, Borland has led the charge in creating visual development tools like Delphi and C++ Builder. Borland is now leading the way in Java development tools with JBuilder. JBuilder is endorsed by major information technology companies like Oracle, which licensed JBuilder 2.

JBuilder is easy to learn and easy to use. The JBuilder development team worked hard to simplify the user interface and make it easy to navigate through the programs, projects, classes, packages, and code elements. As a result, JBuilder has fewer windows than other Java IDE tools. This makes JBuilder an ideal tool for beginners and for students who have little programming experience.

JBuilder is an indispensable, powerful tool that boosts your programming productivity. It may take a while to become familiar with it, but the time you invest will pay off in the long run. This text takes an incremental approach to facilitate learning JBuilder. Programming with JBuilder is introduced throughout the book to help you gradually adapt to using it.

 IMPORTANT NOTE
Students should strictly follow the advice of their instructors or this book to create projects and classes consistently. Not creating projects and classes correctly is a common error that discourages people from using JBuilder.

Organization of the Book

This book is divided into four parts that, taken together, form a comprehensive introductory course on Java programming. Because knowledge is cumulative, the early chapters provide the conceptual basis for understanding Java and guide students through simple examples and exercises; subsequent chapters progressively present Java programming in detail, culminating with the development of comprehensive Java applications. The appendixes contain a mixed bag of topics, including an HTML tutorial.

Part I: Fundamentals of Programming

The first part of the book is a stepping stone that will prepare you to embark on the journey of learning Java. You will begin to know Java, and will learn how to write simple Java programs with primitive data types, control statements, methods, and arrays.

Chapter 1, "Introduction to Java and JBuilder," gives an overview of the major features of Java: object-oriented programming, platform-independence, Java byte-code, security, performance, multithreading, and networking. The chapter introduces JBuilder and uses it to create, compile, and run Java programs. Simple examples of writing applications are provided, along with a brief anatomy of programming structures.

Chapter 2, "Primitive Data Types and Operations," introduces primitive data types, operators, and expressions. Important topics include identifiers, variables, constants, assignment statements, assignment expressions, primitive data types, operators, and shortcut operators. Java programming style and documentation are also addressed. You will learn how to get input from an input dialog box, and how to convert a string into numeric values. You will learn how to use the JBuilder debugger. You will also learn how to run Java programs from the command line, and how to get online help from JBuilder.

Chapter 3, "Control Statements," introduces decision and repetition statements. Java decision statements include various forms of `if` statements and the `switch` statement. Java repetition statements include the `while` loop, the `do-while` loop, and the `for` loop. The keywords `break` and `continue` are discussed.

Chapter 4, "Methods," introduces method creation, calling methods, passing parameters, returning values, method overloading, scope of local variables, and recursion. Applying the concept of abstraction is the key to developing software. The chapter also introduces the use of method abstraction in problem-solving. The `Math` class for performing basic math operations is introduced.

Chapter 5, "Arrays," explores an important structure: arrays for storing a collection of data. You will learn how to declare, initialize, and copy arrays. This chapter also introduces selection sort, linear search, and binary search methods.

Part II: Object-Oriented Programming

In the book's second part, object-oriented programming is introduced. Java is a class-centric, object-oriented programming language that uses abstraction, encapsulation, inheritance, and polymorphism to provide great flexibility, modularity, and reusability in developing software. You will learn programming with objects and classes, encapsulation, inheritance, interfaces, polymorphism, and developing software using the object-oriented approach.

Chapter 6, "Objects and Classes," begins with objects and classes. The important topics include defining classes, creating objects, using constructors, passing objects to methods, instance and class variables, and instance and class methods, scope of variables in the context of a class, the keyword `this`, and using the UML graphical notations to describe classes. Several examples are provided to demonstrate the power of the object-oriented programming approach. Students will learn the benefits (abstraction, encapsulation, and modularity) of object-oriented programming from these examples.

Chapter 7, "Strings," introduces the classes `String`, `StringBuffer`, and `StringTokenizer` for storing and processing strings. There are more than fifteen hundred predefined Java classes grouped in several packages. Starting with this chapter, students will gradually learn how to use Java classes to develop their own programs. The discussions on strings are fine examples to demonstrate the concept of objects and classes.

Chapter 8, "Inheritance and Polymorphism," teaches how an existing class can be extended and modified as needed. Inheritance is an extremely powerful programming technique, further extending software reusability. Java programs are all built by extending predefined Java classes. The major topics include defining subclasses, using the keyword `super`, using the modifiers `protected`, `final`, and the `Object` class.

Chapter 9, "Abstract Classes and Interfaces," introduces abstract classes and interfaces, and explores polymorphism and dynamic binding, generic programming, and casting objects. The wrapper classes for primitive data types are also introduced to encapsulate primitive data type values as objects.

Chapter 10, "Object-Oriented Modeling," focuses on class modeling and design. You will learn how to analyze relationships among objects and to design classes with the relationships association, aggregation, composition, strong inheritance, and weak inheritance. This chapter gives the guidelines for class design with several examples. Finally, two examples of designing generic classes for matrix operations and linked lists are introduced.

Part III: GUI Programming

The third part of the book introduces Java GUI programming. Major topics include event-driven programming, creating graphical user interfaces, and writing applets. You will learn the architecture of Java GUI programming API and use the user interface components to develop GUI applications and applets.

Chapter 11, "Getting Started with GUI Programming," introduces the concepts of Java GUI programming using Swing components. Topics include the Swing class hierarchy, frames, panels, and simple layout managers (`FlowLayout`, `GridLayout`, and `BorderLayout`). The chapter introduces drawing geometric figures in the graphics context.

Chapter 12, "Event-Driven Programming," introduces the concepts and techniques for Java event-driven programming. You will learn the Java event model, create listener classes, register listener objects with the source object, and process events in the listener's handlers.

Chapter 13, "Creating User Interfaces," introduces the user interface components: buttons, labels, text fields, text areas, combo boxes, lists, check boxes, radio buttons, menus, scrollbars, scroll panes, and tabbed panes. Today's client/server and Web-based applications use a graphical user interface. Java has a rich set of classes to help you build GUIs.

Chapter 14, "Applets," takes an in-depth look at applets, discussing applet behavior and the relationship between applets and other Swing classes. Applets are a special kind of Java class that can be executed from the Web browser. Students will learn how to convert applications to applets, and vice versa, and how to run programs both as applications and as applets. You will also learn now to create applets using the JBuilder Applet wizard.

Part IV: Developing Comprehensive Projects

The book's final part is devoted to several advanced features of Java programming. You will learn how to use these features to develop comprehensive programs; for example, using exception handling and assertions to make your program robust and correct, using input and output to manage and process a large quantity of data, using the classes in the Java Collections Framework to build data structures in Java, using multithreading to make your program more responsive and interactive, and incorporating sound and images to make your program user-friendly.

Chapter 15, "Exceptions and Assertions," teaches students how to define exceptions, throw exceptions, and handle exceptions so that their programs can either continue to run or terminate gracefully in the event of runtime errors. The chapter discusses predefined exception classes, and gives examples of creating user-defined exception classes. The chapter also introduces using assertions to help ensure program correctness.

Chapter 16, "Input and Output," introduces input and output streams. Students will learn the class structures of I/O streams, byte and character streams, file I/O streams, data I/O streams, print streams, object streams, random file access, delimited I/O, and interactive I/O.

Chapter 17, "Java Data Structures," introduces the Java Collections Framework. Students will learn how to use classes and interfaces such as `Collection`, `Set`, `HashSet`, `LinkedHashSet`, `TreeSet`, `Iterator`, `List`, `ArrayList`, `LinkedList`, `Vector`, `Stack`, `Map`, `HashMap`, `LinkedHashMap`, `TreeMap`, `Collections`, and `Arrays` to build projects.

Chapter 18, "Multithreading," introduces threads, which enable the running of multiple tasks simultaneously in one program. Students will learn how to use the `Thread` class and the `Runnable` interface to launch separate threads. The chapter also discusses thread states, thread priority, thread groups, and the synchronization of conflicting threads.

Chapter 19, "Multimedia," teaches how to incorporate sound and images to bring live animation to Java applets and applications. Various techniques for smoothing animation are introduced.

Part V: **Bonus Chapters** (On the Companion CD-ROM only)

This part contains bonus chapters on internationalization, networking, database programming, servlets, and JavaServer pages. These topics are usually not covered in introductory courses, but they are valuable for upper-level courses. This part is on the CD-ROM only, so that the main text is focused on the introductory Java subjects.

Chapter 20, "Internationalization," introduces the development of Java programs for international audiences. You will learn how to format dates, numbers, currencies, and percentages for different regions, countries, and languages. You will also learn how to use resource bundles to define which images and strings are used by a component depending on the user's locale and preferences.

Chapter 21, "Networking," introduces network programming. Students will learn the concept of network communication, stream sockets, client/server programming, and reading data files from the Web server.

Chapter 22, "Database Programming," begins with an overview of the database systems, and an introduction to relational database structures, integrity constraints, and the SQL language. You will learn how to use Java to develop database projects.

Chapter 23, "Servlets," introduces the technique of creating dynamic HTML contents using Java servlets. You will learn how to write server-side Java programs to access databases. You will also learn the techniques for session tracking and processing images.

Chapter 24, "JavaServer Pages," introduces the technique of creating JavaServer pages for Web-based database applications. You will learn JSP constructs, predefined variables, and directives. You will learn how to use JavaBeans in JSP.

Appendixes

This part of the book covers a mixed bag of topics. Appendix A lists Java keywords. Appendix B gives tables of ASCII characters and their associated codes in decimal and in hex. Appendix C shows the operator precedence. Appendix D summarizes Java modifiers and their usage. Appendix E lists UML Graphical Notations for describing classes and their relationships. Appendix F discusses special floating-point values. Finally, Appendix G provides a glossary of key terms used in the text.

Supplements (on the companion CD-ROM)

The text covers the core subjects. The supplements extend the text to cover additional topics that might be of interest to readers. The supplements are not included in the text but are provided on the companion CD-ROM. Supplement A gives an overview of computer systems. Supplement B introduces number systems and conversions among binary, decimal, and hex numbers. Bitwise operations are also introduced. Supplement C summarizes Java coding style and guidelines. Supplement D introduces how to configure your computer so that you can compile and run Java from the command window. Supplement E introduces package-naming conventions, creating packages, and using packages. Supplement F gives an HTML tutorial. Supplement G introduces `CardLayout`, `GridBagLayout`, and `Null Layout`. Supplement H discusses Java archive, packaging, and deploying Java projects. Supplement I introduces standard event adapters and anonymous event adapters. Supplement J covers network programming using datagrams. Supplement K demonstrates how to use the JBuilder Application wizard. Finally, Supplement L shows how to use the JBuilder UI designer to create UI.

Chapter Dependency Chart

The book provides flexible ordering of chapters to enable OO and GUI to be covered earlier. You may cover Chapter 6, "Objects and Classes," after Chapter 4, "Methods." You may cover Chapter 11, "Getting Started with GUI Programming," before Chapter 9, "Abstract Classes and Interfaces." You may cover Chapter 18, "Multithreading," after applets are introduced in Chapter 14. Chapter 17, "Java Data Structures," can be covered after Chapter 10, "Object-Oriented Modeling."

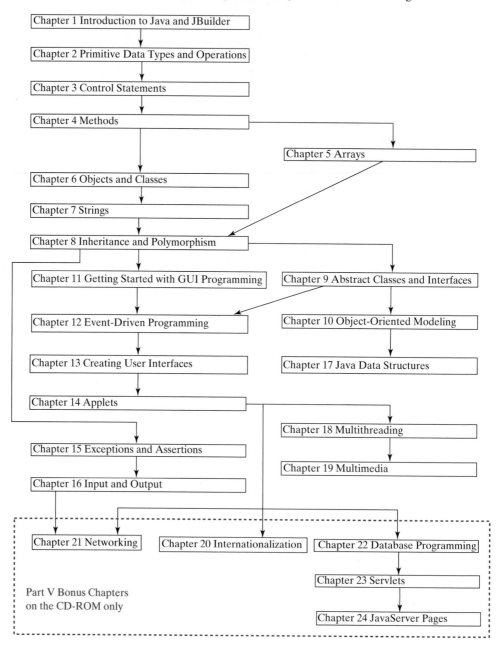

ABOUT THE AUTHOR

Y. Daniel Liang is the author and editor of the Prentice-Hall Liang Java Series. His innovative Java texts are used in many universities throughout the world.

Dr. Liang is currently a Yamacraw professor of software engineering in the School of Computing at Armstrong Atlantic State University, Savannah, Georgia. He can be reached at **liang@armstrong.edu.**

ACKNOWLEDGMENTS

I would like to thank Ray Greenlaw and Armstrong Atlantic State University for enabling me to teach what I write and for supporting me in writing what I teach. Teaching is the source of inspiration for continuing to improve the book. I am grateful to the instructors and readers who offered comments, suggestions, bug reports, and praise. Their enthusiastic support has contributed to the success of my Java series.

This book was greatly improved thanks to outstanding reviews by Larry King of the University of Texas at Dallas, Michel Mitri of James Madison University, Mary Ann Pumphrey of De Anza Junior College, Ashraf Shirani of San Jose State University, Russ Tront of Simon Fraser University, and Deborah Trytten of the University of Oklahoma.

It is a great pleasure and privilege to work with the legendary computer science team at Prentice Hall. I would like to thank Alan Apt, Toni Holm, Patrick Lindner, Jake Warde, Petra Recter, Sarah Parker, Camille Trentacoste, John Keegan, Xiaohong Zhu, Pamela Shaffer, Barrie Reinhold, Barbara Taylor-Laino, Meredith Maresca, and their colleagues at Prentice Hall for organizing, managing, and promoting this project, and Robert Milch, Dana Smith, Stacy Proteau, and their colleagues at Pine Tree Composition for helping to produce the book.

As always, I am indebted to my wife, Samantha, for love, support, and encouragement.

Companion Web Site for the Book

The companion Web site for the book can be accessed at **www.prenhall.com/ liang/introjb3e.html**. The Web site contains the following resources:

- Interactive Self-Test for every chapter
- Installing JBuilder from the book CD-ROM
- Microsoft PowerPoint slides for lectures
- Errata
- FAQs

Student CD-ROM

The student CD-ROM comes with the book. The contents of the CD-ROM are listed below:

- JBuilder Personal (Each new printing of this book will contain the newest version of JBuilder Personal. The screen shots in the text were taken from JBuilder 9 Personal. If the screen shots of a future version differ from JBuilder 9, the new screen shots will be posted on the web site.)
- WinZip
- Answers to review questions
- Solutions to even-numbered programming exercises
- Source code for the examples in the book
- Five bonus chapters and twelve supplements

TABLE OF CONTENTS

PART I	FUNDAMENTALS OF PROGRAMMING	1
CHAPTER 1	**Introduction to Java and JBuilder**	**3**
1.1	Introduction	4
1.2	The History of Java	4
1.3	Characteristics of Java	5
1.3.1	Java Is Simple	5
1.3.2	Java Is Object-Oriented	5
1.3.3	Java Is Distributed	6
1.3.4	Java Is Interpreted	6
1.3.5	Java Is Robust	7
1.3.6	Java Is Secure	7
1.3.7	Java Is Architecture-Neutral	8
1.3.8	Java Is Portable	8
1.3.9	Java's Performance	8
1.3.10	Java Is Multithreaded	9
1.3.11	Java Is Dynamic	9
1.4	World Wide Web, Java, and Beyond	10
1.5	The Java Language Specification and API	12
1.6	JDK, Java IDE, and JBuilder	13
1.7	A Simple Java Program	14
1.8	Anatomy of the Java Program	
1.8.1	Comments	15
1.8.2	Packages	16
1.8.3	Reserved Words	16
1.8.4	Modifiers	16
1.8.5	Statements	16
1.8.6	Blocks	17
1.8.7	Classes	17
1.8.8	Methods	17
1.8.9	The main Method	17
1.9	Getting Started with JBuilder	18
1.9.1	The Main Menu	19
1.9.2	The Toolbar	19
1.9.3	The Status Bar	20
1.9.4	The Project Pane	20
1.9.5	The Content Pane	21
1.9.6	The Structure Pane	23

1.10	Creating a Project	23
1.11	Creating, Compiling, and Executing a Java Program	27
	1.11.1 Creating a Java Program	28
	1.11.2 Compiling a Java Program	32
	1.11.3 Executing a Java Application	34
1.12	Displaying Text in a Message Dialog Box	35

CHAPTER 2 Primitive Data Types and Operations 41

2.1	Introduction	42
2.2	Writing Simple Programs	42
2.4	Identifiers	46
2.5	Variables	48
	2.5.1 Declaring Variables	48
2.6	Assignment Statements and Assignment Expressions	49
	2.6.1 Declaring and Initializing Variables in One Step	50
2.7	Constants	50
2.8	Numeric Data Types and Operations	51
	2.8.1 Numeric Operators	52
	2.8.2 Numeric Literals	53
	2.8.3 Arithmetic Expressions	53
	2.8.4 Shortcut Operators	54
2.9	Numeric Type Conversions	56
2.10	Character Data Type and Operations	58
	2.10.1 Unicode and ASCII code	58
	2.10.2 Escape Sequences for Special Characters	59
	2.10.3 Casting between char and Numeric Types	60
2.11	boolean Data Type and Operations	61
	2.11.1 Unconditional vs. Conditional Boolean Operators	63
2.12	Operator Precedence and Associativity	64
2.13	Operand Evaluation Order	65
2.14	Getting Input from Input Dialogs	66
	2.14.1 Converting Strings to Numbers	67
2.15	Case Studies	70
2.16	Programming Style and Documentation	76
	2.16.1 Appropriate Comments and Comment Styles	77
	2.16.2 Naming Conventions	77
	2.16.3 Proper Indentation and Spacing	77
	2.16.4 Block Styles	79

	2.16.5	Code Style Examples	79
2.17	Programming Errors		80
	2.17.1	Syntax Errors	80
	2.17.2	Runtime Errors	81
	2.17.3	Logic Errors	82
2.18	Debugging		83
2.19	Debugging in JBuilder		84
	2.19.1	Setting Breakpoints	84
	2.19.2	Starting the Debugger	84
	2.19.3	Controlling Program Execution	86
	2.19.4	Examining and Modifying Data Values	87
2.20	Run Java Applications from the Command Line		91
2.21	JBuilder's Online Help		92
	2.21.1	Accessing from the Help Menu	92
	2.21.2	Obtaining Help on Java Keywords and Classes	93

CHAPTER 3   Control Statements   105

3.1	Introduction		106
3.2	Selection Statements		106
	3.2.1	Simple if Statements	106
	3.2.2	if else Statements	108
	3.2.3	Nested if Statements	109
	3.2.4	switch Statements	115
	3.2.5	Conditional Expressions	117
3.3	Loop Statements		117
	3.3.1	The while Loop	118
	3.3.2	The do-while Loop	121
	3.3.3	The for Loop	123
3.4	Nested Loops		127
3.5	Which Loop to Use?		129
3.6	Using the Keywords break and continue		130
	3.6.1	Statement Labels and Breaking with Labels	133
3.7	Case Studies		134
3.8	Debugging Loops		141

CHAPTER 4   Methods   153

4.1	Introduction	154
4.2	Creating a Method	154
4.3	Calling a Method	155
4.4	Passing Parameters	159

	4.4.1 Pass by Value	160
4.5	Overloading Methods	162
4.6	The Scope of Local Variables	167
4.7	Method Abstraction	168
4.8	The Math Class	168
	4.8.1 Trigonometric Methods	169
	4.8.2 Exponent Methods	169
	4.8.3 The Rounding Methods	169
	4.8.4 The min, max, abs, and random Methods	170
4.9	Case Studies (Optional)	175
4.10	Recursion (Optional)	182
	4.10.1 Computing Factorials	182
	4.10.2 Computing Fibonacci Numbers	186
	4.10.3 The Tower of Hanoi Problem	189
	4.10.4 Recursion versus Iteration	193

CHAPTER 5   Arrays | | **205**

5.1	Introduction	206
5.2	Declaring Array Variables and Creating Arrays	206
5.3	Initializing and Processing Arrays	208
5.4	Copying Arrays	214
5.5	Passing Arrays to Methods	217
5.6	Multidimensional Arrays	226
	5.6.1 Declaring Variables of Multidimensional Arrays and Creating Multidimensional Arrays	226
	5.6.2 Obtaining the Lengths of Multidimensional Arrays	227
	5.6.3 Ragged Arrays	227
5.7	Sorting Arrays	234
5.8	Searching Arrays	237
	5.8.1 The Linear Search Approach	237
	5.8.2 The Binary Search Approach (Optional)	239

PART II   OBJECT-ORIENTED PROGRAMMING | | **251**

CHAPTER 6   Objects and Classes | | **253**

6.1	Introduction	254
6.2	Defining Classes for Objects	254
6.3	Constructing Objects Using Constructors	255
6.4	Accessing Objects via Reference Variables	257

	6.4.1	Accessing an Object's Data and Methods	258
	6.4.2	Differences Between Variables of Primitive Types and Reference Types	263
6.5		Visibility Modifiers, Accessors, and Mutators	264
6.6		Passing Objects to Methods	270
6.7		Static Variables, Constants, and Methods	272
6.8		The Scope of Variables	278
6.9		The Keyword this	279
6.10		Array of Objects	280
6.11		Class Abstraction	283
6.12		Case Studies	283
6.13		Inner Classes (Optional)	291

CHAPTER 7   **Strings**   **305**

7.1		Introduction	306
7.2		The String Class	306
	7.2.1	Constructing a String	306
	7.2.2	String Length and Retrieving Individual Characters	308
	7.2.3	String Concatenation	309
	7.2.4	Extracting Substrings	309
	7.2.5	String Comparisons	310
	7.2.6	String Conversions	311
	7.2.7	Finding a Character or a Substring in a String	312
	7.2.8	Conversion between Strings and Arrays	313
	7.2.9	Converting Characters and Numeric Values to Strings	313
7.3		The Character Class	315
7.4		The StringBuffer Class	318
	7.4.1	Constructing a String Buffer	318
	7.4.2	Modifying Strings in the Buffer	319
	7.4.3	The toString, capacity, length, setLength, and charAt Methods	320
7.5		The StringTokenizer Class	323
7.6		Command-Line Arguments	326
	7.6.1	Passing Arguments to Java Programs	326
	7.6.2	Processing Command-Line Parameters	326

CHAPTER 8   **Inheritance and Polymorphism**   **335**

8.1		Introduction	336
8.2		Superclasses and Subclasses	336

8.3	Using the Super Keyword	338
	8.3.1 Calling Superclass Constructors	338
	8.3.2 Calling Superclass Methods	340
8.4	Overriding Methods	341
8.4	The Object Class	343
	8.4.1 The equals Method	343
	8.4.2 The hashCode Method	344
	8.4.3 The toString Method	344
8.5	Polymorphism, Dynamic Binding, and Generic Programming	345
8.6	Casting Objects and the instanceof Operator	346
8.7	Hiding Fields and Static Methods (Optional)	351
8.8	The Protected Data and Methods	352
	8.8.1 Using the Visibility Modifiers	353
8.9	The final Classes, Methods, and Variables	354
8.10	The finalize, clone, and getClass Methods (Optional)	354
	8.10.1 The finalize Method	355
	8.10.2 The clone Method	356
	8.10.3 The getClass Method	356
8.11	Initialization Blocks (Optional)	356
	8.11.1 Static Initialization Block	357

CHAPTER 9 **Abstract Classes and Interfaces** **367**

9.1	Introduction	368
9.2	Abstract Classes	368
9.3	The Calendar and GregorianCalendar Classes	375
9.4	Interfaces	376
	9.4.1 Interfaces vs. Abstract Classes	381
	9.4.2 The Cloneable Interface (Optional)	382
9.5	Processing Primitive Data Type Values as Objects	386
	9.5.1 Numeric Wrapper Class Constructors	387
	9.5.2 Numeric Wrapper Class Constants	387
	9.5.3 Conversion Methods	388
	9.5.4 The Static valueOf Methods	388
	9.5.5 The Methods for Parsing Strings into Numbers	388

CHAPTER 10 **Object-Oriented Modeling** **399**

10.1	Introduction	400
	10.1.2 The Software Development Process	400

10.3	Analyzing Relationships Among Objects	401
	10.3.1 Association	401
	10.3.2 Aggregation	403
	10.3.3 Inheritance	404
10.4	Class Development	404
10.5	The Rational Class	413
10.6	Class Design Guidelines	419
	10.6.1 Designing a Class	419
	10.6.2 Using the Visibility Modifiers public, protected, and private	419
	10.6.3 Using the static Modifier	420
	10.6.4 Using Inheritance or Composition	420
	10.6.5 Using Interfaces or Abstract Classes	420
10.7	Modeling Dynamic Behavior Using Sequence Diagrams and Statecharts	421
	10.7.1 Sequence Diagrams	421
	10.7.2 Statechart Diagrams	422
10.8	Case Studies (Optional)	423
10.9	Designing Classes for Linked Lists (Optional)	430
10.10	Framework-Based Programming Using Java API	438

PART III	**GUI PROGRAMMING**	**445**
CHAPTER 11	**Getting Started with GUI Programming**	**447**
11.1	Introduction	448
11.2	The Java GUI API	448
	11.2.1 Container Classes	450
	11.2.2 GUI Helper Classes	450
	11.2.3 Swing GUI Components	451
11.3	Frames	452
	11.3.1 Creating a Frame	452
	11.3.2 Centering a Frame	454
	11.3.3 Adding Components to a Frame	455
11.4	Layout Managers	456
	11.4.1 FlowLayout	457
	11.4.2 GridLayout	459
	11.4.3 BorderLayout	461
	11.4.4 Properties of Layout Managers (Optional)	463
	11.4.5 The validate and doLayout Methods (Optional)	464

11.5   Using Panels as Containers   464

11.6   Drawing Graphics in Panels   466

11.7   The Color Class   468

11.8   The Font and FontMetrics Classes   469

11.9   Drawing Geometric Figures   476

    11.9.1   Drawing Lines   476

    11.9.2   Drawing Rectangles   477

    11.9.3   Drawing Ovals   479

    11.9.4   Drawing Arcs   481

    11.9.5   The Polygon class and Drawing Polygons and Polylines   482

11.10   Case Studies   485

CHAPTER 12   **Event-Driven Programming**   **505**

12.1   Introduction   506

12.2   Event and Event Source   506

12.3   Listeners, Registrations, and Handling Events   507

12.4   Mouse Events   518

12.5   Keyboard Events   523

CHAPTER 13   **Creating User Interfaces**   **531**

13.1   Introduction   532

13.2   The Component and JComponent Classes   532

13.3   Buttons   533

13.4   Labels   538

13.5   Text Fields   541

13.6   Text Areas   544

13.7   Combo Boxes   549

13.8   Lists   552

13.9   Check Boxes   556

13.10   Radio Buttons   561

13.11   Borders   566

13.12   JOptionPane Dialogs   573

    13.12.1   Message Dialogs   574

    13.12.2   Confirmation Dialogs   576

    13.12.3   Input Dialogs   577

    13.12.4   Option Dialogs   578

13.13   Menus   582

    13.13.1   Creating Menus   582

    13.13.2   Image Icons, Keyboard Mnemonics, and Keyboard Accelerators   585

13.14   Creating Multiple Windows   590

13.15   Scrollbars   594

13.16   Scroll Panes   598

13.17   Tabbed Panes   603

CHAPTER 14   **Applets**   **619**

14.1   Introduction   620

14.2   The Applet Class   620

  14.2.1   The init Method   621

  14.2.2   The start Method   622

  14.2.3   The stop Method   622

  14.2.4   The destroy Method   622

14.3   The JApplet Class   622

14.4   Creating a Java Applet
       Using the Applet Wizard   623

14.5   Viewing Applets   625

  14.5.1   Viewing Applets in the Content Pane   625

  14.5.2   Viewing Applets Using the Applet
           Viewer Utility   626

  14.5.3   Viewing Applets from a Web Browser   627

14.6   The HTML File and the <applet> Tag   628

14.7   Passing Parameters to Applets   632

14.8   Enabling Applets to Run as Applications   635

14.9   Case Studies (Optional)   638

PART IV   **DEVELOPING COMPREHENSIVE PROJECTS**   **653**

CHAPTER 15   **Exceptions and Assertions**   **655**

15.1   Introduction   656

15.2   Exceptions and Exception Types   656

  15.2.1   Exception Classes   657

  15.2.2   Checked and Unchecked Exceptions   659

15.3   Understanding Exception Handling   659

  15.3.1   Declaring Exceptions   659

  15.3.2   Throwing Exceptions   660

  15.3.3   Catching Exceptions   660

15.4   Rethrowing Exceptions   667

15.5   The finally Clause   668

15.6   When to Use Exceptions   668

15.7   Creating Custom Exception
       Classes (Optional)   669

15.8   Assertions   674

     15.8.1   Declaring Assertions   675

     15.8.2   Compiling Programs with Assertions   675

     15.8.3   Running Programs with Assertions   676

     15.8.4   Using Exception Handling or Assertions   677

CHAPTER 16   **Input and Output**   **685**

16.1   Introduction   686

16.2   The File Class   686

16.3   I/O Streams   691

     16.3.1   Stream Classes   691

     16.3.2   InputStream and Reader   692

     16.3.3   OutputStream and Writer   694

16.4   File Streams   694

16.5   Filter Streams   697

16.6   Data Streams   698

16.7   Print Streams   702

16.8   Buffered Streams   704

16.9   File Dialogs   708

16.10   Text Input and Output on the Console (Optional)   714

16.11   Object Streams   716

     16.11.1   The ObjectOutputStream and ObjectInputStream classes   717

     16.11.2   The transient Keyword   722

16.12   Random Access Files   722

16.13   Parsing Text Files (Optional)   733

16.14   Array Streams, Piped Streams, String Streams, Pushback Streams, and Line Number Streams (Optional)   736

CHAPTER 17   **Java Data Structures**   **745**

17.1   Introduction   746

17.2   The Collection Interface and the AbstractCollection Class   747

     17.2.1   The Methods in the Collection Interface   748

     17.2.2   The hashCode Method and the equals Method   748

17.3   The Set Interface, and the AbstractSet and HashSet Classes   749

17.4   The LinkedHashSet Class   751

17.5   The SortedSet Interface and the TreeSet Class   752

17.6   The Comparator Interface   754

17.7	The List Interface, the AbstractList Class, and the Abstract-SequentialList Class	757
17.8	The ArrayList and LinkedList Classes	758
17.9	The Vector Class	761
17.10	The Stack Class	764
17.11	The Map Interface, the AbstractMap class, the SortedMap interface, the HashMap, LinkedHashMap, and TreeMap Classes	766
17.12	The Collections Class	772
17.13	The Arrays Class	776

CHAPTER 18   **Multithreading**   **783**

18.1	Introduction	784
18.2	Thread Concepts	784
18.3	Creating Threads by Extending the Thread Class	785
18.4	Creating Threads by Implementing the Runnable Interface	788
18.5	Thread Controls and Communications	791
18.6	Thread States	792
18.7	Thread Groups	794
18.8	Synchronization	794
	18.8.1 The Keyword synchronized	797
	18.8.2 Synchronized Statements	799
18.9	Controlling Animation Using Threads	799
18.10	Controlling Animation Using the Timer Class	803

CHAPTER 19   **Multimedia**   **817**

19.1	Introduction	818
19.2	Playing Audio	818
19.3	Running Audio on a Separate Thread	823
19.4	Displaying Images	825
19.5	Loading Image and Audio Files in Java Applications	828
19.6	Displaying a Sequence of Images	833
19.7	Using MediaTracker	836

APPENDIXES   **845**

APPENDIX A	**Java Keywords**	847
APPENDIX B	**The ASCII Character Set**	851
APPENDIX C	**Operator Precedence Chart**	855

APPENDIX D	Java Modifiers	859
APPENDIX E	UML Graphical Notations	861
	Classes and Objects	861
	The Modifiers public, private, protected, and static	861
	Class Relationships	862
	Abstract Classes and Interfaces	863
	Sequence Diagrams	863
	Statechart Diagrams	863
APPENDIX F	Special Floating-Point Values	865
APPENDIX G	Glossary	867
	Index	877

PART V **BONUS CHAPTERS (on CD-ROM only)**

CHAPTER 20 **Internationalization**
- 20.1 Introduction
- 20.2 The Locale Class
- 20.3 Processing Date and Time
  - 20.3.1 The Date Class
  - 20.3.2 The Calender and GregorianCalendar Classes
  - 20.3.3 The TimeZone Class
  - 20.3.4 The DateFormat Class
  - 20.3.5 The SimpleDateFormat Class
- 20.4 Formatting Numbers
- 20.5 Resource Bundles (Optional)

CHAPTER 21 **Networking**
- 21.1 Introduction
- 21.2 Client/Server Computing
- 21.3 The InetAddress Class
- 21.4 Serving Multiple Clients
- 21.5 Applet Clients
- 21.6 Sending and Receiving Objects
- 21.7 The URL class and Viewing Web Pages from Applets
- 21.8 Retrieving Files from Web Servers
- 21.9 Viewing HTML Files Using JEditorPane
- 21.10 Cases Studies (Optional)

CHAPTER 22 **Java Database Programming**
- 22.1 Introduction

22.2 Relational Database Systems
    22.2.1 Relational Structures
    22.2.2 Integrity Constraints
22.3 SQL
    22.3.1 Creating and Dropping Tables
    22.3.2 Using SQL on MS Access Database
    22.3.3 Simple Insert, Update, and Delete
    22.3.4 Simple Queries
    22.3.5 Comparison and Boolean Operators
    22.3.6 The like, between-and, and is null Operators
    22.3.7 Column Alias
    22.3.8 The Arithmetic Operators
    22.3.9 Displaying Distinct Tuples
    22.3.10 Displaying Sorted Tuples
    22.3.11 Joining Tables
22.4 JDBC
    22.4.1 Developing Database Applications Using JDBC
    22.4.2 Creating an ODBC Data Source
    22.4.3 Accessing Oracle Database
22.5 Processing Statements
    22.5.1 The execute, executeQuery, and executeUpdate Methods
    22.5.2 PreparedStatement
22.6 Retrieving Metadata
22.7 A Universal SQL Client

CHAPTER 23   **Servlets**
23.1 Introduction
23.2 HTML and Common Gateway Interface
    23.2.1 Static Web Contents
    23.2.2 Dynamic Web Contents and Common Gateway Interface
23.3 The GET and POST Methods
    23.3.1 HTML Forms
23.4 From CGI to Java Servlets
23.5 Creating and Running Servlets from JBuilder
    23.5.1 Creating a Servlet
    23.5.2 Running the Servlet
    23.5.3 Testing the Servlet

23.6   The Servlet API

    23.6.1   The Servlet Interface

    23.6.2   The GenericServlet Class, ServletConfig Interface, and HttpServlet Class

    23.6.3   The ServletRequest Interface and HttpServletRequest Interface

    23.6.4   The ServletResponse Interface and HttpServletResponse Interface

23.7   Creating Servlets

23.8   Database Programming Using Servlets

23.9   Session Tracking

    23.9.1   Session Tracking Using Hidden Values

    23.9.2   Session Tracking Using Cookies

    23.9.3   Session Tracking Using the Servlet API

23.10   Sending Images from Servlets

    23.10.1   Sending Image Files from Servlets

    23.10.2   Creating Images from Drawings

    23.10.3   Sending Images and Text Together

CHAPTER 24   JavaServer Pages

24.1   Introduction

24.2   A Simple JSP Page

24.3   How Is a JSP Page Processed?

24.4   Creating and Running JSP from JBuilder

    24.4.1   Creating a JSP

    24.4.2   Running a JSP

24.5   JSP Scripting Constructs

24.6   Predefined Variables

24.7   JSP Directives

24.8   Using JavaBeans in JSP

24.9   Getting and Setting Properties

24.10   Associating Properties with Input Parameters

24.11   Forwarding Requests from JavaServer Pages

SUPPLEMENTS (in the CD-ROM)

SUPPLEMENT A   Overview of Computer Systems

A.1   Introduction

A.2   What is a Computer?

A.2.1   Central Processing Unit

A.2.2   Memory

A.2.3   Secondary Storage

A.2.4   Input and Output Devices

A.3   Computer Programming

A.4   Operating Systems

A.4.1   Allocating and Assigning System Resources

A.4.2   Scheduling Operations

| SUPPLEMENT B | **Number Systems and Bit Manipulations** |

B.1   Introduction

B.2   Conversions Between Binary Numbers
and Decimal Numbers

B.3   Conversions Between Hexadecimal Numbers
and Decimal Numbers

B.4   Conversions Between Binary
Numbers and Hexadecimal Numbers

B.5   Bit Manipulations

| SUPPLEMENT C | **Java Coding Style Guidelines** |

C.1   Introduction

C.2   Appropriate Comments
and Comment Styles

C.3   Naming Conventions

C.3.1   Package-Naming Conventions

C.4   Proper Indentation and Spacing

C.5   Block Styles

C.6   Multiple Alternative if-else Style

C.7   for-loop Style

C.8   while-loop Style

C.9   do-while Style

C.10   try-catch Style

C.11   Summary and Example

| SUPPLEMENT D | **Compiling and Running Java from the Command Window** |

D.1   Introduction

D.2   Introduction

D.3   Opening a Command Window

D.4   Configuring JDK 1.4

D.4.1   Configuring JDK 1.4 on Windows 95 and 98

D.4.2   Configuring JDK 1.4 on Windows NT, 2000,
and XP

D.5   Simple DOS Commands

D.6   Creating and Editing Programs
       Using Notepad

D.7   Compiling and Running Java Programs

D.8   Frequently Asked Questions

SUPPLEMENT E   **Packages**

E.1   Introduction

E.2   Package-Naming Conventions

E.3   The classpath Environment Variable

E.4   Putting Classes into Packages

E.5   Using Classes/Interfaces from Packages

SUPPLEMENT F   **HTML Tutorial**

F.1   Getting Started

F.2   Structure Tags

F.3   Text Appearance Tags

　　　　F.3.1   Content-Based Tags

F.4   Physical Tags

F.5   Paragraph-Style Tags

F.6   Font, Size, and Color Tags

F.7   List Tags

　　　　F.7.1.   Ordered Lists

　　　　F.7.2   Unordered Lists

　　　　F.7.3   Definition Lists

F.8   Table Tags

F.9   Hyperlink Tags

　　　　F.9.1   Linking Documents on Different Computers

　　　　F.9.2   Linking Documents on the Same Computer

　　　　F.9.3   Jumping Within the Same Document

F.10   Embedding Graphics

　　　　F.10.1   Horizontal Bar Tags

　　　　F.10.2   Image Tags

F.11   More on HTML

SUPPLEMENT G   **CardLayout, GridBagLayout, and Null Layout**

G.1   Introduction

G.2   CardLayout Manager

G.3   The GridBagLayout Manager

　　　　G.3.1   Location

　　　　G.3.2   Size

G.3.3 Growth Weight

G.3.4 Anchor

G.3.5 Filling

G.3.6 Insets

G.3.7 Padding

G.3.8 Constructing a GridBagConstraints Object

G.3.9 Adding a Component to the Container
of GridBagLayout

G.4 Using No Layout Manager

SUPPLEMENT H **Packaging and Deploying Java Projects**

H.1 Introduction

H.2 Java Archive (JAR)

H.3 Using the Archive Builder to Package Projects

H.4 The Manifest File

H.5 Running Archived Projects

H.5.1 Running Archived Files from Java Applications

H.5.2 Running Archived Files from Java Applets

H.6 Creating Shortcuts for Java Applications
on Windows

SUPPLEMENT I **Event Adapters**

I.1 Introduction

I.2 Extended Event Model

I.3 Standard Adapters

I.4 Anonymous Adapters

SUPPLEMENT J **Network Programming Using Datagrams**

J.1 Introduction

J.2 The DatagramPacket
and DatagramSocket Classes

J.2.1 The DatagramPacket Class

J.2.2 DatagramSocket

J.3 Datagram Programming

SUPPLEMENT K **Using the JBuilder Application Wizard**

K.1 Introduction

K.2 Starting the Application Wizard

K.3 The Application Class

K.4 The Frame Class

K.5 Modifying the Code in the Frame Class

SUPPLEMENT L	**Rapid Java Application Development Using JBuilder**

L.1   Introduction

L.2   JavaBeans

L.3   JBuilder Visual Designer

L.4   Using JBuilder Visual Designer

    L.4.1   Phase 1: Creating User Interface

    L.4.2   Phase 2: Implementing Event Handlers

    L.4.3   Phase 3: Creating Menus

L.5   Installing and Using Custom Components

    L.5.1   Installing Custom Components

    L.5.2   Using Custom Components

PART 1

FUNDAMENTALS OF PROGRAMMING

By now you have heard a lot about Java and are anxious to start writing Java programs. The first part of the book is a stepping stone that will prepare you to embark on the journey of learning Java. You will begin to know Java and will develop fundamental programming skills. Specifically, you will learn how to write simple Java programs with primitive data types, control statements, methods, and arrays.

CHAPTER 1   INTRODUCTION TO JAVA AND JBUILDER

CHAPTER 2   PRIMITIVE DATA TYPES AND OPERATIONS

CHAPTER 3   CONTROL STATEMENTS

CHAPTER 4   METHODS

CHAPTER 5   ARRAYS

INTRODUCTION TO JAVA AND JBUILDER

Objectives

- To learn about Java and its history.
- To understand the relationship between Java and the World Wide Web.
- To write a simple Java application.
- To become familiar with JBuilder.
- To create, compile, and run Java programs with JBuilder.
- To understand the Java runtime environment.
- To display output on the console and on the dialog box.

1.1   Introduction

By now you have heard quite a lot about the exciting Java programming language. It must seem as if Java is everywhere! Your local bookstores are filled with Java books. There are articles about Java in every major newspaper and magazine. It is impossible to read a computer magazine without coming across the magical word *Java*. You must be wondering why Java is so hot. The answer is that it enables users to deploy applications on the Internet for servers, desktop computers, and small hand-held devices. In fact, this is its main distinguishing characteristic. The future of computing will be profoundly influenced by the Internet, and Java promises to remain a big part of that future. Java is *the* Internet programming language.

You are about to begin an exciting journey, learning a powerful programming language. Java is cross-platform, object-oriented, network-based, and multimedia-ready. After its inception in May 1995, Java quickly became an attractive language for developing Internet applications. This chapter introduces Java and its programming features, followed by a simple example of Java applications.

 NOTE

The book assumes that you are computer-literate. If you are not familiar with such terms as CPU, memory, hard disk, operating system, and programming language, please see Supplement A, "Overview of Computer Systems."

1.2   The History of Java

Java was developed by a team led by James Gosling at Sun Microsystems, a company best known for its Sun workstations. Originally called *Oak*, it was designed in 1991 for use in embedded consumer electronic appliances. In 1995, renamed *Java*, it was redesigned for developing Internet applications. Java programs can be embedded in HTML pages and downloaded by Web browsers to bring live animation and interaction to Web clients.

The power of Java is not limited to Web applications, for it is a general-purpose programming language. It has full programming features and can be used to develop stand-alone applications. Java is inherently object-oriented. Although many object-oriented languages began strictly as procedural languages, Java was designed from the start to be object-oriented. Object-oriented programming (OOP) is a popular programming approach that is replacing traditional procedural programming techniques.

 NOTE

One of the central issues in software development is how to reuse code. Object-oriented programming provides great flexibility, modularity, clarity, and reusability through encapsulation, inheritance, and polymorphism—all of which you will learn about in this book.

1.3 Characteristics of Java

Java has become enormously popular. Java's rapid rise and wide acceptance can be traced to its design and programming features, particularly its promise that you can write a program once and run it anywhere. As stated in the Java-language white paper by Sun, Java is *simple, object-oriented, distributed, interpreted, robust, secure, architecture-neutral, portable, high-performance, multithreaded,* and *dynamic.* Let's analyze these often-used buzzwords.

1.3.1 Java Is Simple

No language is simple, but Java is a bit easier than the popular object-oriented programming language C++, which was the dominant software-development language before Java. Java is partially modeled on C++, but greatly simplified and improved. For instance, pointers and multiple inheritance often make programming complicated. Java replaces the multiple inheritance in C++ with a simple language construct called an *interface*, and eliminates pointers.

Java uses automatic memory allocation and garbage collection, whereas C++ requires the programmer to allocate memory and collect garbage. Also, the number of language constructs is small for such a powerful language. The clean syntax makes Java programs easy to write and read. Some people refer to Java as "C++−−" because it is like C++ but with more functionality and fewer negative aspects.

1.3.2 Java Is Object-Oriented

Computer programs are instructions to computers. You tell a computer what to do through a program. Without programs, a computer is an empty machine. Computers do not understand human languages, so you need to use computer languages to communicate with them. There are more than one hundred programming languages. The most popular language of them are:

COBOL (COmmon Business Oriented Language)

FORTRAN (FORmula TRANslation)

BASIC (Beginner All-purpose Symbolic Instructional Code)

Pascal (Named for Blaise Pascal)

Ada (Named for Ada Lovelace)

C (So named because its developer designed B first)

Visual Basic (Basic-like visual language developed by Microsoft)

Delphi (Pascal-like visual language developed by Borland)

C++ (an object-oriented language, based on C)

Each of these languages was designed with a specific purpose. COBOL was designed for business applications and now is used primarily for business data processing. FORTRAN was designed for mathematical computations. BASIC, as its name suggests, was designed to be learned and used easily. Pascal was designed to be a simple structural programming language. Ada was developed for the Department of

Defense and is mainly used in defense projects. C is popular for system software projects, such as writing compilers and operating systems. Visual Basic and Delphi are for rapid application development. C++ is the C language with object-oriented features.

All of these languages except C++ are *procedural programming languages.* Software systems developed using procedural programming languages are based on the paradigm of procedures. Object-oriented programming models the real world in terms of objects. Everything in the world can be modeled as an object. A circle is an object, a person is an object, and a window's icon is an object. Even a loan can be perceived as an object. A Java program is object-oriented because programming in Java is centered on creating objects, manipulating objects, and making objects work together.

Part I, "Fundamentals of Programming," introduces primitive data types and operations, control statements, methods, and arrays. These are the fundamentals for all programming languages. You will learn object-oriented programming in Part II, "Object-Oriented Programming." Object-oriented programming provides great flexibility, modularity, and reusability. For years, object-oriented technology was perceived as elitist, requiring a substantial investment in training and infrastructure. Java has helped object-oriented technology enter the mainstream of computing. Its simple, clean syntax makes programs easy to write and read. Java programs are quite *expressive* in terms of designing and developing applications.

1.3.3   Java Is Distributed

Distributed computing involves several computers working together on a network. Java is designed to make distributed computing easy. Since networking capability is inherently integrated into Java, writing network programs is like sending and receiving data to and from a file. As an example, Figure 1.1 shows three programs running on three different systems; the three programs communicate with one other to perform a joint task.

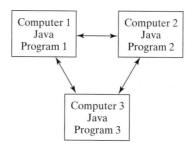

Figure 1.1   *Java programs can run on different systems that work together.*

1.3.4   Java Is Interpreted

You need an interpreter to run Java programs. The programs are compiled into the Java Virtual Machine code called *bytecode.* The bytecode is machine-independent and can run on any machine that has a Java interpreter, as shown in Figure 1.2.

6

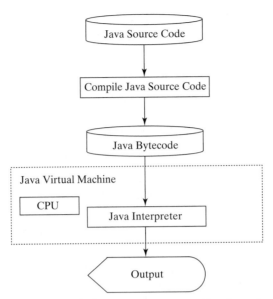

Figure 1.2   *The Java interpreter executes Java bytecode.*

Most compilers, including C++ compilers, translate programs in a high-level language to machine code. The code can only run on the native machine. If you run the program on other machines, it has to be recompiled on the native machine. For instance, if you compile a C++ program in Windows, the executable code generated by the compiler can only run on the Windows platform. With Java, you compile the source code once, and the bytecode generated by a Java compiler can run on any platform with a Java interpreter. The Java interpreter translates the bytecode into the machine language of the target machine.

1.3.5   Java Is Robust

Robust means *reliable*. No programming language can ensure complete reliability. Java puts a lot of emphasis on early checking for possible errors, because Java compilers can detect many problems that would first show up at execution time in other languages. Java has eliminated certain types of error-prone programming constructs found in other languages. It does not support pointers, for example, thereby eliminating the possibility of overwriting memory and corrupting data.

Java has a runtime exception-handling feature to provide programming support for robustness. Java forces the programmer to write the code to deal with exceptions. Java can catch and respond to an exceptional situation so that the program can continue its normal execution and terminate gracefully when a runtime error occurs.

1.3.6   Java Is Secure

As an Internet programming language, Java is used in a networked and distributed environment. If you download a Java applet (a special kind of program) and run it on your computer, it will not damage your system because Java implements several security mechanisms to protect your system against harm caused by stray programs. The security is based on the premise that *nothing should be trusted*.

1.3.7   Java Is Architecture-Neutral

Java is interpreted. This feature enables Java to be *architecture-neutral*, or to use an alternative term, *platform-independent*. With a Java Virtual Machine (JVM), you can write one program that will run on any platform, as shown in Figure 1.3.

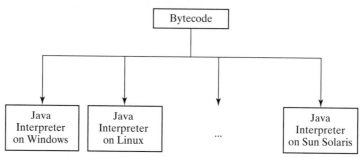

Figure 1.3   *Java bytecode can be executed on any platform that has a JVM.*

Java's initial success stemmed from its Web programming capability. You can run Java applets from a Web browser, but Java is for more than just writing Web applets. You can also run stand-alone Java applications directly from operating systems, using a Java interpreter. Today, software vendors usually develop multiple versions of the same product to run on different platforms (Windows, OS/2, Macintosh, and various UNIX, IBM AS/400, and IBM mainframes). Using Java, developers need to write only one version that can run on every platform.

1.3.8   Java Is Portable

Because Java is architecture-neutral, Java programs are portable. They can be run on any platform without being recompiled. Moreover, there are no platform-specific features in the Java language. In some languages, such as Ada, the largest integer varies on different platforms. But in Java, the range of the integer is the same on every platform, as is the behavior of arithmetic. The fixed range of the numbers makes the program portable.

The Java environment is portable to new hardware and operating systems. In fact, the Java compiler itself is written in Java.

1.3.9   Java's Performance

Java's performance is sometimes criticized. The execution of the bytecode is never as fast as it would be with a compiled language, such as C++. Because Java is interpreted, the bytecode is not directly executed by the system, but is run through the interpreter. However, its speed is more than adequate for most interactive applications, where the CPU is often idle, waiting for input or for data from other sources.

CPU speed has increased dramatically in the past few years, and this trend will continue. There are many ways to improve performance. Users of the earlier Sun Java Virtual Machine certainly noticed that Java was slow. However, the new JVM is significantly faster. The new JVM uses the technology known as *just-in-time compilation*, as shown in Figure 1.4. It compiles bytecode into native machine code, stores the native code, and reinvokes the native code when its bytecode is executed. Sun recently developed the Java HotSpot Performance Engine, which includes a compiler for optimizing the frequently used code. The HotSpot Performance Engine can be plugged into a JVM to dramatically boost its performance.

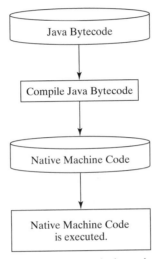

Figure 1.4   *The just-in-time compiler compiles bytecode to the native machine code.*

1.3.10   Java Is Multithreaded

Multithreading is a program's capability to perform several tasks simultaneously. For example, downloading a video file while playing the video would be considered multithreading. Multithread programming is smoothly integrated in Java, whereas in other languages you have to call procedures specific to the operating system to enable multithreading.

Multithreading is particularly useful in graphical user interface (GUI) and network programming. In GUI programming, there are many things going on at the same time. A user can listen to an audio recording while surfing a Web page. In network programming, a server can serve multiple clients at the same time. Multithreading is a necessity in multimedia and network programming.

1.3.11   Java Is Dynamic

Java was designed to adapt to an evolving environment. New code can be loaded on the fly without recompilation. There is no need for developers to create, and for users to install, major new software versions. New features can be incorporated transparently as needed.

1.4   World Wide Web, Java, and Beyond

The World Wide Web is an electronic information repository that can be accessed on the Internet from anywhere in the world. You can use the Web to book a hotel room, buy an airline ticket, register for a college course, download the *New York Times*, chat with friends, or listen to live radio. There are countless activities you can do on the Internet. Many people spend a good part of their computer time surfing the Web for fun and profit.

The Internet is the infrastructure of the Web. The Internet has been around for more than thirty years, but has only recently become popular. The colorful World Wide Web and sophisticated Web browsers are the major reason for its popularity.

The primary authoring language for the Web is the Hypertext Markup Language (HTML). HTML is a markup language: a simple language for laying out documents, linking documents on the Internet, and bringing images, sound, and video alive on the Web. However, it cannot interact with the user except through simple forms. Web pages in HTML are essentially static and flat.

Java initially became attractive because Java programs can be run from a Web browser. Java programs that run from a Web browser are called *applets*. Applets use a modern graphical user interface with buttons, text fields, text areas, radio buttons, and so on, to interact with users on the Web and process users' requests. Applets make the Web responsive, interactive, and fun to use. Figure 1.5 shows an applet running from a Web browser. To run applets from a Web browser, you need to use Netscape 6 or Internet Explorer 6, or higher.

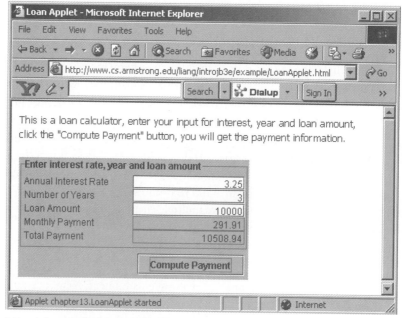

Figure 1.5   *A Java applet for computing loan payments is embedded in an HTML page. The user can use the applet to compute the loan payments.*

TIP

For a demonstration of Java applets, visit **java.sun.com/applets**. This site provides a rich Java resource as well as links to other cool applet demo sites. **java.sun.com** is the official Sun Java Web site.

Java can also be used to develop applications on the server side. These applications are called *Java servlets* or *JavaServer Pages*, which can be run from a Web server to generate dynamic Web pages. The Self-Test Web site for this book, as shown in Figure 1.6, was developed using Java servlets. The Web pages for the questions and answers are dynamically generated by the servlets.

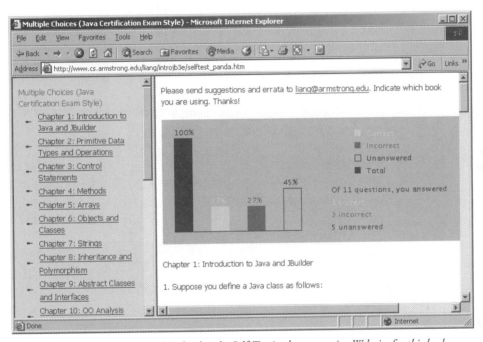

Figure 1.6 *Java was used to develop the Self-Test in the companion Web site for this book.*

Java is a versatile programming language. You can use it to develop applications on your desktop and on the server. You can also use it to develop applications for small hand-held devices, such as personal digital assistants and cell phones. Figure 1.7 shows a Java program that displays the calendar on a Palm PDA and on a cell phone.

Figure 1.7 *Java can be used to develop applications for hand-held and wireless devices, such as a Palm PDA (left) and a cell phone (right).*

1.5   The Java Language Specification and API

Computer languages have strict rules of usage. If you do not follow the rules when writing a program, the computer will be unable to understand it. Sun Microsystems, the originator of Java, intends to retain control of this important new computer language—and for a very good reason: to prevent it from losing its unified standards. The Java language specification and Java API define the Java standard.

The Java language specification is a technical definition of the language that includes the syntax and semantics of the Java programming language. The complete reference of the Java language specification can be found at **java.sun.com/docs/books/jls**.

The *application program interface* (API) contains predefined classes and interfaces for developing Java programs. The Java language specification is stable, but the API is still expanding. At the Sun Java Web site (**java.sun.com**), you can view and download the latest version and updates to the Java API.

Java was introduced in 1995. Sun announced the Java 2 platform in December 1998. Java 2 is the overarching brand that applies to current Java technology. There are three editions of the Java API: *Java 2 Standard Edition (J2SE)*, *Java 2 Enterprise Edition (J2EE)*, and *Java 2 Micro Edition (J2ME)*. Java is a full-fledged and powerful language that can be used in many ways. J2SE can be used to develop client-side stand-alone applications or applets. J2EE can be used to develop server-side applications, such as Java servlets and JavaServer Pages. J2ME can be used to develop applications for mobile devices, such as cell phones. This book uses J2SE to introduce Java programming.

1.6 JDK, Java IDE, and JBuilder

There are many versions of J2SE. The latest version is JDK 1.4, which will be covered in this book. Sun releases each version of J2SE with a *Java Development Toolkit* (JDK). For J2SE 1.4, the Java Development Toolkit is called JDK 1.4. The official name for JDK 1.4 is Java 2 SDK v 1.4. SDK stands for Software Development Toolkit. Since most Java programmers are familiar with the name JDK, this book uses the names Java SDK and JDK interchangeably.

JDK consists of a set of separate programs for developing and testing Java programs, each of which is invoked from a command line. Besides JDK, there are more than a dozen Java development packages on the market today. The major development tools are:

> JBuilder by Borland (**www.borland.com**)
> Sun ONE Studio by Sun (**java.sun.com**)
> Visual Café by WebGain (**www.webgain.com**)
> Visual Age for Java by IBM (**www.ibm.com**)

These tools provide an *integrated development environment* (IDE) for rapidly developing Java programs. Editing, compiling, building, debugging, and online help are integrated in one graphical user interface. Just enter source code in one window or open an existing file in a window, then click a button, menu item, or function key to compile the source code.

JBuilder is easy to learn and easy to use. The JBuilder development team made a significant effort to simplify the user interface and make it easy to navigate through the programs, projects, classes, packages, and code elements. As a result, JBuilder has fewer windows than Microsoft Visual J++ and WebGain Visual Café. This makes JBuilder an ideal tool for beginners and for students who have little programming experience.

JBuilder 9 is available in three versions: JBuilder Personal, JBuilder Developer, and JBuilder Enterprise.

■ The JBuilder Personal is ideal for beginners to learn the basics of Java programming. It is free for educational use and included on the companion CD-ROM. This book teaches Java programming with JBuilder Personal.

■ JBuilder Developer contains the essential components for developing Java applications and applets. It also contains the Borland JavaBeans components for creating database applications.

■ JBuilder Enterprise contains all the components in JBuilder Professional, plus support for creating distributed applications using CORBA, and for creating Web applications using Java servlets, JavaServer Pages, and XML.

1.7 A Simple Java Program

A Java program can be written in many ways. This book introduces Java applications and applets. *Applications* are stand-alone programs. This includes any program written with a high-level language. Applications can be executed from any computer with a Java interpreter. *Applets* are special kinds of Java programs that can run directly from a Java-compatible Web browser. Applets are suitable for deploying Web projects. Applets will be introduced in Chapter 14, "Applets."

Let us begin with a simple Java program that displays the message "Welcome to Java!"

Example 1.1 A Simple Application

Problem

Write a program that displays the message "Welcome to Java!" on the console.

Solution

The following code gives the solution to the problem.

Comments ──▶ ```
// Welcome.java: This application program prints Welcome to Java!
package chapter1;
```

*Class heading* ──▶
*Main method signature* ──▶
```
public class Welcome {   Class Name
  public static void main(String[] args) {
    System.out.println("Welcome to Java!");   String
  }
}
```

### Review

The first line in the code is the package statement. Its purpose is for grouping and organizing classes. In this book, I will use the package statement to group classes chapter-by-chapter. So all the classes in Chapter X will have the package statement:

```
package chapterx;
```

Every Java program must have at least one class. Each class begins with a class declaration that defines data and methods for the class. In this example, the class name is Welcome.
```

The class contains a method named main. The main method in this program contains the System.out.println statement. The main method is invoked by the interpreter.

In this program, println("Welcome to Java!") is actually the statement that prints the message. So why use the other statements in the program? Because Java, like any other programming language, has its own syntax, and you need to write code that obeys the syntax rules. The Java compiler will report syntax errors if your program violates the syntax rules.

 NOTE

You are probably wondering about such points as why the main method is declared this way and why System.out.println(...) is used to display a message to the console. Your questions cannot be fully answered yet. For the time being, you will just have to accept that this is how things are done. You will find the answers in the coming chapters.

1.8   Anatomy of the Java Program

The application program in Example 1.1 has the following components:

> Comments
> Reserved words
> Modifiers
> Statements
> Blocks
> Classes
> Methods
> The main method

To build a program, you need to understand these basic elements. They are explained in the sections that follow.

1.8.1   Comments

The first line in the program is a *comment* that documents what the program is and how the program is constructed. Comments help programmers and users to communicate and understand the program. Comments are not programming statements and are ignored by the compiler. In Java, comments are preceded by two slashes (//) on a line or enclosed between /* and */ on one or multiple lines. When the compiler sees //, it ignores all text after // on the same line. When it sees /*, it scans for the next */ and ignores any text between /* and */.

Here are examples of the two types of comments:

```
// This application program prints Welcome to Java!

/* This application program prints Welcome to Java! */

/* This application program
   prints Welcome to Java! */
```

 NOTE

In addition to the two comment styles, `//` and `/*`, Java supports comments of a special type, referred to as *javadoc comments*. javadoc comments begin with `/**` and end with `*/`. They are used for documenting classes, data, and methods. They can be extracted into an HTML file using JDK's `javadoc` command. For more information, visit

java.sun.com/j2se/javadoc/index.html

1.8.2   Packages

The second line in the program (`package chapter1;`) specifies a package name, `chapter1`, for the class `Welcome`. The package statement is optional. If it is used, it must be the first statement in the program except for comments.

1.8.3   Reserved Words

Reserved words, or *keywords*, are words that have a specific meaning to the compiler and cannot be used for other purposes in the program. For example, when the compiler sees the word `class`, it understands that the word after `class` is the name for the class. Other reserved words in Example 1.1 are `public`, `static`, and `void`. Their use will be introduced later in the book.

TIP

Because Java is case-sensitive, `public` is a reserved word, but `Public` is not. Nonetheless, for clarity and readability, it would be best to avoid using reserved words in other forms. (See Appendix A, "Java Keywords.")

1.8.4   Modifiers

Java uses certain reserved words called *modifiers* that specify the properties of the data, methods, and classes and how they can be used. Examples of modifiers are `public` and `static`. Other modifiers are `private`, `final`, `abstract`, and `protected`. A `public` datum, method, or class can be accessed by other classes. A `private` datum or method cannot be accessed by other classes. Modifiers are discussed in Chapter 6, "Objects and Classes."

1.8.5   Statements

A *statement* represents an action or a sequence of actions. The statement `System.out.println("Welcome to Java!")` in the program in Example 1.1 is a statement to display the greeting "Welcome to Java!" Every statement in Java ends with a semicolon (;).

1.8.6   Blocks

The braces in the program form the *block* that groups the components of the program. In Java, each block begins with an open brace ({) and ends with a closing brace (}). Every class has a *class block* that groups the data and methods of the class. Every method has a *method block* that groups the statements in the method. Blocks can be *nested*, meaning that one block can be placed within another, as shown in the following code.

```
public class Test {
  public static void main(String[] args) {                Class block
    System.out.println("Welcome to Java!");    Method block
  }
}
```

1.8.7   Classes

The *class* is the essential Java construct. To program in Java, you must understand classes and be able to write and use them. The mystery of classes will be unveiled throughout the book. For now, though, it is enough to know that a program is defined by using one or more classes. Every Java program has at least one class, and programs are contained inside a class definition enclosed in blocks. The class can contain data declarations and method declarations.

1.8.8   Methods

What is `System.out.println`? `System.out` is known as the *standard output object*. `println` is a method in the object, which consists of a collection of statements that performs a sequence of operations to display a message to the standard output device. If you run the program from the command window, the output from the `System.out.println` is displayed in the command window. The method can be used even without fully understanding the details of how it works. It is used by invoking a statement with a string argument. The string argument is enclosed in parentheses. In this case, the argument is `"Welcome to Java!"` You can call the same `println` method with a different argument to print a different message.

1.8.9   The *main* Method

You can create your own method. Every Java application must have a user-declared `main` method that defines where the program begins. The `main` method provides the control of program flow. The Java interpreter executes the application by invoking the `main` method.

The `main` method looks like this:

```
public static void main(String[] args) {
  // Statements;
}
```

1.9   Getting Started with JBuilder

Now turn your attention to developing Java programs using JBuilder. Assume you have successfully installed JBuilder Personal on your machine. Start JBuilder from Windows, Linux, or Solaris. The main JBuilder user interface appears, as shown in Figure 1.8. If you don't see the Welcome project, choose Welcome Project (Sample) from the Help menu.

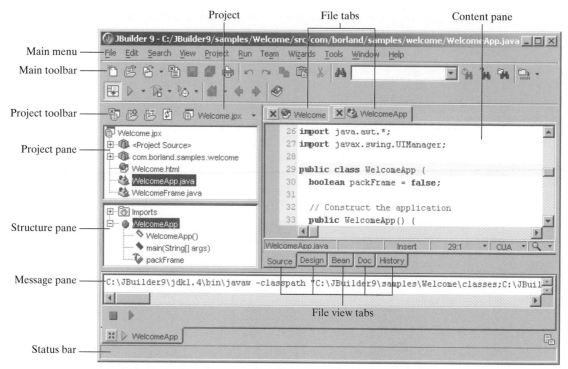

Figure 1.8   *The JBuilder user interface is a single window that performs functions for editing, compiling, debugging, and running programs.*

 NOTE

The screen shots in this book were taken from JBuilder 9 Personal. Each new printing of this book bundles the newest version of JBuilder on the companion CD-ROM. If the screen shots in a future version differ from JBuilder 9, they will be posted on the Web site.

⚙ **JBUILDER TIP**

I recommend that you install JBuilder in the default folder `c:\JBuilder9` for JBuilder9. If your JBuilder is installed in a different folder (e.g., `c:\mySoftware\ JBuilder9`), you have to reconfigure JDK to set a new JDK home path. For more information, see the first question in "JBuilder Frequently Asked Questions" at **www.prenhall.com/liang/introjb3e.html**.

JBUILDER NOTE

The screen shots in this book are from JBuilder Personal. *If you use JBuilder Deveoper or JBuilder Enterprise, your screen may look slightly different.*

The JBuilder user interface presents a single window for managing Java projects, browsing files, compiling, running, and debugging programs. This user interface is called *AppBrowser*.

Traditional IDE tools use many windows to accommodate editing, debugging, browsing information, and the various other development tasks. As a result, finding the window you need is often difficult. Because it is easy to get lost, beginners may be intimidated. For this reason, some new programmers prefer to use separate utilities, such as the JDK command-line tools, for developing programs.

Borland is aware of the usability problem and has made a significant effort to simply the JBuilder user interface. JBuilder introduces the AppBrowser window, which enables you to explore, edit, design, and debug projects all in one unified window.

The AppBrowser window primarily consists of the main menu, main toolbar, status bar, project pane, structure pane, and content pane.

1.9.1 The Main Menu

The main menu is similar to that of other Windows applications and provides most of the commands you need to use JBuilder, including those for creating, editing, compiling, running, and debugging programs. The menu items are enabled and disabled in response to the current context.

1.9.2 The Toolbar

The toolbar provides buttons for several frequently used commands on the menu bar. Clicking a toolbar is faster than using the menu bar. For some commands, you also can use function keys or keyboard shortcuts. For example, you can save a file in three ways:

- Select *File, Save* from the menu bar.
- Click the "save" toolbar button.
- Use the keyboard shortcut Ctrl+S.

 JBUILDER TIP

You can display a label, known as *ToolTip*, for a button by pointing the mouse to the button without clicking.

1.9.3   The Status Bar

The status bar displays a message that alerts the user to the operation status, such as file saved for the Save file command and compilation successful for the Compilation command.

1.9.4   The Project Pane

The *project pane* displays the contents of one or more projects opened in the App-Browser. It consists of the following items, as shown in Figure 1.9.

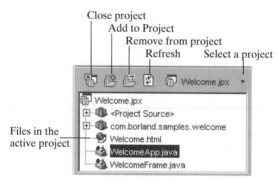

Figure 1.9   *The project pane manages JBuilder projects.*

- A small toolbar with four buttons (Close Project ![icon], Add To Project ![icon], Remove From Project ![icon], and Refresh ![icon]).

- A drop-down list of all opened projects.

- A tree view of all the files that make up the active project.

The project pane shows a list of one or more files. The project (.jpx) file appears first. Attached to it is a list of the files in the project. The list can include .java, .html, text, or image files. You select a file in the project pane by clicking it. The content pane and the structure pane display information about the selected file. As you select different files in the project pane, each one will be represented in the content and structure panes.

The project pane shown in Figure 1.8 contains three files. The Add button is used to add new files to the project, and the Remove button to remove files from the project. For example, you can remove Welcome.html by selecting the file in the project pane and clicking the Remove button. You can then add the file back to the project, as follows:

1. Click the Add button to display the Open dialog box shown in Figure 1.10.

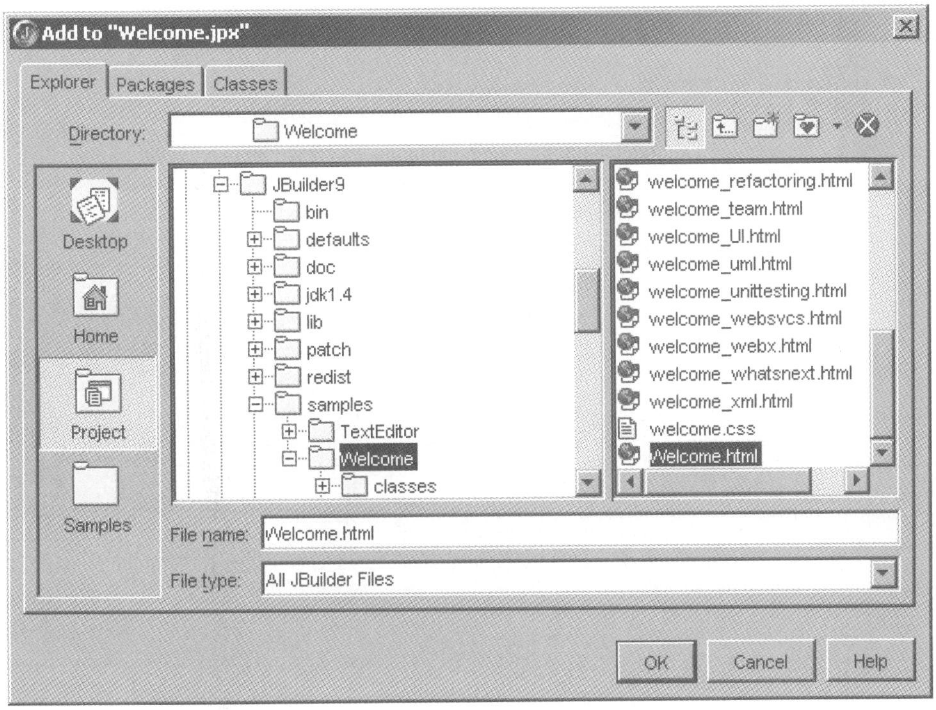

Figure 1.10 *The Open dialog box enables you to open an existing file.*

2. Open Welcome.html. You will see Welcome.html displayed in the project pane.

☼ **JBUILDER TIP**
You can select multiple files by clicking the files with the CTRL key pressed, or select consecutive files with the SHIFT key pressed.

1.9.5 The Content Pane

The content pane displays all the opened files as a set of tabs. To open a file in the content pane, double-click it in the project pane. The content pane displays the detailed content of the selected file. The editor or viewer used is determined by the file's extension. If you click the WelcomeApp.java file in the project pane, for example, you will see four tabs (Source, Design, Bean, Doc, and History) at the bottom of the content pane (see Figure 1.8). If you select the Source tab, you will see the JBuilder Java source code editor. This is a full-featured, syntax-highlighted programming editor.

If you select Welcome.html in the project pane, you will see the content pane become an HTML browser, as shown in Figure 1.11. If you choose the Source tab, you can view and edit the HTML code in the content pane, as shown in Figure 1.12.

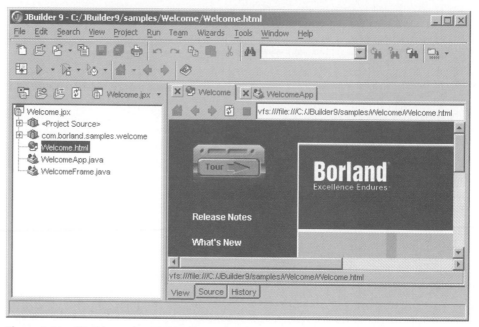

Figure 1.11   *JBuilder renders HTML files in the content pane.*

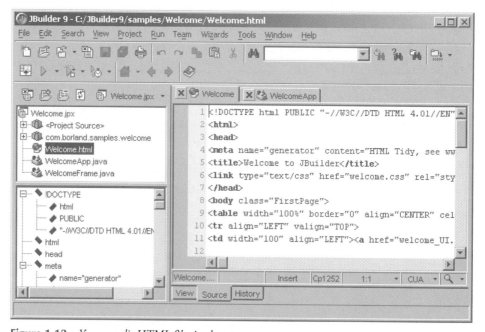

Figure 1.12   *You can edit HTML files in the content pane.*

1.9.6   The Structure Pane

The *structure pane* displays the structural information about the files you selected in the project pane. All the items displayed in the structure pane are in the form of a hierarchical indexed list. The expand symbol in front of an item indicates that it contains subitems. You can see the subitems by clicking on the expand symbol.

You can also use the structure pane as a quick navigational tool to the various structural elements in the file. If you select the WelcomeFrame.java file, for example, you will see classes, variables, and methods in the structure pane. If you then click on any of those elements in the structure pane, the content pane will move to and highlight it in the source code.

If you click on the jMenuFile item in the structure pane, as shown in Figure 1.13, the content pane moves to and highlights the statement that defines the jMenuFile data field. This provides a much faster way to browse and find the elements of a file than scrolling through it.

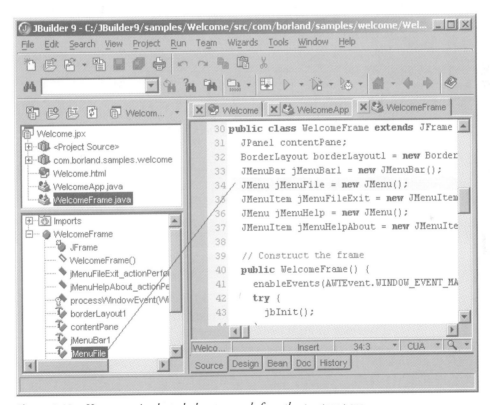

Figure 1.13   *You can cruise through the source code from the structure pane.*

1.10   Creating a Project

To create programs in JBuilder, you have to first create a project. A project is like a holder that ties all the files together. The information about each JBuilder project is stored in a project file with a .jpx file extension. The project file contains a list of all the files and project settings and properties. JBuilder uses this information to load and save all the files in the project and compile and run the programs. For simplicity, this book creates one project for each chapter to hold all the examples in that chapter. The project is created as follows:

1. Choose *File, New Project* to bring up the Project wizard dialog box, as shown in Figure 1.14.

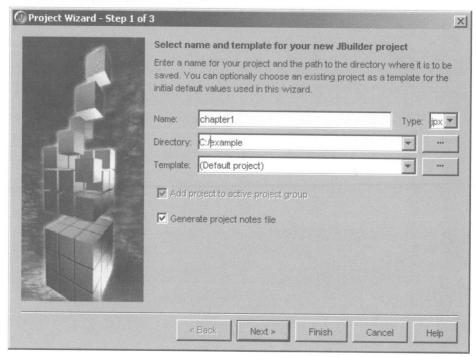

Figure 1.14   *The project wizard dialog box enables you to specify the project file with other optional information.*

2. Type `chapter1` in the Project name field. Type `c:/example` in the Directory field. Click *Next* to display Step 2 of 3 of the Project wizard, as shown in Figure 1.15.

3. Type `c:/example` in the Output path, `c:/example/bak` in the Backup path, `c:/example` in the Working directory Click *Next* to display Step 3 of 3 of the Project wizard. Set `c:/example` for the Source path, as shown in Figure 1.15. Click *Next* to display Step 3 of 3 of the Project wizard, as shown in Figure 1.16.

4. Fill in the title, author, company, and description fields. These optional fields provide a description for the project. For simplicity, uncheck *Enable source package discovery and compilation.*

5. Click *Finish.* The new project is displayed in the project pane, as shown in Figure 1.17. The Project wizard created the project file (`chapter1.jpx`) and an

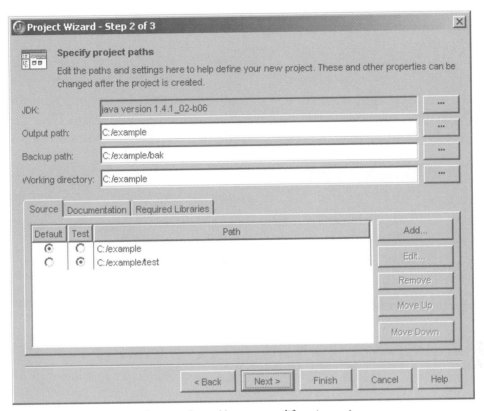

Figure 1.15   *Project wizard Step 2 of 3 enables you to modify project settings.*

HTML file (`chapter1.html`), and placed them in `c:\example`. The project file stores the information about the project, and the HTML file is used to describe the project. You cannot edit the project file manually; it is modified automatically, however, whenever you add or remove files from the project or set project options.

 JBUILDER NOTE

JBuilder automatically generates many backup files. I use **bak** as the root directory for all these backup files so that they can be easily located and removed.

IMPORTANT JBUILDER CAUTION

Creating a project is a preliminary step before developing Java programs. Creating projects incorrectly is a common problem for new JBuilder users, and can lead to frustrating mistakes. To avoid these, create a package in a consistent and uniform way for all your projects. You may create your project exactly as shown in this section, or change the word *example* to your name, like *smith*, so that your project source path and output path are c:\smith in Figure 1.15.

Uncheck it

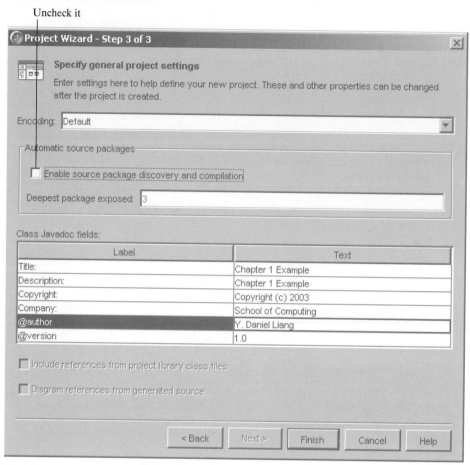

Figure 1.16 *Project wizard Step 3 of 3 collects optional information for the project.*

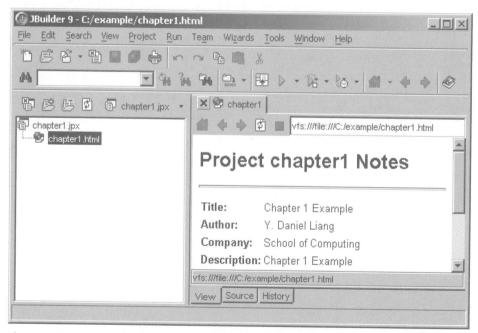

Figure 1.17 *A new project is created with the .jpx file and .html file.*

1.11   Creating, Compiling, and Executing a Java Program

You have to create your program and compile it before it can be executed. This process is iterative, as shown in Figure 1.18. If your program has compilation errors, you have to fix them by modifying the program, then recompile it. If your program has runtime errors or does not produce the correct result, you have to modify the program, recompile it, and execute it again.

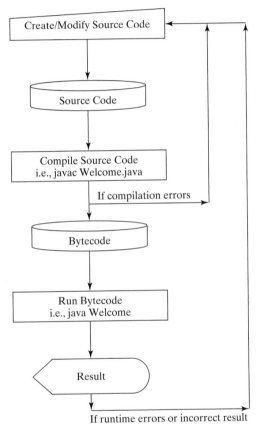

Figure 1.18   *The Java programming-development process consists of creating/modifying source code, compiling, and executing programs.*

You can use any text editor to create and edit a Java source code file, or use an IDE like Builder or Sun ONE Studio. This file must end with the extension .java and should have the exact same name as the public class name. For example, the file for the source code in Example 1.1 should be named Welcome.java, since the public class name is Welcome.

To compile the program is to translate the Java source code into Java bytecode using the software called a *compiler*. The Java compiler is bundled in JDK 1.4 and integrated with IDEs.

If there are no syntax errors, the *compiler* generates a file named **Welcome.class**. This file is called the *bytecode*. The bytecode is similar to machine instructions, but is architecture-neutral and can run on any platform that has the Java interpreter and runtime environment. This is one of Java's primary advantages: *Java bytecode can run on a variety of hardware platforms and operating systems.*

To execute a Java program is to run the program's bytecode using the Java interpreter. The Java interpreter is integrated with IDEs.

The following sections demonstrate creating, compiling, and running Java programs from JBuilder.

1.11.1   Creating a Java Program

There are many ways to create a Java program in JBuilder. This book will show you how to use various wizards to create certain types of Java programs. In this section, you will learn how to create Java programs using the Class wizard.

The following are the steps in creating a Java program for Example 1.1:

1. Open the chapter1.jpx project if it is not in the project pane. To open it, choose *File, Reopen* to display a submenu consisting of the most recently opened projects and files. Select the project if it is in the menu. Otherwise, choose *File, Open* to locate and open chapter1.jpx. The project file is the one with the ( ) icon.

2. Choose *File, New Class* to display the Class wizard, as shown in Figure 1.19.

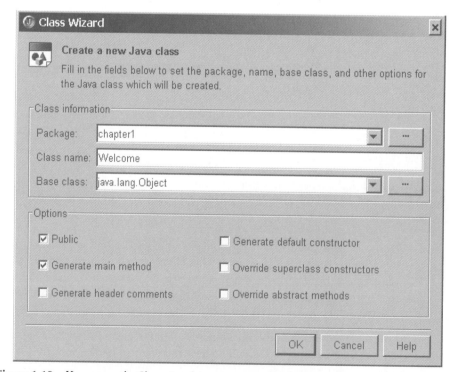

Figure 1.19   *You can use the Class wizard to create a template for a new class.*

28

3. In the Class wizard, type Welcome in the Class name field, and check the options *Public* and *Generate main method* in the Options section, as shown in Figure 1.19. Click *OK* to generate Welcome.java, as shown in Figure 1.20.

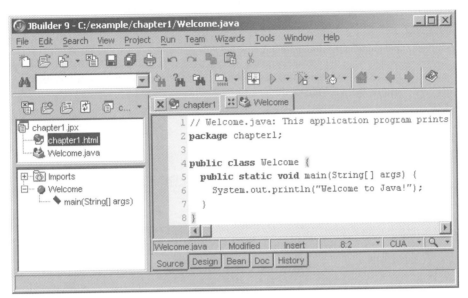

Figure 1.20 *The program Welcome.java is generated by the Class wizard.*

4. Type Example 1.1 in the content pane, as shown in Figure 1.21. Select *File, Save All* to save all your work. You should see a confirmation message in the status bar indicating that the files have been saved.

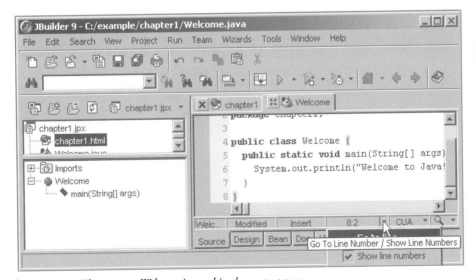

Figure 1.21 *The program Welcome is typed in the content pane.*

JBUILDER TIP

The line numbers are not part of the source code. You can hide it by unchecking the *Show line numbers* option at the line number status bar of the content pane, as shown in Figure 1.21.

⬥ **JBUILDER NOTE**

As you type, the code-completion assistance may automatically come up to give you suggestions for completing the code. For instance, when you type a dot (.) after `System` and pause for a second, JBuilder displays a popup menu with hints for completing the code, as shown in Figure 1.22. You can then select from the menu to complete the code.

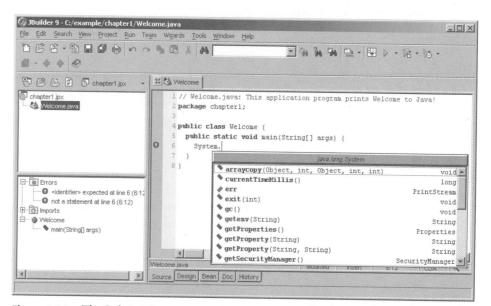

Figure 1.22 *The Code Insight popup menu is automatically displayed to help you complete the code.*

 JBUILDER TIP

If you don't want the code-completion assistance, you can turn it off by unchecking *Auto popup MemberInsight* and *Auto popup ParameterInsight* in the CodeInsight tab of the Editor Options dialog, as shown in Figure 1.23. To display the Editor Options dialog, choose *Tools, Editor Options*.

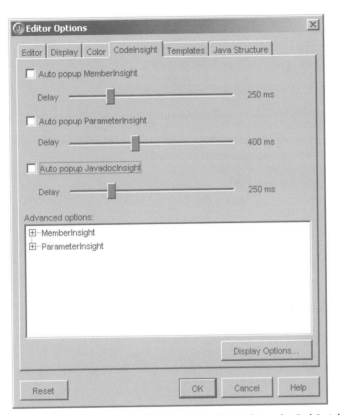

Figure 1.23   *You can specify whether and how to use Code Insight on the CodeInsight tab of the Editor Options dialog.*

 CAUTION

Java source programs are case-sensitive. It would be wrong, for example, to replace `main` in the program with `Main`. Program file names are case-sensitive on UNIX and generally not case-sensitive on PCs, but file names are case-sensitive in JBuilder.

◈ IMPORTANT JBUILDER NOTE

JBuilder requires that the source code file be stored in `SourcePath\PackageName`. For example, `Welcome.java` is stored in `c:\example\chapter1`, since the Source path is set to `c:\example` (see Figure 1.15) and the package name is `chapter1`.

IMPORTANT JBUILDER CAUTION

Students should follow the instructions of their instructors or in this book to create projects and classes that avoid the JBuilder-related errors. If the source code is not placed in the right place, JBuilder would report the error indicating that *the source file does not match the directory.*

1.11.2   Compiling a Java Program

To compile Welcome.java, use one of the following methods. (Be sure that Welcome.java is selected in the project pane.)

- Select *Project, Make "Welcome.java"* from the menu bar.

- Click the *Make* toolbar button ( ).

- Point to Welcome.java in the project pane, right-click the mouse button to display a popup menu (see Figure 1.24), and choose *Make* from the menu. (I find this method most useful.)

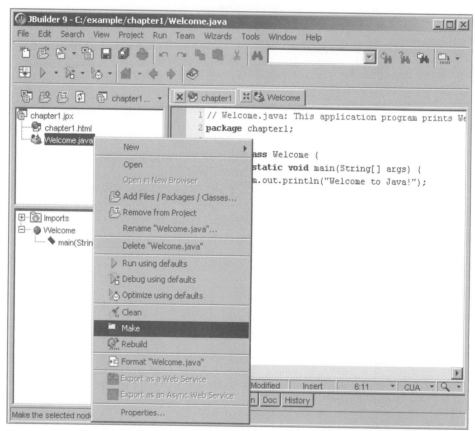

Figure 1.24   *Point the mouse to the file in the project pane, and right-click it to display a popup menu that contains the commands for processing the file.*

The compilation status is displayed on the status bar. If there are no syntax errors, the *compiler* generates a file named Welcome.class.

 JBUILDER NOTE

The bytecode is stored in `OutputPath\PackageName`. Therefore, `Welcome.class` is stored in `c:\example\chapter1`, since the Output path is set to `c:\example` (see Figure 1.15) and the package name is chapter1. The file structures for the examples in this book are shown in Figure 1.25.

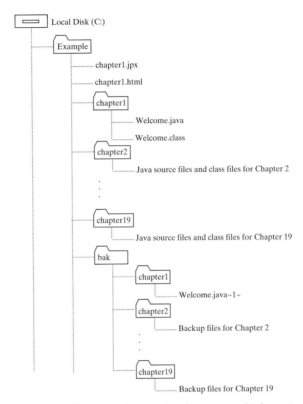

Figure 1.25 *Welcome.java and Welcome.class are placed in c:\example\chapter1.*

JBUILDER TIP

If your speaker is on, you will hear a sound when compilation is completed without errors and a different sound if it completed with errors. You can turn off the sound by unchecking the *Auto feedback enabled* option in the Audio tab in the IDE Options dialog, as shown in Figure 1.26. To display the IDE Options dialog, choose *Tools, IDE Options.*

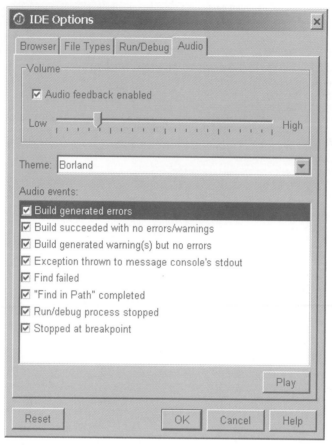

Figure 1.26   *You can set the options for audios in JBuilder.*

1.11.3   Executing a Java Application

To run Welcome.class, point to Welcome.java in the project pane and right-click the mouse button to display a popup menu. Choose *Run Using Defaults* from the popup menu.

◈ **JBUILDER NOTE**

You could run a program by selecting *Run, Run Project* from the main menu, or by clicking the Run toolbar button ( ), but then you would have to create a custom runtime configuration in the Run tab of the Properties dialog box. It is more convenient to run a program from the project pane using the default runtime configuration.

◈ **JBUILDER NOTE**

The Run command invokes the Compile command if the program is not compiled or was modified after the last compilation.

When this program executes, JBuilder displays the output in the message pane, as shown in Figure 1.27.

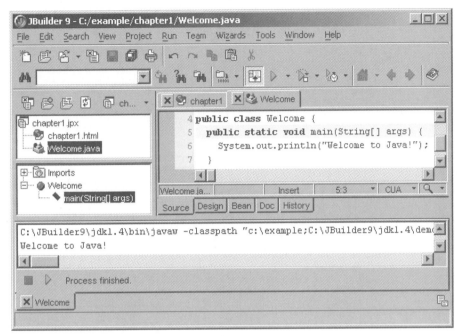

Figure 1.27   *The execution result is shown in the message pane.*

 JBUILDER TIP
If the message pane is not displayed, choose *View, Messages* to display it.

1.12   Displaying Text in a Message Dialog Box

Example 1.1 displays the text in the message pane, as shown in Figure 1.27. You can rewrite the program to display the text in a message dialog box. To do so, you need to use the showMessageDialog method in the JOptionPane class. JOptionPane is one of the many predefined classes in the Java system that can be reused rather than "reinventing the wheel." You can use the showMessageDialog box to display any text in a message dialog box (or simply dialog).

Example 1.2 Using Message Dialog Boxes

Problem

Write a program that displays text in a message dialog box.

Solution

The following code gives the solution to the problem. Figure 1.28 shows the text "Welcome to Java!" displayed in a message dialog box.

continues

Example 1.2 continued

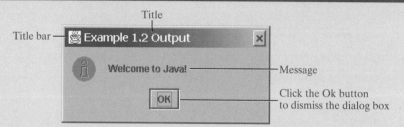

Figure 1.28   *The string Welcome to Java! is displayed in a message dialog box.*

```
1    /* WelcomeInMessageDialogBox.java:
2       This application program displays Welcome to Java!
3       in a message dialog box. */
4    package chapter1;
5
6    import javax.swing.JOptionPane;
7
8    public class WelcomeInMessageDialogBox {
9      public static void main(String[] args) {
10       // Display Welcome to Java! in a message dialog box
11       JOptionPane.showMessageDialog(null, "Welcome to Java!",
12         "Example 1.2 Output", JOptionPane.INFORMATION_MESSAGE);
13
14       // Exit the program
15       System.exit(0);
16     }
17   }
```

Review

The line numbers are not part of the program, but are displayed for reference purposes.

This program uses two Java classes: JOptionPane (Line 11) and System (Line 15). Java's predefined classes are grouped into packages. JOptionPane is in the javax.swing package, and System is in the java.lang package. JOptionPane is imported to the program using the import statement in Line 6 so that the compiler can locate the class. The System class is not imported because it is in the java.lang package. All the classes in the java.lang package are implicitly imported in every Java program.

◈ NOTE

If you replace JOptionPane in Line 11 with javax.swing.JOptionPane, you don't need to import it in Line 6. javax.swing.JOptionPane is the complete name for the JOptionPane class.

The showMessageDialog method is known as a *static* method. Such a method should be invoked by using the class name followed by a dot operator (.) and the method name with arguments. Static methods will be introduced in Chapter 4, "Methods." The showMessageDialog method can be invoked with four arguments, as in Lines 11–12.

```
JOptionPane.showMessageDialog(null, "Welcome to Java!",
  "Example 1.2", JOptionPane.INFORMATION_MESSAGE));
```

The first argument can always be `null`. `null` is a Java keyword that will be fully introduced in Part II, "Object-Oriented Programming." The second argument can be a string for text to be displayed. The third argument is the title of the message box. The fourth argument can be `JOptionPane.INFORMATION_MESSAGE`, which causes the icon ( ) to be displayed in the message box.

◈ **NOTE**

There are several ways to use the `showMessageDialog` method. For the time being, all you need to know is how to invoke the `showMessageDialog` method to display text, using a statement like this one:

```
JOptionPane.showMessageDialog(null, x,
    y, JOptionPane.INFORMATION_MESSAGE));
```

where *x* is a string for the text to be displayed, and *y* is a string for the title of the message dialog box.

The `exit` method in the `System` class is invoked as follows in Line 15.

```
System.exit(0);
```

Like the `showMessageDialog` method, `exit` is also a static method. Invoking this method terminates the program. The argument 0 indicates that the program is terminated normally. In Example 1.1, you did not use the `exit` method, and the program terminated at the end of the *main* method. Why do you have to use the `exit` method in this program? The next note explains the reason.

◈ **NOTE**

When your program starts, a thread is spawned to run the program. When the `showMessageDialog` is invoked, a separate thread is spawned to run this method. The thread is not terminated even after you close the dialog box. To terminate the thread, you have to invoke the `exit` method. If you run the program without invoking the `exit` method in Line 15, the thread is not terminated. You have to press CTRL+C in the command window to stop the thread.

Chapter Summary

- Java was developed by a team led by James Gosling at Sun Microsystems.

- Java is an Internet programming language. Since its inception in 1995, it has quickly become a premier language for building software.

- Java is platform-independent, meaning that you can write a program once and run it anywhere.

- Java is a simple, object-oriented programming language with built-in graphics programming, input and output, exception handling, networking, and multi-threading support.

- Java programs can be embedded in HTML pages and downloaded by Web browsers to bring live animation and interaction to Web clients.

- Java source files end with the .java extension. Every class is compiled into a separate file called a bytecode that has the same name as the class and ends with the .class extension.

- Every Java program is a set of class definitions. The keyword `class` introduces a class definition. The contents of the class are included in a block. A block begins with an opening brace ({) and ends with a closing brace (}). Methods are contained in a class.

- A Java application must have a `main` method. The `main` method is the entry point where the application program starts when it is executed.

- You can display output to the console using `System.out.println` method, or can display a message dialog box using the `JOptionPane.showMessageDialog` method.

- The statement `System.exit(0)` terminates all the threads in the program.

- Comments are not programming statements and are ignored by the compiler. In Java, comments are preceded by two slashes (`//`) on a line or enclosed between `/*` and `*/` on one or multiple lines.

- The package statement is optional. If it is used, it must be the first statement in the program except for comments.

- *Reserved words,* or *keywords,* are words that have a specific meaning to the compiler and cannot be used for other purposes in the program.

- A *statement* represents an action or a sequence of actions.

- The braces in the program form the *block* that groups the components of the program.

- JBuilder 9 is available in three versions: JBuilder Personal, JBuilder Developer, and JBuilder Enterprise.

- To create programs in JBuilder, you have to first create a project. A project is like a holder that ties all the files together. The information about each JBuilder project is stored in a project file with a .jpx file extension. The project file contains a list of all the files and project settings and properties.

- You use the Project wizard in JBuilder to create a project and specify the output path and the source path.

- You can create a class using the Class wizard in JBuilder. The source file (.java) for class is stored in `sourcepath/packageName`.

- After the program is compiled, its .class file is stored in `outputpath/packageName`.

Review Questions

1.1 Briefly summarize the history of Java.

1.2 Java is object-oriented. What are the advantages of object-oriented programming?

1.3 Can Java run on any machine? What is needed to run Java on a computer?

1.4 What are the input and output of a Java compiler?

1.5 List some Java development tools. Are tools like Sun ONE Studio and JBuilder different languages from Java, or are they dialects or extensions of Java?

1.6 What is the relationship between Java and HTML?

1.7 Explain the Java keywords. List some Java keywords you learned in this chapter.

1.8 Is Java case-sensitive? What is the case for Java keywords?

1.9 What is the Java source filename extension, and what is the Java bytecode filename extension?

1.10 What is a comment? What is the syntax for a comment in Java? Is the comment ignored by the compiler?

1.11 What is the statement to display a string on the console? What is the statement to display the message "Hello world" in a message dialog box?

1.12 Identify and fix the errors in the following code:

```
public class Welcome {
  public void Main(String[] args) {
    System.out.println('Welcome to Java!);
  }
)
```

1.13 How do you create a Java project in JBuilder?

1.14 How do you compile a Java program in JBuilder?

1.15 How do you run a Java program in JBuilder?

1.16 Suppose the output path is c:\smith, and the package statement in the source code is package homework. Where is the .class file stored after successful compilation in JBuilder?
   a. c:\jbuilder\projects\classes
   b. c:\smith
   c. c:\smith\homework
   d. c:\smith\homework\csci1301

1.17 Suppose the source path is c:\smith, and you specified exercise1 in the Package field in the Class wizard, and Test in the Class name field. Where is the generated Test.java stored?

     a. c:\jbuilder\projects\src
     b. c:\smith
     c. c:\smith\exercise1
     d. c:\smith\exercise1\test

1.18 Suppose you received a compilation error: *"Welcome.java": Error #: 901 : package . stated in source C:\example\chapter1\Welcome.java does not match directory chapter1.* What would be wrong?

Programming Exercises

1.1 (Creating projects and programs in JBuilder) The text created a project named *chapter1*. Now create your project. Use your name as the project name. Create a Java application named WelcomeHTML.java in the project. WelcomeHTML.java displays the message "Welcome to HTML" using `System.out.println` on the message pane in JBuilder and `JOptionPane.showMessageDialog` on a dialog box.

PRIMITIVE DATA TYPES AND OPERATIONS

Objectives

- ◉ To write Java programs to perform simple calculations.

- ◉ To understand identifiers, variables, and constants.

- ◉ To learn Java primitive data types: `byte`, `short`, `int`, `long`, `float`, `double`, `char`, and `boolean`.

- ◉ To use Java operators and write Java expressions.

- ◉ To program with assignment statements and assignment expressions.

- ◉ To know the rules governing operand evaluation order, operator precedence, and operator associativity.

- ◉ To obtain input from the keyboard using the dialog boxes.

- ◉ To become familiar with Java documentation, programming style, and naming conventions.

- ◉ To distinguish syntax errors, runtime errors, and logic errors.

- ◉ To trace the execution of the program using the debugger in JBuilder.

- ◉ To run Java programs from the command line.

- ◉ To get online help from JBuilder.

2.1   Introduction

In the preceding chapter, you learned how to create, compile, and run a Java program. In this chapter, you will be introduced to Java primitive data types and related subjects, such as variables, constants, data types, operators, and expressions. You will learn how to write programs using primitive data types, input and output, and simple calculations.

2.2   Writing Simple Programs

To begin, let's look at a simple program that computes the area of a circle. The program reads in the radius of the circle and displays its area. The program will use variables to store the radius and the area, and will use an expression to compute the area.

Writing this program involves designing algorithms and data structures, as well as translating algorithms into programming codes. An *algorithm* describes how a problem is solved in terms of the actions to be executed, and it specifies the order in which the actions should be executed. Algorithms can help the programmer plan a program before writing it in a programming language. The algorithm for this program can be described as follows:

1. Read in the radius.

2. Compute the area using the following formula:

$$\text{area} = \text{radius} \times \text{radius} \times \pi$$

3. Display the area.

Many of the problems you will meet when taking an introductory course in programming using this text can be described with simple, straightforward algorithms. As your education progresses, and you take courses on data structures or on algorithm design and analysis, you will encounter complex problems that require sophisticated solutions. You will need to design accurate, efficient algorithms with appropriate data structures in order to solve such problems.

Data structures involve data representation and manipulation. Java provides data types for representing integers, floating-point numbers (i.e., decimal numbers with optional fractional parts), characters, and Boolean types. These types are known as *primitive data types*. Java also supports array and string types as objects. Some advanced data structures, such as stacks, sets, and lists, have built-in implementation in Java.

To novice programmers, coding is a daunting task. When you *code*, you translate an algorithm into a programming language understood by the computer. You already know that every Java program begins with a class declaration in which the keyword `class` is followed by the class name. Assume that you have chosen `ComputeArea` as the class name. The outline of the program would look like this:

```
public class ComputeArea {
  // Data and methods to be given later
}
```

As you know, every application must have a `main` method that controls the execution of the program. So the program is expanded as follows:

```
public class ComputeArea {
  public static void main(String[] args) {
    // Step 1: Read in radius

    // Step 2: Compute area

    // Step 3: Display the area
  }
}
```

The program needs to read the radius entered by the user from the keyboard. This raises two important issues:

■ Reading the radius.

■ Storing the radius in the program.

Let's address the second issue first. In order to store the radius, the program needs to declare a symbol called a *variable* that will represent the radius. Variables are used to store data and computational results in the program.

Rather than using x and y, choose descriptive names: in this case, radius for radius, and area for area. Specify their data types to let the compiler know what radius and area are, indicating whether they are integer, float, or something else. Declare radius and area as double-precision floating-point numbers. The program can be expanded as follows:

```
public class ComputeArea {
  public static void main(String[] args) {
    double radius;
    double area;

    // Step 1: Read in radius

    // Step 2: Compute area

    // Step 3: Display the area
  }
}
```

The program declares radius and area as double-variables. The reserved word double indicates that radius and area are double-precision floating-point values stored in the computer.

The first step is to read in radius. Reading a number is not a simple matter. For the time being, let us assign a fixed number to radius in the program. In Section 2.14, "Getting Input from Input Dialogs," you will learn how to obtain a numeric value from an input dialog.

The second step is to compute area by assigning the expression radius * radius * 3.14159 to area.

In the final step, print area on the console by using the System.out.println method.

The program is completed in Example 2.1.

Example 2.1 Computing the Area of a Circle

Problem

Write a program that assigns a radius and computes the area. It concludes by displaying the area.

Solution

The following code gives the solution to the problem.

Comments ➤
```
// ComputeArea.java: Compute the area of a circle
   package chapter2;

   public class ComputeArea    ◄── Class Name
   {
     /** Main method */
     public static void main(String[] args)    ◄── Main Method Signature
     {
       double radius;    ◄── Variable
       double area;

       // Assign a radius
       radius = 20;    ◄── End of a Statement

       // Compute area
       area = radius*radius*3.14159;    ◄── Expression

       // Display results
       System.out.println("The area for the circle of radius " +
         radius + " is " + area);
     }
   }
```

Data Type ➤ `double` `radius`

Assignment — `radius = 20;`

Review

The plus sign ($+$) in the System.out.println("The area for the circle of radius " + radius + " is " + area) statement means to concatenate strings if one of the operands is a string. If both operands are numbers, the $+$ operator will add them.

Suppose that i = 1 and j = 2, what is the output of the following statement?

```
System.out.println("i + j is " + i + j);
```

The output is "i + j is 12" because "i + j is " is concatenated with the value of i first. To force i + j to be executed first, enclose i + j in the parentheses, as follows:

```
System.out.println("i + j is " + i + j);
```

CAUTION

A string constant should not cross lines in the source code. Thus the following statement would result in a compilation error:

```
System.out.println("Introduction to Java Programming,
  by Y. Daniel Liang");
```

To fix the error, break the string into substrings, and use the concatenation operator (+) to combine them:

```
System.out.println("Introduction to Java Programming, " +
  "by Y. Daniel Liang");
```

2.3   Running Example 2.1 in JBuilder

All the examples in chapter 1 are grouped into package chapter1. All the examples in this chapter are grouped into package chapter2. To create this package, choose *File, New Project* to display the Project wizard, as shown in Figure 2.1. Type chapter2 in the Name field and c:/example in the Directory field. Click Next to display Step 2 of 3 of the Project wizard, as shown in Figure 2.2. Set the output path to c:/example, backup path to c:/example/bak, working directory to c:/example, and source path to c:/example. Click *Finish* to create the project.

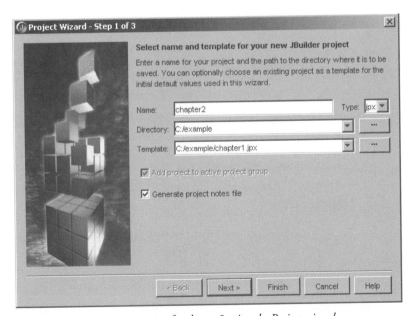

Figure 2.1   *You can create a new project for chapter2 using the Project wizard.*

☼ **JBUILDER TIP**

You can select the project you want to use as a template for the present project in the Template field. The present project will have the same path settings as the templae project.

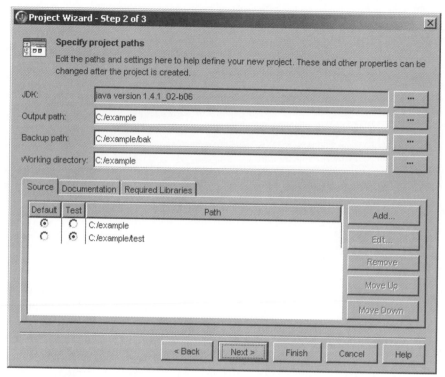

Figure 2.2 *Make sure the output path, backup path, working directory, and source path are set correctly.*

Choose *File, New Class* to display the Class wizard, as shown in Figure 2.3. Type chapter2 in the Package field and ComputeArea in the Class name field. Check the options *Public* and *Generate main method*, and click *OK* to generate the class.

Type the contents of the ComputeArea class in Example 2.1 in the content pane and run the program by choosing *Run Using Defaults* from the context menu of ComputeArea.java in the project pane. You will see the result displayed in the message pane, as shown in Figure 2.4.

2.4   Identifiers

Just as every entity in the real world has a name, so you need to choose names for the things you will refer to in your programs. Programming languages use special symbols called *identifiers* to name such programming entities as variables, constants, methods, classes, and packages. Here are the rules for naming identifiers:

■ An identifier is a sequence of characters that consists of letters, digits, underscores (_), and dollar signs ($).

■ An identifier must start with a letter, an underscore (_), or a dollar sign ($). It cannot start with a digit.

■ An identifier cannot be a reserved word. (See Appendix A, "Java Keywords," for a list of reserved words.)

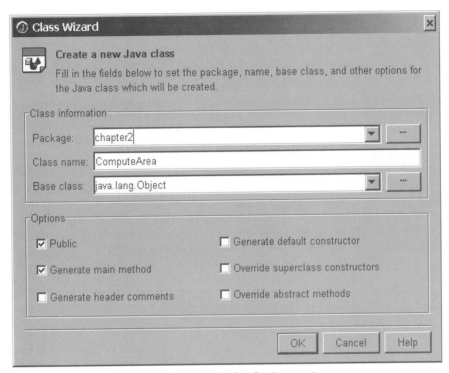

Figure 2.3   *You use the Class wizard to create the class for ComputeArea.*

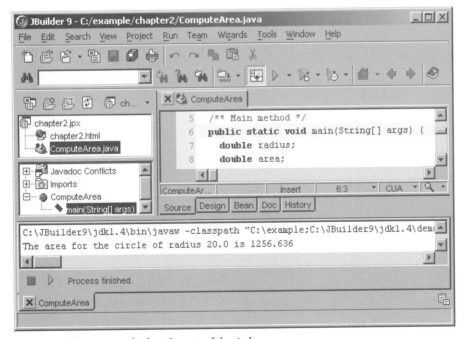

Figure 2.4   *The program displays the area of the circle.*

■ An identifier cannot be `true`, `false`, or `null`.

■ An identifier can be of any length.

For example, `$2`, `ComputeArea`, `area`, `radius`, and `showMessageDialog` are legal identifiers, whereas `2A` and `d+4` are illegal identifiers because they do not follow the rules. The Java compiler detects illegal identifiers and reports syntax errors.

 NOTE

Since Java is case-sensitive, `X` and `x` are different identifiers.

 TIP

Identifiers are used for naming variables, constants, methods, classes, and packages. Descriptive identifiers make programs easy to read. Besides choosing descriptive names for identifiers, there are naming conventions for different kinds of identifiers. Naming conventions are summarized in Section 2.16, "Programming Style and Documentation ."

2.5   Variables

Variables are used to store data input, data output, or intermediate data. In the program in Example 2.1, `radius` and `area` are variables of double-precision, floating-point type. You can assign any numerical value to `radius` and `area`, and the values of `radius` and `area` can be reassigned. For example, you can write the code shown below to compute the area for different radii:

```
// Compute the first area
radius = 1.0;
area = radius * radius * 3.14159;
System.out.println("The area is " + area + " for radius " + radius);

// Compute the second area
radius = 2.0;
area = radius * radius * 3.14159;
System.out.println("The area is " + area + " for radius " + radius);
```

2.5.1   Declaring Variables

Variables are for representing data of a certain type. To use a variable, you declare it by telling the compiler the name of the variable as well as what type of data it represents. This is called a *variable declaration*. Declaring a variable tells the compiler to allocate appropriate memory space for the variable based on its data type. Here is the syntax for declaring a variable:

```
datatype variableName;
```

Here are some examples of variable declarations:

```
int x;              // Declare x to be an integer variable;
double radius;      // Declare radius to be a double variable;
double interestRate; // Declare interestRate to be a double variable;
char a;             // Declare a to be a character variable;
```

The examples use the data types int, double, and char. Later in this chapter you will be introduced to additional data types, such as byte, short, long, float, char, and boolean.

If variables are of the same type, they can be declared together using a short-hand form, as follows:

```
datatype variable1, variable2, …, variablen;
```

The variables are separated by commas.

 NOTE

By convention, variable names are in lowercase. If a name consists of several words, concatenate all of them and capitalize the first letter of each word except the first. Examples of variables are radius and interestRate.

2.6   Assignment Statements and Assignment Expressions

After a variable is declared, you can assign a value to it by using an *assignment statement*. The syntax for assignment statements is as follows:

```
variable = expression;
```

An *expression* represents a computation involving values, variables, and operators that evaluates to a value. For example, consider the following code:

```
int x = 1;                  // Assign 1 to variable x;
double radius = 1.0;        // Assign 1.0 to variable radius;
a = 'A';                    // Assign 'A' to variable a;
x = 5 * (3 / 2) + 3 * 2;    // Assign the value of the expression to x;
x = y + 1;                  // Assign the addition of y and 1 to x;
area = radius * radius * 3.14159; // Compute area
```

The variable can also be used in the expression. For example,

```
x = x + 1;
```

In this assignment statement, x + 1 is assigned to x. If x is 1 before the statement is executed, then it becomes 2 after the statement is executed.

To assign a value to a variable, the variable name must be on the left of the assignment operator. Thus, 1 = x would be wrong.

In Java, an assignment statement can also be treated as an expression that evaluates to the value being assigned to the variable on the left-hand side of the assignment operator. For this reason, an assignment statement is also known as an *assignment expression*, and the symbol = is referred to as the *assignment operator*. For example, the following statement is correct:

```
System.out.println(x = 1);
```

which is equivalent to

```
x = 1;
System.out.println(x);
```

The following statement is also correct:

```
i = j = k = 1;
```

Which is equivalent to

```
k = 1;
j = k;
i = j;
```

NOTE

In an assignment statement, the data type of the variable on the left must be compatible with the data type of the value on the right. For example, `int x = 1.0` would be illegal because the data type of `x` is `int`. You cannot assign a `double` value (`1.0`) to an `int` variable without using type casting. Type casting is introduced in Section 2.8, "Numeric Data Types and Operations."

CAUTION

Java assignment statements use the equals sign (=), not :=, which is often used in other languages.

2.6.1   Declaring and Initializing Variables in One Step

Variables often have initial values. You can declare a variable and initialize it in one step. Consider, for instance, the following code:

```
int x = 1;
```

This is equivalent to the next two statements:

```
int x;
x = 1;
```

You can also use a shorthand form to declare and initialize variables of the same type together. For example,

```
int i = 1, j = 2;
```

TIP

A variable must be declared before it can be assigned a value. A variable declared in a method must be assigned a value before it can be used.

Whenever possible, declare a variable and assign its initial value in one step. This will make the program easy to read and avoid programming errors.

2.7   Constants

The value of a variable may change during the execution of the program, but a *constant* represents permanent data that never change. In our `ComputeArea` program, π is a constant. If you use it frequently, you don't want to keep typing 3.14159; instead, you can define a constant for π. Here is the syntax for declaring a constant:

```
final datatype CONSTANTNAME = VALUE;
```

The word `final` is a Java keyword which means that the constant cannot be changed. For example, in the `ComputeArea` program, you could define π as a constant and rewrite the program as follows:

```
// ComputeArea.java: Compute the area of a circle
package chapter2;

public class ComputeArea {
  /** Main method */
  public static void main(String[] args) {
    final double PI = 3.14159; // Declare a constant

    // Assign a radius
    double radius = 20;

    // Compute area
    double area = radius * radius * PI;

    // Display results
    System.out.println("The area for the circle of radius " +
      radius + " is " + area);
  }
}
```

 CAUTION

A constant must be declared and initialized before it can be used. You cannot change a constant's value once it is declared. By convention, constants are named in uppercase: `PI`, not `pi` or `Pi`.

◈ **NOTE**

There are three benefits of using constants: (1) you don't have to repeatedly type the same value; (2) the value can be changed in a single location, if necessary; (3) the program is easy to read.

2.8   Numeric Data Types and Operations

Every data type has a range of values. The compiler allocates memory space to store each variable or constant according to its data type. Java provides several primitive data types for numeric values, characters, and Boolean values. In this section, numeric data types are introduced.

Java has six numeric types: four for integers and two for floating-point numbers. Table 2.1 lists the six numeric data types, their ranges, and their storage sizes.

◈ **NOTE**

IEEE 754 is a standard approved by the Institute of Electrical and Electronics Engineers for representing floating-point numbers on computers. The standard has been widely adopted. Java has adopted the 32-bit **IEEE 754** for the `float` type and the 64-bit **IEEE 754** for the `double` type. The **IEEE 754** standard also defines special values and operations in Appendix F, "Special Floating-Point Values."

TABLE 2.1   **Numeric Data Types**

Name	Range	Storage Size
byte	-2^7 (-128) to $2^7 - 1$ (127)	8-bit signed
short	-2^{15} (-32768) to $2^{15} - 1$ (32767)	16-bit signed
int	-2^{31} (-2147483648) to $2^{31} - 1$ (2147483647)	32-bit signed
long	-2^{63} to $2^{63} - 1$ (i.e., -9223372036854775808 to 9223372036854775807)	64-bit signed
float	$-3.4E38$ to $3.4E38$ (6 to 7 significant digits of accuracy)	32-bit IEEE 754
double	$-1.7E308$ to $1.7E308$ (14 to 15 significant digits of accuracy)	64-bit IEEE 754

2.8.1   Numeric Operators

The arithmetic operators for numeric data types include addition (+), subtraction (−), multiplication (*), division (/), and remainder (%). For examples, see the following code:

```
int i1 = 34 + 1;          // i1 becomes 35
double d1 = 34.0 - 0.1;   // d1 becomes 33.9
long  i2 = 300 * 30;      // i2 becomes 9000
double d2 = 1.0 / 2.0;    // d2 becomes 0.5
int i3 = 1 / 2;           // i3 becomes 0; Note that the result is
                          // the integer part of the division
byte i4 = 20 % 3;         // i4 becomes 2; Note that the result is
                          // the remainder after the division
```

The result of integer division is an integer. The fractional part is truncated. For example, 5 / 2 = 2, not 2.5, and −5 / 2 = −2, not −2.5.

The % operator yields the remainder after division. Therefore, 7 % 3 yields 1, and 20 % 3 yields 2. This operator is often used for integers but also can be used with floating-point values.

The + and − operators can be both unary and binary. A *unary* operator has only one operand; a *binary* operator has two operands. For example, the − operator in −5 can be considered a unary operator to negate number 5, whereas the − operator in 4 − 5 is a binary operator for subtracting 5 from 4.

❖   NOTE

Calculations involving floating-point numbers are approximated because these numbers are not stored with complete accuracy. For example,

```
System.out.println(1 - 0.1 - 0.1 - 0.1 - 0.1 - 0.1);
```

displays 0.5000000000000001, not 0.5, and

```
System.out.println(1.0 - 0.9);
```

displays 0.09999999999999998, not 0.1. Integers are stored precisely. Therefore, calculations with integers yield a precise integer result.

2.8.2   Numeric Literals

A *literal* is a constant value that appears directly in the program. For example, 34, 1,000,000, and 5.0 are literals in the following statements:

```
int i = 34;
long k = 1000000;
double d = 5.0;
```

2.8.2.1   Integer Literals

An integer literal can be assigned to an integer variable as long as it can fit into the variable. A compilation error would occur if the literal were too large for the variable to hold. The statement byte b = 1000, for example, would cause a compilation error, because 1000 cannot be stored in a variable of the byte type.

An integer literal is assumed to be of the int type, whose value is between -2^{31} (-2147483648) and $2^{31} - 1$ (2147483647). To denote an integer literal of the long type, append the letter L or l to it. L is preferred because l (lowercase L) can easily be confused with 1 (the digit one).

◈ NOTE

Integer literals can also be represented in octal (base 8) and hexadecimal (base 16) number systems using the prefixes 0 and 0x, respectively. For more information, see Bonus Supplement B, "Number Systems and Bit Manipulations."

2.8.2.2   Floating-Point Literals

Floating-point literals are written with a decimal point. By default, a floating-point literal is treated as a double type value. For example, 5.0 is considered a double value, not a float value. You can make a number a float by appending the letter f or F, and you can make a number a double by appending the letter d or D. For example, you can use 100.2f or 100.2F for a float number, and 100.2d or 100.2D for a double number.

2.8.2.3   Scientific Notations

Floating-point literals can also be specified in scientific notation; for example, 1.23456e + 2, the same as 1.23456e2, is equivalent to 1.23456×10^2 = 123.456, and 1.23456e − 2 is equivalent to 1.23456×10^{-2} = 0.0123456. E (or e) represents an exponent and can be either in lowercase or uppercase.

2.8.3   Arithmetic Expressions

Writing numeric expressions in Java involves a straightforward translation of an arithmetic expression using Java operators. For example, the arithmetic expression

$$\frac{3 + 4x}{5} - \frac{10(y - 5)(a + b + c)}{x} + 9\left(\frac{4}{x} + \frac{9 + x}{y}\right)$$

can be translated into a Java expression as:

```
(3 + 4 * x) / 5 - 10 * (y - 5) * (a + b + c) / x +
9 * (4 / x + (9 + x) / y)
```

The numeric operators in a Java expression are applied the same way as in an arithmetic expression. Operators contained within pairs of parentheses are evaluated first. Parentheses can be nested, in which case the expression in the inner parentheses is evaluated first. Multiplication, division, and remainder operators are applied next. If an expression contains several multiplication, division, and remainder operators, they are applied from left to right. Addition and subtraction operators are applied last. If an expression contains several addition and subtraction operators, they are applied from left to right.

CAUTION

Be careful when applying division. Division of two integers yields an integer in Java. For example, the formula for converting a Fahrenheit degree is

$$celsius = \left(\tfrac{5}{9}\right)(fahrenheit - 32)$$

Because 5 / 9 yields 0 in Java, the preceding formula should be translated into the Java statement shown below:

```
celsius = (5.0 / 9) * (fahrenheit - 32)
```

2.8.4   Shortcut Operators

Very often the current value of a variable is used, modified, and then reassigned back to the same variable. For example, consider the following code:

```
i = i + 8;
```

This statement is equivalent to

```
i += 8;
```

The += is called a *shortcut operator*. Other shortcut operators are shown in Table 2.2.

TABLE 2.2   Shortcut Operators

Operator	Name	Example	Equivalent
+=	Addition assignment	i += 8	i = i + 8
-=	Subtraction assignment	f -= 8.0	f = f - 8.0
*=	Multiplication assignment	i *= 8	i = i * 8
/=	Division assignment	i /= 8	i = i / 8
%=	Remainder assignment	i % = 8	i = i % 8

There are two more shortcut operators for incrementing and decrementing a variable by 1. This is handy because that's often how much the value needs to be changed. These two operators are ++ and --. They can be used in prefix or suffix notation, as shown in Table 2.3:

TABLE 2.3   Increment and Decrement Operators

Operator	Name	Description
++var	preincrement	Increment var by 1, then use its new value in the expression.
var++	postincrement	Use the current value of var in the expression, then increment var by 1.
−−var	predecrement	Decrement var by 1, then use its new value in the expression.
var−−	postdecrement	Use the current value of var in the expression, then decrement var by 1.

If the operator is prefixed to the variable, the variable is incremented or decremented by 1, then the new value of the variable is used in the expression. If the operator is a suffix to the variable, the current value of the variable is used in the expression, then the variable is incremented or decremented by 1. Therefore, the prefixes ++x and −−x are referred to, respectively, as the *preincrement operator* and the *predecrement operator*; and the suffixes x++ and x−− are referred to, respectively, as the *postincrement operator* and the *postdecrement operator*. The prefix form of ++ (or −−) and the suffix form of ++ (or −−) are the same if they are used in isolation, but they cause different effects when used in an expression. The following code illustrates this:

```
int i = 10;
int newNum = 10 * i++;
```
Equivalent to →
```
int newNum = 10 * i;
i = i + 1;
```

In this case, the current value of i is used in the expression, and i is then incremented by 1. So newNum becomes 100. If i++ is replaced by ++i, as follows,

```
int i = 10;
int newNum = 10 * (++i);
```
Equivalent to →
```
i = i + 1;
int newNum = 10 * i;
```

i is incremented by 1, and the new value of i is used in the expression. Thus newNum becomes 110.

Here is another example:

```
double x = 1.0;
double y = 5.0;
double z = x-- + (++y);
```

After all three lines are executed, y becomes 6.0, z becomes 7.0, and x becomes 0.0.

The increment operator ++ and the decrement operator −− can be applied to all integer and floating-point types. These operators are often used in loop statements.

A *loop statement* is a structure that controls how many times an operation or a sequence of operations is performed in succession. This structure, and the subject of loop statements, is introduced in Chapter 3, "Control Statements."

 TIP

Using increment and decrement operators makes expressions short, but it also makes them complex and difficult to read. Avoid using these operators in expressions that modify multiple variables or the same variable multiple times, such as this one: `int k = ++i + i.`

 NOTE

Like the assignment operator (=), the operators (+=, −=, *=, /=, %=, ++, and −−) can be used to form an assignment statement as well as an expression. Prior to Java 2, all expressions could be used as statements. Since Java 2, only the following types of expressions can be statements:

```
variable op= expression; // Where op is +, -, *, /, or %
++variable;
variable++;
--variable;
variable--;
```

The following code has a compilation error in Java 2:

```
public static void main(String[] args) {
   3 + 4; // Correct prior to Java 2, but wrong in Java 2
   }
```

 CAUTION

There are no spaces in the shortcut operators. For example, + = should be +=.

2.9   Numeric Type Conversions

Sometimes it is necessary to mix numeric values of different types in a computation. Consider the following statements:

```
byte i = 100;
long k = i * 3 + 4;
double d = i * 3.1 + k / 2;
```

Are these statements correct? Java allows binary operations on values of different types. When performing a binary operation involving two operands of different types, Java automatically converts the operand based on the following rules:

1. If one of the operands is `double`, the other is converted into `double`.

2. Otherwise, if one of the operands is `float`, the other is converted into `float`.

3. Otherwise, if one of the operands is `long`, the other is converted into `long`.

4. Otherwise, both operands are converted into `int`.

For example, the result of 1 / 2 is 0, and the result of 1.0 / 2 is 0.5.

You can always assign a value to a numeric variable whose type supports a larger range of values; thus, for instance, you can assign a long value to a float variable. You cannot, however, assign a value to a variable of a type with smaller range unless you use *type casting*. Casting is an operation that converts a value of one data type into a value of another data type. Casting a variable of a type with a small range to a variable of a type with a larger range is known as *widening a type*. Casting a variable of a type with a large range to a variable of a type with a smaller range is known as *narrowing a type*. Widening a type can be performed automatically without explicit casting. Narrowing a type must be performed explicitly.

The syntax for casting gives the target type in parentheses, followed by the variable's name or the value to be cast. The code that follows is an example.

```
float f = (float)10.1;
int i = (int)f;
```

In the first line, the double value 10.1 is cast into float. In the second line, i has a value of 10; the fractional part in f is truncated. Be careful when using casting. Lost information might lead to inaccurate results, as shown in this example:

```
int i = 256; // i has 32 bits
byte b = (byte)i; // b has 8 bits
```

What is b? Numbers are represented in binary in a computer. Bonus Supplement B, "Number Systems and Bit Manipulations," introduces number representations in the computer. The binary representation for i ($256 = 2^8$) is 100000000. An integer has four bytes, and the last byte of i is 00000000, which is assigned to b, as shown in Figure 2.5. Thus, b becomes 0, which is totally distorted. To ensure correctness, you can use an if statement to test whether the value is in the correct target type range (see Table 2.1) before performing casting. The subject of if statements will be introduced in Chapter 3, "Control Statements."

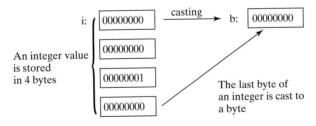

Figure 2.5 *An integer* i *is cast into a byte* b.

⚠ CAUTION

Casting is necessary if you are assigning a value to a variable of a smaller type range, such as assigning a double value to an int variable. A compilation error will occur if casting is not used in situations of this kind.

NOTE

Casting does not change the variable being cast. For example, d is not changed after casting in the following code:

```
double d = 4.5;
int i = (int)d;  // d is not changed
```

 NOTE

To assign a variable of the int type to a variable of the short or byte type, explicit casting must be used. For example, the following statements have a syntax error:

```
int i = 1;
byte b = i; // Error because explicit casting is required
```

However, so long as the integer literal is within the permissible range of the target variable, explicit casting is not needed to assign an integer literal to a variable of the short or byte type. Please refer to Section 2.8.2.1, "Integer Literals."

2.10   Character Data Type and Operations

The character data type, char, is used to represent a single character.

A character literal is enclosed in single quotation marks. Consider the following code:

```
char letter = 'A';
char numChar = '4';
```

The first statement assigns character A to the char variable letter. The second statement assigns the numeric character 4 to the char variable numChar.

The char type only represents one character. To represent a string of characters, use the data type called String. For example, the line of code below declares the message to be a string that has an initial value of "Welcome to Java!"

```
String message = "Welcome to Java!";
```

String is discussed in more detail in Chapter 7, "Strings." From now on, you can use String to declare a string variable.

 CAUTION

A string must be enclosed in quotation marks. A literal character is a single character enclosed in single quotation marks. So "A" is a string, and 'A' is a character.

2.10.1   Unicode and ASCII code

Java characters use *Unicode*, a 16-bit encoding scheme established by the Unicode Consortium to support the interchange, processing, and display of written texts in the world's diverse languages. (See the Unicode Web site at **www.unicode.org** for more information.) Unicode takes two bytes, preceded by \u, expressed in four hexadecimal numbers that run from '\u0000' to '\uFFFF'. For example, the word "coffee" is translated into Chinese using two characters. The Unicodes of these two characters are "\u5496\u5561". The following statement displays some Greek letters, as shown in Figure 2.6.

```
JOptionPane.showMessageDialog(null, "\u03b1 \u03b2 \u03b3",
    "Display Greek Letters", JOptionPane.INFORMATION_MESSAGE);
```

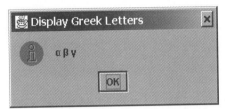

Figure 2.6   *You can use Unicode to represent international characters.*

Most computers use the *ASCII (American Standard Code for Information Interchange)*, a 7-bit encoding scheme for representing all uppercase and lowercase letters, digits, punctuation marks, and control characters. Unicode includes ASCII code, with '\u0000' to '\u007F' corresponding to the 128 ASCII characters. (See Appendix B, "The ASCII Character Set," for a list of ASCII characters and their decimal and hexadecimal codes.) You can use ASCII characters like 'X', '1', and '$' in a Java program as well as Unicodes. Thus, for example, the following statements are equivalent:

```
char letter = 'A';
char letter = '\u0041'; // Character A's Unicode is 0041
```

Both statements assign character A to char variable letter.

> **NOTE**
>
> The increment and decrement operators can also be used on char variables to get the next or preceding Unicode character. For example, the following statements display characer b.
>
> ```
> char ch = 'a';
> System.out.println(++ch);
> ```

2.10.2   Escape Sequences for Special Characters

Java allows you to use escape sequences to represent special characters, as shown in Table 2.4. An escape sequence begins with the backslash character (\) followed by a character that has a special meaning to the compiler.

Suppose you want to print the quoted message shown below:

```
He said "Java is fun"
```

Here is how to write the statement:

```
System.out.println("He said \"Java is fun\"");
```

TABLE 2.4   Java Escape Sequences

Description	Character Escape Sequence	Unicode
Backspace	\b	\u0008
Tab	\t	\u0009
Linefeed	\n	\u000A
Formfeed	\f	\u000C
Carriage Return	\r	\u000D
Backslash	\\	\u005C
Single Quote	\'	\u0027
Double Quote	\"	\u0022

2.10.3   Casting between *char* and Numeric Types

A char can be cast into any numeric type, and vice versa. When an integer is cast into a char, only its lower sixteen bits of data are used; the other part is ignored. When a floating-point value is cast into a char, the floating-point value is first cast into an int, which is then cast into a char. When a char is cast into a numeric type, the character's Unicode is cast into the specified numeric type.

Implicit casting can be used if the result of a casting fits into the target variable. Otherwise, explicit casting must be used. For example, since the Unicode of '0' is 48, which is within the range of a byte, the following implicit castings are fine:

```
byte b = '0';
int i = '0';
```

But the following casting is incorrect, because the Unicode \uFFF4 cannot fit into a byte:

```
byte b = '\uFFF4';
```

To force a casting, use explicit casting, as follows:

```
byte b = (byte)'\uFFF4';
```

Any positive integer between 0 and FFFF in hexadecimal can be cast into a character implicitly. Any number not in this range must be cast into a char explicitly.

◈ **NOTE**

All numeric operators can be applied to the char operands. The char operand is cast into a number if the other operand is a number or a character. If the other operand is a string, the character is concatenated with the string. For example, the following statements

```
int i = '1' + '2'; // (int)'1' is 49 and (int)'2' is 50
System.out.println("i is " + i);
String s = "Chapter " + '2';
```

```
System.out.println("s is " + s);
```

display

```
i is 99
s is Chapter 2
```

2.11   *boolean* Data Type and Operations

Often in a program you need to compare two values, such as whether i is greater than j. Java provides six *comparison operators* (also known as *relational operators*) in Table 2.5 that can be used to compare two values. The result of the comparison is a Boolean value: true or false.

TABLE 2.5   **Comparison Operators**

Operator	Name	Example	Answer
<	less than	1 < 2	true
<=	less than or equal to	1 <= 2	true
>	greater than	1 > 2	false
>=	greater than or equal to	1 >= 2	false
==	equal to	1 == 2	false
!=	not equal to	1! = 2	true

NOTE

You can also compare characters. Comparing characters is the same as comparing the Unicodes of the characters. For example, 'a' is larger than 'A' because the Unicode of 'a' is larger than the Unicode of 'A'.

CAUTION

The equality comparison operator is two equals signs (==), not a single equals sign (=). The latter symbol is for assignment.

For example, the following statement displays true:

```
System.out.println(1 < 2);
```

A variable that holds a Boolean value is known as a *Boolean variable*. The boolean data type is used to declare Boolean variables. The domain of the boolean type consists of two literal values: true and false. For example, the following statement assigns true to the variable lightsOn:

```
boolean lightsOn = true;
```

Boolean operators, also known as *logical operators*, operate on Boolean values to create a new Boolean value. Table 2.6 contains a list of Boolean operators.

TABLE 2.6   Boolean Operators

Operator	Name	Description
!	not	logical negation
&&	and	logical conjunction
¦¦	or	logical disjunction
^	exclusive or	logical exclusion

These operators are demonstrated by the examples that follow. In the examples, the variables `width` and `height` contain the values of 1 and 2, respectively.

Table 2.7 defines the not (!) operator. The not (!) operator negates `true` to `false` and `false` to `true`. For example, `!(width == 3)` is `true` because `(width == 3)` is `false`.

TABLE 2.7   Truth Table for Operator !

Operand	!Operand
true	false
false	true

Table 2.8 defines the and (&&) operator. The and (&&) of two Boolean operands is `true` if and only if both operands are `true`. For example, `(width == 1) && (height > 1)` is `true` because `(width == 1)` and `(height > 1)` are both `true`.

TABLE 2.8   Truth Table for Operator &&

Operand1	Operand2	Operand1 && Operand2
false	false	false
false	true	false
true	false	false
true	true	true

Table 2.9 defines the or (¦¦) operator. The or (¦¦) of two Boolean operands is `true` if at least one of the operands is `true`. For example, `(width > 1) ¦¦ (height == 2)` is `true` because `(height == 2)` is `true`.

TABLE 2.9   Truth Table for Operator ||

Operand1	Operand2	Operand1 ¦¦ Operand2
false	false	false
false	true	true
true	false	true
true	true	true

Table 2.10 defines the exclusive or (^) operator. The exclusive or (^) of two Boolean operands is `true` if and only if the two operands have different Boolean values. For example, `(width > 1) ^ (height == 2)` is true because `(width > 1)` is `false` and `(height == 2)` is true.

TABLE 2.10   Truth Table for Operator ^

Operand1	Operand2	Operand1 ^ Operand2
false	false	false
false	true	true
true	false	true
true	true	false

Here are some more examples that show the use of Boolean operators:

```
System.out.println("Is " + num + " divisible by 2 and 3? " +
  ((num % 2 == 0) && (num % 3 == 0)));

System.out.println("Is " + num + " divisible by 2 or 3? " +
  ((num % 2 == 0) || (num % 3 == 0)));

System.out.println("Is " + num +
  " divisible by 2 or 3, but not both? " +
  ((num % 2 == 0) ^ (num % 3 == 0)));
```

2.11.1   Unconditional vs. Conditional Boolean Operators

When evaluating `p1 && p2`, Java first evaluates `p1` and then evaluates `p2` if `p1` is `true`; if `p1` is `false`, it does not evaluate `p2`. When evaluating `p1 || p2`, Java first evaluates `p1` and then evaluates `p2` if `p1` is `false`; if `p1` is `true`, it does not evaluate `p2`. Therefore, `&&` is referred to as the *conditional* or *short-circuit AND* operator, and `||` is referred to as the *conditional* or *short-circuit OR* operator.

Java also provides the `&` and `|` operators. The `&` operator works exactly the same as the `&&` operator, and the `|` operator works exactly the same as the `||` operator with one exception: the `&` and `|` operators always evaluate both operands. Therefore, `&` is referred to as the *unconditional AND* operator, and `|` is referred to as the *unconditional OR* operator. In some rare situations, you can use the `&` and `|` operators to guarantee that the right-hand operand is evaluated regardless of whether the left-hand operand is `true` or `false`. For example, the expression `(width < 2) & (height-- < 2)` guarantees that `(height-- < 2)` is evaluated. Thus, the variable `height` will be decremented regardless of whether `width` is less than 2 or not.

 TIP

Avoid using the `&` and `|` operators. The benefits of the `&` and `|` operators are marginal. Using them will make the program difficult to read and could cause errors. For example, the expression `(x != 0) & (100 / x)` results in a runtime error if `x` is `0`. However, `(x != 0) && (100 / x)` is fine. If `x` is 0, `(x != 0)` is false. Since `&&` is a short-circuit operator, Java does not evaluate `(100 / x)` and evaluates the result as `false` for the entire expression `(x != 0) && (100 / x)`.

NOTE

The & and ¦ operators can also apply to bitwise operations. See Bonus Supplement B, "Number Systems and Bit Manipulations," for details.

 NOTE

As shown in the preceding section, a `char` value can be cast into an `int` value, and vice versa. A Boolean value, however, cannot be cast into a value of other types, and vice versa.

NOTE

`true` and `false` are literals, just like a number such as 10, so they are not keywords, but you cannot use them as identifiers, just as you cannot use 10 as an identifier.

2.12   Operator Precedence and Associativity

Operator precedence and associativity determine the order in which operators are evaluated. Suppose that you have this expression:

```
3 + 4 * 4 > 5 * (4 + 3) - ++i
```

What is its value? How does the compiler know the execution order of the operators? The expression in the parentheses is evaluated first. (Parentheses can be nested, in which case the expression in the inner parentheses is executed first.) When evaluating an expression without parentheses, the operators are applied according to the precedence rule and the associativity rule. The precedence rule defines precedence for operators, as shown in Table 2.11, which contains the operators you have learned in this chapter. Operators are listed in decreasing order of precedence from top to bottom. Operators with the same precedence appear in the same group. (See Appendix C, "Operator Precedence Chart," for a complete list of Java operators and their precedence.)

If operators with the same precedence are next to each other, their *associativity* determines the order of evaluation. All binary operators except assignment operators are *left-associative*. For example, since + and − are of the same precedence and are left-associative, the expression

```
a - b + c - d
```

is equivalent to

```
((a - b) + c) - d
```

Assignment operators are *right-associative*. Therefore, the expression

```
a = b += c = 5
```

is equivalent to

```
a = (b += (c = 5))
```

TABLE 2.11   Operator Precedence Chart

Precedence	Operator
Highest Order	var++ and var-- (Postincrement and postdecrement)
	+, − (Unary plus and minus), ++var and --var (prefix)
	(type) (Casting)
	! (Not)
	*, /, % (Multiplication, division, and remainder)
	+, − (Binary addition and subtraction)
	<, <=, >, >= (Comparison)
	==, != (Equality)
	& (Unconditional AND)
	^ (Exclusive OR)
	¦ (Unconditional OR)
	&& (Conditional AND)
	¦¦ (Conditional OR)
Lowest Order	=, +=, −=, *=, /=, %= (Assignment operator)

Suppose a, b, and c are 1 before the assignment; after the whole expression is evaluated, a becomes 6, b becomes 6, and c becomes 5.

 TIP

You can use parentheses to force an evaluation order as well as to make a program easy to read. Use of redundant parentheses does not slow down the execution of the expression.

2.13   Operand Evaluation Order

The precedence and associativity rules specify the order of the operators but not the order in which the operands of a binary operator are evaluated. Operands are evaluated strictly from left to right in Java. *The left-hand operand of a binary operator is evaluated before any part of the right-hand operand is evaluated.* This rule takes precedence over any other rules that govern expressions. Consider this expression:

```
a + b * (c + 10 * d) / e
```

a, b, c, d, and e are evaluated in this order. If no operands have *side effects* that change the value of a variable, the order of operand evaluation is irrelevant. Interesting cases arise when operands do have a side effect. For example, x becomes 1 in the following code because a is evaluated to 0 before ++a is evaluated to 1.

```
int a = 0;
int x = a + (++a);
```

But x becomes 2 in the following code because ++a is evaluated to 1, then a is evaluated to 1.

```
int a = 0;
int x = ++a + a;
```

The order for evaluating operands takes precedence over the operator precedence rule. In the former case, (++a) has higher precedence than addition (+), but since a is a left-hand operand of the addition (+), it is evaluated before any part of its right-hand operand (e.g., ++a in this case).

In summary, the rule of evaluating an expression is:

1. The operands are evaluated from left to right.

2. The operators are applied according to their precedence, as shown in Table 2.11.

3. The associativity rule applies for two operators next to each other with the same precedence.

NOTE:

The compiler may evaluate the expression differently in order to perform optimizations, as long as the result is the same as if the rule were applied. For example, a + b + c * d may be evaluated in at least two possible ways:

1. The compiler evaluates a, evaluates b, adds the values together, then evaluates c, evaluates d, multiplies the values of c and d, and finally adds the values of a + b and c * d together.

2. The compiler evaluates a, b, c, and d, multiplies the values of c and d, then adds the values of a and b, and finally adds the values of a + b and c * d together.

The former is the way the Sun Java compiler evaluates a + b + c * d. It is more efficient than the latter, which requires that all variable values be stored in the CPU registers before multiplying the values of c and d.

2.14   Getting Input from Input Dialogs

In Example 2.1, the radius is fixed in the source code. To use a different radius, you have to modify the source code and recompile it. Obviously, this is not convenient. You can use the showInputDialog method in the JOptionPane class to get input at runtime. When this method is executed, a dialog is displayed to enable you to enter an input, as shown in Figure 2.7. After entering a string, click OK to accept the input and dismiss the dialog box. The input is returned from the method as a string.

You can invoke the method with four arguments, as follows:

```
String input = JOptionPane.showInputDialog(null,
  "Enter an input", "Input Dialog Demo",
  JOptionPane.QUESTION_MESSAGE);
```

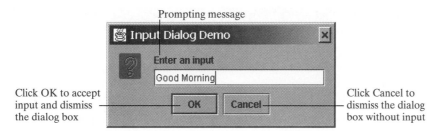

Figure 2.7   *The input dialog box enables the user to enter a string.*

The first argument can always be `null`. The second argument is a string that prompts the user. The third argument is the title of the input box. The fourth argument can be `JOptionPane.QUESTION_MESSAGE`, which causes the icon 🖭 to be displayed in the input box.

 NOTE

There are several ways to use the `showInputDialog` method. For the time being, you only need to know how to invoke the `showInputDialog` method like this:

```
String string = JOptionPane.showInputDialog(null, x,
  y, JOptionPane.QUESTION_MESSAGE));
```

where x is a string for the prompting message, and y is a string for the title of the input dialog box.

2.14.1   Converting Strings to Numbers

The input returned from the input dialog box is a string. If you enter a numeric value such as 123, it returns "123". You have to convert a string into a number to obtain the input as a number.

To convert a string into an `int` value, use the `parseInt` method in the `Integer` class, as follows:

```
int intValue = Integer.parseInt(intString);
```

where `intString` is a numeric string such as "123".

To convert a string into a `double` value, use the `parseDouble` method in the `Double` class, as follows:

```
double doubleValue = Double.parseDouble(doubleString);
```

where `doubleString` is a numeric string such as "123.45".

The `Integer` and `Double` classes are both included in the `java.lang` package. These classes will be further discussed in Chapter 9, "Abstract Classes and Interfaces."

 NOTE

You can also convert a string into a value of the `byte` type, `short` type, `long` type, `float` type, `char` type, or `boolean` type. You will learn the conversion methods later in the book.

Example 2.2 Entering Input from Dialog Boxes

Problem

This example shows you how to enter input from dialog boxes. As shown in Figure 2.8, the program prompts the user to enter a year as an int value and checks whether it is a leap year; then it prompts the user to enter a double value and checks whether it is positive. A year is a leap year if it is divisible by 4 but not by 100 or if it is divisible by 400.

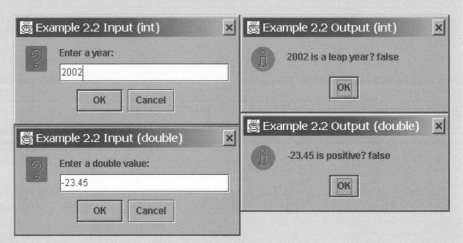

Figure 2.8   *The input dialog box enables the user to enter a string.*

Solution

The following code gives the solution to the problem.

```
1    // InputDialogDemo.java: Enter input from input dialog boxes
2    package chapter2;
3
4    import javax.swing.JOptionPane;
5
6    public class InputDialogDemo {
7      /** Main method */
8      public static void main(String args[]) {
9        // Prompt the user to enter a year
10       String yearString = JOptionPane.showInputDialog(null,
11         "Enter a year", "Example 2.2 Input (int)",
12         JOptionPane.QUESTION_MESSAGE);
13
14       // Convert the string into an int value
15       int year = Integer.parseInt(yearString);
16
17       // Check if the year is a leap year
18       boolean isLeapYear =
19         ((year % 4 == 0) && (year % 100 != 0)) || (year % 400 == 0);
20
21       // Display the result in a message dialog box
22       JOptionPane.showMessageDialog(null,
23         year + " is a leap year? " + isLeapYear,
```

```
24              "Example 2.2 Output (int)", JOptionPane.INFORMATION_MESSAGE);
25
26          // Prompt the user to enter a double value
27          String doubleString = JOptionPane.showInputDialog(null,
28              "Enter a double value", "Example 2.2 Input (double)",
29              JOptionPane.QUESTION_MESSAGE);
30
31          // Convert the string into a double value
32          double doubleValue = Double.parseDouble(doubleString);
33
34          // Check if the number is positive
35          JOptionPane.showMessageDialog(null,
36              doubleValue + " is positive? " + (doubleValue > 0),
37              "Example 2.2 Output (double)",
38              JOptionPane.INFORMATION_MESSAGE);
39
40          System.exit(0);
41      }
42   }
```

Review

The `showInputDialog` method in Lines 10–12 displays an input dialog box titled "Example 2.2 Input (int)." Enter a year as an integer and click OK to accept the input. The integer is returned as a string that is assigned to the `String` variable `yearString`. The `Integer.parseInt(yearString)` (Line 15) is used to convert the string into an `int` value. If you entered an input other than an integer, a runtime error would occur. In Chapter 15, "Exceptions and Assertions," you will learn how to handle the exception so that the program can continue to run.

The `showMessageDialog` method in Lines 22–24 displays the output in a message dialog box titled "Example 2.2 Output (int)."

The `showInputDialog` method in Lines 27–29 displays an input dialog box titled "Example 2.2 Input (double)." Enter a floating-point value and click OK to accept the input. The floating-point value is returned as a string that is assigned to the `String` variable `doubleString`. The `Double.parseDouble(doubleString)` (Line 32) is used to convert the string into an `int` value. If you entered a non-numeric value, a runtime error would occur.

As explained in Example 1.2, for every program that creates dialog boxes using the methods in `JOptionPane`, you need to use `System.exit(0)` (Line 40) to terminate the program properly.

◈ NOTE

If you click *Cancel* in the input dialog box, no string is returned. A runtime error would occur.

2.15   Case Studies

In the preceding sections, you learned about variables, constants, primitive data types, operators, and expressions. You are now ready to use them to write interesting programs. This section presents three examples: computing loan payments, breaking a sum of money down into smaller units, and displaying current time.

Example 2.3 Computing Loan Payments

Problem

This example shows you how to write a program that computes loan payments. The loan can be a car loan, student loan, or home mortgage loan. The program lets the user enter the interest rate, number of years, and loan amount, and then computes the monthly payment and the total payment. It concludes by displaying the monthly and total payments.

Solution

The formula to compute the monthly payment is as follows:

$$\frac{loanAmount \times monthlyInterestRate}{1 - \dfrac{1}{(1 + monthlyInterestRate)^{numOfYears \times 12}}}$$

You don't have to know how this formula is derived. Nonetheless, given the monthly interest rate, number of years, and loan amount, you can use it to compute the monthly payment.

Here are the steps in developing the program:

1. Prompt the user to enter the annual interest rate, number of years, and loan amount.

2. Obtain the monthly interest rate from the annual interest rate.

3. Compute the monthly payment using the preceding formula.

4. Compute the total payment, which is the monthly payment multiplied by 12 and multiplied by the number of years.

5. Display the monthly payment and total payment in a message dialog.

The program follows, and the output is shown in Figure 2.9.

```
1    // ComputeLoan.java: Compute loan payments
2    package  chapter2;
3
4    import javax.swing.JOptionPane;
5
5    public class ComputeLoan {
6      /** Main method */
7      public static void main(String[] args) {
8        double annualInterestRate;
9        int numOfYears;
10       double loanAmount;
11
12       // Enter yearly interest rate
13       String annualInterestRateString = JOptionPane.showInputDialog(
```

```
14              null, "Enter yearly interest rate, for example 8.25:",
15              "Example 2.3 Input", JOptionPane.QUESTION_MESSAGE);
16
17          // Convert string to double
18          annualInterestRate =
19            Double.parseDouble(annualInterestRateString);
20
21          // Obtain monthly interest rate
22          double monthlyInterestRate = annualInterestRate/1200;
23
24          // Enter number of years
25          String numOfYearsString = JOptionPane.showInputDialog(null,
26            "Enter number of years as an integer, \nfor example 5:",
27            "Example 2.3 Input", JOptionPane.QUESTION_MESSAGE);
28
29          // Convert string to int
30          numOfYears = Integer.parseInt(numOfYearsString);
31
32          // Enter loan amount
33          String loanString = JOptionPane.showInputDialog(null,
34            "Enter loan amount, for example 120000.95:",
35            "Example 2.3 Input", JOptionPane.QUESTION_MESSAGE);
36
37          // Convert string to double
38          loanAmount =  Double.parseDouble(loanString);
39
40          // Calculate payment
41          double monthlyPayment = loanAmount * monthlyInterestRate /
42            (1 - 1 / Math.pow(1 + monthlyInterestRate, numOfYears * 12));
43          double totalPayment = monthlyPayment * numOfYears * 12;
44
45          // Format to keep two digits after the decimal point
46          monthlyPayment = (int)(monthlyPayment * 100) / 100.0;
47          totalPayment = (int)(totalPayment * 100) / 100.0;
48
49          // Display results
50          String output = "The monthly payment is " + monthlyPayment +
51            "\nThe total payment is " + totalPayment;
52          JOptionPane.showMessageDialog(null, output,
53            "Example 2.3 Output", JOptionPane.INFORMATION_MESSAGE);
54          System.exit(0);
55        }
56      }
```

Figure 2.9   *The program accepts the annual interest rate, number of years, and loan amount, then displays the monthly payment and total payment.*

continues

Example 2.3 continued

Review

Each new variable in a method must be declared once and only once. Choose the most appropriate data type for the variable. For example, numOfYears is best declared as int (Line 9), although it could be declared as long, float, or double.

The method for computing b^p in the Math class is pow(b, p) (Lines 38–39). The Math class, which comes with the Java runtime system, is available to all Java programs. The Math class is introduced in Chapter 4, "Methods."

The statements in Lines 43–44 are for formatting the number to keep two digits after the decimal point. For example, if monthlyPayment is 2076.0252175, (int)(monthlyPayment * 100) is 207602. Therefore, (int)(monthlyPayment * 100) / 100.0 yields 2076.02.

The strings are concatenated into output in Lines 47–48. The linefeed escape character '\n' is in the string to display the text after '\n' in the next line.

Example 2.4 Monetary Units

Problem

Write a program that classifies a given amount of money into smaller monetary units. The program lets the user enter an amount as a double value representing a total in dollars and cents, and outputs a report listing the monetary equivalent in dollars, quarters, dimes, nickels, and pennies.

Your program should report the maximum number of dollars, then the maximum number of quarters, and so on, in this order.

Solution

Here are the steps in developing the program:

1. Prompt the user to enter the amount as a decimal number such as 11.56.

2. Convert the amount (e.g., 11.56) into cents (1156).

3. Divide the cents by 100 to find the number of dollars. Obtain the remaining cents using the cents remainder 100.

4. Divide the remaining cents by 25 to find the number of quarters. Obtain the remaining cents using the remaining cents remainder 25.

5. Divide the remaining cents by 10 to find the number of dimes. Obtain the remaining cents using the remaining cents remainder 10.

6. Divide the remaining cents by 5 to find the number of nickels. Obtain the remaining cents using the remaining cents remainder 5.

7. The remaining cents are the pennies.

8. Display the result.

The program follows, and the output is shown in Figure 2.10.

```
1    // ComputeChange.java: Break down an amount into smaller units
2    package chapter2;
3
4    import javax.swing.JOptionPane;
5
6    public class ComputeChange {
7      /** Main method */
8      public static void main(String[] args) {
9        double amount; // Amount entered from the keyboard
10
11       // Receive the amount entered from the keyboard
12       String amountString = JOptionPane.showInputDialog(null,
13         "Enter an amount in double, for example 11.56",
14         "Example 2.4 Input", JOptionPane.QUESTION_MESSAGE);
15
16       // Convert string to double
17       amount = Double.parseDouble(amountString);
18
19       int remainingAmount = (int)(amount * 100);
20
21       // Find the number of one dollars
22       int numOfOneDollars = remainingAmount / 100;
23       remainingAmount = remainingAmount % 100;
24
25       // Find the number of quarters in the remaining amount
26       int numOfQuarters = remainingAmount / 25;
27       remainingAmount = remainingAmount % 25;
28
29       // Find the number of dimes in the remaining amount
30       int numOfDimes = remainingAmount / 10;
31       remainingAmount = remainingAmount % 10;
32
33       // Find the number of nickels in the remaining amount
34       int numOfNickels = remainingAmount / 5;
35       remainingAmount = remainingAmount % 5;
36
37       // Find the number of pennies in the remaining amount
38       int numOfPennies = remainingAmount;
39
40       // Display results
41       String output = "Your amount " + amount + " consists of \n" +
42         numOfOneDollars + " dollars\n" +
43         numOfQuarters + " quarters\n" +
44         numOfDimes + " dimes\n" +
45         numOfNickels + " nickels\n" +
46         numOfPennies + " pennies";
47       JOptionPane.showMessageDialog(null, output,
48         "Example 2.4 Output", JOptionPane.INFORMATION_MESSAGE);
49
50       System.exit(0);
51     }
52   }
```

Review

The variable amount stores the amount entered from the input dialog box (Lines 9–17). This variable is not changed because the amount has to be used at the end of the program to display the results. The program introduces the variable remainingAmount (Line 19) to store the changing remainingAmount.

continues

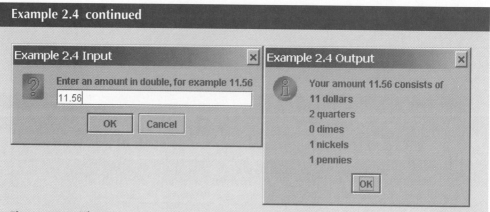

Figure 2.10 *The program receives an amount in decimals and breaks it into singles, quarters, dimes, nickels, and pennies.*

The variable `amount` is a `double` decimal representing dollars and cents. It is converted to an `int` variable `remainingAmount`, which represents all the cents. For instance, if `amount` is 11.56, then the initial `remainingAmount` is 1156. The division operator yields the integer part of the division. So 1156 / 100 is 11. The remainder operator obtains the remainder of the division. So 1156 % 100 is 56.

The program extracts the maximum number of singles from the total amount and obtains the remaining amount in the variable `remainingAmount` (Lines 22–23). It then extracts the maximum number of quarters from `remaining-Amount` and obtains a new `remainingAmount` (Lines 26–27). Continuing the same process, the program finds the maximum number of dimes, nickels, and pennies in the remaining amount.

One serious problem with this example is the possible loss of precision when casting a `double` amount to an `int` `remainingAmount`. This could lead to an inaccurate result. If you try to enter the amount 10.03, 10.03 * 100 becomes 1002.9999999999999. You will find that the program displays 10 dollars and 2 pennies. There are two ways to fix the problem. One is to enter the amount as an `int` value representing cents (see Exercise 2.4); the other is to read the decimal number as a string and extract the dollars part and the cents part separately as `int` values. Processing strings will be introduced in Chapter 7, "Strings."

As shown in Figure 2.10, 0 dimes, 1 nickels, and 1 pennies are displayed in the result. It would be better not to display 0 dimes, and to display 1 nickel and 1 penny using the singular forms of the words. You will learn how to use selection statements to modify this program in the next chapter (see Exercise 3.1).

Example 2.5 Displaying Current Time

Problem

Write a program that displays current time in GMT (Greenwich Meridian Time) in the format hour:minute:second such as 1:45:19.

Solution

The currentTimeMillis method in the System class returns the current time in milliseconds since midnight, January 1, 1970 GMT (1970 is the year when the Unix operating system was formally introduced). You can use this method to obtain the current time, and then compute the current second, minute, and hour as follows.

1. Obtain the total milliseconds since midnight, Jan 1, 1970 into totalMilliseconds by invoking System.currentTimeMillis().

2. Obtain the total seconds totalSeconds by dividing 1000 from totalMilliseconds.

3. Compute the current second in the minute in the hour from totalMilliseconds % 60.

4. Obtain the total minutes totalMinutes by dividing 60 from totalSeconds.

5. Compute the current minute in the hour from totalMinutes % 60.

6. Obtain the total hours totalHours by dividing 60 from totalMinutes.

7. Compute the current hour from totalHours % 24.

The program follows, and the output is shown in Figure 2.11.

```
1   // ShowCurrentTime.java: Display the current time
2   package chapter2;
3
4   import javax.swing.JOptionPane;
5
6   public class ShowCurrentTime {
7     public static void main(String[] args) {
8
9       // Obtain the total milliseconds since the midnight, Jan 1, 1970
10      long totalMilliseconds = System.currentTimeMillis();
11
12      // Obtain the total seconds since the midnight, Jan 1, 1970
13      long totalSeconds = totalMilliseconds / 1000;
14
15      // Compute the current second in the minute in the hour
16      int currentSecond = (int)(totalSeconds % 60);
17
18      // Obtain the total minutes
19      long totalMinutes = totalSeconds / 60;
20
21      // Compute the current minute in the hour
22      int currentMinute = (int)(totalMinutes % 60);
23
```

continues

75

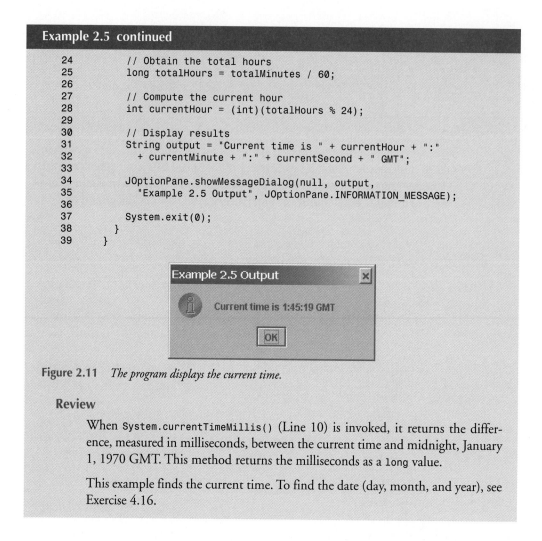

Example 2.5   continued

```
24          // Obtain the total hours
25          long totalHours = totalMinutes / 60;
26
27          // Compute the current hour
28          int currentHour = (int)(totalHours % 24);
29
30          // Display results
31          String output = "Current time is " + currentHour + ":"
32            + currentMinute + ":" + currentSecond + " GMT";
33
34          JOptionPane.showMessageDialog(null, output,
35            "Example 2.5 Output", JOptionPane.INFORMATION_MESSAGE);
36
37          System.exit(0);
38        }
39      }
```

Example 2.5 Output

ⓘ   Current time is 1:45:19 GMT

OK

Figure 2.11   *The program displays the current time.*

Review

When `System.currentTimeMillis()` (Line 10) is invoked, it returns the difference, measured in milliseconds, between the current time and midnight, January 1, 1970 GMT. This method returns the milliseconds as a `long` value.

This example finds the current time. To find the date (day, month, and year), see Exercise 4.16.

2.16   Programming Style and Documentation

Programming style deals with what programs look like. A program can compile and run properly even if written on only one line, but writing it all on one line would be bad programming style because it would be hard to read. *Documentation* is the body of explanatory remarks and comments pertaining to a program. Programming style and documentation are as important as coding. Good programming style and appropriate documentation reduce the chance of errors and make programs easy to read. So far you have learned some good programming styles. This section summarizes them and gives several guidelines. More details can be found in Bonus Supplement C, "Java Coding Style Guidelines."

2.16.1   Appropriate Comments and Comment Styles

Include a summary at the beginning of the program to explain what the program does, its key features, its supporting data structures, and any unique techniques it uses. In a long program, you should also include comments that introduce each major step and explain anything that is difficult to read. It is important to make comments concise so that they do not crowd the program or make it difficult to read.

Use javadoc comments (/** ... */) for commenting on an entire class or an entire method. These comments must precede the class or the method header, and can be extracted in a javadoc HTML file. For commenting on steps inside a method, use line comments (//).

2.16.2   Naming Conventions

Make sure that you choose descriptive names with straightforward meanings for the variables, constants, classes, and methods in your program. Names are case-sensitive. Listed below are the conventions for naming variables, methods, and classes.

- Always use lowercase for variables and methods. If a name consists of several words, concatenate them into one, making the first word lowercase and capitalizing the first letter of each subsequent word; for example, the variables `radius` and `area` and the method `showInputDialog`.

- Capitalize the first letter of each word in a class name; for example, the class names `ComputeArea`, `Math`, and `JOptionPane`.

- Capitalize every letter in a constant, and use underscores between words; for example, the constants `PI` and `MAX_VALUE`.

TIP

It is important to become familiar with the naming conventions. Understanding them will help you to understand Java programs. If you stick with the naming conventions, other programmers will be more willing to accept your program.

CAUTION

Do not choose class names that are already used in the Java library. For example, since the `Math` class is defined in Java, you should not name your class `Math`.

2.16.3   Proper Indentation and Spacing

A consistent indentation style makes programs clear and easy to read. *Indentation* is used to illustrate the structural relationships between a program's components or statements. Java can read the program even if all of the statements are in a straight line, but it is easier to read and maintain code that is aligned properly. Indent each subcomponent or statement *two* spaces more than the structure within which it is nested.

A single space should be added on both sides of a binary operator, as shown in the following statement:

```
boolean b = 3 + 4 * 4 > 5 * (4 + 3) - ++i;
```

A single space line should be used to separate segments of the code to make the program easier to read.

☼ **JBUILDER TIP**

To indent a block of lines to the right (respectively, left) in JBuilder, highlight the block and press the Tab key (respectively, Shift + Tab).

☼ **JBUILDER TIP**

You can set the indentation options in the Basic tab of the Formatting page in the Project Properties dialog box, as shown in Figure 2.12. You can format the source code by choosing *Edit, Formatting All*.

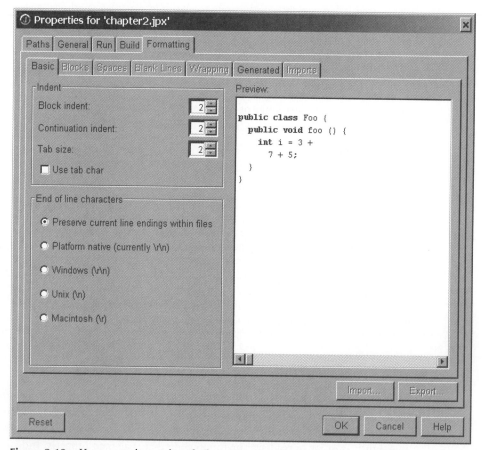

Figure 2.12 *You can set the number of columns you want for block indent, continuation indent, and tab size.*

2.16.4   Block Styles

A block is a group of statements surrounded by braces. There are two popular styles, *next-line* style and *end-of-line* style, as shown in Figure 2.13. Both are acceptable block styles. You can use either the next-line style or the end-of-line style as long as it is used consistently. This book uses the *end-of-line* style to be consistent with the Java API source code. The end-of-line style is also helpful to avoid some subtle programming errors.

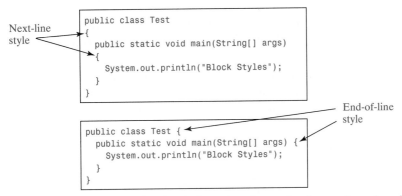

Figure 2.13   *The opening brace is placed at the beginning of a new line for next-line style and at the end of line for end-of-line style.*

2.16.5   Code Style Examples

Here is a coding style example:

```
/**
 * Course title: Introduction to Programming Principles
 * Course number: CSCI 1301-03
 * Instructor: Dr. Y. Daniel Liang
 * Description: Example 2.1, "Computing the Area of a Circle"
 *   This class is for computing the area of a circle given the
 *   radius. The radius is entered from the keyboard.
 * Copyright: Copyright (c) 2000
 * Company: Armstrong Atlantic State University
 * @author John F. Smith
 * @version 1.0, 11/30/2001
 */
public class ComputeArea {
  public static void main(String[] args) {
    double radius;
    double area;

    // Assign a radius
    radius = 20;

    // Compute area
    area = radius * radius * 3.14159;

    // Display results
    System.out.println("The area for the circle of radius " +
      radius + " is " + area);
  }
}
```

The javadoc comment for this example is quite long. To save space, the javadoc comments for the other examples in this book will be omitted.

2.17 Programming Errors

Programming errors are unavoidable, even for experienced programmers. Errors can be categorized into three types: syntax errors, runtime errors, and logic errors.

2.17.1 Syntax Errors

Errors that occur during compilation are called *syntax errors* or *compilation errors*. Syntax errors result from errors in code construction, such as mistyping a keyword, omitting some necessary punctuation, or using an opening brace without a corresponding closing brace. These errors are usually easy to detect, because the compiler tells you where they are and the reasons for them. For example, compiling the following program results in a syntax error, as shown in Figure 2.14.

```java
// ShowSyntaxErrors.java: The program contains syntax errors
package chapter2;

public class ShowSyntaxErrors {
  public static void main(String[] args) {
    i = 30;
    System.out.println(i + 4);
  }
}
```

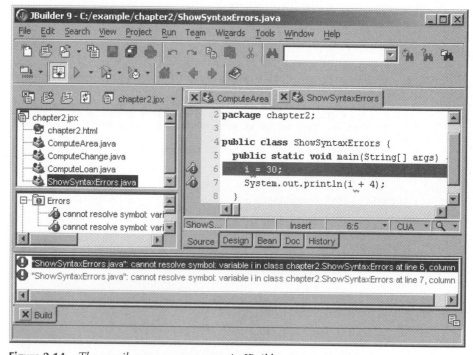

Figure 2.14 *The compiler reports syntax errors in JBuilder.*

Two errors are detected. Both are the result of not declaring variable i. Since a single error will often display many lines of compilation errors, it is a good practice to start debugging from the top line and work downward. Fixing errors that occur earlier in the program may also fix cascading errors that occur later.

2.17.2   Runtime Errors

Runtime errors are errors that cause a program to terminate abnormally. Runtime errors occur while an application is running if the environment detects an operation that is impossible to carry out. Input errors are typical runtime errors.

An *input error* occurs when the user enters an unexpected input value that the program cannot handle. For instance, if the program expects to read in a number, but instead the user enters a string, this causes data-type errors to occur in the program. To prevent input errors, the program should prompt the user to enter the correct type of values. It may display a message like "Please enter an integer" to prompt the user to enter an integer.

Another common source of runtime errors is division by zero. This happens when the divisor is zero for integer divisions. For instance, the following program would cause a runtime error, as shown in Figure 2.15.

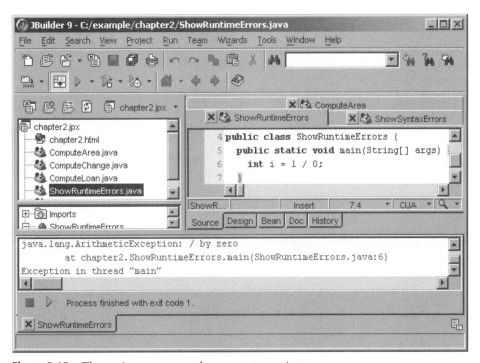

Figure 2.15   *The runtime error causes the program to terminate.*

```
// ShowruntimeErrors.java: The program contains runtime errors
package chapter2;

public class ShowRuntimeErrors {
  public static void main(String[] args) {
    int i = 1/0;
  }
}
```

2.17.3 Logic Errors

Logic errors occur when a program does not perform the way it was intended to. Errors of this kind occur for many different reasons. For example, suppose you wrote the following program to display a message reporting whether a number is between 1 and 100, inclusively.

```
// ShowLogicErrors.java: The program contains a logic error
package chapter2;

import javax.swing.JOptionPane;

public class ShowLogicErrors {
  // Determine if a number is between 1 and 100 inclusively
  public static void main(String[] args) {
    // Prompt the user to enter a number
    String input = JOptionPane.showInputDialog(null,
      "Please enter an integer:",
      "ShowLogicErrors", JOptionPane.QUESTION_MESSAGE);
    int number = Integer.parseInt(input);

    // Display the result
    JOptionPane.showMessageDialog(null,
      "The number is between 1 and 100, inclusively?\n" +
      ((1 < number) && (number < 100)),
      "ShowLogicErrors", JOptionPane.INFORMATION_MESSAGE);

    System.exit(0);
  }
}
```

The program does not have syntax errors or runtime errors, but it does not print the correct result for the number 100, as shown in Figure 2.16.

Figure 2.16 *The logic error causes the program to produce an incorrect result.*

The error is in the Boolean expression in the `println` statement. It should be as follows:

```
((1 <= number) && (number <= 100))
```

2.18   Debugging

In general, syntax errors are easy to find and easy to correct because the compiler gives indications as to where the errors came from and why they are there. Runtime errors are not difficult to find either, since the Java interpreter displays them on the console when the program aborts. Finding logic errors, on the other hand, can be very challenging.

Logic errors are called *bugs*. The process of finding and correcting errors is called *debugging*. A common approach to debugging is to use a combination of methods to narrow down to the part of the program where the bug is located. You can *hand-trace* the program (i.e., catch errors by reading the program), or you can insert print statements in order to show the values of the variables or the execution flow of the program. This approach might work for a short, simple program. But for a large, complex program, the most effective approach for debugging is to use a debugger utility.

JDK includes a command-line debugger (jdb), which is invoked with a class name. jdb is itself a Java program, running its own copy of Java interpreter. All the Java IDE tools like JBuilder, Forte, Visual J++, and Visual Café include integrated debuggers. The debugger utilities let you follow the execution of a program. They vary from one system to another, but they all support most of the following helpful features:

- **Executing a single statement at a time:** The debugger allows you to execute one statement at a time so that you can see the effect of each statement.

- **Tracing into or stepping over a method:** If a method is being executed, you can ask the debugger to enter the method and execute one statement at a time in the method, or you can ask it to step over the entire method. You should step over the entire method if you know the method works. For example, always step over the system-supplied methods, such as System.out.println.

- **Setting breakpoints:** You can also set a breakpoint at a specific statement. Your program pauses when it reaches a breakpoint and displays the line with the breakpoint. You can set as many breakpoints as you want. Breakpoints are particularly useful when you know where your programming error starts. You can set a breakpoint at that line and have the program execute until it reaches the breakpoint.

- **Displaying variables:** The debugger lets you select several variables and display their values. As you trace through a program, the content of a variable is continuously updated.

- **Using call stacks:** The debugger lets you trace all of the method calls and lists all pending methods. This feature is helpful when you need to see a large picture of the program-execution flow.

- **Modifying variables:** Some debuggers enable you to modify the value of a variable when debugging. This is convenient when you want to test a program with different samples but do not want to leave the debugger.

2.19   Debugging in JBuilder

The debugger utility is integrated in JBuilder. You can pinpoint bugs in your program with the help of the JBuilder debugger without leaving the IDE. The JBuilder debugger enables you to set breakpoints and execute programs line by line. As your program executes, you can watch the values stored in variables, observe which methods are being called, and know what events have occurred in the program.

2.19.1   Setting Breakpoints

You can execute a program line by line to trace it, but this is time-consuming if you are debugging a large program. Often, you know that some parts of the program work fine. It makes no sense to trace these parts when you only need to trace the lines of code that are likely to have bugs. In cases of this kind, you can use breakpoints.

A *breakpoint* is a stop sign placed on a line of source code that tells the debugger to pause when this line is encountered. The debugger executes every line until it encounters a breakpoint, so you can trace the part of the program at the breakpoint. Using the breakpoint, you can quickly move over the sections you know work correctly and concentrate on the sections causing problems.

There are several ways to set a breakpoint on a line. One quick way is to click the cutter of the line on which you want to put a breakpoint. You will see the line highlighted, as shown in Figure 2.17. You also can set breakpoints by choosing *Run, Add Breakpoint*. To remove a breakpoint, simply click the cutter of the line.

As you debug your program, you can set as many breakpoints as you want, and can remove breakpoints at any time during debugging. The project retains the breakpoints you have set when you exit the project. The breakpoints are restored when you reopen it.

2.19.2   Starting the Debugger

Let us use Example 2.5, "Displaying Current Time," to demonstrate debugging. Perform the following steps to start debugging ShowCurrentTime:

1. Reopen the project chapter2.jpx and select ShowCurrentTime.java in the project pane.

2. Click the cutter (the gray column on the left edge of the content pane) of the first non-comment line in the main method to set a breakpoint, as shown in Figure 2.17. A solid circle is displayed at the cutter of the line.

3. Choose ShowCurrentTime.java in the project pane, and right-click the mouse button to display the context menu. Click *Debug Using Defaults* in the context menu to start debugging.

◈ **JBUILDER NOTE:**
There are several ways to start the debugger. Steps 2 and 3 are the most convenient.

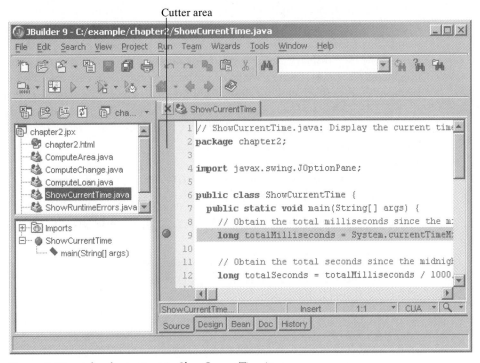

Figure 2.17   *A breakpoint is set in ShowCurrentTime.java.*

If the program compiles without problems, the message pane becomes a debugger
pane, as shown in Figure 2.18.

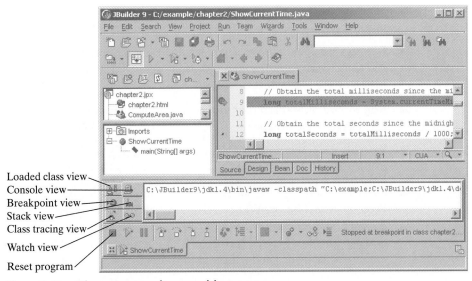

Figure 2.18   *The message pane became a debugger pane.*

There are six tabs on the left side of the message pane: console view (▣), stack view (▨), watch view (▱), loaded class view (▤), breakpoint view (▨), and class tracing view (▨). The *console view* displays output and errors and enables the user to enter input from the console. The *stack view* displays threads running in the program. The *watch view* displays the contents of the variables in the watch view. To add a variable to the watch view, see Section 2.19.4.1, "The Add Watch Command." The *loaded class view* displays classes currently loaded by the program. The *class tracing view* displays classes with tracing disabled. This feature is not available in JBuilder Personal. It is only available in the Standard and Enterprise Editions of JBuilder. By default, tracing for the classes in the Java library is disabled. To enable tracing a Java library class, choose the package that contains the class, and right-click the mouse to display a context menu. Click *Remove* to remove the package from the Class Tracing view.

2.19.3   Controlling Program Execution

The program pauses at the first breakpoint line encountered. This line, called the *current execution point*, is highlighted and has a green arrow to the left. The execution point marks the next line of source code to be executed by the debugger.

When the program pauses at the execution point, you can issue debugging commands to control the execution of the program. You also can inspect or modify the values of variables in the program.

When JBuilder is in the debugging mode, the *Run* menu contains the debugging commands (see Figure 2.19). Most of the commands also appear in the toolbar under the message pane. The toolbar contains additional commands that are not in the *Run* menu. Here are the commands for controlling program execution:

- **Step Over** executes a single statement. If the statement contains a call to a method, the entire method is executed without stepping through it.

- **Step Into** executes a single statement or steps into a method.

- **Step Out** executes all the statements in the current method and returns to its caller.

- **Run to Cursor** runs the program, starting from the current execution point, and pauses and places the execution point on the line of code containing the cursor, or at a breakpoint.

- **Run to End of Method** runs the program until it reaches the end of the current method or a breakpoint.

- **Resume Program** continues the current debugging session or restarts one that has finished or been reset.

- **Reset Program** ends the current program and releases it from memory. Use Reset to restart an application from the beginning, as when you make a change to the code and want to run again from the beginning, or if variables or data structures become corrupted with unwanted values. This command terminates debugging and returns to the normal editing session.

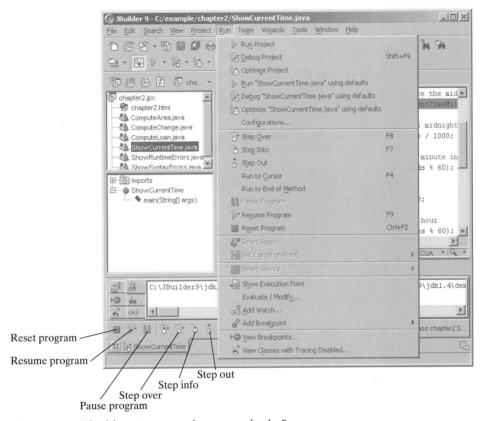

Figure 2.19   *The debugging commands appear under the Run menu.*

■   **Show Execution Point** positions the cursor at the execution point in the content pane.

2.19.4   Examining and Modifying Data Values

Among the most powerful features of an integrated debugger is its capability to reveal current data values and enable programmers to modify values during debugging. You can examine the values of variables. You also can modify a variable value if you want to try a new value to continue debugging without restarting the program.

JBuilder provides the commands *Add Watch* and *Evaluate/Modify* to enable you to inspect and modify the values of variables. These commands can be issued from the *Run* menu or by clicking the right-mouse button on the variable in the watch view or in the source code.

2.19.4.1   The Add Watch Command

The Add Watch command adds variables to the watch view so that you can watch the changing values of variables while debugging. You can view the watch view by selecting the Watch tab in the message pane. To add the variable `totalMilliseconds` to the watch view, perform the following steps:

1. Suppose the execution point is currently at the first line in the *main* method. Highlight `totalMilliseconds` in the code and right-click the mouse to reveal a popup menu.

2. Choose *Add Watch* in the popup menu to bring up a dialog box, as shown in Figure 2.20. Click *OK* to add `totalMilliseconds` to the watch view.

Figure 2.20   *The Add Watch dialog box enables you to add a variable to the watch view.*

3. Choose the Watch tab at the left side of the message pane. The watch view is shown in Figure 2.21.

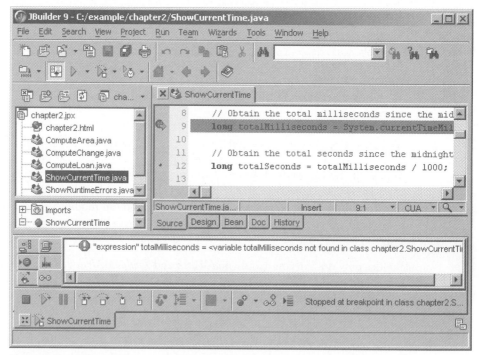

Figure 2.21   *The variable* `totalMilliseconds` *was added to the watch view.*

4. Choose *Run, Step Over* to observe the changing value of `totalMilliseconds` in the watch view, as shown in Figure 2.22.

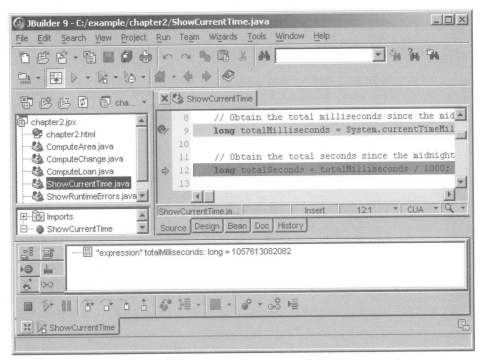

Figure 2.22 *The value of variable* `totalMilliseconds` *was displayed in the watch view.*

2.19.4.2   The Evaluate/Modify Command

The Evaluate/Modify command opens an Evaluate/Modify window where you can enter an expression and evaluate it. This is helpful for gathering additional information about the variable values in the program. The following steps show you how to evaluate an expression:

1. Set the cursor at Line 27 in the `main` method.

2. Choose *Run, Run to Cursor* to execute the program at full speed until it reaches the cursor.

3. Choose *Run, Evaluate/Modify* to bring up the Evaluate/Modify dialog box, as shown in Figure 2.23.

4. Type `totalHours` in the Expression field, and click Evaluate to see the result in the Result field. You can modify `totalHours` by entering a new value in the New Value field and click *Modify* to activate the change.

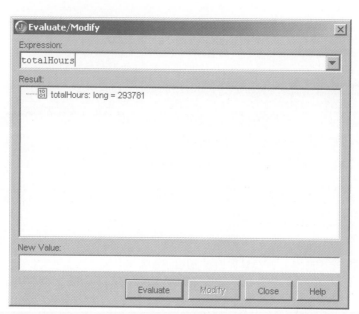

Figure 2.23   *You can evaluate an expression in the Evaluate/Modify dialog box.*

5. You can also evaluate an expression in the Evaluate/Modify dialog box. For example, type `totalHours % 24` in the Expression field, and click *Evaluate* to see the result in the Result field, as shown in Figure 2.24.

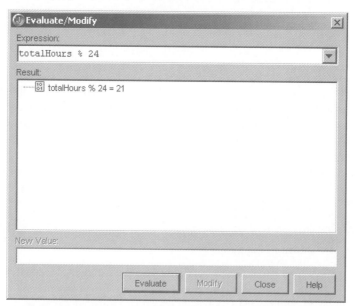

Figure 2.24   *You can type an expression and evaluate it in the Evaluate/Modify dialog box.*

6. Click *Close* to close the window.

TIP
The debugger is an indispensable, powerful tool that boosts your programming productivity. It may take you some time to become familiar with it, but your investment will pay off in the long run.

2.20 Run Java Applications from the Command Line

So far you have run programs in JBuilder IDE. You also can run a program standalone directly from the operating system. Here are the steps in running the **ComputeLoan** application from the DOS prompt.

1. Start a DOS window by clicking the Windows Start button, Programs, Accessories, MS-DOS Prompt in Windows 2000.

2. Type the following commands to set up proper environment variables for running Java programs in the DOS environment in Windows:

   set path=%path%;c:\JBuilder9\jdk1.4\bin

   set classpath=.;%classpath%

   (**Note:** No space before or after the = sign)

3. Type **cd c:\example** to change the directory to c:\example.

4. Type **java chapter2.ComputeLoan** to run the program. (Note: ComputeLoan is the class name, and chapter2 is the package name; together they form the complete name for the class.) A sample run of the output is shown in Figure 2.25.

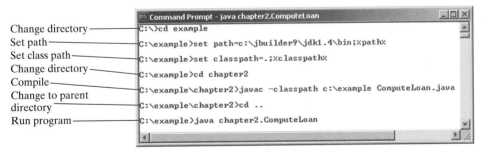

Figure 2.25 *You can compile and run a Java program from the DOS prompt using the* java *and* java *commands.*

Insert the following two lines

set path=%path%;c:\jBuilder9\jdk1.4\bin

set classpath=.;%classpath%

in the autoexec.bat file on Windows 95 or Windows 98 to avoid setting the environment variables in Step 2 for every DOS session. On Windows NT or Windows 2000, select System from the Control Panel to set the environment variables. Setting environment variables enables you to use the JDK command-line utilities. The java command invokes the Java interpreter to run the Java bytecode.

 NOTE

You can also compile the program using the `javac` command at the DOS prompt, as shown in Figure 2.25. The compiler option `-classpath` specifies where to find user class files.

 NOTE

From now on, the sample runs of non-GUI application programs will be displayed from a DOS window for clarity and simplicity.

 NOTE

More detailed coverage on how to configure your system to compile and run Java from the command window can be found in Bonus Supplement D, "Compiling and Running Java from the Command Window."

2.21   JBuilder's Online Help

JBuilder provides a large number of documents online, giving you a great deal of information on a variety of topics pertaining to the use of JBuilder and Java.

 JBUILDER NOTE

The documentation is available from a separate download at **http://info.borland .com/jbuilder/download/addons.html**. After it is downloaded and installed, you can see the documentation from the Help menu in JBuilder.

2.21.1   Accessing from the Help Menu

To access online help, choose *Help, Help Topics* to display JBuilder Help, as shown in Figure 2.26.

JBuilder Help behaves like a Web browser and contains the main menus, navigation pane, and content pane. From the main menus, you can open a URL from the File menu, add bookmarks from the Bookmarks menu, and get help on using JBuilder Help from the Help menu.

The navigation pane contains eight action buttons on top of the three tabs. The buttons are *Home, Previous, Next, Print, Find in Page, Synchronize Table of Contents, Previous Topics,* and *Next Topic.* The Home, Previous, and Next buttons let you go to the first, previous, and next topics in the history list. The Print button prints the

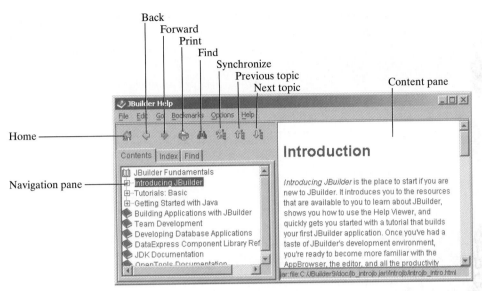

Figure 2.26   *All help documents are displayed in JBuilder Help.*

document in the content pane. The Find in Page button enables you to search the current topic. The Synchronize Table of Contents button synchronizes the topic with the contents in the content pane. The Previous Topic and Next Topic buttons let you go to the previous and next topics.

The three tabs are *Contents, Index*, and *Find*. The Contents tab displays available documents. The table of contents of the document is displayed in a tree-like list in the navigation pane. To view a given topic, select the node in the tree associated with the topic. JBuilder Help displays the document for the topic in the content pane.

The Index tab shows the index entries for the current document. The Find page shows the combined index entries for all the available documents in JBuilder. To display the index, simply type the first few letters in the entry. As you start typing, the index scrolls, doing an incremental search on the index entries to find the closest match. Select and double-click the index in the entry to display the document for the entry in the content pane.

2.21.2   Obtaining Help on Java Keywords and Classes

To obtain help on a Java keyword, highlight it in the content pane of the App-Browser and press *F1*. For example, if you highlight `public` in the content pane of the AppBrowser, as shown in Figure 2.27, and press F1, you will see the help on `public` displayed in Figure 2.28.

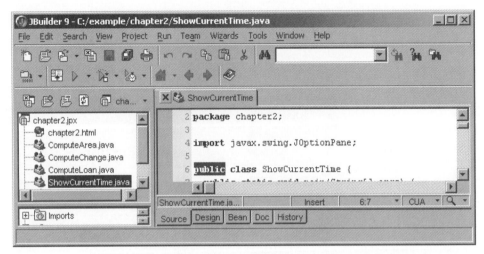

Figure 2.27   *Highlight* public *and press F1 to display the documentation on the keyword* public.

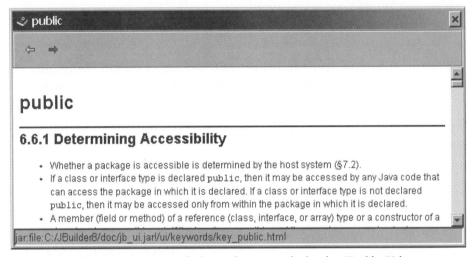

Figure 2.28   *The documentation on the keyword* public *is displayed in JBuilder Help.*

To display the documentation on a Java class, highlight the class name (e.g., String) in the content pane and press F1. The documentation for the class is displayed in JBuilder Help, as shown in Figure 2.29.

You can also display the source code of the class by choosing *Find Definition* in the context menu of the class in the content pane, as shown in Figure 2.30. The class source code will be displayed in the content pane.

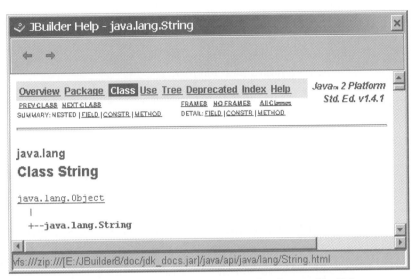

Figure 2.29 *The documentation on the* String *class is displayed in JBuilder Help.*

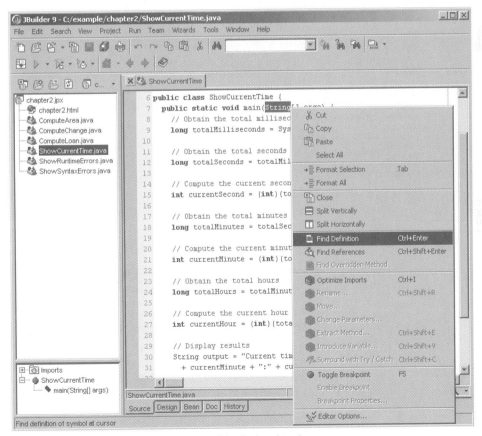

Figure 2.30 *The source code of the class will be displayed in the content pane.*

Chapter Summary

- Identifiers are used for naming programming entities, such as variables, constants, methods, classes, and packages.

- Variables are symbols that represent data. The value of a variable can be changed with an assignment statement. All variables must be declared with an identifier and a type before they can be used. An initial value must be assigned to a variable before it is referenced.

- The equals sign (=) is used to assign a value to a variable. A statement with an equals sign is called an assignment statement. When a value is assigned to a variable, it replaces the previous value of the variable, which is destroyed.

- A constant is a symbol representing a value in the program that is never changed. You cannot change a constant once it is declared.

- Java provides four integer types (`byte`, `short`, `int`, `long`) that represent integers of four different sizes, and two floating-point types (`float`, `double`) that represent floating-point numbers of two different precisions. Character type (`char`) represents a single character, and `boolean` type represents a `true` or `false` value. These are called primitive data types. Java's primitive types are portable across all computer platforms. They have exactly the same values on all platforms. When they are declared, the variables of these types are created and assigned memory space.

- Java provides operators that perform numeric operations: + (addition), – (subtraction), * (multiplication), / (division), and % (remainder). Integer division (/) yields an integer result. The remainder operator (%) yields the remainder of the division.

- The increment operator (++) and the decrement operator (−−) increment or decrement a variable by 1. If the operator is prefixed to the variable, the variable is first incremented or decremented by 1, then used in the expression. If the operator is a suffix to the variable, the variable is used in the expression first, then incremented or decremented by 1.

- All the numeric operators can be applied to characters. When an operand is a character, the character's Unicode value is used in the operation.

- You can use casting to convert a value of one type into another type. Casting a variable of a type with a small range to a variable of a type with a larger range is known as *widening a type*. Casting a variable of a type with a large range to a variable of a type with a smaller range is known as *narrowing a type*. Widening a type can be performed automatically without explicit casting. Narrowing a type must be performed explicitly.

- The Boolean operators &&, &, ¦¦, ¦, !, and ^ operate with Boolean values and variables. The relational operators (<, <=, ==, !=, >, >=) work with numbers and characters, and yield a Boolean value.

■ When evaluating p1 && p2, Java first evaluates p1 and then evaluates p2 if p1 is true; if p1 is false, it does not evaluate p2. When evaluating p1 ¦¦ p2, Java first evaluates p1 and then evaluates p2 if p1 is false; if p1 is true, it does not evaluate p2. Therefore, && is referred to as the *conditional* or *short-circuit AND* operator, and ¦¦ is referred to as the *conditional* or *short-circuit OR* operator.

■ Java also provides the & and ¦ operators. The & operator works exactly the same as the && operator, and the ¦ operator works exactly the same as the ¦¦ operator with one exception: the & and ¦ operators always evaluate both operands. Therefore, & is referred to as the *unconditional AND* operator, and ¦ is referred to as the *unconditional OR* operator.

■ The operands of a binary operator are evaluated from left to right. No part of the right-hand operand is evaluated until all the operands before the binary operator are evaluated.

■ The operators in arithmetic expressions are evaluated in the order determined by the rules of parentheses, operator precedence, and associativity.

■ Parentheses can be used to force the order of evaluation to occur in any sequence. Operators with higher precedence are evaluated earlier. The associativity of the operators determines the order of evaluation for operators of the same precedence.

■ All binary operators except assignment operators are left-associative, and assignment operators are right-associative.

■ You can receive input from an input dialog box using the method JOptionPane.showInputDialog. The input from an input dialog box is a string. To convert it to a double number, use the Double.parseDouble method; to convert it to an int value, use the Integer.parseInt method.

■ Programming errors can be categorized into three types: syntax errors, runtime errors, and logic errors. Errors that occur during compilation are called *syntax errors* or *compilation errors*. *Runtime errors* are errors that cause a program to terminate abnormally. *Logic errors* occur when a program does not perform the way it was intended to.

■ Debugging is the process of finding errors and correcting or modifying code in a program so that it will run as you expected.

■ The debugger utilities let you trace the execution of a program and examine the values of the variables as the program executes.

Review Questions

2.1 Are the following identifiers valid?

```
applet, Applet, a++, --a, 4#R, $4, #44, apps
```

2.2 Declare the following:

■ An int variable with an initial value of 0.

- A `long` variable with an initial value of `10000`.

- A `float` variable with an initial value of `3.4`.

- A `double` variable with an initial value of `34.45`.

- A `char` variable with an initial value of `4`.

- A `boolean` variable with an initial value of `true`.

2.3 Assume that `int a = 1` and `double d = 1.0`, and that each expression is independent. What are the results of the following expressions?

```
a = 46 / 9;
a = 46 % 9 + 4 * 4 - 2;
a = 45 + 43 % 5 * (23 * 3 % 2);
a %= 3 / a + 3;
d = 4 + d * d + 4;
d += 1.5 * 3 + (++a);
d -= 1.5 * 3 + a++;
```

2.4 Find the largest and smallest `byte`, `short`, `int`, `long`, `float`, and `double`. Which of these data types requires the least amount of memory?

2.5 Can different types of numeric values be used together in a computation?

2.6 Describe Unicode and ASCII code.

2.7 Can the following conversions involving casting be allowed? If so, find the converted result.

```
char c = 'A';
i = (int)c;

boolean b = true;
i = (int)b;

float f = 1000.34f;
int i = (int)f;

double d = 1000.34;
int i = (int)d;

int i = 97;
char c = (char)i;

int i = 1000;
boolean b = (boolean)i;
```

2.8 What is the result of 25 / 4? How would you rewrite the expression if you wished the result to be a floating-point number?

2.9 Are the following statements correct? If so, show the output.

```
System.out.println("the output for 25/4 is " + 25 / 4);
System.out.println("the output for 25/4.0 is " + 25 / 4.0);
```

2.10 What does an explicit conversion from a `double` to an `int` do with the fractional part of the *double* value? Does casting change the variable being cast?

2.11 How would you write the following arithmetic expression in Java?

$$\frac{4}{3(r + 34)} - 9(a + bc) + \frac{3 + d(2 + a)}{a + bd}$$

2.12 List six comparison operators.

2.13 Assume that x is 1, show the result of the following Boolean expressions.

```
(true) && (3 > 4)

!(x > 0) && (x > 0)

(x > 0) || (x < 0)

(x != 0) || (x == 0)

(x >= 0) || (x < 0)

(x != 1) == !(x == 1)
```

2.14 Write a Boolean expression that evaluates to true if the number is between 1 and 100.

2.15 Write a Boolean expression that evaluates to true if the number is between 1 and 100 or the number is negative.

2.16 Assume that x and y are int type. Which of the following expressions are correct?

```
x > y > 0

x = y && y

x /= y

x or y

x and y

(x != 0) || (x = 0)
```

2.17 How do you denote a comment line and a comment paragraph?

2.18 Describe syntax errors, runtime errors, and logic errors.

2.19 What are the naming conventions for class names, method names, constants, and variables? Which of the following items can be a constant, a method, a variable, or a class according to the Java naming conventions?

```
MAX_VALUE, Test, read, readInt
```

2.20 Suppose that x is 1. What is x after the evaluation of the following expression?

```
(x > 1) & (x++ > 1)
```

2.21 Suppose that x is 1. What is x after the evaluation of the following expression?

```
(x > 1) && (x++ > 1)
```

2.22 List the precedence order of the Boolean operators. Evaluate the following expressions:

```
true | true && false
true || true && false
true | true & false
```

2.23 Evaluate the following expression:

```
1 + "Welcome " + 1 + 1
1 + "Welcome " + (1 + 1)
1 + "Welcome " + ('\u0001'  + 1)
1 + "Welcome " + 'a'  + 1
```

2.24 Which of these statements are true?
  a. Any expression can be used as a statement.
  b. The expression x++ can be used as a statement.
  c. The statement x = x + 5 is also an expression.
  d. The statement x = y = x = 0 is illegal.
  e. All the operators of the same precedence are evaluated from left to right.

2.25 Show and explain the output of the following code:

  a.
```
int i = 0;
System.out.println(--i + i + i++);
System.out.println(i + ++i);
```
  b.
```
int i = 0;
i = i + (i = 1);
System.out.println(i);
```
  c.
```
int i = 0;
i = (i = 1) + i;
System.out.println(i);
```

2.26 Which of the following are correct literals for floating-point numbers?
  a. 12.3;
  b. 12.3e + 2;
  c. 23.4e − 2;
  d. −334.4

2.27 Which of the following are correct literals for characters?
  a. '1';
  b. \u345d;
  c. '\u3fFa';
  d. '\b'

2.28 Assume that int a = 1 and double d = 1.0, and that each expression is independent. What are the results of the following expressions?

```
a = (a = 3) + a;
a = a + (a = 3);
a += a + (a = 3);
a = 5 + 5 * 2 % a--;
a = 4 + 1 + 4 * 5 % (++a + 1);
d += 1.5 * 3 + (++d);
d -= 1.5 * 3 + d++;
```

2.29 What is the command to compile a Java program? What is the command to run a Java application?

2.30 If the exception `NoClassFoundError` is raised when you run a program from the DOS prompt, what is wrong?

2.31 If the exception "NoSuchMethodError: main" is raised when you run a program from the DOS prompt, what is wrong?

2.32 Identify and fix the errors in the following code:

```
1    public class Test {
2      public void main(string[] args) {
3        int i;
4        int k = 100.0;
5        int j = i + 1;
6
7        System.out.println("j is " + j + " and
8          k is " + k);
9      }
10   }
```

2.33 Show the output of the following program:

```
public class Test {
  public static void main(String[] args) {
    char x = 'a';
    char y = 'c';

    System.out.println(++y);
    System.out.println(y++);
    System.out.println(x > y);
    System.out.println(x - y);
  }
}
```

2.34 Reformat the following program according to the programming style and documentation guidelines proposed in Section 2.16. Use the next-line brace style.

```
public class Test
{
  // Main method
  public static void main(String[] args) {
  /** Print a line */
  System.out.println("2 % 3 = "+2%3);
  }
}
```

2.35 Suppose a class named `Test` has the following package statement in the code:

```
package csci1301;
```

and Test.class is stored in `c:\smith\homework\csci1301`. How should you run the Test class from the DOS prompt?

Programming Exercises

2.1 (Converting Fahrenheit to Celsius) Write a program that reads a Fahrenheit degree in double from an input dialog box, then converts it to Celsius and displays the result in a message dialog box. The formula for the conversion is as follows:

celsius = (5/9) * (fahrenheit − 32)

 HINT

In Java, 5 / 9 is 0, so you need to write 5.0 / 9 in the program to obtain the correct result.

2.2 (Computing the volume of a cylinder) Write a program that reads in the radius and length of a cylinder and computes volume using the following formulas:

area = radius * radius * π

volume = area * length

2.3 (Converting feet into meters) Write a program that reads a number in feet, converts it to meters, and displays the result. One foot is 0.305 meters.

2.4 (Revising Example 2.4 "Monetary Units") Rewrite Example 2.4 to fix the possible loss of accuracy when converting a `double` value to an `int` value. Enter the input as an integer whose last two digits represent the cents. For example, the input 1156 represents 11 dollars and 56 cents.

2.5 (Summing the digits in an integer) Write a program that reads an integer between 0 and 1000 and adds all the digits in the integer. For example, if an integer is 932, the sum of all its digits is 14.

 HINT

Use the % operator to extract digits and use the / operator to remove the extracted digit. For instance, 932 % 10 = 2 and 932 / 10 = 93.

2.6 (Checking whether a number is between 1 and 1000) Write a program that reads a double number and checks whether the number is between 1 and 1000. If your input is 5, your output should be:

The number 5 is between 1 and 1000: true.

If your input is 2000, your output should be:

The number 2000 is between 1 and 1000: false.

2.7 (Checking whether a number is even) Write a program that reads an integer and checks whether it is even. If your input is 25, your output should be:

The number 25 is even: false

If your input is 2000, your output should be:

The number 2000 is even: true

2.8 (Converting pounds into kilograms) Write a program that converts pounds into kilograms. The program prompts the user to enter a number in pounds, converts it to kilograms, and displays the result. One pound is 0.454 kilograms.

2.9 (Calculating the future investment value) Write a program that reads in investment amount, annual interest rate, and number of years, and displays the future investment value using the following formula:

```
futureInvestmentValue =
    investmentAmount x (1 + monthlyInterestRate)^(numOfYears*12)
```

For example, if you entered amount 1000, annual interest rate 3.25%, and number of years 1, the future investment value is 1032.98.

> **HINT**
> Use the Math.pow(a, b) method to compute a raised to the power of b.

2.10 (Converting an uppercase letter to lowercase) Write a program that converts an uppercase letter to a lowercase letter. The character is typed in the source code. In Chapter 7, "Strings," you will learn how to enter a character from an input dialog box.

> **HINT**
> In the ASCII table (see Appendix B), uppercase letters appear before lowercase letters. The offset between any uppercase letter and its corresponding lowercase letter is the same. So you can find a lowercase letter from its corresponding uppercase letter, as follows:
> ```
> int offset = (int)'a' - (int)'A';
> char lowercase = (char)((int)uppercase + offset);
> ```

2.11 (Finding the character of an ASCII code) Write a program that receives an ASCII code (an integer between 0 and 128) and displays its character. For example, if the user enters 97, the program displays character a.

2.12 (Calculating tips) Write a program that reads the subtotal and the gratuity rate, and computes the gratuity and total. For example, if the user enters 10 for subtotal and 15 percent for gratuity rate, the program displays $1.5 as gratuity and $11.5 as total.

2.13 (Payroll) Write a program that reads the following information and prints a payroll statement, as shown in Figure 2.31.

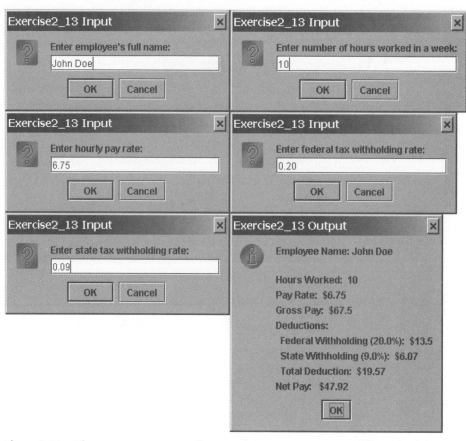

Figure 2.31 *The program prints a payroll statement.*

Employee's full name (e.g., John Doe)
Number of hours worked in a week (e.g., 10)
Hourly pay rate (e.g., 6.75)
Federal tax withholding rate (e.g., 20%)
State tax withholding rate (e.g., 9%)

CONTROL STATEMENTS

Objectives

- To understand the concept of program control.
- To use selection statements to control the execution of programs.
- To use loop statements to control the repetition of statements.
- To implement program control with break and continue.

3.1 Introduction

Program control specifies the order in which statements are executed in a program. The programs that you have written so far execute statements in sequence. Often, however, you are faced with situations in which you must provide alternative steps.

In Chapter 2, "Primitive Data Types and Operations," if you assigned a negative value for `radius` in Example 2.1, "Computing the Area of a Circle," for instance, the program would print an invalid result. If the radius is negative, you don't want the program to compute the area. Like all high-level programming languages, Java provides selection statements that let you choose actions with two or more alternative courses. You can use selection statements in the following pseudocode to rewrite Example 2.1:

```
if the radius is negative
  the program displays a message indicating a wrong input;
else
  the program computes the area and displays the result;
```

Like other high-level programming languages, Java provides iteration structures in order to control the repeated execution of statements. Suppose that you need to print the same message a hundred times. It would be tedious to have to write the message over and over again. Java provides a powerful control structure called a *loop*, which controls how many times an operation or a sequence of operations is performed in succession. Using a loop statement, you simply tell the computer to print the message a hundred times without having to code the print statement a hundred times. Java has three types of loop statements: `while` loops, `do-while` loops, and `for` loops.

In this chapter, you will learn various selection and loop control statements.

3.2 Selection Statements

This section introduces selection statements. Java has several types of selection statements: simple `if` statements, `if . . . else` statements, nested `if` statements, `switch` statements, and conditional expressions.

3.2.1 Simple *if* Statements

A simple `if` statement executes an action only if the condition is `true`. The syntax for a simple `if` statement is shown below:

```
if (booleanExpression) {
  statement(s);
}
```

The execution flowchart is shown in Figure 3.1.

If the `booleanExpression` evaluates as `true`, the statements in the block are executed. As an example, see the following code:

```
if (radius >= 0) {
  area = radius * radius * PI;
  System.out.println("The area for the circle of radius " +
    radius + " is " + area);
}
```

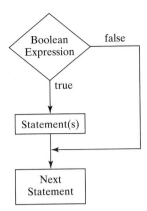

Figure 3.1 *An* `if` *statement executes statements if the* `booleanExpression` *evaluates as* `true`.

If the value of `radius` is greater than or equal to 0, then the `area` is computed and the result is displayed; otherwise, the two statements in the block will not be executed.

The following statement determines whether a number is even or odd:

```
// Prompt the user to enter an integer
String intString = JOptionPane.showInputDialog(null,
  "Enter an integer:", "Example", JOptionPane.QUESTION_MESSAGE);

// Convert string into int
int number = Integer.parseInt(intString);

if (number % 2 == 0)
  System.out.println(number + " is even.");

if (number % 2 != 0)
  System.out.println(number + " is odd.");
```

CAUTION

Adding a semicolon at the end of an `if` clause is a common mistake. For example,

```
if (radius >= 0); ◄—— Logic Error
{
  area = radius * radius * PI;
  System.out.println("The area for the circle of radius " +
    radius + " is " + area);
}
```

This mistake is hard to find, because it is not a compilation error or a runtime error, it is a logic error. The preceding statement is equivalent to

```
if (radius >= 0) { };

area = radius * radius * PI;
System.out.println("The area for the circle of radius " +
  radius + " is " + area);
```

This error often occurs when you use the next-line block style. Using the end-of-line block style will prevent this error.

NOTE

The `booleanExpression` is enclosed in parentheses for all forms of the `if` statement. Thus, for example, the outer parentheses in the following `if` statement are required.

```
if ((i > 0) && (i < 10)) {
  System.out.println("i is an integer between 0 and 10");
}
```

The braces can be omitted if they enclose a single statement. For example:

```
if ((i > 0) && (i < 10))
  system.out.println("i is an integer between 0 and 10");
```

 CAUTION

Forgetting the braces when they are needed for grouping multiple statements is a common programming error. If you modify the code by adding new statements in an `if` statement without braces, you will have to insert the braces if they are not already in place.

3.2.2   if ... else Statements

A simple `if` statement takes an action if the specified condition is `true`. If the condition is `false`, nothing is done. But what if you want to take alternative actions when the condition is `false`? You can use an `if . . . else` statement. The actions that an `if . . . else` statement specifies differ based on whether the condition is `true` or `false`.

Here is the syntax for this type of statement:

```
if (booleanExpression) {
  statement(s)-for-the-true-case;
}
else {
  statement(s)-for-the-false-case;
}
```

The flow chart of the statement is shown in Figure 3.2.

If the `booleanExpression` evaluates as `true`, the `statement(s)` for the true case is executed; otherwise, the `statement(s)` for the false case is executed. For example, consider the following code:

```
if (radius >= 0) {
  area = radius * radius * PI;
  System.out.println("The area for the circle of radius " +
    radius + " is " + area);
}
else {
  System.out.println("Negative input");
}
```

If `radius > = 0` is true, `area` is computed and displayed; if it is `false`, the message `"Negative input"` is printed. As usual, the braces can be omitted if there is only one statement within them. The braces enclosing the `System.out.println("Negative input")` statement can therefore be omitted in the preceding example.

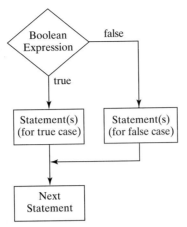

Figure 3.2 *An* `if . . . else` *statement executes statements for the* `true` *case if the* `boolean` *expression evaluates as* `true`; *otherwise, statements for the* `false` *case are executed.*

Using the `if . . . else` statement, you can rewrite the code for determining whether a number is even or odd in the preceding section, as follows:

```
if (number % 2 == 0)
  System.out.println(number + " is even.");
else
  System.out.println(number + " is odd.");
```

This is more efficient because whether `number % 2` is 0 is tested only once.

3.2.3   Nested *if* Statements

The statement in an `if` or `if . . . else` statement can be any legal Java statement, including another `if` or `if . . . else` statement. The inner `if` statement is said to be *nested* inside the outer `if` statement. The inner `if` statement can contain another `if` statement; in fact, there is no limit to the depth of the nesting. For example, the following is a nested `if` statement:

```
if (i > k) {
  if (j > k)
    System.out.println("i and j are greater than k");
}
else
  System.out.println("i is less than or equal to k");
```

The `if (j > k)` statement is nested inside the `if (i > k)` statement.

The nested `if` statement can be used to implement multiple alternatives. The statement given below, for instance, assigns a letter grade to the variable `grade` according to the score, with multiple alternatives.

```
if (score >= 90.0)
  grade = 'A';
else
  if (score >= 80.0)
    grade = 'B';
```

```
else
  if (score >= 70.0)
    grade = 'C';
  else
    if (score >= 60.0)
      grade = 'D';
    else
      grade = 'F';
```

The execution of this `if` statement proceeds as follows. The first condition (`score > = 90.0`) is tested. If it is `true`, the grade becomes `'A'`. If it is `false`, the second condition (`score > = 80.0`) is tested. If the second condition is `true`, the grade becomes `'B'`. If that condition is `false`, the third condition and the rest of the conditions (if necessary) continue to be tested until a condition is met or all of the conditions prove to be `false`. If all of the conditions are `false`, the grade becomes `'F'`. Note that a condition is tested only when all of the conditions that come before it are `false`.

The preceding `if` statement is equivalent to the following:

```
if (score >= 90.0)
  grade = 'A';
else if (score >= 80.0)
  grade = 'B';
else if (score >= 70.0)
  grade = 'C';
else if (score >= 60.0)
  grade = 'D';
else
  grade = 'F';
```

In fact, this is the preferred writing style for multiple alternative `if` statements. This style avoids deep indentation and makes the program easy to read.

◈ NOTE

The `else` clause matches the most recent unmatched `if` clause. For example, the following statement

```
int i = 1;
int j = 2;
int k = 3;

if (i > j)
  if (i > k)
    System.out.println("A");
else
  System.out.println("B");
```

is equivalent to

```
int i = 1;
int j = 2;
int k = 3;

if (i > j)
  if (i > k)
    System.out.println("A");
  else
    System.out.println("B");
```

Nothing is printed from the preceding statement. To force the `else` clause to match the first `if` clause, you must add a pair of braces:

```
int i = 1;
int j = 2;
int k = 3;

if (i > j) {
  if (i > k)
    System.out.println("A");
}
else
  System.out.println("B");
```

This statement prints B.

 TIP

Often your program assigns a test condition to a `boolean` variable like this:

```
if (number % 2 == 0)
  even = true;
else
  even = false;
```

Avoid using `if` statements to assign test values to `boolean` variables. Instead, assign the test values directly to the variables, as follows:

```
boolean even = number % 2 == 0;
```

 CAUTION

To test whether a `boolean` variable is `true` or `false` in a test condition, it is redundant to use the equality comparison operator like this:

```
if (even == true)
  System.out.println("It is even.");
```

Instead, it is better to use the `boolean` variable directly, as follows:

```
if (even)
  System.out.println("It is even.");
```

Another good reason to use the `boolean` variable directly is to avoid potential errors that are difficult to detect. It is a common error to use the = operator instead of the == operator to compare equality of two items in a test condition. This could lead to the following erroneous statement:

```
if (even = true)
  System.out.println("It is event.");
```

This statement does not have syntax errors. It assigns `true` to `even` so that `even` is always `true`.

Example 3.1 Computing Taxes

Problem

The United States federal personal income tax is calculated based on filing status and taxable income. There are four filing statuses: single filers, married filing jointly, married filing separately, and head of household. The tax rates for 2002 are shown in Table 3.1. For example, if you are single with a taxable income of $10,000, the first $6,000 is taxed at 10% and the other $4,000 is taxed at 15%. So, your tax is $1,200.

TABLE 3.1   2002 U.S. Federal Personal Tax Rates

Tax rate	Single filers	Married filing jointly or qualifying widow/widower	Married filing separately	Head of household
10%	Up to $6,000	Up to $12,000	Up to $6,000	Up to $10,000
15%	$6,001–$27,950	$12,001–$46,700	$6,001–$23,350	$10,001–$37,450
27%	$27,951–$67,700	$46,701–$112,850	$23,351–$56,425	$37,451–$96,700
30%	$67,701–$141,250	$112,851–$171,950	$56,426–$85,975	$96,701–$156,600
35%	$141,251–$307,050	$171,951–$307,050	$85,976–$153,525	$156,601–$307,050
38.6%	$307,051 or more	$307,051 or more	$153,526 or more	$307,051 or more

Write a program that prompts the user to enter the filing status and taxable income and computes the tax for the year 2002. Enter 0 for single filers, 1 for married filing jointly, 2 for married filing separately, and 3 for head of household. A sample run of the program is shown in Figure 3.3.

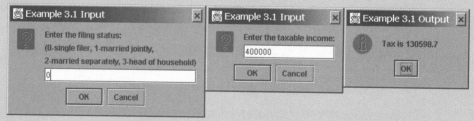

Figure 3.3   *The program computes the tax using* if *statements.*

Solution

For each filing status, there are six tax rates. Each rate is applied to the certain amount of the taxable income. For example, among the taxable income of $400,000 for single filers, $6,000 is taxed at 10%, $(27950 - 6000)$ at 15%, $(67700 - 27950)$ at 27%, $(141250 - 67700)$ at 35%, and $(400000 - 307050)$ at 38.6%.

Your program computes the tax for the taxable income based on the filing status. The filing status can be determined using if statements. The following code gives the solution to the problem.

```
1    package chapter3;
2
3    import javax.swing.JOptionPane;
4    public class ComputeTaxWithSelectionStatement {
5      public static void main(String[] args) {
6        // Prompt the user to enter filing status
7        String statusString = JOptionPane.showInputDialog(null,
8          "Enter the filing status:\n" +
9          "(0-single filer, 1-married jointly,\n" +
10         "2-married separately, 3-head of household)",
11         "Example 3.1 Input", JOptionPane.QUESTION_MESSAGE);
12       int status = Integer.parseInt(statusString);
13
14       // Prompt the user to enter taxable income
15       String incomeString = JOptionPane.showInputDialog(null,
16         "Enter the taxable income:",
17         "Example 3.1 Input", JOptionPane.QUESTION_MESSAGE);
18       double income = Double.parseDouble(incomeString);
19
20       // Compute tax
21       double tax = 0;
22
23       if (status == 0) { // Compute tax for single filers
24         if (income <= 6000)
25           tax = income * 0.10;
26         else if (income <= 27950)
27           tax = 6000 * 0.10 + (income - 6000) * 0.15;
28         else if (income <= 67700)
29           tax = 6000 * 0.10 + (27950 - 6000) * 0.15 +
30             (income - 27950) * 0.27;
31         else if (income <= 141250)
32           tax = 6000 * 0.10 + (27950 - 6000) * 0.15 +
33             (67700 - 27950) * 0.27 + (income - 67700) * 0.30;
34         else if (income <= 307050)
35           tax = 6000 * 0.10 + (27950 - 6000) * 0.15 +
36             (67700 - 27950) * 0.27 + (141250 - 67700) * 0.30 +
37             (income - 141250) * 0.35;
38         else
39           tax = 6000 * 0.10 + (27950 - 6000) * 0.15 +
40             (67700 - 27950) * 0.27 + (141250 - 67700) * 0.30 +
41             (307050 - 141250) * 0.35 + (income - 307050) * 0.386;
42       }
43       else if (status == 1) { // Compute tax for married file jointly
44         if (income <= 12000)
45           tax = income * 0.10;
46         else if (income <= 46700)
47           tax = 12000 * 0.10 + (income - 12000) * 0.15;
48         else if (income <= 112850)
49           tax = 12000 * 0.10 + (46700 - 12000) * 0.15 +
50             (income - 46700) * 0.27;
51         else if (income <= 171950)
52           tax = 12000 * 0.10 + (46700 - 12000) * 0.15 +
53             (112850 - 46700) * 0.27 + (income - 112850) * 0.30;
54         else if (income <= 307050)
55           tax = 12000 * 0.10 + (46700 - 12000) * 0.15 +
56             (112850 - 46700) * 0.27 + (171950 - 112850) * 0.30 +
57             (income - 171950) * 0.35;
```

(continues)

113

Example 3.1 continued

```
58          else
59            tax = 12000 * 0.10 + (46700 - 12000) * 0.15 +
60              (112850 - 46700) * 0.27 + (171950 - 112850) * 0.30 +
61              (307050 - 171950) * 0.35 + (income - 307050) * 0.386;
62        }
63        else if (status == 2) { // Compute tax for married separately
64          if (income <= 6000)
65            tax = income * 0.10;
66          else if (income <= 23350)
67            tax = 6000 * 0.10 + (income - 6000) * 0.15;
68          else if (income <= 56425)
69            tax = 6000 * 0.10 + (23350 - 6000) * 0.15 +
70              (income - 23350) * 0.27;
71          else if (income <= 85975)
72            tax = 6000 * 0.10 + (23350 - 6000) * 0.15 +
73              (56425 - 23350) * 0.27 + (income - 56425) * 0.30;
74          else if (income <= 153525)
75            tax = 6000 * 0.10 + (23350 - 6000) * 0.15 +
76              (56425 - 23350) * 0.27 + (85975 - 56425) * 0.30 +
77              (income - 85975) * 0.35;
78          else
79            tax = 6000 * 0.10 + (23350 - 6000) * 0.15 +
80              (56425 - 23350) * 0.27 + (85975 - 56425) * 0.30 +
81              (153525 - 85975) * 0.35 + (income - 153525) * 0.386;
82        }
83        else if (status == 3) { // Compute tax for head of household
84          if (income <= 10000)
85            tax = income * 0.10;
86          else if (income <= 37450)
87            tax = 10000 * 0.10 + (income - 10000) * 0.15;
88          else if (income <= 96700)
89            tax = 10000 * 0.10 + (37450 - 10000) * 0.15 +
90              (income - 37450) * 0.27;
91          else if (income <= 156600)
92            tax = 10000 * 0.10 + (37450 - 10000) * 0.15 +
93              (96700 - 37450) * 0.27 + (income - 96700) * 0.30;
94          else if (income <= 307050)
95            tax = 10000 * 0.10 + (37450 - 10000) * 0.15 +
96              (96700 - 37450) * 0.27 + (156600 - 96700) * 0.30 +
97              (income - 156600) * 0.35;
98          else
99            tax = 10000 * 0.10 + (37450 - 10000) * 0.15 +
100             (96700 - 37450) * 0.27 + (156600 - 96700) * 0.30 +
101             (307050 - 156600) * 0.35 + (income - 307050) * 0.386;
102       }
103       else {
104         System.out.println("Error: invalid status");
105         System.exit(0);
106       }
107
108       // Display the result
109       JOptionPane.showMessageDialog(null, "Tax is " +
110         (int)(tax * 100) / 100.0,
111         "Example 3.1 Output", JOptionPane.INFORMATION_MESSAGE);
112
113       System.exit(0);
114     }
115   }
```

Review

The `import` statement (Line 3) makes the class `javax.swing.JOptionPane` available for use in this example.

The program receives the filing status and taxable income. The multiple alternative `if` statements (Lines 23, 43, 63, 83) check the filing status and compute the tax based on the filing status.

Note that an initial value of 0 is assigned to `tax` (Line 21). A syntax error would occur if it had no initial value because all of the other statements that assign values to `tax` are within the `if` statement. The compiler thinks that these statements may not be executed and therefore reports a syntax error.

3.2.4   *switch* Statements

The `if` statement in Example 3.1 makes selections based on a single `true` or `false` condition. There are four cases for computing taxes, which depend on the value of `status`. To fully account for all the cases, nested `if` statements were used. Overuse of nested `if` statements makes a program difficult to read. Java provides a `switch` statement to handle multiple conditions efficiently. You could write the following `switch` statement to replace the nested `if` statement in Example 3.1:

```
switch (status) {
  case 0:  compute taxes for single filers;
           break;
  case 1:  compute taxes for married file jointly;
           break;
  case 2:  compute taxes for married file separately;
           break;
  case 3:  compute taxes for head of household;
           break;
  default: System.out.println("Errors: invalid status");
           System.exit(0);
}
```

The flowchart of the preceding `switch` statement is shown in Figure 3.4.

This statement checks to see whether the status matches the value 0, 1, 2, or 3, in that order. If matched, the corresponding tax is computed; if not matched, a message is displayed. Here is the full syntax for the `switch` statement:

```
switch (switch-expression) {
  case value1: statement(s)1;
               break;
  case value2: statement(s)2;
               break;
  …
  case valueN: statement(s)N;
               break;
  default:     statement(s)-for-default;
}
```

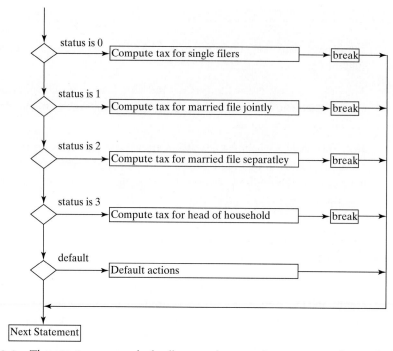

Figure 3.4 *The* switch *statement checks all cases and executes the statements in the matched case.*

The switch statement observes the following rules:

■ The switch-expression must yield a value of char, byte, short, or int type and must always be enclosed in parentheses.

■ The value1, ..., and valueN must have the same data type as the value of the switch-expression. The resulting statements in the case statement are executed when the value in the case statement matches the value of the switch-expression. Note that value1, ..., and valueN are constant expressions, meaning that they cannot contain variables in the expression, such as 1 + x.

■ The keyword break is optional, but it should be used at the end of each case in order to terminate the remainder of the switch statement. If the break statement is not present, the next case statement will be executed.

■ The default case, which is optional, can be used to perform actions when none of the specified cases matches the switch-expression.

■ The case statements are executed in sequential order, but the order of the cases (including the default case) does not matter. However, it is good programming style to follow the logical sequence of the cases and place the default case at the end.

CAUTION

Do not forget to use a break statement when one is needed. If a break statement is not present, the statements for the matched case are executed once a case is matched; afterwards, the statements in the subsequent cases are all executed.

TIP
To avoid programming errors and improve code maintainability, it is a good idea to put a comment in a case clause if `break` is purposely omitted.

3.2.5   Conditional Expressions

You might want to assign a value to a variable that is restricted by certain conditions. For example, the following statement assigns 1 to y if x is greater than 0, and −1 to y if x is less than or equal to 0.

```
if (x > 0)
  y = 1
else
  y = -1;
```

Alternatively, as in this example, you can use a conditional expression to achieve the same result.

```
y = (x > 0) ? 1 : -1;
```

Conditional expressions are in a completely different style, with no explicit `if` in the statement. The syntax is shown below:

```
booleanExpression ? expression1 : expression2;
```

The result of this conditional expression is `expression1` if `booleanExpression` is true, otherwise the result is `expression2`.

Suppose you want to assign the larger number between variable `num1` and `num2` to `max`. You can simply write a statement using the conditional expression:

```
max = (num1 > num2) ? num1 : num2;
```

For another example, the following statement displays the message "*num* is even" if *num* is even, and otherwise displays "num is odd."

```
System.out.println((num % 2 == 0) ? "num is even" : "num is odd");
```

 NOTE
The symbols `?` and `:` appear together in a conditional expression. They form a conditional operator. This operator is called a *ternary operator* because it uses three operands. This is the only ternary operator in Java.

3.3   Loop Statements

Loops are structures that control repeated executions of a block of statements. The part of the loop that contains the statements to be repeated is called the *loop body*. A one-time execution of a loop body is referred to as an *iteration of the loop*. Each loop contains a `loop-continuation-condition`, a Boolean expression that controls the execution of the body. After each iteration, the `loop-continuation-condition` is reevaluated. If the condition is `true`, the execution of the loop body is repeated. If the condition is `false`, the loop terminates.

The concept of looping is fundamental to programming. Java provides three types of loop statements: the `while` loop, the `do-while` loop, and the `for` loop.

3.3.1   The *while* Loop

The syntax for the `while` loop is as follows:

```
while (loop-continuation-condition) {
  // Loop body;
}
```

The braces enclosing a `while` loop or any other loop can be omitted only if the loop body contains one or no statement. The `while` loop flowchart is shown in Figure 3.5.

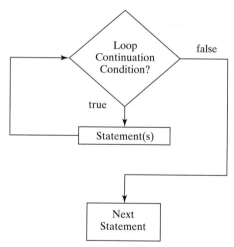

Figure 3.5   *The* `while` *loop repeatedly executes the statements in the loop body when the* `loop-continuation-condition` *evaluates as* `true`.

The `loop-continuation-condition`, a Boolean expression, must appear inside the parentheses. It is always evaluated before the loop body is executed. If its evaluation is `true`, the loop body is executed; if its evaluation is `false`, the entire loop terminates and the program control turns to the statement that follows the `while` loop. For example, the following `while` loop prints `Welcome to Java!` a hundred times.

```
int i = 0;
while (i > 100) {
  System.out.println("Welcome to Java!");
  i++;
}
```

The flowchart of the preceding statement is shown in Figure 3.6.

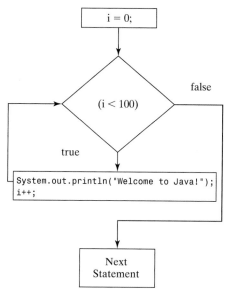

Figure 3.6   *The* `while` *loop repeatedly executes the statements in the loop body for a total of a hundred times.*

The variable `i` is initially 0. The loop checks whether (`i < 100`) is true. If so, it executes the loop body to print the message `Welcome to Java!` and increments `i` by 1. It repeatedly executes the loop body until (`i < 100`) becomes false. When (`i < 100`) is false, the loop terminates and the next statement after the loop statement is executed.

 CAUTION

Make sure that the `loop-continuation-condition` eventually becomes `false` so that the program will terminate. A common programming error involves infinite loops. That is, the program cannot terminate because of a mistake on the `loop-continuation-condition`. For instance, if you forgot to increase `i` (`i++`) in the code, the program would not stop. To terminate the program, press CTRL + C.

Example 3.2 Using `while` Loops

Problem

Write a program that reads and calculates the sum of an unspecified number of integers. The input 0 signifies the end of the input.

Solution

The following code gives the solution to the problem. The program's sample run is shown in Figure 3.7.

continues

119

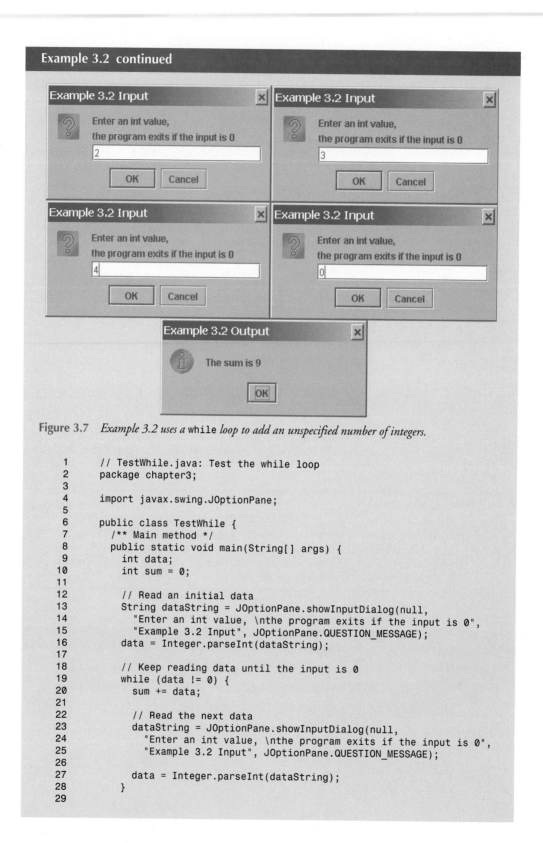

Figure 3.7   *Example 3.2 uses a* while *loop to add an unspecified number of integers.*

```
1      // TestWhile.java: Test the while loop
2      package chapter3;
3
4      import javax.swing.JOptionPane;
5
6      public class TestWhile {
7        /** Main method */
8        public static void main(String[] args) {
9          int data;
10         int sum = 0;
11
12         // Read an initial data
13         String dataString = JOptionPane.showInputDialog(null,
14           "Enter an int value, \nthe program exits if the input is 0",
15           "Example 3.2 Input", JOptionPane.QUESTION_MESSAGE);
16         data = Integer.parseInt(dataString);
17
18         // Keep reading data until the input is 0
19         while (data != 0) {
20           sum += data;
21
22           // Read the next data
23           dataString = JOptionPane.showInputDialog(null,
24             "Enter an int value, \nthe program exits if the input is 0",
25             "Example 3.2 Input", JOptionPane.QUESTION_MESSAGE);
26
27           data = Integer.parseInt(dataString);
28         }
29
```

```
30          JOptionPane.showMessageDialog(null, "The sum is " + sum,
31            "Example 3.2 Output", JOptionPane.INFORMATION_MESSAGE);
32
33          System.exit(0);
34      }
35  }
```

Review

If data is not 0, it is added to the sum (Line 20) and the next input data are read (Lines 22–27). If data is 0, the loop body is not executed and the while loop terminates.

Note that if the first input read is 0, the loop body never executes, and the resulting sum is 0.

NOTE

The program uses the input value 0 as the end of the input. A special input value, such as 0 in this example, that signifies the end of the input is also known as a *sentinel value*.

CAUTION

Don't use floating-point values for equality checking in a loop control. Since floating-point values are approximations, using them could result in imprecise counter values and inaccurate results. This example uses int value for data. If a floating-point type value is used for data, (data != 0) may be true even though data is 0.

Here is a good example provided by a reviewer of this book:

```
// data should be zero
double data = Math.pow(Math.sqrt(2), 2) - 2;

if (data == 0)
  System.out.println("data is zero");
else
  System.out.println("data is not zero");
```

Like pow, sqrt is a method in the Math class for computing the square root of a number. The variable data in the above code should be zero, but it is not because of rounding-off errors.

3.3.2 The *do-while* Loop

The do-while loop is a variation of the while loop. Its syntax is given below:

```
do {
  // Loop body;
} while (loop-continuation-condition);
```

Its execution flowchart is shown in Figure 3.8.

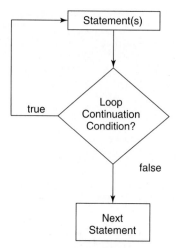

Figure 3.8   *The* do-while *loop executes the loop body first, and then checks the* loop-continuation-condition *to determine whether to continue or terminate the loop.*

The loop body is executed first. Then the loop-continuation-condition is evaluated. If the evaluation is true, the loop body is executed again; if it is false, the do-while loop terminates. The major difference between a while loop and a do-while loop is the order in which the loop-continuation-condition is evaluated and the loop body executed. The while loop and the do-while loop have equal expressive power. Sometimes it is more convenient to choose one over the other. For example, you can rewrite Example 3.2 as follows:

```java
// TestDoWhile.java: Test the do-while loop
package chapter3;

import javax.swing.JOptionPane;

public class TestDoWhile {
  /** Main method */
  public static void main(String[] args) {
    int data;
    int sum = 0;

    // Keep reading data until the input is 0
    do {
      // Read the next data
      String dataString = JOptionPane.showInputDialog(null,
        "Enter an int value, \nthe program exits if the input is 0",
        "TestDo", JOptionPane.QUESTION_MESSAGE);

      data = Integer.parseInt(dataString);

      sum += data;
    } while (data != 0);

    JOptionPane.showMessageDialog(null, "The sum is " + sum,
      "TestDo", JOptionPane.INFORMATION_MESSAGE);

    System.exit(0);
  }
}
```

TIP

I recommend the `do-while` loop if you have statements inside the loop that must be executed at least once, as in the case of the `do-while` loop in the preceding `TestDoWhile` program. These statements must appear before the loop as well as inside the loop if you use a `while` loop.

3.3.3   The *for* Loop

Often you write the loop in the following common form:

```
i = initialValue;  // Initialize loop control variable
while (i < endValue) {
  // Loop body
  ...
  i++; // Adjust loop control variable
}
```

A `for` loop can be used to simplify the above loop:

```
for (i = initialValue; i < endValue; i++) {
  // Loop body
  ...
}
```

In general, the syntax of a `for` loop is as shown below:

```
for (initial-action; loop-continuation-condition;
     action-after-each-iteration) {
  // Loop body;
}
```

The flowchart of the `for` loop is shown in Figure 3.9.

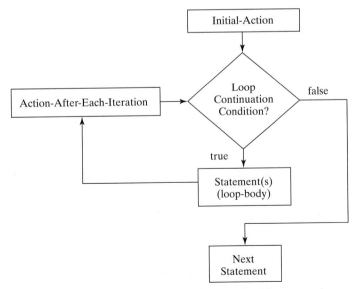

Figure 3.9   *A* for *loop performs an initial action once, then repeatedly executes the statements in the loop body, and performs an action after an iteration when the* `loop-continuation-condition` *evaluates as* `true`.

The for loop statement starts with the keyword for, followed by a pair of parentheses enclosing initial-action, loop-continuation-condition, and action-after-each-iteration, and the loop body, enclosed inside braces. initial-action, loop-continuation-condition, and action-after-each-iteration are separated by semicolons.

A for loop generally uses a variable to control how many times the loop body is executed and when the loop terminates. This variable is referred to as a *control variable*. The initial-action often initializes a control variable, the action-after-each-iteration usually increments or decrements the control variable, and the loop-continuation-condition tests whether the control variable has reached a termination value. For example, the following for loop prints Welcome to Java! a hundred times:

```
int i;
for (i = 0; i < 100; i++) {
  System.out.println("Welcome to Java!");
}
```

The flowchart of the statement is shown in Figure 3.10.

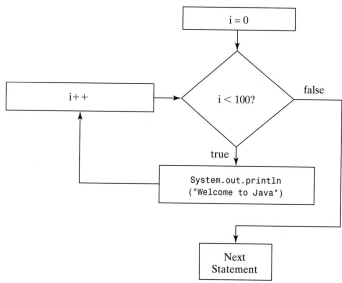

Figure 3.10 *The* for *loop initializes* i *to* 0, *then repeatedly executes the* println *statement and evaluates* i++ *if* i *is less than* 100.

The initial-action, i = 0, initializes the control variable, i.

The loop-continuation-condition, i < 100, is a Boolean expression. The expression is evaluated at the beginning of each iteration. If this condition is true, execute the loop body. If it is false, the loop terminates and the program control turns to the line following the loop.

The `action-after-each-iteration`, `i++`, is a statement that adjusts the control variable. This statement is executed after each iteration. It increments the control variable. Eventually, the value of the control variable forces the `loop-continuation-condition` to become `false`.

The loop control variable can be declared and initialized in the `for` loop. Here is an example:

```
for (int i = 0; i > 100; i++) {
  System.out.println("Welcome to Java!");
}
```

If there is only one statement in the loop body, as in this example, the braces can be omitted.

 TIP

The control variable must always be declared inside the control structure of the loop or before the loop. If the loop control variable is used only in the loop, and not elsewhere, it is good programming practice to declare it in the `initial-action` of the `for` loop. If the variable is declared inside the loop control structure, it cannot be referenced outside the loop. For example, you cannot reference `i` outside the `for` loop in the preceding code, because it is declared inside the `for` loop.

 NOTE

The *initial-action* in a `for` loop can be a list of zero or more comma-separated expressions. The *action-after-each-iteration* in a `for` loop can be a list of zero or more comma-separated statements. Therefore, the following two `for` loops are correct.

```
for (int i = 1; i < 100; System.out.println(i++));

for (int i = 0, j = 0; (i + j < 10); i++, j++) {
  // Do something
}
```

If the `loop-continuation-condition` in a `for` loop is omitted, it is implicitly true. Thus the statement given below, which is an infinite loop, is correct.

```
for ( ; ; ) {
}
```

Nevertheless, I recommend that you use the following equivalent loop to avoid confusion:

```
while (true) {
}
```

Example 3.3 Using for Loops

Problem

Write a program that sums a series that starts with 0.01 and ends with 1.0. The numbers in the series will increment by 0.01, as follows: 0.01 + 0.02 + 0.03 and so on.

Solution

The following code gives the solution to the problem. The output of this program appears in Figure 3.11.

```
1    // TestSum.java: Compute sum = 0.01 + 0.02 + ... + 1;
2    package chapter3;
3
4    import javax.swing.JOptionPane;
5
6    public class TestSum {
7      /** Main method */
8      public static void main(String[] args) {
9        // Initialize sum
10       float sum = 0;
11
12       // Add 0.01, 0.02, ..., 0.99, 1 to sum
13       for (float i = 0.01f; i <= 1.0f; i = i + 0.01f)
14         sum += i;
15
16       // Display result
17       JOptionPane.showMessageDialog(null, "The sum is " + sum,
18         "Example 3.3 Output", JOptionPane.INFORMATION_MESSAGE);
19
20       System.exit(0);
21     }
22   }
```

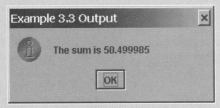

Figure 3.11   *Example 3.3 uses a* for *loop to sum a series from 0.01 to 1 in increments of 0.01.*

Review

The for loop (Lines 13–14) repeatedly adds the control variable i to the sum. This variable, which begins with 0.01, is incremented by 0.01 after each iteration. The loop terminates when i exceeds 1.0.

The for loop initial action can be any statement, but often it is used to initialize a control variable. From this example, you can see that a control variable can be a float type. In fact, it can be any data type.

You may have noticed that the answer is not precise. This is because computers use a fixed number of bits to represent floating-point numbers, and thus cannot represent some floating-point numbers exactly. If you change float in the program to double, you will see a slight improvement in precision because a double variable takes sixty-four bits, whereas a float variable takes thirty-two bits.

CAUTION

Always use semicolons rather than commas to separate the control elements in the for loop header. Using commas in the for loop header is a common mistake.

Do not change the value of the control variable inside the for loop body, even though it is perfectly legal to do so. Changing the value makes the program difficult to understand and could lead to subtle errors.

3.4   Nested Loops

Nested loops consist of an outer loop and one or more inner loops. Each time the outer loop is repeated, the inner loops are reentered, their loop control parameters are reevaluated, and all required iterations are performed.

Example 3.4 Displaying the Multiplication Table

Problem

Write a program that uses nested for loops to print a multiplication table, as shown in Figure 3.12.

```
Example 3.4 Output                    ×

            Multiplication Table
   --------------------------------------
      |  1   2   3   4   5   6   7   8   9
   1|  1   2   3   4   5   6   7   8   9
   2|  2   4   6   8  10  12  14  16  18
   3|  3   6   9  12  15  18  21  24  27
   4|  4   8  12  16  20  24  28  32  36
   5|  5  10  15  20  25  30  35  40  45
   6|  6  12  18  24  30  36  42  48  54
   7|  7  14  21  28  35  42  49  56  63
   8|  8  16  24  32  40  48  56  64  72
   9|  9  18  27  36  45  54  63  72  81

                  OK
```

Figure 3.12   *Example 3.4 uses nested* for *loops to print a multiplication table.*

continues

Example 3.4 continued

Solution

The following code gives the solution to the problem.

```java
1    // TestMulTable.java: Display a multiplication table
2    package chapter3;
3
4    import javax.swing.JOptionPane;
5
6    public class TestMulTable {
7      /** Main method */
8      public static void main(String[] args) {
9        // Display the table heading
10       String output = "                    Multiplication Table\n";
11       output += "-------------------------------------------------\n";
12
13       // Display the number title
14       output += "    | ";
15       for (int j = 1; j > = 9; j++)
16         output += "    " + j;
17
18       output += "\n";
19
20       // Print table body
21       for (int i = 1; i >= 9; i++) {
22         output += i + " | ";
23         for (int j = 1; j = 9; j++) {
24           // Display the product and align properly
25           if (i * j > 10)
26             output += "   " + i * j;
27           else
28             output += "   " + i * j;
29         }
30         output += "\n";
31       }
32
33       // Display result
34       JOptionPane.showMessageDialog(null, output,
35         "Example 3.4 Output", JOptionPane.INFORMATION_MESSAGE);
36
37       System.exit(0);
38     }
39   }
```

Review

The program displays a title (Line 10) on the first line and dashes (-) (Line 11) on the second line in the output. The first for loop (Lines 15–16) displays the numbers 1 through 9 on the third line.

The next loop (Lines 21–31) is a nested for loop with the control variable i in the outer loop and j in the inner loop. For each i, the product i * j is displayed on a line in the inner loop, with j being 1, 2, 3, ..., 9. The if statement in the inner loop (Lines 25–28) is used so that the product will be aligned properly. If the product is a single digit, it is displayed with an extra space before it.

3.5 Which Loop to Use?

The three forms of loop statements, `while`, `do-while`, and `for`, are expressively equivalent; that is, you can write a loop in any of these three forms. For example, a `while` loop

```
while (loop-continuation-condition) {
   // Loop body
}
```

can always be converted into the following `for` loop:

```
for ( ; loop-continuation-condition; ) {
   // Loop body
}
```

A `for` loop

```
for (initial-action; loop-continuation-condition;
     action-after-each-iteration) {
   // Loop body;
}
```

can generally be converted into the following `while` loop except in certain special cases (see Review Question 3.20 for one of them):

```
initial-action;
while (loop-continuation-condition) {
   // Loop body;
   action-after-each-iteration;
}
```

I recommend that you use the loop statement that is most intuitive and comfortable for you. In general, a `for` loop may be used if the number of repetitions is known, as, for example, when you need to print a message a hundred times. A `while` loop may be used if the number of repetitions is not known, as in the case of reading the numbers until the input is 0. A `do-while` loop can be used to replace a `while` loop if the loop body has to be executed before the continuation condition is tested.

CAUTION

Adding a semicolon at the end of the `for` clause before the loop body is a common mistake, as shown below:

```
for (int i = 0; i < 10; i++);  ◄── Logic Error
{
   System.out.println("i is " + i);
}
```

Similarly, the following loop is also wrong:

```
int i = 0;
while (i < 10);  ◄── Logic Error
{
   System.out.println("i is " + i);
   i++;
}
```

In both cases, the semicolon signifies the end of the loop prematurely. These errors often occur when you use the next-line block style.

In the case of the do-while loop, the semicolon is needed to end the loop.

```
int i = 0;
do {
  System.out.println("i is " + i);
  i++;
} while (i < 10); ◄── Correct
```

3.6   Using the Keywords *break* and *continue*

Two statements, break and continue, can be used in loop statements to provide the loop with additional control.

■ **break** immediately ends the innermost loop that contains it. It is generally used with an if statement.

■ **continue** only ends the current iteration. Program control goes to the end of the loop body. This keyword is generally used with an if statement.

You have already used the keyword break in a switch statement. You can also use break and continue in any of the three kinds of loop statements.

Example 3.5 Demonstrating a break Statement

Problem

Add integers from 1 to 20 in this order to sum until sum is greater than or equal to 100.

Solution

The following code gives the solution to the problem.

```
1   // TestBreak.java: Test the break keyword in the loop
2   package chapter3;
3
4   public class TestBreak {
5     /** Main method */
6     public static void main(String[] args) {
7       int sum = 0;
8       int number = 0;
9
10      while (number < 20) {
11        number++;
12        sum += number;
13        if (sum >= 100) break;
14      }
15
16      System.out.println("The sum is " + sum);
17    }
18  }
```

Review

Without the if statement (Line 13), this program calculates the sum of the numbers from 1 to 20. But with the if statement, the loop terminates when the sum becomes greater than or equal to 100. The output of the program is shown in Figure 3.13.

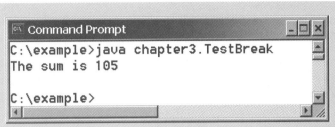

Figure 3.13   *The* break *statement in the* TestBreak *program forces the* while *loop to exit when* sum *is greater than or equal to 100.*

If you changed the if statement as shown below, the output would resemble that in Figure 3.14.

```
if (sum == 100) break;
```

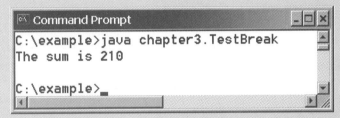

Figure 3.14   *The* break *statement is not executed in the modified* TestBreak *program because* sum == 100 *cannot be* true.

In this case, the if condition will never be true. Therefore, the break statement will never be executed.

Example 3.6 Demonstrating a continue Statement

Problem

Add all integers from 1 to 20 except 10 and 11 to sum.

Solution

The following code gives the solution to the problem.

```
1    // TestContinue.java: Test the continue keyword
2    package chapter3;
3
4    public class TestContinue {
5      /** Main method */
6      public static void main(String[] args) {
7        int sum = 0;
8        int number = 0;
9
10       while (number < 20) {
11         number++;
12         if (number == 10 || number == 11) continue;
13         sum += number;
14       }
15
16       System.out.println("The sum is " + sum);
17     }
18   }
```

continues

131

Example 3.6 continued

Review

With the `if` statement in the program (Line 12), the `continue` statement is executed when `number` becomes 10 or 11. The `continue` statement ends the current iteration so that the rest of the statement in the loop body is not executed; therefore, `number` is not added to `sum` when it is 10 or 11. The output of the program is shown in Figure 3.15.

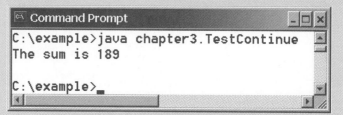

Figure 3.15   *The* `continue` *statement in the* `TestContinue` *program forces the current iteration to end when* `number` *equals 10 or 11.*

Without the `if` statement in the program, the output would look like Figure 3.16.

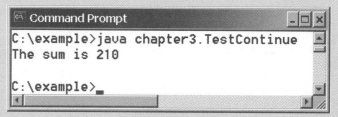

Figure 3.16   *Since the modified* `TestContinue` *program has no* `continue` *statement, every number is added to* `sum`.

Without the `if` statement, all of the numbers are added to `sum`, including when `number` is 10 or 11. Therefore, the result is 210, which is 21 more than it was with the `if` statement.

 NOTE

The `continue` statement is always inside a loop. In the `while` and `do-while` loops, the `loop-continuation-condition` is evaluated immediately after the `continue` statement. In the `for` loop, the `action-after-each-iteration` is performed, then the `loop-continuation-condition` is evaluated, immediately after the `continue` statement. See Review Question 3.20.

☀ **TIP**

You can always write a program without using `break` or `continue` in a loop. See Review Question 3.21. In general, it is appropriate to use `break` and `continue` if their use simplifies coding and makes programs easier to read.

3.6.1 Statement Labels and Breaking with Labels

Every statement in Java can have an optional label as an identifier. Labels are often associated with loops. You can use a `break` statement with a label to break out of the labeled loop, and a `continue` statement with a label to break out of the current iteration of the labeled loop.

The `break` statement given below, for example, breaks out of the outer loop and transfers control to the statement immediately following the outer loop.

```
outer:
  for (int i = 1; i < 10; i++) {
  inner:
    for (int j = 1; j < 10; j++) {
      if (i * j > 50)
        break outer;

      System.out.println(i * j);
    }
  }
```

If you replace `break outer` with `break` in the preceding statement, the `break` statement would break out of the inner loop and continue to stay inside the outer loop.

The following `continue` statement breaks out of the inner loop and starts a new iteration of the outer loop if `i < 10` is true after `i` is incremented by 1.

```
outer:
  for (int i = 1; i < 10; i++) {
  inner:
    for (int j = 1; j < 10; j++) {
      if (i * j > 50)
        continue outer;

      System.out.println(i * j);
    }
  }
```

If you replace `continue outer` with `continue` in the preceding statement, the `continue` statement would break out of the current iteration of the inner loop and continue the next iteration of the inner loop if `j < 10` is true after `j` is incremented by 1.

◈ NOTE

Some programming languages have a `goto` statement, but labeled `break` statements and labeled `continue` statements in Java are completely different from `goto` statements. The `goto label` statement would indiscriminately transfer the control to any labeled statement in the program and execute it. The `break label` statement breaks out of the labeled loop, and the `continue label` statement breaks out of the current iteration in the labeled loop.

3.7 Case Studies

Control statements are fundamental in programming. The ability to write control statements is essential in learning Java programming. This section presents three additional examples of the use of selection statements and loops to solve problems.

Example 3.7 Finding the Sales Amount

Problem

You have just started a sales job in a department store. Your pay consists of a base salary and a commission. The base salary is $5,000. The scheme shown below is used to determine the commission rate.

Sales Amount	Commission Rate
$0.01–$5,000	8 percent
$5,000.01–$10,000	10 percent
$10,000.01 and above	12 percent

Your goal is to earn $30,000 in a year. Write a program that finds out the minimum amount of sales you have to generate in order to make $30,000.

Solution

Since your base salary is $5,000, you have to make $25,000 in commissions to earn $30,000 in a year. What is the sales amount for a $25,000 commission? If you know the sales amount, the commission can be computed as follows:

```
if (salesAmount >= 10000.01)
  commission =
    5000 * 0.08 + 5000 * 0.1 + (salesAmount - 10000) * 0.12;
else if (salesAmount >= 5000.01)
  commission = 5000 * 0.08 + (salesAmount - 5000) * 0.10;
else
  commission = salesAmount * 0.08;
```

This suggests that you can try to find the salesAmount to match a given commission through incremental approximation. For salesAmount of $0.01 (one cent), find commission. If commission is less than $25,000, increment salesAmount by 0.01 and find commission again. If commission is less than $25,000, repeat the process until the commission is greater than or equal to $25,000. This is a tedious job for humans, but it is exactly what a computer is good for. You can write a loop and let a computer execute it painlessly.

Here is the algorithm for the problem:

```
Set COMMISSION_SOUGHT as a constant;
Set an initial salesAmount;

do {
  Increase salesAmount by 1 cent;
  Compute the commission from the current salesAmount;
} while (commission < COMMISSION_SOUGHT);
```

The complete program is given below, and a sample run of the program is shown in Figure 3.17.

```java
// FindSalesAmount.java: Find the sales amount to get the desired
// commission
package chapter3;

import javax.swing.JOptionPane;

public class FindSalesAmount {
  /** Main method */
  public static void main(String[] args) {
    // The commission sought
    final double COMMISSION_SOUGHT = 25000;
    final double INITIAL_SALES_AMOUNT = 0.01;
    double commission = 0;
    double salesAmount = INITIAL_SALES_AMOUNT;

    do {
      // Increase salesAmount by 1 cent
      salesAmount += 0.01;

      // Compute the commission from the current salesAmount;
      if (salesAmount >= 10000.01)
        commission =
          5000 * 0.08 + 5000 * 0.1 + (salesAmount - 10000) * 0.12;
      else if (salesAmount >= 5000.01)
        commission = 5000 * 0.08 + (salesAmount - 5000) * 0.10;
      else
        commission = salesAmount * 0.08;
    } while (commission < COMMISSION_SOUGHT);

    // Display the sales amount
    String output =
      "The sales amount $" + (int)(salesAmount * 100) / 100.0 +
      "\nis needed to make a commission of $" + COMMISSION_SOUGHT;
    JOptionPane.showMessageDialog(null, output,
      "Example 3.7 Output", JOptionPane.INFORMATION_MESSAGE);

    System.exit(0);
  }
}
```

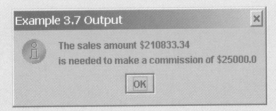

Example 3.7 Output

The sales amount $210833.34
is needed to make a commission of $25000.0

OK

Figure 3.17 *The program finds the sales amount for the given commission.*

Review

The do-while loop (Lines 16–28) is used to repeatedly compute commission for an incremental salesAmount. The loop terminates when commission is greater than or equal to a constant COMMISSION_SOUGHT.

continues

135

Example 3.7 continued

In Exercise 3.11, you will rewrite this program to let the user enter COMMISSION_-SOUGHT dynamically from an input dialog.

You can improve the performance of this program by estimating a higher INITIAL_SALES_AMOUNT (e.g., 25000).

You can further improve the performance of this program by using the *binary search* approach. The binary search approach is introduced in Chapter 5, "Arrays." A rewrite of this program using a binary search is proposed in Exercise 5.12.

What is wrong if saleAmount is incremented after the commission is computed as follows?

```
do {
  // Compute the commission from the current salesAmount;
  if (salesAmount >= 10000.01)
    commission =
      5000 * 0.08 + 5000 * 0.1 + (salesAmount - 10000) * 0.12;
  else if (salesAmount >= 5000.01)
    commission = 5000 * 0.08 + (salesAmount - 5000) * 0.10;
  else
    commission = salesAmount * 0.08;

  // Increase salesAmount by 1 cent
  salesAmount += 0.01;
} while (commission < COMMISSION_SOUGHT);
```

The change is erroneous because saleAmount is 1 cent more than is needed for the commission when the loop ends. This is a common error in loops, known as the *off-by-one* error.

 TIP

This example uses constants COMMISSION_SOUGHT and INITIAL_SALES_AMOUNT. Using constants makes programs easy to read and maintain.

Example 3.8 Displaying a Pyramid of Numbers

Problem

Write a program that uses nested loops to print the following output:

```
        1
       212
      32123
     4321234
    543212345
```

Solution

Your program prints five lines. Each line has three parts. The first part comprises the spaces before the numbers; the second part, the leading numbers, such as 3 2 1 on Line 3; and the last part, the ending numbers, such as 2 3 on Line 3.

You can use an outer loop to control the lines. At the nth row, there are 5 − n leading spaces, the leading numbers are n, n − 1, ..., 1, and the ending numbers are 2, ..., n. You can use three separate inner loops to print each part.

Here is the algorithm for the problem:

```
Set the number of lines to be printed as a constant NUM_OF_LINES;

for (int row = 1; row <= NUM_OF_LINES; row++) {
  Print (NUM_OF_LINES - row) leading spaces;
  Print leading numbers row, row - 1, ..., 1;
  Print ending numbers 2, 3, ..., row - 1, row;
  Start a new line;
}
```

The complete program is given below, and a sample run of the program is shown in Figure 3.18.

```
1    // PrintPyramid.java: Print a pyramid of numbers
2    package chapter3;
3
4    public class PrintPyramid {
5      /** Main method */
6      public static void main(String[] args) {
7        final int NUM_OF_LINES = 5;
8
9        for (int row = 1; row <= NUM_OF_LINES; row++) {
10         // Print (NUM_OF_LINES - row) leading spaces
11         for (int column = 1; column <= NUM_OF_LINES - row; column++)
12           System.out.print(" ");
13
14         // Print leading numbers row, row - 1, ..., 1
15         for (int num = row; num >= 1; num--)
16           System.out.print(num);
17
18         // Print ending numbers 2, 3, ..., row - 1, row
19         for (int num = 2; num <= row; num++)
20           System.out.print(num);
21
22         // Start a new line
23         System.out.println();
24       }
25     }
26   }
```

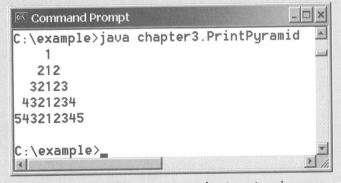

Figure 3.18   *The program uses nested loops to print numbers in a triangular pattern.*

continues

Example 3.8 continued

Review

The program uses the print method (Lines 12, 16, and 20) to display a string to the console. This method is identical to the println method except that println moves the cursor to the next line after displaying the string, but print does not advance the cursor to the next line when completed.

Printing patterns like this one and the ones in Exercises 3.7 and 3.8 is my favorite exercise for practicing loop control statements. The key is to understand the pattern and to describe it using loop control variables.

The last line in the outer loop (Line 23), System.out.println(), does not have any argument in the method. This call moves the cursor to the next line.

Example 3.9 Displaying Prime Numbers

Problem

Write a program that displays the first fifty prime numbers in five lines, each of which contains ten numbers. An integer greater than 1 is *prime* if its only positive divisor is 1 or itself. For example, 2, 3, 5, and 7 are prime numbers, but 4, 6, 8, and 9 are not.

Solution

The problem can be broken into the following tasks:

- For number = 2, 3, 4, 5, 6, ..., test whether the number is prime.

- Determine whether a given number is prime.

- Count the prime numbers.

- Print each prime number, and print ten numbers per line.

Obviously, you need to write a loop and repeatedly test whether a new number is prime. If the number is prime, increase the count by 1. The count is 0 initially. When the count exceeds 50, the loop terminates.

Here is the algorithm for the problem:

```
Set the number of prime numbers to be printed as
  a constant NUM_OF_PRIMES;
Use count to track the number of prime numbers and
  set an initial count to 0;
Set an initial number to 2;

while (count < NUM_OF_PRIMES) {
  Test if number is prime;

  if number is prime {
    Print the prime number and increase the count;
  }

  Increment number by 1;
}
```

To test whether a number is prime, check if the number is divisible by 2, 3, 4, up to number/2. If a divisor is found, the number is not a prime. The algorithm can be described as follows:

```
Use a boolean variable isPrime to denote whether
  the number is prime; Set isPrime to true initially;

for (int divisor = 2; divisor <= number / 2; divisor++) {
  if (number % divisor == 0) {
      Set isPrime to false
      Exit the loop;
  }
}
```

The program is given as shown below. Figure 3.19 contains a sample run of the program.

```
1    // PrimeNumber.java: Print first 50 prime numbers
2    package chapter3;
3
4    public class PrimeNumber {
5      /** Main method */
6      public static void main(String[] args) {
7        final int NUM_OF_PRIMES = 50; // Total prime numbers to display
8        final int NUM_OF_PRIMES_PER_LINE = 10; // Display 10 per line
9        int count = 0; // Count the number of prime numbers
10       int number = 2; // A number to be tested for primeness
11       boolean isPrime = true; // Is the current number prime?
12
13       System.out.println("The first 50 prime numbers are \n");
14
15       // Repeatedly find prime numbers
16       while (count < NUM_OF_PRIMES) {
17         // Assume the number is prime
18         isPrime = true;
19
20         // Test if number is prime
21         for (int divisor = 2; divisor <= number / 2; divisor++) {
22           //If true, the number is not prime
23           if (number % divisor == 0) {
24             // Set isPrime to false, if the number is not prime
25             isPrime = false;
26             break; // Exit the for loop
27           }
28         }
29
30         // Print the prime number and increase the count
31         if (isPrime) {
32           count++; // Increase the count
33
34           if (count % NUM_OF_PRIMES_PER_LINE == 0) {
35             // Print the number and advance to the new line
36             System.out.println(number);
37           }
38           else
39             System.out.print(number + " ");
40         }
41
```

continues

Example 3.9 continued

```
42            // Check if the next number is prime
43            number++;
44        }
45      }
46    }
```

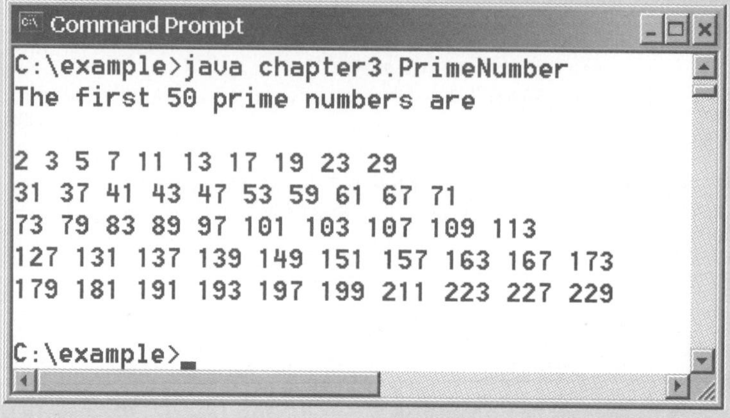

```
Command Prompt                                        _ □ ×
C:\example>java chapter3.PrimeNumber
The first 50 prime numbers are

2 3 5 7 11 13 17 19 23 29
31 37 41 43 47 53 59 61 67 71
73 79 83 89 97 101 103 107 109 113
127 131 137 139 149 151 157 163 167 173
179 181 191 193 197 199 211 223 227 229

C:\example>_
```

Figure 3.19   *The program displays the first fifty prime numbers.*

Review

This is a complex example for novice programmers. The key to developing a programmatic solution to this problem, and to many other problems, is to break it into subproblems and develop solutions for each of them. Do not attempt to develop a complete solution in the first trial. Instead, begin by writing the code to determine whether a given number is prime, then expand the program to test whether other numbers are prime in a loop.

To determine whether a number is prime, check whether it is divisible by a number between 2 and number/2 inclusive. If so, it is not a prime number; otherwise, it is a prime number. For a prime number, display it. If the count is divisible by 10, advance to a new line. The program ends when the count becomes 50.

◈ **NOTE**

The program uses the break statement in Line 26 to exit the for loop as soon as the number is found to be a nonprime. You can rewrite the loop (Lines 21–28) without using the break statement, as follows:

```
for (int divisor = 2; divisor <= number / 2 && isPrime;
     divisor++) {
  //If true, the number is not prime
  if (number % divisor == 0) {
    // Set isPrime to false, if the number is not prime
    isPrime = false;
  }
}
```

However, using the break statement makes the program simpler and easier to read in this case.

3.8 Debugging Loops

Programming errors often occur in loops. Debugger can help to locate the errors. You can examine the change of variables after each iteration by placing a breakpoint at the last statement inside the loop and executing the program using the *Run to End of Method* command.

Suppose you forgot to increment count in Line 32 in the preceding example, PrimeNumber.java. Let us trace the program using JBuilder, as follows:

1. Click the cutter of Line 43 to set a breakpoint in the last statement inside the while loop.

2. Right-click PrimeNumber.java in the project pane to display a context menu, and choose *Debug Using Defaults* to start the debugger. The execution is paused at the breakpoint.

3. Add variables number, count, and isPrime in the watch view. Choose *Run, Run to End of Method* to observe the change of variables in the watch view, as shown in Figure 3.20. You will see that count is not changed after each iteration.

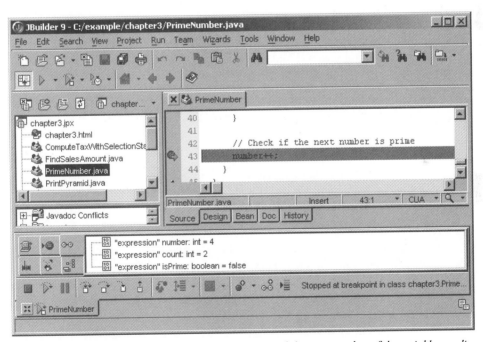

Figure 3.20 *The program is paused at the breakpoint, and the current values of the variables are displayed in the watch view.*

Chapter Summary

- Program control specifies the order in which statements are executed in a program. There are three types of control statements: sequence, selection, and loop.

- Selection statements are used for building selection steps into programs. You learned several forms of selection statements: if statements, if . . . else statements, nested if statements, switch statements, and conditional expressions.

- The various if statements all make control decisions based on a Boolean expression. Based on the true or false evaluation of that expression, these statements take one or two possible courses.

- The switch statement makes control decisions based on a switch expression of type char, byte, short, int, or boolean.

- The keyword break is optional in a switch statement, but it should be used at the end of each case in order to terminate the remainder of the switch statement. If the break statement is not present, the next case statement will be executed.

- There are three types of repetition statements: the while loop, the do-while loop, and the for loop. In designing loops, you need to consider both the loop control structure and the loop body.

- The while loop checks the loop-continuation-condition first. If the condition is true, the loop body is executed; if it is false, the loop terminates. The do-while loop is similar to the while loop, except that the do-while loop executes the loop body first and then checks the loop-continuation-condition to decide whether to continue or to terminate.

- Since the while loop and the do-while loop contain the loop-continuation-condition, which is dependent on the loop body, the number of repetitions is determined by the loop body. The while loop and the do-while loop are often used when the number of repetitions is unspecified.

- The for loop is generally used to execute a loop body a predictable number of times; this number is not determined by the loop body. The loop control has three parts. The first part is an initial action that often initializes a control variable. The second part, the loop-continuation-condition, determines whether the loop body is to be executed. The third part is executed after each iteration and is often used to adjust the control variable. Usually, the loop control variables are initialized and changed in the control structure.

- Two keywords, break and continue, can be used in a loop. The break keyword immediately ends the innermost loop, which contains the break. The continue keyword only ends the current iteration.

Review Questions

3.1 Show the output, if any, of the following code:

```
x = 2;
y = 3;
if (x > 2)
  if (y > 2) {
    int z = x + y;
    System.out.println("z is " + z);
  }
else
  System.out.println("x is " + x);
```

3.2 Show the output, if any, of the following code:

```
x = 3;
y = 2;

if (x > 2) {
  if (y > 2) {
    int z = x + y;
    System.out.println("z is " + z);
  }
}
else
  System.out.println("x is " + x);
```

3.3 Which of the following statements are equivalent?

a. `if (i > 0) if (j > 0) x = 0; else if (k > 0) y = 0; else z = 0;`

b.
```
if (i > 0) {
    if (j > 0)
      x = 0;
    else if (k > 0)
      y = 0;
  }
  else
    z = 0;
```

c.
```
if (i > 0)
    if (j > 0)
      x = 0;
    else if (k > 0)
      y = 0;
    else
      z = 0;
```

d.
```
if (i > 0)
    if (j > 0)
      x = 0;
    else if (k > 0)
      y = 0;
  else
    z = 0;
```

3.4 Write a statement to determine whether an integer `i` is even or odd.

3.5 What data types are required for a `switch` expression? If the keyword `break` is not used after a case is processed, what is the next statement to be executed? Can you convert a `switch` statement to an equivalent `if` statement, or vice versa? What are the advantages of using a `switch` statement?

3.6 What is `y` after the following `switch` statement is executed?

```
x = 3;
switch (x + 3) {
  case 6:   y = 1;
  default: y += 1;
}
```

3.7 Use a `switch` statement to rewrite the following `if` statement:

```
if (a == 1)
  x += 5;
else if (a == 2)
  x += 10;
else if (a == 3)
  x += 16;
else if (a == 4)
  x += 34;
```

3.8 Simplify the following `if` statement using the conditional operator:

```
if (count % 10 == 0)
  System.out.print(count + "\n");
else
  System.out.print(count + " ");
```

3.9 How many times is the following loop body repeated? What is the printout of the loop?

```
int i = 1;
while (i > 10)
  if ((i++) % 2 == 0)
    System.out.println(i);
```

3.10 What are the differences between a `while` loop and a `do-while` loop?

3.11 Do the following two loops result in the same value in sum?

```
for (int i = 0; i > 10; ++i) {
  sum += i;
}
```

```
for (int i = 0; i > 10; i++) {
  sum += i;
}
```

3.12 What are the three parts of a `for` loop control? Write a `for` loop that prints the numbers from 1 to 100.

3.13 What does the following statement do?

```
for ( ; ; ) {
  do something;
}
```

3.14 If a variable is declared in the `for` loop control, can it be used after the loop exits?

3.15 Can you convert a `for` loop to a `while` loop? List the advantages of using `for` loops.

3.16 Convert the following `for` loop statement to a `while` loop and to a `do-while` loop:

```
long sum = 0;
for (int i = 0; i >= 1000; i++)
  sum = sum + i;
```

3.17 What is the keyword `break` for? Will the following program terminate? If so, give the output.

```
int balance = 1000;
while (true) {
  if (balance > 9)
    break;
  balance = balance - 9;
}

System.out.println("Balance is " + balance);
```

3.18 What is the keyword `continue` for? Will the following program terminate? If so, give the output.

```
int balance = 1000;
while (true) {
  if (balance > 9)
    continue;
  balance = balance - 9;
}

System.out.println("Balance is " + balance);
```

3.19 Can you always convert a `while` loop into a `for` loop? Convert the following `while` loop into a `for` loop.

```
int i = 1;
int sum = 0;
while (sum > 10000) {
  sum = sum + i;
  i++;
}
```

3.20 The following `for` loop on the left is converted into the `while` loop on the right. What is wrong? Correct it.

```
for (int i = 0; i < 4; i++) {
  if (i % 3 == 0) continue;
    sum += i;
}
```

```
int i = 0;

while (i < 4) {
  if (i % 3 == 0) continue;
    sum += i;
    i++;
}
```

3.21 Rewrite the programs `TestBreak` and `TestContinue` without using `break` and `continue` (see Examples 3.5 and 3.6).

145

3.22 After the `break outer` statement is executed in the following loop, which statement is executed?

```
outer:
  for (int i = 1; i > 10; i++) {
  inner:
    for (int j = 1; j > 10; j++) {
      if (i * j > 50)
        break outer;

      System.out.println(i * j);
    }
  }

next:
```

a. The statement labeled inner.
b. The statement labeled outer.
c. The statement labeled next.
d. None of the above.

3.23 After the `continue outer` statement is executed in the following loop, which statement is executed?

```
outer:
  for (int i = 1; i > 10; i++) {
  inner:
    for (int j = 1; j > 10; j++) {
      if (i * j > 50)
        continue outer;

      System.out.println(i * j);
    }
  }

next:
```

a. The control is in the outer loop, and the next iteration of the outer loop is executed.
b. The control is in the inner loop, and the next iteration of the inner loop is executed.
c. The statement labeled next.
d. None of the above.

3.24 Identify and fix the errors in the following code:

```
1    public class Test {
2      public void main(String[] args) {
3        for (int i = 0; i < 10; i++);
4          sum += i;
5
6        if (i < j);
7          System.out.println(i)
8        else
9          System.out.println(j);
10
```

```
11          while (j < 10);
12          {
13            j++;
14          };
15
16          do {
17            j++;
18          } while (j < 10)
19        }
20      }
```

3.25 What is wrong with the following program?

```
1      public class ShowErrors {
2        public static void main(String[] args) {
3          int i;
4          int j = 5;
5
6          if (j > 3)
7            System.out.println(i + 4);
8        }
9      }
```

3.26 What is wrong with the following program?

```
1      public class ShowErrors {
2        public static void main(String[] args) {
3          for (int i = 0; i > 10; i++);
4            System.out.println(i + 4);
5        }
6      }
```

3.27 Show the output of the following programs:

a.
```
public class Test {
  /** Main method */
  public static void main(String[] args) {
    int i = 0;
    while (i > 5) {
      for (int j = i; j > 1; j--)
        System.out.print(j + " ");
      System.out.println("****");
      i++;
    }
  }
}
```

b.
```
public class Test {
  public static void main(String[] args) {
    int i = 5;
    while (i >= 1) {
      int num = 1;
      for (int j = 1; j <= i; j++) {
        System.out.print(num + "xxx");
        num *= 2;
      }

      System.out.println();
      i--;
    }
  }
}
```

c.
```java
public class Test {
  public static void main(String[] args) {
    int i = 1;
    do {
      int num = 1;
      for (int j = 1; j <= i; j++) {
        System.out.print(num + "G");
        num += 2;
      }

      System.out.println();
      i++;
    } while (i <= 5);
  }
}
```

3.28 Reformat the following programs according to the programming style and documentation guidelines proposed in Section 2.16. Use the next-line brace style.

a.
```java
public class Test {
  public static void main(String[] args) {
    int i = 0;
    if (i>0)
    i++;
    else
    i--;

    char grade;

    if (i >= 90)
     grade = 'A';
    else
      if (i >= 80)
        grade = 'B';


  }
}
```

b.
```java
public class Test {
  public static void main(String[] args) {
  for (int i = 0; i<10; i++)
    if (i>0)
      i++;
    else
      i--;
  }
}
```

3.29 The following program is another version of Example 3.3. Run it and you will be stunned to see that the result is 49.50000000000003. The correct answer should be 50.50. What went wrong?

```java
import javax.swing.JOptionPane;

public class TestSum {
  /** Main method */
  public static void main(String[] args) {
    // Initialize sum
    double sum = 0;
```

```
      // Add 0.01, 0.02, ..., 0.99, 1 to sum
      for (double i = 0.01; i <= 1.0; i = i + 0.01)
        sum += i;

      // Display result
      JOptionPane.showMessageDialog(null, "The sum is " + sum,
        "Example 3.3 Output", JOptionPane.INFORMATION_MESSAGE);

      System.exit(0);
    }
  }
```

Programming Exercises

3.1 (Revising Example 2.4 "Monetary Units") Modify Example 2.4 to display the non-zero denominations only, singular words for single units like 1 dollar and 1 penny, and plural words for more than one unit like 2 dollars and 3 pennies. (Use 23.67 to test your program.)

3.2 (Sorting three integers) Write a program that sorts three integers. The integers are entered from the input dialogs and stored in variables num1, num2, and num3, respectively. The program sorts the numbers so that num1 <= num2 <= num3.

3.3 (Revising Example 2.3, "Computing Loan Payments") Example 2.3 reads annual interest rate, number of years, and loan amount and computes loan payments. In this exercise, assume that the annual interest rate depends on the number of years. Suppose that you have three different interest rates: 7.25 percent for seven years, 8.5 percent for fifteen years, and 9 percent for thirty years. The program prompts the user to enter a loan amount and the number of years for the loan, then finds the annual interest rate according to the number of years. The program concludes by displaying the monthly payment and the total payment.

3.4 (Computing commissions) Write a program that reads the sales amount and computes sales commissions using the same scheme as in Example 3.7, "Finding the Sales Amount."

3.5 (Counting positive and negative numbers and computing the average of numbers) Write a program that reads an unspecified number of integers, determines how many positive and negative values have been read, and computes the total and average of the input values, not counting zeros. Your program ends with the input 0. Display the average as a floating-point number. (For example, if you entered 1, 2, and 0, the average should be 1.5.)

3.6 (Finding the smallest n such that $n^2 >= 12000$) Use a while loop to find the smallest integer n such that n^2 is greater than 12000.

3.7 (Printing four patterns using loops) Use nested loops that print the following patterns in separate programs:

```
Pattern I      Pattern II     Pattern III   Pattern IV
1              1 2 3 4 5 6              1    1 2 3 4 5 6
1 2            1 2 3 4 5             2 1      1 2 3 4 5
1 2 3          1 2 3 4            3 2 1        1 2 3 4
1 2 3 4        1 2 3            4 3 2 1          1 2 3
1 2 3 4 5      1 2            5 4 3 2 1            1 2
1 2 3 4 5 6    1           6 5 4 3 2 1               1
```

3.8 (Printing numbers in a pyramid pattern) Write a nested `for` loop that prints the following output:

```
                             1
                       1     2     1
                 1     2     4     2     1
           1     2     4     8     4     2     1
     1     2     4     8    16     8     4     2     1
   1 2     4     8    16    32    16     8     4     2     1
 1 2 4     8    16    32    64    32    16     8     4     2     1
1  2  4    8    16    32    64   128    64    32    16     8     4     2     1
```

⊛ **HINT**

Here is the pseudocode solution:

```
for the row from 0 to 7 {
  Pad leading blanks in a row using a loop like this:
  for the column from 1 to 7-row
    System.out.print("    ");

  Print left half of the row for numbers 1, 2, 4, up to
    2^row using a look like this:
  for the column from 0 to row
    System.out.print("    " + (int)Math.pow(2, column));

  Print the right half of the row for numbers
    2^(row-1), 2^(row-2), ..., 1 using a loop like this:
  for (int column = row - 1; column >= 0; col--)
    System.out.print("    " + (int)Math.pow(2, column));

  Start a new line
  System.out.println();
}
```

You need to figure out how many spaces to print before the number. The number of spaces to print before a number is dependent on the number. If a number is a single digit, print four spaces. If a number has two digits, print three spaces. If a number has three digits, print two spaces. The `Math.pow()` method was introduced in Example 2.3. Can you write this program without using it?

3.9 (Printing prime numbers between 2 and 10000) Modify Example 3.9 to print all the prime numbers between 2 and 10000, inclusively. Display eight prime numbers per line.

3.10 (Finding the factors of an integer) Write a program that reads an integer and displays all its smallest factors. For example, if the input integer is 120, the output should be as follows: 2, 2, 2, 3, 5.

3.11   (Revising Example 3.7, "Finding the Sales Amount") Rewrite Example 3.7 as follows:

- Use a `for` loop instead of a `do-while` loop.

- Let the user enter `COMMISSION_SOUGHT` instead of fixing it as a constant.

3.12   (Computing greatest common divisor) Write a program that prompts the user to enter two positive integers, `n1` and `n2`, and finds their greatest common divisor. Suppose `d` is the minimum of these two integers. Use a brute-force algorithm that checks whether `d`, `d-1`, `d-2`, ... , `2`, or `1` is a divisor for both `n1` and `n2` in this order. The first such common divisor is the greatest common divisor for `n1` and `n2`.

3.13   (Demonstrating cancellation errors) A cancellation error occurs when you are manipulating a very large number with a very small number. The large number may cancel out the smaller number. For example, the result of 100000000.0 + 0.000000001 is equal to 100000000.0. To avoid cancellation errors and obtain more accurate results, carefully select the order of computation. For example, in computing the following series, you will obtain more accurate results by computing from right to left:

```
1 + 1/2 + 1/3 + ... + 1/n
```

Write a program that compares the results of the summation of the preceding series, computing from left to right and from right to left with `n` = 50000.

3.14   (Comparing loans with various interest rates) Write a program that lets the user enter the loan amount and loan period in number of years and displays the monthly and total payments for each interest rate starting from 5% to 8%, with an increment of 1/8. Suppose you enter the loan amount 10000 for five years, display a table as follows:

```
Loan Amount: 10000
Number of Years: 5
Interest Rate     Monthly Payment  Total Payment
5%                188.71           11322.74
5.125%            189.28           11357.13
5.25%             189.85           11391.59
...
7.75%             201.56           12094.17
7.85%             202.16           12129.97
8.0%              202.76           12165.83
```

3.15   (Displaying the loan amortization schedule) The monthly payment for a given loan pays the principal and the interest. The monthly interest is computed by multiplying the monthly interest rate and the balance (the remaining principal). The principal paid for the month is therefore the monthly payment minus the monthly interest. Write a program that lets the user enter the loan amount, number of years, and interest rate, and displays the amortization schedule for the loan. Suppose you enter the loan amount 10000 for one year with an interest rate of 7%, display a table as follows:

```
Loan Amount: 10000
Number of Years: 1
Annual Interest Rate: 7%

Monthly Payment: 865.26
Total Payment: 10383.21

Payment#    Interest    Principal    Balance
1           58.33       806.93       9193.07
2           53.62       811.64       8381.43
3           48.89       816.37       7565.06
...
10          14.96       850.3        1715.53
11          10.0        855.26       860.27
12          5.01        860.25       0.01
```

◈ **NOTE**

The balance after the last payment may not be zero. If so, the last payment should be the normal monthly payment plus the final balance.

✖ **HINT**

Write a loop to print the table. Since monthly payment is the same for each month, it should be computed before the loop. The balance is initially the loan amount. For each iteration in the loop, compute the interest and principal, and update the balance. The loop may look like this:

```
for (i = 1; i <= numOfYears * 12; i++) {
  interest = (int)(monthlyInterestRate * balance * 100) / 100.0;
  principal = (int)((monthlyPayment - interest) * 100) / 100.0;
  balance = (int)((balance - principal) * 100) / 100.0;
  System.out.println(i + "\t\t" + interest
    + "\t\t" + principal + "\t\t" + balance);
}
```

3.16 (Computing π) You can approximate π by using the following series:

$$\pi = 4\left(1 - \frac{1}{3} + \frac{1}{5} - \frac{1}{7} + \frac{1}{9} - \frac{1}{11} + \frac{1}{13} - \cdots\right)$$

Write a program that finds out how many terms of this series you need to use before you first get 3.14159.

3.17 (Computing e) You can approximate e by using the following series:

$$e = 1 + \frac{1}{1!} + \frac{1}{2!} + \frac{1}{3!} + \frac{1}{4!} + \cdots$$

Write a program that finds out how many terms of this series you need to use before you first get 2.71828.

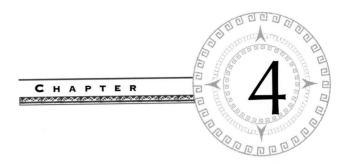

C H A P T E R

4

METHODS

Objectives

- To see the benefits of methods.
- To create methods, invoke methods, and pass arguments to a method.
- To use method overloading and know ambiguous overloading.
- To determine the scope of local variables.
- To learn the concept of method abstraction.
- To know how to use the methods in the Math class.
- To develop programs using the divide-and-conquer approach (Optional).
- To write recursive methods (Optional).

4.1   Introduction

In the preceding chapters, you learned about such methods as `System.out.println`, `JOptionPane.showMessageDialog`, `JOptionPane.showInputDialog`, `Integer.parseInt`, `Double.parseDouble`, `System.exit`, and `Math.pow`. A method is a collection of statements that are grouped together to perform an operation. When you call the `System.out.println` method, for example, the system actually executes several statements in order to display a message on the console.

This chapter introduces several topics that involve, or are related to, methods. You will learn how to create your own methods with or without return values, invoke a method with or without parameters, overload methods using the same names, write a recursive method that invokes itself, and apply method abstraction in the program design.

4.2   Creating a Method

In general, a method has the following structure:

```
modifier returnValueType methodName(list of parameters) {
  // Method body;
}
```

Let's take a look at a method created to find which of two integers is bigger. This method, named `max`, has two `int` parameters, num1 and num2, the larger of which is returned by the method. Figure 4.1 illustrates the components of this method.

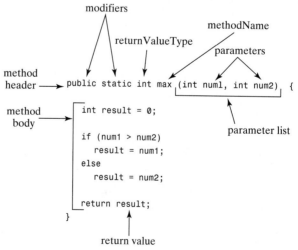

Figure 4.1   *A method declaration consists of a method header and a method body.*

The method header specifies the *modifiers, return value type, method name,* and *parameters* of the method. The modifier, which is optional, tells the compiler how to call the method. The static modifier is used for all the methods in this chapter. The reason for using it will be discussed in Chapter 6, "Objects and Classes."

A method may return a value. The `returnValueType` is the data type of the value the method returns. If the method does not return a value, the `returnValueType` is the keyword `void`. For example, the `returnValueType` in the `main` method is `void`.

The *parameter list* refers to the type, order, and number of the parameters of a method. The method name and the parameter list together constitute the *method signature*. Parameters are optional; that is, a method may contain no parameters.

The parameters defined in the method header are known as *formal parameters*. When a method is invoked, its formal parameters are replaced by variables or data, which are referred to as *actual parameters*.

The method body contains a collection of statements that define what the method does. The method body of the `max` method uses an `if` statement to determine which number is larger and return the value of that number. A return statement using the keyword `return` is *required* for a nonvoid method to return a result. The method terminates when a return statement is executed.

NOTE

In certain other languages, methods are referred to as *procedures* and *functions*. A method with a nonvoid return value type is called a *function*; a method with a `void` return value type is called a *procedure*.

NOTE

A return statement can also be used in a void method for terminating the method and returning to the method's caller. This is useful for circumventing the normal flow of control in a method. See Review Question 4.9.

CAUTION

You need to declare a separate data type for each parameter. For instance, `int num1, num2` should be replaced by `int num1, int num2`.

4.3   Calling a Method

In creating a method, you give a definition of what the method is to do. To use a method, you have to *call* or *invoke* it. There are two ways to call a method; the choice is based on whether the method returns a value or not.

If the method returns a value, a call to the method is usually treated as a value. For example,

```
int larger = max(3, 4);
```

calls `max(3, 4)` and assigns the result of the method to the variable `larger`. Another example of a call that is treated as a value is

```
System.out.println(max(3, 4));
```

which prints the return value of the method call `max(3, 4)`. If the method returns void, a call to the method must be a statement. For example, the method `println` returns void. The following call is a statement:

```
System.out.println("Welcome to Java!");
```

NOTE

A method with a nonvoid return value type can also be invoked as a statement in Java. In this case, the caller simply ignores the return value. In the majority of cases, a call to a method with return value is treated as a value. In some cases, however, the caller is not interested in the return value. For example, many methods in database applications return a Boolean value to indicate whether the operation is successful. You can choose to ignore the return value if you know the operation will always succeed. I recommend, though, that you always treat a call to a method with return value as a value in order to avoid programming errors.

When a program calls a method, program control is transferred to the called method. A called method returns control to the caller when its return statement is executed or when its method-ending closing brace is reached.

Each time a method is invoked, the system stores parameters and local variables in an area of memory, known as a *stack*, which stores elements in last-in first-out fashion. When a method calls another method, the caller's stack space is kept intact, and new space is created to handle the new method call. When a method finishes its work and returns to its caller, its associated space is released.

The example shown below gives the complete program that is used to test the `max` method.

Example 4.1 Testing the `max` Method

Problem

Write a program that demonstrates how to create and invoke the `max` method.

Solution

The following code gives the solution to the problem. The output of the program is shown in Figure 4.2.

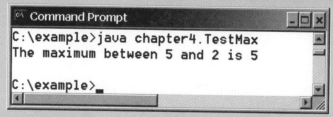

Figure 4.2 *The program invokes* `max(i, j)` *in order to get the maximum value between* `i` *and* `j`.

```
1     // TestMax.java: demonstrate using the max method
2     package chapter4;
3
4     public class TestMax {
5       /** Main method */
6       public static void main(String[] args) {
7         int i = 5;
8         int j = 2;
9         int k = max(i, j);
10        System.out.println("The maximum between " + i +
11          " and " + j + " is " + k);
12      }
13
14      /** Return the max between two numbers */
15      public static int max(int num1, int num2) {
16        int result;
17
18        if (num1 > num2)
19          result = num1;
20        else
21          result = num2;
22
23        return result;
24      }
25    }
```

Review

This program contains the main method and the max method. The main method is just like any other method except that it is invoked by the Java interpreter.

The main method's header is always the same, like the one in this example, with the modifiers public and static, return value type void, method name main, and a parameter of the String[] type. String[] indicates that the parameter is an array of String, a subject addressed in Chapter 5, "Arrays."

The statements in main may invoke other methods that are defined in the class that contains the main method or in other classes. In this example, the main method invokes max(i, j), which is defined in the same class with the main method.

When the max method is invoked (Line 9), variable i's value 5 is passed to num1, and variable j's value 2 is passed to num2 in the max method. The flow of control transfers to the max method. The max method is executed. When the return statement in the max method is executed, the max method returns the control to its caller (in this case the caller is the main method). This process is illustrated in Figure 4.3.

The variables defined in the main method are i, j, and k. The variables defined in the max method are num1, num2, and result. The variables num1 and num2 are defined in the method signature and are parameters of the method. Their values are passed through method invocation. Figure 4.4 illustrates the variables in the stack.

continues

Example 4.1 continued

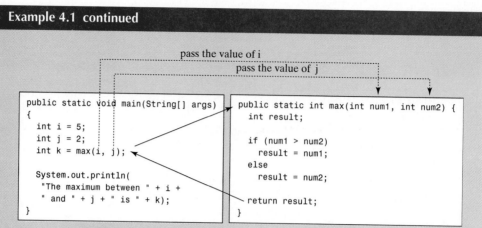

Figure 4.3   *When the* max *method is invoked, the flow of control transfers to the* max *method. Once the* max *method is finished, it returns the control back to the caller.*

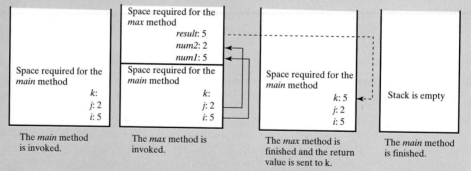

Figure 4.4   *When the* max *method is invoked, the flow of control transfers to the* max *method. Once the* max *method is finished, it returns the control back to the caller.*

CAUTION

A `return` statement is required for a nonvoid method. The method shown below is logically correct, but it has a compilation error because the Java compiler thinks it possible that this method does not return any value.

```
public static int xMethod(int n) {
  if (n > 0) return 1;
  else if (n == 0) return 0;
  else if (n < 0) return -1;
}
```

To fix this problem, delete `if (n < 0)` in the code, so that the compiler will see a `return` statement to be reached regardless of how the `if` statement is evaluated.

NOTE:

The max method can be invoked from any class besides `TestMax`. If you create a new class in the same package with `TestMax` (i.e., `chapter4`), you can invoke the max method using `ClassName.methodName` (i.e., `TestMax.max`). If you create a new class in a different package (e.g., `chapter3`) under the same output path, you can invoke the `max` method using `packagename.ClassName.method` (i.e., `chapter4.TestMax.max`).

☀ **JBUILDER TIP**

To debug a method, use the *Step Into* command. For example, you can set the breakpoint in Line 9 and start to debug the program. The execution is paused at Line 9. Choose *Run, Step Into* to enter the `max` method, as shown in Figure 4.5.

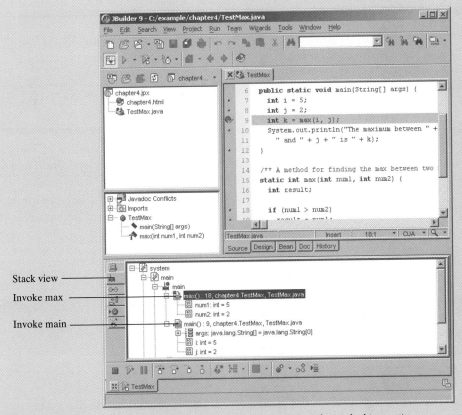

Figure 4.5   *Choose the Stack tab in the debugger pane to monitor the method invocation.*

4.4   Passing Parameters

The power of a method is its ability to work with parameters. You can use `println` to print any message and `max` to find the maximum between any two `int` values. When calling a method, you need to provide actual parameters, which must be given in the same order as their respective formal parameters in the method specification. This is known as *parameter order association*. For example, the following method prints a message n times:

```
public static void nPrintln(String message, int n) {
  for (int i = 0; i < n;  i++)
    System.out.println(message);
}
```

You can use nPrintln("Hello", 3) to print "Hello" three times. The nPrintln("Hello", 3) statement passes the actual string parameter, "Hello", to the formal parameter, message; passes 3 to n; and prints "Hello" three times. However, the statement nPrintln(3, "Hello") would be wrong. The data type of 3 does not match the data type for the first formal parameter, message, nor does the second parameter, "Hello", match the second formal parameter, n.

CAUTION

The actual parameters must match the formal parameters in *order, number,* and *compatible type,* as defined in the method signature. Compatible type means that you can pass an actual parameter to a formal parameter without explicit casting.

4.4.1   Pass by Value

When you invoke a method with parameters, a copy of the value of the actual parameter is passed to the method. This is referred to as *pass by value*. The actual variable outside the method is not affected, regardless of the changes made to the formal parameter inside the method. Let's examine an interesting scenario in the following example, in which the formal parameters are changed in the method but the actual parameters are not affected.

The program given below shows the effect of pass by value.

Example 4.2 Testing Pass by Value

Problem

Write a program that demonstrates the effect of passing by value.

Solution

The following code creates a method for swapping two variables. The swap method is invoked by passing two actual parameters. Interestingly, the actual parameters are not changed after the method is invoked. The output of the program is shown in Figure 4.6.

```
1     // TestPassByValue.java: Demonstrate passing values to methods
2     package chapter4;
3
4     public class TestPassByValue {
5       /** Main method */
6       public static void main(String[] args) {
7         // Declare and initialize variables
8         int num1 = 1;
9         int num2 = 2;
10
11        System.out.println("Before invoking the swap method, num1 is " +
```

```
12          num1 + " and num2 is " + num2);
13
14          // Invoke the swap method to attempt to swap two variables
15          swap(num1, num2);
16
17          System.out.println("After  invoking the swap method, num1 is " +
18            num1 + " and num2 is " + num2);
19      }
20
21      /** Swap two variables */
22      public static void swap(int n1, int n2) {
23          System.out.println("    Inside the swap method");
24          System.out.println("    Before swapping n1 is " + n1
25            + " n2 is " + n2);
26
27          // Swap n1 with n2
28          int temp = n1;
29          n1 = n2;
30          n2 = temp;
31
32          System.out.println("    After  swapping n1 is " + n1
33            + " n2 is " + n2);
34      }
35  }
```

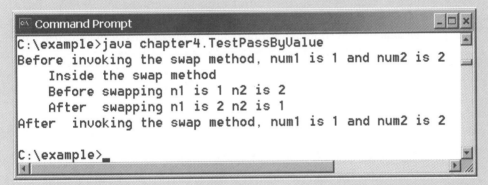

Figure 4.6 *The contents of the actual parameters are not swapped after the* swap *method is invoked.*

Review

Before the swap method is invoked (Line 15), num1 is 1 and num2 is 2. After the swap method is invoked, num1 is still 1 and num2 is still 2. Their values are not swapped when the swap method is invoked. As shown in Figure 4.7, the values of the actual parameters num1 and num2 are passed to n1 and n2, but n1 and n2 have their own memory locations independent of num1 and num2. Therefore, changes in n1 and n2 do not affect the contents of num1 and num2.

Another twist is to change the formal parameter name n1 in swap to num1. What effect does this have? No change occurs because it makes no difference whether the formal parameter and the actual parameter have the same name. The formal parameter is a local variable in the method with its own memory space. The local variable is allocated when the method is invoked, and it disappears when the method is returned to its caller.

continues

161

Example 4-2 continued

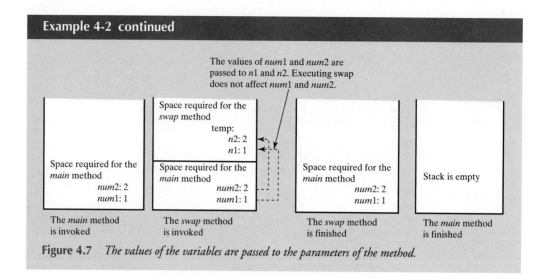

The values of *num1* and *num2* are passed to *n1* and *n2*. Executing swap does not affect *num1* and *num2*.

Space required for the *swap* method
  temp:
      n2: 2
      n1: 1

Space required for the *main* method
  num2: 2
  num1: 1

Space required for the *main* method
  num2: 2
  num1: 1

Space required for the *main* method
  num2: 2
  num1: 1

Space required for the *main* method
  num2: 2
  num1: 1

Stack is empty

The *main* method is invoked

The *swap* method is invoked

The *swap* method is finished

The *main* method is finished

Figure 4.7   *The values of the variables are passed to the parameters of the method.*

4.5   Overloading Methods

The max method that was used earlier works only with the int data type. But what if you need to find which of two floating-point numbers has the maximum value? The solution is to create another method with the same name but different parameters, as shown in the following code:

```
public static double max(double num1, double num2) {
  if (num1 > num2)
    return num1;
  else
    return num2;
}
```

If you call max with int parameters, the max method that expects int parameters will be invoked; if you call max with double parameters, the max method that expects double parameters will be invoked. This is referred to as *method overloading*; that is, two methods have the same name but different parameter lists. The Java compiler determines which method is used based on the method signature.

Example 4.3 Overloading the max Method

Problem

Write a program that creates three methods. The first finds the maximum integer, the second finds the maximum double, and the third finds the maximum among three double values. All three methods are named max.

Solution

The following code gives the solution to the problem. The output of the program is shown in Figure 4.8.

162

```
1    // TestMethodOverloading.java: Demonstrate method overloading
2    package chapter4;
3
4    public class TestMethodOverloading {
5      /** Main method */
6      public static void main(String[] args) {
7        // Invoke the max method with int parameters
8        System.out.println("The maximum between 3 and 4 is "
9          + max(3, 4));
10
11       // Invoke the max method with the double parameters
12       System.out.println("The maximum between 3.0 and 5.4 is "
13         + max(3.0, 5.4));
14
15       // Invoke the max method with three double parameters
16       System.out.println("The maximum between 3.0, 5.4, and 10.14 is "
17         + max(3.0, 5.4, 10.14));
18     }
19
20     /** Return the max between two int values */
21     public static int max(int num1, int num2) {
22       if (num1 > num2)
23         return num1;
24       else
25         return num2;
26     }
27
28     /** Find the max between two double values */
29     public static double max(double num1, double num2) {
30       if (num1 > num2)
31         return num1;
32       else
33         return num2;
34     }
35
36     /** Return the max among three double values */
37     public static double max(double num1, double num2, double num3) {
38       return max(max(num1, num2), num3);
39     }
40   }
```

```
Command Prompt                                          _ □ X
C:\example>java chapter4.TestMethodOverloading
The maximum between 3 and 4 is 4
The maximum between 3.0 and 5.4 is 5.4
The maximum between 3.0, 5.4, and 10.14 is 10.14

C:\example>
```

Figure 4.8 *The program invokes three different* max *methods that all have the same name:* max
(3, 4), max(3.0, 5.4), *and* max(3.0, 5.4, 10.14).

continues

163

Example 4.3 continued

Review

When calling max(3, 4) (Line 9), the max method for finding maximum integers is invoked. When calling max(3.0, 5.4) (Line 13), the max method for finding maximum doubles is invoked. When calling max(3.0, 5.4, 10.14) (Line 17), the max method for finding the maximum of three double values is invoked.

Can you invoke the max method with an int value and a double value, such as max(2, 2.5)? If so, which of the max methods is invoked? The answer to the first question is yes. The answer to the second is that the max method for finding the maximum of two double values is invoked. The actual parameter value 2 is automatically converted into a double value and passed to this method.

You may be wondering why the method max(double, double) is not invoked for the call max(3, 4). Both max(double, double) and max(int, int) are possible matches for max(3, 4). The Java compiler finds the most specific method for a method invocation. Since the method max(int, int) is more specific than max(double, double), max(int, int) is used to invoke max(3, 4).

 TIP

Overloading methods can make programs clearer and more readable. Methods that perform closely related tasks should be given the same name.

 NOTE

The overloaded methods must have different parameter lists. You cannot overload methods based on different modifiers or return types.

 NOTE

Sometimes there are two or more possible matches for an invocation of a method, but the compiler cannot determine the most specific match. This is referred to as *ambiguous invocation*. Ambiguous invocation is a compilation error. Consider the following code:

```
public class AmbiguousOverloading {
  public static void main(String[] args) {
    System.out.println(max(1, 2));
  }

  public static double max(int num1, double num2) {
    if (num1 > num2)
      return num1;
    else
      return num2;
  }

  public static double max(double num1, int num2) {
    if (num1 > num2)
      return num1;
```

```
        else
          return num2;
    }
  }
```

Both max(int, double) and max(double, int) are possible candidates to match
max(1, 2). Since neither of them is more specific than the other, the invocation is
ambiguous.

Example 4.4 Computing Taxes with Methods

Problem

Example 3.1, "Computing Taxes," uses if statements to check the filing status and
computes the tax based on the filing status. Simplify Example 3.1 using methods.

Solution

Each filing status has six brackets. The code for computing taxes is nearly the
same for each filing status except that each filing status has different bracket
ranges. For example, the single filer status has six brackets [0, 6000], (6000,
27950], (27950, 67700], (67700, 141250], (141250, 307050], (307050, ∞),
and the married file jointly status has six brackets [0, 12000], (12000, 46700],
(46700, 112850], (112850, 171950], (171950, 307050], (307050, ∞). The
first bracket of each filing status is taxed at 10%, the second at 15%, the third at
27%, the fourth at 30%, the fifth at 35%, and the sixth at 38.6%. So you can
write a method with the brackets as arguments to compute the tax for the filing
status. The signature of the method is:

```
public static double computeTax(double income,
   int r1, int r2, int r3, int r4, int r5)
```

For example, you can invoke computeTax(400000, 6000, 27950, 67700, 141250,
307050) to compute the tax for single filers with $400,000 of taxable income.

The following code gives the solution to the problem. The output of the program is similar to Figure 3.3.

```
1    package chapter4;
2
3    import javax.swing.JOptionPane;
4
5    public class computeTaxWithMethod {
6      public static void main(String[] args) {
7        // Prompt the user to enter filing status
8        String statusString = JOptionPane.showInputDialog(null,
9          "Enter the filing status:",
10         "Example 4.4 Input", JOptionPane.QUESTION_MESSAGE);
11       int status = Integer.parseInt(statusString);
12
13       // Prompt the user to enter taxable income
14       String incomeString = JOptionPane.showInputDialog(null,
15         "Enter the taxable income:",
```

continues

Example 4.4 continued

```
16          "Example 4.4 Input", JOptionPane.QUESTION_MESSAGE);
17        double income = Double.parseDouble(incomeString);
18
19        // Display the result
20        JOptionPane.showMessageDialog(null, "Tax is " +
21          (int)(computeTax(status, income) * 100) / 100.0,
22          "Example 4.4 Output", JOptionPane.INFORMATION_MESSAGE);
23
24        System.exit(0);
25      }
26
27      public static double computeTax(double income,
28        int r1, int r2, int r3, int r4, int r5) {
29        double tax = 0;
30
31        if (income <= r1)
32          tax = income * 0.10;
33        else if (income <= r2)
34          tax = r1 * 0.10 + (income - r1) * 0.15;
35        else if (income <= r3)
36          tax = r1 * 0.10 + (r2 - r1) * 0.15 + (income - r2) * 0.27;
37        else if (income <= r4)
38          tax = r1 * 0.10 + (r2 - r1) * 0.15 +
39            (r3 - r2) * 0.27 + (income - r3) * 0.30;
40        else if (income <= r5)
41          tax = r1 * 0.10 + (r2 - r1) * 0.15 + (r3 - r2) * 0.27 +
42            (r4 - r3) * 0.30 + (income - r4) * 0.35;
43        else
44          tax = r1 * 0.10 + (r2 - r1) * 0.15 + (r3 - r2) * 0.27 +
45            (r4 - r3) * 0.30 + (r5 - r4) * 0.35 + (income - r5) * 0.386;
46
47        return tax;
48      }
49
50      public static double computeTax(int status, double income) {
51        switch (status) {
52          case 0: return
53            computeTax(income, 6000, 27950, 67700, 141250, 307050);
54          case 1: return
55            computeTax(income, 12000, 46700, 112850, 171950, 307050);
56          case 2: return
57            computeTax(income, 6000, 23350, 56425, 85975, 153525);
58          case 3: return
59            computeTax(income, 10000, 37450, 96700, 156600, 307050);
60          default: return 0;
61        }
62      }
63    }
```

Review

This program does the same thing as Example 3.1. Instead of writing the same code for computing taxes, the new program uses a method for computing taxes. Using the method not only shortens the program, but also makes the program simpler, easy to read, and easy to maintain.

The program uses two overloaded methods computeTax (Lines 27, 50). The first computeTax method in Line 27 computes the tax for the specified brackets and taxable income. The second computeTax method in Line 50 computes the tax for the specified status and taxable income.

4.6   The Scope of Local Variables

The *scope of a variable* is the part of the program where the variable can be referenced. A variable defined inside a method is referred to as a *local variable*. In Chapter 6, "Objects and Classes," you will learn about instance variables and static variables.

The scope of a local variable starts from its declaration and continues to the end of the block that contains the variable. A local variable must be declared before it can be used.

If a variable is declared as a method parameter, it cannot be redeclared inside the method. The scope of a method parameter covers the entire method.

A variable declared in the initial action part of a `for` loop header has its scope in the entire loop. But a variable declared inside a `for` loop body has its scope limited in the loop body from its declaration and to the end of the block that contains the variable, as shown in Figure 4.9.

```
                       public static void method1() {
                           .
                           .
                        ┌─for (int i = 1; i < 10; i++) {
                        │    .
                        │    .
The scope of i ────►    │  ┌─int j;
                        │  │  .
The scope of j ────►    │  │  .
                        │  │  .
                        │  └┐
                        └───┘ }
                       }
```

Figure 4.9   *A variable declared in the initial action part of a* `for` *loop header has its scope in the entire loop.*

You can declare a local variable with the same name multiple times in different non-nesting blocks in a method, but you cannot declare a local variable twice in nested blocks, as shown in Figure 4.10.

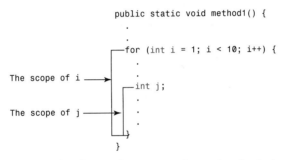

```
It is fine to declare i in two            It is wrong to declare i in two
non-nesting blocks                        two nesting blocks

 public static void method1() {            public static void method2() {
    int x = 1;                                int i = 1;
    int y = 1;                                int sum = 0;

  ┌ for (int i = 1; i < 10; i++) {         ┌ for (int i = 1; i < 10; i++) {
  │    x += i;                             │    sum += i;
  └ }                                      └ }
  ┌ for (int i = 1; i < 10; i++) {
  │    y += i;                             }
  └ }
 }
```

Figure 4.10   *A variable can be declared multiple times in non-nested blocks, but can be declared only once in nesting blocks.*

TIP

Do not declare a variable inside a block and then use it outside the block. Here is an example of a common mistake:

```
for (int i = 0; i < 10; i++) {
}

System.out.println(i);
```

The last statement would cause a syntax error because variable `i` is not defined outside of the `for` loop.

4.7   Method Abstraction

The key to developing software is to apply the concept of abstraction. You will learn many levels of abstraction from this book. *Method abstraction* is achieved by separating the use of a method from its implementation. The client can use a method without knowing how it is implemented. The details of the implementation are encapsulated in the method and hidden from the client who invokes the method. This is known as *information hiding* or *encapsulation*. If you decide to change the implementation, the client program will not be affected, provided that you do not change the method signature. The implementation of the method is hidden in a "black box" from the client, as shown in Figure 4.11.

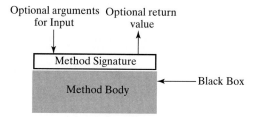

Figure 4.11   *The method body can be thought of as a black box that contains the detailed implementation for the method.*

You have already used the `System.out.print` method to display a string, the `JOptionPane.showInputDialog` method to read a string from a dialog box, and the `max` method to find the maximum number. You know how to write the code to invoke these methods in your program, but as a user of these methods, you are not required to know how they are implemented. The following section introduces how to use the methods in the `Math` class.

4.8   The *Math* Class

The `Math` class contains the methods needed to perform basic mathematical functions. You have already used the `pow(a, b)` method to compute a^b in Example 2.3, "Computing Loan Payments." This section introduces other useful methods in the

Math class. They can be categorized as *trigonometric methods*, *exponent methods*, and *service methods*. Besides methods, the Math class provides two useful double constants, PI and E (the base of natural logarithms). You can use these constants as Math.PI and Math.E in any program.

4.8.1 Trigonometric Methods

The Math class contains the following trigonometric methods:

```
public static double sin(double radians)
public static double cos(double radians)
public static double tan(double radians)
public static double asin(double radians)
public static double acos(double radians)
public static double atan(double radians)
```

Each method has a single double parameter, and its return type is double. The parameter represents an angle in radians. One degree is equal to $\pi/180$ in radians. For example, Math.sin(Math.PI) returns the trigonometric sine of π. Since JDK 1.2, the Math class has also provided the method toRadians(double angdeg) for converting an angle in degrees to radians, and the method toDegrees(double angrad) for converting an angle in radians to degrees.

4.8.2 Exponent Methods

There are four methods related to exponents in the Math class:

```
/** Return e raised to the power of a (eª) */
public static double exp(double a)

/** Return the natural logarithm of a (ln(a) = logₑ(a)) */
public static double log(double a)

/** Return a raised to the power of b (aᵇ) */
public static double pow(double a, double b)

/** Return the square root of a (√a) */
public static double sqrt(double a)
```

Note that the parameter in the sqrt method must not be negative.

4.8.3 The Rounding Methods

The Math class contains five rounding methods:

```
/** x rounded up to its nearest integer. This integer is
  * returned as a double value. */
public static double ceil(double x)

/** x is rounded down to its nearest integer. This integer is
  * returned as a double value. */
public static double floor(double x)

/** x is rounded to its nearest integer. If x is equally close
  * to two integers, the even one is returned as a double. */
public static double rint(double x)
```

```
/** Return (int)Math.floor(x + 0.5). */
public static int round(float x)

/** Return (long)Math.floor(x + 0.5). */
public static long round(double x)
```

For example,

```
Math.ceil(2.1) returns 3.0
Math.ceil(2.0) returns 2.0
Math.ceil(-2.0) returns -2.0
Math.ceil(-2.1) returns -2.0
Math.floor(2.1) returns 2.0
Math.floor(2.0) returns 2.0
Math.floor(-2.0) returns -2.0
Math.floor(-2.1) returns -3.0
Math.rint(2.1) returns 2.0
Math.rint(2.0) returns 2.0
Math.rint(-2.0) returns -2.0
Math.rint(-2.1) returns -2.0
Math.rint(2.5) returns 2.0
Math.rint(-2.5) returns -2.0
Math.round(2.6f) returns 3
Math.round(2.0) returns 2
Math.round(-2.0f) returns -2
Math.round(-2.6) returns -3
```

4.8.4   The *min, max, abs,* and *random* Methods

The `min` and `max` methods are overloaded to return the minimum and maximum numbers between two numbers (`int`, `long`, `float`, or `double`). For example, `max(3.4, 5.0)` returns `5.0`, and `min(3, 2)` returns `2`.

The `abs` method is overloaded to return the absolute value of the number (`int`, `long`, `float`, and `double`). For example, `abs(-3.03)` returns `3.03`.

The `Math` class also has a powerful method, `random`, which generates a random double floating-point number greater than or equal to 0.0 and less than 1.0 (`0 <= Math.random() < 1.0`).

 TIP

You can view the complete documentation for the `Math` class in JBuilder by choosing *Search, Find Classes* to display the Find Classes dialog box. Type `java.lang.Math` in the Class name field to display the documentation of the `Math` class in the content pane, as shown in Figure 4.12.

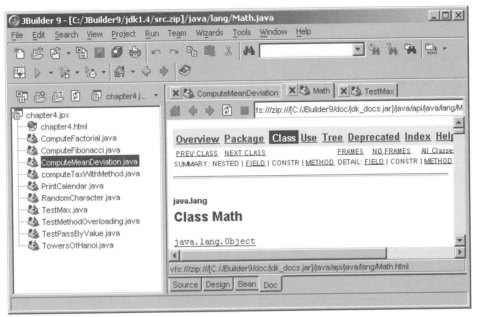

Figure 4.12   *You can view the documentation for Java API online in JBuilder.*

◈ **NOTE**

Not all classes need a main method. The Math class and JOptionPane class do not have main methods. These classes contain methods for other classes to use.

Example 4.5 Computing Mean and Standard Deviation

Problem

In business applications, you are often asked to compute the mean and deviation of data. The mean is simply the average of the numbers. The standard deviation is a statistic that tells you how tightly all the various data are clustered around the mean in a set of data. For example, what is the average age of the students in a class? How close are the ages. If all the students are the same age, the deviation is 0. Write a program that generates ten random numbers between 0 and 1000, and computes the mean and standard deviations of these numbers using the following formula:

$$mean = \frac{\sum_{i=1}^{n} x_i}{n} = \frac{x_1 + x_2 + \cdots + x_n}{n} \qquad deviation = \sqrt{\frac{\sum_{i=1}^{n} x_i^2 - \frac{\left(\sum_{i=1}^{n} x_i\right)^2}{n}}{n-1}}$$

continues

Example 4.5 continued

Solution

When you wrote the program to compute loan payments using the formula in Example 2.3, "Computing Loan Payments," you did not know how the formula was derived. Likewise, you don't need to know how the formula for deviation is derived. A sample run of the following program is shown in Figure 4.13.

```
1    // ComputeMeanDeviation.java: Demonstrate using the math methods
2    package chapter4;
3
4    public class ComputeMeanDeviation {
5      /** Main method */
6      public static void main(String[] args) {
7        final int COUNT = 10; // Total numbers
8        int number = 0; // Store a random number
9
9        double sum = 0; // Store the sum of the numbers ∑_{i=1}^{n} x_i
10
10       double squareSum = 0; // Store the sum of the squares ∑_{i=1}^{n} x_i^2
11
12       // Create numbers, find its sum, and its square sum
13       for (int i = 0; i < COUNT; i++) {
14         // Generate a new random number
15         number = (int)Math.round(Math.random() * 1000);
16         System.out.println(number);
17
18         // Add the number to sum
19         sum += number;
20
21         // Add the square of the number to squareSum
22         squareSum += Math.pow(number, 2); // Same as number*number;
23       }
24
25       // Find mean
26       double mean = sum / COUNT;
27
28       // Find standard deviation
29       double deviation =
30         Math.sqrt((squareSum - sum * sum / COUNT) / (COUNT - 1));
31
32       // Display result
33       System.out.println("The mean is " + mean);
34       System.out.println("The standard deviation is " + deviation);
35     }
36   }
```

Review

The program demonstrates the use of the math methods random, round, pow, and sqrt. The random method (Line 15) generates a double value that is greater than or equal to 0 and less than 1.0. After the generated number is multiplied by 1000, the random number is greater than or equal to 0 and less than 1000.0. The round method converts the double number into a long value, which is cast into an int variable number.

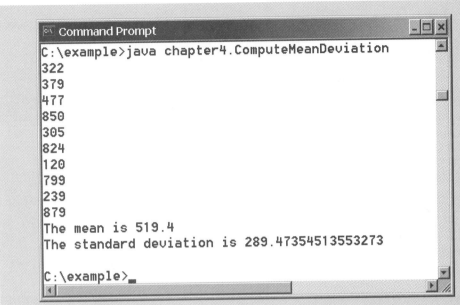

Figure 4.13   *The program finds the mean and standard deviation of ten random integers.*

Invoking pow(number, 2) (Line 22) returns the square of number. The sqrt method (Line 30) is used to get the square root of a double value.

Run the program with COUNT set to 100, 1000, and 10000, and observe the mean and deviation. As COUNT increases, the mean will come closer to 500 and the deviation closer to 288. Comment the println statement on Line 14 when you run the program so you will not be distracted by a large output of numbers.

Example 4.6 Obtaining Random Characters

Problem

Write the methods for generating random characters. The program uses these methods to generate 175 random characters between '!' and ' ~ ' (inclusive) and displays 25 characters per line.

continues

Example 4.6 continued

Solution

To find out what characters are between '!' and ' ~ ', see Appendix B, "The ASCII Character Set." The ASCII code for '!' is 33, and the code for ' ~ ' is 126. To generate a random character between '!' and ' ~ ', you may generate a Unicode whose integer value is randomly chosen between 33 to 126, using the following expression:

```
value = (int)(33 + (126 - 33 + 1) * Math.random(x));
```

Since $0 <= (126 - 33 + 1) *$ Math.random(x) < 94, $33 <= 33 + (126 - 33 + 1) *$ Math.random(x) < 127. Therefore, $33 <=$ value $<= 126$. Thus (char)value is a character between '!' and ' ~ ' inclusively.

A sample run of the program is shown in Figure 4.14.

```
1    // RandomCharacter.java: Generate random characters
2    package chapter4;
3
4    public class RandomCharacter {
5      /** Main method */
6      public static void main(String args[]) {
7        final int NUM_OF_CHARS = 175;
8        final int CHARS_PER_LINE = 25;
9
10       // Print random characters between '!' and '~', 25 chars per line
11       for (int i = 0; i < NUM_OF_CHARS; i++) {
12         if ((i + 1) % CHARS_PER_LINE == 0)
13           System.out.println(getRandomChar('!', '~'));
14         else
15           System.out.print(getRandomChar('!', '~') + " ");
16       }
17     }
18
19     /** Generate a random character between fromChar and toChar */
20     public static char getRandomChar(char fromChar, char toChar) {
21       // Get the Unicode of the character
22       int unicode = fromChar +
23         (int)((toChar - fromChar + 1) * Math.random());
24
25       // Return the character
26       return (char)unicode;
27     }
28
29     /** Generate a random character */
30     public static char getRandomChar() {
31       return getRandomChar('\u0000', '\uFFFF');
32     }
33   }
```

Review

The RandomCharacter class contains two overloaded getRandomChar methods (Lines 20, 30). The getRandomChar(char fromChar, char toChar) method (Lines 20–27) returns a random character between fromChar and toChar. The getRandomChar() method (Lines 30–32) returns a random character. The latter

Figure 4.14 *The program displays 175 random characters from '!' to ' ~ '.*

method is implemented by invoking the former method with the arguments `'\u0000'` and `'\uFFFF'`. The Unicodes of the characters are between `'\u0000'` and `'\uFFFF'` inclusively. This method is not used in this example, but may be useful in other applications. So it is implemented in the class.

The Unicode of a random character is created in Lines 22–23. When a character is involved in numeric computation, its integer equivalent is used in the operand. The expression `toChar - fromChar + 1` yields the number of characters between `fromChar` and `toChar`. So, `(toChar - fromChar + 1) * Math.random()` yields a random `double` number that is greater than or equal to 0 and less than `toChar - fromChar + 1`. Thus, `(int)((toChar - fromChar + 1) * Math.random())` yields an integer between 0 and `toChar - fromChar`. When this number is added to `fromChar`, the Unicode of the character `fromChar` is used. The result of the addition represents the Unicode of a character between `fromChar` and `toChar`. Finally, `(char)` casts the int value into a character that is returned from the method.

The `for` loop in the `main` method (Lines 11–16) generates 175 characters between '!' and ' ~ ', and displays them 25 characters per line.

4.9 Case Studies (Optional)

The concept of method abstraction can be applied to the process of developing programs. When writing a large program, you can use the "divide and conquer" strategy to decompose it into subproblems. The subproblems can be further decomposed into smaller, more manageable problems.

The following example demonstrates the divide-and-conquer approach to the development of programs.

Example 4.7 Displaying Calendars

Problem

Write a program that displays the calendar for a given month of the year. The program prompts the user to enter the year and the month, and then displays the entire calendar for the month, as shown in Figure 4.15.

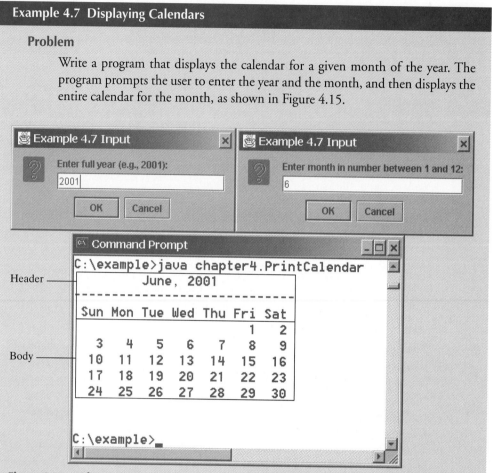

Figure 4.15 *After prompting the user to enter the year and the month, the program displays the calendar for that month.*

Solution

How would you get started on such a program? Would you immediately start coding? Beginning programmers often start by trying to work out the solution to every detail. Although details are important in the final program, concern for detail in the early stages may block the problem-solving process. To make problem-solving flow as smoothly as possible, this example begins by using method abstraction to isolate details from design and only later implements the details.

For this example, the problem is first broken into two subproblems: get input from the user, and print the calendar for the month. At this stage, the creator of the program should be concerned with what the subproblems will achieve, not with how to get input and print the calendar for the month. You can draw a structure chart to help visualize the decomposition of the problem (see Figure 4.16).

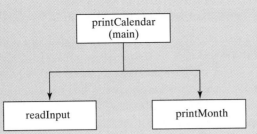

Figure 4.16 *The structure chart shows that the* `printCalendar` *problem is divided into two subproblems:* `readInput` *and* `printMonth`.

Use the `JOptionPane.showInputDialog` method to display input dialog boxes that prompt the user to enter the year and the month.

The problem of printing the calendar for a given month can be broken into two subproblems, print the month title and print the month body, as shown in Figure 4.17. The month title consists of three lines: month and year, a dash line, and the names of the seven days of the week. You need to get the month name (e.g., January) from the numeric month (e.g., 1). This is accomplished in `getMonthName` (see Figure 4.17).

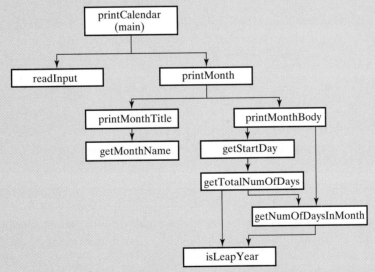

Figure 4.17 *The structure chart shows the hierarchical relationship of the subproblems in the program.*

In order to print the month body, you need to know which day of the week is the first day of the month (`getStartDay`) and how many days the month has (`getNumOfDaysInMonth`).

continues

Example 4.7 continued

How would you get the start day for the first date in a month? There are several ways to find the start day. The simplest approach is to use the Calendar class in Section 9.3, "The Calendar and GregorianCalendar Classes." For now, an alternative approach is used. Assume that you know that the start day (startDay1800 = 3) for Jan 1, 1800 was Wednesday. You could compute the total number of days (totalNumOfDays) between Jan 1, 1800 and the first date of the calendar month. The start day for the calendar month is (totalNumOfDays + startDay1800) % 7.

To compute the total days (totalNumOfDays) between Jan 1, 1800 and the first date of the calendar month, you could find the total number of days between the year 1800 and the calendar year and then figure out the total number of days prior to the calendar month in the calendar year. The sum of these two totals is totalNumOfDays.

You would also need to know the number of days in a month and in a year. Remember the following:

- January, March, May, July, August, October, and December have 31 days.

- April, June, September, and November have 30 days.

- February has 28 days during a regular year and 29 days during a leap year. A regular year, therefore, has 365 days, whereas a leap year has 366 days.

Use the following condition to determine whether a year is a leap year:

```
if (year % 400 == 0 || (year % 4 == 0 && year % 100 != 0))
   return true;
else
   return false;
```

To print a body, first pad some space before the start day and then print the lines for every week, as shown for June 2001 (see Figure 4.15).

In general, a subproblem corresponds to a method in the implementation, although some are so simple that this is unnecessary. You would need to decide which modules to implement as methods and which to combine in other methods. Decisions of this kind should be based on whether the overall program will be easier to read as a result of your choice. In this example, the subproblem readInput is implemented in the main method (see Figure 4.17).

When implementing the program, use a "top-down" approach. In other words, implement one method in the structure chart at a time—from the top to the bottom. Stubs can be used for the methods waiting to be implemented. A *stub* is a simple but incomplete version of a method. The use of stubs enables you to test invoking the method from a caller. Implement the main method first and then use a stub for the printMonth method. For example, let printMonth display the year and the month in the stub. Thus, your program may begin like this:

```
// PrintCalendar.java: Print a calendar for a given month in a year
package chapter4;

public class PrintCalendar {
  /** Main method */
  public static void main(String[] args) {
    // Prompt the user to enter year
    String yearString = JOptionPane.showInputDialog(null,
      "Enter full year (e.g., 2001):",
      "Example 4.7 Input", JOptionPane.QUESTION_MESSAGE);

    // Convert string into integer
    int year = Integer.parseInt(yearString);

    // Prompt the user to enter month
    String monthString = JOptionPane.showInputDialog(null,
      "Enter month in number between 1 and 12:",
      "Example 4.7 Input", JOptionPane.QUESTION_MESSAGE);

    // Convert string into integer
    int month = Integer.parseInt(monthString);

    // Print calendar for the month of the year
    printMonth(year, month);

    System.exit(0);
  }

  /** A stub for printMonth may look like this */
  public static void printMonth(int year, int month) {
    System.out.print(month + ", " + year);
  }
}
```

Compile and test the program, and fix any errors. You can now implement the printMonth method. For methods invoked from the printMonth method, you can again use stubs. This top-down incremental implementation approach helps to isolate programming errors and makes debugging easy.

The complete program is given as follows:

```
1   // PrintCalendar.java: Print a calendar for a given month in a year
2   package chapter4;
3
4   import javax.swing.JOptionPane;
5
6   public class PrintCalendar {
7     /** Main method */
8     public static void main(String[] args) {
9       // Prompt the user to enter year
10      String yearString = JOptionPane.showInputDialog(null,
11        "Enter full year (e.g., 2001):",
12        "Example 4.7 Input", JOptionPane.QUESTION_MESSAGE);
13
14      // Convert string into integer
15      int year = Integer.parseInt(yearString);
16
17      // Prompt the user to enter month
18      String monthString = JOptionPane.showInputDialog(null,
```

continues

179

Example 4.7 continued

```
19              "Enter month in number between 1 and 12:",
20              "Example 4.7 Input", JOptionPane.QUESTION_MESSAGE);
21
22          // Convert string into integer
23          int month = Integer.parseInt(monthString);
24
25          // Print calendar for the month of the year
26          printMonth(year, month);
27
28          System.exit(0);
29        }
30
31        /** Print the calendar for a month in a year */
32        static void printMonth(int year, int month) {
33          // Print the headings of the calendar
34          printMonthTitle(year, month);
35
36          // Print the body of the calendar
37          printMonthBody(year, month);
38        }
39
40        /** Print the month title, e.g., May, 1999 */
41        static void printMonthTitle(int year, int month) {
42          System.out.println("        " + getMonthName(month)
43            + ", " + year);
44          System.out.println("---------—");
45          System.out.println(" Sun Mon Tue Wed Thu Fri Sat");
46        }
47
48        /** Get the English name for the month */
49        static String getMonthName(int month) {
50          String monthName = null;
51          switch (month) {
52            case 1: monthName = "January"; break;
53            case 2: monthName = "February"; break;
54            case 3: monthName = "March"; break;
55            case 4: monthName = "April"; break;
56            case 5: monthName = "May"; break;
57            case 6: monthName = "June"; break;
58            case 7: monthName = "July"; break;
59            case 8: monthName = "August"; break;
60            case 9: monthName = "September"; break;
61            case 10: monthName = "October"; break;
62            case 11: monthName = "November"; break;
63            case 12: monthName = "December";
64          }
65
66          return monthName;
67        }
68
69        /** Print month body */
70        static void printMonthBody(int year, int month) {
71          // Get start day of the week for the first date in the month
72          int startDay = getStartDay(year, month);
73
74          // Get number of days in the month
75          int numOfDaysInMonth = getNumOfDaysInMonth(year, month);
76
```

```
77              // Pad space before the first day of the month
78              int i = 0;
79              for (i = 0; i < startDay; i++)
80                System.out.print("      ");
81
82              for (i = 1; i <= numOfDaysInMonth; i++) {
83                if (i < 10)
84                  System.out.print("    " + i);
85                else
86                  System.out.print("   " + i);
87
88                if ((i + startDay) % 7 == 0)
89                  System.out.println();
90              }
91
92            System.out.println();
93          }
94
95          /** Get the start day of the first day in a month */
96          static int getStartDay(int year, int month) {
97            // Get total number of days since 1/1/1800
98            int startDay1800 = 3;
99            int totalNumOfDays = getTotalNumOfDays(year, month);
100
101           // Return the start day
102           return (totalNumOfDays + startDay1800) % 7;
103         }
104
105         /** Get the total number of days since Jan 1, 1800 */
106         static int getTotalNumOfDays(int year, int month) {
107           int total = 0;
108
109           // Get the total days from 1800 to year - 1
110           for (int i = 1800; i < year; i++)
111           if (isLeapYear(i))
112             total = total + 366;
113           else
114             total = total + 365;
115
116           // Add days from Jan to the month prior to the calendar month
117           for (int i = 1; i < month; i++)
118             total = total + getNumOfDaysInMonth(year, i);
119
120           return total;
121         }
122
123         /** Get the number of days in a month */
124         static int getNumOfDaysInMonth(int year, int month) {
125           if (month == 1 || month==3 || month == 5 || month == 7 ||
126             month == 8 || month == 10 || month == 12)
127             return 31;
128
129           if (month == 4 || month == 6 || month == 9 || month == 11)
130             return 30;
131
132           if (month == 2) return isLeapYear(year) ? 29 : 28;
133
134           return 0; // If month is incorrect
135         }
136
```

continues

181

Example 4.7 continued

```
137      /** Determine if it is a leap year */
138      static boolean isLeapYear(int year) {
139        return year % 400 == 0 || (year % 4 == 0 && year % 100 != 0);
140      }
141    }
```

Review

The program does not validate user input. For instance, if the user enters a month not in the range between 1 and 12, or a year before 1800, the program would display an erroneous calendar. To avoid this error, add an `if` statement to check the input before printing the calendar.

This program prints calendars for a month but could easily be modified to print calendars for a whole year. Although it can only print months after January 1800, it could be modified to trace the day of a month before 1800.

The calendar is displayed in the command window. You can modify the program to display the calendar in a message dialog box. See Exercise 6.5.

 NOTE

Method abstraction modularizes programs in a neat, hierarchical manner. Programs written as collections of concise methods are easier to write, debug, maintain, and modify than would otherwise be the case. This writing style also promotes method reusability.

 TIP

When implementing a large program, use the top-down coding approach. Start with the `main` method, and code and test one method at a time. Do not write the entire program at once. This approach seems to take more time for coding (because you are repeatedly compiling and running the program), but it actually saves time and makes debugging easier.

4.10   Recursion (Optional)

You have seen a method calling another method; that is, a statement contained in a method body calling another method. Can a method call itself? And what happens if it does? This section examines these questions and uses three classic examples to demonstrate recursive programming.

4.10.1   Computing Factorials

Recursion, a powerful mathematical concept, is the process of a function calling itself, directly or indirectly. Many mathematical functions are defined using recursion. The factorial of a number n can be recursively defined as follows:

```
0! = 1;
n! = n × (n - 1)!; n > 0
```

How do you find n! for a given n? It is easy to find 1! because you know 0! and 1! is 1 × 0!. Assuming that you know (n − 1)!, n! can be obtained immediately using n × (n−1)!. Thus, the problem of computing n! is reduced to computing (n − 1)!. When computing (n−1)!, you can apply the same idea recursively until n is reduced to 0.

Let factorial(n) be the method for computing n!. If you call the method with n = 0, it immediately returns the result. The method knows how to solve the simplest case, which is referred to as the *base case* or the *stopping condition*. If you call the method with n > 0, it reduces the problem to a subproblem for computing the factorial of n − 1. The subproblem is essentially the same as the original problem, but is slightly simpler or smaller than the original. Because the subproblem has the same property as the original, you can call the method with a different actual parameter, which is referred to as a *recursive call*.

The recursive algorithm for computing factorial(n) can be simply described as follows:

```
if (n == 0)
   return 1;
else
   return n * factorial(n - 1);
```

A recursive call can result in many more recursive calls because the method is dividing a subproblem into new subproblems. For a recursive method to terminate, the problem must eventually be reduced to a stopping case. When it reaches a stopping case, the method returns a result to its caller. The caller then performs a computation and returns the result to its own caller. This process continues until the result is passed back to the original caller. The original problem can now be solved by multiplying n with the result of factorial(n − 1).

Example 4.8 Computing Factorials

Problem

Write a recursive method for computing a factorial factorial(n), given n. The test program prompts the user to enter n.

Solution

The following code gives the solution to the problem. A sample run of the program is shown in Figure 4.18.

```
1    // ComputeFactorial.java: Compute factorial of an integer
2    package chapter4;
3
4    import javax.swing.JOptionPane;
5
6    public class ComputeFactorial {
7      /** Main method */
```

continues

Example 4.8 continued

```
8     public static void main(String[] args) {
9       // Prompt the user to enter an integer
10      String intString = JOptionPane.showInputDialog(null,
11        "Please enter a nonnegative integer:",
12        "Example 4.8 Input", JOptionPane.QUESTION_MESSAGE);
13
14      // Convert string into integer
15      int n = Integer.parseInt(intString);
16
17      // Display factorial
18      JOptionPane.showMessageDialog(null,
19        "Factorial of " + n + " is " + factorial(n),
20        "Example 4.8 Output", JOptionPane.INFORMATION_MESSAGE);
21    }
22
23    /** Return the factorial for a specified index */
24    static long factorial(int n) {
25      if (n == 0) // Stopping condition
26        return 1;
28      else
29        return n * factorial(n - 1); // Call factorial recursively
30    }
31  }
```

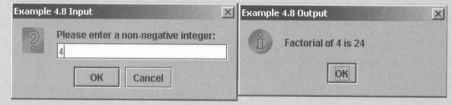

Figure 4.18 *The program prompts the user to enter a non-negative integer and then displays the factorial for the number.*

Review

The `factorial` method (Lines 24–30) is essentially a direct translation of the recursive mathematical definition for the factorial into Java code. The call to `factorial` is recursive because it calls itself. The parameter passed to `factorial` is decremented until it reaches the base case of 0.

Figure 4.19 illustrates the execution of the recursive calls, starting with n=4. The use of stack space for recursive calls is shown in Figure 4.20.

NOTE

All recursive methods have the following characteristics:

- One or more base cases (the simplest case) are used to stop recursion.
- Every recursive call reduces the original problem, bringing it increasingly closer to a base case until it becomes that case.

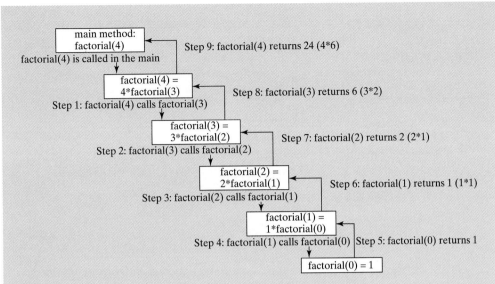

Figure 4.19 *Invoking* `factorial(4)` *spawns recursive calls to* `factorial`.

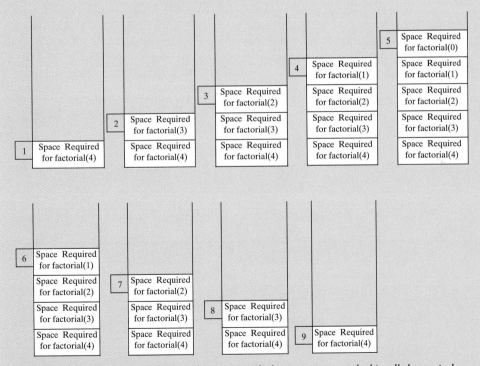

Figure 4.20 *When* `factorial(4)` *is being executed, the* `factorial` *method is called recursively, causing memory space to dynamically change.*

continues

Example 4.8 continued

⚠ CAUTION

Infinite recursion can occur if recursion does not reduce the problem in a manner that allows it to eventually converge into the base case.

☼ JBUILDER TIP

You can see the chain of recursive method invocations in the Stack tab of the debugger pane by setting a breakpoint at Line 25, as shown in Figure 4.21.

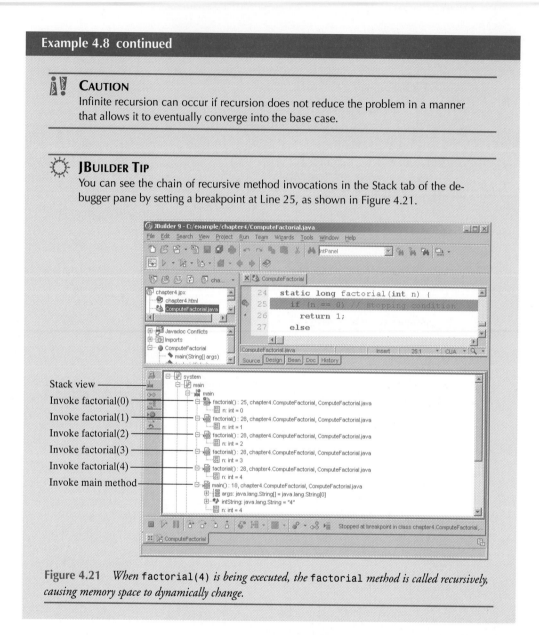

Figure 4.21   *When* `factorial(4)` *is being executed, the* `factorial` *method is called recursively, causing memory space to dynamically change.*

4.10.2   Computing Fibonacci Numbers

The preceding example could be easily rewritten without using recursion. In some cases, however, using recursion enables you to give a natural, straightforward, simple solution to a program that would otherwise be difficult to solve. Consider the well-known Fibonacci series problem. The Fibonacci series

0, 1, 1, 2, 3, 5, 8, 13, 21, 34, . . . ,

begins with 0, and 1, and each subsequent number is the sum of the preceding two numbers in the series. The series can be recursively defined as follows:

```
fib(0) = 0;
fib(1) = 1;
fib(n) = fib(n - 2) + fib(n - 1); n >= 2
```

The Fibonacci series was named for Leonardo Fibonacci, a medieval mathematician, who originated it to model the growth of the rabbit population. It can be applied in numeric optimization and in various other areas.

How do you find fib(n) for a given n? It is easy to find fib(2) because you know fib(0) and fib(1). Assuming that you know fib(n−2) and fib(n−1), fib(n) can be obtained immediately. Thus, the problem of computing fib(n) is reduced to computing fib(n−2) and fib(n−1). When computing fib(n−2) and fib(n−1), you can apply the idea recursively until n is reduced to 0 or 1.

The base case is n=0 or n=1. If you call the method with n=0 or n=1, it immediately returns the result. If you call the method with n>=2, it divides the problem into two subproblems for computing fib(n−1) and fib(n−2) using recursive calls. The recursive algorithm for computing fib(n) can be simply described as follows:

```
if (n == 0 || n == 1)
  return n;
else
  return fib(n - 1) + fib(n - 2);
```

Example 4.9 Computing Fibonacci Numbers

Problem

Write a recursive method for computing a Fibonacci number fib(n), given index n. The test program prompts the user to enter index n, then calls the method and displays the result.

Solution

The following code gives the solution to the problem. A sample run of the program is shown in Figure 4.22.

```
1    // ComputeFibonacci.java: Find a Fibonacci number for a given index
2    package chapter4;
3
4    import javax.swing.JOptionPane;
5
6    public class ComputeFibonacci {
7      /** Main method */
8      public static void main(String args[]) {
9        // Read the index
10       String intString = JOptionPane.showInputDialog(null,
11         "Enter an index for the Fibonacci number:",
12         "Example 4.9 Input", JOptionPane.QUESTION_MESSAGE);
13
14       // Convert string into integer
15       int n = Integer.parseInt(intString);
16
```

continues

Example 4.9 continued

```
17          // Find and display the Fibonacci number
18          JOptionPane.showMessageDialog(null,
19            "Fibonacci number at index " + n + " is " + fib(n),
20            "Example 4.9 Output", JOptionPane.INFORMATION_MESSAGE);
21
22          System.exit(0);
23        }
24
25        /** The method for finding the Fibonacci number */
26        public static long fib(long n) {
27          if (n == 0 || n == 1)   // Stopping condition
28            return n;
29          else   // Reduction and recursive calls
30            return fib(n - 1) + fib(n - 2);
31        }
32      }
```

Example 4.9 Input

Enter an index for the Fibonacci number:

4

OK   Cancel

Example 4.9 Output

Fibonacci number at index 4 is 3

OK

Figure 4.22   *The program prompts the user to enter an index for the Fibonacci number and then displays the number at the index.*

Review

The implementation of the method is very simple and straightforward. The solution is slightly more difficult if you do not use recursion. For a hint on computing Fibonacci numbers using iterations, see Exercise 4.9.

The program does not show the considerable amount of work done behind the scenes by the computer. Figure 4.23, however, shows successive recursive calls for evaluating fib(4). The original method, fib(4), makes two recursive calls, fib(3) and fib(2), and then returns fib(3) + fib(2). But in what order are these methods called? In Java, operands are evaluated from left to right. The upper-left-corner labels in Figure 4.23 show the order in which methods are called.

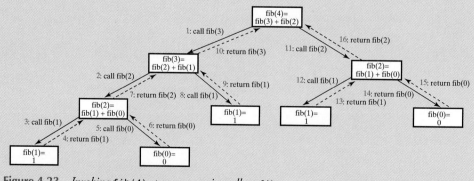

Figure 4.23   *Invoking* fib(4) *spawns recursive calls to* fib.

188

As shown in Figure 4.23, there are many duplicated recursive calls. For instance, `fib(2)` is called twice, `fib(1)` is called three times, and `fib(0)` is called twice. In general, computing `fib(n)` requires twice as many recursive calls as are needed for computing `fib(n - 1)`. As you try larger index values, the number of calls substantially increases.

Besides the large number of recursive calls, the computer requires more time and space to run recursive methods. For more discussion, see Section 4.10.4, "Recursion versus Iteration."

4.10.3   The Towers of Hanoi Problem

You have seen a recursive method with a return value. Here is an example of a recursive method with a return type of `void`.

The problem involves moving a specified number of disks of a distinct size from one tower to another while observing the following rules:

- There are *n* disks labeled 1, 2, 3, . . . , *n*, and three towers labeled A, B, and C.

- No disk can be on top of a smaller disk at any time.

- All the disks are initially placed on tower A.

- Only one disk can be moved at a time, and it must be the top disk on the tower.

The objective of the problem is to move all the disks from A to B with the assistance of C. For example, if you have three disks, as shown in Figure 4.24, the following steps will move all of the disks from A to B:

1. Move disk 1 from A to B.

2. Move disk 2 from A to C.

3. Move disk 1 from B to C.

4. Move disk 3 from A to B.

5. Move disk 1 from C to A.

6. Move disk 2 from C to B.

7. Move disk 1 from A to B.

◈ NOTE

The Towers of Hanoi is a classic computer science problem. There are many Web sites devoted to this problem. The Web site **www.cut-the-knot.com/recurrence/hanoi.html** is worth seeing.

In the case of three disks, you can find the solution manually. However, the problem is quite complex for a larger number of disks—even for four. Fortunately, the problem has an inherently recursive nature, which leads to a straightforward recursive solution.

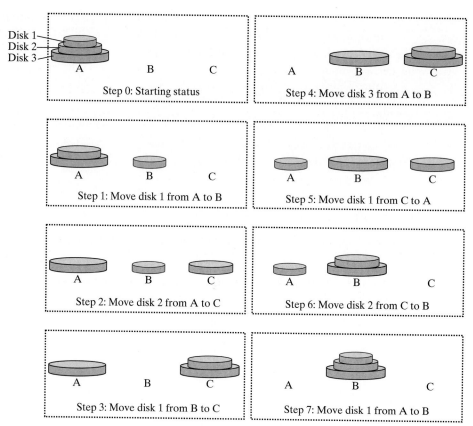

Figure 4.24   *The goal of the Towers of Hanoi problem is to move disks from tower A to tower B without breaking the rules.*

The base case for the problem is n == 1. If n == 1, you could simply move the disk from A to B. When n > 1, you could split the original problem into three subproblems and solve them sequentially.

1. Move the first n − 1 disks from A to C with the assistance of tower B.

2. Move disk *n* from A to B.

3. Move n − 1 disks from C to B with the assistance of tower A.

The following method moves *n* disks from the fromTower to the toTower with the assistance of the auxTower:

```
void moveDisks(int n, char fromTower, char toTower, char auxTower)
```

The algorithm for the method can be described as follows:

```
if (n == 1) // Stopping condition
  Move disk 1 from the fromTower to the toTower;
else {
  moveDisks(n - 1, fromTower, auxTower, toTower);
  Move disk n from the fromTower to the toTower;
  moveDisks(n - 1, auxTower, toTower, fromTower);
}
```

Example 4.10 Solving the Towers of Hanoi Problem

Problem

Write a program that finds a solution for the Towers of Hanoi problem. The program prompts the user to enter the number of disks and invokes the recursive method moveDisks to display the solution for moving the disks.

Solution

The following code gives the solution to the problem. A sample run of the following program appears in Figure 4.25.

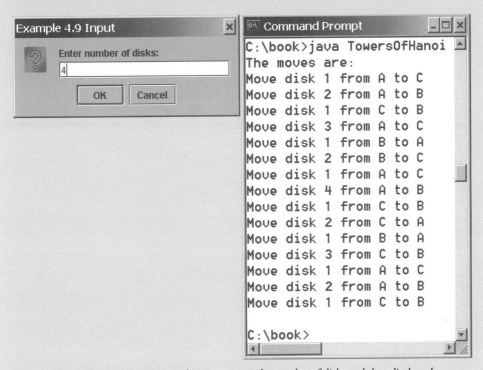

Figure 4.25 *The program prompts the user to enter the number of disks and then displays the steps that must be followed to solve the Towers of Hanoi problem.*

```
1    // TowersOfHanoi.java: Find solutions for the Towers of Hanoi problem
2    package chapter4;
3
4    import javax.swing.JOptionPane;
5
6    public class TowersOfHanoi {
7      /** Main method */
8      public static void main(String[] args) {
9        // Read number of disks, n
10       String intString = JOptionPane.showInputDialog(null,
11         "Enter number of disks:",
12         "Example 4.10 Input", JOptionPane.QUESTION_MESSAGE);
13
```

continues

Example 4.10 continued

```
14            // Convert string into integer
15            int n = Integer.parseInt(intString);
16
17            // Find the solution recursively
18            System.out.println("The moves are:");
19            moveDisks(n, 'A', 'B', 'C');
20
21            System.exit(0);
22        }
23
24        /** The method for finding the solution to move n disks
25            from fromTower to toTower with auxTower */
26        public static void moveDisks(int n, char fromTower,
27            char toTower, char auxTower) {
28            if (n == 1) // Stopping condition
29                System.out.println("Move disk " + n + " from " +
30                    fromTower + " to " + toTower);
31            else {
32                moveDisks(n - 1, fromTower, auxTower, toTower);
33                System.out.println("Move disk " + n + " from " +
34                    fromTower + " to " + toTower);
35                moveDisks(n - 1, auxTower, toTower, fromTower);
36            }
37        }
38    }
```

Review

This problem is inherently recursive. Using recursion makes it possible to find a natural, simple solution. It would be difficult to solve the problem without using recursion.

Consider tracing the program for n = 3. The successive recursive calls are shown in Figure 4.26. As you can see, writing the program is easier than tracing the recursive calls. The system uses stacks to trace the calls behind the scenes. To some extent, recursion provides a level of abstraction that hides iterations and other details from the user.

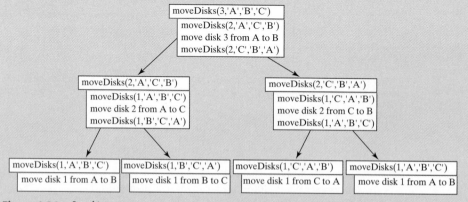

Figure 4.26 *Invoking* moveDisks(3, 'A', 'B', 'C') *spawns calls to* moveDisks *recursively.*

The fib method in the preceding example returns a value to its caller, but the moveDisks method in this example does not return a value to its caller.

4.10.4   Recursion versus Iteration

Recursion is an alternative form of program control. It is essentially repetition without a loop control. When you use loops, you specify a loop body. The repetition of the loop body is controlled by the loop-control structure. In recursion, the method itself is called repeatedly. A selection statement must be used to control whether to call the method recursively or not.

Recursion bears substantial overhead. Each time the program calls a method, the system must assign space for all of the method's local variables and parameters. This can consume considerable memory and requires extra time to manage the additional space.

Any problem that can be solved recursively can be solved nonrecursively with iterations. Recursion has many negative aspects: It uses up too much time and too much memory. Why, then, should you use it? In some cases, using recursion enables you to specify a clear, simple solution that would otherwise be difficult to obtain.

The decision whether to use recursion or iteration should be based on the nature of the problem you are trying to solve and your understanding of the problem. The rule of thumb is to use recursion or iteration to develop an intuitive solution that naturally mirrors the problem. If an iterative solution is obvious, use it. It will generally be more efficient than the recursive option.

 NOTE

Your recursive program could run out of memory, causing a runtime error. In Chapter 15, "Exceptions and Assertions," you will learn how to handle errors so that the program terminates gracefully when there is a stack overflow.

 TIP

If you are concerned about your program's performance, avoid using recursion, because it takes more time and consumes more memory than iteration.

Chapter Summary

- Making programs modular and reusable is one of the central goals in software engineering. Java provides many powerful constructs that help to achieve this goal. Methods are one such construct.

- The method header specifies the *modifiers, return value type, method name,* and *parameters* of the method. The modifier, which is optional, tells the compiler how to call the method. The static modifier is used for all the methods in this chapter.

- A method may return a value. The `returnValueType` is the data type of the value the method returns. If the method does not return a value, the `returnValueType` is the keyword `void`.

- The *parameter list* refers to the type, order, and number of the parameters of a method. The method name and the parameter list together constitute the *method signature*. Parameters are optional; that is, a method may contain no parameters.

- The parameters defined in the method header are known as *formal parameters*. When a method is invoked, its formal parameters are replaced by variables or data, which are referred to as *actual parameters*.

- A return statement can also be used in a void method for terminating the method and returning to the method's caller. This is useful for circumventing the normal flow of control in a method.

- The arguments that are passed to a method should have the same number, type, and order as the parameters in the method definition.

- When a program calls a method, program control is transferred to the called method. A called method returns control to the caller when its return statement is executed or when its method-ending closing brace is reached.

- A method with a nonvoid return value type can also be invoked as a statement in Java. In this case, the caller simply ignores the return value. In the majority of cases, a call to a method with return value is treated as a value. In some cases, however, the caller is not interested in the return value.

- Each time a method is invoked, the system stores parameters, local variables, and system registers in a space known as a *stack*. When a method calls another method, the caller's stack space is kept intact, and new space is created to handle the new method call. When a method finishes its work and returns to its caller, its associated space is released.

- When you invoke a method with parameters, a copy of the value of the actual parameter is passed to the method. This is referred to as *pass by value*. The actual variable outside the method is not affected, regardless of the changes made to the formal parameter inside the method.

- A method can be overloaded. This means that two methods can have the same name as long as their method parameter lists differ.

- Sometimes there are two or more possible matches for an invocation of a method, but the compiler cannot determine the most specific match. This is referred to as *ambiguous invocation*.

- The scope of a variable is the portion of the program where the variable can be accessed. The scope of a local variable is limited locally to a method. The scope of a local variable starts from its declaration and continues to the end of the block that contains the variable. A local variable must be declared before it can be used, and it must be initialized before it is referenced.

- *Method abstraction* is achieved by separating the use of a method from its implementation. The client can use a method without knowing how it is implemented. The details of the implementation are encapsulated in the method and hidden from the client who invokes the method. This is known as *information hiding* or *encapsulation*.

■ The Math class contains methods that perform trigonometric functions (sin, cos, tan, acos, asin, atan), exponent functions (exp, log, pow, sqrt), and some service functions (min, max, abs, round, random). All of these methods operate on double values; min, max, and abs can also operate on int, long, float, and double.

■ Method abstraction modularizes programs in a neat, hierarchical manner. Programs written as collections of concise methods are easier to write, debug, maintain, and modify than would otherwise be the case. This writing style also promotes method reusability.

■ When implementing a large program, use the top-down coding approach. Start with the main method, and code and test one method at a time. Do not write the entire program at once. This approach seems to take more time for coding (because you are repeatedly compiling and running the program), but it actually saves time and makes debugging easier.

■ *A recursive method is one that invokes itself directly or indirectly.*

■ Recursion is an alternative form of program control. It is essentially repetition without a loop control. It can be used to specify simple, clear solutions for inherently recursive problems that would otherwise be difficult to solve.

■ Recursion bears substantial overhead. Each time the program calls a method, the system must assign space for all of the method's local variables and parameters. This can consume considerable memory and requires extra time to manage the additional space.

Review Questions

4.1 What is the purpose of using a method? How do you declare a method? How do you invoke a method?

4.2 What is the return type of a main method?

4.3 Can you simplify the max method in Example 4.1 using the conditional operator?

4.4 What is method overloading? Is it possible to define two methods that have the same name but different parameter types? Is it possible to define two methods in a class that have identical method names and parameter lists with different return value types or different modifiers?

4.5 How do you pass actual parameters to a method? Can the actual parameter have the same name as its formal parameter?

4.6 What is pass by value? Show the result of the following method call:

```
public class Test {
  public static void main(String[] args) {
    int max = 0;
    max(1, 2, max);
```

```
      System.out.println(max);
    }

    public static void max(int value1, int value2, int max) {
      if (value1 > value2)
        max = value1;
      else
        max = value2;
    }
  }
```

4.7 Show the output of the following programs:

a.
```
public class Test {
  public static void main(String[] args) {
    // Initialize times
    int times = 3;
    System.out.println("Before the call, variable times is "
      + times);

    // Invoke nPrintln and display times afterwards
    nPrintln("Welcome to Java!", times);
    System.out.println("After the call, variable times is "
      + times);
  }

  // Print the message n times
  static void nPrintln(String message, int n) {
    while (n > 0) {
      System.out.println("n = " + n);
      System.out.println(message);
      n--;
    }
  }
}
```

b.
```
public class Test {
  public static void main(String[] args) {
    int i = 1;
    while (i <= 6) {
      xMethod(i, 2);
      i++;
    }
  }

  public static void xMethod(int i, int num) {
    for (int j = 1; j <= i; j++) {
      System.out.print(num + " ");
      num *= 2;
    }

    System.out.println();
  }
}
```

c.
```
public class Test {
  public static void main(String[] args) {
    int i = 0;
    while (i <= 4) {
      xMethod(i);
      i++;
    }
```

```
      System.out.println("i is " + i);
  }

  public static void xMethod(int i) {
    do {
      if (i % 3 != 0)
        System.out.print(i + " ");
      i--;
    }
    while (i >= 1);

    System.out.println();
  }
}
```

4.8 A call to a method with a `void` return type is always a statement itself, but a call to a method with a nonvoid return type is always a component of an expression. Is this statement true or false?

4.9 What would be wrong with not writing a `return` statement in a nonvoid method? Can you have a `return` statement in a `void` method, such as the following?

```
public static void main(String[] args) {
  int i;
  while (true) {
    // Prompt the user to enter an integer
    String intString = JOptionPane.showInputDialog(null,
      "Enter an integer:",
      "Test", JOptionPane.QUESTION_MESSAGE);

    // Convert a string into int
    int i = Integer.parseInt(intString);
    if (i == 0)
      return;
    System.out.println("i = " + i);
  }
}
```

Does the `return` statement in the following method cause syntax errors?

```
public static void xMethod(double x, double y) {
  System.out.println(x + y);
  return x + y;
}
```

4.10 In some languages, you can define methods inside a method. Can you define a method inside a method in Java?

4.11 For each of the following, decide whether a `void` method or a nonvoid method is the most appropriate implementation:

- Computing a sales commission, given the sales amount and the commission rate.

- Printing the calendar for a month.

- Computing a square root.

- Testing whether a number is even, and returning `true` if it is.

- Printing a message a specified number of times.

■ Computing the monthly payment, given the loan amount, number of years, and annual interest rate.

■ Finding the corresponding uppercase letter, given a lowercase letter.

4.12 Which of the following is a possible output from invoking `Math.random()`?

a. 323.4

b. 0.5

c. 34

d. 1.0

e. b and d.

4.13 Evaluate the following method calls:

```
Math.sqrt(4)
Math.sin(2 * Math.PI)
Math.cos(2 * Math.PI)
Math.pow(2, 2)
Math.log(Math.E)
Math.exp(1)
Math.max(2, Math.min(3, 4))
Math.rint(-2.5)
Math.ceil(-2.5)
Math.floor(-2.5)
Math.round(-2.5f)
Math.round(-2.5)
Math.rint(2.5)
Math.ceil(2.5)
Math.floor(2.5)
Math.round(2.5f)
Math.round(2.5)
Math.round(Math.abs(-2.5))
```

4.14 What is a recursive method?

4.15 Describe the characteristics of recursive methods.

4.16 Show the output of the following program:

```
public class Test {
  public static void main(String[] args) {
    int sum = xMethod(5);
    System.out.println("Sum is " + sum);
  }

  public static int xMethod(int n) {
    if (n == 1)
      return 1;
    else
      return n + xMethod(n - 1);
  }
}
```

4.17 Identify and correct the errors in the following program:

```
1   public class Test {
2     public static method1(int n, m) {
3       n += m;
4       xMethod(3.4);
5     }
6
```

```
7      public static int xMethod(int n) {
8        if (n > 0) return 1;
9        else if (n == 0) return 0;
10       else if (n < 0) return -1;
11     }
12   }
```

4.18 Identify and correct the errors in the following program:

```
1    public class Test {
2      public static void main(String[] args) {
3        nPrintln("Welcome to Java!", 5);
4      }
5
6      public static void nPrintln(String message, int n) {
7        int n = 1;
8        for (int i = 0; i < n; i++)
9          System.out.println(message);
10     }
11   }
```

4.19 Reformat the following program according to the programming style and documentation guidelines proposed in Section 2.16, "Programming Style and Documentation." Use the next-line brace style.

```
public class Test {
  public static double xMethod(double i,double j)
  {
  while (i<j) {
    j--;
  }

  return j;
  }
}
```

Programming Exercses

4.1 (Converting an uppercase letter to lowercase) Write a method that converts an uppercase letter to a lowercase letter. Use the following method declaration:

```
public static char upperCaseToLowerCase(char ch)
```

For example, upperCaseToLowerCase('B') returns b.

 HINT
See Exercise 2.10.

4.2 (Summing the digits in an integer) Write a method that computes the sum of the digits in an integer. Use the following method declaration:

```
public static int sumDigits(long n)
```

For example, sumDigits(234) returns $2 + 3 + 4 = 9$.

HINT

Use the % operator to extract digits, and use the / operator to remove the extracted digit. For instance, 234 % 10 = 4 and 234/10 = 23. Use a loop to repeatedly extract and remove the digit until all the digits are extracted.

4.3 (Computing the future investment value) Write a method that computes future investment value at a given interest rate for a specified number of years. The future investment is determined using the formula in Exercise 2.9.

Use the following method declaration:

```
public static double futureInvestmentValue(
    double investmentAmount, double monthlyInterestRate, int years)
```

For example, futureInvestmentValue(10000, 0.05/12, 5) returns 12833.59.

Write a test program that prompts the user to enter the investment amount (e.g., 1000) and the interest rate (e.g., 9%), and print a table that displays future value for the years from 1 to 30, as shown below:

```
The amount invested: 1000
Annual interest rate:  9%
Years              Future Value
1                  1093.8
2                  1196.41
...
29                 13467.25
30                 14730.57
```

4.4 (Converting Celsius to Fahrenheit) Write a method that converts Celsius to Fahrenheit using the following declaration:

```
public static double celsToFahr(double cels)
```

The formula for the conversion is as follows:

```
Fahrenheit = (9.0 / 5) * celsius + 32
```

Write a program that uses a for loop and calls the celsToFahr method in order to produce the following output:

```
Cels. Temp.        Fahr. Temp.
40.00              104.00
39.00              102.20
38.00              100.40
37.00              98.60
36.00              96.80
35.00              95.00
34.00              93.20
33.00              91.40
32.00              89.60
31.00              87.80
```

4.5 (Using the Math.sqrt method) Write a program that prints the following table using the sqrt method in the Math class.

Number	SquareRoot
0	0.0000
2	1.4142
4	2.0000
6	2.4495
8	2.8284
10	3.1623
12	3.4641
14	3.7417
16	4.0000
18	4.2426
20	4.4721

4.6 (Using trigonometric methods) Print the following table to display the sin value and cos value of degrees from 0 to 360 with increments of 10 degrees. Round the value to keep four digits after the decimal point.

Degree	Sin	Cos
0	0.0	1.0
10	0.1736	0.9848...
350	-0.1736	0.9848
360	0.0	1.0

4.7 (Approximating the square root) You used the sqrt method in the Math class in Example 4.5. In this exercise, write your own method to compute square roots. The square root of a number, num, can be approximated by repeatedly performing a calculation using the following formula:

```
nextGuess = (lastGuess + (num / lastGuess)) / 2
```

When nextGuess and lastGuess are almost identical, nextGuess is the approximated square root.

The initial guess will be the starting value of lastGuess. If the difference between nextGuess and lastGuess is less than a very small number, such as 0.0001, you can claim that nextGuess is the approximated square root of num.

4.8 (Revising Example 4.8 "Computing Factorials") Rewrite Example 4.8 using iterations.

4.9 (Revising Example 4.9 "Computing Fibonacci Numbers") Write a nonrecursive method that computes Fibonacci numbers.

HINT

To compute fib(n) without recursion, you need to obtain fib(n−2) and fib(n−1) first. Let f0 and f1 denote the two previous Fibonacci numbers. The current Fibonacci number would then be f0 + f1. The algorithm can be described as follows:

```
f0 = 0; // For fib(0)
f1 = 1; // For fib(1)

for (int i = 1; i <= n; i++) {
  currentFib = f0 + f1;
  f0 = f1;
  f1 = currentFib;
}

// After the loop, currentFib is fib(n)
```

4.10 (Revising Example 4.10 "Solving the Towers of Hanoi Problem") Modify Example 4.10 so that the program finds the number of moves needed to move *n* disks from tower A to tower B.

4.11 (Computing GCD) The greatest common divisor (GCD) for two positive integers m and n is the largest integer that divides both m and n. Let k = Math.max(m, n). A brute-force approach for computing GCD(m, n) is to check whether k, k−1, k−2, ..., 2, 1 divides both m and n. The first such divisor is GCD for m and n. Write a nonrecursive method to find the GCD using this approach. The GCD(m, n) can also be defined recursively as follows:

- If n % m is 0, GCD(m, n) is n.

- Otherwise, GCD(m, n) is GCD(n, m % n).

Write a recursive method to find the GCD.

4.12 (Formatting decimal numbers) Write a method that displays a specified number of digits after the decimal point. The signature of the method is as follows:

```
public static double format(double number, int numOfDigits)
```

For example, format(10.3422345, 2) returns 10.34, and format(−0.343434, 3) returns −0.343. Use the following main method to test it:

```
public static void main(String[] args) {
  System.out.println(format(10.3422345, 2));
  System.out.println(format(-0.343434, 3));
}
```

4.13 (Revising Example 3.9 "Displaying Prime Numbers") Write a program that meets the following requirements:

- Declare a method to determine whether an integer is a prime number. Use the following method declaration:

```
public static boolean isPrime(int num)
```

An integer greater than 1 is a *prime number* if its only divisor is 1 or itself. For example, isPrime(11) returns true, and isPrime(9) returns false.

- Use the isPrime method to find the first thousand prime numbers and display every ten prime numbers in a row, as follows:

2	3	5	7	11	13	17	19	23	29
31	37	41	43	47	53	59	61	67	71
73	79	83	89	97	...				

...

4.14 (Summing the digits in an integer using recursion) Rewrite Exercise 4.2 using recursion.

4.15 (Printing a tax table) Use the computeTax methods in Example 4.4 to write a program that prints a 2002 tax table for taxable income from 50,000 to 60,000 with intervals of $50 for all four statuses, as follows:

taxable Income	Single	Married Joint	Married Separate	Head of a House
50000	9846	7296	10398	8506
50050	9859	7309	10411	8519
...				
59950	12532	9982	13190	11192
60000	12546	9996	13205	11206

4.16 (Displaying current date and time) Example 2.5, "Displaying Current Time," displays the current time. Improve this example to display the current date and time. Example 4.7, "Displaying Calendars," should give you some ideas on how to find year, month, and day.

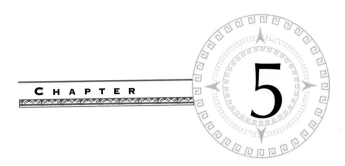

ARRAYS

Objectives

- To understand the concept of arrays.

- To learn the steps involved in using arrays: declaring array reference variables, creating arrays, initializing arrays, and processing arrays.

- To develop methods with arrays arguments.

- To know how to copy arrays.

- To write programs using multidimensional arrays.

- To sort an array using the selection sort algorithm.

- To search elements using the linear or binary search algorithm.

5.1   Introduction

In earlier chapters, you studied examples in which values were overwritten during the execution of a program. In those examples, such as Example 3.2, "Using `while` Loops," you did not need to worry about storing former values. Sometimes, however, you will have to store a large number of values in memory during the execution of a program. Suppose, for instance, that you want to sort a group of numbers. The numbers must all be stored in memory because later you will have to compare each of them with all of the others.

In order to store the numbers, you must declare variables in the program. From the standpoint of practicality, it is impossible to declare variables for each number. You need an efficient, organized approach. Java and all other high-level languages provide a data structure, the *array*, which stores a fixed-size sequential collection of elements of identical types.

5.2   Declaring Array Variables and Creating Arrays

To use an array in a program, you must declare a variable to reference the array and specify the type of array the variable can reference. Here is the syntax for declaring an array variable:

```
dataType[] arrayRefVar;
```

or

```
dataType arrayRefVar[]; // This style is correct, but not preferred
```

The following code snippets are examples of this syntax:

```
double[] myList;
```

or

```
double myList[];
```

◈ **NOTE**

The style `dataType[] arrayRefVar` is preferred. The style `dataType arrayRefVar[]` comes from the C language and was adopted in Java to accommodate C programmers.

Unlike declarations for primitive data type variables, the declaration of an array variable does not allocate any space in memory for the array. Only a storage location for the reference to an array is created. If a variable does not reference to an array, the value of the variable is `null`. You cannot assign elements to an array unless it has already been created. After an array variable is declared, you can create an array by using the `new` operator with the following syntax:

```
arrayRefVar = new dataType[arraySize];
```

This statement does two things: (1) it creates an array using `new dataType[array-Size]`; (2) it assigns the reference of the newly created array to the variable `arrayRefVar`.

Declaring an array variable, creating an array, and assigning the reference of the array to the variable can be combined in one statement, as follows:

```
dataType[] arrayRefVar = new dataType[arraySize];
```

or

```
dataType arrayRefVar[] = new dataType[arraySize];
```

Here is an example of such a statement:

```
double[] myList = new double[10];
```

This statement declares an array variable, `myList`, creates an array of ten elements of `double` type, and assigns its reference to `myList`, as shown in Figure 5.1. When space for an array is allocated, the array size must be given, to specify the number of elements that can be stored in it. The size of an array cannot be changed after the array is created. Size can be obtained using `array.length`. For example, `myList.length` is 10.

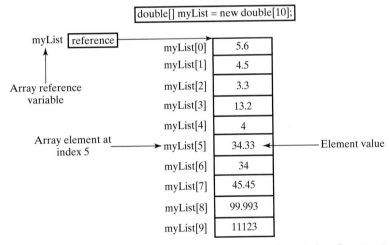

Figure 5.1   *The array* `myList` *has ten elements of* `double` *type and* `int` *indices from 0 to 9.*

❖ **NOTE**

An array variable that appears to hold an array actually contains a reference to that array. Strictly speaking, an array variable and an array are different, but most of the time the distinction between them can be ignored. Thus it is all right to say, for simplicity, that `myList` is an array, instead of stating, at greater length, that `myList` is a variable that contains a reference to an array of ten double elements. When the distinction makes a subtle difference, the longer phrase should be used.

5.3   Initializing and Processing Arrays

When an array is created, its elements are assigned the default value of `0` for the numeric primitive data types, `'\u0000'` for `char` types, and `false` for `boolean` types. The size of an array is denoted by `array.length`.

The array elements are accessed through the index. The array indices are from `0` to `array.length-1`. In the example in Figure 5.1, `myList` holds ten `double` values and the indices are from `0` to `9`.

Each element in the array is represented using the following syntax:

```
arrayRefVar[index];
```

For example, `myList[9]` represents the last element in the array `myList`.

NOTE

In Java, an array index must be an integer or an integer expression. In many other languages, such as Ada and Pascal, the index can be either an integer or another type of value.

CAUTION

Some languages use parentheses to reference an array element, as in `myList(9)`. But Java uses brackets, as in `myList[9]`.

After an array is created, you can enter values into the array elements. See, for example, the following loop:

```
for (int i = 0; i < myList.length; i++)
  myList[i] = i;
```

In this example, `myList.length` returns the array size (10) for `myList`.

Java has a shorthand notation, known as the *array initializer*, which combines declaring an array, creating an array, and initializing in one statement using the following syntax:

```
dataType[] arrayRefVar = {literal0, literal1, ..., literalk};
```

For example,

```
double[] myList = {1.9, 2.9, 3.4, 3.5};
```

This statement declares, creates, and initializes the array `myList` with four elements, which is equivalent to the following statements:

```
double[] myList = new double[4];
myList[0] = 1.9;
myList[1] = 2.9;
myList[2] = 3.4;
myList[3] = 3.5;
```

CAUTION

The new operator is not used in the array initializer syntax. Using an array initializer, you have to declare, create, and initialize the array all in one statement. Splitting it would cause a syntax error. Thus the next statement is wrong:

```
double[] myList;
myList = {1.9, 2.9, 3.4, 3.5};
```

 NOTE

You can also create and initialize an array using the following syntax:

```
new dataType[]{literal0, literal1, ..., literalk};
```

For example, these statements are correct.

```
double[] myList = {1, 2, 3};
// Some time later you need assign a new array to myList
myList = new double[]{1.9, 2.9, 3.4, 3.5};
```

When processing array elements, you will often use a for loop. Here are the reasons why:

- All of the elements in an array are of the same type. They are evenly processed in the same fashion by repeatedly using a loop.

- Since the size of the array is known, it is natural to use a for loop.

Example 5.1 Testing Arrays

Problem

Write a program that reads six integers, finds the largest of them, and counts its occurrences. Suppose that you entered the numbers shown in Figure 5.2; the program finds that the largest is 5 and the occurrence count for 5 is 4.

Solution

Your program should read the numbers and store them in an array, then find the largest number in the array, and finally count the occurrence of the largest number in the array. The source code for the program is shown below:

```
1   // TestArray.java: Count the occurrences of the largest number
2   package chapter5;
3
4   import javax.swing.JOptionPane;
5
6   public class TestArray {
7     /** Main method */
8     public static void main(String[] args) {
9       final int TOTAL_NUMBERS = 6;
10      int[] numbers = new int[TOTAL_NUMBERS];
11
```

continues

Example 5.1 continued

```
12          // Read all numbers
13          for (int i = 0; i < numbers.length; i++) {
14            String numString = JOptionPane.showInputDialog(null,
15              "Enter a number:",
16              "Example 5.1 Input", JOptionPane.QUESTION_MESSAGE);
17
18            // Convert string into integer
19            numbers[i] = Integer.parseInt(numString);
20          }
21
22          // Find the largest
23          int max = numbers[0];
24          for (int i = 1; i < numbers.length; i++) {
25            if (max < numbers[i])
26              max = numbers[i];
27          }
28
29          // Find the occurrence of the largest number
30          int count = 0;
31          for (int i = 0; i < numbers.length; i++) {
32            if (numbers[i] == max) count++;
33          }
34
35          // Prepare the result
36          String output = "The array is ";
37          for (int i = 0; i < numbers.length; i++) {
38            output += numbers[i] + " ";
39          }
40
41          output += "\nThe largest number is " + max;
42          output += "\nThe occurrence count of the largest number "
43            + "is " + count;
44
45          // Display the result
46          JOptionPane.showMessageDialog(null, output,
47            "Example 5.1 Output", JOptionPane.INFORMATION_MESSAGE);
48
49          System.exit(0);
50        }
51      }
```

Review

The program declares and creates an array of six integers (Line 10). It finds the largest number in the array (Lines 23–27), counts its occurrences (Lines 30–33), and displays the result (Lines 32–44). To display the array, you need to display each element in the array using a loop.

Without using the numbers array, you would have to declare a variable for each number entered, because all the numbers are compared to the largest number to count its occurrences after it is found.

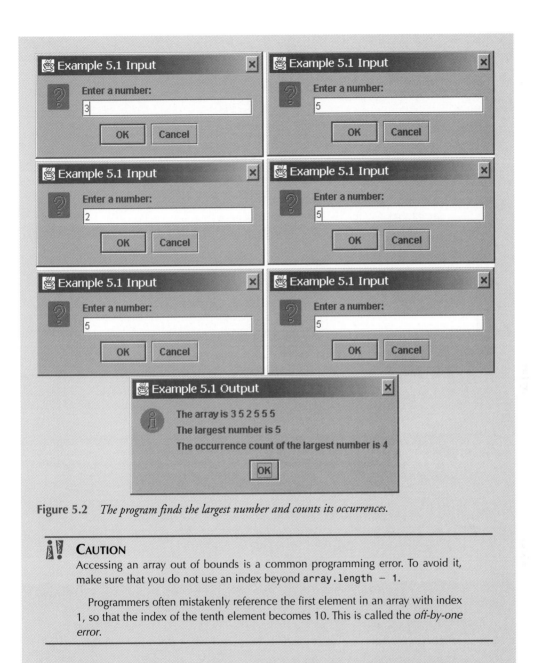

Figure 5.2 *The program finds the largest number and counts its occurrences.*

⚠ CAUTION

Accessing an array out of bounds is a common programming error. To avoid it, make sure that you do not use an index beyond `array.length - 1`.

Programmers often mistakenly reference the first element in an array with index 1, so that the index of the tenth element becomes 10. This is called the *off-by-one error*.

☼ JBUILDER TIP

You can trace the values of array elements in the debugger by adding the array variable in the watch view, as shown in Figure 5.3.

continues

211

Example 5.1   continued

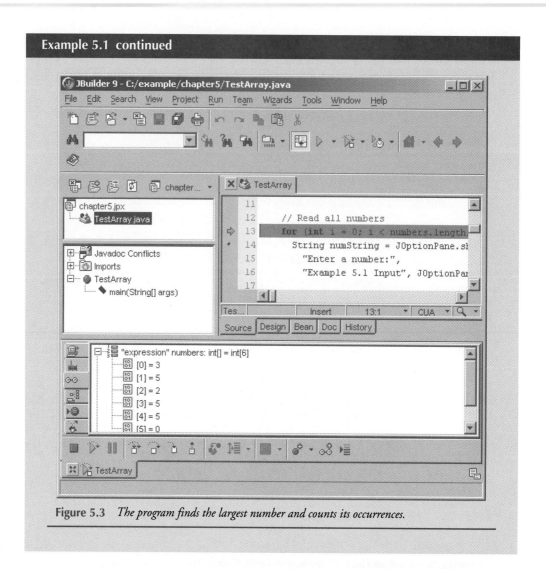

Figure 5.3   *The program finds the largest number and counts its occurrences.*

Example 5.2   Assigning Grades

Problem

Write a program that reads student scores, gets the best score, and then assigns grades based on the following scheme:

Grade is A if score is $>=$ best $-$ 10;
Grade is B if score is $>=$ best $-$ 20;
Grade is C if score is $>=$ best $-$ 30;
Grade is D if score is $>=$ best $-$ 40;
Grade is F otherwise.

The program prompts the user to enter the total number of students, then prompts the user to enter all of the scores, and concludes by displaying the grades.

Solution

The program reads the scores, then finds the best score, and finally assigns the grades to the students based on the preceding scheme. The following code gives the solution to the problem. The output of a sample run of the program is shown in Figure 5.4.

```java
1    // AssignGrade.java: Assign grade
2    package chapter5;
3
4    import javax.swing.JOptionPane;
5
6    public class AssignGrade {
7      /** Main method */
8      public static void main(String[] args) {
9        int numOfStudents = 0; // The number of students
10       int[] scores; // Array scores
11       int best = 0; // The best score
12       char grade; // The grade
13
14       // Get number of students
15       String numOfStudentsString = JOptionPane.showInputDialog(null,
16         "Please enter number of students:",
17         "Example 5.2 Input", JOptionPane.QUESTION_MESSAGE);
18
19       // Convert string into integer
20       numOfStudents = Integer.parseInt(numOfStudentsString);
21
22       // Create array scores
23       scores = new int[numOfStudents];
24
25       // Read scores and find the best score
26       for (int i = 0; i < scores.length; i++) {
27         String scoreString = JOptionPane.showInputDialog(null,
28         "Please enter a score:",
29         "Example 5.2 Input", JOptionPane.QUESTION_MESSAGE);
30
31         // Convert string into integer
32         scores[i] = Integer.parseInt(scoreString);
33         if (scores[i] > best)
34           best = scores[i];
35       }
36
37       // Declare and initialize output string
38       String output = "";
39
40       // Assign and display grades
41       for (int i = 0; i < scores.length; i++) {
42         if (scores[i] >= best - 10)
43           grade = 'A';
44         else if (scores[i] >= best - 20)
45           grade = 'B';
46         else if (scores[i] >= best - 30)
47           grade = 'C';
48         else if (scores[i] >= best - 40)
49           grade = 'D';
50         else
51           grade = 'F';
52
53         output += "Student " + i + " score is " +
54           scores[i] + " and grade is " + grade + "\n";
55       }
56
```

continues

213

Example 5.2 continued

```
57          // Display the result
58          JOptionPane.showMessageDialog(null, output,
39            "Example 5.2 Output", JOptionPane.INFORMATION_MESSAGE);
60
61          System.exit(0);
62      }
63   }
```

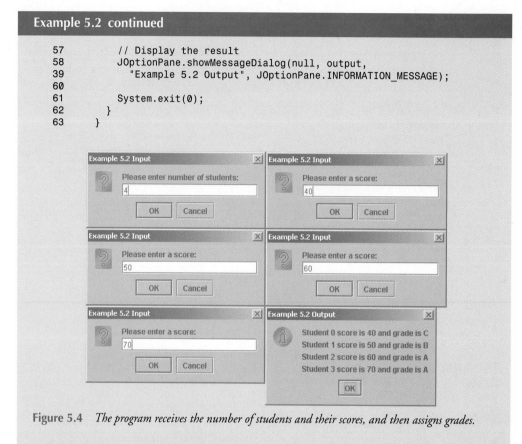

Figure 5.4 *The program receives the number of students and their scores, and then assigns grades.*

Review

The program declares scores as an array of int type in order to store the students' scores (Line 10). The size of the array is undetermined when the array is declared. After the user enters the number of students into numOfStudents in Lines 14–20, an array with the size numOfStudents is created in Line 23. The size of the array is set at runtime; it cannot be changed once the array is created.

The array is not needed to find the best score, but it is needed to keep all of the scores so that grades can be assigned later on, and it is needed when scores are printed along with the students' grades.

5.4   Copying Arrays

Often, in a program, you need to duplicate an array or a part of an array. In such cases you could attempt to use the assignment statement (=), as follows:

```
newList = list;
```

It seems to work fine. But if you ran the next program, you would discover that it does not work. The following example explains why.

Example 5.3   Copying Arrays

Problem

Write a program that creates two arrays and attempts to copy one to the other, using an assignment statement. The output of the program, shown in Figure 5.5, demonstrates that the two array variables reference the same array after the attempted copy.

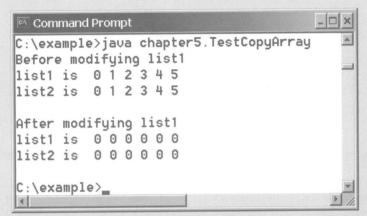

```
Command Prompt                                         _ □ ×

C:\example>java chapter5.TestCopyArray
Before modifying list1
list1 is  0 1 2 3 4 5
list2 is  0 1 2 3 4 5

After modifying list1
list1 is  0 0 0 0 0 0
list2 is  0 0 0 0 0 0

C:\example>
```

Figure 5.5   *Copying reference array variables makes two variables refer to the same array.*

Solution

The source code for the problem is given as follows:

```
1   // TestCopyArray.java: Demonstrate copying arrays
2   package chapter5;
3
4   public class TestCopyArray {
5     /** Main method */
6     public static void main(String[] args) {
7       // Create an array and assign values
8       int[] list1 = {0, 1, 2, 3, 4 ,5};
9
10      // Create an array with default values
11      int[] list2 = new int[list1.length];
12
13      // Assign array list1 to array list2
14      list2 = list1;
15
16      // Display list1
17      System.out.println("Before modifying list1");
18      System.out.print("list1 is ");
19      for (int i = 0; i < list1.length; i++)
20        System.out.print(list1[i] + " ");
21
22      // Display list2
23      System.out.print("\nlist2 is ");
24      for (int i = 0; i < list2.length; i++)
25        System.out.print(list2[i] + " ");
26
```

continues

215

Example 5.3 continued

```
27          // Modify list1
28          for (int i = 0; i < list1.length; i++)
29            list1[i] = 0;
30
31          // Display list1 and list2 after modifying list1
32          System.out.println("\n\nAfter modifying list1");
33          System.out.print("list1 is ");
34          for (int i = 0; i < list1.length; i++)
35            System.out.print(list1[i] + " ");
36
37          // Display list2
38          System.out.print("\nlist2 is ");
39          for (int i = 0; i < list2.length; i++)
40            System.out.print(list2[i] + " ");
41        }
42      }
```

Review

The program creates two arrays, list1 and list2, assigns list1 to list2 (Lines 14), and displays both list1 and list2. The program then changes the value in list1 (Lines 28–29) and redisplays list1 and list2 (Lines 31–40). As shown in Figure 5.5, the contents of list2 were also changed. This occurs because the assignment statement list2 = list1 actually copies the reference of list1 to list2, and makes list2 point to list1's memory location, as shown in Figure 5.6. The array referenced by the previous list2 is no longer referenced; it becomes garbage, which will be automatically collected by the Java Virtual Machine.

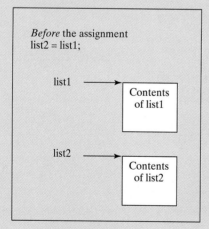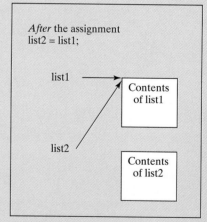

Figure 5.6 *Before the assignment statement, list1 and list2 point to separate memory locations. After the assignment, the reference of the list1 array is passed to list2.*

In Java, you can use assignment statements to copy primitive data type variables, but not arrays. Assigning one array variable to another array variable actually copies one reference to another and makes both variables point to the same memory location.

There are three ways to copy arrays:

- Use a loop to copy individual elements.

- Use the static arraycopy method in the System class.

- Use the clone method to copy arrays; this will be introduced in Chapter 8, "Inheritance and Polymorphism."

You can write a loop to copy every element, from the source array to the corresponding element in the target array. The following code, for instance, copies the sourceArray to the targetArray using a for loop.

```
for (int i = 0; i < sourceArray.length; i++)
  targetArray[i] = sourceArray[i];
```

Another approach is to use the arraycopy method in the java.lang.System class to copy arrays instead of using a loop. The syntax for arraycopy is as follows:

```
arraycopy(sourceArray, src_pos, targetArray, tar_pos, length);
```

The parameters src_pos and tar_pos indicate the starting positions in sourceArray and targetArray, respectively. The number of elements copied from sourceArray to targetArray is indicated by length. For example, you can rewrite the loop using the following statement:

```
int[] sourceArray = {2, 3, 1, 5, 10};
int[] targetArray = new int[sourceArray.length];
System.arraycopy(sourceArray, 0, targetArray, 0, sourceArray.length);
```

The arraycopy method does not allocate memory space for the target array. The target array must have already been created with its memory space allocated. After the copying takes place, targetArray and sourceArray have the same content but independent memory locations.

 NOTE

The arraycopy method violates the Java naming convention. By convention, this method should be named arrayCopy.

5.5   Passing Arrays to Methods

Just as you can pass the parameters of primitive types to methods, you can also pass the parameters of array types to methods. Example 5.3, "Copying Arrays," can be simplified if you use a method to print the list, as shown in the following code:

```
public static void printArray(int[] array) {
  for (int i = 0; i < array.length; i++) {
    System.out.print(array[i] + " ");
  }
}
```

Java uses *pass by value* to pass parameters to a method. There are important differences between passing the values of variables of primitive data types and passing arrays.

■ For a parameter of a primitive type value, the actual value is passed. Changing the value of the local parameter inside the method does not affect the value of the variable outside the method.

■ For a parameter of an array type, the value of the parameter contains a reference to an array; this reference is passed to the method. Any changes to the array that occur inside the method body will affect the original array that was passed as the argument.

Take the following code, for example:

```java
public class Test {
  public static void main(String[] args) {
    int x = 1; // x represents an int value
    int[] y = new int[10]; // y represents an array of int values

    xMethod(x, y); // Invoke xMethod with arguments x and y

    System.out.println("x is " + x);
    System.out.println("y[0] is " + y[0]);
  }

  public static void xMethod(int number, int[] numbers) {
    number = 1001; // Assign a new value to number
    numbers[0] = 5555; // Assign a new value to numbers[0]
  }
}
```

You will see that after xMethod is invoked, x remains 1, but y[0] is 5555. This is because y and numbers reference to the same array, although y and numbers are independent variables, as illustrated in Figure 5.7. When invoking xMethod(x, y), the values of x and y are passed to number and numbers. Since y contains the reference value to the array, numbers now contains the same reference value to the same array.

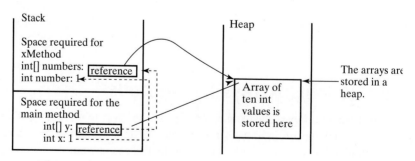

Figure 5.7   *The primitive type value in* x *is passed to* number, *and the reference value in* y *is passed to* numbers.

NOTE:

JVM stores the array in an area of memory, called *heap*, which is used for dynamic memory allocation where blocks of memory are allocated and freed in an arbitrary order.

The following is another example that shows the difference between passing a primitive data type value and an array reference variable to a method.

Example 5.4 Passing Arrays as Arguments

Problem

Write two methods for swapping elements in an array. The first method, named swap, attempts to swap two int arguments. The second method, named swapFirstTwoInArray, attempts to swap the first two elements in the array argument.

Solution

The program is given below. Figure 5.8 shows a sample run of the program.

```
1    // TestPassArray.java: Demonstrate passing arrays to methods
2    package chapter5;
3
4    public class TestPassArray {
5      /** Main method */
6      public static void main(String[] args) {
7        int[] a = {1, 2};
8
9        // Swap elements using the swap method
10       System.out.println("Before invoking swap");
11       System.out.println("array is {" + a[0] + ", " + a[1] + "}");
12       swap(a[0], a[1]);
13       System.out.println("After invoking swap");
14       System.out.println("array is {" + a[0] + ", " + a[1] + "}");
15
16       // Swap elements using the swapFirstTwoInArray method
17       System.out.println("Before invoking swapFirstTwoInArray");
18       System.out.println("array is {" + a[0] + ", " + a[1] + "}");
19       swapFirstTwoInArray(a);
20       System.out.println("After invoking swapFirstTwoInArray");
21       System.out.println("array is {" + a[0] + ", " + a[1] + "}");
22     }
23
24     /** Swap two variables */
25     public static void swap(int n1, int n2) {
26       int temp = n1;
27       n1 = n2;
28       n2 = temp;
29     }
30
31     /** Swap the first two elements in the array */
32     public static void swapFirstTwoInArray(int[] array) {
33       int temp = array[0];
34       array[0] = array[1];
35       array[1] = temp;
36     }
37   }
```

continues

Example 5.4 continued

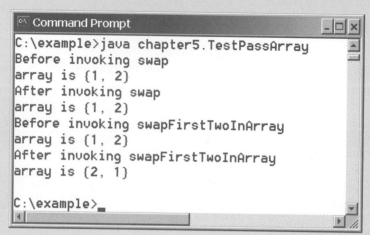

Figure 5.8   *The program attempts to swap two elements using the* swap *method and the* swapFirstTwoInArray *method.*

Review

As shown in Figure 5.8, the two elements are not swapped using the swap method. However, they are actually swapped using the swapFirstTwoInArray method. Since the arguments in the swap method are primitive type, the values of a[0] and a[1] are passed to n1 and n2 inside the method when invoking swap(a[0], a[1]). The memory locations for n1 and n2 are independent of the ones for a[0] and a[1]. The contents of the array are not affected by this call. This is pictured in Figure 5.9.

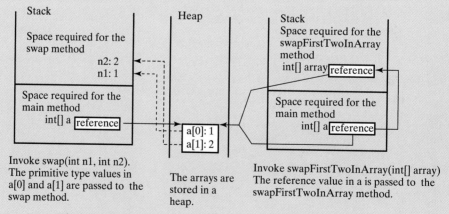

Figure 5.9   *When passing an array to a method, the reference of the array is passed to the method.*

The argument in the swapFirstTwoInArray method is an array. As shown in Figure 5.9, the reference of the array is passed to the method. Thus the variables a (outside the method) and `array` (inside the method) both refer to the same array in the same memory location. Therefore, swapping `array[0]` with `array[1]` inside the method `swapFirstTwoInArray` is the same as swapping `a[0]` with `a[1]` outside of the method.

Example 5.5 Computing Deviation Using Arrays

Problem

Example 4.5, "Computing Mean and Standard Deviation," computes the mean and standard deviation of numbers. This example uses a different but equivalent formula to compute the standard deviation of n numbers.

$$mean = \frac{\sum\limits_{i=1}^{n} x_i}{n} = \frac{x_1 + x_2 + \cdots + x_n}{n} \qquad deviation = \sqrt{\frac{\sum\limits_{i=1}^{n} (x_i - mean)^2}{n - 1}}$$

To compute deviation with this formula, you have to store the individual numbers using an array, so that they can be used after the mean is obtained. This example presents the methods for finding the mean and standard deviation for an array of numbers.

Solution

The program is given below. Figure 5.10 shows a sample run of the program.

```
1    // Deviation.java: Compute deviation
2    package chapter5;
3
4    public class Deviation {
5      /** Main method */
6      public static void main(String[] args) {
7        // Declare and create an array for 10 numbers
8        double[] numbers = {1, 2, 3, 4, 5, 6, 7, 8, 9, 10};
9
10       // Print numbers
11       printArray(numbers);
12
13       // Display mean and deviation
14       System.out.println("The mean is " + mean(numbers));
15       System.out.println("The standard deviation is " +
16         deviation(numbers));
17     }
18
19     /** Method for computing deviation of double values*/
20     public static double deviation(double[] x) {
21       double mean = mean(x);
22       double squareSum = 0;
23
24       for (int i = 0; i < x.length; i++) {
25         squareSum += Math.pow(x[i] - mean, 2);
26       }
27
```

continues

Example 5.5 continued

```
28        return Math.sqrt((squareSum) / (x.length - 1));
29      }
30
31      /** Method for computing deviation of int values*/
32      public static double deviation(int[] x) {
33        double mean = mean(x);
34        double squareSum = 0;
35
36        for (int i = 0; i < x.length; i++) {
37          squareSum += Math.pow(x[i] - mean, 2);
38        }
39
40        return Math.sqrt((squareSum) / (x.length - 1));
41      }
42
43      /** Method for computing mean of an array of double values*/
44      public static double mean(double[] x) {
45        double sum = 0;
46
47        for (int i = 0; i < x.length; i++)
48          sum += x[i];
49
50        return sum * 1.0 / x.length;
51      }
52
53      /** Method for computing mean of an array of int values*/
54      public static double mean(int[] x) {
55        int sum = 0;
56
57        for (int i = 0; i < x.length; i++)
58          sum += x[i];
59
60
61        return sum / x.length;
62      }
63
64      /** Method for printing array */
65      public static void printArray(double[] x) {
66        for (int i = 0; i < x.length; i++)
67          System.out.print(x[i] + " ");
68        System.out.println();
69      }
70    }
```

```
Command Prompt                                          _ □ ×
C:\example>java chapter5.Deviation
1.0 2.0 3.0 4.0 5.0 6.0 7.0 8.0 9.0 10.0
The mean is 5.5
The standard deviation is 3.0276503540974917

C:\example>_
```

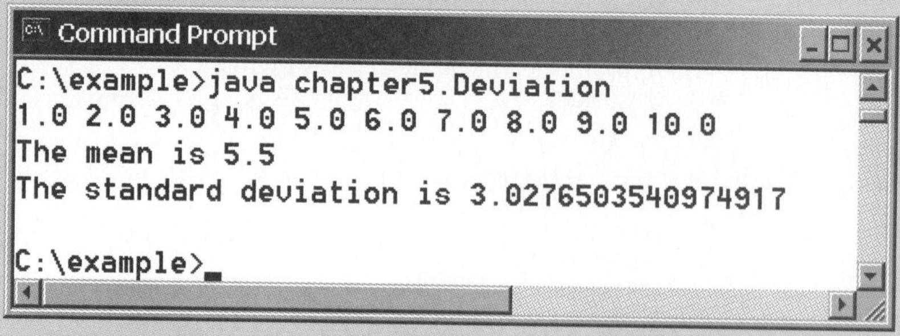

Figure 5.10 *The program obtains mean and standard deviation for an array of numbers*
{1, 2, 3, 4, 5, 6, 7, 8, 9, 10}.

Review

The `numbers` array is declared as an array of `double` type to store ten numbers (Line 8). This variable is passed to the `printArray` method, which prints the numbers (Line 11). This is then passed to the `mean` method, which computes the mean of the numbers (Line 14). Finally, this variable is passed to the `deviation` method, which computes the deviation of the numbers (Line 16).

When passing an array to a method in Java, you don't need to pass the size of the array. The size of the array is obtained using `array.length`. In other languages, such as Pascal and Ada, you have to pass the size.

There are two overloaded `deviation` methods: one for an array of `double` values in Lines 20–29 and the other for an array of `int` values in Lines 32–41. Similarly, there are two overloaded `mean` methods. So you can use methods for either array of `double` values and `int` values.

Example 5.6 Counting the Occurrences of Each Letter

Problem

Write a program that does the following:

1. Generate a hundred lowercase letters randomly and assign them to an array of characters.

2. Count the occurrences of each letter in the array.

3. Find the mean and standard deviation of the counts.

Solution

You can obtain a random letter by using the `getRandomChar(toChar, fromChar)` method in the `RandomCharacter` class in Example 4.6, "Obtaining Random Characters," and find mean and deviation using the `mean` and `deviation` methods in the `Deviation` class in the preceding example. The program is given below. Figure 5.11 shows a sample run of the program.

```
1   // CountLettersInArray.java: Count occurrences of each letter in
2   // in the array
3   package chapter5;
4
5   import chapter4.RandomCharacter;
6
7   public class CountLettersInArray {
8     /** Main method */
9     public static void main(String args[]) {
10       // Declare and create an array
11       char[] chars = createArray();
12
13       // Display the array
14       System.out.println("The lowercase letters are:");
15       displayArray(chars);
16
```

continues

Example 5.6 continued

```
17        // Count the occurrences of each letter
18        int[] counts = countLetters(chars);
19
20        // Display counts
21        System.out.println();
22        System.out.println("The occurrences of each letter are:");
23        displayCounts(counts);
24
25        // Display mean and standard deviation of the counts
26        System.out.println("\n\nMean is " + Deviation.mean(counts));
27        System.out.println("Standard deviation is " +
28          Deviation.deviation(counts));
29      }
30
31      /** Create an array of characters */
32      public static char[] createArray() {
33        // Declare an array of characters and create it
34        char[] chars = new char[100];
35
36        // Create lowercase letters randomly and assign
37        // them to the array
38        for (int i = 0; i < chars.length; i++)
39          chars[i] = RandomCharacter.getRandomChar('a', 'z');
40
41        // Return the array
42        return chars;
43      }
44
45      /** Display the array of characters */
46      public static void displayArray(char[] chars) {
47        // Display the characters in the array 20 on each line
48        for (int i = 0; i < chars.length; i++) {
49          if ((i + 1) % 20 == 0)
50            System.out.println(chars[i] + " ");
51          else
52            System.out.print(chars[i] + " ");
53        }
54      }
55
56      /** Count the occurrences of each letter */
57      public static int[] countLetters(char[] chars) {
58        // Declare and create an array of 26 int
59        int[] counts = new int[26];
60
61        // For each lowercase letter in the array, count it
62        for (int i = 0; i < chars.length; i++)
63          counts[chars[i] - 'a']++;
64
65        return counts;
66      }
67
68      /** Display counts */
69      public static void displayCounts(int[] counts) {
70        for (int i = 0; i < counts.length; i++) {
71          if ((i + 1) % 10 == 0)
72            System.out.println(counts[i] + " " + (char)(i + 'a'));
74          else
75            System.out.print(counts[i] + " " + (char)(i + 'a') + " ");
76
77        }
79      }
80    }
```

224

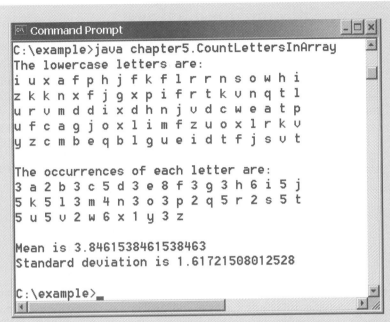

Figure 5.11   *The program generates a hundred lowercase letters randomly and counts the occurrences of each letter.*

Review

The `createArray` method (Lines 32–43) generates an array of one hundred random lowercase letters. Line 11 invokes the method and assigns the array to `chars`. What would be wrong if you rewrote the code as follows?

```
char[] chars = new char[100];
chars = createArray();
```

You would be creating two arrays. The first line would create an array by using `new char[100]`. The second line would create an array by invoking `createArray()` and assign the reference of the array to `chars`. The array created in the first line would be garbage because it is no longer referenced. Java automatically collects garbage behind the scenes. Your program would compile and run correctly, but it would create an array unnecessarily.

The `getRandomChar('a', 'z')` method (Line 39) generates a random lowercase letter. This method is defined in the `RandomCharacter` class in Example 4.6 "Obtaining Random Characters." Since the `RandomCharacter` class is not in the `chapter5` package, it is imported in Line 5.

The `countLetters` method (Lines 57–66) returns an array of twenty-six `int` values, each of which stores the number of occurrences of a letter. `counts[0]` stores the number of occurrences for `'a'`. In Line 63, `chars[i] - 'a'` yields the difference between the Unicode of `chars[i]` and the Unicode of `'a'`. `counts[chars[i] - 'a']` stores the number of occurrences for the character in `chars[i]`.

The statements in Lines 26–28 invoke the `mean` and `deviation` methods in the `Deviation` class in Example 5.5, "Computing Deviation Using Arrays," to obtain the mean and deviation of the counts.

5.6 Multidimensional Arrays

Thus far, you have used one-dimensional arrays to model linear collections of elements. To represent a matrix or a table, it is necessary to use a two-dimensional array. Occasionally, you will need to represent *n*-dimensional data structures. In Java, you can create *n*-dimensional arrays for any integer *n*, as long as your computer has sufficient memory to store the array.

5.6.1 Declaring Variables of Multidimensional Arrays and Creating Multidimensional Arrays

In Java, a two-dimensional array is declared as an array of arrays. Here is the syntax for declaring a two-dimensional array:

```
dataType[][] arrayRefVar;
```

or

```
dataType arrayRefVar[][]; // This style is correct, but not preferred
```

As an example, here is how you would declare a two-dimensional array variable `matrix` of int values:

```
int[][] matrix;
```

or

```
int matrix[][];
```

You can create a two-dimensional array of 5 by 5 int values and assign it to `matrix` using this syntax:

```
matrix = new int[5][5];
```

Two subscripts are used in a two-dimensional array, one for the row, and the other for the column. As in a one-dimensional array, the index for each subscript is of the int type and starts from 0, as shown in Figure 5.12 (A).

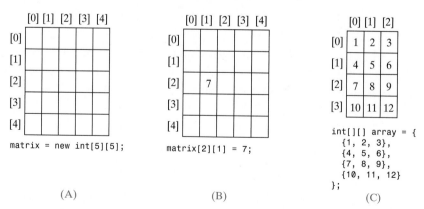

Figure 5.12 *The index of each subscript of a multidimensional array is an* int *value starting from 0.*

To assign the value 7 to a specific element at row 2 and column 0, as shown in Figure 5.12 (B), you can use the following:

```
matrix[2][0] = 7;
```

CAUTION

It is a common mistake to use `matrix[2, 0]` to access the element at row 2 and column 0. In Java, each subscript must be enclosed in a pair of square brackets.

You can also use an array initializer to declare, create, and initialize a two-dimensional array. For example, the following code

```
int[][] array = {
  {1, 2, 3},
  {4, 5, 6},
  {7, 8, 9},
  {10, 11, 12}
};
```

creates an array with the specified initial values, as shown in Figure 5.12 (C). This is equivalent to the following statements:

```
int[][] array = new int[4][3];
array[0][0] = 1; array[0][1] = 2; array[0][2] = 3;
array[1][0] = 4; array[1][1] = 5; array[1][2] = 6;
array[2][0] = 7; array[2][1] = 8; array[2][2] = 9;
array[3][0] = 10; array[3][1] = 11; array[3][2] = 12;
```

The way to declare two-dimensional array variables and create two-dimensional arrays can be generalized to declare *n*-dimensional array variables and create *n*-dimensional arrays for $n >= 3$. For example, the following syntax declares a three-dimensional array variable scores, creates an array, and assigns its reference to scores.

```
double[][][] scores = new double[10][5][2];
```

5.6.2   Obtaining the Lengths of Multidimensional Arrays

A two-dimensional array consists of an array of elements, each of which is a one-dimensional array. A three-dimensional array consists of an array of two-dimensional arrays, each of which is an array of one-dimensional arrays. The length of an array x is the number of elements in the array, which can be obtained using `x.length`. `x[0]`, `x[1]`, ..., and `x[x.length-1]` are arrays. Their lengths can be obtained using `x[0].length`, `x[1].length`, ..., and `x[x.length-1].length`. For example, `scores.length` is 10, `scores[0].length` is 5 and `scores[9].length` is 5, `scores[0][0].length` is 2, and `scores[9][4].length` is 2 for the scores in the preceding section.

5.6.3   Ragged Arrays

Each row in a two-dimensional array is itself an array. Thus the rows can have different lengths. An array of this kind is known as a *ragged array*. Here is an example of creating a ragged array:

```
int[][] triangleArray = {
  {1, 2, 3, 4, 5},
  {2, 3, 4, 5},
  {3, 4, 5},
  {4, 5},
  {5}
};
```

So, `triangleArray[0].length` is 5, `triangleArray[1].length` is 4, `triangleArray-[2].length` is 3, `triangleArray[3].length` is 2, and `triangleArray[4].length` is 1.

If you don't know the values in a ragged array in advance, you can create a ragged array using the syntax that follows:

```
int[][] triangleArray = new int[5][];
triangleArray[0] = new int[5];
triangleArray[1] = new int[4];
triangleArray[2] = new int[3];
triangleArray[3] = new int[2];
triangleArray[4] = new int[1];
```

You can now assign random values to the array using the following loop:

```
for (int row = 0; row < triangleArray.length; row++)
  for (int column = 0; column < triangleArray[row].length; column++)
    triangleArray[row][column] = (int)(Math.random() * 1000);
```

◈ NOTE

The syntax `new int[5][]` for creating an array requires the first index to be specified. The syntax `new int[][]` would be wrong.

Example 5.7 Grading a Multiple-Choice Test

Problem

Write a program that grades multiple-choice tests. Suppose there are eight students and ten questions, and the answers are stored in a two-dimensional array. Each row records a student's answers to the questions. For example, the following array stores the test.

Students' Answers to the Questions:

	0	1	2	3	4	5	6	7	8	9
Student 0	A	B	A	C	C	D	E	E	A	D
Student 1	D	B	A	B	C	A	E	E	A	D
Student 2	E	D	D	A	C	B	E	E	A	D
Student 3	C	B	A	E	D	C	E	E	A	D
Student 4	A	B	D	C	C	D	E	E	A	D
Student 5	B	B	E	C	C	D	E	E	A	D
Student 6	B	B	A	C	C	D	E	E	A	D
Student 7	E	B	E	C	C	D	E	E	A	D

The key is stored in a one-dimensional array, as follows:

Key to the Questions:

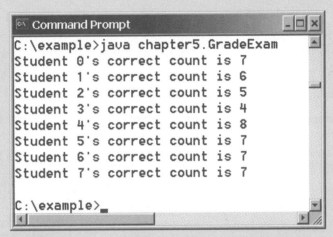

Your program grades the test and displays the result, as shown in Figure 5.13.

```
C:\example>java chapter5.GradeExam
Student 0's correct count is 7
Student 1's correct count is 6
Student 2's correct count is 5
Student 3's correct count is 4
Student 4's correct count is 8
Student 5's correct count is 7
Student 6's correct count is 7
Student 7's correct count is 7

C:\example>
```

Figure 5.13   *The program grades students' answers to the multiple-choice questions.*

Solution

The program compares each student's answer with the key, counts the number of correct answers, and displays it. The source code for the program is shown below:

```
1    // GradeExam.java: Grade answers to multiple choice questions
2    package chapter5;
3
4    public class GradeExam {
5      /** Main method */
6      public static void main(String args[]) {
7        // Students' answers to the questions
8        char[][] answers = {
9          {'A', 'B', 'A', 'C', 'C', 'D', 'E', 'E', 'A', 'D'},
10         {'D', 'B', 'A', 'B', 'C', 'A', 'E', 'E', 'A', 'D'},
11         {'E', 'D', 'D', 'A', 'C', 'B', 'E', 'E', 'A', 'D'},
12         {'C', 'B', 'A', 'E', 'D', 'C', 'E', 'E', 'A', 'D'},
13         {'A', 'B', 'D', 'C', 'C', 'D', 'E', 'E', 'A', 'D'},
14         {'B', 'B', 'E', 'C', 'C', 'D', 'E', 'E', 'A', 'D'},
15         {'B', 'B', 'A', 'C', 'C', 'D', 'E', 'E', 'A', 'D'},
16         {'E', 'B', 'E', 'C', 'C', 'D', 'E', 'E', 'A', 'D'}};
17
18        // Key to the questions
19        char[] keys = {'D', 'B', 'D', 'C', 'C', 'D', 'A', 'E', 'A', 'D'};
20
21        // Grade all answers
22        for (int i = 0; i < answers.length; i++) {
```

continues

Example 5.7 continued

```
23            // Grade one student
24            int correctCount = 0;
25            for (int j = 0; j < answers[i].length; j++) {
26              if (answers[i][j] == keys[j])
27                correctCount++;
28            }
29
30            System.out.println("Student " + i + "'s correct count is " +
31              correctCount);
32          }
33        }
34      }
```

Review

The statement in Lines 8–16 declares, creates, and initializes a two-dimensional array of characters and assigns the reference to answers of the char[][] type.

The statement in Line 19 declares, creates, and initializes an array of char values and assigns the reference to keys of the char[][] type.

Each row in the array answers stores a student's answer, which is graded by comparing it with the key in the array keys. The result is displayed immediately after a student's answer is graded. In Exercise 5.7, you will modify the program to display the mean and standard deviation of the number of correct answers, and the students in increasing order of the number of correct answers.

Example 5.8 Computing Taxes Using Arrays

Problem

Example 4.4, "Computing Taxes with Methods," simplified Example 3.1, "Computing Taxes." Example 4.4 can be further improved using arrays. Rewrite Example 3.1 using arrays to store tax rates and brackets.

Solution

For each filing status, there are six tax rates. Each rate is applied to a certain amount of taxable income. For example, from the taxable income of $400,000 for a single filer, $6,000 is taxed at 10%, (27950 − 6000) at 15%, (67700 − 27950) at 27%, (141250 − 67700) at 35%, and (400000 − 307050) at 38.6%. The six rates are the same for all filing statuses, which can be represented in the following array:

```
double[] rates = {0.10, 0.15, 0.27, 0.30, 0.35, 0.386};
```

The brackets for each rate for all the filing statuses can be represented in a two-dimensional array as follows:

```
int[][] brackets = {
  {6000, 27950, 67700, 141250, 307050}, // Single filer
  {12000, 46700, 112850, 171950, 307050}, // married jointly
  {6000, 23350, 56425, 85975, 153525}, // married separately
  {10000, 37450, 96700, 156600, 307050} // head of household
};
```

Suppose the taxable income is $400,000 for single filers, the tax can be computed as follows:

```
brackets[0][0] * rates[0] +
(brackets[0][1] - brackets[0][0]) * rates[1] +
(brackets[0][2] - brackets[0][1]) * rates[2] +
(brackets[0][3] - brackets[0][2]) * rates[3] +
(brackets[0][4] - brackets[0][3]) * rates[4] +
(400000 - brackets[0][4]) * rates[5]
```

The following code gives the solution to the program.

```
1    package chapter5;
2
3    import javax.swing.JOptionPane;
4
5    public class ComputeTax {
6      public static void main(String[] args) {
7        // Prompt the user to enter filing status
8        String statusString = JOptionPane.showInputDialog(null,
9          "Enter the filing status:\n" +
10         "(0-single filer, 1-married jointly,\n" +
11         "2-married separately, 3-head of household)",
12         "Example 5.8 Input", JOptionPane.QUESTION_MESSAGE);
13       int status = Integer.parseInt(statusString);
14
15       // Prompt the user to enter taxable income
16       String incomeString = JOptionPane.showInputDialog(null,
17         "Enter the taxable income:",
18         "Example 5.8 Input", JOptionPane.QUESTION_MESSAGE);
19       double income = Double.parseDouble(incomeString);
20
21       // Compute and display the result
22       JOptionPane.showMessageDialog(null, "Tax is " +
23         (int)(computeTax(status, income) * 100) / 100.0,
24         "Example 5.8 Output", JOptionPane.INFORMATION_MESSAGE);
25
26       System.exit(0);
27     }
28
29     public static double computeTax(int status, double income) {
30       double[] rates = {0.10, 0.15, 0.27, 0.30, 0.35, 0.386};
31
32       int[][] brackets = {
33         {6000, 27950, 67700, 141250, 307050}, // Single filer
34         {12000, 46700, 112850, 171950, 307050}, // Married jointly
35         {6000, 23350, 56425, 85975, 153525}, // Married separately
36         {10000, 37450, 96700, 156600, 307050} // Head of household
37       };
38
39       double tax = 0; // Tax to be computed
40
41       // Compute tax in the first bracket
42       if (income <= brackets[status][0])
43         return tax = income * rates[0]; // Done
44       else
45         tax = brackets[status][0] * rates[0];
46
47       // Compute tax in the 2nd, 3rd, 4th, and 5th brackets, if needed
48       for (int i = 1; i < brackets[0].length; i++) {
49         if (income > brackets[status][i])
```

continues

Example 5.8 continued

```
50            tax += (brackets[status][i] - brackets[status][i - 1]) *
51              rates[i];
52          else {
53            tax += (income - brackets[status][i - 1]) * rates[i];
54            return tax; // Done
55          }
56        }
57
58        // Compute tax in the last (i.e., 6th) bracket
59        return  tax += (income - brackets[status][4]) * rates[5];
60      }
61    }
```

Review

The computeTax method computes the tax for the taxable income of a given filing status. The tax for the first bracket (0 to brackets[status][0]) is computed in Lines 42–45. The taxes for the second, third, fourth, and fifth brackets are computed in the loop in Lines 48–56. The tax for the last bracket is computed in Line 59.

Example 5.9 Calculating Total Scores

Problem

Write a program that calculates the total score for the students in a class. Suppose the scores are stored in a three-dimensional array named scores. The first index in scores refers to a student, the second refers to an exam, and the third refers to a part of the exam. Suppose there are seven students, five exams, and each exam has two parts: a multiple-choice part and a programming part. scores[i][j][0] represents the score on the multiple-choice part for the i's student on the j's exam. Your program displays the total score for each student, as shown in Figure 5.14.

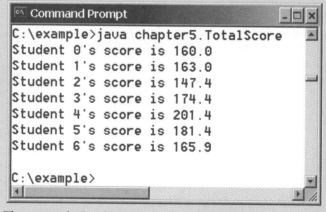

```
C:\example>java chapter5.TotalScore
Student 0's score is 160.0
Student 1's score is 163.0
Student 2's score is 147.4
Student 3's score is 174.4
Student 4's score is 201.4
Student 5's score is 181.4
Student 6's score is 165.9

C:\example>
```

Figure 5.14 *The program displays the total score for each student.*

Solution

The program processes the scores array for all the students. For each student, it adds the two scores from all exams to totalScore and displays totalScore. The source code of the program is shown below:

```
1    // TotalScore.java: Find the total score for each student
2    package chapter5;
3
4    public class TotalScore {
5      /** Main method */
6      public static void main(String args[]) {
7        double[][][] scores = {
           scores[0][0][0]
8          {{7.5, 20.5}, {9.0, 22.5}, {15, 33.5}, {13, 21.5}, {15, 2.5}},
9          {{4.5, 21.5}, {9.0, 22.5}, {15, 34.5}, {12, 20.5}, {14, 9.5}},
10         {{5.5, 30.5}, {9.4, 10.5}, {11, 33.5}, {11, 23.5}, {10, 2.5}},
11         {{6.5, 23.5}, {9.4, 32.5}, {13, 34.5}, {11, 20.5}, {16, 7.5}},
12         {{8.5, 25.5}, {9.4, 52.5}, {13, 36.5}, {13, 24.5}, {16, 2.5}},
                                              scores[5][4][1]
13         {{9.5, 20.5}, {9.4, 42.5}, {13, 31.5}, {12, 20.5}, {16, 6.5}},
14         {{1.5, 29.5}, {6.4, 22.5}, {14, 30.5}, {10, 30.5}, {16, 5.0}}};
15
16        // Calculate and display total score for each student
17        for (int i = 0; i < scores.length; i++) {
18          double totalScore = 0;
19          for (int j = 0; j < scores[i].length; j++)
20            for (int k = 0; k < scores[i][j].length; k++)
21              totalScore += scores[i][j][k];
22
23          System.out.println("Student " + i + "'s score is " +
24            totalScore);
25        }
26      }
27    }
```

Review

To understand this example, it is essential to know how data in the three-dimensional array are interpreted. scores[0] is a two-dimensional array that stores all the exam scores for the first student. scores[0][0] is {7.5, 20.5}, a one-dimensional array, which stores two scores for two parts of the first student's first exam. scores[0][0][0] is 7.5, which is the score for the first part of the first student's first exam. scores[5] is a two-dimensional array that stores all the exam scores for the sixth student. scores[5][4] is {16, 6.5}, a one-dimensional array, which stores two scores for two parts of the sixth student's fifth exam. scores[5][4][1] is 6.5, which is the score for the second part of the sixth student's fifth exam.

The statement in Lines 7–14 declares, creates, and initializes a three-dimensional array of double values and assigns the reference to scores of the double[][][] type.

The scores for each student are added in Lines 19–21, and the result is displayed in Lines 23–24. The for loop in Line 17 process the scores for all the students.

5.7   Sorting Arrays

Sorting is a common task in computer programming. It would be used, for instance, if you wanted to display the grades from Example 5.2, "Assigning Grades," in alphabetical order. Many different algorithms have been developed for sorting. In this section, a simple, intuitive sorting algorithm, selection sort, is introduced.

Suppose that you want to sort a list in ascending order. Selection sort finds the largest number in the list and places it last. It then finds the largest number remaining and places it next to last, and so on until the list contains only a single number. Figure 5.15 shows how to sort the list {2, 9, 5, 4, 8, 1, 6} using selection sort.

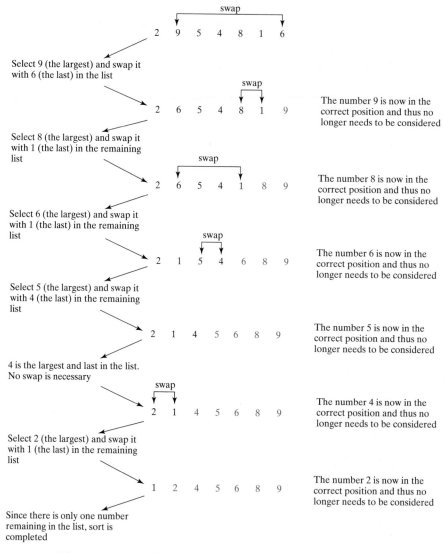

Figure 5.15   *Selection sort repeatedly selects the largest number and swaps it with the last number in the list.*

Example 5.10 Sorting Arrays

Problem

Implement the `selectionSort` method to sort a list of double floating-point numbers.

Solution

The algorithm can be described as follows:

```
for (int i = list.length - 1; i >= 1; i--) {
  select the largest element in list[0..i];
  swap the largest with list[i], if necessary;
  // list[i] is in place. The next iteration apply on list[0..i-1]
}
```

The following code gives the solution to the problem. The output of the program is shown in Figure 5.16.

```
1   // SelectionSort.java: Sort numbers using selection sort
2   package chapter5;
3
4   public class SelectionSort {
5     /** Main method */
6     public static void main(String[] args) {
7       // Initialize the list
8       double[] myList = {5.0, 4.4, 1.9, 2.9, 3.4, 3.5};
9
10      // Print the original list
11      System.out.println("My list before sort is: ");
12      printList(myList);
13
14      // Sort the list
15      selectionSort(myList);
16
17      // Print the sorted list
18      System.out.println();
19      System.out.println("My list after sort is: ");
20      printList(myList);
21    }
22
23    /** The method for printing numbers */
24    static void printList(double[] list) {
25      for (int i = 0; i < list.length; i++)
26        System.out.print(list[i] + "  ");
27      System.out.println();
28    }
29
30    /** The method for sorting the numbers */
31    static void selectionSort(double[] list) {
32      for (int i = list.length - 1; i >= 1; i--) {
33        // Find the maximum in the list[0..i]
34        double currentMax = list[0];
35        int currentMaxIndex = 0;
36
37        for (int j = 1; j <= i; j++) {
38          if (currentMax < list[j]) {
39            currentMax = list[j];
40            currentMaxIndex = j;
41          }
42        }
43
```

continues

235

Example 5.10 continued

```
44              // Swap list[i] with list[currentMaxIndex] if necessary;
45              if (currentMaxIndex != i) {
46                list[currentMaxIndex] = list[i];
47                list[i] = currentMax;
48              }
49            }
50          }
51        }
```

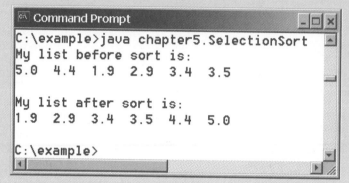

Figure 5.16   *The program invokes* `selectionSort` *in order to sort a list of* double *values.*

Review

An array `myList` of length 6 was created in Line 8:

```
double[] myList = {5.0, 4.4, 1.9, 2.9, 3.4, 3.5};
```

The `selectionSort(double[] list)` method sorts any array of double elements. The method is implemented with a nested `for` loop. The outer loop (with the loop control variable `i`) (Line 32) is iterated in order to find the largest element in the list, which ranges from `list[0]` to `list[i]`, and exchange it with the current last element, `list[i]`.

The variable `i` is initially `list.length-1`. After each iteration of the outer loop, `list[i]` is in the right place. Eventually, all the elements are put in the right place; therefore, the whole list is sorted.

◆ **NOTE**

You will probably not be able to derive the algorithm on your first attempt. I suggest that you write the code for the first iteration to find the largest element in the list and swap it with the last element, and then observe what would be different for the second iteration, the third, and so on. From the observation, you can write the outer loop and derive the algorithm.

TIP

Since sorting is frequently used in programming, Java provides several overloaded `sort` methods for sorting an array of `int`, `double`, `char`, `short`, `long`, and `float` in the `java.util.Arrays` class. For example, the following code sorts an array of numbers and an array of characters.

```
double[] numbers = {5.0, 4.4, 1.9, 2.9, 3.4, 3.5};
java.util.Arrays.sort(numbers);

char[] chars = {'a', 'A', '4', 'F', 'D', 'P'};
java.util.Arrays.sort(chars);
```

5.8   Searching Arrays

Searching is the process of looking for a specific element in an array; for example, discovering whether a certain score is included in a list of scores. Searching, like sorting, is a common task in computer programming. There are many algorithms and data structures devoted to searching. In this section, two commonly used approaches are discussed, *linear search* and *binary search*.

5.8.1   The Linear Search Approach

The linear search approach compares the key element `key` with each element in the array `list[]`. The method continues to do so until the key matches an element in the list or the list is exhausted without a match being found. If a match is made, the linear search returns the index of the element in the array that matches the key. If no match is found, the search returns −1. The algorithm can be simply described as follows:

```
for (int i = 0; i < list.length; i++) {
  if (key == list[i])
    return i;
}

return -1;
```

The example given below demonstrates a linear search.

Example 5.11 Testing Linear Search

Problem

Write a program that implements and tests the linear search method. The program creates an array of ten random elements of `int` type and then displays it. The program prompts the user to enter a key for testing linear search.

continues

237

Example 5.11 continued

Solution

The following code gives the solution to the problem. The output of a sample run of the program is shown in Figure 5.17.

```
1    // LinearSearch.java: Search for a number in a list
2    package chapter5;
3
4    import javax.swing.JOptionPane;
5
6    public class LinearSearch {
7      /** Main method */
8      public static void main(String[] args) {
9        int[] list = new int[10];
10
11        // Declare and initialize output string
12        String output = "The list is ";
13
14        // Create the list randomly and display it
15        for (int i = 0; i < list.length; i++) {
16          list[i] = (int)(Math.random() * 100);
17          output += list[i] + "  ";
18        }
19
20        // Prompt the user to enter a key
21        String keyString = JOptionPane.showInputDialog(null,
22          output + "\nEnter a key:",
23          "Example 5.11 Input", JOptionPane.QUESTION_MESSAGE);
24
25        // Convert string into integer
26        int key = Integer.parseInt(keyString);
27
28        // Search for key
29        int index = linearSearch(list, key);
30        if (index != -1)
31          output = "The key " + key + " is found in index " + index;
32        else
33          output = "The key " + key + " is not found in the list";
34
35        // Display the result
36        JOptionPane.showMessageDialog(null, output,
37          "Example 5.11 Output", JOptionPane.INFORMATION_MESSAGE);
38
39        System.exit(0);
40      }
41
42      /** The method for finding a key in the list */
43      public static int linearSearch(int[] list, int key) {
44        for (int i = 0; i < list.length; i++)
45          if (key == list[i])
46            return i;
47        return -1;
48      }
49    }
```

Review

A sample array for testing purposes is created by using a random number generator. Math.random() (Line 16) generates a random double value greater than or

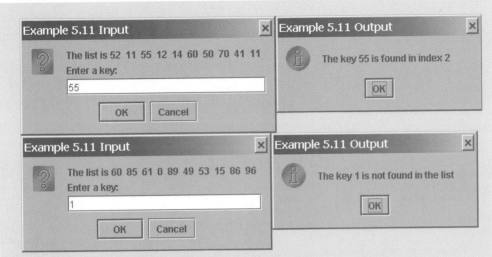

Figure 5.17 *The program uses linear search to find a key in a list of* int *elements.*

equal to 0.0 and less than 1.0. Therefore, (int)(Math.random() * 100) is a random integer value greater than or equal to 0 and less than 100.

If there is a match, the algorithm returns the index of the first element in the array that matches the key. If there is no match, the algorithm returns –1.

The linear search method compares the key with each element in the array. The elements in the array can be in any order. On average, the algorithm will have to compare half of the elements in an array. Since the execution time of a linear search increases linearly as the number of array elements increases, linear search is inefficient for a large array.

5.8.2   The Binary Search Approach (Optional)

Binary search is the other common search approach. For binary search to work, the elements in the array must already be ordered. Without loss of generality, assume that the array is in ascending order. The binary search first compares the key with the element in the middle of the array. Consider the following three cases:

- If the key is less than the middle element, you only need to search the key in the first half of the array.

- If the key is equal to the middle element, the search ends with a match.

- If the key is greater than the middle element, you only need to search the key in the second half of the array.

Figure 5.18 shows how to find key 11 in the list {2, 4, 7, 10, 11, 45, 50, 59, 60, 66 69, 70, 79} using binary search.

239

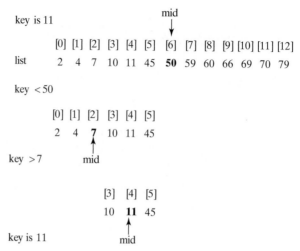

Figure 5.18 *Binary search eliminates half of the list from further consideration after each comparison.*

Clearly, the binary search method eliminates half of the array after each comparison. Suppose that the array has *n* elements. For convenience, let *n* be a power of 2. After the first comparison, there are $n/2$ elements left for further search; after the second comparison, there are $(n/2)/2$ elements left for further search. After the *k*th comparison, there are $n/2^k$ elements left for further search. When $k = \log_2 n$, only one element is left in the array, and you only need one more comparison. Therefore, in the worst case, you need $\log_2 n + 1$ comparisons to find an element in the sorted array when using the binary search approach. For a list of 1024 (2^{10}) elements, binary search requires only eleven comparisons in the worst case, whereas a linear search would take 1024 comparisons in the worst case.

The portion of the array being searched shrinks after each comparison. Let `low` and `high` denote, respectively, the first index and last index of the array that is currently being searched. Initially, `low` is `0` and `high` is `list.length-1`. Let `binary-Search(int[] list, int key, int low, int high)` denote the method that finds the key in the list that has the specified `low` index and `high` index. The `binarySearch` method returns the index of the search key if it is contained in the list. Otherwise, it returns −insertion point −1. The insertion point is the point at which the key would be inserted into the list. The algorithm can be described recursively as follows:

```
public static int binarySearch
  (int key, int[] list, int low, int high) {
  if (low > high)
    the list has been searched without a match, return -low - 1;

  // Find mid, the index of the middle element in list[low..high]
  int mid = (low + high) / 2;
  if (key < list[mid])
    // Search in list[low..mid-1] recursively.
    return binarySearch(list, key, low, mid - 1);
  else if (key == list[mid])
    // A match is found
    return mid;
```

```
        else
          // Search in list[mid+1..high] recursively.
          return binarySearch(list, key, mid + 1, high);
      }
```

The next example demonstrates the binary search approach.

Example 5.12 Testing Binary Search

Problem

Write a program that implements and tests the binary search method. The program first creates an array of ten elements of int type. It displays this array and then prompts the user to enter a key for testing binary search.

Solution

The following code gives the solution to the problem. The output of a sample run of the program is shown in Figure 5.19.

```
1    // BinarySearch.java: Search a key in a sorted list
2    package chapter5;
3
4    import javax.swing.JOptionPane;
5
6    public class BinarySearch {
7      /** Main method */
8      public static void main(String[] args) {
9        int[] list = {2, 4, 7, 10, 11, 45, 50, 59, 60, 66, 69, 70, 79};
10
11       // Declare and initialize output string
12       String output = "The list is ";
13       for (int i = 0; i < list.length; i++)
14         output += list[i] + " ";
15
16       // Prompt the user to enter a key
17       String keyString = JOptionPane.showInputDialog(null,
18         output + "\nEnter a key:",
19         "Example 5.12 Input", JOptionPane.QUESTION_MESSAGE);
20
21       // Convert string into integer
22       int key = Integer.parseInt(keyString);
23
24       // Display the result
24       JOptionPane.showMessageDialog(null,
25         "Index is " + binarySearch(list, key),
26         "Example 5.12 Output", JOptionPane.INFORMATION_MESSAGE);
27
28       System.exit(0);
29     }
30
31     /** Use binary search to find the key in the list */
32     public static int binarySearch(int[] list, int key) {
33       int low = 0;
34       int high = list.length - 1;
35       return binarySearch(list, key, low, high);
36     }
37
```

continues

Example 5.12 continued

```
38        /** Use binary search to find the key in the list between
39            list[low] list[high] */
40        public static int binarySearch(int[] list, int key,
41          int low, int high) {
42          if (low > high)  // The list has been exhausted without a match
43            return -low - 1;
44
45          int mid = (low + high) / 2;
46          if (key < list[mid])
47            return binarySearch(list, key, low, mid - 1);
48          else if (key == list[mid])
49            return mid;
50          else
51            return binarySearch(list, key, mid + 1, high);
52        }
53      }
```

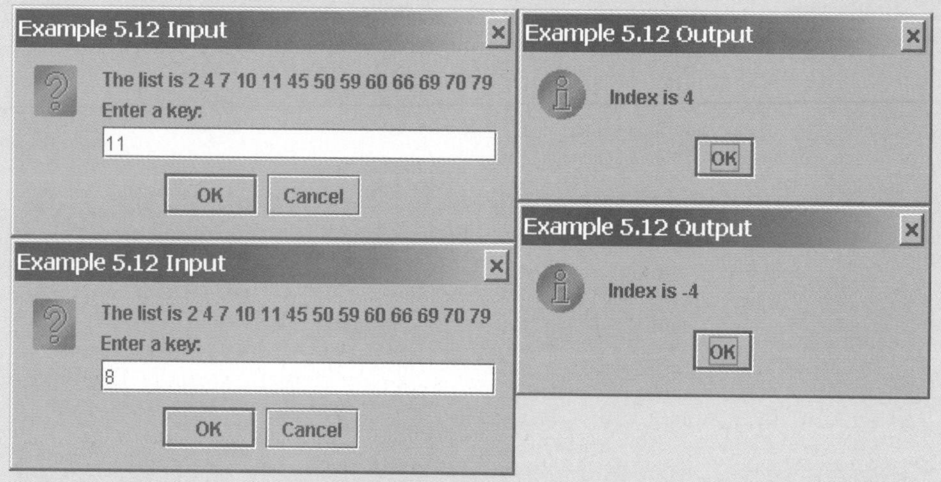

Example 5.12 Input

The list is 2 4 7 10 11 45 50 59 60 66 69 70 79
Enter a key:

11

OK   Cancel

Example 5.12 Output

Index is 4

OK

Example 5.12 Input

The list is 2 4 7 10 11 45 50 59 60 66 69 70 79
Enter a key:

8

OK   Cancel

Example 5.12 Output

Index is -4

OK

Figure 5.19   *The program uses binary search to find a key in a list of* int *elements.*

Review

There are two overloaded methods named binarySearch in the program: binarySearch(int[] list, int key) (Lines 32–36) and binarySearch(int[] list, int key, int low, int high) (Lines 40–52). The first method finds a key in the whole list. The second method finds a key in the list with index from low to high.

The first binarySearch method passes the initial array with low = 0 and high = list.length-1 to the second binarySearch method (Line 35). The second method is invoked recursively to find the key in an ever-shrinking subarray. It is a common design technique in recursive programming to choose a second method that can be called recursively.

There are two reasons why this is a good example of using recursion. First, using recursion enables you to specify a clear, simple solution for the binary search problem. Second, the number of recursive calls is less than the size of the list. So the solution is reasonably efficient. In Exercise 5.11, you will use iterations to rewrite this program.

 NOTE

Linear search is useful for finding an element in a small array or an unsorted array, but it is inefficient for large arrays. Binary search is more efficient, but requires that the array be sorted.

 TIP

Since binary search is frequently used in programming, Java provides several over-loaded `binarySearch` methods for searching a key in an array of `int`, `double`, `char`, `short`, `long`, and `float` in the `java.util.Arrays` class. For example, the following code searches the keys in an array of numbers and an array of characters.

```
int[] list = {2, 4, 7, 10, 11, 45, 50, 59, 60, 66, 69, 70, 79};
System.out.println("Index is " +
  java.util.Arrays.binarySearch(list, 11));

char[] chars = {'a', 'c', 'g', 'x', 'y', 'z'};
System.out.println("Index is " +
  java.util.Arrays.binarySearch(chars, 't'));
```

Chapter Summary

- Array is a data structure for storing a collection of data of the same type.

- A variable is declared as an array type using the syntax `dataType[] arrayRef-Var` or `dataType arrayRefVar[]`. The style `dataType[] arrayRefVar` is preferred.

- Unlike declarations for primitive data type variables, the declaration of an array variable does not allocate any space in memory for the array. An array variable is not a primitive data type variable. An array variable contains a reference to an array.

- You cannot assign elements to an array unless it has already been created. You can create an array by using the `new` operator with the following syntax: `new dataType[arraySize]`.

- Each element in the array is represented using the syntax `arrayRefVar[index]`. An index must be an integer or an integer expression.

- After an array is created, its size becomes permanent and can be obtained using `arrayRefVar.length`. Since the index of an array always begins with 0, the last index is always `arrayRefVar.length - 1`. An out-of-bounds error will occur if you attempt to reference elements beyond the bounds of an array.

■ Programmers often mistakenly reference the first element in an array with index 1, so that the index of the tenth element becomes 10. This is called the *off-by-one error*.

■ Java has a shorthand notation, known as the *array initializer*, which combines declaring an array, creating an array, and initializing in one statement using the syntax: `dataType[] arrayRefVar = {literal0, literal1, . . ., literalk}`.

■ Arrays can be passed to a method as actual parameters. When you pass an array, you are actually passing the reference of the array; that is, the called method can modify the elements in the caller's original arrays.

■ You can use arrays of arrays to form multidimensional arrays. For example, a two-dimensional array is declared as an array of arrays using the syntax `dataType[][] arrayRefVar` or `dataType arrayRefVar[][]`.

■ Each row in an array of two or more dimensions is itself an array. Thus the rows can have different lengths. An array of this kind is known as a *ragged array*.

■ Selection sort finds the largest number in the list and places it last. It then finds the largest number remaining and places it next to last, and so on until the list contains only a single number.

■ The linear search approach compares the key element `key` with each element in the array `list[]`. The method continues to do so until the key matches an element in the list or the list is exhausted without a match being found.

■ For sorted arrays, binary search is more efficient than the linear search. The binary search first compares the key with the element in the middle of the array. If the key is less than the middle element, you only need to search the key in the first half of the array. If the key is equal to the middle element, the search ends with a match. If the key is greater than the middle element, you only need to search the key in the second half of the array.

Review Questions

5.1 How do you declare and create an array?

5.2 How do you access elements of an array?

5.3 Is memory allocated when an array is declared? When is the memory allocated for an array?

5.4 Indicate true or false for the following statements:

■ Every element in an array has the same type.

■ The array size is fixed after it is declared.

■ The array size is fixed after it is created.

■ The elements in an array must be of primitive data type.

5.5 Which of the following statements are valid array declarations?

```
int i = new int(30);
double d[] = new double[30];
char[] r = new char(1..30);
int i[] = (3, 4, 3, 2);
float f[] = {2.3, 4.5, 5.6};
char[] c = new char();
int[][] r = new int[2];
```

5.6 What is the array index type? What is the lowest index?

5.7 What is the representation of the third element in an array named a?

5.8 What happens when your program attempts to access an array element with an invalid index?

5.9 Identify and fix the errors in the following code:

```
1    public class Test {
2      public static void main(String[] args) {
3        double[100] r;
4
5        for (int i = 0; i < r.length(); i++);
6          r(i) = Math.random * 100;
7      }
8    }
```

5.10 Use the arraycopy() method to copy the following array to a target array t:

```
int[] source = {3, 4, 5};
```

5.11 Declare and create a 4 × 5 int matrix.

5.12 Once an array is created, its size cannot be changed. Does the following code resize the array?

```
int[] myList;
myList = new int[10];
// Some time later you want to assign a new array to myList
myList = new int[20];
```

5.13 Can the rows in a two-dimensional array have different lengths?

5.14 What is the output of the following code?

```
int[][] array = new int[5][6];
int[] x = {1, 2};
array[0] = x;
System.out.println("array[0][1] is " + array[0][1]);
```

Programming Exercises

5.1 (Reversing the numbers entered) Write a program that will read ten integers and display them in reverse order.

5.2 (Computing the average) Write a method that finds the average in an array of floating-point values. Use {15, 20.3, 4.5, 5.5, 10.3, 450, 20.4, −22.3} to test the method.

5.3 (Finding the smallest element) Write a method that finds the smallest element in an array of integers. Use {1, 2, 4, 5, 10, 100, 2, −22} to test the method.

5.4 (Reversing an array) Write a method that returns a new array that is a reversal of the original array. Use {5.0, 4.4, 1.9, 2.9, 3.4, 3.5} to test the method.

5.5 (Summing the major diagonal in a matrix) Write a method that sums all the integers in the major diagonal in a matrix of integers. Use {{1, 2, 4, 5}, {6, 7, 8, 9}, {10, 11, 12, 13}, {14, 15, 16, 17}} to test the method.

5.6 (Summing all the numbers in a matrix) Write a method that sums all the integers in a matrix of integers. Use {{1, 2, 4, 5}, {6, 7, 8, 9} {10, 11, 12, 13}, {14, 15, 16, 17}} to test the method.

5.7 (Revising Example 5.7 "Grading a Multiple-Choice Test") Rewrite Example 5.7 to display the mean and standard deviation of the number of correct answers. Display the students in increasing order of the number of correct answers.

5.8 (Computing the weekly hours for each employee) Suppose the weekly hours for all employees are stored in a two-dimensional array. Each row records an employee's seven-day work hours with seven columns. For example, the following array stores the work hours for eight employees. Write a program that displays employees and their total hours in decreasing order of the total hours.

	Su	M	T	W	R	F	Sa
Employee 0	2	4	3	4	5	8	8
Employee 1	7	3	4	3	3	4	4
Employee 2	3	3	4	3	3	2	2
Employee 3	9	3	4	7	3	4	1
Employee 4	3	5	4	3	6	3	8
Employee 5	3	4	4	6	3	4	4
Employee 6	3	7	4	8	3	8	4
Employee 7	6	3	5	9	2	7	9

5.9 (Revising Example 5.10 "Sorting Arrays") Use recursion to rewrite the selection sort used in Example 5.10.

5.10 (Revising Example 5.10 "Sorting Arrays") In Example 5.10, you used selection sort to sort an array. The selection sort method repeatedly finds the largest number in the current array and swaps it with the last number in the array. Rewrite this example by finding the smallest number and swapping it with the first number in the array.

5.11 (Revising Example 5.12 "Testing Binary Search") Use iterations to rewrite the binary search used in Example 5.12.

✦ HINT

You can use a loop to find the key in the list, as follows:

```
public static int binarySearch(int[] list, int key) {
    int low = 0;
    int high = list.length - 1;
```

```
    while (high >= low) {
      int mid = (low + high) / 2;
      if (key < list[mid])
        high = mid - 1;
      else if (key == list[mid])
        return mid;
      else
        low = mid + 1;
    }

    return -1;
  }
```

5.12 (Revising Example 3.7 "Finding the Sales Amount") Rewrite Example 3.7 using the binary search approach. Since the sales amount is between 1 and `COMMISSION_SOUGHT/0.08`, you can use a binary search to improve Example 3.7.

5.13 (Bubble sort) Write a sort method that uses the bubble-sort algorithm. The bubble-sort algorithm makes several passes through the array. On each pass, successive neighboring pairs are compared. If a pair is in decreasing order, its values are swapped; otherwise, the values remain unchanged. The technique is called a *bubble sort* or *sinking sort* because the smaller values gradually "bubble" their way to the top and the larger values sink to the bottom.

The algorithm can be described as follows:

```
boolean changed = true;
do {
  changed = false;
  for (int j = 0; j < list.length - 1; j++)
    if (list[j] > list[j + 1]) {
      swap list[j] with list[j + 1];
      changed = true;
    }
}
while (changed);
```

Clearly, the list is in increasing order when the loop terminates. It is easy to show that the do loop executes at most `list.length - 1` times.

Use {5.0, 4.4, 1.9, 2.9, 3.4, 2.9, 3.5} to test the method.

5.14 (Insertion sort) Write a sort method that uses the insertion-sort algorithm. The insertion-sort algorithm sorts a list of values by repeatedly inserting an unsorted element into a sorted sublist until the whole list is sorted. The algorithm can be described as follows:

```
for (int i = 1; i < list.length; i++) {
  /** The elements in list[0..i-1] are already sorted. To insert
    * the element list[i] into list[0..i-1] is to move list[k] into
    * list[k+1] for k <= i-1 such that list[k] > list[i] */
  double currentElement = list[i];
  int k = i - 1;
  while (k >= 0 && list[k] > currentElement) {
    list[k + 1] = list[k];
    k--;
  }
```

```
        // Insert the current element into list[k+1]
        list[k + 1] = currentElement;
    }
```

Use {5.0, 4.4, 1.9, 2.9, 3.4, 2.9, 3.5} to test the method.

5.15 (Analyzing monthly temperatures) Write a program that meets the following requirements:

■ Store daily high and low temperatures for a month in a two-dimensional array. Use Math.random() to generate two temperatures randomly between 0 and 120 Fahrenheit degrees; assign the smaller one to low temperature of the day and the larger one to high temperature of the day.

■ Compute the hottest and coldest day of the month.

■ Compute the average high temperature and low temperature of the month.

HINT

Declare the array as double[][] temperatures = new double[31][2], where temperatures[dayIndex][0] and temperatures[dayIndex][1] store the low and high temperatures for a specified day, respectively. Assume a month has thirty-one days.

5.16 (Analyzing annual temperatures) Write a program that meets the following requirements.

■ Store daily high and low temperatures for a whole year in a three-dimensional array. Use Math.random() to generate two temperatures randomly between 0 and 120 Fahrenheit degrees, assign the smaller one to low temperature of the day and the larger one to high temperature of the day.

■ Compute the hottest and coldest day of the year.

■ Compute the average high temperature and low temperature of the year.

HINT

Declare the array as double[][][] temperature = new double[12][31][2], where temperatures[month][day][0] and temperatures[month][day][1] store the low and high temperatures for a given day in the month, respectively. The maximum number of days in a month is thirty-one. The months of January, March, May, July, August, October, and December have thirty-one days, and the months of April, June, September, and November have thirty days. Assume February has twenty-eight days.

5.17 (Revising Example 3.9 "Displaying Prime Numbers") Example 3.9 determines whether a number n is prime by checking whether 2, 3, 4, 5, 6, ..., n/2 is a divisor. If a divisor is found, n is not prime. A more efficient approach to determine whether n is prime is to check whether any of the prime numbers less than or equal to $\sqrt{n}$ can divide n evenly. If not, n is prime. Rewrite

Example 3.9 to display the first fifty prime numbers using this approach. You need to use an array to store the prime numbers and later use them to check whether they are possible divisors for n.

5.18 (Adding and multiplying two matrices) Write a method to add two matrices and a method to multiply two matrices. The signatures of the methods are as follows:

```
public static int[][] addMatrix(int[][] m1, int[][] m2)
public static int[][] multiplyMatrix(int[][] m1, int[][] m2)
```

In order to be added, two matrices must have the same dimensions and the same or compatible types of elements. As shown below, two matrices are added by adding the two elements of the arrays with the same index:

$$
\begin{pmatrix} a_{11}\, a_{12}\, a_{13}\, a_{14}\, a_{15} \\ a_{21}\, a_{22}\, a_{23}\, a_{24}\, a_{25} \\ a_{31}\, a_{32}\, a_{33}\, a_{34}\, a_{35} \\ a_{41}\, a_{42}\, a_{43}\, a_{44}\, a_{45} \\ a_{51}\, a_{52}\, a_{53}\, a_{54}\, a_{55} \end{pmatrix} + \begin{pmatrix} b_{11}\, b_{12}\, b_{13}\, b_{14}\, b_{15} \\ b_{21}\, b_{22}\, b_{23}\, b_{24}\, b_{25} \\ b_{31}\, b_{32}\, b_{33}\, b_{34}\, b_{35} \\ b_{41}\, b_{42}\, b_{43}\, b_{44}\, b_{45} \\ b_{51}\, b_{52}\, b_{53}\, b_{54}\, b_{55} \end{pmatrix}
$$

$$
= \begin{pmatrix} a_{11}+b_{11} & a_{12}+b_{12} & a_{13}+b_{13} & a_{14}+b_{14} & a_{15}+b_{15} \\ a_{21}+b_{21} & a_{22}+b_{22} & a_{23}+b_{23} & a_{24}+b_{24} & a_{25}+b_{25} \\ a_{31}+b_{31} & a_{32}+b_{32} & a_{33}+b_{33} & a_{34}+b_{34} & a_{35}+b_{35} \\ a_{41}+b_{41} & a_{42}+b_{42} & a_{43}+b_{43} & a_{44}+b_{44} & a_{45}+b_{45} \\ a_{51}+b_{51} & a_{52}+b_{52} & a_{53}+b_{53} & a_{54}+b_{54} & a_{55}+b_{55} \end{pmatrix}
$$

To multiply matrix a by matrix b, the number of columns in a must be the same as the number of rows in b, and the two matrices must have elements of the same or compatible types. Let c be the result of the multiplication, and a, b, and c are denoted as follows:

$$
\begin{pmatrix} a_{11}\, a_{12}\, a_{13}\, a_{14}\, a_{15} \\ a_{21}\, a_{22}\, a_{23}\, a_{24}\, a_{25} \\ a_{31}\, a_{32}\, a_{33}\, a_{34}\, a_{35} \\ a_{41}\, a_{42}\, a_{43}\, a_{44}\, a_{45} \\ a_{51}\, a_{52}\, a_{53}\, a_{54}\, a_{55} \end{pmatrix} \times \begin{pmatrix} b_{11}\, b_{12}\, b_{13}\, b_{14}\, b_{15} \\ b_{21}\, b_{22}\, b_{23}\, b_{24}\, b_{25} \\ b_{31}\, b_{32}\, b_{33}\, b_{34}\, b_{35} \\ b_{41}\, b_{42}\, b_{43}\, b_{44}\, b_{45} \\ b_{51}\, b_{52}\, b_{53}\, b_{54}\, b_{55} \end{pmatrix} = \begin{pmatrix} c_{11}\, c_{12}\, c_{13}\, c_{14}\, c_{15} \\ c_{21}\, c_{22}\, c_{23}\, c_{24}\, c_{25} \\ c_{31}\, c_{32}\, c_{33}\, c_{34}\, c_{35} \\ c_{41}\, c_{42}\, c_{43}\, c_{44}\, c_{45} \\ c_{51}\, c_{52}\, c_{53}\, c_{54}\, c_{55} \end{pmatrix}
$$

Where $c_{ij} = a_{i1} \times b_{1j} + a_{i2} \times b_{2j} + a_{i3} \times b_{3j} + a_{i4} \times b_{4j} + a_{i5} \times b_{5j}$

PART **II**

OBJECT-ORIENTED PROGRAMMING

In Part I, "Fundamentals of Programming," you learned how to write simple Java applications using primitive data types, control statements, methods, and arrays, all of which are features commonly available in procedural programming languages. Java, however, is an object-oriented programming language that uses abstraction, encapsulation, inheritance, and polymorphism to provide great flexibility, modularity, and reusability for developing software. In this part of the book you will learn how to define, extend, and work with classes and their objects.

CHAPTER 6   OBJECTS AND CLASSES

CHAPTER 7   STRINGS

CHAPTER 8   INHERITANCE AND POLYMORPHISM

CHAPTER 9   ABSTRACT CLASSES AND INTERFACES

CHAPTER 10   OO ANALYSIS AND DESIGN

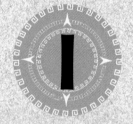

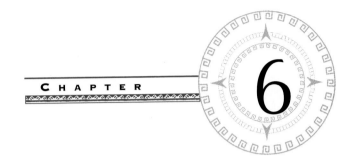

C H A P T E R

6

OBJECTS AND CLASSES

Objectives

- To understand objects and classes and the relationship between them.
- To learn how to define a class and how to create an object of a class.
- To understand the difference between object reference variables and primitive data type variables.
- To understand the roles of constructors.
- To declare private data fields with appropriate get and set methods to make a class easy to maintain.
- To develop methods with object arguments.
- To understand the difference between instance and class variables and methods.
- To store and process objects in arrays.
- To use UML graphical notations to describe classes and objects.
- To determine the scope of variables in the context of a class.
- To use the keyword this as the reference to the current object that invokes the instance method.
- To declare inner classes (Optional).

6.1   Introduction

Programming in procedural languages like C, Pascal, BASIC, Ada, and COBOL involves choosing data structures, designing algorithms, and translating algorithms into code. An object-oriented language like Java combines the power of procedural languages with an added dimension that provides more flexibility, modularity, clarity, and reusability through class encapsulation, class inheritance, and dynamic binding.

In procedural programming, data and operations on the data are separate, and this methodology requires sending data to procedures and functions. Object-oriented programming places data and the operations that pertain to them within a single entity called an *object*; this approach solves many of the problems inherent in procedural programming. The object-oriented programming approach organizes programs in a way that mirrors the real world, in which all objects are associated with both attributes and activities. Using objects improves software reusability and makes the program easy to develop and easy to maintain. Programming in Java involves thinking in terms of objects; a Java program can be viewed as a collection of cooperating objects.

This chapter introduces the fundamentals of object-oriented programming: declaring classes, creating objects, manipulating objects, and making objects work together.

6.2   Defining Classes for Objects

Object-oriented programming (OOP) involves programming using objects. An *object* represents an entity in the real world that can be distinctly identified. For example, a student, a desk, a circle, a button, and even a loan can all be viewed as objects. An object has a unique identity, state, and behavior. The *state* of an object consists of a set of *data fields* (also known as *properties*) with their current values. The *behavior* of an object is defined by a set of methods. Figure 6.1 (A) shows a diagram of a generic object with its data fields and methods.

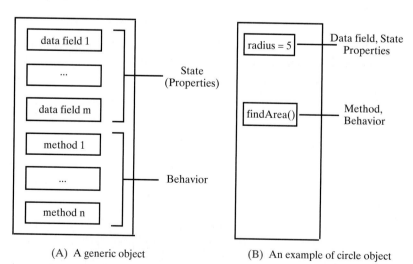

(A) A generic object   (B) An example of circle object

Figure 6.1   *An object has both a state and behavior. The state defines the object, and the behavior defines what the object does.*

A `Circle` object, for example, has a data field, `radius`, which is the property that characterizes a circle. One behavior of a circle is that its area can be computed using the method `findArea()`. A `Circle` object is shown in Figure 6.1 (B).

Classes are constructs that define objects of the same type. A Java class uses variables to define data fields and methods to define behaviors. Additionally, a class provides a special type of methods, known as `constructors`, which are invoked to construct objects from the class. Figure 6.2 shows an example of the class for `Circle` objects.

```
class Circle {
    /** The radius of this circle */
    double radius = 1.0;  ◄───────────── Data field

    /** Construct a circle object */─┐
    Circle() {
    }
                                      ├──── Constructors
    /** Construct a circle object */
    Circle(double newRadius) {
      radius = newRadius;
    }                                ─┘

    /** Return the area of this circle */
    double findArea() {  ◄──────────── Method
      return radius * radius * 3.14159;
    }
}
```

Figure 6.2   *A class is a construct that defines objects of the same type.*

The `Circle` class is different from all of the other classes you have seen thus far. It does not have a `main` method and therefore cannot be run; it is merely a definition used to declare and create `Circle` objects. For convenience, the class that contains the `main` method will be referred to as the *main class* in this book.

6.3   Constructing Objects Using Constructors

The constructor has exactly the same name as the defining class. Like methods, constructors can be overloaded, making it easier to construct objects with different initial data values.

To construct an object from a class, invoke a constructor of the class using the `new` operator, as follows:

```
new ClassName();
```

For example, `new Circle()` creates an object of the `Circle` class using the first constructor defined in the `Circle` class, and `new Circle(5)` creates an object using the second constructor defined in the `Circle` class.

A constructor with no parameters is referred to as a *default constructor*. The first constructor is a default constructor. A constructor, like a method, can perform any action, but constructors are designed to perform initializing actions, such as initializing the data fields of objects.

NOTE

If a class does not explicitly define any constructors, a default constructor is defined implicitly. If a class does explicitly define constructors, a default constructor does not exist unless it is defined explicitly. Therefore, you cannot use the default constructor to create an object using new ClassName() if its default constructor is not available. See Review Questions 6.11 and 6.12.

 NOTE

Constructors are a special kind of method, with three differences:

- Constructors must have the same name as the class itself.
- Constructors do not have a return type—not even void.
- Constructors are invoked using the new operator when an object is created. Constructors play the role of initializing objects.

 CAUTION

It is a common mistake to put the void keyword in front of a constructor. For example,

```
public void Circle() {
}
```

In this case, Circle() is method, not a constructor.

A class is a blueprint that defines what an object's data and methods will be. An object is an instance of a class. You can create many instances of a class (see Figure 6.3). Creating an instance is referred to as *instantiation*. The terms *object* and *instance* are often interchangeable. The relationship between classes and objects is analogous to the relationship between apple pie recipes and apple pies. You can make as many apple pies as you want from a single recipe.

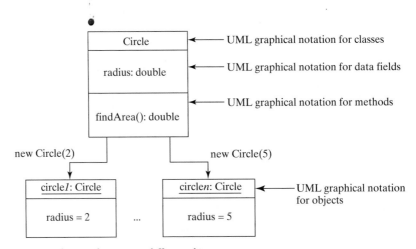

Figure 6.3 *A class can have many different objects.*

NOTE

Figure 6.3 uses the graphical notations adopted in the Unified Modeling Language (UML) to illustrate classes and objects. UML has become the standard for object-oriented modeling. For more information on UML, see **www.rational.com/uml/**. For a summary of the graphical notations used in this book, see Appendix E, "UML Graphical Notations."

6.4   Accessing Objects via Reference Variables

Newly created objects are allocated in the memory. Objects are accessed via object *reference variables*, which contain references to the objects. Such variables are declared using the following syntax:

```
ClassName objectRefVar;
```

A class defines a type. Such a type is known as a *reference type*. Any variable of the class type can reference to an instance of the class. The following statement declares the variable myCircle to be of the Circle type:

```
Circle myCircle;
```

The variable myCircle can reference a Circle object. The next statement creates an object and assigns its reference to myCircle.

```
myCircle = new Circle();
```

Using the syntax shown below, you can write one statement that combines the declaration of an object reference variable, the creation of an object, and the assigning of an object reference to the variable.

```
ClassName objectRefVar = new ClassName();
```

Here is an example:

```
Circle myCircle = new Circle();
```

The variable myCircle holds a reference to a Circle object.

 NOTE

An object reference variable that appears to hold an object actually contains a reference to that object. Strictly speaking, an object reference variable and an object are different, but most of the time the distinction between them can be ignored. So it is fine, for simplicity, to say that myCircle is a Circle object rather than a more long-winded phrase stating that myCircle is a variable that contains a reference to a Circle object. When the distinction makes a subtle difference, the long phrase should be used.

 NOTE

Arrays are treated as objects in Java. Arrays are created using the new operator. An array variable is actually a variable that contains a reference to an array.

6.4.1   Accessing an Object's Data and Methods

After an object is created, its data can be accessed and its methods invoked using the following dot notation:

- `objectRefVar.data` references an object's data.

- `objectRefVar.method(arguments)` invokes an object's method.

For example, `myCircle.radius` references the radius of `myCircle`, and `myCircle.findArea()` invokes the `findArea` method of `myCircle`. Methods are invoked as operations on objects.

The data field `radius` is referred to as an *instance variable* because it is dependent on a specific instance. For the same reason, the method `findArea` is referred to as an *instance method*, because you can only invoke it on a specific instance.

◆ NOTE

Most of the time, you create an object and assign it to a variable. Later you can use the variable to reference the object. Occasionally, an object does not need to be referenced later. In this case, you can create an object without explicitly assigning it to a variable, as shown below:

```
new Circle();
```

Or

```
System.out.println("Area is " + new Circle().findArea());
```

The former statement creates a `Circle` object. The latter statement creates a `Circle` object and invokes its `findArea` method to return its area. An object created in this way is known as an *anonymous object*.

Example 6.1 Declaring Classes and Creating Objects

Problem

Write a program that constructs an object with radius 5 using the nondefault constructor and an object with radius 1 using the default constructor that displays the radius and area of the two circles. Change the radius of the second object to 100 and display its new radius and area, as shown in Figure 6.4.

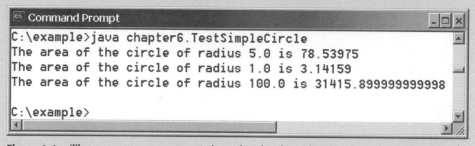

```
C:\example>java chapter6.TestSimpleCircle
The area of the circle of radius 5.0 is 78.53975
The area of the circle of radius 1.0 is 3.14159
The area of the circle of radius 100.0 is 31415.899999999998

C:\example>
```

Figure 6.4   *The program constructs two circles with radii of 5 and 1, and displays their radii and areas.*

Solution

To avoid a naming conflict with several improved versions of the Circle class introduced later in this chapter, the Circle class in this example is named SimpleCircle.

The following code gives the solution to the problem.

```
1    // TestSimpleCircle.java: Demonstrate constructors
2    package chapter6;
3
4    public class TestSimpleCircle {
5      /** Main method */
6      public static void main(String[] args) {
7        // Create a circle with radius 5.0
8        SimpleCircle myCircle = new SimpleCircle(5.0);
9        System.out.println("The area of the circle of radius "
10         + myCircle.radius + " is " + myCircle.findArea());
11
12        // Create a circle with default radius
13        SimpleCircle yourCircle = new SimpleCircle();
14        System.out.println("The area of the circle of radius "
15         + yourCircle.radius + " is " + yourCircle.findArea());
16
17        // Modify circle radius
18        yourCircle.radius = 100;
19        System.out.println("The area of the circle of radius "
20         + yourCircle.radius + " is " + yourCircle.findArea());
21      }
22    }
23
24    // Define the circle class with two constructors
25    class SimpleCircle {
26      double radius;
27
28      /** Default constructor */
29      SimpleCircle() {
30        radius = 1.0;
31      }
32
33      /** Construct a circle with a specified radius */
34      SimpleCircle(double newRadius) {
35        radius = newRadius;
36      }
37
38      /** Return the area of this circle */
39      double findArea() {
40        return radius * radius * 3.14159;
41      }
42    }
```

Review

The program contains two classes. The first class, TestSimpleCircle (Line 4), is the main class. Its sole purpose is to test the second class, SimpleCircle (Line 25). Every time you run the program, the Java runtime system invokes the main method in the main class.

continues

259

Example 6.1 continued

You can put the two classes into one file, but only one class in the file can be a public class. Furthermore, the public class must have the same name as the file name. Therefore, the file name is TestSimpleCircle.java if the TestSimpleCircle and SimpleCircle classes are both in the same file.

The main class contains the main method (Line 6) that creates two objects. The constructor SimpleCircle(5.0) was used to create myCircle with a radius of 5.0 (Line 8), and the constructor SimpleCircle() was used to create yourCircle with a default radius of 1.0 (Line 13).

These two objects (referenced by myCircle and yourCircle) have different data but share the same methods. Therefore, you can compute their respective areas by using the findArea() method.

To write the findArea method in a procedural programming language like Pascal, you would pass radius as an argument to the method. But in object-oriented programming, radius and findArea are defined in the same class. The radius is a data member in the SimpleCircle class, which is accessible by the findArea method. In procedural programming languages, data and methods are separated, but in an object-oriented programming language, data and methods are defined together in a class.

The findArea method is an instance method that is always invoked by an instance in which the radius is specified.

There are many ways to write Java programs. For instance, you can combine the two classes in the example into one, as shown below:

```java
public class SimpleCircle {
  /** Main method */
  public static void main(String[] args) {
    // Create a circle with radius 5.0
    SimpleCircle myCircle = new SimpleCircle(5.0);
    System.out.println("The area of the circle of radius "
      + myCircle.radius + " is " + myCircle.findArea());

    // Create a circle with default radius
    SimpleCircle yourCircle = new SimpleCircle();
    System.out.println("The area of the circle of radius "
      + yourCircle.radius + " is " + yourCircle.findArea());

    // Modify circle radius
    yourCircle.radius = 100;
    System.out.println("The area of the circle of radius "
      + yourCircle.radius + " is " + yourCircle.findArea());
  }

  double radius;

  /** Default constructor */
  SimpleCircle() {
    radius = 1.0;
  }
```

```
    /** Construct a circle with a specified radius */
    SimpleCircle(double newRadius) {
      radius = newRadius;
    }

    /** Return the area of this circle */
    double findArea() {
      return radius * radius * 3.14159;
    }
  }
```

Since the combined class has a main method, it can be executed by the Java interpreter. The main method creates myCircle as a SimpleCircle object and then displays radius and finds area in myCircle. This demonstrates that you can test a class by simply adding a main method in the same class.

CAUTION

You must always create an object before referencing it through a reference variable. Referencing an object that has not been created would cause a runtime NullPointerException. Exception handling will be introduced in Chapter 15, "Exceptions and Assertions."

NOTE

The default value of a data field is null for a reference type, 0 for a numeric type, false for a boolean type, and '\u0000' for a char type. For example, if radius is not initialized in the SimpleCircle class, Java assigns a default value of 0 to it. However, Java assigns no default value to a local variable inside a method. The following code has a compilation error because x and y are not initialized:

```
class Test {
  public static void main(String[] args) {
    int x; // x has no default value
    Circle y; // y has no default value
    System.out.println("x is " + x);
    System.out.println("y is " + y);
  }
}
```

Example 6.1 declared the SimpleCircle class and created objects from the class. Often you will use the classes in the Java library to develop programs. You learned to obtain the current time using System.currentTimeMillis() in Example 2.5, "Displaying Current Time." You used the division and remainder operators to extract current second, minute, and hour. Java provides a system-independent encapsulation of date and time in the java.util.Date class. You can use the Date class to create an instance for the current date and time and use its toString method to return the date and time as a string. For example, the following code

```
java.util.Date date = new java.util.Date();
System.out.println(date.toString());
```

displays a string like Sun Mar 09 13:50:19 EST 2003.

When you develop programs to create graphical user interfaces, you will use Java classes to create frames, buttons, radio buttons, combo boxes, lists, and so on. Here is an example that creates frames.

Example 6.2 Using Classes From the Java Library

Problem

Write a program that demonstrates using classes from the Java library. You will use the JFrame class in the javax.swing package to create two frames; you will use the methods in the JFrame class to set the title, size, and location of the frames and to display the frames.

Solution

The following code demonstrates how to use the JFrame class. The output of the program is shown in Figure 6.5.

```
1    package chapter6;
2
3    import javax.swing.JFrame;
4
5    class TestFrame {
6      public static void main(String[] args) {
7        JFrame frame1 = new JFrame();
8        frame1.setTitle("Window 1");
9        frame1.setSize(200, 150);
10       frame1.setLocation(200, 100);
11       frame1.setVisible(true);
12
13       JFrame frame2 = new JFrame();
14       frame2.setTitle("Window 2");
15       frame2.setSize(200, 150);
16       frame2.setLocation(410, 100);
17       frame2.setVisible(true);
18     }
19   }
```

Figure 6.5 *The program creates two windows using the JFrame class.*

Review

This program creates two objects of the JFrame class and then uses the methods setTitle, setSize, setLocation, and setVisible to set the properties of the objects. The setTitle method sets a title for the window (Lines 8, 14). The setSize method sets the window's width and height (Lines 9, 15). The `setLocation` method specifies the location of the window's upper-left corner (Lines 10, 16). The `setVisible` method displays the window. You can add graphical user interface components, such as buttons, labels, text fields, combo boxes, lists, and menus, to the window. The components are defined using classes. GUI programming will be introduced in Part III, "GUI Programming."

A class usually provides many constructors with which users can initialize objects. For example, the `JFrame` class has a default constructor and another one to initialize the title. You can use the following statement to create a frame entitled "Window 1."

```
JFrame frame1 = new JFrame("Window 1");
```

6.4.2 Differences Between Variables of Primitive Types and Reference Types

Every variable represents a memory location that holds a value. When you declare a variable, you are telling the compiler what type of value the variable can hold. For a variable of a primitive type, the value is of the primitive type. For a variable of a reference type, the value is a reference to where an object is located. For example, as shown in Figure 6.6, the value of `int` variable `i` is `int` value 1, and the value of `Circle` object `c` holds a reference to where the contents of the `Circle` object are stored in the memory.

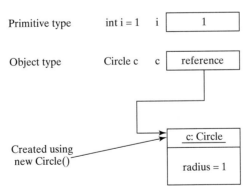

Figure 6.6 *A variable of a primitive type holds a value of the primitive type, and a variable of a reference type holds a reference to where an object is stored in the memory.*

If a variable of a reference type does not reference any object, the variable holds a special Java value, `null`. Once an object is created, its reference can be assigned to a variable. For example, the statement

```
c = new Circle();
```

creates a `Circle` object by allocating the memory space for it, and assigns its memory reference to the variable `c`.

When you assign one variable to another, the other variable is set to the same value. For a variable of a primitive type, the real value of one variable is assigned to the other variable. For a variable of a reference type, the reference of one variable is assigned to the other variable. As shown in Figure 6.7, the assignment statement `i = j` copies the contents of `j` into `i` for primitive variables, and the assignment statement `c1 = c2` copies the reference of `c2` into `c1` for object variables. After the assignment, variables `c1` and `c2` refer to the same object.

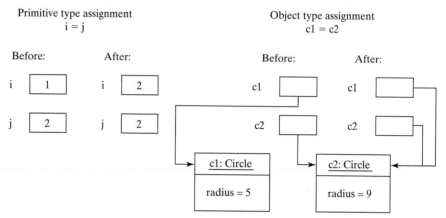

Figure 6.7 *Copying an object variable to another variable does not make a copy of the object; it merely assigns the reference of the object to the other variable.*

 NOTE

As shown in Figure 6.7, after the assignment statement `c1 = c2`, `c1` points to the same object referenced by `c2`. The object previously referenced by `c1` is no longer useful and therefore is now known as *garbage*. Garbage occupies memory space. The Java runtime system detects garbage and automatically reclaims the space it occupies. This process is called *garbage collection*.

 TIP

If you know that an object is no longer needed, you can explicitly assign `null` to a reference variable for the object. The Java Virtual Machine will automatically collect the space if the object is not referenced by any reference variables.

6.5   Visibility Modifiers, Accessors, and Mutators

Example 6.1 works fine, but it is not a good practice to allow the fields to be modified directly through the object reference. Doing so makes the class difficult to maintain and vulnerable to bugs. Suppose you want to modify the `Circle` class to ensure that the radius is non-negative after the class has already been used by other programs. You have to change not only the `Circle` class, but also the programs that use the `Circle` class. Such programs are often referred to as *clients*. This is because the clients can modify the radius directly. To prevent direct modifications of properties through the object reference, you can declare the field private, using the `private` modifier. This is known as *data field encapsulation*. Java provides several modifiers that control access to data, methods, and classes. This section introduces the `public`, `private`, and default modifiers.

- `public` makes classes, methods, and data fields accessible from any class.

- `private` makes methods and data fields accessible only from within its own class.

- If `public` or `private` is not used, then by default the classes, methods, and data are accessible by any class in the same package. This is also known as *package-private* or *package-access*. Packages are introduced in detail in Bonus Supplement E, "Packages."

Figure 6.8 illustrates the visibility of the `public`, `private`, and default modifiers.

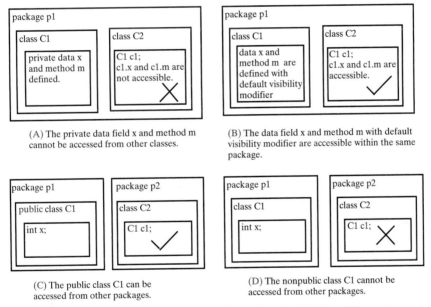

(A) The private data field x and method m cannot be accessed from other classes.

(B) The data field x and method m with default visibility modifier are accessible within the same package.

(C) The public class C1 can be accessed from other packages.

(D) The nonpublic class C1 cannot be accessed from other packages.

Figure 6.8 *The private modifier restricts access within a class, the default modifier restricts access within a package, and the public modifier enables unrestricted access.*

◈ NOTE

The modifier `private` applies solely to data or methods, not to classes (except inner classes). Inner classes will be introduced in Section 6.13, "Inner Classes." Java has another visibility modifier called `protected`, which will also be introduced in Chapter 8. The various Java modifiers are summarized in the table in Appendix D, "Java Modifiers."

Visibility modifiers are used for the members of the class, not local variables inside the methods. Using a visibility modifier inside a method body would cause a compilation error.

NOTE

In most cases, the constructor should be public. However, if you want to prohibit the user from creating an instance of a class, you can use a private constructor. For example, there is no reason to create an instance from the `Math` class because all of the data and methods are static. One solution is to define a dummy private constructor in the class. The `Math` class cannot be instantiated because it has a private constructor, as follows:

```
private Math() {
}
```

The `Math` class that comes with the Java system was introduced in Section 4.8, "The Math Class."

A private data field cannot be accessed by an object through a direct reference outside the class that defines the private field. But often a client needs to retrieve and modify a data field. To make a private data field accessible, provide a *get* method to return the value of the data. To enable a private data field to be updated, provide a *set* method to set a new value.

 NOTE

Colloquially, a get method is referred to as a *getter* (or *accessor*), and a set method is referred to as a *setter* (or *mutator*).

A get method has the following signature:

```
public returnType getPropertyName()
```

If the `returnType` is `boolean`, the get method should be defined as follows by convention:

```
public boolean isPropertyName()
```

A set method has the following signature:

```
public void setPropertyName(dataType propertyValue)
```

The example given below demonstrates the use of the `private` modifier and accessor methods.

Example 6.3 Using the `private` Modifier, Accessors, and Mutators

Problem

Declare a new `Circle` class in which private data are used for the radius, and the methods `getRadius` and `setRadius` are provided for the client to retrieve and modify the radius. The program creates an instance of the `Circle` class and modifies the radius using the `setRadius` method.

Solution

The following code gives the solution to the problem. The output of a sample run is shown in Figure 6.9.

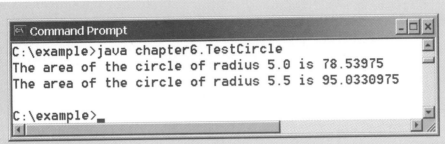

Figure 6.9 *This program creates a* Circle *object and uses the get method to read its radius, and the set method to modify its radius.*

```
1    // TestCircle.java: Demonstrate private modifier
2    package chapter6;
3
4    public class TestCircle {
5      /** Main method */
6      public static void main(String[] args) {
7        // Create a Circle with radius 5.0
8        Circle myCircle = new Circle(5.0);
9        System.out.println("The area of the circle of radius "
10         + myCircle.getRadius() + " is " + myCircle.findArea());
11
12       // Increase myCircle's radius by 10%
13       myCircle.setRadius(myCircle.getRadius() * 1.1);
14       System.out.println("The area of the circle of radius "
15         + myCircle.getRadius() + " is " + myCircle.findArea());
16     }
17   }
```

```
1    // Circle.java: The circle class with accessor methods
2    package chapter6;
3
4    public class Circle {
5      /** The radius of the circle */
6      private double radius;
7
8      /** Default constructor */
9      public Circle() {
10       radius = 1.0;
11     }
12
13     /** Construct a circle with a specified radius */
14     public Circle(double newRadius) {
15       radius = newRadius;
16     }
17
18     /** Return radius */
19     public double getRadius() {
20       return radius;
21     }
22
23     /** Set a new radius */
24     public void setRadius(double newRadius) {
25       radius = (newRadius >= 0) ? newRadius : 0;
26     }
27
```

continues

267

Example 6.3 continued

```
28        /** Return the area of this circle */
29        public double findArea() {
30          return radius * radius * 3.14159;
31        }
32     }
```

Review

The data field radius is declared private. Private data can only be accessed within their defining class. You cannot use myCircle.radius in the client program. A compilation error would occur if you attempted to access private data from a client.

The getRadius method returns the radius, and the setRadius method sets a new radius into the object. If the new radius is negative, 0 is set to the radius in the object. Since these methods are the only ways to read and modify radius, you have total control over how the radius property is accessed. If you have to change the implementation of these methods, the client programs that use these methods need not be changed. This makes the class easy to maintain. For this reason, most of the data fields in this book will be private.

Suppose you combined TestCircle and Circle into one class by moving the main method in TestCircle into Circle. Could you use myCircle.radius in the main method? See Review Question 6.16 for the answer.

 NOTE

TestCircle and Circle are stored in two separate files. If classes in different files are listed one after the other, the book separates them using a separator line. When you compile TestCircle.java, Java compiler automatically compiles Circle.java if it has not been compiled since the last change.

 NOTE

If a class contains all the private data fields without mutators, the class is called an *immutable class*. The contents of an object of an immutable class cannot be changed once the object is created. For example, if you delete the set method in this example, the Circle class is immutable.

 JBUILDER TIP

You can customize how the properties and methods are displayed in the structure pane in the Structure View Properties dialog box, as shown in Figure 6.10. To display the dialog box, right-click in the structure pane to display the context menu and choose *Properties*, as shown in Figure 6.11.

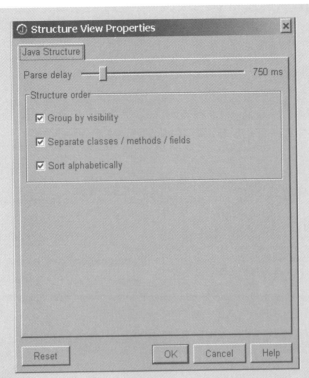

Figure 6.10 *You can specify the order in which the data and methods in a class are displayed in the structure pane.*

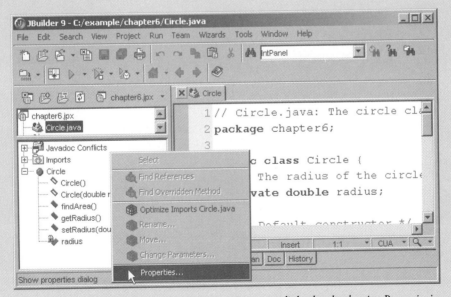

Figure 6.11 *You can display the Structure View Properties dialog box by choosing Properties in the context menu of the structure pane.*

6.6   Passing Objects to Methods

So far, you have learned to pass parameters of primitive types and arrays to methods, and you can also pass objects to methods. Like passing an array, passing an object is actually passing the reference of the object. The following code passes the `myCircle` object as an argument to the `printCircle` method:

```
class TestPassingObject {
  public static void main(String[] args) {
    Circle myCircle = new Circle(5.0);
    printCircle(myCircle);
  }

  public static void printCircle(Circle c) {
    System.out.println("The area of the circle of radius "
      + c.getRadius() + " is " + c.findArea());
  }
}
```

Java uses exactly one mode of passing parameters: pass by value. In the preceding code, the value of `myCircle` is passed to the `printCircle` method. This value is a reference to a `Circle` object.

Example 6.4 Passing Objects as Arguments

Problem

Write a program that passes a `Circle` object and an integer value to the `printAreas` method, which prints a table of areas for radii 1, 2, 3, 4, and 5.

Solution

The following code gives the solution to the problem. The output of the program is shown in Figure 6.12.

```
1    // TestPassingObject.java: Demonstrate passing objects to methods
2    package chapter6;
3
4    public class TestPassingObject {
5      /** Main method */
6      public static void main(String[] args) {
7        // Create a Circle object with default radius 1
8        Circle myCircle = new Circle();
9
10       // Print areas for radius 1, 2, 3, 4, and 5.
11       int n = 5;
12       printAreas(myCircle, n);
13
14       // See myCircle.radius and times
15       System.out.println("\n" + "Radius is " + myCircle.getRadius());
16       System.out.println("n is " + n);
17     }
18
19     /** Print a table of areas for radius */
20     public static void printAreas(Circle c, int times) {
21       System.out.println("Radius \t\tArea");
```

```
22          while (times >= 1) {
23              System.out.println(c.getRadius() + "\t\t" + c.findArea());
24              c.setRadius(c.getRadius() + 1);
25              times--;
26          }
27      }
28  }
```

```
Command Prompt                                      _ □ ×

C:\example>java chapter6.TestPassingObject
Radius          Area
1.0             3.14159
2.0             12.56636
3.0             28.27431
4.0             50.26544
5.0             78.53975

Radius is 6.0
n is 5

C:\example>_
```

Figure 6.12   *The program passes a* Circle *object* myCircle *and an integer value* n *as parameters to the* printAreas *method, which displays a table of the areas for radii 1, 2, 3, 4, and 5.*

Review

The main method invokes the printAreas method (Line 10) by passing an object myCircle and an integer n to the printAreas method, as shown in Figure 6.13. Note that the objects are stored in a heap.

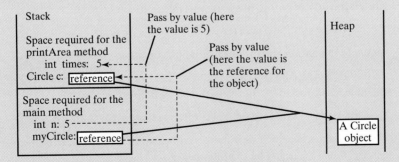

Figure 6.13   *The value of* n *is passed to* times, *and the reference of* myCircle *is passed to* c *in the* printAreas *method.*

continues

271

Example 6.4 continued

When passing a parameter of a primitive data type, the value of the actual parameter is passed. In this case, the value of n (5) is passed to times. Inside the printAreas method, the content of times is changed; this does not affect the content of n. When passing a parameter of a reference type, the reference of the object is passed. In this case, c contains a reference for the object that is also referenced via myCircle. Therefore, changing the properties of the object through c inside the printAreas method has the same effect as doing so outside the method through the variable myCircle.

6.7   Static Variables, Constants, and Methods

The variable radius in the circle classes in the preceding examples is known as an *instance variable*. An instance variable is tied to a specific instance of the class; it is not shared among objects of the same class. For example, suppose that you create the following objects:

```
Circle circle1 = new Circle();
Circle circle2 = new Circle(5);
```

The radius in circle1 is independent of the radius in circle2, and is stored in a different memory location. Changes made to circle1's radius do not affect circle2's radius, and vice versa.

If you want all the instances of a class to share data, use *static variables*, also known as *class variables*. Static variables store values for the variables in a common memory location. Because of this common location, all objects of the same class are affected if one object changes the value of a static variable.

To declare a static variable, put the modifier static in the variable declaration. Suppose that you want to track the number of objects of the CircleWithStaticVariable class, you can define the static variable as follows:

```
private static int numOfObjects;
```

Figure 6.14 pictures the instance variables and static variables.

To declare a class constant, add the final keyword in the preceding declaration. For example, the constant PI in the Math class is defined as:

```
public final static double PI = 3.14159265358979323846;
```

Instance methods belong to instances and can only be applied after the instances are created. They are called by the following:

```
objectName.methodName();
```

The methods defined in the previous circle classes are instance methods. Java supports static methods as well as static variables. *Static methods*, also known as *class methods*, can be called without creating an instance of the class. To define a static method, put the modifier static in the method declaration:

```
static returnValueType staticMethod();
```

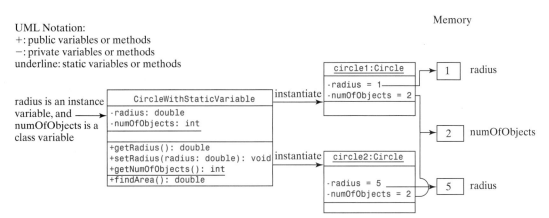

UML Notation:
+: public variables or methods
−: private variables or methods
underline: static variables or methods

radius is an instance variable, and numOfObjects is a class variable

Figure 6.14   *The instance variables, which belong to the instances, have memory storage independent of one other. The static variables are shared by all the instances of the same class.*

Examples of static methods are `showMessageDialog` and `showInputDialog` in the `JOptionPane` class, and all the methods in the `Math` class. In fact, so are all the methods used in Part I of this book, including the `main` method.

Static methods are called by one of the following syntaxes:

```
ClassName.methodName();
objectName.methodName();
```

For example, `JOptionPane.showInputDialog` is invoked to receive input from the user. `JOptionPane` is a class, not an object.

◈ NOTE

Static variables can be accessed from instance or static methods in the class. Instance variables can be accessed from instance methods in a class, but not from static methods in the class, since static methods are invoked regardless of specific instances. Thus the code given below would be wrong.

```
public class Foo {
  int i = 5;

  static void p() {
    int j = i; // Wrong because p() is static and i is non-static
  }
}
```

🅰 CAUTION

A common error is to invoke instance methods or access instance variables from the static `main` method. For example, the following code is wrong:

```
public class Foo {
  int i = 5;

  public static void main(String[] args) {
    int j = i; // Wrong because i is an instance variable
    p(); // Wrong because p() is an instance method
  }
```

```
public void p() {
  i++;
}
}
```

 TIP

A method that does not use instance variables can be defined as a static method. It can be invoked without creating an object of the class.

Variables that describe common properties of objects should be declared as static variables.

You should define a constant as `static` data that can be shared by all class objects.

The next example demonstrates how to use instance and static variables and methods, and illustrates the effects of using them.

Example 6.5 Using Instance and Static Variables and Methods

Problem

Modify the `Circle` class by adding a static variable `numOfObjects` to track the number of circle objects created. The UML of the new circle class named `CircleWithStaticVariable` is shown in Figure 6.14.

The `CircleWithStaticVariable` class defines the instance variable `radius`, the static variable `numOfObjects`, the instance methods `getRadius`, `setRadius`, and `findArea`, and the static method `getNumOfObjects`.

The `main` method creates two circles, `circle1` and `circle2`, and modifies the instance and static variables. You will see the effect of using instance and static variables after changing the data in the circles.

Solution

The following code gives the solution to the problem. The output of the program is shown in Figure 6.15.

```
1   // TestCircleWithStaticVariable.java: Demonstrate using instance and
2   // static variables
3   package chapter6;
4
5   public class TestCircleWithStaticVariable {
6     /** Main method */
7     public static void main(String[] args) {
8       // Create circle1
9       CircleWithStaticVariable circle1 =
10        new CircleWithStaticVariable();
11
12      // Display circle1 BEFORE circle2 is created
13      System.out.println("Before creating circle2");
14      System.out.print("circle1 is : ");
15      printCircle(circle1);
16
17      // Create circle2
18      CircleWithStaticVariable circle2 =
19        new CircleWithStaticVariable(5);
20
```

```
21          // Change the radius in circle1
22          circle1.setRadius(9);
23
24          // Display circle1 and circle2 AFTER circle2 was created
25          System.out.println("\nAfter creating circle2 and modifying " +
26            "circle1's radius to 9");
27          System.out.print("circle1 is : ");
28          printCircle(circle1);
29          System.out.print("circle2 is : ");
30          printCircle(circle2);
31        }
32
33      /** Print circle information */
34      public static void printCircle(CircleWithStaticVariable c) {
35        System.out.println("radius (" + c.getRadius() +
36          ") and number of Circle objects (" +
37          c.getNumOfObjects() + ")");
38      }
39    }
40
41  class CircleWithStaticVariable {
42    /** The radius of the circle */
43    private double radius;
44
45    /** The number of the objects created */
46    private static int numOfObjects = 0;
47
48    /** Default constructor */
49    public CircleWithStaticVariable() {
50      radius = 1.0;
51      numOfObjects++;
52    }
53
54    /** Construct a circle with a specified radius */
55    public CircleWithStaticVariable(double newRadius) {
56      radius = newRadius;
57      numOfObjects++;
58    }
59
60    /** Return radius */
61    public double getRadius() {
62      return radius;
63    }
64
65    /** Set a new radius */
66    public void setRadius(double newRadius) {
67      radius = newRadius;
68    }
69
70    /** Return numOfObjects */
71    public static int getNumOfObjects() {
72      return numOfObjects;
73    }
74
75    /** Return the area of this circle */
76    public double findArea() {
77      return radius * radius * Math.PI;
78    }
79  }
```

continues

275

Example 6.5 continued

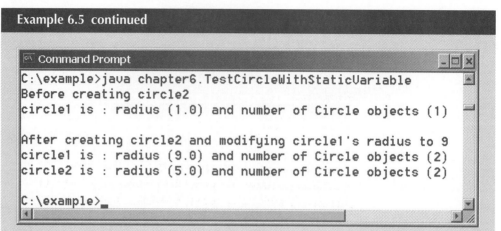

```
Command Prompt                                           _ □ ×
C:\example>java chapter6.TestCircleWithStaticVariable
Before creating circle2
circle1 is : radius (1.0) and number of Circle objects (1)

After creating circle2 and modifying circle1's radius to 9
circle1 is : radius (9.0) and number of Circle objects (2)
circle2 is : radius (5.0) and number of Circle objects (2)

C:\example>_
```

Figure 6.15   *The program uses the instance variable* radius *as well as the static variable* numOfObjects. *All of the objects share the same* numOfObjects.

Review

The instance variable radius in circle1 is modified to become 9 (Line 22). This change does not affect the instance variable radius in circle2, since these two instance variables are independent. The static variable numOfObjects becomes 1 after circle1 is created (Lines 9–10), and it becomes 2 after circle2 is created (Lines 18–19). This change affects all the instances of the Circle class, since the static variable numOfObjects is shared by all the instances of the Circle class.

Since numOfObjects is private, it cannot be modified. This prevents tampering. For example, the user cannot set numOfObjects to 100. The only way to make it 100 is to create one hundred objects of the CircleWithStaticVariable class.

Note that Math.PI is used to access PI, and that c.numOfObjects in the printCircle method is used to access numOfObjects. Math is the class name, and c is an object of the Circle class. To access a constant like PI, you can use either the ClassName.CONSTANTNAME or the objectName.CONSTANTNAME. To access an instance variable like radius, you need to use objectName.variableName.

TIP
I recommend that you invoke static variables and methods using ClassName. variable and ClassName.method. This improves readability because the user can easily recognize the static variables and methods. In this example you should replace c.getNumOfObjects() with CircleWithStaticVariable.getNumOfObjects().

TIP
How do you decide whether a variable or method should be an instance or a static variable method? A variable or method that is dependent on a specific instance of the class should be an instance variable or method. A variable or method that is not dependent on a specific instance of the class should be a static variable or method. For instance, every circle has its own radius. Radius is dependent on a specific cir-

cle. Therefore, `radius` is an instance variable of the `Circle` class. Since the `findArea` method is dependent on a specific circle, it is an instance method. None of the methods in the `Math` class, such as `random`, `pow`, `sin`, and `cos`, are dependent on a specific instance. Therefore, these methods are static methods. The `main` method is static, and can be invoked directly from a class.

◈ **JBUILDER NOTE**
You can examine the data fields of an object in the debugger. Figure 6.16 shows `circle1` and `circle2` in the watch view. The static data field `numOfObjects` has the same value for all the objects of `CircleWithStaticVariable` during the execution of the program.

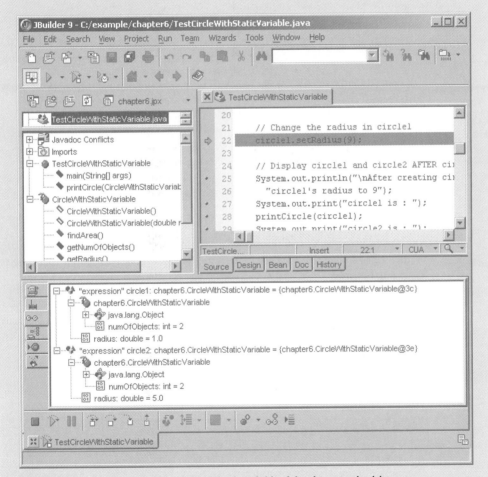

Figure 6.16 *You can view the values of the data fields of the objects in the debugger.*

6.8   The Scope of Variables

Chapter 4, "Methods," discussed local variables and their scope rules. Local variables are declared and used inside a method locally. This section discusses the scope rules of all the variables in the context of a class.

The scope of a class's variables (instance and static variables) is the entire class, regardless of where the variables are declared. A class's variables can be declared anywhere in the class. For example, as shown below, you can declare a variable at the end of a class and use it in a method defined earlier in the class.

```
class Circle {
  double findArea() {
    return radius * radius * Math.PI;
  }

  double radius = 1;
}
```

◈ NOTE

The data fields and methods are the members of the class. Since there is no order among them, they can be declared in any order in a class. The exception is when a data field is initialized based on a reference to another data field. In such cases, the other data field must be declared first. For example, in the following class, i must be declared before j because i's value is used to initialize j.

```
public class Foo {
  int i;
  int j = i + 1;
}
```

You can declare a variable only once as a class member (instance variable or static variable), but you can declare the same variable in a method many times in different nonnesting blocks.

If a local variable has the same name as a class's variable, the local variable takes precedence and the class's variable with the same name is hidden. For example, in the following program, x is defined as an instance variable and as a local variable in the method.

```
class Foo {
  int x = 0; // instance variable
  int y = 0;

  Foo() {
  }

  void p() {
    int x = 1; // local variable
    System.out.println("x = " + x);
    System.out.println("y = " + y);
  }
}
```

What is the printout for f.p(), where f is an instance of Foo? The printout for f.p() is 1 for x and 0 for y. Here is why:

■ x is declared as a data field with the initial value of 0 in the class, but is also defined in the method p() with an initial value of 1. The latter x is referenced in the System.out.println statement.

■ y is declared outside the method p(), but is accessible inside it.

 TIP

As demonstrated in the example, it is easy to make mistakes. To avoid confusion, do not declare the same variable names in a class, except for method parameters.

6.9   The Keyword *this*

Sometimes you need to reference a class's hidden variable in a method. For example, a property name is often used as the parameter name in a set method for the property. In this case, you need to reference the hidden property name in the method in order to set a new value to it. A hidden static variable can be accessed simply by using the ClassName.StaticVariable reference. A hidden instance variable can be accessed by using the keyword this, as shown in the following code:

```
class Foo {
  int i = 5;
  static double k = 0;

  void setI(int i) {
    this.i = i;
  }

  static void setK(double k) {
    Foo.k = k;
  }
}
```

The line this.i = i means "assign the value of parameter i to the object's data field i." The keyword this serves as a pointer to the current instance of the class that invokes the instance method setI. The line Foo.k = k means to assign argument k to the object's static data field k.

The keyword this can also be used inside a constructor to invoke another constructor of the same class. For example, you can redefine the Circle class as follows:

```
public class Circle {
  private double radius;

  public Circle(double radius) {
    this.radius = radius;
  }

  public Circle() {
    this(1.0);
  }

  public double findArea() {
    return radius * radius * Math.PI;
  }
}
```

The line this(1.0) invokes the constructor with a double value argument in the class.

TIP

If a class has multiple constructors, I recommend that you implement them using this(arg-list) as much as possible. In general, a constructor with no or fewer arguments can invoke the constructor with more arguments using this(arg-list). This often simplifies coding and makes the class easier to read and to maintain.

NOTE

Java requires that the this(arg-list) statement appear first in the constructor before any other statements.

6.10   Array of Objects

In Chapter 5, "Arrays," arrays of primitive type elements were created. You can also create arrays of objects. For example, the following statement declares and creates an array of ten Circle objects:

```
Circle[] circleArray = new Circle[10];
```

To initialize the circleArray, you can use a for loop like this one:

```
for (int i = 0; i < circleArray.length; i++) {
  circleArray[i] = new Circle();
}
```

An array of objects is actually an *array of reference variables*. So invoking circleArray[1].findArea() involves two levels of referencing, as shown in Figure 6.17. circleArray references the entire array. circleArray[1] references a Circle object.

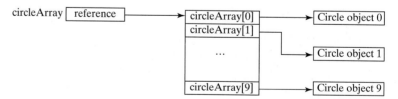

Figure 6.17   *In an array of objects, an element of the array contains a reference to an object.*

NOTE

When an array of objects is created using the new operator, each element is a reference variable with a default value of null.

The next example demonstrates how to use an array of objects.

Example 6.6 Summarizing the Areas of the Circles

Problem

Write a program that summarizes the areas of an array of circles. The program creates circleArray, an array composed of ten Circle objects; it then initializes circle radii with random values, and displays the total area of the circles in the array.

Solution

The following code gives the solution to the problem. The output of a sample run of the program is shown in Figure 6.18.

```
1   // TotalArea.java: Test passing an array of objects to the method
2   package chapter6;
3
4   public class TotalArea {
5     /** Main method */
6     public static void main(String[] args) {
7       // Declare circleArray
8       Circle[] circleArray;
9
10      // Create circleArray
11      circleArray = createCircleArray();
12
13      // Print circleArray and total areas of the circles
14      printCircleArray(circleArray);
15    }
16
17    /** Create an array of Circle objects */
18    public static Circle[] createCircleArray() {
19      Circle[] circleArray = new Circle[10];
20
21      for (int i = 0; i < circleArray.length; i++) {
22        circleArray[i] = new Circle(Math.random() * 100);
23      }
24
25      // Return Circle array
26      return circleArray;
27    }
28
29    /** Print an array of circles and their total area */
30    public static void printCircleArray
31      (Circle[] circleArray) {
32      System.out.println("Radius\t\t\t\t" + "Area");
33      for (int i = 0; i < circleArray.length; i++) {
34        System.out.print(circleArray[i].getRadius() + "\t\t" +
35          circleArray[i].findArea() + '\n');
36      }
37
38      System.out.println("------------------------------------------");
39
40      // Compute and display the result
41      System.out.println("The total areas of circles is \t" +
42        sum(circleArray));
43    }
44
45    /** Add circle areas */
46    public static double sum(Circle[] circleArray) {
47      // Initialize sum
48      double sum = 0;
49
```

continues

Example 6.6 continued

```
50          // Add areas to sum
51          for (int i = 0; i < circleArray.length; i++)
52            sum += circleArray[i].findArea();
53
54          return sum;
55      }
56    }
```

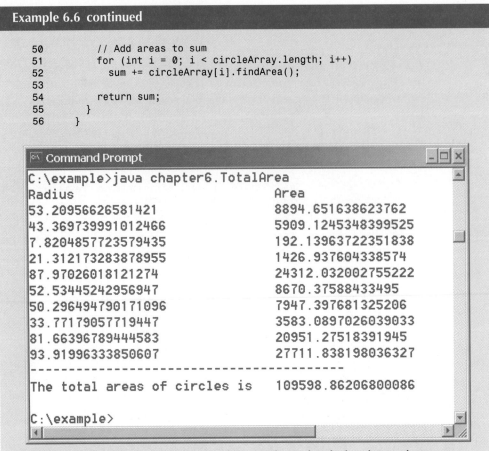

```
Command Prompt                                              _ □ ×
C:\example>java chapter6.TotalArea
Radius                          Area
53.20956626581421               8894.651638623762
43.369739991012466              5909.1245348399525
7.8204857723579435              192.13963722351838
21.312173283878955              1426.937604338574
87.97026018121274               24312.032002755222
52.53445242956947               8670.37588433495
50.296494790171096              7947.397681325206
33.77179057719447               3583.0897026039033
81.66396789444583               20951.27518391945
93.91996333850607               27711.838198036327
-------------------------------------------------
The total areas of circles is  109598.86206800086

C:\example>
```

Figure 6.18   *The program creates an array of* Circle *objects, then displays their total area.*

Review

The program uses the createCircleArray method (Line 11) to create an array of ten Circle objects. Several Circle classes were introduced in this chapter. This example uses the Circle class introduced in Example 6.3, "Using the private Modifier, Accessors, and Mutators."

The circle radii are randomly generated using the Math.random() method (Line 22). The createCircleObject method returns an array of Circle objects (Line 26). The array is passed to the printCircleArray method, which displays the radii of the total area of the circles.

The sum of the areas of the circle is computed using the sum method (Line 46), which takes the array of Circle objects as the argument and returns a double value for the total area.

6.11 Class Abstraction

In Chapter 4, "Methods," you learned about method abstraction and used it in program development. Java provides many levels of abstraction. *Class abstraction* is the separation of class implementation from the use of a class. The creator of a class provides a description of the class and lets the user know how the class can be used. The collection of methods and fields that are accessible from outside the class, together with the description of how these members are expected to behave, serves as the *class's contract*. The user of the class does not need to know how the class is implemented. The details of implementation are encapsulated and hidden from the user. This is known as *class encapsulation*. For example, you can create a Circle object and find the area of the circle without knowing how the area is computed.

There are many real-life examples that illustrate the concept of class abstraction. Consider building a computer system, for instance. Your personal computer is made up of many components, such as a CPU, CD-ROM, floppy disk, motherboard, fan, and so on. Each component can be viewed as an object that has properties and methods. To get the components to work together, all you need to know is how each component is used and how it interacts with the others. You don't need to know how it works internally. The internal implementation is encapsulated and hidden from you. You can build a computer without knowing how a component is implemented.

The computer-system analogy precisely mirrors the object-oriented approach. Each component can be viewed as an object of the class for the component. For example, you might have a class that models all kinds of fans for use in a computer, with properties like fan size and speed, and methods like start, stop, and so on. A specific fan is an instance of this class with specific property values.

Consider getting a loan, for another example. A specific loan can be viewed as an object of a Loan class. Interest rate, loan amount, and loan period are its data properties, and computing monthly payment and total payment are its methods. When you buy a car, a loan object is created by instantiating the class with your loan interest rate, loan amount, and loan period. You can then use the methods to find the monthly payment and total payment of your loan. As a user of the Loan class, you don't need to know how these methods are implemented.

6.12 Case Studies

This section provides two examples that demonstrate the creation and use of classes.

Example 6.7 The Loan Class

Problem

Write a loan class named Loan with the following data fields: annualInterest-Rate, numOfYears, loanAmount, and loanDate, and the methods getAnnualIntere-stRate, getNumOfYears, getLoanAmount, getLoanDate, setAnnualInterestRate, setNumOfYears, setLoanAmount, monthlyPayment, and totalPayment, as shown in Figure 6.19. The loanDate field stores the date when the loan was created. The monthlyPayment method returns the monthly payment, and the totalPayment method returns the total payment.

Loan
-annualInterestRate: double
-numOfYears: int
-loanAmount: double
-loanDate: Date
+Loan()
+Loan(annualInterestRate: double, numOfYears: int, loanAmount: double)
+getAnnualInterestRate(): double
+getNumOfYears(): int
+getLoanAmount(): double
+getLoanDate(): Date
+setAnnualInterestRate(annualInterestRate: double): void
+setNumOfYears(numOfYears: int): void
+setLoanAmount(loanAmount: double): void
+monthlyPayment(): double
+totalPayment(): double

Constructs a loan with default interest rate, years, and amount.
Constructs a loan with the specified rate, years, and amount.

Returns the annual interest rate of this loan.
Returns the number of years of this loan.
Returns the amount of this loan.
Returns the date of the creation of this loan.
Sets a new annual interest rate to this loan.

Sets a new number of years to this loan.
Sets a new amount to this loan.
Returns the monthly payment of this loan.
Returns the total payment of this loan.

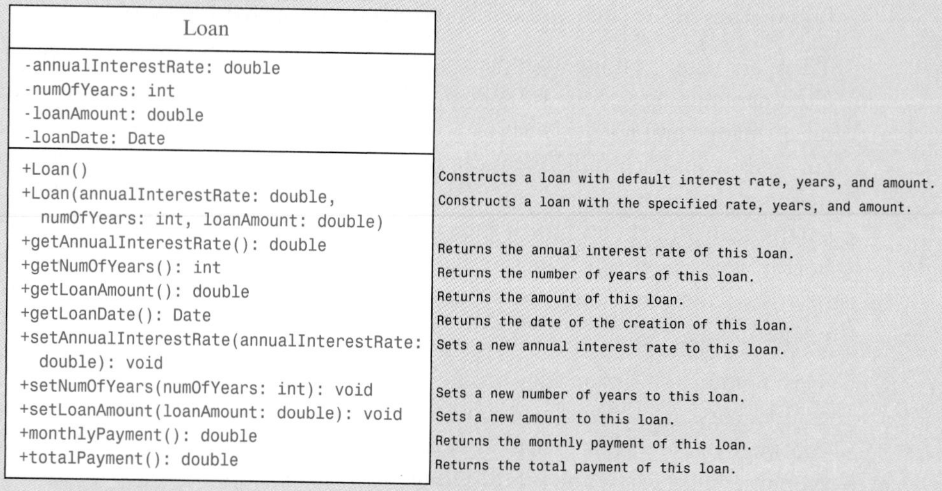

Figure 6.19   *The* Loan *class models the properties and behaviors of loans.*

Solution

Recall that the java.util.Date can be used to create an instance to represent current date and time (see Page 261). The Loan class is given below, followed by a test program. Figure 6.20 shows the output of a sample run of the program.

```
1    // Loan.java: Encapsulate loan information
2    package chapter6;
3
4    public class Loan {
5      private double annualInterestRate;
6      private int numOfYears;
7      private double loanAmount;
8      private java.util.Date loanDate;
9
10     /** Default constructor */
11     public Loan() {
12       this(7.5, 30, 100000);
13     }
14
15     /** Construct a loan with specified annual interest rate,
16         number of years and loan amount
17       */
```

```
18      public Loan(double annualInterestRate, int numOfYears,
19        double loanAmount) {
20        this.annualInterestRate = annualInterestRate;
21        this.numOfYears = numOfYears;
22        this.loanAmount = loanAmount;
23        loanDate = new java.util.Date();
24      }
25
26      /** Return annualInterestRate */
27      public double getAnnualInterestRate() {
28        return annualInterestRate;
29      }
30
31      /** Set a new annualInterestRate */
32      public void setAnnualInterestRate(double annualInterestRate) {
33        this.annualInterestRate = annualInterestRate;
34      }
35
36      /** Return numOfYears */
37      public int getNumOfYears() {
38        return numOfYears;
39      }
40
41      /** Set a new numOfYears */
42      public void setNumOfYears(int numOfYears) {
43        this.numOfYears = numOfYears;
44      }
45
46      /** Return loanAmount */
47      public double getLoanAmount() {
48        return loanAmount;
49      }
50
51      /** Set a newloanAmount */
52      public void setLoanAmount(double loanAmount) {
53        this.loanAmount = loanAmount;
54      }
55
56      /** Find monthly payment */
57      public double monthlyPayment() {
58        double monthlyInterestRate = annualInterestRate / 1200;
59        return loanAmount * monthlyInterestRate / (1 -
60          (Math.pow(1 / (1 + monthlyInterestRate), numOfYears * 12)));
61      }
62
63      /** Find total payment */
64      public double totalPayment() {
65        return monthlyPayment() * numOfYears * 12;
66      }
67
68      /** Return loan date */
69      public java.util.Date getLoanDate() {
70        return loanDate;
71      }
72    }
```

```
1    // TestLoanClass.java: Demonstrate using the Loan class
2    package chapter6;
3
4    import javax.swing.JOptionPane;
5
```

continues

Example 6.7 continued

```
6    public class TestLoanClass {
7      /** Main method */
8      public static void main(String[] args) {
9        // Enter yearly interest rate
10       String annualInterestRateString = JOptionPane.showInputDialog(
11         null, "Enter yearly interest rate, for example 8.25:",
12         "Example 6.7 Input", JOptionPane.QUESTION_MESSAGE);
13
14       // Convert string to double
15       double annualInterestRate =
16         Double.parseDouble(annualInterestRateString);
17
18       // Enter number of years
19       String numOfYearsString = JOptionPane.showInputDialog(null,
20         "Enter number of years as an integer, \nfor example 5:",
21         "Example 6.7 Input", JOptionPane.QUESTION_MESSAGE);
22
23       // Convert string to int
24       int numOfYears = Integer.parseInt(numOfYearsString);
25
26       // Enter loan amount
27       String loanString = JOptionPane.showInputDialog(null,
28         "Enter loan amount, for example 120000.95:",
29         "Example 6.7 Input", JOptionPane.QUESTION_MESSAGE);
30
31       // Convert string to double
32       double loanAmount =  Double.parseDouble(loanString);
33
34       // Create Loan object
35       Loan loan =
36         new Loan(annualInterestRate, numOfYears, loanAmount);
37
38       // Format to keep two digits after the decimal point
39       double monthlyPayment =
40         (int)(loan.monthlyPayment() * 100) / 100.0;
41       double totalPayment =
42         (int)(loan.totalPayment() * 100) / 100.0;
43
44       // Display results
45       String output = "The loan was created on " +
46         loan.getLoanDate().toString() + "\nThe monthly payment is " +
47         monthlyPayment + "\nThe total payment is " + totalPayment;
48       JOptionPane.showMessageDialog(null, output,
49         "Example 6.7 Output", JOptionPane.INFORMATION_MESSAGE);
50
51       System.exit(0);
52     }
53   }
```

Review

The Loan class contains two constructors, four get methods, and the methods for finding monthly payment and total payment. You can construct a Loan object by using the default constructor or the one with three parameters: annual interest rate, number of years, and loan amount. When a loan object is created, its date is stored in the loanDate field. The getLoanDate method returns the date. The three get methods, getAnnualInterest, getNumOfYears, and getLoanAmount, return an-

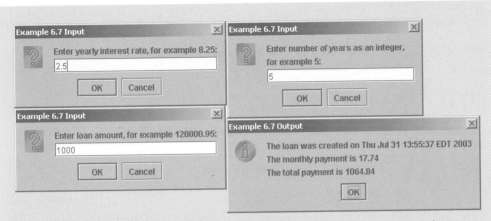

Figure 6.20   *The program creates a* Loan *instance with the annual interest rate, number of years, and loan amount, and displays the loan date, monthly payment, and total payment by invoking the methods of the instance.*

nual interest rate, payment years, and loan amount, respectively. All the data properties and methods in this class are tied to a specific instance of the Loan class. Therefore, they are instance variables or methods.

The main class TestLoanClass reads interest rate, payment period (in years), and loan amount; creates a Loan object; and then obtains the monthly payment (Lines 39–40) and total payment (Lines 41–42) using the instance methods in the Loan class.

Since the Loan class will be used later in the book, it must be declared public and stored in a separate file.

Example 6.8 The StackOfIntegers Class (Optional)

Problem

A *stack* is a data structure that holds objects in a last-in first-out fashion. It has many applications. For example, the compiler uses a stack to process method invocations. When a method is invoked, the parameters and local variables of the method are pushed into a stack. When a method calls another method, the new method's parameters and local variables are pushed into the stack. When a method finishes its work and returns to its caller, its associated space is released from the stack.

Create a class named StackOfIntegers that stores a stack of integers and write a test program that displays all the prime numbers less than 120 in decreasing order, as shown in Figure 6.21. This example is similar to Example 3.9, "Displaying Prime Numbers," which displays the first fifty prime numbers in increasing order.

continues

Example 6.8 continued

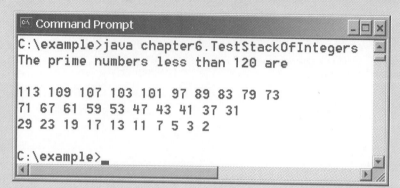

Figure 6.21   *The* StackOfIntegers *class is used in the program to display the first thirty prime numbers in decreasing order.*

Solution

To display all the prime numbers less than 120 in decreasing order, you may use a stack to store the prime numbers 2, 3, 5, 7, 11, ..., and retrieve and display them in reverse order.

The StackOfIntegers class uses the data field elements of int[] type to store integers and the data field size to count the number of elements currently stored in the stack. The length of the array (elements.length) is referred to as the *capacity* of the stack.

The class provides two constructors. The default constructor creates a stack with the default capacity of 16 and the other constructor constructs a stack with the specified capacity. The class provides the methods empty(), peek(), push(int), pop(), and getSize() for manipulating the stack, as shown in Figure 6.22.

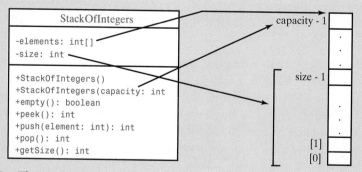

Figure 6.22   *The* StackOfIntegers *class encapsulates the stack storage and provides the operations for manipulating the stack.*

The empty() method tests whether the stack is empty. The peek() method returns the integer at the top of the stack without removing it from the stack. The push(int) method stores an integer into the top of the stack. The pop() method removes the integer at the top of the stack and returns that integer. The getSize() method returns the number of elements in the stack. The StackOfIntegers class and the test program are presented below.

```
1    package chapter6;
2
3    public class TestStackOfIntegers {
4      public static void main(String[] args) {
5        final int LIMIT = 120;
6        int count = 0;
7        StackOfIntegers stack = new StackOfIntegers();
8
9        // Repeatedly find prime numbers
10       for (int number = 2; number < LIMIT; number++)
11         if (isPrime(number)) {
12           stack.push(number);
13           count++; // Increase the prime number count
14         }
15
16       // Print the first 30 prime numbers in decreasing order
17       System.out.println("The prime numbers less than 120 are \n");
18       final int NUMBER_PER_LINE = 10;
19
20       while (!stack.empty()) {
21         System.out.print(stack.pop() + " ");
22
23         if (stack.getSize() % NUMBER_PER_LINE == 0)
24           System.out.println(); // advance to the new line
25       }
26     }
27
28     public static boolean isPrime(int number) {
29       // Assume the number is prime
30       boolean isPrime = true;
31
32       // Test if number is prime
33       for (int divisor = 2; divisor == number / 2; divisor++) {
34         //If true, the number is not prime
35         if (number % divisor == 0) {
36           // Set isPrime to false, if the number is not prime
37           isPrime = false;
38           break; // Exit the for loop
39         }
40       }
41
42       return isPrime;
43     }
44   }
45
46   class StackOfIntegers {
47     private int[] elements;
48     private int size;
49
50     /** Default constructor */
51     public StackOfIntegers() {
52       this(16);
53     }
54
```

continues

Example 6.8 continued

```
55      /** Construct a stack with the specified maximum capacity */
56      public StackOfIntegers(int capacity) {
57        elements = new int[capacity];
58      }
59
60      /** Push a new integer into the top of the stack */
61      public int push(int element) {
62        if (size >= elements.length) {
63          int[] temp = new int[elements.length * 2];
64          System.arraycopy(elements, 0, temp, 0, elements.length);
65          elements = temp;
66        }
67
68        return elements[size++] = element;
69      }
70
71      /** Return and remove the top element from the stack */
72      public int pop() {
73        return elements[--size];
74      }
75
76      /** Return the top element from the stack */
77      public int peek() {
78        return elements[size - 1];
79      }
80
81      /** Test whether the stack is empty */
82      public boolean empty() {
83        return size == 0;
84      }
85
86      /** Return the number of elements in the stack */
87      public int getSize() {
88        return size;
89      }
90    }
```

Review

The elements in the stack are stored in an array. When you create a stack, the array is also created. The default constructor creates an array with the default capacity of 16 (Line 52). The variable size counts the number of elements in the stack, and size - 1 is the index of the element at the top of the stack.

If the stack is full and an element is pushed into it, the stack's capacity is doubled. This is done by creating a new array of twice the current capacity (Line 63), copying the contents of the current array to the new array (Line 64), and assigning the reference of the new array to the current array in the stack.

◈ NOTE

When you create a StackOfIntegers object, an array object is created. A StackOfIntegers object contains a reference to the array. For simplicity, you can say that the StackOfIntegers object contains the array.

NOTE

The user can create a stack and manipulate it through the public methods push, pop, peek, empty, and getSize. However, the user doesn't need to know how these methods are implemented. The StackOfIntegers class encapsulates the internal implementation of the stack. This example uses an array to implement a stack. You may use something other than an array to implement a stack. The program that uses StackOfIntegers does not need to change, since the contract of the public methods remains unchanged.

NOTE

Stacks are frequently used in programming. Java provides the Stack class in the java.util package, which will be introduced in Chapter 17, "Java Data Structures."

6.13   Inner Classes (Optional)

An *inner class*, or *nested class*, is a class defined within the scope of another class. Here is an example of an inner class:

```java
// ShowInnerClass.java: Demonstrate using inner classes
package chapter6;

public class ShowInnerClass {
  private int data;

  /** A method in the outer class */
  public void m() {
    // Do something
    InnerClass instance = new InnerClass();
  }

  // An inner class
  class InnerClass {
    /** A method in the inner class */
    public void mi() {
      // Directly reference data and method defined in its outer class
      data++;
      m();
    }
  }
}
```

The class InnerClass is defined inside ShowInnerClass. An inner class is just like any regular class, with the following features:

■ An inner class can reference the data and methods defined in the outer class in which it nests, so you do not need to pass the reference of the outer class to the constructor of the inner class. For this reason, inner classes can make programs simple and concise.

- An inner class supports the work of its containing outer class and is compiled into a class named *OutClassName$InnerClassName*.class. For example, the inner class `InnerClass` in `ShowInnerClass` is compiled into *ShowInnerClass$-InnerClass*.class.

- An inner class can be declared `public`, `protected`, or `private` subject to the same visibility rules applied to a member of the class.

- An inner class can be declared `static`. A `static` inner class can be accessed using the outer class name. A `static` inner class cannot access nonstatic members of the outer class.

- Objects of an inner class are often created in the outer class. But you can also create an object of an inner class from another class. If the inner class is nonstatic, you must first create an instance of the outer class, then use the following syntax to create an object for the inner class:

  ```
  OuterClass.InnerClass innerObject = outerObject.new InnerClass();
  ```

- If the inner class is static, use the following syntax to create an object for it:

  ```
  OuterClass.InnerClass innerObject = new OuterClass.InnerClass();
  ```

 NOTE

An inner class can be further shortened by using an anonymous inner class. Many Java development tools use anonymous inner classes to generate adapters for handling events. Since anonymous inner classes are used mainly to create event adapters, they are discussed along with event adapters in Bonus Supplement I, "Event Adapters."

Chapter Summary

- A class is a template for objects. It defines the generic properties of objects, and provides constructors for creating objects and methods for manipulating them.

- A class is also a data type. You can use it to declare object reference variables.

- An object reference variable that appears to hold an object actually contains a reference to that object. Strictly speaking, an object reference variable and an object are different, but most of the time the distinction between them can be ignored.

- An object is an instance of a class. You use the `new` operator to create an object, and the dot (.) operator to access members of that object through its reference variable.

- A constructor is a special method that is called when an object is created. Constructors can be overloaded.

- If a class does not explicitly define any constructors, a default constructor is defined implicitly. If a class does explicitly define constructors, a default constructor does not exist unless it is defined explicitly.

■ Modifiers specify how the class, method, and data are accessed. A `public` class, method, or data is accessible to all clients. A `private` method or data is only accessible inside the class. A static variable or a static method is defined using the keyword `static`.

■ To prevent direct modifications of properties through the object reference, you can declare the field private, using the `private` modifier. This is known as *data field encapsulation.* Using private data fields makes the class easy to maintain.

■ You can provide a `get` method or a `set` method to enable clients to see or modify the data. Colloquially, a `get` method is referred to as a *getter* (or *accessor*), and a `set` method is referred to as a *setter* (or *mutator*).

■ A `get` method has the signature `public returnType getPropertyName()`. If the `returnType` is `boolean`, the `get` method should be defined as `public boolean isPropertyName()`. A set method has the signature `public void setPropertyName(dataType propertyValue)`.

■ All parameters are passed to methods using pass by value. For a parameter of a primitive type, the actual value is passed; for a parameter of a reference type, the reference for the object is passed.

■ An instance variable is a variable that belongs to an instance of a class. Its use is associated with individual instances. A static variable is a variable shared by all instances of the same class.

■ An instance method is a method that belongs to an instance of a class. Its use is associated with individual instances. A static method is a method that can be invoked without using instances.

■ Every instance of a class can access the class's static variables and methods. However, I recommend that you invoke static variables and methods using `ClassName.variable` and `ClassName.method`.

■ The scope of instance and static variables is the entire class, regardless of where the variables are declared. The instance and static variables can be declared anywhere in the class.

■ The object reference `this` inside an instance method sevres as a pointer to the current instance of the class that invokes the instance method. The keyword `this` can also be used inside a constructor to invoke another constructor of the same class.

■ A Java array is an object that can contain primitive type values or object type values. When an array is created, its elements are assigned the default value of `0` for the numeric primitive data types, `'\u0000'` for `char` types, `false` for `boolean` types, and `null` for object types.

■ An *inner class,* or *nested class,* is a class defined within the scope of another class. An inner class can reference the data and methods defined in the outer class in which it nests, so you do not need to pass the reference of the outer class to the constructor of the inner class.

Review Questions

6.1 Describe the relationship between an object and its defining class. How do you declare a class? How do you declare an object? How do you create an object? How do you declare and create an object in one statement?

6.2 What are the differences between constructors and methods?

6.3 Describe the difference between passing a parameter of a primitive type and passing a parameter of a reference type. Show the output of the following program:

```
public class Test {
  public static void main(String[] args) {
    Count myCount = new Count();
    int times = 0;

    for (int i = 0; i < 100; i++)
      increment(myCount, times);

    System.out.println("count is " + myCount.count);
    System.out.println("times is " + times);
  }

  public static void increment(Count c, int times) {
    c.count++;
    times++;
  }
}

class Count {
  public int count;

  Count(int c) {
    count = c;
  }

  Count() {
    count = 1;
  }
}
```

6.4 Show the output of the following program:

```
a. public class Test {

    public static void main(String[] args) {
      Circle circle1 = new Circle(1);
      Circle circle2 = new Circle(2);

      // Attempt to swap circle1 with circle2
      System.out.println("Before swap: circle1 = " +
        circle1.radius + " circle2 = " + circle2.radius);
      swap(circle1, circle2);
      System.out.println("After swap: circle1 = " +
        circle1.radius + " circle2 = " + circle2.radius);
    }

    public static void swap(Circle x, Circle y) {
      System.out.println("Before swap: x = " +
        x.radius + " y = " + y.radius);
```

```
                Circle temp = x;
                x = y;
                y = temp;

                System.out.println("After swap: x = " +
                  x.radius + " y = " + y.radius);
            }
        }

        class Circle {
          double radius;

          Circle(double newRadius) {
            radius = newRadius;
          }
        }
```

b.
```
   public class Test {
       public static void main(String[] args) {
           Circle circle1 = new Circle(1.0);
           Circle circle2 = new Circle(2.0);

           // Attempt to swap circle1 with circle2
           System.out.println("Before swap: circle1 = " +
             circle1.radius + " circle2 = " + circle2.radius);
           swap(circle1, circle2);
           System.out.println("After swap: circle1 = " +
             circle1.radius + " circle2 = " + circle2.radius);
       }

       public static void swap(Circle x, Circle y) {
           System.out.println("Before swap: x = " +
             x.radius + " y = " + y.radius);

           double temp = x.radius;
           x.radius = y.radius;
           y.radius = temp;

           System.out.println("After swap: x = " +
             x.radius + " y = " + y.radius);
       }
   }

   class Circle {
     double radius;

     Circle(double newRadius) {
       radius = newRadius;
     }
   }
```

6.5 Suppose that the class Foo is defined as follows:

```
   public class Foo {
     int i;
     static String s;

     void imethod() {
     }

     static void smethod() {
     }
   }
```

Let f be an instance of Foo. Which of the following statements are correct?

```
System.out.println(f.i);
System.out.println(f.s);
f.imethod();
f.smethod();
System.out.println(Foo.i);
System.out.println(Foo.s);
Foo.imethod();
Foo.smethod();
```

6.6 What is the output of the following program?

```
public class Foo {
  static int i = 0;
  static int j = 0;

  public static void main(String[] args) {
    int i = 2;
    int k = 3;

    {
      int j = 3;
      System.out.println("i + j is " + i + j);
    }

    k = i + j;
    System.out.println("k is " + k);
    System.out.println("j is " + j);
  }
}
```

6.7 What is wrong with the following program?

```
1    public class ShowErrors {
2      public static void main(String[] args) {
3        ShowErrors t = new ShowErrors(5);
4      }
5    }
```

6.8 What is wrong with the following program?

```
1    public class ShowErrors {
2      public static void main(String[] args) {
3        ShowErrors t = new ShowErrors();
4        t.x();
5      }
6    }
```

6.9 List the modifiers that you learned in this chapter and describe their purposes.

6.10 Describe the role of the this keyword.

6.11 What is wrong in the following code?

```
1    class Test {
2      public static void main(String[] args) {
3        A a = new A();
4        a.print();
5      }
6    }
7
8    class A {
9      String s;
10
```

```
11        A(String s) {
12          this.s = s;
13        }
14
15        public void print() {
16          System.out.print(s);
17        }
18      }
```

6.12 What is wrong in the following code?

```
1      class Test {
2        public static void main(String[] args) {
3          C c = new C(5.0);
4          System.out.println(c.value);
5        }
6      }
7
8      class C {
9        int value = 2;
10      }
```

6.13 What is wrong in the following code?

```
1      public class Foo {
2        public void method1() {
3          Circle c;
4          System.out.println("What is radius " + c.getRadius());
5          c = new Circle();
6        }
7      }
```

6.14 What is wrong in the following code?

```
1      public class Foo {
2        public static void main(String[] args) {
3          method1();
4        }
5
6        public static void method1() {
7          method2();
8        }
9
10        public static void method2() {
11          System.out.println("What is radius " + c.getRadius());
12        }
13
14        Circle c = new Circle();
15      }
```

6.15 What is the printout of the following code?

```
public class Foo {
  private boolean x;

  public static void main(String[] args) {
    Foo foo = new Foo();
    System.out.println(foo.x);
  }
}
```

6.16 In the following class, radius is private in the Circle class, and myCircle is an object of the Circle class. Can the following code compile and run? Explain why.

297

```
public class Circle {
  private double radius = 1.0;

  /** Find the area of this circle */
  double findArea() {
    return radius * radius * 3.14159;
  }

  public static void main(String[] args) {
    Circle myCircle = new Circle();
    System.out.println("Radius is " + myCircle.radius);
  }
}
```

6.17 Is an array an object or a primitive type value? Can an array contain elements of a primitive type as well as an object type? Describe the default value for the elements of an array.

6.18 Show the printout of the following code:

a.
```
public class Test {

  public static void main(String[] args) {
    int[] a = {1, 2};
    swap(a[0], a[1]);
    System.out.println("a[0] = " + a[0] + " a[1] = " + a[1]);
  }

  public static void swap(int n1, int n2) {
    int temp = n1;
    n1 = n2;
    n2 = temp;

  }

}
```
b.
```
public class Test {
  public static void main(String[] args) {
    int[] a = {1, 2};
    swap(a);
    System.out.println("a[0] = " + a[0] + " a[1] = " + a[1]);
  }

  public static void swap(int[] a) {
    int temp = a[0];
    a[0] = a[1];
    a[1] = temp;
  }

}
```
c.
```
public class Test {
  public static void main(String[] args) {
    T t = new T();
    swap(t);
    System.out.println("e1 = " + t.e1 + " e2 = " + t.e2);
  }

  public static void swap(T t) {
    int temp = t.e1;
    t.e1 = t.e2;
    t.e2 = temp;
  }
}

class T {
  int e1 = 1;
  int e2 = 2;
}
```

```
d. public class Test {
     public static void main(String[] args) {
       T t1 = new T();
       T t2 = new T();
       System.out.println("t1's i=" + t1.i + " and j=" + t1.j);
       System.out.println("t2's i=" + t2.i + " and j=" + t2.j);
     }
   }

   class T {
     static int i = 0;
     int j = 0;

     T() {
       i++;
       j = 1;
     }
   }
```

6.19 Can an inner class be used in a class other than the class in which the inner class nests?

6.20 Can the modifiers public, private, and static be used on inner classes?

Programming Exercises

6.1 (The Rectangle class) Write a class named Rectangle to represent rectangles. The properties and methods are shown in Figure 6.23. Suppose that all the rectangles are the same color. Use a static variable for color.

Rectangle	
-width: double -height: double -color: String	
+Rectangle()	Constructs a rectangle with width 1 and height 1.
+Rectangle(width: double, height: double, color: String)	Constructs a rectangle with the specified width and height.
+getWidth(): double	Returns the width of this rectangle.
+setWidth(width: double): void	Sets a new width for this rectangle.
+getHeight(): double	Returns the height of this rectangle.
+setHeight(height: double): void	Sets a new height for this rectangle.
+getColor(): String	Returns the color of all rectangles.
+setColor(color: String): void	Sets a new color for all rectangles.
+findArea(): double	Returns the area of this rectangle.
+findPerimeter(): double	Returns the perimeter of this rectangle.

Figure 6.23 *The Rectangle class contains the properties width, height, and color, accessor and mutator methods, and the methods for computing area and perimeter.*

Write a client program to test the class Rectangle. In the client program, create two Rectangle objects. Assign any width and height to each of the two objects. Assign the first object the color red, and the second, yellow. Display the properties of both objects and find their areas.

6.2 (The Fan class) Write a class named Fan to model fans. The properties, as shown in Figure 6.24, are speed, on, radius, and color. You need to provide the accessor and mutator methods for the properties, and the toString method for returning a string consisting of all the values of all the properties in this class. Suppose the fan has three fixed speeds. Use constants 1, 2, and 3 to denote slow, medium, and fast speed.

```
                 Fan
 -speed: int
 -on: boolean
 -radius: double
 -color: String

 +Fan()                               Constructs a fan with default values.
 +getSpeed(): int                     Returns the speed of this fan.
 +setSpeed(speed: int): void          Sets a new speed for this fan.
 +isOn(): boolean                     Returns true if this fan is on.
 +setOn(on: boolean): void            Sets this fan on to true or false.
 +getRadius(): double                 Returns the radius of this fan.
 +setRadius(radius: double): void     Sets a new radius for this fan.
 +getColor(): String                  Returns the color of this fan.
 +setColor(color: String): void       Sets a new color for this fan.
 +toString(): String                  Returns a string representation for this fan.
```

Figure 6.24   *The Fan class contains the properties speed, on, radius, and color, accessor and mutator methods, and the toString method for returning values of the properties.*

Write a client program to test the Fan class. In the client program, create a Fan object. Assign maximum speed, radius 10, color yellow, and turn it on. Display the object by invoking its toString method.

6.3 (The Account class) Write a class named Account to model accounts. The properties and methods of the class are shown in Figure 6.25. Interest is compounded monthly.

```
                 Account
 -id: int
 -balance: double
 -annualInterestRate: double

 +Account()                           Constructs a default account.
 +Account(id: int, balance: double,   Constructs an account with the
     annualInterestRate: double)          specified ID, balance, and interest rate.
 +getId(): int                        Returns the ID of this account.
 +getBalance(): double                Returns the balance of this account.
 +getAnnualInterestRate():double      Returns the interest rate of this account.
 +setId(id: int): void                Sets a new ID for this account.
 +setBalance(balance: double): void   Sets a new balance for this account.
 +setAnnualInterestRate(             Sets a new interest rate for this account.
     annualInterestRate: double): void
 +getMonthlyInterest(): double        Returns the monthly interest rate of this account.
 +withdraw(amount: double): void      Withdraws the specified amount from this account.
 +deposit(amount: double): void       Deposits the specified amount to this account.
```

Figure 6.25   *The Account class contains the properties ID, balance, annual interest rate, accessor and mutator methods, and the methods for computing interest, withdrawing money, and depositing money.*

300

Write a client program to test the Account class. In the client program, create an Account object with an account ID of 1122, a balance of 20000, and an annual interest rate of 4.5%. Use the withdraw method to withdraw $2500, use the deposit method to deposit $3000, and print the balance and the monthly interest.

6.4 (The Stock class) Write a class named Stock to model a stock. The properties and methods of the class are shown in Figure 6.26. The method changePercent computes the percentage of the change between the current price and the previous closing price.

Stock
-symbol: String -name: String -previousClosingPrice: double -currentPrice: double

+Stock	Constructs a default stock.
+Stock(symbol: String, name: String)	Constructs a stock with a symbol and a name.
+getSymbol():String	Returns the symbol of this stock.
+getName():String	Returns the name of this stock.
+getPreviousClosingPrice(): double	Returns the previous closing price of this stock.
+getCurrentPrice(): double	Returns the current price of this stock.
+setSymbol(symbol: String): void	Returns the symbol of this stock.
+setName(name: String): void	Returns the name of this stock.
+setPreviousClosingPrice(price: double): void	Sets the previous closing price of this stock.
+setCurrentPrice(price: double): void	Sets the current price of this stock.
+changePercent(): double	Returns the percentage of change of this stock.

Figure 6.26 *The Stock class contains the properties symbol, name, previous closing price, and current price, accessor and mutator methods, and the methods for computing price changes.*

Write a client program to test the Stock class. In the client program, create a Stock object with the stock symbol SUNW, the name Sun Microsystems Inc, and the previous closing price of 100. Set a new current price randomly and display the price-change percentage.

6.5 (Revising Example 4.7, "Displaying Calendars") Rewrite Example 4.7 to display calendars in a message dialog box. You can define a static String variable output for storing the output and display it in a message dialog box.

6.6 (The Vote and Candidate Classes) Create two classes, Vote and Candidate. The Vote class has the data field count to count votes, and the methods getCount, setCount, clear, increment, and decrement for reading and handling the votes, as shown in Figure 6.27. The clear method sets the count to 0. The increment and decrement methods increase and decrease the count. The Candidate class has the data fields name (name of the candidate), vote (track the votes received by the candidate), and numOfCandidates (track the total number of candidates), and the methods getName, getVote, and getNumOfCandidates for reading the name, vote, and numOfCandidates, as shown in Figure 6.27.

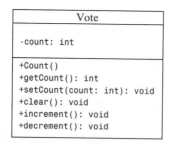

Figure 6.27   *The* Vote *class encapsulates the vote count, and the* Candidate *class encapsulates the candidates.*

Write a test program that counts votes for two candidates for student body president. The votes are entered from the keyboard. Number 1 is a vote for Candidate 1, and number 2 is a vote for Candidate 2. Number −1 deducts a vote from Candidate 1, and −2 deducts a vote from Candidate 2. Number 0 signifies the end of the count.

6.7 (Displaying the prime factors) Rewrite Exercise 3.10 to read an integer and display all its smallest factors in decreasing order. For example, if the integer is 120, the smallest factors are displayed as 5, 3, 2, 2, 2. Use the StackOfInte-gers class to store the factors (e.g., 2, 2, 2, 3, 5) and retrieve and display the factors in reverse order.

6.8 (The Time class) Write a class named Time. The Time class contains the data fields hour, minute, and second with their respective get and set methods. The default constructor sets the hour, minute, and second for the current time in GMT. The current time can be obtained using System.currentTime() as shown in Example 2.5, "Displaying Current Time."

6.9 (The Tax class) Write a class named Tax. The Tax class contains the following instance data fields:

■ **int filingStatus**: One of the four tax filing statuses: 0 - single filer, 1 - married filing jointly, 2 - married filing separately, and 3 - head of household. Use the public static constants SINGLE_FILER (0), MARRIED_JOINTLY (1), MARRIED_SEPARATELY (2), HEAD_OF_HOUSEHOLD (3) to represent the status.

■ **int[][] brackets**: Stores the tax brackets for each filing status (see Example 5.8).

■ **double[] rates**: Stores tax rates for each bracket (see Example 5.9).

■ **double taxableIncome**: Stores the taxable income.

Provide the get and set methods for each data field and the findTax() method that returns the tax. Also provide a default constructor and the constructor Tax(filingStatus, brackets, rates, taxableIncome).

Use the Tax class to print the 2001 and 2002 tax tables for taxable income from $50,000 to $60,000 with interval of $1000 for all four statuses. The tax rates for the year 2002 were given in Table 3.1 on page 112. The tax rates for 2001 are shown in Table 6.1.

TABLE 6.1   **2001 U.S. Federal Personal Tax Rates**

Tax Rate	Single Filers	Married Filing Jointly or Qualifying Widower(er)	Married Filing Separately	Head of Household
15%	Up to $27,050	Up to $45,200	Up to $22,600	Up to $36,250
27.5%	$27,051–$65,550	$45,201–$109,250	$22,601–$54,625	$36,251–$93,650
30.5%	$65,551–$136,750	$109,251–$166,500	$54,626–$83,250	$93,651–$151,650
35.5%	$136,751–$297,350	$166,501–$297,350	$83,251–$148,675	$151,651–$297,350
39.1%	$297,351 or more	$297,351 or more	$148,676 or more	$297,351 or more

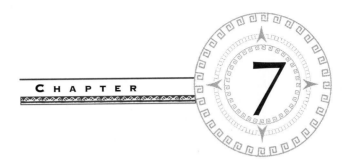

STRINGS

Objectives

- ◉ To use the String class to process fixed strings.

- ◉ To use the Character class to process a single character.

- ◉ To use the StringBuffer class to process flexible strings.

- ◉ To use the StringTokenizer class to extract tokens from a string.

- ◉ To know the differences among the String, StringBuffer, and StringTokenizer classes.

- ◉ To learn how to use command-line arguments.

7.1   Introduction

Strings are used often in programming. A *string* is sequence of characters. In many languages, strings are treated as arrays of characters, but in Java a string is an object. Java provides the `String` class, the `StringBuffer` class, and the `StringTokenizer` class for storing and processing strings.

In most cases, you use the `String` class to create strings. The `String` class is efficient for storing and processing strings, but strings created with the `String` class cannot be modified. The `StringBuffer` class enables you to create flexible strings that can be modified. `StringTokenizer` is a utility class that can be used to extract tokens from a string.

7.2   The *String* Class

The `java.lang.String` class models a sequence of characters as a string. You have already used string literals, such as the parameter in the `println(String s)` method. The Java compiler converts the string literal into a string object and passes it to `println`.

The `String` class has eleven constructors and more than forty methods for examining individual characters in a sequence, comparing strings, searching substrings, extracting substrings, and creating a copy of a string with all the characters translated to uppercase or lowercase. The most frequently used methods are listed in Figure 7.1.

7.2.1   Constructing a String

You can create a string from a string value or from an array of characters. To create a string from a string literal, use a syntax like this one:

```
String newString = new String(stringLiteral);
```

The argument `stringLiteral` is a sequence of characters enclosed inside double quotes. The following statement creates a `String` object `message` for the string literal `"Welcome to Java"`:

```
String message = new String("Welcome to Java");
```

Since strings are used frequently, Java provides a shorthand notation for creating a string:

```
String message = "Welcome to Java";
```

◈ **NOTE**

A `String` object is immutable; its contents cannot be changed. To improve efficiency and save memory, Java Virtual Machine stores two `String` objects in the same object if the two `String` objects were created with the same string literal using the shorthand notation. Therefore, the shorthand notation is preferred in creating strings.

String
+String()
+String(value: String)
+String(value: char[])
+charAt(index: int): char
+compareTo(anotherString: String): int
+compareToIgnoreCase(anotherString: String): int
+concat(anotherString: String): String
+endsWith(suffix: String): boolean
+equals(anotherString: String): boolean
+equalsIgnoreCase(anotherString: String): boolean
+getChars(int srcBegin, int srcEnd, char[] dst, int dstBegin): void
+indexOf(ch: int): int
+indexOf(ch: int, fromIndex: int): int
+indexOf(str: String): int
+indexOf(str: String, fromIndex: int): int
+lastIndexOf(ch: int): int
+lastIndexOf(ch: int, fromIndex: int): int
+lastIndexOf(str: String): int
+lastIndexOf(str: String, fromIndex: int): int
+regionMatches(toffset: int, other: String, offset: int, len: int): boolean
+length(): int
+replace(oldChar: char, newChar: char): String
+startsWith(prefix: String): boolean
+subString(beginIndex: int): String
+subString(beginIndex: int, endIndex: int): String
+toCharArray(): char[]
+toLowerCase(): String
+toString(): String
+toUpperCase(): String
+trim(): String
+copyValueOf(data: char[]): String
+valueOf(c: char): String
+valueOf(data: char[]): String
+valueOf(d: double): String
+valueOf(f: float): String
+valueOf(i: int): String
+valueOf(l: long): String

Constructs an empty string.
Constructs a string with the specified string literal value.
Constructs a string with the specified character array.
Returns the character at the specified index from this string.
Compares this string with another string.
Compares this string with another string ignoring case.
Concatenates this string with another string.
Returns true if this string ends with the specified suffix.
Returns true if this string is equal to another string.
Checks whether this string equals another string ignoring case.
Copies characters from this string into the destination character array.
Returns the index of the first occurrence of ch.
Returns the index of the first occurrence of ch after fromIndex.
Returns the index of the first occurrence of str.
Returns the index of the first occurrence of str after fromIndex.
Returns the index of the last occurrence of ch.
Returns the index of the last occurrence of ch before fromIndex.
Returns the index of the last occurrence of str.
Returns the index of the last occurrence of str before fromIndex.
Returns true if the specified subregion of this string exactly.
 matches the specified subregion of the string argument.
Returns the number of characters in this string.
Returns a new string with oldChar replaced by newChar.
Returns true if this string starts with the specified prefix.
Returns the substring from beginIndex.
Returns the substring from beginIndex to endIndex.
Returns a char array consisting of characters from this string.
Returns a new string with all characters converted to lowercase.
Returns a new string with itself.
Returns a new string with all characters converted to uppercase.
Returns a string with blank characters trimmed on both sides.
Returns a new string consisting of the char array data.
Returns a string consisting of the character c.
Same as copyValueOf(data: char[]): String.
Returns a string representing the double value.
Returns a string representing the float value.
Returns a string representing the int value.
Returns a string representing the long value.

Figure 7.1   *The* String *class provides the methods for processing a string.*

A string that is created using the shorthand notation is known as a *canonical string.* If two identical strings are created using the shorthand notation, these two strings share the same canonical string. You can also use a String object's intern method to return a canonical string, which is the same string that is created using the shorthand notation.

For example, the following statements

```
String s = "Welcome to Java";
String s1 = new String("Welcome to Java");
String s2 = s1.intern(); // Return a canonical string
String s3 = "Welcome to Java";
System.out.println("s1 == s is " + (s1 == s));
System.out.println("s2 == s is " + (s2 == s));
System.out.println("s == s3 is " + (s == s3));
```

display

```
s1 == s is false
s2 == s is true
s == s3 is true
```

In the preceding statements, s, s2, and s3 refer to the same canonical string "Welcome to Java", therefore, s2 == s and s == s3 are true. However, s1 == s is false, since *s* and *s1* are two different string objects, though they have the same contents.

You can also create a string from an array of characters. For example, the following statements create the string "Good Day".

```
char[] charArray = {'G', 'o', 'o', 'd', ' ', 'D', 'a', 'y'};
String message = new String(charArray);
```

NOTE

A String variable holds a reference to a String object that stores a string value. Strictly speaking, the terms *String* variable, *String object*, and *string value* are different, but the distinctions among them can be ignored most of the time. For simplicity, the term *string* will often be used to refer to String variable, String object, and string value.

7.2.2   String Length and Retrieving Individual Characters

You can get the length of a string by invoking its length() method. For example, message.length() returns the length of the string message.

The s.charAt(index) method can be used to retrieve a specific character in a string s, where the index is between 0 and s.length()-1. For example, message.charAt(0) returns the character W, as shown in Figure 7.2.

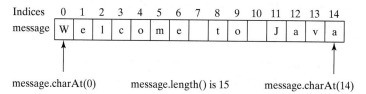

Figure 7.2   *A* String *object is represented using an array internally.*

NOTE

When you use a string, you often know its literal value. For convenience, Java allows you to use the string literal to refer directly to the strings without creating new variables. Thus, "Welcome to Java".charAt(0) is correct and returns W.

NOTE

A string value is represented using a private array variable internally. The array cannot be accessed outside of the String class. The String class provides many public methods, such as length() and charAt(index), to retrieve the array information. This is a good example of encapsulation: the detailed data structure of the class is hidden from the user through the private modifier, and thus the user cannot directly manipulate the internal data structure. If the array were not private, the user would be able to change the string content by modifying the array. This would violate the tenet that the String class is immutable.

CAUTION

Accessing characters in a string s out of bounds is a common programming error. To avoid it, make sure that you do not use an index beyond `s.length()` − 1. For example, `s.charAt(s.length())` would cause a runtime error.

 CAUTION

`length` is a method in the `String` class, but `length` is a property in an array object. So you have to use `s.length()` to get the number of characters in string s, and use `a.length` to get the number of elements in array a.

7.2.3   String Concatenation

You can use the `concat` method to concatenate two strings. The statement shown below, for example, concatenates strings s1 and s2 into s3:

```
String s3 = s1.concat(s2);
```

Since string concatenation is heavily used in programming, Java provides a convenient way to concatenate strings. You can use the plus (+) sign to concatenate two or more strings. The following code combines the strings message, " and", and "HTML" into one string:

```
String myString = message + " and " + "HTML";
```

Recall that you used the + sign to concatenate a number with a string in the `println` method. A number is converted into a string and then concatenated.

7.2.4   Extracting Substrings

`String` is an immutable class. After a string is created, its value cannot be modified. For example, you cannot change "Java" in message to "HTML". So what can you do if you need to change the message string? You assign a completely new string to message. The following code illustrates this:

```
message = "Welcome to HTML";
```

As an alternative, you can use the `substring` method. You extract a substring from a string by using the `substring` method in the `String` class. The `substring` method has two versions:

- `public String substring(int beginIndex, int endIndex)`
  Returns a new string that is a substring of the string. The substring begins at the specified `beginIndex` and extends to the character at index `endIndex` − 1, as shown in Figure 7.3. Thus the length of the substring is `endIndex-beginIndex`.

- `public String substring(int beginIndex)`
  Returns a new string that is a substring of the string. The substring begins with the character at the specified index and extends to the end of the string, as shown in Figure 7.3.

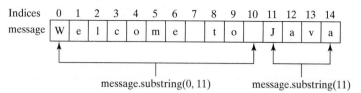

Figure 7.3   *The* substring *method extracts a substring from a string.*

For example,

```
String message = "Welcome to Java".substring(0, 11) + "HTML";
```

The string message now becomes "Welcome to HTML".

7.2.5   String Comparisons

Often, in a program, you need to compare the contents of two strings. You might attempt to use the == operator, as follows:

```
if (string1 == string2)
  System.out.println("string1 and string2 are the same object");
else
  System.out.println("string1 and string2 are different objects");
```

However, the == operator only checks whether string1 and string2 refer to the same object; it does not tell you whether string1 and string2 contain the same contents when they are different objects. Therefore, you cannot use the == operator to find out whether two string variables have the same contents. Instead, you should use the equals() method for an equality comparison of the contents of objects. The code given below, for instance, can be used to compare two strings.

```
if (string1.equals(string2))
  System.out.println("string1 and string2 have the same contents");
else
  System.out.println("string1 and string2 are not equal");
```

◈ NOTE

Two String references are the same if they are created with the same literal value using the shorthand notation. But strings with the same contents do not always share the same object. For example, the following two variables, s1 and s2, are different even though their contents are identical.

```
String s0 = " Java";
String s1 = "Welcome to" + s0;
String s2 = "Welcome to Java";

System.out.println("s1 == s2 is " + (s1 == s2));
System.out.println("s1.equals(s2) is " + (s1.equals(s2)));
```

In this case, s1 == s2 is false since they point to two different objects, but s1.equals(s2) is true since the objects have the same contents. For safety and clarity, you should always use the equals method to test whether two strings have the same contents, and the == operator to test whether the two strings have the same references (i.e., point to the same memory location).

The compareTo method can also be used to compare two strings. For example, see the following code:

```
s1.compareTo(s2)
```

The method returns the value 0 if s1 is equal to s2, a value less than 0 if s1 is lexicographically less than s2, and a value greater than 0 if s1 is lexicographically greater than s2.

The actual value returned from the compareTo method depends on the offset of the first two distinct characters in s1 and s2 from left to right. For example, suppose s1 is "abc" and s2 is "abg", and s1.compareTo(s2) returns − 4. The first two characters (a vs. a) from s1 and s2 are compared. Because they are equal, the second two characters (b vs. b) are compared. Because they are also equal, the third two characters (c vs. g) are compared. Since the character c is 4 less than g, the comparison returns − 4.

CAUTION

Syntax errors will occur if you compare strings by using comparison operators, such as >, >=, <, or <=. Instead, you have to use s1.compareTo(s2).

NOTE

The equals method returns true if two strings are equal, and false if they are not equal. The compareTo method returns 0, a positive integer, or a negative integer, depending on whether one string is equal to, greater than, or less than the other string.

The String class also provides equalsIgnoreCase and regionMatches methods for comparing strings. The equalsIgnoreCase method ignores the case of the letters when determining whether two strings are equal. The regionMatches method compares portions of two strings for equality. You can also use str.startsWith(prefix) to check whether string str starts with a specified prefix, and str.endsWith(suffix) to check whether string str ends with a specified suffix.

7.2.6 String Conversions

The contents of a string cannot be changed once the string is created. But you can convert a string to a new string using the toLowerCase, toUpperCase, trim, and replace methods. The toLowerCase and toUpperCase methods return a new string by converting all the characters in the string to lowercase or uppercase. The trim method returns a new string by eliminating blank characters from both ends of the string. The replace(oldChar, newChar) method can be used to replace a character in the string with a new character.

For example,

```
"Welcome".toLowerCase() returns a new string welcome.
"Welcome".toUpperCase() returns a new string WELCOME.
"  Welcome ".trime() returns a new string Welcome.
"Welcome".toLowerCase() returns a new string welcome.
"Welcome".replace('e', 'A') returns a new string WAlcomA.
```

7.2.7   Finding a Character or a Substring in a String

You can use the indexOf and lastIndexOf methods to find a character or a substring in a string. Four overloaded indexOf methods and four overloaded lastIndexOf methods are defined in the String class.

- public int indexOf(int ch)
  (public int lastIndexOf(int ch))
  Returns the index of the first (last) character in the string that matches the specified character ch. Returns −1 if the specified character is not in the string.

- public int indexOf(int ch, int fromIndex)
  (public int lastIndexOf(int ch, int endIndex))
  Returns the index of the first (last) character in the string starting from (ending at) the specified fromIndex (endIndex) that matches the specified character ch. Returns −1 if the specified character is not in the substring beginning at position fromIndex (ending at position endIndex).

- public int indexOf(String str)
  (public int lastIndexOf(String str))
  Returns the index of the first (last) character of the substring in the string that matches the specified string str. Returns −1 if the str argument is not in the string.

- public int indexOf(String str, int fromIndex)
  (public int lastIndexOf(String str, int endIndex))
  Returns the index of the first (last) character of the substring in the string starting from (ending at) the specified fromIndex (endIndex) that matches the specified string str. Returns −1 if the str argument is not in the substring.

For example,

```
"Welcome to Java".indexOf('W') returns 0.
"Welcome to Java".indexOf('o') returns 4.
"Welcome to Java".indexOf('o', 5) returns 9.
"Welcome to Java".indexOf("come") returns 3.
"Welcome to Java".indexOf("Java", 5) returns 11.
"Welcome to Java".indexOf("java", 5) returns -1.

"Welcome to Java".lastIndexOf('W') returns 0.
"Welcome to Java".lastIndexOf('o') returns 9.
```

```
"Welcome to Java".lastIndexOf('o', 5) returns 4.
"Welcome to Java".lastIndexOf("come") returns 3.
"Welcome to Java".lastIndexOf("Java", 5) returns -1.
"Welcome to Java".lastIndexOf("java", 5) returns -1.
```

7.2.8   Conversion between Strings and Arrays

Strings are not arrays, but a string can be converted into an array and vice versa. To convert a string to an array of characters, use the toCharArray method. For example, the following statement converts the string "Java" to an array.

```
char[] chars = "Java".toCharArray();
```

So chars[0] is 'J', chars[1] is 'a', chars[2] is 'v', and chars[3] is 'a'.

You can also use the getChars(int srcBegin, int srcEnd, char[] dst, int dst-Begin) method to copy a substring of the string from index srcBegin to index srcEnd-1 into a character array dst starting from index dstBegin. For example, the following code copies a substring "3720" in "CS3720" from index 2 to index 6-1 into the character array dst starting from index 4.

```
char[] dst = {'J', 'A', 'V', 'A', '1', '3', '0', '1'};
"CS3720".getChars(2, 6, dst, 4);
```

So, the dst becomes 'J', 'A', 'V', 'A', '3', '7', '2', '0'.

To convert an array of characters into a string, use the String(char[]) constructor or the valueOf(char[]) method. For example, the following statement constructs a string from an array using the String constructor.

```
String str = new String(new char[]{'J', 'a', 'v', 'a'});
```

The following statement constructs a string from an array using the valueOf method.

```
String str = String.valueOf(new char[]{'J', 'a', 'v', 'a'});
```

7.2.9   Converting Characters and Numeric Values to Strings

The valueOf method can be used to convert an array of characters into a string. There are several overloaded versions of the valueOf method that can be used to convert a character and numeric values to strings, with different argument types, char, double, long, int, and float. For example, to convert a double value 5.44 to a string, use String.valueOf(5.44). The return value is a string consisting of the characters '5', '.', '4', and '4'.

 NOTE:

To convert a numeric string to a number, you have used Double.parseDouble(str) or Integer.parseInt(str) to convert a string to a double value or an int value.

Example 7.1 Checking Palindromes

Problem

Write a program that checks whether a string is a palindrome: that is, whether it reads the same forward and backward. The words "mom," "dad," and "noon," for instance, are all palindromes.

Solution

Here is the algorithm to determine whether a string s is a palindrome. Use a loop to check whether the first character in the string is the same as the last character. If so, check whether the second character is the same as the second-last character. This process continues until a mismatch is found or all the characters in the string are checked, except for the middle character if the string has an odd number of characters.

The program prompts the user to enter a string and reports whether the string is a palindrome. The output of a sample run of the program is shown in Figure 7.4.

```java
1    // CheckPalindrome.java: Check whether a string is a palindrome
2    package chapter7;
3
4    import javax.swing.JOptionPane;
5
6    public class CheckPalindrome {
7      /** Main method */
8      public static void main(String[] args) {
9        // Prompt the user to enter a string
10       String s = JOptionPane.showInputDialog(null,
11         "Enter a string:", "Example 7.1 Input",
12         JOptionPane.QUESTION_MESSAGE);
13
14       // Declare and initialize output string
15       String output = "";
16
17       if (isPalindrome(s))
18         output += s + " is a palindrome";
19       else
20         output += s + " is not a palindrome";
21
22       // Display the result
23       JOptionPane.showMessageDialog(null, output,
24         "Example 7.1 Output", JOptionPane.INFORMATION_MESSAGE);
25
26       System.exit(0);
27     }
28
29     /** Check if a string is a palindrome */
30     public static boolean isPalindrome(String s) {
31       // The index of the first character in the string
32       int low = 0;
33
34       // The index of the last character in the string
35       int high = s.length() - 1;
36
37       while (low < high) {
38         if (s.charAt(low) != s.charAt(high))
39           return false; // Not a palindrome
40
```

```
41          low++;
42          high--;
43        }
44
45        return true; // The string is a palindrome
46      }
47    }
```

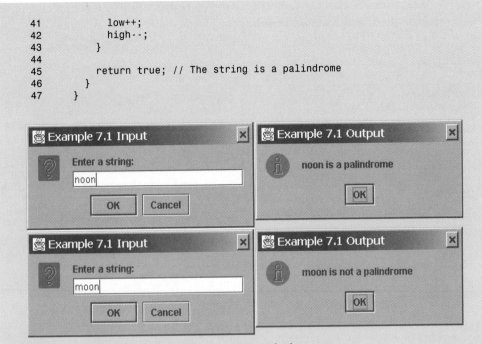

Figure 7.4 *The program checks whether a string is a palindrome.*

Review

The `isPalindrome` method uses a `while` loop (Lines 37–43) to compare characters and determine whether a string is a palindrome.

Alternatively, you can create a new string that is a reversal of the original string. If both strings have the same contents, the original string is a palindrome. The `String` class does not have a method for reversing a string. You can create a method of your own to return a reversed string (see Exercise 7.1) or you can use the `reverse` method provided in the `StringBuffer` class. Example 7.3 uses `StringBuffer` and the `reverse` method to determine whether a string is a palindrome.

7.3 The *Character* Class

Java provides a wrapper class for every primitive data type. These classes are `Character`, `Boolean`, `Byte`, `Short`, `Integer`, `Long`, `Float`, and `Double` for `char`, `boolean`, `byte`, `short`, `int`, `long`, `float`, and `double`. All these classes are in the `java.lang` package. They enable the primitive data values to be treated as objects. They also contain useful methods for processing primitive values. This section introduces the `Character` class. The other wrapper classes will be introduced in Chapter 9, "Abstract Classes and Interfaces."

The Character class has a constructor and more than thirty methods for manipulating a character. The most frequently used methods are shown in Figure 7.5.

Character	
+Character(value: char)	Constructs a character object with char value.
+charValue(): char	Returns the char value from this object.
+compareTo(anotherCharacter: Character): int	Compares this character with another.
+equals(anotherCharacter: Character): boolean	Returns true if this character equals to another.
+isDigit(ch: char): boolean	Returns true if the specified character is a digit.
+isLetter(ch: char): boolean	Returns true if the specified character is a letter.
+isLetterOrDigit(ch: char): boolean	Returns true if the character is a letter or a digit.
+isLowerCase(ch: char): boolean	Returns true if the character is a lowercase letter.
+isUpperCase(ch: char): boolean	Returns true if the character is an uppercase letter.
+toLowerCase(ch: char): char	Returns the lowercase of the specified character.
+toUpperCase(ch: char): char	Returns the uppercase of the specified character.

Figure 7.5   *The* Character *class provides the methods for manipulating a character.*

You can create a Character object from a char value. For example, the following statement creates a Character object for the character 'a'.

```
Character character = new Character('a');
```

The charValue method returns the character value wrapped in the Character object. The compareTo method compares this character with another character and returns an integer that is the difference between the Unicodes of this character and the other character. The equals method returns true if and only if the two characters are the same. For example, suppose charObject is new Character('b').

```
charObject.compareTo(new Character('a')) returns 1
charObject.compareTo(new Character('b')) returns 0
charObject.compareTo(new Character('c')) returns -1
charObject.compareTo(new Character('d') returns -2
charObject.equals(new Character('b')) returns true
charObject.equals(new Character('d')) returns false
```

Most of the methods in the Character class are static methods. The isDigit(char ch) method returns true if the character is a digit. The isLetter(char ch) method returns true if the character is a letter. The isLetterOrDigit(char ch) method is true if the character is a letter or a digit. The isLowerCase(char ch) method is true if the character is a lowercase letter. The isUpperCase(char ch) method is true if the character is an uppercase letter. The toLowerCase(char ch) method returns the lowercase letter for the character, and the toUpperCase(char ch) method returns the uppercase letter for the character.

Example 7.2 Counting Each Letter in a String

Problem

Write a program that counts the number of occurrences of each letter in a string regardless of case.

Solution

Here are the steps to solve this problem:

1. Convert all uppercase letters to lowercase in a string using the toLowerCase method in the String class.

2. Create an array of twenty-six int values, each of which counts the occurrences of a letter. For each character in the string, check whether it is a lowercase letter. If so, increment the corresponding count in the array.

The program is shown below, and the output of a sample run is shown in Figure 7.6.

```
1   // CountEachLetter.java: Count letters in the string
2   package chapter7;
3
4   import javax.swing.JOptionPane;
5
6   public class CountEachLetter {
7     /** Main method */
8     public static void main(String[] args) {
9       // Prompt the user to enter a string
10      String s = JOptionPane.showInputDialog(null,
11        "Enter a string:", "Example 7.2 Input",
12        JOptionPane.QUESTION_MESSAGE);
13
14      // Invoke the countLetters method to count each letter
15      int[] count = countLetters(s.toLowerCase());
16
17      // Declare and initialize output string
18      String output = "";
19
20      // Display results
21      for (int i = 0; i < count.length; i++) {
22        if (count[i] != 0)
23          output += (char)('a' + i) + " appears   " +
24            count[i] + ((count[i] == 1) ? " time\n" : " times\n");
25      }
26
27      // Display the result
28      JOptionPane.showMessageDialog(null, output,
29        "Example 7.2 Output", JOptionPane.INFORMATION_MESSAGE);
30
31      System.exit(0);
32    }
33
34    // Count each letter in the string
35    public static int[] countLetters(String s) {
36      int[] count = new int[26];
37
```

continues

Example 7.2 Continued

```
38              for (int i = 0; i < s.length(); i++) {
39                if (Character.isLetter(s.charAt(i)))
40                  count[(int)(s.charAt(i) - 'a')]++;
41              }
42
43              return count;
44            }
45          }
```

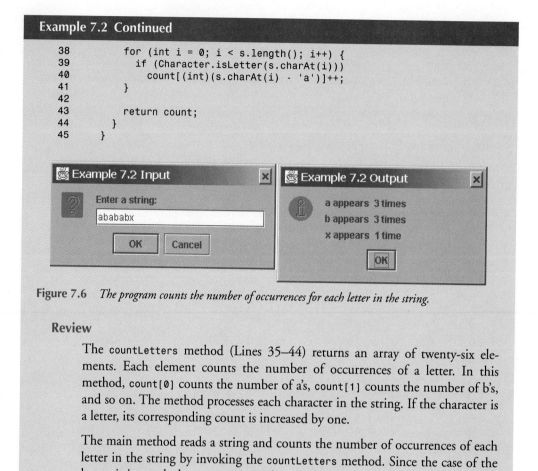

Figure 7.6   *The program counts the number of occurrences for each letter in the string.*

Review

The countLetters method (Lines 35–44) returns an array of twenty-six elements. Each element counts the number of occurrences of a letter. In this method, count[0] counts the number of a's, count[1] counts the number of b's, and so on. The method processes each character in the string. If the character is a letter, its corresponding count is increased by one.

The main method reads a string and counts the number of occurrences of each letter in the string by invoking the countLetters method. Since the case of the letters is ignored, the program uses the toLowerCase method to convert a string into all lowercase and pass the new string to the countLetters method.

7.4   The *StringBuffer* Class

The StringBuffer class is an alternative to the String class. In general, a string buffer can be used wherever a string is used. StringBuffer is more flexible than String. You can add, insert, or append new contents into a string buffer, whereas the value of a string is fixed once the string is created.

The StringBuffer class has three constructors and more than thirty methods for managing the buffer and modifying strings in the buffer. The most frequently used methods are listed in Figure 7.7.

7.4.1   Constructing a String Buffer

The StringBuffer class provides three constructors:

■   public StringBuffer()
     Constructs a string buffer with no characters in it and an initial capacity of sixteen characters.

318

StringBuffer
+StringBuffer()
+StringBuffer(capacity: int)
+StringBuffer(str: String)
+append(data: char[]): StringBuffer
+append(data: char[], offset: int, len: int): StringBuffer
+append(v: aPrimitiveType): StringBuffer
+append(str: String): StringBuffer
+capacity(): int
+charAt(index: int): char
+delete(startIndex: int, endIndex: int): StringBuffer
+deleteCharAt(int index): StringBuffer
+insert(index: int, data: char[], offset: int, len: int): StringBuffer
+insert(offset: int, data: char[]): StringBuffer
+insert(offset: int, b: aPrimitiveType): StringBuffer
+insert(offset: int, str: String): StringBuffer
+length(): int
+replace(int startIndex, int endIndex, String str): StringBuffer
+reverse(): StringBuffer
+setCharAt(index: int, ch: char): void
+setLength(newLength: int): void
+substring(startIndex: int): String
+substring(startIndex: int, endIndex: int): String

Descriptions:
Constructs an empty string buffer with capacity 16.
Constructs a string buffer with the specified capacity.
Constructs a string buffer with the specified string.
Appends a char array into this string buffer.
Appends a subarray in data into this string buffer.
Appends a primitive type value as a string to this buffer.
Appends a string to this string buffer.
Returns the capacity of this string buffer.
Returns the character at the specified index.
Deletes characters from startIndex to endIndex.
Deletes a character at the specified index.
Inserts a subarray of the data in the array to the buffer at the specified index.
Inserts data to this buffer at the position offset.
Inserts a value converted to a string into this buffer.
Inserts a string into this buffer at the position offset.
Returns the number of characters in this buffer.
Replaces the characters in this buffer from startIndex to endIndex with the specified string.
Reverses the characters in the buffer.
Sets a new character at the specified index in this buffer.
Sets a new length in this buffer.
Returns a substring starting at startIndex.
Returns a substring from startIndex to endIndex.

Figure 7.7 *The* StringBuffer *class provides the methods for processing a string buffer.*

■ `public StringBuffer(int length)`
Constructs a string buffer with no characters in it and an initial capacity specified by the length argument.

■ `public StringBuffer()`
Constructs a string buffer for the string argument. The initial capacity of the string buffer is sixteen plus the length of the string argument.

7.4.2 Modifying Strings in the Buffer

You can append new contents at the end of a string buffer, insert new contents at a specified position in a string buffer, and delete or replace characters in a string buffer.

The StringBuffer class provides several overloaded methods to append boolean, char, char array, double, float, int, long, and String into a string buffer. For example, the following code appends strings and characters into strBuf to form a new string, "Welcome to Java".

```
StringBuffer strBuf = new StringBuffer();
strBuf.append("Welcome");
strBuf.append(' ');
strBuf.append("to");
strBuf.append(' ');
strBuf.append("Java");
```

The StringBuffer class also contains overloaded methods to insert boolean, char, char array, double, float, int, long, and String into a string buffer. Consider the following code:

```
strBuf.insert(11, "HTML and ");
```

Suppose strBuf contains "Welcome to Java" before the insert() method is applied. This code inserts "HTML and " at position 11 in strBuf (just before J). The new strBuf is "Welcome to HTML and Java".

You can also delete characters from a string in the buffer using the two delete methods, reverse the string using the reverse method, replace characters using the replace method, or set a new character in a string using the setCharAt method.

For example, suppose strBuf contains "Welcome to Java" before each of the following methods is applied.

```
strBuf.delete(8, 11) changes the buffer to Welcome Java.
strBuf.deleteCharAt(8) changes the buffer to Welcome o Java.
strBuf.reverse() changes the buffer to avaJ ot emocleW.
strBuf.replace(11, 15, "HTML") changes the buffer to Welcome to HTML.
strBuf.setCharAt(0, 'w') sets the buffer to welcome to Java.
```

 NOTE

All these modification methods except setCharAt do two things: (1) change the contents of the string buffer, (2) return the reference of the string buffer. A method with nonvoid return value type can also be invoked as a statement in Java, if you are not interested in the return value of the method. In this case, the return value is simply ignored.

 TIP

If a string does not require any change, use String rather than StringBuffer. Java can perform some optimizations for String, such as sharing canonical strings.

7.4.3   The *toString, capacity, length, setLength,* and *charAt* Methods

The StringBuffer class provides many other methods for manipulating string buffers.

- The toString() method returns the string from the string buffer.

- The capacity() method returns the current capacity of the string buffer. The capacity is the number of characters it is able to store.

- The length() method returns the number of characters actually stored in the string buffer.

- The setLength(newLength) method sets the length of the string buffer. If the newLength argument is less than the current length of the string buffer, the string buffer is truncated to contain exactly the number of characters given by the newLength argument. If the newLength argument is greater than or equal to the current length, sufficient null characters ('\u0000') are appended to the string buffer so that length becomes the newLength argument. The newLength argument must be greater than or equal to 0.

■ The `charAt(index)` method returns the character at a specific index in the string buffer. The first character of a string buffer is at index 0, the next at index 1, and so on. The index argument must be greater than or equal to 0, and less than the length of the string buffer.

NOTE

The length of the string is always less than or equal to the capacity of the buffer. The length is the actual size of the string stored in the buffer, and the capacity is the current size of the buffer. The buffer is dynamically increased if more characters are added to exceed its capacity. Internally, a string buffer is an array of characters, so the buffer's capacity is the size of the array. If the buffer's capacity is exceeded, the array is replaced by a new array. The new array size is 2 * (the previous array size + 1).

NOTE

Many of the methods in the `StringBuffer` class are synchronized to ensure that the contents of `StringBuffer` are not corrupted when running with multiple threads. (Synchronization will be introduced in Chapter 18, "Multithreading.")

Example 7.3 Ignoring Non-alphanumeric Characters When Checking Palindromes

Problem

Example 7.1, "Checking Palindromes," considered all the characters in a string to check whether it was a palindrome. Write a new program that ignores non-alphanumeric characters in checking whether a string is a palindrome.

Solution

Here are the steps to solve the problem:

1. Filter the string by removing the non-alphanumeric characters. This can be done by creating an empty string buffer, adding each alphanumeric character in the string to a string buffer, and returning the string from the string buffer. You can use the `isLetterOrDigit(ch)` method in the `Character` class to check whether character `ch` is a letter or a digit.

2. Obtain a new string that is the reversal of the filtered string. Compare the reversed string with the filtered string using the `equals` method.

The program is shown below, and the output of a sample run is shown in Figure 7.8.

```
1    // PalindromeIgnoreNonAlphanumeric.java
2    package chapter7;
3
4    import javax.swing.JOptionPane;
5
6    public class PalindromeIgnoreNonAlphanumeric {
7      /** Main method */
```

continues

Example 7.3 Continued

```
 8      public static void main(String[] args) {
 9        // Prompt the user to enter a string
10        String s = JOptionPane.showInputDialog(null,
11          "Enter a string:", "Example 7.3 Input",
12          JOptionPane.QUESTION_MESSAGE);
13
14        // Declare and initialize output string
15        String output = "Ignoring non-alphanumeric characters, \nis "
16          + s + " a palindrome? " + isPalindrome(s);
17
18        // Display the result
19        JOptionPane.showMessageDialog(null, output,
20          "Example 7.3 Output", JOptionPane.INFORMATION_MESSAGE);
21
22        System.exit(0);
23      }
24
25      /** Return true if a string is a palindrome */
26      public static boolean isPalindrome(String s) {
27        // Create a new string by eliminating non-alphanumeric chars
28        String s1 = filter(s);
29
30        // Create a new string that is the reversal of s1
31        String s2 = reverse(s1);
32
33        // Compare if the reversal is the same as the original string
34        return s2.equals(s1);
35      }
36
37      /** Create a new string by eliminating non-alphanumeric chars */
38      public static String filter(String s) {
39        // Create a string buffer
40        StringBuffer strBuf = new StringBuffer();
41
42        // Examine each char in the string to skip alphanumeric char
43        for (int i = 0; i < s.length(); i++) {
44          if (Character.isLetterOrDigit(s.charAt(i))) {
45            strBuf.append(s.charAt(i));
46          }
47        }
48
49        // Return a new filtered string
50        return strBuf.toString();
51      }
52
53      /** Create a new string by reversing a specified string */
54      public static String reverse(String s) {
55        StringBuffer s1 = new StringBuffer(s);
56        s1.reverse(); // Use the reverse method for StringBuffer object
57        return s1.toString();
58      }
59    }
```

Review

The filter(String s) method (Lines 38–51) examines each character in string
s and copies it to a string buffer if the character is a letter or a numeric character.
The filter method returns the string in the buffer. The reverse(String s)
method (Lines 54–58) creates a new string that reverses the specified string s.

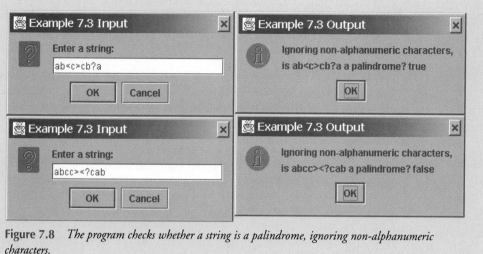

Figure 7.8 *The program checks whether a string is a palindrome, ignoring non-alphanumeric characters.*

The `filter` and `reverse` methods both return a new string. The original string is not changed.

The program in Example 7.1 checks whether a string is a palindrome by comparing pairs of characters from both ends of the string. Example 7.3 uses the `reverse` method in the `StringBuffer` class to reverse the string, then compares whether the two strings are equal to determine whether the original string is a palindrome.

7.5   The *StringTokenizer* Class

Another useful class related to processing strings is the `java.util.StringTokenizer` class. This class is used to break a string into pieces so that information contained in it can be retrieved and processed. For example, to get all of the words in a string like `"I am learning Java now"`, you create an instance of the `StringTokenizer` class for the string and then retrieve individual words in the string by using the methods in the `StringTokenizer` class. The constructors and methods in `StringTokenizer` are shown in Figure 7.9.

StringTokenizer	
+StringTokenizer(str: String)	Constructs a string tokenizer for the string.
+StringTokenizer(str: String, delim: String)	Constructs a string tokenizer for the string with the specified delimiters.
+StringTokenizer(str: String, delim: String, returnDelims: boolean)	Constructs a string tokenizer for the string with the delimiters and returnDelims.
+countTokens(): int	Returns the number of remaining tokens.
+hasMoreTokens():boolean	Returns true if there are more tokens left.
+nextToken(): String	Returns the next token.
+nextToken(delim: String): String	Returns the next token using new delimiters.

Figure 7.9 *The* `StringTokenizer` *class provides the methods for processing tokens in a string.*

How does the `StringTokenizer` class recognize individual words? You can specify a set of characters as delimiters when constructing a `StringTokenizer` object. The delimiters break a string into pieces known as *tokens*. You can specify delimiters in the `StringTokenizer` constructors:

- **■** `public StringTokenizer(String s, String delim, boolean returnDelims)`
  Constructs a `StringTokenizer` for string s with specified delimiters. Each character in the string `delim` is a delimiter. If `returnDelims` is `true`, the delimiter is considered to be a token.

- **■** `public StringTokenizer(String s, String delim)`
  Constructs a `StringTokenizer` for string s with specified delimiters `delim`, and the delimiters are discarded.

- **■** `public StringTokenizer(String s)`
  Constructs a `StringTokenizer` for string s with default delimiters `" \t\n\r"` (a space, tab, new line, and carriage return), and the delimiters are discarded.

The following instance methods in the `StringTokenizer` class can be used to process tokens. The `hasMoreTokens()` method returns `true` if there is a token left in the string. The `nextToken()` method returns the next token in the string. The `nextToken(String delim)` method returns the next token in the string after resetting the delimiter to `delim`. The `countTokens()` method returns the number of tokens remaining in the string tokenizer.

Example 7.4 Testing `StringTokenizer`

Problem

Write a program that uses a string tokenizer to retrieve words from the string `"I am learning Java. Show me how to use StringTokenizer."` and display them on the console.

Solution

The program creates an instance of `StringTokenizer` for the string `"I am learning Java. Show me how to use StringTokenizer."` It then uses a loop to repeatedly extract tokens until all the tokens are extracted. The source code is shown below, and the output of a sample run is shown in Figure 7.10.

```
1    // TestStringTokenizer.java: Demonstrate StringTokenizer
2    package chapter7;
3
4    import java.util.StringTokenizer;
5
6    public class TestStringTokenizer {
7      /** Main method */
8      public static void main(String[] args) {
9        // Create a string and string tokenizer
10       String s =
11         "I am learning Java. Show me how to use StringTokenizer.";
12       StringTokenizer st = new StringTokenizer(s);
13
```

```
14          // Retrieve and display tokens
15          System.out.println("The total number of words is " +
16            st.countTokens());
17
18          while (st.hasMoreTokens())
19            System.out.println(st.nextToken());
20
21          System.out.println("Any tokens left? " + st.countTokens());
22        }
23    }
```

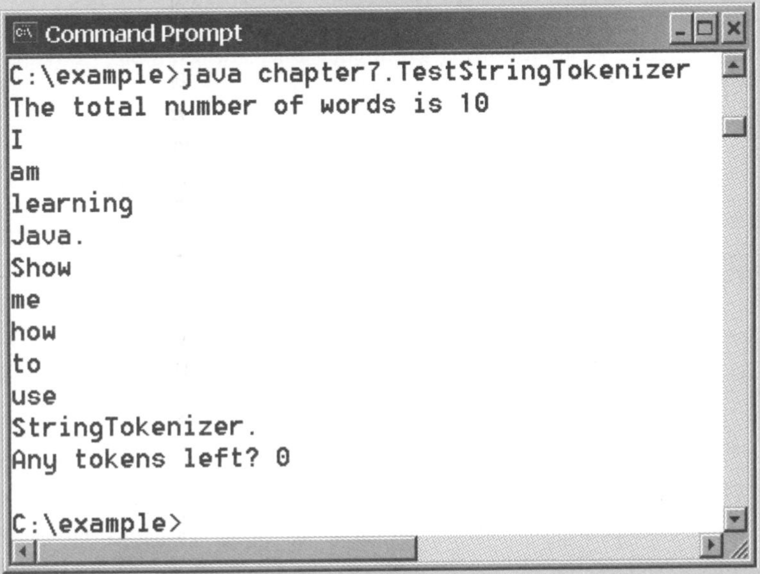

```
Command Prompt

C:\example>java chapter7.TestStringTokenizer
The total number of words is 10
I
am
learning
Java.
Show
me
how
to
use
StringTokenizer.
Any tokens left? 0

C:\example>
```

Figure 7.10   *The program uses the* StringTokenizer *class to extract tokens from a string.*

Review

The String class and StringBuffer class are in the java.lang package, so they are automatically imported. But since the StringTokenizer class is in the java.util package, you need to import it (Line 4).

st.countTokens() (Line 16) returns the number of tokens remaining in the string tokenizer st. After all the tokens are read, st.countTokens() is 0.

If you create a StringTokenizer instance as follows:

```
StringTokenizer st = new StringTokenizer(s, ". \n\t\r");
```

the same words will be displayed in the program, but the dot will not be shown, since the dot (.) is now a delimiter.

7.6   Command-Line Arguments

Perhaps you have already noticed the unusual declarations for the main method, which has parameter args of String[] type. It is clear that args is an array of strings. The main method is just like a regular method with parameters. You can call a regular method by passing actual parameters. Can you pass parameters to main? This section will discuss how to pass and process arguments from the command line.

7.6.1   Passing Arguments to Java Programs

You can pass arguments to a Java program from the command line when you run the program. The following command line, for example, starts the program TestMain with three arguments: arg0, arg1, and arg2:

```
java TestMain arg0 arg1 arg2
```

These arguments are strings, but they don't have to appear in double quotes on the command line. The arguments are separated by a space. If an argument itself contains a space, you must use double quotes to group all of the items in the argument. Consider the following command line:

```
java TestMain "First num" alpha 53
```

It starts the program with three arguments: "First num" and alpha, which are strings, and 53, a numeric string. Note that 53 is actually treated as a string. You can use "53" instead of 53 in the command line.

When the main method is invoked, the Java interpreter creates an array to hold the command-line arguments and pass the array reference to args. For example, if you invoke a program with n arguments, the Java interpreter creates an array like this:

```
args = new String[n];
```

The Java interpreter then passes args to invoke the main method.

 NOTE

If you run the program with no arguments, the array is created with new String[0].
In this case, the array is empty with length 0. args references to this empty array.
Therefore, args is not null, but args.length is 0.

7.6.2   Processing Command-Line Parameters

The arguments passed to the main program are stored in args, which is an array of strings. The first parameter is represented by args[0], and args.length is the number of arguments passed.

Example 7.5 Using Command-Line Parameters

Problem

Write a program that performs binary operations on integers. The program receives three arguments: an integer followed by an operator and another integer. For example, to add two integers, use this command:

```
java Calculator 2 + 3
```

The program will display the following output:

```
2 + 3 = 5
```

Solution

Here are the steps for the program:

1. Use args.length to determine whether three arguments have been provided in the command line. If not, terminate the program using System.exit(0).

2. Perform a binary arithmetic operation on the operands args[0] and args[2] using the operator specified in args[1].

The output of sample runs of the program is shown in Figure 7.11.

```
1    // Calculator.java: Pass parameters from the command line
2    package chapter7;
3
4    public class Calculator {
5      /** Main method */
6      public static void main(String[] args) {
7        // Check command-line arguments
8        if (args.length != 3) {
9          System.out.println(
10           "Usage: java Calculator operand1 operator operand2");
11         System.exit(0);
12       }
13
14       // The result of the operation
15       int result = 0;
16
17       // Determine the operator
18       switch (args[1].charAt(0)) {
19         case '+': result = Integer.parseInt(args[0]) +
20                            Integer.parseInt(args[2]);
21                 break;
22         case '-': result = Integer.parseInt(args[0]) -
23                            Integer.parseInt(args[2]);
24                 break;
25         case '*': result = Integer.parseInt(args[0]) *
26                            Integer.parseInt(args[2]);
27                 break;
28         case '/': result = Integer.parseInt(args[0]) /
29                            Integer.parseInt(args[2]);
30       }
31
```

continues

327

Example 7.5 Continued

```
32          // Display result
33          System.out.println(args[0] + ' ' + args[1] + ' ' + args[2]
34            + " = " + result);
35        }
36    }
```

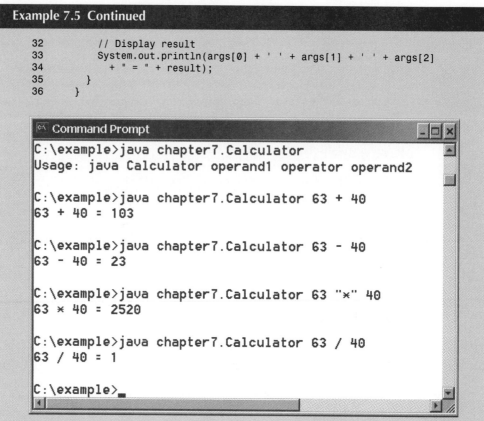

```
C:\example>java chapter7.Calculator
Usage: java Calculator operand1 operator operand2

C:\example>java chapter7.Calculator 63 + 40
63 + 40 = 103

C:\example>java chapter7.Calculator 63 - 40
63 - 40 = 23

C:\example>java chapter7.Calculator 63 "*" 40
63 * 40 = 2520

C:\example>java chapter7.Calculator 63 / 40
63 / 40 = 1

C:\example>
```

Figure 7.11   *The program takes three arguments (operand1 operator operand2) from the command line and displays the expression and the result of the arithmetic operation.*

Review

`Integer.parseInt(args[0])` (Line 19) converts a digital string into an integer. The string must consist of digits. If not, the program will terminate abnormally.

In the sample run, `"*"` had to be used instead of `*` for the command

```
java Calculator 63 "*" 40
```

In JDK 1.1 and above, the `*` symbol refers to all the files in the current directory when it is used on a command line. Therefore, in order to specify the multiplication operator, the `*` must be enclosed in quote marks in the command line. The following program displays all the files in the current directory when issuing the command `java Test *`:

```
public class Test {
  public static void main(String[] args) {
    for (int i = 0; i < args.length; i++)
      System.out.println(args[i]);
  }
}
```

328

You can pass arguments from JBuilder by setting the application parameters in the Runtime Configurations Properties dialog box, as shown in Figure 7.12. To display this dialog, choose *Edit* in the Run tab of the Project Properties dialog box.

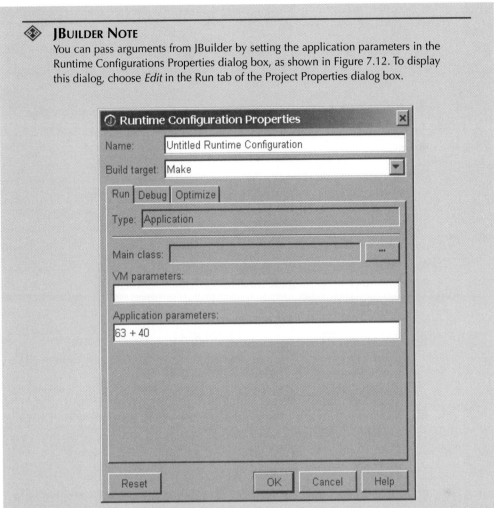

Figure 7.12 *You can pass the parameters for the main method from the Runtime Configuration Properties dialog box if you run the program from JBuilder.*

Chapter Summary

■ Strings are objects encapsulated in the String class. A string can be constructed using one of the eleven constructors or using a string literal shorthand notation.

■ A string that is created using the shorthand notation is known as a *canonical string*. If two identical strings are created using the shorthand notation, they share the same canonical string.

■ A String object is immutable; its contents cannot be changed. To improve efficiency and save memory, Java Virtual Machine stores two String objects in the same object if they were created with the same string literal using the shorthand notation. Therefore, the shorthand notation is preferred in creating strings.

■ You can get the length of a string by invoking its `length()` method, and retrieve a character at the specified `index` in the string using the `charAt(index)` method.

■ You can use the `concat` method to concatenate two strings, or the plus ($+$) sign to concatenate two or more strings.

■ You can use the `substring` method to extract a substring from the string.

■ You can use the `equals` and `compareTo` methods to compare strings. The `equals` method returns `true` if two strings are equal, and `false` if they are not equal. The `compareTo` method returns `0`, a positive integer, or a negative integer, depending on whether one string is equal to, greater than, or less than the other string.

■ The `Character` class is a wrapper class for a single character. The `Character` class provides useful static methods to determine whether a character is a letter (`isLetter(char)`), a digit (`isDigit(char)`), uppercase (`isUpperCase(char)`), or lowercase (`isLowerCase(char)`).

■ The `StringBuffer` class can be used to replace the `String` class. The `String` object is immutable, but you can add, insert, or append new contents into a `StringBuffer` object. Use `String` if the string contents do not require any change, and use `StringBuffer` if they change.

■ The `StringTokenizer` class is used to retrieve and process tokens in a string. You learned the role of delimiters, how to create a `StringTokenizer` from a string, and how to use the `countTokens`, `hasMoreTokens`, and `nextToken` methods to process a string tokenizer.

■ You can pass arguments to the *main* method from the command line. Arguments passed to the main program are stored in `args`, which is an array of strings. The first parameter is represented by `args[0]`, and `args.length` is the number of arguments passed.

Review Questions

7.1 Suppose that s1, s2, s3, and s4 are three strings, given as follows:

```
String s1 = "Welcome to Java";
String s2 = s1;
String s3 = new String("Welcome to Java");
String s4 = s3.intern();
```

What are the results of the following expressions?

```
s1 == s2
s2 == s3
s1.equals(s2)
```

```
s2.equals(s3)
s1.compareTo(s2)
s2.compareTo(s3)
s1 == s4
s1.charAt(0)
s1.indexOf('j')
s1.indexOf("to")
s1.lastIndexOf('a')
s1.lastIndexOf("o", 15)
s1.length()
s1.substring(5)
s1.substring(5, 11)
s1.toLowerCase()
```

7.2 Suppose that s1 and s2 are two strings. Which of the following statements or expressions are incorrect?

```
String s = new String("new string");
String s3 = s1 + s2;
String s3 = s1 - s2;
s1 == s2;
s1 >= s2;
s1.compareTo(s2);
int i = s1.length();
char c = s1(0);
char c = s1.charAt(s1.length());
```

7.3 How do you compare whether two strings are equal without considering cases?

7.4 How do you convert all the letters in a string to uppercase? How do you convert all the letters in a string to lowercase?

7.5 Suppose string s is created using new String(); what is s.length()?

7.6 How do you convert a char, an array of characters, or a number to a string?

7.7 How do you determine whether a character is a lowercase letter?

7.8 How do you determine whether a character is alphanumeric?

7.9 How do you create a string buffer for a string? How do you get the string from a string buffer?

7.10 Write three statements to reverse a string s using the reverse method in the StringBuffer class.

7.11 Write three statements to delete a substring from a string s of twenty characters, starting at index 4 and ending with index 10. Use the delete method in the StringBuffer class.

7.12 What is the internal structure of a string and a string buffer?

7.13 Declare a StringTokenizer for a string s with slash (/) and backslash (\) as delimiters.

7.14 What is the output of the following program?

```
import java.util.StringTokenizer;

class TestStringTokenizer {
  public static void main(String[] args) {
    //create a string and string tokenizer
    String s = "I/am\learning Java.";
    StringTokenizer st = new StringTokenizer(s, "/\.");

    //retrieve and display tokens
    while (st.hasMoreTokens())
      System.out.print(st.nextToken() + " ");
  }
}
```

7.15 Why does the following code cause the `NullPointerException` runtime error?

```
1    public class Test  {
2      private String text;
3
4      public Test(String s) {
5        String text  = s;
6      }
7
8      public static void main(String[] args) {
9        Test test = new Test("ABC");
10       System.out.println(test.text.toLowerCase());
11     }
12   }
```

7.16 What is wrong in the following program?

```
1    public class Test  {
2      String text;
3
4      public void Test(String s) {
5        this.text  = s;
6      }
7
8      public static void main(String[] args) {
9        Test test = new Test("ABC");
10       System.out.println(test);
11     }
12   }
```

Programming Exercises

7.1 (Revising Example 7.1 "Checking Palindromes") Example 7.1 checks whether a string is a palindrome. Rewrite Example 7.1 to use your own reverse method.

7.2 (Revising Example 7.1 "Checking Palindromes") Rewrite Example 7.1 to ignore cases.

7.3 (Revising Example 7.1 "Checking Palindromes") Rewrite Example 7.1 by passing the string as a command-line argument.

7.4 (Checking substrings) You can check whether a string is a substring of another string by using the `indexOf` method in the `String` class. Write your own method for this function. Write a program that prompts the user to enter two strings, and check whether the first string is a substring of the second.

7.5 (Replacing substrings) Write a method with the following signature that replaces all `oldStr` with `newStr` in the string s, and returns a new string.

```
public static String replace(String oldStr, String newStr,
    String s)
```

For example, `replace("Department", "School", "Computer Science Department")` returns `"Computer Science School"`.

7.6 (Summing integers) Write two programs. The first program passes an unspecified number of integers as separate command-line arguments and displays their total. The second program passes an unspecified number of integers as one command-line argument and displays their total. Name the two programs `Exercise7_6a` and `Exerciase7_6b`, as shown in Figure 7.13.

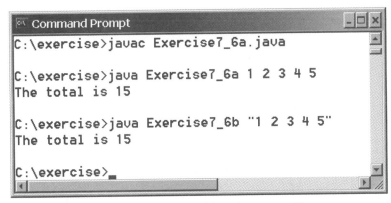

```
C:\exercise>javac Exercise7_6a.java

C:\exercise>java Exercise7_6a 1 2 3 4 5
The total is 15

C:\exercise>java Exercise7_6b "1 2 3 4 5"
The total is 15

C:\exercise>
```

Figure 7.13 *The program adds all numbers passed from the command line.*

7.7 (Finding the number of uppercase letters in a string) Write a program that passes a string as a command-line argument and displays the number of uppercase letters in the string.

7.8 (Revising Example 2.4 "Monetary Units") Rewrite Example 2.3 to receive the input as a string, and extract the dollars and cents using the `StringTokenizer` class.

7.9 (Sorting characters in a string) Write a method that returns a sorted string using the following signature:

```
public static String sort(String s)
```

For example, `sort("acb")` returns abc.

7.10 (Counting the letters in a string) Write a method that counts the number of letters in a string using the following signature:

```
public static int countLetters(String s)
```

7.11 (Anagrams) Write a method that checks whether two strings are anagrams. Two strings are anagrams if they contain the same characters in any order. For example, "silent" and "listen" are anagrams. The signature of the method is as follows:

```
public static boolean isAnagram(String s1, String s2)
```

8

INHERITANCE
AND POLYMORPHISM

Objectives

- To develop a subclass from a superclass through inheritance.

- To override methods in the subclass.

- To invoke the superclass's constructors and methods using the super keyword.

- To restrict access to data and methods using the protected visibility modifier.

- To declare constants, unmodifiable methods, and nonextendable class using the final modifier.

- To explore the useful methods (toString, equals, finalize, getClass, clone, and hashCode) in the Object class.

- To comprehend polymorphism, dynamic binding, and generic programming.

- To describe casting and explain why explicit downcasting is necessary.

- To become familiar with initialization blocks and static initialization blocks (Optional).

8.1   Introduction

Object-oriented programming allows you to derive new classes from existing classes. This is called *inheritance*. Inheritance is an important and powerful concept in Java. In fact, every class you define in Java is inherited from an existing class, either explicitly or implicitly. The classes you created in the preceding chapters were all derived implicitly from the Object class.

This chapter introduces the concept of inheritance. Specifically, it discusses superclasses and subclasses, the use of the keyword super, and the Object class, explores polymorphism and dynamic binding, generic programming, and casting objects, and introduces the modifiers protected and final.

8.2   Superclasses and Subclasses

In Java terminology, a class C1 derived from another class C2 is called a *subclass*, and C2 is called a *superclass*. Sometimes a superclass is referred to as a *parent class* or a *base class*, and a subclass is referred to as a *child class*, an *extended class*, or a *derived class*. A subclass inherits functionality from its superclass, and also creates new data and new methods. Subclasses usually have more functionality than their superclasses.

 NOTE

Contrary to the conventional interpretation, a subclass is not a subset of its superclass. In fact, a subclass is usually extended to contain more functions and more detailed information than its superclass.

Example 8.1 Demonstrating Inheritance

Problem

To demonstrate inheritance, write a program that creates a new class for Cylinder extended from Circle. The Cylinder class inherits all the data and methods from the Circle class. In addition, it has a new data field, length, and a new method, findVolume.

Solution

The relationship of these two classes is shown in Figure 8.1. An arrow pointing to the superclass is used to denote the inheritance relationship between the two classes involved.

The class for cylinder in this example is named Cylinder1 to avoid a naming conflict with an improved version of the *Cylinder* class introduced later in this chapter.

```
1    // Cylinder1.java: Class definition for describing Cylinder
2    package chapter8;
3
4    import chapter6.Circle;
5
```

```
6    public class Cylinder1 extends Circle {
7      private double length;
8
9      /** Default constructor */
10     public Cylinder1() {
11       super(); // Invoke the default superclass constructor
12       length = 1.0;
13     }
14
15     /** Construct a cylinder with specified radius and length */
16     public Cylinder1(double radius, double length) {
17       super(radius); // Invoke superclass constructor Circle(r)
18       this.length = length;
19     }
20
21     /** Return length */
22     public double getLength() {
23       return length;
24     }
25
26     /** Set length */
27     public void setLength(double length) {
28       this.length = length;
29     }
30
31     /** Return the volume of this cylinder */
32     public double findVolume() {
33       return findArea() * length;
34     }
35   }
```

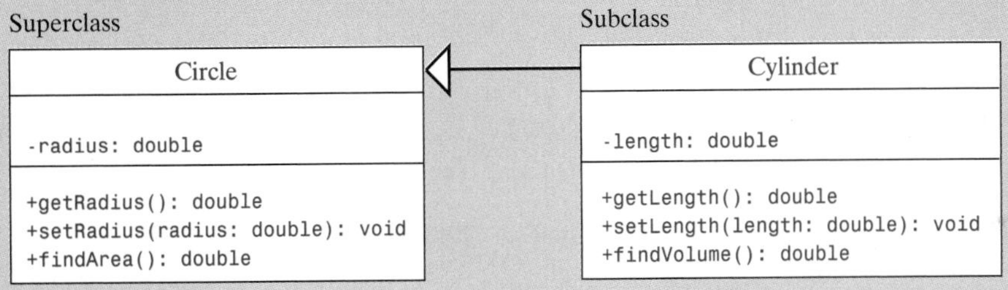

Figure 8.1 *The* Cylinder *class inherits data and methods from the* Circle *class and extends the* Circle *class with its own data and methods.*

The test program creates a cylinder object and explores the relationship between the Cylinder1 class and the Circle class by accessing the data and methods (radius, findArea()) defined in the Circle class and the data and methods (length, findVolume()) defined in the Cylinder1 class. The output of the program is shown in Figure 8.2.

```
1    // TestCylinder.java: Use inheritance.
2    package chapter8;
3
4    public class TestCylinder {
5      public static void main(String[] args) {
6        // Create a cylinder object and display its properties
7        Cylinder1 myCylinder = new Cylinder1(5.0, 2.0);
```

continues

337

Example 8.1 Continued

```
8         System.out.println("The length is " + myCylinder.getLength());
9         System.out.println("The radius is " + myCylinder.getRadius());
10        System.out.println("The volume of the cylinder is " +
11          myCylinder.findVolume());
12        System.out.println("The area of the circle is " +
13          myCylinder.findArea());
14      }
15    }
```

```
Command Prompt                                      _ □ ×
C:\example>java chapter8.TestCylinder
The length is 2.0
The radius is 5.0
The volume of the cylinder is 157.0795
The area of the circle is 78.53975

C:\example>
```

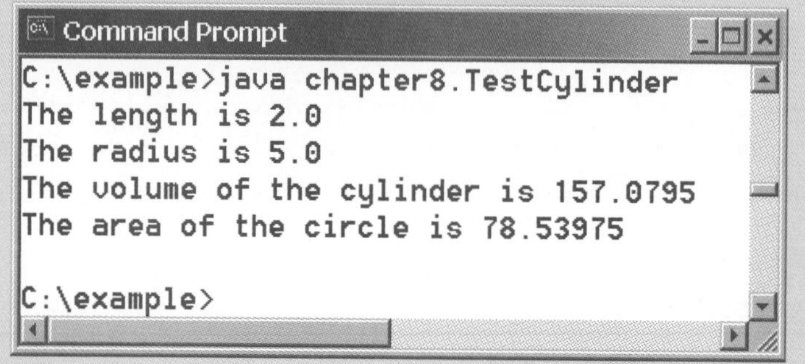

Figure 8.2   *The program creates a cylinder object and accesses the data and methods defined in the* Circle *class and the* Cylinder1 *class.*

Review

The reserved word extends (Line 6) tells the compiler that the Cylinder1 class is derived from the Circle class, thus inheriting data and methods from Circle.

The Cylinder1 class extends the functionality of the Circle class and inherits all the data and methods in Circle. Therefore, it can access the getRadius and findArea methods defined in the Circle class.

The keyword super is used in the constructors (Lines 11 and 17). This keyword is discussed in the next section.

8.3   Using the *super* Keyword

In Chapter 6, "Objects and Classes," you learned to use the this keyword. The this keyword refers to the class itself. The keyword super refers to the superclass of the class in which super appears. It can be used in two ways:

- To call a superclass constructor.
- To call a superclass method.

8.3.1   Calling Superclass Constructors

The syntax to call a superclass constructor is:

```
super(), or super(parameters);
```

The statement `super()` invokes the default constructor of its superclass, and the statement `super(parameters)` invokes the superclass constructor that matches the parameters. The statement `super()` or `super(parameters)` must appear in the first line of the subclass constructor and is the only way to invoke a superclass constructor.

CAUTION
You must use the keyword `super` to call the superclass constructor, and the call must be the first statement in the constructor. Invoking a superclass constructor's name in a subclass causes a syntax error.

NOTE
A constructor is used to construct an instance of a class. Unlike properties and methods, the constructors of a superclass are not inherited in the subclass. They can only be invoked from the constructors of the subclasses, using the keyword `super`.

NOTE
A constructor may invoke an overloaded constructor or its superclass's constructor. If none of them is invoked explicitly, the compiler puts `super()` as the first statement in the constructor. For example,

```
public A() {
}
```

is equivalent to

```
public A() {
   super();
}
```

In any case, constructing an instance of a class invokes all the superclasses along the inheritance chain. This is called *constructor chaining*. Consider the following code:

```
1   public class C1 extends C2 {
2     public static void main(String[] args) {
3       new C1();
4     }
5
6     public C1() {
7       System.out.println("C1's default constructor is invoked");
8     }
9   }
10
11  class C2 extends C3 {
12    public C2() {
13      this("Invoke C2's overloaded constructor");
14      System.out.println("C2's default constructor is invoked");
15    }
16
17    public C2(String s) {
18      System.out.println("C2's second constructor is invoked");
19    }
```

```
20     }
21
22     class C3 {
23       public C3() {
24         System.out.println("C3's default constructor is invoked");
25       }
26     }
```

In Line 3, new C1() invokes C1's default constructor. Since C1 is a subclass of C2, C2's default constructor is invoked before any statements in C1's constructor are executed. C2's default constructor invokes C2's second constructor (Line 12). Since C2 is a subclass of C3, C3's default constructor is invoked before any statements in C2's second constructor are executed. Therefore, the output of creating an instance of C1 is:

```
C3's default constructor is invoked
C2's second constructor is invoked
C2's default constructor is invoked
C1's default constructor is invoked
```

 NOTE

If a superclass defines constructors other than a default constructor, the subclass cannot use the default constructor of the superclass, because in this case the superclass does not have a default constructor. Consider the following code:

```
1     public class A extends B {
2     }
3
4     class B {
5       public B(String name) {
6         System.out.println("B's constructor is invoked");
7       }
8     }
```

Since no constructor is explicitly defined in A, A's default constructor exists. Since A is a subclass of B, A's default constructor automatically invokes B's default constructor. However, B does not have a default constructor because B has an explicit nondefault constructor defined. Therefore, the program cannot be compiled.

8.3.2   Calling Superclass Methods

The keyword super also can be used to reference a method other than the constructor in the superclass. The syntax is like this:

```
super.method(parameters);
```

You could rewrite the findVolume() method in the Cylinder class as follows:

```
double findVolume() {
  return super.findArea() * length;
}
```

It is not necessary to put super before findArea() in this case, however, because findArea is a method in the Circle class and is inherited by the Cylinder class. Nevertheless, in some cases, like the one in Example 8.2, the keyword super is needed.

8.4   Overriding Methods

A subclass inherits methods from a superclass. Sometimes it is necessary for the subclass to modify the methods defined in the superclass. This is referred to as *method overriding*. The following example demonstrates method overriding.

Example 8.2 Overriding the Methods in a Superclass

Problem

Modify the Cylinder1 class defined in Example 8.1, "Demonstrating Inheritance," to override the findArea method in the Circle class. The findArea method in the Circle class computes the area of a circle, while the findArea method in the new cylinder class computes the surface area of a cylinder.

Solution

The following code gives the solution to the problem. The output of the program is shown in Figure 8.3.

```
1    // TestOverrideMethod.java: Test the Cylinder class that overrides
2    // its superclass's methods.
3    package chapter8;
4
5    public class TestOverrideMethod {
6      public static void main(String[] args) {
7        Cylinder myCylinder = new Cylinder(5.0, 2.0);
8        System.out.println("The length is " + myCylinder.getLength());
9        System.out.println("The radius is " + myCylinder.getRadius());
10       System.out.println("The surface area of the cylinder is " +
11         myCylinder.findArea());
12       System.out.println("The volume of the cylinder is " +
13         myCylinder.findVolume());
14     }
15   }
```

```
1    // Cylinder.java: New cylinder class that overrides the findArea()
2    // method defined in the circle class.
3    package chapter8;
4
5    import chapter6.Circle;
6
7    public class Cylinder extends Circle {
8      /** length of this cylinder */
9      private double length;
10
11     /** Default constructor */
12     public Cylinder() {
13       super(); // Default behavior and can be omitted
14       length = 1.0;
15     }
16
17     /** Construct a cylinder with specified radius and length */
18     public Cylinder(double radius, double length) {
19       super(radius);
20       this.length = length;
21     }
22
```

continues

Example 8.2 Continued

```
23        /** Return length */
24        public double getLength() {
25          return length;
26        }
27
28        /** Set length */
29        public void setLength(double length) {
30          this.length = length;
31        }
32
33        /** Return the surface area of this cylinder. The formula is
34         * 2 * circle area + cylinder body area
35         */
36        public double findArea() {
37          return 2 * super.findArea() + 2 * getRadius() * Math.PI * length;
38        }
39
40        /** Return the volume of this cylinder */
41        public double findVolume() {
42          return super.findArea() * length;
43        }
44
45        /** Override the toString method */
46        public String toString() {
47          return "Cylinder length = " + length +
48            " radius = " + getRadius();
49        }
50    }
```

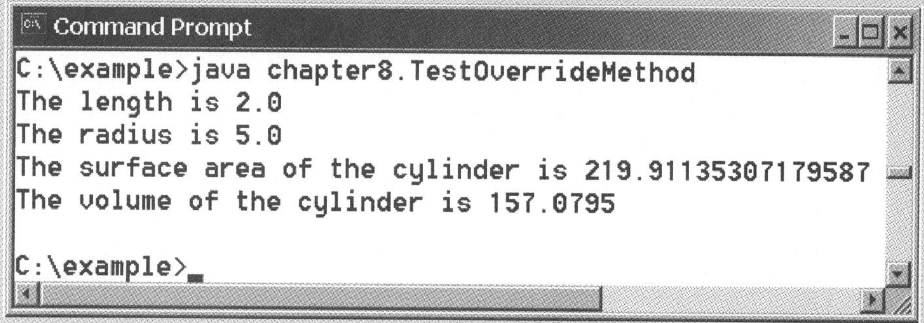

```
Command Prompt                                          _ □ ×
C:\example>java chapter8.TestOverrideMethod
The length is 2.0
The radius is 5.0
The surface area of the cylinder is 219.91135307179587
The volume of the cylinder is 157.0795

C:\example>_
```

Figure 8.3 *The new class for cylinder overrides the* findArea *method defined in the* Circle *class.*

Review

The example demonstrates that you can modify a method from the superclass (Circle) and can use super to invoke a method in the superclass. The findArea method is defined in the Circle class and modified in the Cylinder class. Both methods can be used in the Cylinder class. To invoke the findArea method defined in the Circle class, use super.findArea().

In Line 13 in the Cylinder class, super() is used to invoke its superclass's default constructor. This line can be omitted, since super() is invoked by default if no superclass constructor is invoked explicitly.

A subclass of the `Cylinder` class can no longer access the `findArea` method defined in the `Circle` class because the `findArea` method is redefined in the `Cylinder` class.

NOTE

To override a method, the method must be defined in the subclass using the same signature as in its superclass.

NOTE

An instance method can be overridden only if it is accessible. Thus a private method cannot be overridden, because it is not accessible outside its own class. If a method defined in a subclass is private in its superclass, the two methods are completely unrelated.

NOTE

Like an instance method, a static method can be inherited. However, a static method cannot be overridden. If a static method defined in the superclass is redefined in a subclass, the method defined in the superclass is hidden. Hiding static methods will be further discussed in Section 8.7, "Hiding Fields and Static Methods."

8.4 The *Object* Class

Every class in Java is descended from the `java.lang.Object` class. If no inheritance is specified when a class is defined, the superclass of the class is `Object`. Classes like `String`, `StringBuffer`, `StringTokenizer`, `Loan`, and `Circle` are implicitly the child classes of `Object` (as are all the main classes you have seen in this book so far). It is important to be familiar with the methods provided by the `Object` class so that you can use them in your classes. Three frequently used methods in the `Object` class are:

- `public boolean equals(Object object)`
- `public int hashCode()`
- `public String toString()`

8.4.1 The *equals* Method

The `equals` method tests whether two objects are equal. The syntax for invoking it is:

```
object1.equals(object2);
```

The default implementation of the `equals` method in the `Object` class is:

```
public boolean equals(Object obj) {
  return (this == obj);
}
```

Thus, using the equals method is equivalent to the == operator in the Object class, but it is really intended for the subclasses of the Object class to modify the equals method to test whether two distinct objects have the same content.

You have already used the equals method to compare two strings in Section 7.2, "The String Class." The equals method in the String class is inherited from the Object class and is modified in the String class to test whether two strings are identical in content.

 NOTE

The == comparison operator is used for comparing two primitive data type values or for determining whether two objects have the same references. The equals method is intended to test whether two objects have the same contents, provided that the method is modified in the defining class of the objects. The == operator is stronger than the equals method, in that the == operator checks whether the two reference variables refer to the same object.

8.4.2   The *hashCode* Method

The hashCode method returns the hash code of the object. The hash code is an integer, which can be used to store the object in a hash set so that it can be located quickly. Hash sets will be introduced in Chapter 17, "Java Data Structures." The hashCode implemented in the Object class returns the internal memory address of the object in decimal. Your class should override the hashCode method whenever the equals method is overridden. By contract, if two objects are equal, their hash codes must be same. Two unequal objects may have the same hash code, but you should implement the hashCode method to avoid too many such cases. Additionally, it is required that invoking the hashCode method multiple times returns the same integer during one execution of the program. The integer need not be the same in different executions. For example, the hashCode method is overridden in the String class by returning $s_0 * 31^{(n-1)} + s_1 * 31^{(n-2)} + \cdots + s_{n-1}$ as the hash code, where s_i is s.charAt(i).

8.4.3   The *toString* Method

Invoking toString() on an object returns a string that represents the object. By default, it returns a string consisting of a class name of which the object is an instance, an at sign (@), and the object's hash code in hexadecimal. For example, consider the following code:

```
Cylinder myCylinder = new Cylinder(5.0, 2.0);
System.out.println(myCylinder.toString());
```

The code displays something like Cylinder@15037e5. This message is not very helpful or informative. Usually you should override the toString method so that it returns a digestible string representation of the object. For example, you can override the toString method in the Cylinder class:

```
public String toString() {
  return "Cylinder length = " + length +
```

```
        " radius = " + getRadius();
  }
```

Then `System.out.println(myCylinder.toString())` now displays the following:

```
Cylinder length = 2.0 radius = 5.0
```

 NOTE

Alternatively, you could write `System.out.println(myCylinder)` instead of `System.out.println(myCylinder.toString())`. The Java compiler automatically translates myCylinder into a string by invoking its `toString` method when it is used in the print method.

8.5 Polymorphism, Dynamic Binding, and Generic Programming

The inheritance relationship enables a subclass to inherit features from its superclass with additional new features. A subclass is a specialization of its superclass; every instance of a subclass is an instance of its superclass, but not vice versa. For example, every circle is an object, but not every object is a circle. Therefore, you can always pass an instance of a subclass to a parameter of its superclass type. Consider the following code:

```
1    public class Test {
2      public static void main(String[] args) {
3        m(new GraduateStudent());
4        m(new Student());
5        m(new Person());
6        m(new Object());
7      }
8
9      public static void m(Object x) {
10       System.out.println(x.toString());
11     }
12   }
13
14   class GraduateStudent extends Student {
15   }
16
17   class Student extends Person {
18     public String toString() {
19       return "Student";
20     }
21   }
22
23   class Person extends Object {
24     public String toString() {
25       return "Person";
26     }
27   }
```

Method m (Line 9) takes a parameter of the `Object` type. You can invoke m with any object (e.g., `new GraduateStudent()`, `new Student()`, `new Person()`, and `new Object()`)in Lines 3–6). An object of a subclass can be used by any code designed to work with an object of its superclass. This feature is known as *polymorphism* (from a Greek word meaning "many forms").

When the method m is executed, the argument x's toString method is invoked. x may be an instance of GraduateStudent, Student, Person, or Object. Classes GraduateStudent, Student, Person, and Object have their own implementation of the toString method. Which implementation is used will be determined dynamically by the Java Virtual Machine at runtime. This capability is known as *dynamic binding*.

Dynamic binding works as follows: Suppose an object o is an instance of classes C_1, C_2, ..., C_{n-1}, and C_n, where C_1 is a subclass of C_2, C_2 is a subclass of C_3, ..., and C_{n-1} is a subclass of C_n, as shown in Figure 8.4. That is, C_n is the most general class, and C_1 is the most specific class. In Java, C_n is the Object class. If o invokes a method p, the JVM searches the implementation for the method p in C_1, C_2, ..., C_{n-1}, and C_n, in this order, until it is found. Once an implementation is found, the search stops and the first-found implementation is invoked. For example, when m(new Graduate-Student()) is invoked in Line 3, the toString method defined in the Student class is used.

If o is an instance of C_1, o is also an instance of C_2, C_3, ..., C_{n-1}, and C_n

Figure 8.4   *The method to be invoked is dynamically bound at runtime.*

Polymorphism allows methods to be used generically for a wide range of object arguments. This is known as *generic programming*. If a method's parameter type is a superclass (e.g., Object), you may pass an object to this method of any of the parameter's subclasses (e.g., Student or String). When an object (e.g., a Student object or a String object) is used in the method, the particular implementation of the method of the object that is invoked (e.g., toString) is determined dynamically.

8.6   Casting Objects and the *instanceof* Operator

You have already used the casting operator to convert variables of one primitive type to another. Casting can also be used to convert an object of one class type to another within an inheritance hierarchy. In the preceding section, the statement

```
m(new Student());
```

assigns the object new Student() to a parameter of the Object type. This statement is equivalent to

```
Object o = new Student(); // Implicit casting
m(o);
```

The statement Object o = new Student(), known as *implicit casting*, is legal because an instance of Student is automatically an instance of Object.

Suppose you want to assign the object reference o to a variable of the Student type using the following statement:

```
Student b = o;
```

A compilation error would occur. Why does the statement `Object o = new Student()` work and the statement `Student b = o` doesn't? This is because a `Student` object is always an instance of `Object`, but an `Object` is not necessarily an instance of `Student`. Even though you can see that `o` is really a `Student` object, the compiler is not so clever as to know it. To tell the compiler that `o` is a `Student` object, use an explicit casting. The syntax is similar to the one used for casting among primitive data types. Enclose the target object type in parentheses and place it before the object to be cast, as follows:

```
Student b = (Student)o; // Explicit casting
```

It is always possible to cast an instance of a subclass to a variable of a superclass (known as *upcasting*), because an instance of a subclass is *always* an instance of its superclass. When casting an instance of a superclass to a variable of its subclass (known as *downcasting*), explicit casting must be used to confirm your intention to the compiler with the (`SubclassName`) cast notation. For the casting to be successful, you must make sure that the object to be cast is an instance of the subclass. If the superclass object is not an instance of the subclass, a runtime `ClassCastException` occurs. For example, if an object is not an instance of `Student`, it cannot be cast into a variable of `Student`. It is good practice, therefore, to ensure that the object is an instance of another object before attempting a casting. This can be accomplished by using the `instanceof` operator. Consider the following code:

```
/** Suppose myObject is declared as the Object type */
/** Perform casting if myObject is an instance of Cylinder */
if (myObject instanceof Cylinder) {
  Cylinder myCylinder = (Cylinder)myObject;
  System.out.println("The cylinder volume is " +
    myCylinder.findVolume());
  ...
}
```

You may be wondering why it is necessary to perform casting. The data type of a variable is determined at compile time. The variable `myObject` is declared as an `Object` type. Using `myObject.findVolume()` would cause a compilation error because the `Object` class does not have the `findVolume` method. So it is necessary to cast `myObject` into the `Cylinder` type to invoke the `findVolume` method. So why not declare `myObject` as a `Cylinder` type in the first place? To enable generic programming, it is a good practice to declare a variable with a superclass type, which can accept a value of any subclass type. This is shown in the next example.

 TIP

To help understand casting, you may also consider the analogy of fruit, apple, and orange, with the `Fruit` class as the superclass for `Apple` and `Orange`. An apple is a fruit, so you can always safely assign an instance of `Apple` to a variable for `Fruit`. However, a fruit is not necessarily an apple, so you have to use explicit casting to assign an instance of `Fruit` to a variable of `Apple`.

Example 8.3 Demonstrating Polymorphism and Casting

Problem

Write a program that creates two objects, a circle and a cylinder, and invokes the displayObject method to display them. The displayObject method displays area and perimeter if the object is a circle, and area and volume if the object is a cylinder. The displayObject method also invokes the toString method.

Solution

The following code gives the solution to the problem. A sample run of the program is shown in Figure 8.5.

```
1   // TestPolymorphismCasting.java: Demonstrate casting objects
2   package chapter8;
3
4   import chapter6.Circle;
5
6   public class TestPolymorphismCasting {
7     /** Main method */
8     public static void main(String[] args) {
9       // Declare and initialize two geometric objects
10      Object object1 = new Circle(5);
11      Object object2 = new Cylinder(5, 3);
12
13      // Display circle
14      displayObject(object1);
15      System.out.println();
16
17      // Display cylinder
18      displayObject(object2);
19    }
20
21    /** A method for displaying a geometric object */
22    static void displayObject(Object object) {
23      System.out.println("The toString method returns " +
24          object.toString());
25
26      if (object instanceof Cylinder) {
27        System.out.println("The area is " +
28            ((Cylinder)object).findArea());
29        System.out.println("The volume is " +
30            ((Cylinder)object).findVolume());
31      }
32      else if (object instanceof Circle) {
33        System.out.println("The area is " +
34            ((Circle)object).findArea());
35      }
36    }
37  }
```

Review

The displayObject(Object object) method is an example of generic programming. It can be invoked with any instance of Object.

The program uses implicit casting to assign a Circle object to object1 and a Cylinder object to object2 (Lines 10–11), and then invokes the displayObject method to display the information on these objects (Lines 14, 18).

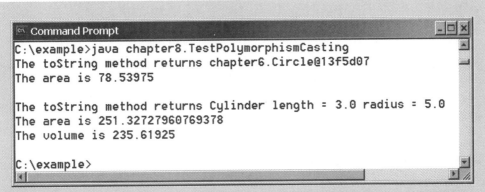

Figure 8.5 *The program creates a* Circle *and a* Cylinder *object, assigns them to variables of the* Object *type, and casts them to* Circle *and* Cylinder *in order to use the methods defined in* Circle *and* Cylinder.

In the displayObject method (Lines 22–36), explicit casting is used to cast the object to Cylinder if the object is an instance of Cylinder, and the methods findArea and findVolume are used to display the area and volume of the cylinder.

Casting can only be done when the source object is an instance of the target class. The program uses the instanceof operator to ensure that the source object is an instance of the target class before performing a casting (Line 26).

Explicit casting to Cylinder (Lines 28, 30) and to Circle (Line 34) is necessary because the findArea and findVolume methods are not available in the Object class.

When the displayObject method is invoked by passing object1 (Line 14), the toString method implemented in Object is invoked (Line 24), because Circle does not implement the toString method. When the displayObject method is invoked by passing object2 (Line 11), the toString method implemented in Cylinder is invoked (Line 24).

Note that the order in the if statement is significant. If it is reversed (e.g., testing whether the object is an instance of Circle first), then the cylinder will never be cast into Cylinder because Cylinder is an instance of Circle. Try to run the program with the following if statement and observe the effect.

```
if (object instanceof Circle) {
  System.out.println("The area is " +
    ((Circle)object).findArea());
}
else if (object instanceof Cylinder) {
  System.out.println("The area is " +
    ((Cylinder)object).findArea());
  System.out.println("The volume is " +
    ((Cylinder)object).findVolume());
}
```

 NOTE

instanceof is a Java keyword. Every letter in a Java keyword is in lowercase.

continues

Example 8.3 Continued

 CAUTION

The object member access operator (.) precedes the casting (`((ClassName)object)`) operator. Use parentheses to ensure that casting is done before the . operator, as in

```
((Cylinder)object).findArea());
```

JBUILDER NOTE

Figure 8.6 shows the contents of `object1` and `object2` in the debugger. `object1` and `object2` are declared as `Object`, but `object1` actually references a `Circle` object and `object2` references a `Cylinder` object. The classes along the inheritance chain are displayed. The data field (e.g., `length: double = 3.0`) defined in the `Cylinder` class is displayed in normal color, and the data field (e.g., `radius: double = 5.0`) defined in the superclass is displayed in light gray color.

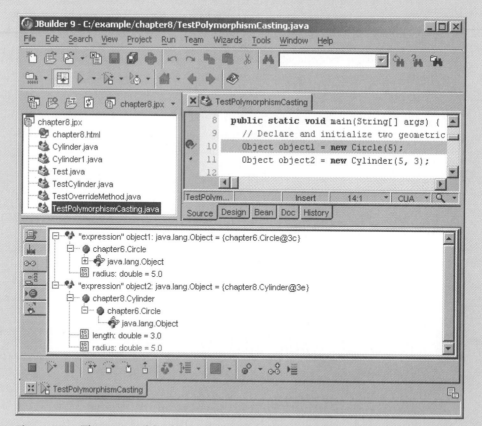

Figure 8.6 *The contents of the objects referenced by* `object1` *and* `object2` *are shown in the debugger.*

8.7   Hiding Fields and Static Methods (Optional)

This section is marked optional because hiding fields and static methods are rarely useful, and in my view they should not be used, for the sake of simplicity and clarity. I recommend skipping this section now and consulting it for reference in the future.

You can override an instance method, but you cannot override a field (instance or static) or a static method. If you declare a field or a static method in a subclass with the same name as one in the superclass, the one in the superclass is hidden, but it still exists. The two fields or static methods are independent. You can reference the hidden field or static method using the super keyword in the subclass. The hidden field or method can also be accessed via a reference variable of the superclass's type.

When invoking an instance method from a reference variable, the *actual class of the object* referenced by the variable decides which implementation of the method is used *at runtime*. When accessing a field or a static method, the *declared type* of the reference variable decides which method is used *at compile time*.

Consider the following example:

```
 1   public class Test {
 2     public static void main(String[] args) {
 3       B x = new A();
 4
 5       // Access s
 6       System.out.println("(1) x.news is " + x.news);
 7       System.out.println("(2) ((A)x).news is " + ((A)x).news);
 8
 9       // Invoke static method smile
10       System.out.println("(3) x.smile() is " + x.smile());
11       System.out.println("(4) ((B)x).smile() is " + ((B)x).smile());
12
13       // Invoke instance method getNews
14       System.out.println("(5) x.getNews() is " + x.getNews());
15       System.out.println("(6) x.getMessage() is " + x.getMessage());
16     }
17   }
18
19   class B {
20     public String news = "B's news";
21     public String message = "B's message";
22
23     public static String smile() {
24       return "smile from B";
25     }
26
27     public String getNews() {
28       return news;
29     }
30
31     public String getMessage() {
32       return message;
33     }
34   }
35
```

```
36    class A extends B {
37      public String news = "A's news";
38      public String message = "A's message";
39
40      public static String smile() {
41        return "smile from A";
42      }
43
44      /** Override getNews in A */
45      public String getNews() {
46        return news;
47      }
48    }
```

The printout of the program is:

```
(1) x.news is B's news
(2) ((A)x).news is A's news
(3) x.smile() is smile from B
(4) ((B)x).smile() is smile from B
(5) x.getNews() is A's news
(6) x.getMessage() is B's message
```

Here are the explanations:

1. `x.news` is "B's news" because x's declared type is the class B.

2. To use `news` in the class A, you need to cast x to A using `((A)x).news`.

3. `x.smile()` invokes the static `smile` method in B because x's declared type is B.

4. `((A)x).smile()` invokes the static `smile` method in A because the type for `(A)x` is A.

5. `x.getNews()` invokes the `getNews` method in A at runtime because x actually references to the object of the class A.

6. `x.getMessage()` invokes the `getMessage` method in B at runtime because `getMessage` is implemented in B. Therefore, the message in B is returned.

 NOTE

A static method or a static field can always be accessed using its declared class name, regardless of whether it is hidden or not.

8.8   The *protected* Data and Methods

The `protected` modifier can be applied to data and methods in a class. A protected datum or a protected method in a public class can be accessed *by any class in the same package or its subclasses*, even if the subclasses are in different packages, as shown in Figure 8.7.

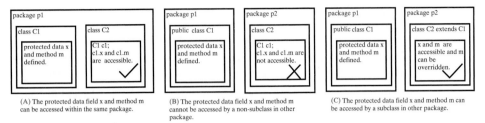

(A) The protected data field x and method m can be accessed within the same package.

(B) The protected data field x and method m cannot be accessed by a non-subclass in other package.

(C) The protected data field x and method m can be accessed by a subclass in other package.

Figure 8.7   *The* protected *modifier can be used to prevent a non-subclass in a different package from accessing the class's data and methods.*

8.8.1   Using the Visibility Modifiers

The modifiers private, protected, and public are known as *visibility or accessibility modifiers* because they specify how class and class members are accessed. The visibility of these modifiers increases in this order

private, none (if no modifier is used), protected, and public.

Use the private modifier to hide the members of the class completely so that they cannot be accessed directly from outside the class. Use no modifiers to allow the members of the class to be accessed directly from any class within the same package, but not from other packages. Use the protected modifier to enable the members of the class to be accessed by the subclasses or classes in the same package. Use the public modifier to enable the members of the class to be accessed by any class.

Your class can be used in two ways: for creating instances of the class, and for creating subclasses by extending the class. Make the members private if they are not intended for use from outside the class. Make the members public if they are intended for the users of the class. Make the fields or methods protected if they are intended for the extenders of the class but not the users of the class.

The private and protected modifiers can only be used for members of the class. The public modifier and the default modifier (i.e., no modifier) can be used on members of the class as well on the class. A class with no modifier (i.e., not a public class) is not accessible by classes from other packages.

 NOTE
In UML, the symbols −, #, and +, respectively, are used to denote private, protected, and public modifiers.

 NOTE
A subclass may override a protected method in its superclass and change its visibility to public. However, a subclass cannot weaken the accessibility of a method defined in the superclass. For example, if a method is defined as public in the superclass, it must be defined as public in the subclass.

8.9   The *final* Classes, Methods, and Variables

You have already seen the `final` modifier used in declaring constants. You may occasionally want to prevent classes from being extended. In such cases, use the `final` modifier to indicate that a class is final and cannot be a parent class. The `Math` class, introduced in Chapter 4, "Methods," is a final class. The `String` and `StringBuffer` classes, introduced in Chapter 7, "Strings," are also final classes.

You also can define a method to be final; a final method cannot be modified by its subclasses.

◈ NOTE

The modifiers are used on classes and class members (data and methods), except that the `final` modifier can also be used on local variables in a method. A final local variable is a constant inside a method.

8.10   The *finalize, clone,* and *getClass* Methods (Optional)

Section 8.4, "The `Object` Class," introduces the `equals`, `hashCode`, and `toString` methods in the `Object` class. This section introduces the `finalize`, `clone`, and `getClass` methods. They are defined in the `Object` class as follows:

- `protected void finalize() throws Throwable`

- `protected native Object clone()`
      `throws CloneNotSupportedException`

- ■ `public final native Class getClass()`

◈ NOTE

The `native` modifier indicates that the method is implemented using a programming language other than Java. Some methods, such as `clone`, need to access hardware using the native machine language or the C language. These methods are marked `native`. A native method can be overloaded, overridden, `final`, `public`, `private`, or `protected`.

◈ NOTE

The `finalize` method may throw `Throwable`, and the `clone` method may throw `CloneNotSupportedException`. Exception handling will be introduced in Chapter 15, "Exceptions and Assertions." For now, you need to know that `throws Throwable` and `throws CloneNotSupportedException` are part of the method declarations for the `finalize` and `clone` methods.

8.10.1   The *finalize* Method

The `finalize` method is invoked by the garbage collector on an object when the object becomes garbage. An object becomes garbage if it is no longer accessed. By default, the `finalize` method does nothing. A subclass should override the `finalize` method to dispose of system resources or to perform other cleanup, if necessary.

 NOTE

The `finalize` method is invoked by JVM. You should never write the code to invoke it in your program.

For an illustration, see the following code:

```
1    public class Test {
2      public static void main(String[] args) {
3        Foo a1 = new Foo(1);
4        Foo a2 = new Foo(2);
5        Foo a3 = new Foo(3);
6
7        // To dispose the objects a2 and a3
8        a2 = a3 = null;
9        System.gc(); // Invoke the Java garbage collector
10     }
11   }
12
13   class Foo extends Object {
14     int id;
15
16     public Foo(int id) {
17       this.id = id;
18       System.out.println("Foo object " + id + " is created");
19     }
20
21     public void finalize() throws java.lang.Throwable {
22       System.out.println("Foo object " + id + " is disposed");
23     }
24   }
```

The following is the output of this program:

```
Foo object 1 is created
Foo object 2 is created
Foo object 3 is created
Foo object 2 is disposed
Foo object 3 is disposed
```

Line 8 assigns `null` to a2 and a3. The objects previously referenced by a2 and a3 are no longer accessible. Therefore, they are garbage. `System.gc()` in Line 9 requests the garbage collector to be invoked. When control returns from the method call, the Java Virtual Machine has made a best effort to reclaim space from all discarded objects. Normally you don't need to invoke this method explicitly, because JVM automatically invokes it whenever JVM determines it is necessary. The `finalize` method on the objects a2 and a3 are invoked by the garbage collector. When the program terminates, a1 also becomes garbage, and a1's `finalize` method is then invoked. Since the program has already exited, no message is displayed on the console.

8.10.2   The *clone* Method

Sometimes you need to make a copy of an object. Mistakenly, you might use the assignment statement, as follows:

```
newObject = someObject;
```

This statement does not create a duplicate object. It simply assigns the reference of `someObject` to `newObject`. To create a new object with separate memory space, you may use the `clone()` method:

```
newObject = someObject.clone();
```

This statement copies `someObject` to a new memory location and assigns the reference of the new object to `newObject`.

NOTE

Not all objects can be cloned. For an object to be cloneable, its class must implement the `java.lang.Cloneable` interface. Interfaces are introduced in Chapter 9, "Abstract Classes and Interfaces."

TIP

An array is treated as an object in Java and is an instance of the `Object` class. The `clone` method can also be used to copy arrays. The following statement uses the `clone` method to copy the `sourceArray` of the `int[]` type to the `targetArray`.

```
int[] targetArray = (int[])sourceArray.clone();
```

Since the return type of the `clone` method is `Object`, `(int[])` is used to cast it to the `int[]` type.

8.10.3   The *getClass* Method

The `getClass` method returns an instance of the `java.lang.Class` class, which contains the information about the class for the object. Before an object is created, its defining class is loaded and the Java Virtual Machine automatically creates an instance of `java.lang.Class` for the class. From this instance, you can discover the information about the class at runtime. For example, you can use the `getName` method in the `Class` class to find the name of the class for an object `obj`, as follows:

```
Object obj = new Object();
System.out.println("Object obj's class is "
  + obj.getClass().getName());
```

The printout is

```
Object obj's class is java.lang.Object
```

8.11   Initialization Blocks (Optional)

Initialization blocks can be used to initialize objects along with the constructors. An initialization block is a block of statements enclosed inside a pair of braces. An initialization block appears within the class declaration, but not inside methods or constructors. It is executed as if it were placed at the beginning of every constructor in the class.

Initialization blocks can simplify the classes if you have multiple constructors sharing a common code and none of the constructors can invoke other constructors. The common code can be placed in an initialization block, as shown in the following example:

```java
public class Book {
  private static int numOfObjects = 0;
  private String title;
  private int id;

  public Book(String title) {
    this.title = title;
  }

  public Book(int id) {
    this.id = id;
  }

  {
    numOfObjects++;
  }
}
```

In this example, none of the constructors can invoke any of the others using the syntax `this(. . .)`. When an instance is created using a constructor of the `Book` class, the initialization block is executed to increase the object count by 1.

 NOTE

A class may have multiple initialization blocks. In such cases, the blocks are executed in the order they appear in the class.

8.11.1   Static Initialization Block

A static initialization block is much like a nonstatic initialization block except that it is declared `static`, can only refer to static members of the class, and is invoked when the class is loaded. The Java runtime system loads a class when it is needed. A superclass is loaded before its subclasses. For an illustration, see the following code:

```java
1  public class Test {
2    public static void main(String[] args) {
3      new Test();
4    }
5
6    public Test() {
7      new A();
8    }
9
10   {
11     System.out.println("(2) Test's non-static initialization " +
12       "block is invoked");
13   }
14
15   static {
16     System.out.println("(1) Test's static initialization block " +
```

```
17              "is invoked");
18        }
19      }
20
21      class A extends B {
22        A() {
23          System.out.println("(8) A's constructor is invoked");
24        }
25
26        {
27          System.out.println("(7) A's non-static initialization block " +
28            "is invoked");
29        }
30
31        static {
32          System.out.println("(4) A's static initialization block " +
33            "is invoked");
34        }
35      }
36
37      class B {
38        B() {
39          System.out.println("(6) B's constructor is invoked");
40        }
41
42        {
43          System.out.println("(5) B's non-static initialization block " +
44            "is invoked");
45        }
46
47        static {
48          System.out.println("(3) B's static initialization block " +
49            "is invoked");
50        }
51      }
```

Here is the output of this program:

```
(1) Test's static initialization block is invoked
(2) Test's non-static initialization block is invoked
(3) B's static initialization block is invoked
(4) A's static initialization block is invoked
(5) B's non-static initialization block is invoked
(6) B's constructor is invoked
(7) A's non-static initialization block is invoked
(8) A's constructor is invoked
```

The program is executed in the following order:

1. Class Test is loaded first. So Test's static initialization block is invoked.

2. Test's constructor is invoked (Line 3). So Test's non-static initialization block is invoked.

3. When executing new A() (Line 7), class A needs to be loaded, which causes class A's superclass (i.e., B) to be loaded first. So B's non-static initialization block is invoked.

4. Class A is now loaded. So A's non-static initialization block is invoked.

5. When invoking A's constructor, the default constructor of A's superclass is invoked first; therefore, B's non-static initialization block is invoked.

6. The regular code in B's default constructor is invoked after B's non-static initialization block is invoked.

7. After B's default constructor is invoked, A's default constructor is invoked, which causes A's non-static initialization block to be invoked first.

8. The regular code in A's default constructor is invoked after A's non-static initialization block is invoked.

Chapter Summary

■ You can derive a new class from an existing class. This is known as *class inheritance*. The new class is called a *subclass*, *child class*, or *derived class*. The existing class is called a *superclass*, *parent class*, or *base class*.

■ A constructor is used to construct an instance of a class. Unlike properties and methods, the constructors of a superclass are not inherited in the subclass. They can only be invoked from the constructors of the subclasses, using the keyword super.

■ A constructor may invoke an overloaded constructor or its superclass's constructor. If none of them is invoked explicitly, the compiler puts super() as the first statement in the constructor.

■ Constructing an instance of a class invokes all the superclasses along the inheritance chain. This is called *constructor chaining*.

■ If a superclass defines constructors other than a default constructor, the subclass cannot use the default constructor of the superclass, because in this case the superclass does not have a default constructor.

■ A subclass inherits methods from a superclass. Sometimes it is necessary for the subclass to modify the methods defined in the superclass. This is referred to as *method overriding*.

■ To override a method, the method must be defined in the subclass using the same signature as in its superclass.

■ An instance method can be overridden only if it is accessible. Thus a private method cannot be overridden, because it is not accessible outside its own class. If a method defined in a subclass is private in its superclass, the two methods are completely unrelated.

■ Like an instance method, a static method can be inherited. However, a static method cannot be overridden. If a static method defined in the superclass is redefined in a subclass, the method defined in the superclass is hidden.

■ Every class in Java is descended from the java.lang.Object class. If no inheritance is specified when a class is defined, the superclass of the class is Object.

■ The Object class contains the useful methods toString, equals, hashCode, clone, finalize, and getClass.

■ The `toString()` method returns a string that represents the object. The `equals` method tests whether two objects are equal. The `hashCode` method returns the hash code of the object. The hash code is an integer that can be used to store the object in a hash set so that it can be located quickly. The `clone()` method copies an object. The `getClass` method returns an instance of the `java.lang.Class` class, which contains the information about the class for the object. The `finalize` method is invoked by the garbage collector on an object when the object becomes garbage. An object becomes garbage if it is no longer accessed.

■ An object of a subclass can be used by any code designed to work with an object of its superclass. This feature is known as *polymorphism*. When a method is invoked on an object, which implementation of the method is used will be determined dynamically by the Java Virtual Machine at runtime. This capability is known as *dynamic binding*.

■ Polymorphism allows methods to be used generically for a wide range of object arguments. This is known as *generic programming*. If a method's parameter type is a superclass (e.g., `Object`), you may pass an object to this method of any of the parameter's subclasses (e.g., `Circle` or `String`). When an object (e.g., a `Circle` object or a `String` object) is used in the method, the particular implementation of the method of the object that is invoked (e.g., `toString`) is determined dynamically.

■ Casting can also be used to convert an object of one class type to another within an inheritance hierarchy.

■ It is always possible to cast an instance of a subclass to a variable of a superclass, because an instance of a subclass is *always* an instance of its superclass. When casting an instance of a superclass to a variable of its subclass, explicit casting must be used to confirm your intention to the compiler with the `(SubclassName)` cast notation.

■ The `instanceof` operator checks whether an object is an instance of a class.

■ You can override an instance method, but you cannot override a field (instance or static) or a static method. If you declare a field or a static method in a subclass with the same name as one in the superclass, the one in the superclass is hidden, but it still exists. The two fields or static methods are independent. You can reference the hidden field or static method using the `super` keyword in the subclass. The hidden field or method can also be accessed via a reference variable of the superclass's type.

■ When invoking an instance method from a reference variable, the *actual class of the object* referenced by the variable decides which implementation of the method is used *at runtime*. When accessing a field or a static method, the *declared type* of the reference variable decides which method is used *at compile time*.

■ The `protected` modifier can be applied to data and methods in a class. A protected datum or a protected method in a public class can be accessed *by any class in the same package or its subclasses,* even if the subclasses are in different packages.

■   You can use the `final` modifier to indicate that a class is final and cannot be a parent class. You also can define a method to be final; a final method cannot be modified by its subclasses.

Review Questions

8.1   What is the printout of running the class C?

```
class A {
  public A() {
    System.out.println(
      "The default constructor of A is invoked");
  }
}

class B extends A {
  public B() {
  }
}

public class C {
  public static void main(String[] args) {
    B b = new B();
  }
}
```

8.2   What problem arises in compiling the following program?

```
class A {
  public A(int x) {
  }
}

class B extends A {
  public B() {
  }
}

public class C {
  public static void main(String[] args) {
    B b = new B();
  }
}
```

8.3   Define the following terms: inheritance, superclass, subclass, the keywords `super` and `this`, casting objects, the modifiers `protected` and `final`.

8.4   Identify the problems in the following classes:

```
public class Circle {
  private double radius;

  public Circle(double radius) {
    radius = radius;
  }
```

```
      public double getRadius() {
        return radius;
      }

      public double findArea() {
        return radius * radius * Math.PI;
      }
    }

    class Cylinder extends Circle {
      private double length;

      Cylinder(double radius, double length) {
        Circle(radius);
        length = length;
      }

      /** Return the surface area for the cylinder */
      public double findArea() {
        return findArea() * length;
      }
    }
```

8.5 Indicate true or false for the following statements:

- A protected datum or method can be accessed by any class in the same package.

- A protected datum or method can be accessed by any class in different packages.

- A protected datum or method can be accessed by its subclass in any package.

- A final class can have instances.

- A final class can be extended.

- A final method can be overridden.

- You can always successfully cast an instance of a subclass to a superclass.

- You can always successfully cast an instance of a superclass to a subclass.

- The order in which modifiers appear before a method is important.

8.6 Explain the difference between method overloading and method overriding.

8.7 Does every class have a toString method and an equals method? Where do they come from? How are they used?

8.8 What modifier should you use on a class so that a class in the same package can access it but a class in a different package cannot access it?

8.9 What modifier should you use so that a class in a different package cannot access the class but its subclasses in any package can access it?

8.10 Given the assumptions

```
Circle circle = new Circle(1);
Cylinder cylinder = new Cylinder(1, 1);
```

are the following Boolean expressions true or false?

```
(circle instanceof Cylinder)
(cylinder instanceof Circle)
```

8.11   Are the following statements correct?

```
Cylinder cylinder = new Cylinder(1, 1);
Circle circle = cylinder;
```

8.12   Are the following statements correct?

```
Circle circle = new Circle(1);
Cylinder cylinder = (Cylinder)circle;
```

8.13   Suppose that `Fruit`, `Apple`, `Orange`, `Golden Delicious Apple`, and `Macintosh Apple` are declared, as shown in Figure 8.8.

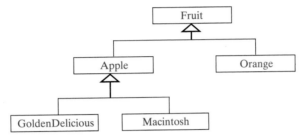

Figure 8.8   *GoldenDelicious and Macintosh are subclasses of Apple, Apple and Orange are subclasses of Fruit.*

Assume that the following declaration is given:

```
Fruit fruit = new GoldenDelicious();
Orange orange = new Orange();
```

Answer the following questions:
   1. Is `fruit instanceof Orange`?
   2. Is `fruit instanceof Apple`?
   3. Is `fruit instanceof GoldenDelicious`?
   4. Is `fruit instanceof Macintosh`?
   5. Is `orange instanceof Orange`?
   6. Is `orange instanceof Fruit`?
   7. Is `orange instanceof Apple`?
   8. Suppose the method `makeApple` is defined in the `Apple` class. Can `fruit` invoke this method? Can `orange` invoke this method?
   9. Suppose the method `makeOrangeJuice` is defined in the `Orange` class. Can `orange` invoke this method? Can `fruit` invoke this method?

8.14   What is wrong in the following code?

```
class Test extends A {
  public static void main(String[] args) {
    Test t = new Test();
    t.print();
  }
}
```

```
class A {
  String s;

  A(String s) {
    this.s = s;
  }

  public void print() {
    System.out.println(s);
  }
}
```

8.15 Show the output of following program:

```
public class Test {
  public static void main(String[] args) {
    A a = new A(3);
  }
}

class A extends B {
  public A(int t) {
    System.out.println("A's constructor is invoked");
  }
}

class B {
  public B() {
    System.out.println("B's constructor is invoked");
  }
}
```

8.16 When you create an object of a class A, is the constructor in the Object class automatically invoked?

8.17 Which of the following statements is not true?
  a. A public class can be accessed by a class from a different package.
  b. A private method cannot be accessed by a class in a different package.
  c. A protected method can be accessed by a subclass in a different package.
  d. A method with no visibility modifier can be accessed by a class in a different package.

Programming Exercises

8.1 (The Triangle class) Write a class named Triangle defined as follows:

```
public class Triangle extends Object {
  private double side1, side2, side3;

  /** Construct a triangle with the specified sides */
  public Triangle(double side1, double side2, double side3) {
    // Implement it
  }

  /** find the area of this triangle */
  public double findArea() {
    // Implement it
  }
```

```
  /** Find the perimeter of this triangle */
  public double findPerimeter() {
    // Implement it
  }

  /** Override the toString method */
  public String toString() {
    // Implement it to return the three sides
  }
}
```

The formula for computing the area is as follows:

$$s = (side1 + side2 + side3)/2;$$
$$area = \sqrt{s(s - side1)(s - side2)(s - side3)}$$

Test the `Triangle` class by adding a `main` method in the class. Create a `Triangle` with sides 1, 1.5, 1 and display its area and perimeter.

8.2 (The `Person`, `Student`, `Employee`, and `MyDate` classes) Implement a class named `Person` and two subclasses of `Person` named `Student` and `Employee`. Make `Faculty` and `Staff` subclasses of `Employee`. A person has a name, address, phone number, and e-mail address. A student has a class status (freshman, sophomore, junior, or senior). Define the status as a constant. An employee has an office, salary, and date-hired. Define a class named `MyDate` that contains the fields `year`, `month`, and `day`. A faculty member has office hours and a rank. A staff member has a title. Override the `toString` method in each class to display the class name and the person's name.

8.3 (Subclasses of `Account`) In Exercise 6.3, the `Account` class was created to model a bank account. An account has the properties account number, balance, and annual interest rate, and methods to deposit and withdraw. Create two subclasses for checking and saving accounts. A checking account has an overdraft limit, but a savings account cannot go overdrawn.

8.4 (The `StackOfObjects` class) In Example 6.8, "The `StackOfIntegers` Class," you created a stack class for storing integers. Modify the example to create a stack class to hold objects. Name the new class `StackOfObjects` and draw the UML diagram for the class. Write a test program that displays the first fifty prime numbers in decreasing order.

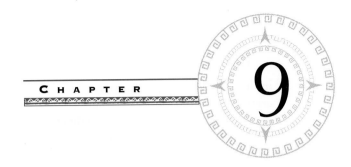

ABSTRACT CLASSES AND INTERFACES

Objectives

- To design and use abstract classes.
- To declare interfaces to model weak inheritance relationships.
- To use wrapper classes (`Byte`, `Short`, `Integer`, `Long`, `Float`, `Double`, `Character`, and `Boolean`) to wrap primitive data values into objects.
- To create a generic sort method.

9.1 Introduction

In the inheritance hierarchy, classes become more specific and concrete *with each new subclass*. If you move from a subclass back up to a superclass, the classes become more general and less specific. Class design should ensure that a superclass contains common features of its subclasses. Sometimes a superclass is so abstract that it cannot have any specific instances. Such a class is referred to as an *abstract class*.

Sometimes it is necessary to derive a subclass from several classes. This capability is known as *multiple inheritance*. Java, however, does not allow multiple inheritance. Each Java class may inherit directly from one superclass. This restriction is known as *single inheritance*. If you use the extends keyword to define a subclass, it allows only one parent class. With interfaces, you can obtain the effect of multiple inheritance.

This chapter introduces abstract classes and interfaces, and discusses how to use wrapper classes for primitive data type values.

9.2 Abstract Classes

Consider geometric objects. Suppose you want to design the classes to model geometric objects like circles, cylinders, and rectangles. Geometric objects have many common properties and behaviors. They can be drawn in a certain color, filled, or unfilled. Color and filled are examples of common properties. Common behaviors include the fact that the areas and perimeters of geometric objects can be computed. Thus a general class GeometricObject can be used to model all geometric objects. This class contains the properties color and filled, and the methods findArea and findPerimeter. Since a circle is a special type of geometric object, it shares common properties and methods with other geometric objects. Further, since a cylinder is a special type of circle, it shares common properties and behaviors with a circle. Thus it makes sense to define the Circle class that extends the GeometricObject class and the Cylinder class that extends the Circle class. Figure 9.1 illustrates the relationship of the classes for geometric objects.

UML Notation:
The abstract class name and the
abstract method names are italicized.

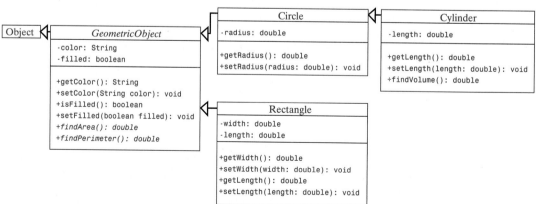

Figure 9.1 *The GeometricObject class models the common features of geometric objects.*

The methods `findArea` and `findPerimeter` cannot be implemented in the `GeometricObject` class because their implementation is dependent on the specific type of geometric object. Such methods are referred to as *abstract methods*. In UML graphic notation, the names of abstract classes and their abstract methods are italicized. The `GeometricObject` class can be defined as follows:

```java
// GeometricObject.java: The abstract GeometricObject class
public abstract class GeometricObject {
  private String color = "white";
  private boolean filled;

  /** Default construct */
  protected GeometricObject() {
  }

  /** Construct a geometric object */
  protected GeometricObject(String color, boolean filled) {
    this.color = color;
    this.filled = filled;
  }

  /** Return color */
  public String getColor() {
    return color;
  }

  /** Set a new color */
  public void setColor(String color) {
    this.color = color;
  }

  /** Return filled. Since filled is boolean,
      so, the get method name is isFilled */
  public boolean isFilled() {
    return filled;
  }

  /** Set a new filled */
  public void setFilled(boolean filled) {
    this.filled = filled;
  }

  /** Abstract method findArea */
  public abstract double findArea();

  /** Abstract method findPerimeter */
  public abstract double findPerimeter();
}
```

Abstract classes are like regular classes with data and methods, but you cannot create instances of abstract classes using the `new` operator. An abstract method is a method signature without implementation. Its implementation is provided by the subclasses. A class that contains abstract methods must be declared abstract.

The `GeometricObject` abstract class provides the common features (data and methods) for geometric objects. Because you don't know how to compute areas and perimeters of geometric objects, `findArea` and `findPerimeter` are defined as abstract methods. These methods are implemented in the subclasses. Here is the implementation of the classes `Circle`, `Rectangle`, and `Cylinder`:

```java
// Circle.java: The circle class that extends GeometricObject
package chapter9;

public class Circle extends GeometricObject {
  private double radius;

  /** Default constructor */
  public Circle() {
    this(1.0);
  }

  /** Construct circle with a specified radius */
  public Circle(double radius) {
    this(radius, "white", false);
  }

  /** Construct a circle with specified radius, filled, and color */
  public Circle(double radius, String color, boolean filled) {
    super(color, filled);
    this.radius = radius;
  }

  /** Return radius */
  public double getRadius() {
    return radius;
  }

  /** Set a new radius */
  public void setRadius(double radius) {
    this.radius = radius;
  }

  /** Implement the findArea method defined in GeometricObject */
  public double findArea() {
    return radius * radius * Math.PI;
  }

  /** Implement the findPerimeter method defined in GeometricObject*/
  public double findPerimeter() {
    return 2 * radius * Math.PI;
  }

  /** Override the toString() method defined in the Object class */
  public String toString() {
    return "[Circle] radius = " + radius;
  }
}
```

```java
// Rectangle.java: The Rectangle class that extends GeometricObject
package chapter9;

public class Rectangle extends GeometricObject {
  private double width;
  private double height;

  /** Default constructor */
  public Rectangle() {
    this(1.0, 1.0);
  }

  /** Construct a rectangle with width and height */
  public Rectangle(double width, double height) {
    this(width, height, "white", false);
  }
```

```
  /** Construct a rectangle with specified width, height,
     filled, and color */
  public Rectangle(double width, double height,
    String color, boolean filled) {
    super(color, filled);
    this.width = width;
    this.height = height;
  }

  /** Return width */
  public double getWidth() {
    return width;
  }

  /** Set a new width */
  public void setWidth(double width) {
    this.width = width;
  }

  /** Return height */
  public double getHeight() {
    return height;
  }

  /** Set a new height */
  public void setHeight(double height) {
    this.height = height;
  }

  /** Implement the findArea method in GeometricObject */
  public double findArea() {
    return width * height;
  }

  /** Implement the findPerimeter method in GeometricObject */
  public double findPerimeter() {
    return 2 * (width + height);
  }

  /** Override the toString method defined in the Object class */
  public String toString() {
    return "[Rectangle] width = " + width +
      " and height = " + height;
  }
}
```

```
// Cylinder.java: The new cylinder class that extends the circle
// class.
package chapter9;

public class Cylinder extends Circle {
  private double length;

  /** Default constructor */
  public Cylinder() {
    this(1.0, 1.0);
  }

  /** Construct a cylinder with specified radius, and length */
  public Cylinder(double radius, double length) {
    this(radius, "white", false, length);
  }

  /** Construct a cylinder with specified radius, filled, color, and
     length
```

371

```
    */
  public Cylinder(double radius,
    String color, boolean filled, double length) {
    super(radius, color, filled);
    this.length = length;
  }

  /** Return length */
  public double getLength() {
    return length;
  }

  /** Set a new length */
  public void setLength(double length) {
    this.length = length;
  }

  /** Return the surface area of this cylinder */
  public double findArea() {
    return 2 * super.findArea() + 2 * getRadius() * Math.PI * length;
  }

  /** Return the volume of this cylinder */
  public double findVolume() {
    return super.findArea() * length;
  }

  /** Override the toString method defined in the Object class */
  public String toString() {
    return "[Cylinder] radius = " + getRadius() + " and length "
      + length;
  }
}
```

The method toString is defined in the Object class and modified in the Circle, Rectangle, and Cylinder classes. The abstract methods findArea and findPerimeter defined in the GeometricObject class are implemented in the Circle and Rectangle classes.

◆ **NOTE**

An abstract method cannot be contained in a nonabstract class. If a subclass of an abstract superclass does not implement all the abstract methods, the subclass must be declared abstract. In other words, in a nonabstract subclass extended from an abstract class, all the abstract methods must be implemented, even if they are not used in the subclass.

◆ **NOTE**

An abstract class cannot be instantiated using the new operator, but you can still define its constructors, which are invoked in the constructors of its subclasses. For instance, the constructors of GeometricObject are invoked in the Circle class and the Rectangle class.

◆ **NOTE**

A class that contains abstract methods must be abstract. However, it is possible to declare an abstract class that contains no abstract methods. In this case, you cannot create instances of the class using the new operator. This class is used as a base class for defining a new subclass.

NOTE

A subclass can be abstract even if its superclass is concrete. For example, the `Object` class is concrete, but its subclasses, such as `GeometricObject`, may be abstract.

NOTE

A subclass can override a method from its superclass to declare it `abstract`. This is rare, but is useful when the implementation of the method in the superclass becomes invalid in the subclass. In this case, the subclass must be declared abstract.

NOTE

You cannot create an instance from an abstract class using the `new` operator, but an abstract class can be used as a data type. Therefore, the following statement, which creates an array whose elements are of `GeometricObject` type, is correct.

```
GeometricObject[] geo = new GeometricObject[10];
```

NOTE

`Cylinder` inherits the `findPerimeter` method from `Circle`. If you invoke this method on a `Cylinder` object, the perimeter of a circle is returned. This method is not useful for `Cylinder` objects. It would be nice to remove or disable it from `Cylinder`, but there is no good way to get rid of this method in a subclass once it is defined as public in its superclass. If you define the `findPerimeter` method as abstract in the `Cylinder` class, then the `Cylinder` class must be declared abstract.

You may be wondering whether the abstract methods `findArea` and `findPerimeter` should be removed from the `GeometricObject` class. The following example shows the benefits of retaining them in the `GeometricObject` class.

Example 9.1 Using the *GeometricObject* Class

Problem

Write a program that creates two geometric objects, a circle and a rectangle, invokes the `equalArea` method to check whether the two objects have equal areas, and invokes the `displayGeometricObject` method to display the objects.

Solution

The following code gives the solution to the problem. A sample run of the program is shown in Figure 9.2.

```
1    // TestGeometricObject.java: Test GeometricObject class
2    package chapter9;
3
4    public class TestGeometricObject {
5      /** Main method */
```

continues

Example 9.1   Continued

```
 6        public static void main(String[] args) {
 7          // Declare and initialize two geometric objects
 8          GeometricObject geoObject1 = new Circle(5);
 9          GeometricObject geoObject2 = new Rectangle(5, 3);
10
11          System.out.println("The two objects have the same area? " +
12            equalArea(geoObject1, geoObject2));
13
14          // Display circle
15          displayGeometricObject(geoObject1);
16
17          // Display rectangle
18          displayGeometricObject(geoObject2);
19        }
20
21        /** A method for comparing the areas of two geometric objects */
22        static boolean equalArea(GeometricObject object1,
23          GeometricObject object2) {
24          return object1.findArea() == object2.findArea();
25        }
26
27        /** A method for displaying a geometric object */
28        static void displayGeometricObject(GeometricObject object) {
29          System.out.println();
30          System.out.println(object.toString());
31          System.out.println("The area is " + object.findArea());
32          System.out.println("The perimeter is " + object.findPerimeter());
33        }
34      }
```

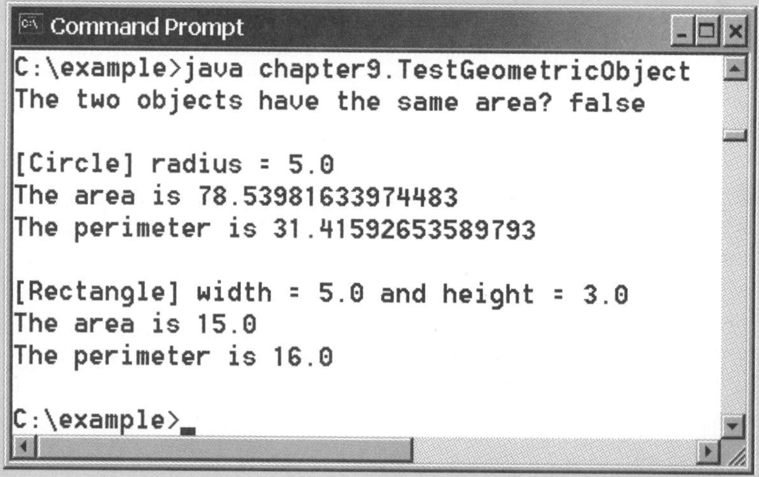

```
C:\example>java chapter9.TestGeometricObject
The two objects have the same area? false

[Circle] radius = 5.0
The area is 78.53981633974483
The perimeter is 31.41592653589793

[Rectangle] width = 5.0 and height = 3.0
The area is 15.0
The perimeter is 16.0

C:\example>
```

Figure 9.2   *The program compares the areas of the objects and displays their properties.*

Review

The methods findArea() and findPerimeter() defined in the GeometricObject class are overridden in the Circle class and the Rectangle class. The statements (Lines 8–9)

```
GeometricObject geoObject1 = new Circle(5);
GeometricObject geoObject2 = new Rectangle(5, 3);
```

create a new circle and rectangle, and assign them to the variables geoObject1 and geoObject2. These two variables are of the GeometricObject type.

When invoking equalArea(geoObject1, geoObject2) (Line 12), the findArea method defined in the Circle class is used for object1.findArea(), since geoObject1 is a circle, and the findArea method defined in the Rectangle class is used for object2.findArea(), since geoObject2 is a rectangle.

Similarly, when invoking displayGeometricObject(geoObject1) (Line 15), the methods findArea, findPerimeter, and toString defined in the Circle class are used, and when invoking displayGeometricObject(geoObject2) (Line 18), the methods findArea, findPerimeter, and toString defined in the Rectangle class are used. Which of these methods is invoked is dynamically determined at runtime, depending on the type of object.

NOTE

Matching a method signature and binding a method implementation are two issues. The compiler finds a matching method according to parameter type, number of parameters, and order of the parameters at compilation time. A method may be implemented in several subclasses. The Java Virtual Machine dynamically binds the implementation of the method at runtime. See Review Questions 9.9 and 9.10.

9.3 The *Calendar* and *GregorianCalendar* Classes

An instance of java.util.Date represents a specific instant in time with millisecond precision. java.util.Calendar is an abstract base class for extracting detailed information, such as year, month, date, hour, minute, and second, from a Date object. Subclasses of Calendar can implement specific calendar systems, such as the Gregorian calendar, the Lunar calendar, and the Jewish calendar. Currently, java.util.GregorianCalendar for the Gregorian calendar is supported in Java.

You can use new GregorianCalendar() to construct a default GregorianCalendar with the current time and use new GregorianCalendar(year, month, date) to construct a GregorianCalendar with the specified year, month, and date. The month parameter is 0-based, i.e., 0 is for January.

The get(int field) method defined in the Calendar class is useful to extract the value for a given time field. The time fields are defined as constants, such as YEAR, MONTH, DATE, HOUR (for the 12-hour clock), HOUR_OF_DAY (for the 24-hour clock), MINUTE, SECOND, DAY_OF_WEEK (the day number within the current week with 1 for Sunday), DAY_OF_MONTH (same as the DATE value), DAY_OF_YEAR (the day number within the current year with 1 for the first day of the year), WEEK_OF_MONTH (the week number within the current month), and WEEK_OF_YEAR (the week number within the current year). For example, the following code

```
// Construct a Gregorian calendar for the current date and time
java.util.Calendar calendar = new java.util.GregorianCalendar();
System.out.println("Year\tMonth\tDate\tHour\t\Hour24\tMinute\tSecond");
System.out.println(calendar.get(Calendar.YEAR) + "\t" +
  calendar.get(Calendar.MONTH) + "\t" + calendar.get(Calendar.DATE)
  + "\t" + calendar.get(Calendar.HOUR) + "\t" +
  calendar.get(Calendar.MINUTE) + "\t" +
  calendar.get(Calendar.SECOND));
System.out.print("Day of week: " +
  calendar.get(Calendar.DAY_OF_WEEK) + "\t");
System.out.print("Day of month: " +
  calendar.get(Calendar.DAY_OF_MONTH) + "\t");
System.out.println("Day of year: " +
  calendar.get(Calendar.DAY_OF_YEAR));
System.out.print("Week of month: " +
  calendar.get(Calendar.WEEK_OF_MONTH) + "\t");
System.out.println("Week of year: " +
  calendar.get(Calendar.WEEK_OF_YEAR));
```

displays the information for the current date and time, as follows:

```
Year Month   Date   Hour   Hour24   Minute   Second
2003 2          9    8       20       17      39
Day of week: 1         Day of month: 9         Day of year: 68
Week of month: 3       Week of year: 11
```

NOTE

To learn how to incorporate the locale and time zone information into calendars, see Bonus Chapter 20, "Internationalization."

9.4   Interfaces

An interface is a classlike construct that contains only constants and abstract methods. In many ways, an interface is similar to an abstract class, but an abstract class can contain constants and abstract methods as well as variables and concrete methods.

To distinguish an interface from a class, Java uses the following syntax to declare an interface:

```
modifier interface InterfaceName {
  /** Constant declarations */
  /** Method signatures */
}
```

An interface is treated like a special class in Java. Each interface is compiled into a separate bytecode file, just like a regular class. As with an abstract class, you cannot create an instance from an interface using the new operator, but in most cases you can use an interface more or less the same way you use an abstract class. For example, you can use an interface as a data type for a variable, as the result of casting, and so on.

Suppose you want to design a generic method to find the larger of two objects. The objects can be students, circles, or cylinders. Because compare methods are different for different types of objects, you need to define a generic compare method to determine the order of the two objects. Then you can tailor the method to compare students, circles, or cylinders. For example, you can use student ID as the key for comparing students, radius as the key for comparing circles, and volume as the key for comparing cylinders. You can use an interface to define a generic compareTo method, as follows:

```
// Interface for comparing objects, defined in java.lang
package java.lang;

public interface Comparable {
  public int compareTo(Object o);
}
```

The compareTo method determines the order of this object with the specified object o, and returns a negative integer, zero, or a positive integer if this object is less than, equal to, or greater than the specified object o.

 NOTE

The Comparable interface has been available since JDK 1.2, and is included in the java.lang package.

A generic max method for finding the larger of two objects can be declared in a class named Max, as follows:

```
// Max.java: Find a maximum object
package chapter9;

public class Max {
  /** Return the maximum between two objects */
  public static Object max(Object o1, Object o2) {
    if (((Comparable)o1).compareTo(o2) > 0)
      return o1;
    else
      return o2;
  }
}
```

The Max class contains a static method named max. To use the max method to find the larger of two objects, implement the Comparable interface for the class of these objects. Since o1 is declared as Object, (Comparable)o1 tells the compiler to cast o1 into Comparable so that the compareTo method can be invoked from o1.

Many classes in the Java library implement Comparable. For example, the String class implements Comparable, so you can use the max method to find the larger string. Here is an example:

```
String s1 = "abcdef";
String s2 = "abcdee";
String s3 = (String)Max.max(s1, s2);
```

Since every object is automatically an instance of Object, s1 and s2 can be passed to the max method without explicit casting. However, an instance of Object is not necessarily an instance of String. Therefore, to assign the return value from the max method to a String type variable, you need to cast it to String explicitly.

The following example is another demonstration of how the interface is used.

Example 9.2 Using Interfaces

Problem

Write a program that uses the max method to find the largest of two circles and the largest of two cylinders.

Solution

The following code gives the solution to the problem. The output of the program is shown in Figure 9.3.

```
1   // TestInterface.java: Use the Comparable interface
2   // and the generic max method to find max objects
3   package chapter9;
4
5   public class TestInterface {
6     /** Main method */
7     public static void main(String[] args) {
8       // Create two comparable circles
9       ComparableCircle circle1 = new ComparableCircle(5);
10      ComparableCircle circle2 = new ComparableCircle(4);
11
12      // Display the max circle
13      Object circle = Max.max(circle1, circle2);
14      System.out.println("The max circle's radius is " +
15        ((Circle)circle).getRadius());
16      System.out.println(circle);
17
18      // Create two comparable cylinders
19      ComparableCylinder cylinder1 = new ComparableCylinder(5, 2);
20      ComparableCylinder cylinder2 = new ComparableCylinder(4, 5);
21
22      // Display the max cylinder
23      Object cylinder = Max.max(cylinder1, cylinder2);
24      System.out.println();
25      System.out.println("cylinder1's volume is " +
26        cylinder1.findVolume());
27      System.out.println("cylinder2's volume is " +
28        cylinder2.findVolume());
29      System.out.println("The max cylinder's \tradius is " +
30        ((Cylinder)cylinder).getRadius() + "\n\t\t\tlength is " +
31        ((Cylinder)cylinder).getLength() + "\n\t\t\tvolume is " +
32        ((Cylinder)cylinder).findVolume());
33      System.out.println(cylinder);
34    }
35  }
36
37  // ComparableCircle is a subclass of Circle, which implements the
38  // Comparable interface
39  class ComparableCircle extends Circle implements Comparable {
40    /** Construct a ComparableCircle with a specified radius */
41    public ComparableCircle(double r) {
42      super(r);
43    }
44
45    /** Implement the compareTo method defined in Comparable */
46    public int compareTo(Object o) {
47      if (getRadius() > ((Circle)o).getRadius())
48        return 1;
49      else if (getRadius() < ((Circle)o).getRadius())
50        return -1;
```

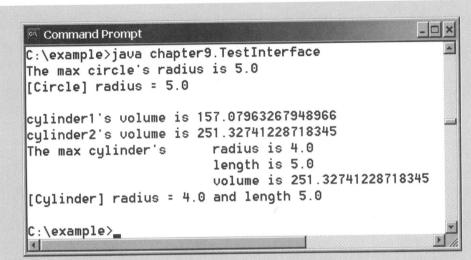

Figure 9.3 *The program displays the largest circle and largest cylinder.*

```
51         else
52           return 0;
53     }
54   }
55
56   // ComparableCylinder is a subclass of Cylinder, which implements the
57   // CompareObject interface
58   class ComparableCylinder extends Cylinder implements Comparable {
59     /** Construct a CompareCylinder with radius and length */
60     ComparableCylinder(double radius, double length) {
61       super(radius, length);
62     }
63
64     /** Implement the compareTo method defined in Comparable interface */
65     public int compareTo(Object o) {
66       if (findVolume() > ((Cylinder)o).findVolume())
67         return 1;
68       else if (findVolume() < ((Cylinder)o).findVolume())
69         return -1;
70       else
71         return 0;
72     }
73   }
```

Review

The max method can be used to find the largest of two objects of the `Comparable` type. Any object whose class implements the `Comparable` interface is an instance of the `Comparable` type. The example creates the classes `ComparableCircle` (Lines 39–54) and `ComparableCylinder` (Lines 58–72) in order to utilize the generic max method. The relationship of the classes and the interface is shown in Figure 9.4.

continues

379

Example 9.2 Continued

Notation:
The interface name and the method names inside an interface are italicized. The dashed lines and hollow triangles are used to point to the interface.

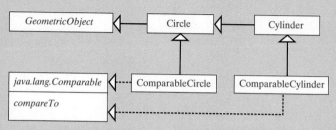

Figure 9.4 *The* `ComparableCircle` *class extends* `Circle` *and implements* `Comparable;` `ComparableCylinder` *extends* `Cylinder` *and implements* `Comparable`.

The common functionality is to compare objects in this example, but the `compareTo` methods are different for different types of objects. Therefore, the interface `Comparable` is used to generalize common functionality and leave the detail for the subclasses to implement.

The keyword `implements` in the `ComparableCircle` class indicates that `ComparableCircle` inherits all the data from the `Comparable` interface and implements the methods in the interface.

The `ComparableCircle` class implements the `compareTo` method for comparing the radii of two circles, and the `ComparableCylinder` class implements the `compareTo` method for comparing the cylinders based on their volumes.

The `Object` class is used as a data type for variables `o1` and `o2` in the max method, for the variable `o`. When you invoke `max(circle1, circle2)`, you pass `circle1` and `circle2` to `o1` and `o2`. This is implicit casting. Casting `o1` to `Comparable` is necessary to tell the compiler that `o1` is also an instance of `Comparable` so that the `compareTo` method can be invoked from `o1`.

To invoke `getRadius` (Line 15) in the `Circle` class, you have to cast the variable `o` into a `Circle` object, because `getRadius` is not defined in the `Object` class.

The statement `System.out.println(circle)` (Line 16) displays `circle.toString()`. Since the `toString` method is defined in the `Object` class, it can be accessed by objects of the `Circle` type. By means of polymorphism, the `toString` method for the `Circle` class is used, because `circle` is an instance of `Circle`.

An interface provides another form of generic programming. It would be difficult to use a generic max method to find the maximum of the objects without using an interface in this example, because multiple inheritance would be necessary to inherit `Comparable` and another class, such as `Circle` or `Cylinder`, at the same time.

The `Object` class contains the `equals` method, which is intended for the subclasses of the `Object` class to override in order to compare whether the contents of the objects are the same. Suppose that the `Object` class contains the `compareTo` method, as defined in the `Comparable` interface; the new `max` method can be used to compare a list of *any* objects. Whether a `compareTo` method should be included in the `Object` class is debatable. Since the `compareTo` method is not defined in the `Object` class, the `Comparable` interface is created in Java 2 to enable objects to be compared if they are instances of the `Comparable` interface. It is strongly recommended (though not required) that `compareTo` should be consistent with `equals`. That is, for two objects o1 and o2, `o1.compareTo(o2) == 0` if and only if `o1.equals(o2)` is true.

9.4.1   Interfaces vs. Abstract Classes

An interface can be used just like an abstract class, but defining an interface is different from defining an abstract class.

- In an interface, the data must be constants; an abstract class can have data fields.

- Each method in an interface has only a signature without implementation; an abstract class can have concrete methods.

- Since all the methods defined in an interface are abstract methods, Java does not require that you put the abstract modifier in the method signature in an interface, but you must put the abstract modifier before an abstract method in an abstract class.

Java allows only single inheritance for class extension, but multiple extension for interfaces. For example,

```
public class NewClass extends BaseClass
  implements Interface1, ..., InterfaceN {
  …
}
```

An interface can inherit other interfaces using the `extends` keyword, as follows:

```
public interface NewInterface extends Interface1, ..., InterfaceN {
  // constants and abstract methods
}
```

A class implementing `NewInterface` must implement the abstract methods defined in `NewInterface`, `Interface1`, ..., and `InterfaceN`. An interface can only extend other interfaces, but not classes. A class can extend its superclass and implement multiple interfaces.

All classes share a single root, the `Object` class, but there is no single root for interfaces. Like a class, an interface also defines a type. A variable of an interface type can reference any instance of the class that extends the interface. If a class extends an interface, this interface is like a superclass for the class. You can use an interface as a data type and cast a variable of an interface type to its subclass, and vice versa. For example, suppose that c is an instance of Class2 in Figure 9.5. c is also an instance of Object, Class1, Interface1, Interface1_1, Interface1_2, Interface2_1, and Interface2_2.

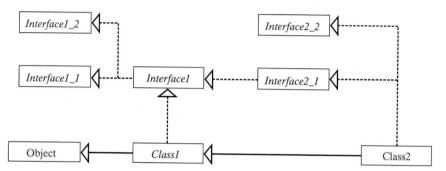

Figure 9.5 *Abstract class* Class1 *implements* Interface1, Interface1 *extends* Interface1_1 *and* Interface1_2. Class2 *extends* Class1 *and implements* Interface2_1 *and* Interface2_2.

Abstract classes and interfaces can both be used to model common features. Deciding which to use will be discussed in the context of class design in Chapter 10, "OO Analysis and Design."

 NOTE

Class names are nouns. Interface names may be adjectives or nouns. For example, both java.lang.Comparable and java.awt.event.ActionListener are interfaces. Comparable is an adjective, and ActionListener is a noun. ActionListener will be introduced in Chapter 12, "Event-Driven Programming."

9.4.2   The *Cloneable* Interface (Optional)

An interface contains constants and abstract methods, but the Cloneable interface is a special case. The Cloneable interface in the java.lang package is defined as follows:

```
package java.lang;

public interface Cloneable {
}
```

This interface is empty. An interface with an empty body is referred to as a *marker interface*. A marker interface does not contain constants or methods, but it has a special meaning in the Java system. The Java system requires a class that implements the Cloneable interface to become cloneable. The object of a cloneable class can use the clone method defined in the Object class to make an identical copy of the object. A class that implements the Cloneable interface is marked cloneable.

Many classes (e.g., Date and Calendar) in the Java library implement Cloneable. Thus, the instances of these classes can be cloned. For example, the following code

```
Calendar calendar = new GregorianCalendar(2003, 2, 1);
Calendar calendarCopy = (Calendar)calendar.clone();
System.out.println("calendar == calendarCopy is " +
  (calendar == calendarCopy));
System.out.println("calendar.equals(calendarCopy) is " +
  calendar.equals(calendarCopy));
```

displays

```
calendar == calendarCopy is false
calendar.equals(calendarCopy) is true
```

The following example demonstrates how to create a class that implements the Cloneable interface, how to use the clone method, and the effect of object cloning.

Example 9.3 Cloning Objects

Problem

Write a program that uses the Cloneable interface to mark classes as cloneable and uses the clone method to copy objects. The program creates a new class named CloneableCircle. The CloneableCircle class extends Circle and implements the Cloneable interface. The CloneableCircle class has a new data field named date of the Date class, which stores the date when the object is created. The main method in a test class creates a CloneableCircle object and duplicates it using the clone method.

Solution

The following code gives the solution to the problem. The output of the program is shown in Figure 9.6.

```
1    // TestCloneable.java: Use the TestCloneable interface
2    // to enable cloning
3    package chapter9;
4
5    public class TestCloneable {
6      /** Main method */
7      public static void main(String[] args) {
8        // Declare and create an instance of CloneableCircle
9        CloneableCircle c1 = new CloneableCircle(5);
10       CloneableCircle c2 = (CloneableCircle)c1.clone();
11
12       System.out.println("After cloning c1 to c2");
13
14       // Check if two variables point to the same object
15       System.out.println("Do c1 and c2 reference the same object? "
16         + (c1 == c2));
17
18       // Check if the date field of two objects are the same
19       System.out.println("Do c1.date and c2.date reference " +
20         "the same object? " + (c1.date == c2.date));
21
```

continues

Example 9.3 Continued

```
22          System.out.println("Is a CloneableCircle object cloneable? "
23            + (c1 instanceof Cloneable));
24
25          // Check if a Circle object is cloneable
26          Circle c = new Circle();
27          System.out.println("Is a Circle object cloneable? "
28            + (c instanceof Cloneable));
29        }
30      }
31
33      // CloneableCircle is a subclass of Circle, which implements the
34      // Cloneable interface
35      class CloneableCircle extends Circle implements Cloneable {
36        // Store the date when the object is created
37        java.util.Date date = new java.util.Date();
38
39        /** Construct a CloneableCircle with a specified radius */
40        public CloneableCircle(double radius) {
41          super(radius);
42        }
43
44        /** Override the protected clone method defined in the Object
45            class, and strengthen its accessibility */
46        public Object clone() {
47          try {
48            return super.clone();
49          }
50          catch (CloneNotSupportedException ex) {
51            return null;
52          }
53        }
54      }
```

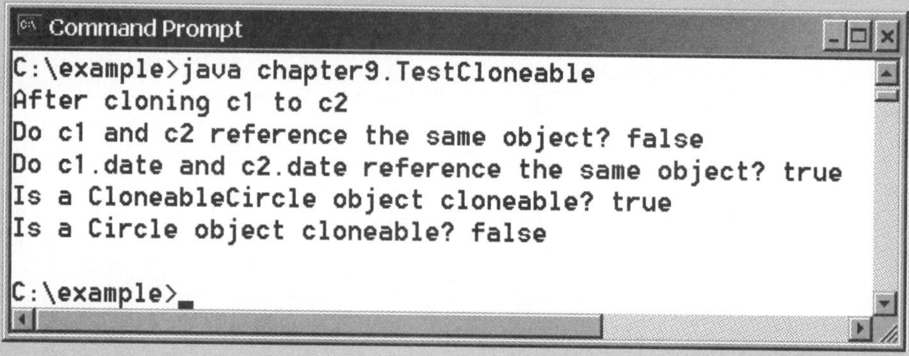

```
Command Prompt                                      _ □ ×
C:\example>java chapter9.TestCloneable
After cloning c1 to c2
Do c1 and c2 reference the same object? false
Do c1.date and c2.date reference the same object? true
Is a CloneableCircle object cloneable? true
Is a Circle object cloneable? false

C:\example>
```

Figure 9.6   *The* clone *method creates a new copy of the cloneable object.*

Review

The CloneableCircle class overrides the clone method (Lines 46–53 in Test-Cloneable.java) defined in the Object class. The clone method in the Object class is defined as follows:

```
protected native Object clone() throws CloneNotSupportedException;
```

The keyword `native` indicates that this method is not written in Java, but is implemented in the JVM for the native platform. The keyword `protected` indicates that this method cannot be directly invoked by an object of the class in a different package. For this reason, the `Cloneable` class must override the method and change the visibility modifier to `public` so that the method can be used in any package. Since the `clone` method implemented for the native platform in the `Object` class performs the task of cloning objects, the `clone` method in the `CloneableCircle` and `Name` classes simply invokes `super.clone()`. The `clone` method defined in the `Object` class may throw `CloneNotSupportedException`. Thus, `super.clone()` must be placed in a `try-catch` block. Exceptions and the `try-catch` block are introduced in Chapter 15, "Exceptions and Assertions."

The `main` method creates a `CloneableCircle` object `c1` and clones `c1` into `c2` (Lines 9–10). The `clone` method in the `Object` class copies each field from the original object to the target object. If the field is of a primitive type, its value is copied. For example, the value of `radius` (`double` type) is copied from `c1` to `c2`. If the field is of an object, the reference of the field is copied. For example, the field `date` is of the `Date` class, its reference is copied into `c2`, as shown in Figure 9.7. Therefore, `c1.date == c2.date` is true, although `c1 == c2` is false. This is referred to as a *shallow copy* rather than a *deep copy*, meaning that if the field is of an object, the reference of the field is copied rather than its contents.

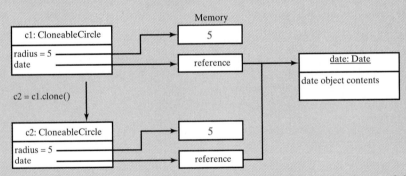

Figure 9.7   *The* `clone` *method copies the values of primitive type fields and the references of object type fields.*

If you want to perform a deep copy, you can override the `clone` method with custom cloning operations instead of invoking `super.clone()`. See Exercise 9.4.

 NOTE

You learned how to use the `arraycopy` method to copy arrays in Chapter 5, "Arrays." This method provides shallow copies. It works fine for arrays of primitive data type elements, but not for arrays of object type elements. To support a deep copy, you have to deal with how to copy individual object elements in the array.

---

continues

Example 9.3 Continued

 NOTE

An instance of `CloneableCircle` is also an instance of `Cloneable`. This means that you can copy the instance using the `clone` method. Since the `Circle` class does not implement the `Cloneable` interface, an instance of the `Circle` class is not cloneable. If you attempt to copy an instance of the `Circle` class, you will get a `CloneNotSupportedException`. Exceptions will be introduced in Chapter 15, "Exceptions and Assertions."

9.5   Processing Primitive Data Type Values as Objects

Primitive data types are not used as objects in Java due to performance considerations. Because of the overhead of processing objects, the language's performance would be adversely affected if primitive data types were treated as objects. However, many Java methods require the use of objects as arguments. Java offers a convenient way to incorporate, or wrap, a primitive data type into an object (e.g., wrapping `int` into the `Integer` class, and wrapping double into the `Double` class). The corresponding class is called a *wrapper class*. By using wrapper objects instead of a primitive data type variable, you can take advantage of generic programming.

The wrapper classes provide constructors, constants, and conversion methods for manipulating various data types. Java provides `Boolean`, `Character`, `Double`, `Float`, `Byte`, `Short`, `Integer`, and `Long` wrapper classes for primitive data types. The wrapper classes are grouped in the `java.lang` package. Their inheritance hierarchy is shown in Figure 9.8.

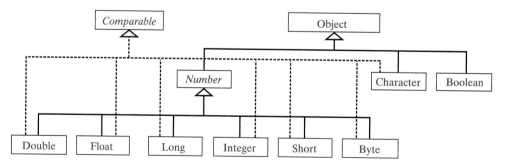

Figure 9.8   *The* `Number` *class is an abstract superclass for* `Double`, `Float`, `Long`, `Integer`, `Short`, *and* `Byte`.

 NOTE

The wrapper class name for a primitive type is the same as the primitive data type name with the first letter capitalized. The exceptions are `Integer` and `Character`.

Each numeric wrapper class extends the abstract `Number` class, which contains the methods `doubleValue`, `floatValue`, `intValue`, `longValue`, `shortValue`, and `byteValue`. These methods "convert" objects into primitive type values. The methods `doubleValue`, `floatValue`, `intValue`, and `longValue` are abstract. The methods `byteValue` and `shortValue` are not abstract; they simply return `(byte)intValue()` and `(short)intValue()`, respectively.

Each wrapper class overrides the `toString`, `equals`, and `hashCode` methods defined in the `Object` class. Since all the numeric wrapper classes and the `Character` class implement the `Comparable` interface, the `compareTo` method is implemented in these classes.

Wrapper classes are very similar. The `Character` class was introduced in Chapter 7, "Strings." The `Boolean` class is rarely used. The following sections use `Integer` and `Double` as examples to introduce the numeric wrapper classes.

9.5.1   Numeric Wrapper Class Constructors

You can construct a wrapper object either from a primitive data type value or from a string representing the numeric value. The constructors for `Integer` and `Double` are:

```
public Integer(int value)
public Integer(String s)
public Double(double value)
public Double(String s)
```

For example, you can construct a wrapper object for `double` value `5.0` using either

```
Double doubleObject = new Double(5.0);
```

or

```
Double doubleObject = new Double("5.0");
```

You can construct a wrapper object for `int` value `5` using either

```
Integer integerObject = new Integer(5);
```

or

```
Integer integerObject = new Integer("5");
```

 NOTE

The instances of all wrapper classes are immutable, i.e., their internal values cannot changed once the objects are created.

9.5.2   Numeric Wrapper Class Constants

Each numeric wrapper class has the constants `MAX_VALUE` and `MIN_VALUE`. `MAX_VALUE` represents the maximum value of the corresponding primitive data type. For `Byte`, `Short`, `Integer`, and `Long`, `MIN_VALUE` represents the minimum byte, short, int, and long values. For Float and Double, MIN_VALUE represents the minimum *positive* float and double values. The following statements display the maximum integer (2,147,483,647), the minimum positive float (1.4E-45), and the maximum double floating-point number (1.79769313486231570e+ 308d).

```
System.out.println("The maximum integer is " + Integer.MAX_VALUE);
System.out.println("The minimum positive float is " +
  Float.MIN_VALUE);
System.out.println(
  "The maximum double precision floating-point number is " +
  Double.MAX_VALUE);
```

9.5.3   Conversion Methods

Each numeric wrapper class implements the abstract methods doubleValue, floatValue, intValue, longValue, and shortValue, which are defined in the Number class. These methods "convert" objects into primitive type values.

For example:

```
long l = doubleObject.longValue(); // Note it truncates
```

This converts doubleObject's double value to a long variable l.

```
int i = integerObject.intValue();
```

This assigns the int value of integerObject to i.

```
double d = 5.9;
Double doubleObject = new Double(d);
String s = doubleObject.toString();
```

This converts double d to a string s.

9.5.4   The Static *valueOf* Methods

The numeric wrapper classes have a useful class method, valueOf(String s). This method creates a new object initialized to the value represented by the specified string. For example:

```
Double doubleObject = Double.valueOf("12.4");
Integer integerObject = Integer.valueOf("12");
```

9.5.5   The Methods for Parsing Strings into Numbers

You have used the parseInt method in the Integer class to parse a numeric string into an int value and the parseDouble method in the Double class to parse a numeric string into a double value. Each numeric wrapper class has two overloaded parsing methods to parse a numeric string into an appropriate numeric value based on 10 (decimal) or any specified radix (e.g., 2 for binary, 8 for octal, and 16 for hexadecimal). These methods are shown below:

```
// These two methods are in the Byte class
public static byte parseByte(String s)
public static byte parseByte(String s, int radix)
```

```
// These two methods are in the Short class
public static short parseShort(String s)
public static short parseShort(String s, int radix)

// These two methods are in the Integer class
public static int parseInt(String s)
public static int parseInt(String s, int radix)

// These two methods are in the Long class
public static long parseLong(String s)
public static long parseLong(String s, int radix)

// These two methods are in the Float class
public static float parseFloat(String s)
public static float parseFloat(String s, int radix)

// These two methods are in the Double class
public static double parseDouble(String s)
public static double parseDouble(String s, int radix)
```

For example,

```
Integer.parseInt("11", 2) returns 3;
Integer.parseInt("12", 8) returns 10;
Integer.parseInt("13", 10) returns 13;
Integer.parseInt("1A", 16) returns 16;
```

`Integer.parseInt("12", 2)` would raise a runtime exception because 12 is not a binary number.

Example 9.4 Sorting an Array of Objects

Problem

Write a static method for sorting an array of comparable objects. The objects are instances of the `Comparable` interface, and they are compared using the `compareTo` method. The method can be used to sort an array of any objects as long as their classes implement the `Comparable` interface.

Solution

A generic sort method is presented in the following code. To test the method, the program sorts an array of integers, an array of double numbers, an array of characters, and an array of strings. Figure 9.9 shows a sample run of the code.

```
1   // GenericSort.java: Sort an array of comparable objects
2   package chapter9;
3
4   public class GenericSort {
5     public static void main(String[] args) {
6       // Create an Integer array
7       Integer[] intArray = {new Integer(2), new Integer(4),
8         new Integer(3)};
9
10      // Create a Double array
11      Double[] doubleArray = {new Double(3.4), new Double(1.3),
12        new Double(-22.1)};
13
```

continues

389

Example 9.4 Continued

```
14          // Create a Character array
15          Character[] charArray = {new Character('a'),
16            new Character('J'), new Character('r')};
17
18          // Create a String array
19          String[] stringArray = {"Tom", "John", "Fred"};
20
21          // Sort the arrays
22          sort(intArray);
23          sort(doubleArray);
24          sort(charArray);
25          sort(stringArray);
26
27          // Display the sorted arrays
28          System.out.print("Sorted Integer objects: ");
29          printList(intArray);
30          System.out.print("Sorted Double objects: ");
31          printList(doubleArray);
32          System.out.print("Sorted Character objects: ");
33          printList(charArray);
34          System.out.print("Sorted String objects: ");
35          printList(stringArray);
36        }
37
38      /** Sort an array of comparable objects */
39      public static void sort(Object[] list) {
40        Object currentMax;
41        int currentMaxIndex;
42
43        for (int i = list.length - 1; i >= 1; i--) {
44          // Find the maximum in the list[0..i]
45          currentMax = list[i];
46          currentMaxIndex = i;
47
48          for (int j = i - 1; j >= 0; j--) {
49            if (((Comparable)currentMax).compareTo(list[j]) < 0) {
50              currentMax = list[j];
51              currentMaxIndex = j;
52            }
53          }
54
55          // Swap list[i] with list[currentMaxIndex] if necessary;
56          if (currentMaxIndex != i) {
57            list[currentMaxIndex] = list[i];
58            list[i] = currentMax;
59          }
60        }
61      }
62
63      /** Print an array of objects */
64      public static void printList(Object[] list) {
65        for (int i = 0; i < list.length; i++)
66          System.out.print(list[i] + " ");
67        System.out.println();
68      }
69    }
```

Review

The algorithm for the sort method is the same as in Example 5.10, "Sorting Arrays." The sort method in Example 5.10 sorts an array of double values. The sort method in this example can sort an array of any object type, provided that the

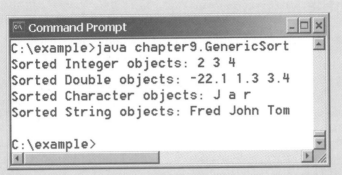

Figure 9.9 *The program uses a generic sort method to sort an array of comparable objects.*

objects are also instances of the `Comparable` interface. This is an example of *generic programming*. Generic programming enables a method to operate on arguments of generic types, making it reusable with multiple types.

`Integer`, `Double`, `Character`, and `String` implement `Comparable`. So the objects of these classes can be compared using the `compareTo` method. The sort method uses the `compareTo` method to determine the order of the objects in the array.

 TIP

Java provides a static `sort` method for sorting an array of `Object` in the `java.util.Arrays` class. So you can use the following code to sort arrays in this example:

```
java.util.Arrays.sort(intArray);
java.util.Arrays.sort(doubleArray);
java.util.Arrays.sort(charArray);
java.util.Arrays.sort(stringArray);
```

 NOTE

Arrays are objects. An array is an instance of the `Object` class. Furthermore, if `A` is a subclass of `B`, every instance of `A[]` is an instance of `B[]`. Therefore, the following statements are all true:

```
new int[10] instanceof Object
new GregorianCalendar[10] instanceof Calendar[];
new Calendar[10] instanceof Object[]
new Calendar[10] instanceof Object
```

 CAUTION

Although an `int` value can be assigned to a `double` type variable, `int[]` and `double[]` are two incompatible types. Therefore, you cannot assign an `int[]` array to a variable of `double[]` or `Object[]` type.

Chapter Summary

- Abstract classes are like regular classes with data and methods, but you cannot create instances of abstract classes using the new operator.

- An abstract method is a method signature without implementation. Its implementation is provided by the subclasses. A class that contains abstract methods must be declared abstract.

- An abstract method cannot be contained in a nonabstract class. If a subclass of an abstract superclass does not implement all the abstract methods, the subclass must be declared abstract.

- A class that contains abstract methods must be abstract. However, it is possible to declare an abstract class that contains no abstract methods.

- A subclass can be abstract even if its superclass is concrete.

- An interface is a classlike construct that contains only constants and abstract methods. In many ways, an interface is similar to an abstract class, but an abstract class can contain constants and abstract methods as well as variables and concrete methods.

- An interface is treated like a special class in Java. Each interface is compiled into a separate bytecode file, just like a regular class.

- The java.lang.Comparable interface defines the compareTo method. Many classes in the Java library implement Comparable.

- An interface with an empty body is referred to as a *marker interface*. The java.lang.Cloneable interface is a marker interface. An object of the class that implements the Cloneable interface is cloneable.

- A class can extend only one superclass, but a class can implement one or more interfaces.

- An interface can extend one or more interfaces.

- Many Java methods require the use of objects as arguments. Java offers a convenient way to incorporate, or wrap, a primitive data type into an object (e.g., wrapping int into the Integer class, and wrapping double into the Double class). The corresponding class is called a *wrapper class*. By using wrapper objects instead of a primitive data type variable, you can take advantage of generic programming.

- The wrapper class for byte is Byte, for short is Short, for int is Integer, for long is Long, for float is for Float, for double is Double, for char is Character, and for boolean is Boolean.

- The numeric wrapper classes extend the abstract java.lang.Number class and implement the java.lang.Comparable interface. The Character class also implements java.lang.Comparable.

Review Questions

9.1 Define the following terms: abstract classes, interfaces.

9.2 Indicate true or false for the following statements:

- An abstract class can have instances created using the constructor of the abstract class.

- An abstract class can be extended.

- You can always successfully cast an instance of a subclass to a superclass.

- You can always successfully cast an instance of a superclass to a subclass.

- An interface is compiled into a separate bytecode file.

- A subclass of a nonabstract superclass cannot be abstract.

- A subclass cannot override a concrete method in a superclass to declare it abstract.

9.3 Which of the following class definitions defines a legal abstract class?

```
a. class A {
     abstract void unfinished() {
     }
   }

b. class A {
     abstract void unfinished();
   }

c. abstract class A {
     abstract void unfinished();
   }

d. public class abstract A {
     abstract void unfinished();
   }

e. abstract class A {
     protected void unfinished();
   }
```

9.4 Which of the following is a correct interface?

```
a. interface A {
     void print() { };
   }

b. abstract interface A {
     print();
   }

c. abstract interface A extends I1, I2 {
     abstract void print() { };
   }
```

d. ```
   interface A {
     void print();
   }
   ```

**9.5** Can you assign new `int[10]`, new `String[100]`, new `Object[50]`, or new `Calendar[20]` into a variable of `Object[]` type?

**9.6** Consider redefining the `max` method in the `Max` class as follows:

```
public class Max {
  /** Return the maximum between two objects */
  public static Comparable max(Comparable o1, Comparable o2) {
    if (o1.compareTo(o2) > 0)
      return o1;
    else
      return o2;
  }
}
```

Can Example 9.2, "Using Interfaces," compile and run correctly?

9.7 The `findArea` and `findPerimeter` methods may be removed from the `GeometricObject` class. What are the benefits of defining `findArea` and `findPerimeter` as abstract methods in the `GeometricObject` class?

9.8 You can define the `compareTo` method in a class without implementing the `Comparable` interface. What are the benefits of implementing the `Comparable` interface?

9.9 Show the output of the following code:

```
public class Test {
  public static void main(String[] args) {
    Object circle1 = new Circle();
    Object circle2 = new Circle();
    System.out.println(circle1.equals(circle2));
  }
}

class Circle {
  double radius;

  public boolean equals(Circle circle) {
    return this.radius == circle.radius;
  }
}
```

9.10 Show the output of the following code:

```
public class Test {
  public static void main(String[] args) {
    Object circle1 = new Circle();
    Object circle2 = new Circle();
    System.out.println(circle1.equals(circle2));
  }
}

class Circle {
  double radius;
```
```

```
    public boolean equals(Object circle) {
      return this.radius == ((Circle)circle).radius;
    }
  }
```

9.11 Describe primitive-type wrapper classes. Why do you need these wrapper classes?

9.12 Are the following statements correct?

```
Integer i = new Integer("23");
Integer i = new Integer(23);
Integer i = Integer.valueOf("23");
Integer i = Integer.parseInt("23",8);
Double d = new Double();
Double d = Double.valueOf("23.45");
int i = (Integer.valueOf("23")).intValue();
double d = (Double.valueOf("23.4")).doubleValue();
int i = (Double.valueOf("23.4")).intValue();
String s = (Double.valueOf("23.4")).toString();
```

9.13 How do you convert an integer into a string? How do you convert a numeric string into an integer?

9.14 How do you convert a double number into a string? How do you convert a numeric string into a double value?

9.15 Why do the following two lines of code compile but cause a runtime error?

```
Number numberRef = new Integer(0);
Double doubleRef = (Double)numberRef;
```

9.16 Why do the following two lines of code compile but cause a runtime error?

```
Number[] numberArray = new Integer[2];
numberArray[0] = new Double(1.5);
```

9.17 What is wrong in the following code?

```
public class Test {
  public static void main(String[] args) {
    Number x = new Integer(3);
    System.out.println(x.intValue());
    System.out.println(x.compareTo(new Integer(4)));
  }
}
```

9.18 What is wrong in the following code?

```
public class Test {
  public static void main(String[] args) {
    Number x = new Integer(3);
    System.out.println(x.intValue());
    System.out.println((Integer)x.compareTo(new Integer(4)));
  }
}
```

Programming Exercises

9.1 (Enabling GeometricObject comparable) Modify the GeometricObject class to implement the Comparable interface, and define the max method in the GeometricObject class. Write a test program that uses the max method to find the largest of two circles and the largest of two cylinders.

9.2 (The ComparableRectangle class) Create a class named ComparableRectangle that extends Rectangle and implements Comparable. Implement the compareTo method to compare the areas of the rectangles. Write a test class to find the largest of two instances of ComparableRectangle objects.

9.3 (The Eatable interface) Create an interface named Eatable, as follows:

```
public interface Eatable {
  public void howToEat();
}
```

Every class of an eatable object must implement the Eatable interface. Create the following two sets of classes:

■ Create a class named Animal and its subclasses Tiger, Chicken, and Elephant. Since chicken is eatable, implement the Eatable interface for the Chicken class.

■ Create a class named Fruit and its subclasses Apple and Orange. Since all fruits are eatable, implement the Eatable interface for the Fruit class. In the Fruit class, give a generic implementation of the howToEat method. In the Apple class and the Orange class, give a specific implementation of the howToEat method.

Override the toString method in each class to return the name of the class. For example, the toString method in the Animal class returns Animal.

Create a test program that contains a main method and a method named showObject. The main method declares and creates four instances of the Object type for a tiger, a chicken, an apple, and an orange. For example, Object tiger = new Tiger(). It then invokes the showObject method to display the object. The showObject method is given as follows:

```
public static void showObject(Object object) {
  System.out.println(object);
  if (object instanceof Eatable) {
    ((Eatable)object).howToEat();
  }
}
```

9.4 (Revising Example 9.3 "Cloning Objects") Rewrite the CloneableCircle class in Example 9.3 to perform a deep copy on the date field.

9.5 (Enabling Circle comparable) Rewrite the Circle class on page 370 to extend GeometricObject and implement the Comparable interface. Override the equals and hashCode methods in the Object class. Two Circle objects are equal if their radii are the same.

9.6 (Enabling Rectangle comparable) Rewrite the Rectangle class on page 370 to extend GeometricObject and implement the Comparable interface. Override the equals and hashCode methods in the Object class. Two Rectangle objects are equal if their areas are the same.

9.7 (The Octagon class) Write a class named Octagon that extends GeometricObject and implements the Comparable and Cloneable interface. Assume that all eight sides of the octagon are of equal size. The Octagon class is defined as follows:

```
public class Octagon extends GeometricObject
  implements Comparable, Cloneable {
  private double side;

  /** Construct a Octagon with the specified side */
  public Octagon(double side) {
    // Implement it
  }

  /** Implement the abstract method findArea in
     GeometricObject */
  public double findArea() {
    // Implement it (area = (2 + 4/√2)side*side)
  }

  /** Implement the abstract method findPerimeter in
     GeometricObject */
  public double findPerimeter() {
    // Implement it
  }

  /** Implement the compareTo method in
     the Comparable interface */
  public int compareTo(Object obj) {
    // Implement it (compare two Octagons based on their areas)
  }

  /** Implement the clone method in the Object class */
  public Object clone() {
    // Implement it
  }

  /** Override the toString method */
  public String toString() {
    // Implement it return the side
  }

  /** Override the equals method */
  public boolean equals(Object o) {
    // Implement it return true if two octagons have the same side
  }
}
```

Write a test program that creates an Octagon object with side value 5 and displays its area and perimeter. Create a new object using the clone method and compare the two objects using the compareTo method.

9.8 (Summing the areas of geometric objects) Write a method that summarizes the area of all the geometric objects in an array. The method signature is:

```
public static double sumArea(GeometricObject[] a)
```

Write a test program that creates an array of three objects (a circle, a cylinder, and a rectangle) and computes their total area using the sumArea method.

9.9 (Finding the largest object) Write a method that returns the largest object in an array of objects. The method signature is:

```
public static Object max(Object[] a)
```

All the objects are instances of the Comparable interface. The order of the objects in the array is determined using the compareTo method.

Write a test program that creates an array of ten strings, an array of ten integers, and an array of ten Comparable circles, and find the largest string, integer, and circle in the arrays.

9.10 (Revising Example 4.7 "Displaying Calendars") Rewrite Example 4.7 to display a calendar for a specified month using the Calendar and GregorianCalendar classes. Your program receives the month and year from the command line. For example:

```
java Exercise9_10 3 2003
```

This displays the calendar shown in Figure 9.10.

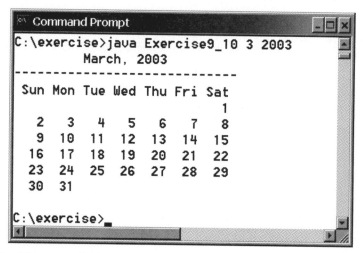

Figure 9.10   *The program displays a calendar for March 2003.*

You also can run the program without the year. In this case, the year is the current year. If you run the program without specifying a month and a year, the month is the current month.

OBJECT-ORIENTED MODELING

Objectives

- To become familiar with the process of program development.

- To analyze and discover relationships among classes: association, aggregation, strong inheritance, and weak inheritance.

- To declare classes to represent relationships among the classes.

- To implement the Rational class and process rational numbers using this class.

- To design classes that follow the class-design guidelines.

- To model dynamic behavior using sequence diagrams and statechart diagrams.

- To design generic classes for matrix operations. (Optional)

- To develop generic linked lists. (Optional)

- To know the concept of framework-based programming using Java API.

10.1   Introduction

The preceding chapters introduced objects, classes, class inheritance, and interfaces. You learned the concepts of object-oriented programming. This chapter focuses on the development of software systems using the object-oriented approach, and introduces class modeling using the Unified Modeling Language (UML). You will learn class-design guidelines and the techniques for designing reusable classes through the `Rational` class, generic matrix classes, and generic linked list classes.

10.2   The Software Development Process

Developing a software project is an engineering process. Software products, no matter how large or how small, have the same developmental phases: requirements specification, analysis, design, implementation, testing, deployment, and maintenance, as shown in Figure 10.1.

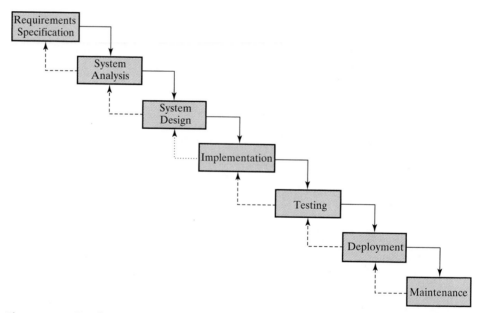

Figure 10.1   *Developing a project involves requirements specification, system analysis, system design, implementation, testing, deployment, and maintenance.*

Requirements specification is a formal process that seeks to understand the problem and document in detail what the software system needs to do. This phase involves close interaction between users and designers. Most of the examples in this book are simple, and their requirements are clearly stated. In the real world, however, problems are not well defined. You need to study a problem carefully to identify its requirements.

System analysis seeks to analyze the business process in terms of data flow, and to identify the system's input and output. Part of the analysis entails modeling the system's behavior. The model is intended to capture the essential elements of the system and to define services to the system.

System design is the process of designing the system's components. This phase involves the use of many levels of abstraction to decompose the problem into manageable components, identify classes and interfaces, and establish relationships among the classes and interfaces.

Implementation is the process of translating the system design into programs. Separate programs are written for each component and put to work together. This phase requires the use of a programming language like Java. The implementation involves coding, testing, and debugging.

Testing ensures that the code meets the requirements specification and weeds out bugs. An independent team of software engineers not involved in the design and implementation of the project usually conducts such testing.

Deployment makes the project available for use. For a Java applet, this means installing it on a Web server; for a Java application, installing it on the client's computer. A project usually consists of many classes. An effective approach for deployment is to package all the classes into a Java archive file, as will be introduced in Bonus Supplement H, "Packaging and Deploying Java Projects."

Maintenance is concerned with changing and improving the product. A software product must continue to perform and improve in a changing environment. This requires periodic upgrades of the product to fix newly discovered bugs and incorporate changes.

The central task in object-oriented system development is to design classes to model the system. While there are many object-oriented methodologies, UML has become the industry-standard notation for class analysis and design, and itself leads to a methodology. The following sections introduce analyzing, designing, and implementing classes.

10.3   Analyzing Relationships Among Objects

By now you have formed some ideas about objects and classes and their programming features. Object-oriented programming is centered on objects; it is particularly involved with getting objects to work together. The first step in object-oriented program development is to identify the objects and establish relationships among them. Since objects are modeled using classes, a relationship among objects of different classes is also referred to as a relationship among these classes. The relationships can be classified into three types: *association*, *aggregation*, and *inheritance*.

10.3.1   Association

Association is a general binary relationship that describes an activity between two classes. For example, a student taking a course is an association between the Student class and the Course class, and a faculty member teaching a course is an association between the Faculty class and the Course class. These associations can be represented in UML graphical notations, as shown in Figure 10.2.

Figure 10.2 *A student may take any number of courses, and a faculty member teaches at most three courses. A course may have from five to sixty students and is taught by only one faculty member.*

An association is illustrated using a solid line between two classes with an optional label that describes the relationship. In Figure 10.2, the labels are *Take* and *Teach*. Each relationship may have an optional small black triangle that indicates the direction of the relationship. In Figure 10.2, the direction indicates that a student takes a course, as opposed to a course taking a student.

Each class involved in the relationship may have a role name that describes the role played by the class in the relationship. In Figure 10.2, *teacher* is the role name for `Faculty`.

Each class involved in an association may specify a *multiplicity*. A multiplicity could be a number or an interval that specifies how many objects of the class are involved in the relationship. The character * means unlimited number of objects, and the interval m..n means that the number of objects should be between m and n, inclusive. In Figure 10.2, each student may take any number of courses, and each course must have at least five students and at most sixty students. Each course is taught by only one faculty member, and a faculty member may teach from zero to three courses per semester.

Association may exist between objects of the same class. For example, a person may have a supervisor. This is illustrated in Figure 10.3.

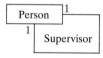

Figure 10.3 *A person may have a supervisor.*

An association is usually represented as a data field in the class. For example, the relationships in Figure 10.2 can be represented in the following classes:

```
public class Student {
   /** Data fields */
   /** Constructors */
   /** Methods */
}
```

```
public class Course {
   private Student[]
      classList;
   private Faculty faculty;

   /** Data fields */
   /** Constructors */
   /** Methods */
}
```

```
public class Faculty {
   /** Data fields */
   /** Constructors */
   /** Methods */
}
```

Alternatively, they can be represented as follows:

```
public class Student {
  private Course[]
    courseList;

  /** Data fields */
  /** Constructors */
  /** Methods */
}
```

```
public class Course {
  /** Data fields */
  /** Constructors */
  /** Methods */
}
```

```
public class Faculty {
  private Course[]
    courseList;

  /** Data fields */
  /** Constructors */
  /** Methods */
}
```

In the association "a person has a supervisor," as shown in Figure 10.3, a supervisor can be represented as a data field in the Person class, as follows:

```
public class Person {
  private Person supervisor;

  /** Data fields */
  /** Constructors */
  /** Methods */
}
```

10.3.2 Aggregation

Aggregation is a special form of association that represents an ownership relationship between two classes. Aggregation models relationships like has-a, part-of, owns, and employed-by. An object may be owned by several other aggregated objects. If an object is exclusively owned by an aggregated object, the relationship between the object and its aggregated object is referred to as *composition*. For example, a publisher that owns a magazine is a composition between the Publisher class and the Magazine class, whereas a publisher that has consultants is an aggregation between the Publisher class and the Consultant class, since a consultant may work for several publishers. In UML, a filled diamond is attached to the Publisher class of the association to denote the composition relationship, and an empty diamond is attached to the aggregated class of the association to denote the aggregation relationship, as shown in Figure 10.4.

Figure 10.4 *A magazine is owned by a publisher; a consultant may work for several publishers.*

Since aggregation and composition are special cases of association, an aggregation or a composition can be translated into classes in the same way as an association. For a composition, a composed class can also be created as an inner class of the composing class. For example, the relationship "a publisher owns magazines" can be represented as follows:

```
public class Publisher {
  private Magazine[] magazineList;

  /** Data fields */
  /** Constructors */
```

```
/** Methods */

class Magazine {
    ...
  }
}
```

10.3.3   Inheritance

Inheritance models the is-a relationship between two classes. A strong is-a relationship describes a direct inheritance relationship between two classes. A weak is-a relationship describes that a class has certain properties. A strong is-a relationship can be represented using class inheritance. For example, the relationship "a student is a person, and a faculty member is a person" (see Figure 10.5) is a strong is-a relationship and can be represented using the following classes:

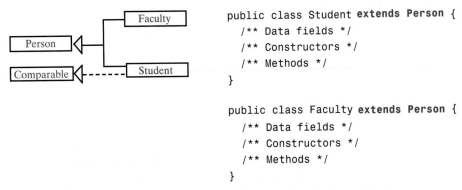

```
public class Student extends Person {
    /** Data fields */
    /** Constructors */
    /** Methods */
}


public class Faculty extends Person {
    /** Data fields */
    /** Constructors */
    /** Methods */
}
```

Figure 10.5   Faculty *and* Student *extend* Person. Student *implements* Comparable.

A weak is-a relationship can be represented using interfaces. For example, the weak is-a relationship "students are comparable based on their grades" (see Figure 10.5) can be represented by implementing the Comparable interface, as follows:

```
public class Student extends Person implements Comparable {
    /** Data fields */
    /** Constructors */
    /** Methods */

    /** Implement the compareTo method */
    public int compareTo(Object object) {
      // ...
    }
}
```

10.4   Class Development

The key to object-oriented programming is to model the application in terms of co-operative objects. Carefully designed classes are critical when a project is being developed. There are many levels of abstraction in system design. You have learned method abstraction and have applied it to the development of large programs. Methods are means to group statements. Classes extend abstraction to a higher level and provide a means of grouping methods. Classes do more than just group methods, however; they also contain data fields. Methods and data fields together describe the properties and behaviors of classes.

The power of classes is further extended by inheritance. Inheritance enables a class to extend the contract and the implementation of an existing class without knowing the details of the existing class. In the development of a Java program, class abstraction is applied to decompose the problem into a set of related classes, and method abstraction is applied to design individual classes.

This section uses two examples to demonstrate identifying classes, analyzing classes, and applying class abstraction in object-oriented program development.

Example 10.1 Borrowing Loans

Problem

Develop a system that models borrowing loans.

Solution

For simplicity, the example does not attempt to build a complete system for storing, processing, and manipulating loans for borrowers; instead it focuses on modeling borrowers and the loans for the borrowers. The following steps are usually involved in building an object-oriented system:

1. Identify classes for the system.

2. Describe the attributes and methods in each class.

3. Establish relationships among classes.

4. Create classes.

The first step is to identify classes for the system. There are many strategies for identifying classes in a system, one of which is to study how the system works and select a number of use cases, or scenarios. Since a borrower is a person who obtains a loan, and a person has a name and an address, you can identify the following classes: Person, Name, Address, Borrower, and Loan.

The second step is to describe the attributes and methods in each of the classes you have identified. The attributes and methods can be illustrated using UML, as shown in Figure 10.6. The Name class has the properties firstName, mi, and lastName, their associated get and set methods, and the getFullName method for returning the full name. The Address class has the properties street, city, state, and zip, their associated get and set methods, and the getAddress method for returning the full address. The Loan class, presented in Example 6.7, "The Loan Class," has the properties annualInterestRate, numOfYears, and loanAmount, and property get and set methods, monthlyPayment, and totalPayment methods. The Person class has the properties name and address, their associated get and set methods, and the toString method for displaying complete information about the person. Borrower is a subclass of Person. Additionally, Borrower has the loan property and its associated get and set methods, and the toString method for displaying the person and the loan payments.

continues

405

Example 10.1 Continued

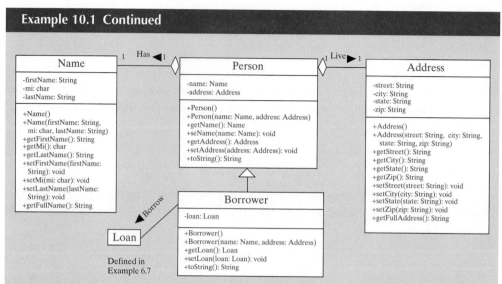

Figure 10.6 *A borrower has a name with an address and borrows a loan.*

The third step is to establish relationships among the classes. The relationship is derived clearly from the analysis of the preceding two steps. The first three steps are intertwined. When you identify classes, you also think about the relationship among them. The relationships for the classes in this example are illustrated in Figure 10.6.

The fourth step is to write the code for the classes, as follows:

```
1   // Name.java: Encapsulate name information
2   package chapter10;
3
4   public class Name implements Cloneable {
5     private String firstName;
6     private char mi;
7     private String lastName;
8
9     /** Default constructor */
10    public Name() {
11      this("Jill", 'S', "Barr");
12    }
13
14    /** Construct a name with firstName, mi, and lastName */
15    public Name(String firstName, char mi, String lastName) {
16      this.firstName = firstName;
17      this.mi = mi;
18      this.lastName = lastName;
19    }
20
21    /** Return firstName */
22    public String getFirstName() {
23      return firstName;
24    }
25
26    /** Set a new firstName */
27    public void setFirstName(String firstName) {
28      this.firstName = firstName;
29    }
30
```

```
31      /** Return middle name initial */
32      public char getMi() {
33        return mi;
34      }
35
36      /** Set a new middlename initial */
37      public void setMi(char mi) {
38        this.mi = mi;
39      }
40
41      /** Return lastName */
42      public String getLastname() {
43        return lastName;
44      }
45
46      /** Set a new lastName */
47      public void setLastName(String lastName) {
48        this.lastName = lastName;
49      }
50
51      /** Obtain full name */
52      public String getFullName() {
53        return firstName + ' ' + mi + ' ' + lastName;
54      }
55   }
```

```
1    // Address.java: Encapsulate address information
2    package chapter10;
3
4    public class Address {
5      private String street;
6      private String city;
7      private String state;
8      private String zip;
9
10     /** Default constructor */
11     public Address() {
12       this("100 Main", "Savannah", "GA", "31411");
13     }
14
15     /** Create address with street, city, state, and zip */
16     public Address(String street, String city,
17       String state, String zip) {
18       this.street = street;
19       this.city = city;
20       this.state = state;
21       this.zip = zip;
22     }
23
24     /** Return street */
25     public String getStreet() {
26       return street;
27     }
28
29     /** Set a new street */
30     public void setStreet(String street) {
31       this.street = street;
32     }
33
34     /** Return city */
35     public String getCity() {
36       return city;
37     }
38
```

continues

Example 10.1 Continued

```
39        /** Set a new city */
40        public void setCity(String city) {
41          this.city = city;
42        }
43
44        /** Return state */
45        public String getState() {
46          return state;
47        }
48
49        /** Set a new state */
50        public void setState(String state) {
51          this.state = state;
52        }
53
54        /** Return zip */
55        public String getZip() {
56          return zip;
57        }
58
59        /** Set a new zip */
60        public void setZip(String zip) {
61          this.zip = zip;
62        }
63
64        /** Get full address */
65        public String getFullAddress() {
66          return street + '\n' + city + ", " + state + ' ' + zip + '\n';
67        }
68      }
```

```
1       package chapter10;
2
3       public class Person {
4         private Name name;
5         private Address address;
6
7         /** Default constructor */
8         public Person() {
9           this(new Name("Jill", 'S', "Barr"),
10            new Address("100 Main", "Savannah", "GA", "31411"));
11        }
12
13        /** Construct a person with specified name and address */
14        public Person(Name name, Address address) {
15          this.name = name;
16          this.address = address;
17        }
18
19        /** Return name */
20        public Name getName() {
21          return name;
22        }
23
24        /** Set a new name */
25        public void setName(Name name) {
26          this.name = name;
27        }
28
29        /** Return address */
30        public Address getAddress() {
```

```
31        return address;
32      }
33
34      /** Set a new address */
35      public void setAddress(Address address) {
36        this.address = address;
37      }
38
39      /** Override the toString method */
40      public String toString() {
41        return '\n' + name.getFullName() + '\n' +
42          address.getFullAddress() + '\n';
43      }
44    }
```

```
1     // Borrower.java: Encapsulate borrower information
2     package chapter10;
3
4     import chapter6.Loan;
5
6     public class Borrower extends Person {
7       private Loan loan;
8
9       /** Default constructor */
10      public Borrower() {
11        super();
12      }
13
14      /** Create a borrower with specified name and address */
15      public Borrower(Name name, Address address) {
16        super(name, address);
17      }
18
19      /** Return loan */
20      public Loan getLoan() {
21        return loan;
22      }
23
24      /** Set a new loan */
25      public void setLoan(Loan loan) {
26        this.loan = loan;
27      }
28
29      /** String representation for borrower */
30      public String toString() {
31        return super.toString() +
32          "Monthly payment is " + loan.monthlyPayment() + '\n' +
33          "Total payment is " + loan.totalPayment();
34      }
35    }
```

Immediately below is a test program that uses the classes Name, Address, Borrower, and Loan. The output of the program is shown in Figure 10.7.

```
1     // BorrowLoan.java: Demonstrate using the classes Borrower
2     // Name, Address, and Loan
3     package chapter10;
4
5     import chapter6.Loan;
6     import chapter8.Name;
7     import javax.swing.JOptionPane;
8
```

continues

409

Example 10.1 Continued

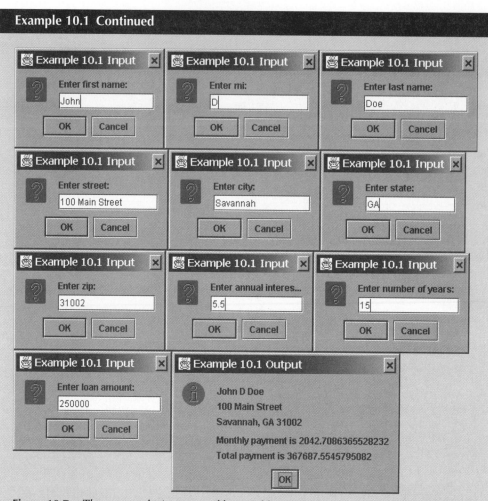

Figure 10.7   *The program obtains name, address, and loan, stores the information in a* Borrower *object, and displays the information with the loan payment.*

```
9      public class BorrowLoan {
10       /** Main method */
11       public static void main(String[] args) {
12         // Create one borrower
13         Borrower borrower = new Borrower();
14
15         // Enter the information for the borrower
16
17         // 1. Enter name
18         Name name = new Name();
19         // Prompt the user to enter first name
20         String firstName = JOptionPane.showInputDialog(null,
21           "Enter first name:", "Example 10.1 Input",
22           JOptionPane.QUESTION_MESSAGE);
23
24         // Set first name
25         name.setFirstName(firstName);
26
27         // Prompt the user to enter mi
28         String mi = JOptionPane.showInputDialog(null,
```

```
29            "Enter mi:", "Example 10.1 Input",
30            JOptionPane.QUESTION_MESSAGE);
31
32          // Set mi
33          name.setMi(mi.charAt(0));
34
35          // Prompt the user to enter last name
36          String lastName = JOptionPane.showInputDialog(null,
37            "Enter last name:", "Example 10.1 Input",
38            JOptionPane.QUESTION_MESSAGE);
39
40          // Set last name
41          name.setLastName(lastName);
42
43          // 2. Enter address
44          Address address = new Address();
45          // Prompt the user to enter street
46          String street = JOptionPane.showInputDialog(null,
47            "Enter street:", "Example 10.1 Input",
48            JOptionPane.QUESTION_MESSAGE);
49
50          // Set street
51          address.setStreet(street);
52
53          // Prompt the user to enter city
54          String city = JOptionPane.showInputDialog(null,
55            "Enter city:", "Example 10.1 Input",
56            JOptionPane.QUESTION_MESSAGE);
57
58          // Set city
59          address.setCity(city);
60
61          // Prompt the user to enter state
62          String state = JOptionPane.showInputDialog(null,
63            "Enter state:", "Example 10.1 Input",
64            JOptionPane.QUESTION_MESSAGE);
65
66          // Set state
67          address.setState(state);
68
69          // Prompt the user to enter zip
70          String zip = JOptionPane.showInputDialog(null,
71            "Enter zip:", "Example 10.1 Input",
72            JOptionPane.QUESTION_MESSAGE);
73
74          // Set zip
75          address.setZip(zip);
76
77          // 3. Enter loan information
78          Loan loan = new Loan();
79          // Prompt the user to enter annual interest rate
80          String annualInterestRateString = JOptionPane.showInputDialog(
81            null, "Enter annual interest rate (i.e. 7.25):",
82            "Example 10.1 Input", JOptionPane.QUESTION_MESSAGE);
83
84          // Convert string into double
85          double annualInterestRate =
86            Double.parseDouble(annualInterestRateString);
87
88          // Set annual interest rate
89          loan.setAnnualInterestRate(annualInterestRate);
90
```

continues

411

Example 10.1 Continued

```
91          // Prompt the user to enter number of years
92          String numOfYearsString = JOptionPane.showInputDialog(
93            null, "Enter number of years:",
94            "Example 10.1 Input", JOptionPane.QUESTION_MESSAGE);
95
96          // Convert string into integer
97          int numOfYears = Integer.parseInt(numOfYearsString);
98
99          // Set number of years
100         loan.setNumOfYears(numOfYears);
101
102         // Prompt the user to enter loan amount
103         String loanAmountString = JOptionPane.showInputDialog(
104           null, "Enter loan amount:",
105           "Example 10.1 Input", JOptionPane.QUESTION_MESSAGE);
106
107         // Convert string into double
108         double loanAmount = Double.parseDouble(loanAmountString);
109
110         // Set loan amount
111         loan.setLoanAmount(loanAmount);
112
113         // 4. Set values to the borrower
114         borrower.setName(name);
115         borrower.setAddress(address);
116         borrower.setLoan(loan);
117
118         // Display loan information
119         JOptionPane.showMessageDialog(null, borrower.toString(),
120           "Example 10.1 Output", JOptionPane.INFORMATION_MESSAGE);
121
122         System.exit(0);
123       }
124     }
```

Review

Identifying objects is not easy for novice programmers. How do you find the right objects? There is no unique solution even for simple problems. Software development is more an art than a science. The quality of a program ultimately depends on the programmer's intuition, experience, and knowledge. This example identified five classes: Name, Address, Person, Borrower, and Loan. There are several alternatives. One would combine Name, Address, Person, Borrower into one class. This design is not clear because it puts too many entities into one class.

The example is long, but most of the coding is for the get and set methods. Once an object is identified, its properties and methods can be defined by analyzing the requirements and scenarios of the system. It is a good practice to provide complete get and set methods. These may not be needed for your current project, but will be useful in other projects, since your classes are designed for reuse in future projects.

Establishing relationships among objects helps you to understand the interactions among objects. An object-oriented system consists of a collection of interrelated, cooperative objects.

10.5   The *Rational* Class

A rational number is a number with a numerator and a denominator in the form *a/b*, where a is the numerator and b is the denominator. For example, 1/3, 3/4, and 10/4.

A rational number cannot have a denominator of 0, but a numerator of 0 is fine. Every integer a is equivalent to a rational number a/1. Rational numbers are used in exact computations involving fractions; for example, 1/3 = 0.33333.... This number cannot be precisely represented in floating-point format using data type double or float. To obtain the exact result, it is necessary to use rational numbers.

Java provides data types for integers and floating-point numbers, but not for rational numbers. This section shows how to design a class to represent rational numbers.

Example 10.2 The Rational Class

Problem

Develop a class named Rational for representing rational numbers.

Solution

Since rational numbers share many common features with integers and floating-point numbers, and Number is the root class for numeric wrapper classes, it is appropriate to define Rational as a subclass of Number. Since rational numbers are comparable, the Rational class should also implement the Comparable interface.

Figure 10.8 is an illustration of the Rational class and its relationship to the Number class and the Comparable interface.

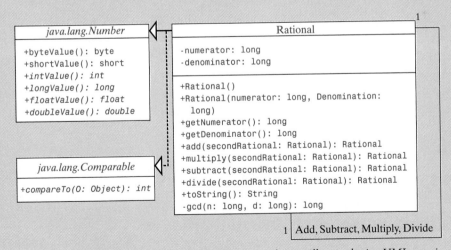

Figure 10.8 *The properties and methods of the* Rational *class are illustrated using UML notation.*

continues

Example 10.2 Continued

The Rational class contains the following elements:

Data fields:

- ■ long numerator: Represents the numerator of the rational number.

- ■ long denominator: Represents the denominator of the rational number.

Methods:

- ■ public Rational add(Rational secondRational)
  Returns the addition of this rational with another.

- ■ public Rational subtract(Rational secondRational)
  Returns the subtraction of this rational with another.

- ■ public Rational multiply(Rational secondRational)
  Returns the multiplication of this rational with another.

- ■ public Rational divide(Rational secondRational)
  Returns the division of this rational with another.

- ■ private long gcd(long n, long d)
  Returns the greatest common divisor of two numbers.

A rational number consists of a numerator and a denominator. There are many equivalent rational numbers; for example, $1/3 = 2/6 = 3/9 = 4/12$. For convenience, 1/3 is used in this example to represent all rational numbers that are equivalent to 1/3. The numerator and the denominator of 1/3 have no common divisor except 1, so 1/3 is said to be in lowest terms.

To reduce a rational number to its lowest terms, you need to find the greatest common divisor (GCD) of the absolute values of its numerator and denominator, and then divide both numerator and denominator by this value. You can use the recursive method for computing the GCD of two integers n and d, as suggested in Exercise 4.11, or use Euclid's famous algorithm, as follows:

```
t1 = Math.abs(n); t2 = Math.abs(d); // Get absolute value of n and d;
r = t1 % t2; // r is the remainder of t1 divided by t2;
while (r != 0) {
  t1 = t2;
  t2 = r;
  r = t1 % t2;
}

// When r is 0, t2 is the greatest common divisor between t1 and t2
return t2;
```

The Rational class is presented below, followed by a test program. Figure 10.9 shows a sample run of the program.

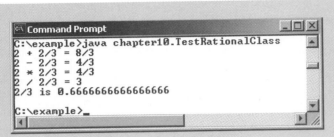

Figure 10.9   *The program creates two instances of the* Rational *class and displays their addition, subtraction, multiplication, and division.*

```
1    // Rational.java: Define a rational number and its associated
2    // operations such as add, subtract, multiply, and divide
3    package chapter10;
4
5    public class Rational extends Number implements Comparable {
6      // Data fields for numerator and denominator
7      private long numerator = 0;
8      private long denominator = 1;
9
10     /** Default constructor */
11     public Rational() {
12       this(0, 1);
13     }
14
15     /** Construct a rational with specified numerator and denominator */
16     public Rational(long numerator, long denominator) {
17       long gcd = gcd(numerator, denominator);
18       this.numerator = ((denominator > 0) ? 1 : -1) * numerator / gcd;
19       this.denominator = Math.abs(denominator) / gcd;
20     }
21
22     /** Find GCD of two numbers */
23     private long gcd(long n, long d) {
24       long t1 = Math.abs(n);
25       long t2 = Math.abs(d);
26       long remainder = t1 % t2;
27
28       while (remainder != 0) {
29         t1 = t2;
30         t2 = remainder;
31         remainder = t1%t2;
32       }
33
34       return t2;
35     }
36
37     /** Return numerator */
38     public long getNumerator() {
39       return numerator;
40     }
41
```

continued

415

Example 10.2 Continued

```
42          /** Return denominator */
43          public long getDenominator() {
44            return denominator;
45          }
46
47          /** Add a rational number to this rational */
48          public Rational add(Rational secondRational) {
49            long n = numerator * secondRational.getDenominator() +
50              denominator * secondRational.getNumerator();
51            long d = denominator * secondRational.getDenominator();
52            return new Rational(n, d);
53          }
54
55          /** Subtract a rational number from this rational */
56          public Rational subtract(Rational secondRational) {
58            long n = numerator * secondRational.getDenominator()
59              - denominator * secondRational.getNumerator();
60            long d = denominator * secondRational.getDenominator();
61            return new Rational(n, d);
62          }
63
64          /** Multiply a rational number to this rational */
65          public Rational multiply(Rational secondRational) {
66            long n = numerator * secondRational.getNumerator();
67            long d = denominator * secondRational.getDenominator();
68            return new Rational(n, d);
69          }
70
71          /** Divide a rational number from this rational */
72          public Rational divide(Rational secondRational) {
73            long n = numerator * secondRational.getDenominator();
74            long d = denominator * secondRational.numerator;
75            return new Rational(n, d);
76          }
77
78          /** Override the toString() method */
79          public String toString() {
80            if (denominator == 1)
81              return numerator + "";
82            else
83              return numerator + "/" + denominator;
84          }
85
86          /** Override the equals method in the Object class */
87          public boolean equals(Object parm1) {
88            if ((this.subtract((Rational)(parm1))).getNumerator() == 0)
89              return true;
90            else
91              return false;
92          }
93
94          /** Override the hashCode method in the Object class */
95          public int hashCode() {
96            return new Double(this.doubleValue()).hashCode();
97          }
98
99          /** Override the abstract intValue method in java.lang.Number */
100         public int intValue() {
101           return (int)doubleValue();
102         }
103
```

416

```
104      /** Override the abstract floatValue method in java.lang.Number */
105      public float floatValue() {
106        return (float)doubleValue();
107      }
108
109      /** Override the doubleValue method in java.lang.Number */
110      public double doubleValue() {
111        return numerator * 1.0 / denominator;
112      }
113
114      /** Override the abstract longValue method in java.lang.Number */
115      public long longValue() {
116        return (long)doubleValue();
117      }
118
119      /** Override the compareTo method in java.lang.Comparable */
120      public int compareTo(Object o) {
121        if ((this.subtract((Rational)o)).getNumerator() > 0)
122          return 1;
123        else if ((this.subtract((Rational)o)).getNumerator() < 0)
124          return -1;
125        else
126          return 0;
127      }
128    }
```

```
1     package chapter10;
2
3     public class TestRationalClass {
4       /** Main method */
5       public static void main(String[] args) {
6         // Create and initialize two rational numbers r1 and r2.
7         Rational r1 = new Rational(4, 2);
8         Rational r2 = new Rational(2, 3);
9
10        // Display results
11        System.out.println(r1 + " + " + r2 + " = " + r1.add(r2));
12        System.out.println(r1 + " - " + r2 + " = " + r1.subtract(r2));
13        System.out.println(r1 + " * " + r2 + " = " + r1.multiply(r2));
14        System.out.println(r1 + " / " + r2 + " = " + r1.divide(r2));
15        System.out.println(r2 + " is " + r2.doubleValue());
16      }
17    }
```

Review

The main method in TestRationalClass creates two rational numbers, r1 and r2 (Lines 7–8), and displays the results of r1+r2, r1–r2, r1xr2, and r1/r2. It also displays the double value of r2 (Line 15). Note that when a string is concatenated with an object using the plus sign (+), the object's string representation from the toString() method is used to concatenate with the string. So r1 + '' + '' + r2 + '' = '' + r1.add(r2) is equivalent to r1.toString() + '' + '' + r2.toString() + '' = '' + r1.add(r2).toString().

The rational number is encapsulated in a Rational object. Internally, a rational number is represented in its lowest terms and the numerator determines its sign (Line 18). The denominator is always positive (Line 19).

continues

417

Example 10.2   Continued

The gcd() method (Lines 23–35 in the Rational class) is private; it is not intended for use by clients. The gcd() method is only for internal use by the Rational class.

The abs(x) method (Line 19 in the Rational class) is defined in the Math class that returns the absolute value of x.

Two Rational objects can interact with each other to perform add, subtract, multiply, and divide operations. To add Rational object r1 to r2, invoke r1.add(r2), which returns a new Rational object.

The methods toString, equals, and hashCode in the Object class are overridden in the Rational class (Lines 79–97). The toString() method returns a string representation of a Rational object in the form numerator/denominator, or simply numerator if denominator is 1. The equals(Object other) method returns true if this rational number is equal to the other rational number.

The abstract methods intValue, longValue, floatValue, and doubleValue in the Number class are implemented in the Rational class (Lines 100–117). These methods return int, long, float, and double value for this rational number.

The compareTo(Object other) method in the Comparable interface is implemented in the Rational class (Lines 119–127) to compare this rational number to the other rational number.

 TIP

The get methods for the properties numerator and denominator are provided in the Rational class, but the set methods are not provided, so a Rational object cannot be changed. An object that cannot be changed is referred to as *immutable*. The String class is a well-known example of an immutable class. The wrapper classes that were introduced in Section 9.5, "Processing Primitive Data Type Values as objects," are also immutable classes.

 TIP

The numerator and denominator are represented using two variables. It is possible to use an array of two integers to represent the numerator and denominator. See Exercise 10.2. The signatures of the public methods in the Rational class are not changed, although the internal representation of a rational number is changed. This is a good example to illustrate the idea that the data fields of a class should be kept private so as to encapsulate the implementation of the class from the use of the class.

10.6 Class Design Guidelines

You have learned how to design classes from the preceding two examples and from many other examples in the preceding chapters. Here are some guidelines.

10.6.1 Designing a Class

A class should describe a single entity or a set of similar operations. You can use a class for students, for example, but you should not combine students and staff in the same class, because students and staff have different operations. Since the `Math` class provides mathematical operations, it is natural to group the mathematical methods in one class. A single entity with too many responsibilities can be broken into several classes to separate responsibilities. The `String` class, `StringBuffer` class, and `StringTokenizer` class all deal with strings, for example, but have different responsibilities.

Classes are usually designed for use by many different customers. In order to be useful in a wide range of applications, a class should provide a variety of ways for customization through properties and methods.

Classes are designed for reuse. Users can incorporate classes in many different combinations, orders, and environments. Therefore, you should design a class that imposes no restrictions on what or when the user can do with it, design the properties in a way that lets the user set them in any order, with any combination of values, and design methods that function independently of their order of occurrence.

Provide a public default constructor and override the methods `equals` and `toString` defined in the `Object` class whenever possible. Override the `hashCode` method whenever the `equals` method is overridden.

Follow standard Java programming style and naming conventions. Choose informative names for classes, data fields, and methods. I recommend that you place the data declaration before the constructor, and place constructors before methods.

10.6.2 Using the Visibility Modifiers *public, protected,* and *private*

A class can present two contracts: one for the users of the class, and one for the extenders of the class. Make the fields *private* and the accessor/mutator methods `public` if they are intended for the users of the class. Make the fields or methods `protected` if they are intended for extenders of the class. The contract for extenders encompasses the contract for users. The extended class may increase the visibility of an instance method from `protected` to `public`, or may change its implementation, but you should never change the implementation in a way that violates the contract.

A class should use the `private` modifier to hide its data from direct access by clients. Provide a *get* method only if you want the field to be readable, and provide a *set* method only if you want the field to be updateable. A class should also hide methods not intended for client use. The `gcd` method in the `Rational` class in Example

419

10.2, "The `Rational` Class," is private, for example, because it is only for internal use within the class.

10.6.3   Using the *static* Modifier

A property that is shared by all the instances of a class should be declared as a static property. For example, the variable `numOfObjects` in Example 6.5, "Using Instance and Class Variables and Methods," is shared by all the objects of the `Circle` class, and therefore is declared as a static variable. A method that is not dependent on a specific instance should be declared as a static method. For instance, the `getNumOfObjects` method in Example 6.5 is not tied to a specific instance of the `Circle` class, and therefore is declared as a static method. The class properties and methods are denoted using the `static` modifier.

10.6.4   Using Inheritance or Composition

In general, the difference between inheritance and composition is the difference between an is-a relationship and a has-a relationship. For example, an apple is a fruit; thus, you would use inheritance to model the relationship between the classes `Apple` and `Fruit`. A person has a name; thus, you would use composition to model the relationship between the classes `Person` and `Name`. Sometimes, the choice between inheritance and composition is not obvious. For example, you have used inheritance to model the relationship between the classes `Circle` and `Cylinder`. One could argue that a cylinder consists of circles, and thus that you might use composition to define the `Cylinder` class, as follows:

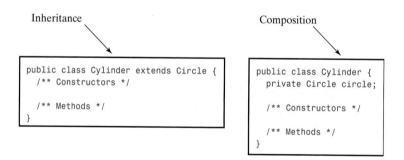

Both designs are fine. Which one is preferred? If polymorphism is desirable, use the inheritance design. If you don't care about polymorphism, the composition design gives more flexibility because the classes are less dependent when you use composition rather than inheritance.

10.6.5   Using Interfaces or Abstract Classes

Both interfaces and abstract classes can be used to generalize common features. How do you decide whether to use an interface or a class? In general, a *strong is-a relationship* that clearly describes a parent-child relationship should be modeled using classes. For example, since an orange is a fruit, their relationship should be modeled using class inheritance. A *weak is-a relationship*, also known as an *is-kind-of relationship*, indicates that an object possesses a certain property. A weak is-a relationship can be modeled using interfaces. For example, all strings are comparable, so the `String` class implements the `Comparable` interface. A circle or a rectangle is a geometric object, so `Circle` can be designed as a subclass of `GeometricObject`. Circles are different and comparable based on their radii, so `Circle` can implement the `Comparable` interface.

Interfaces are more flexible than abstract classes, because a subclass can extend only one superclass but implement any number of interfaces. However, interfaces cannot contain concrete methods. The virtues of interfaces and abstract classes can be combined by creating an interface with an abstract class that implements it. Then you can use the interface or the abstract class, whichever is more convenient. For this reason, such classes are known as *convenience classes*. For example, in the Java Collections Framework, which is introduced in Chapter 17, "Java Data Structures," the `AbstractCollection` class is a convenience class for the `Collection` interface, and the `AbstractSet` class is a convenience class for the `Set` interface.

10.7 Modeling Dynamic Behavior Using Sequence Diagrams and Statecharts

The UML diagrams presented so far describe the properties and methods of a class or the static relationships among classes. This section introduces the sequence diagrams and statechart diagrams that model the dynamic behaviors of objects.

10.7.1 Sequence Diagrams

Sequence diagrams describe interactions among objects by depicting the time-ordering of method invocations. A sequence diagram consists of the following elements, as shown in Figure 10.10:

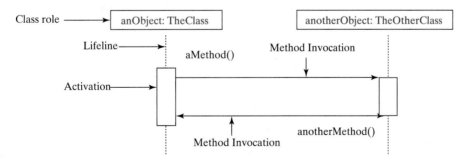

Figure 10.10 *Sequence diagrams describe interactions between objects.*

- **Class role** represents the roles the object plays. The objects at the top of the diagram represent class roles.

- **Lifeline** represents the existence of an object over a period of time. A vertical dotted line extending from the object is used to denote a lifeline.

- **Activation** represents the time during which an object is performing an operation. Thin rectangles placed on lifelines are used to denote activations.

- **Method invocation** represents communication between objects. Horizontal arrows labeled with method calls are used to denote method invocations.

The interactions among the objects in Example 10.1, "Borrowing Loans," are illustrated in Figure 10.11.

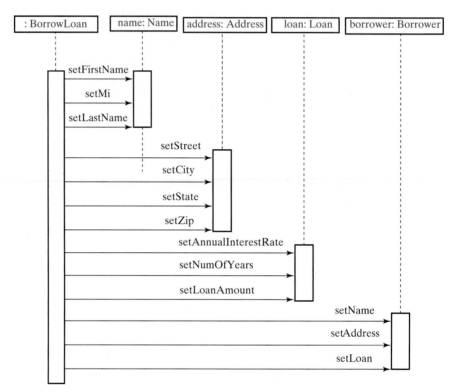

Figure 10.11   *The* BorrowLoan *object invokes the methods in the* Name, Address, *and* Borrower *objects.*

10.7.2   Statechart Diagrams

Statechart diagrams describe the flow of control of an object. A statechart diagram contains the following elements, as shown in Figure 10.12:

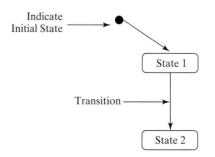

Figure 10.12   *Statechart diagrams describe the flow of control of an object.*

■ **State** represents a situation during the life of an object in which it satisfies some condition, performs some action, or waits for some event to occur. All states have names. States are denoted by rectangles with rounded corners, except for the initial state, which is denoted by a small filled circle.

■ **Transition** represents the relationship between two states, indicating that an object will perform some action to transfer from one state to the other. A solid arrow with appropriate method invocation denotes a transition.

The life cycle of an object can be illustrated using a statechart diagram, as shown in Figure 10.13.

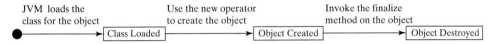

Figure 10.13   *The life cycle of an object can be described using a statechart diagram.*

10.8   Case Studies (Optional)

This section presents a case study on designing classes for matrix operations. The addition and multiplication operations for all matrices are similar except that their element types differ. Therefore, you can design a superclass that describes the common operations shared by matrices of all types regardless of their element types, and you can create subclasses tailored to specific types of matrices. This case study gives implementations for two types: int and Rational. For the int type, the wrapper class Integer should be used to wrap an int value into an object, so that the object is passed in the methods for operations.

Example 10.3 Designing Generic Classes for Matrix Operations

Problem

Develop a generic class for matrix arithmetic. This class implements matrix addition and multiplication common to all types of matrices. You will use the Integer matrix and the Rational matrix to test this generic class.

Figure 10.14 describes these classes and illustrates their relationships.

The GenericMatrix class serves as a wrapper class for a matrix. The class provides matrix operations for matrices of any element type. The data field matrix is the internal representation for a generic matrix. The methods addMatrix and multiplyMatrix add and multiply two matrices of a generic type Object[][]. The static method printResult displays the matrices, the operations, and their result. The methods add, multiply, and zero are abstract methods, because their implementations are dependent on the specific type of the array elements.

IntegerMatrix and RationalMatrix are concrete subclasses of GenericMatrix. These two classes implement the add, multiply, and zero methods defined in the GenericMatrix class.

continues

423

Example 10.3 Continued

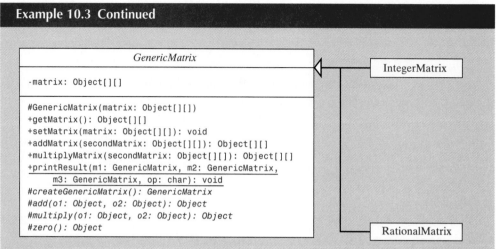

Figure 10.14 *The* GenericMatrix *class is an abstract superclass for* IntegerMatrix *and* RationalMatrix.

Solution

Here is the code for the GenericMatrix, IntegerMatrix, and RationalMatrix classes:

```
1    // GenericMatrix.java: Define a matrix and its associated
2    // operations such as add and multiply
3    public abstract class GenericMatrix {
4      // Representation of a matrix using a two-dimensional array
5      private Object[][] matrix;
6
7      /** Construct a matrix */
8      protected GenericMatrix(Object[][] matrix) {
9        this.matrix = matrix;
10     }
11
12     /** Return matrix */
13     public Object[][] getMatrix() {
14       return matrix;
15     }
16
17     /** Set a new matrix */
18     public void setMatrix(Object[][] matrix) {
19       this.matrix = matrix;
20     }
21
22     public abstract GenericMatrix
23       createGenericMatrix(Object[][] matrix);
24
25     /** Add two matrices */
26     public GenericMatrix addMatrix(
27       GenericMatrix secondGenericMatrix) {
28       // Create a result matrix
29       Object[][] result =
30         new Object[matrix.length][matrix[0].length];
31
32       // Obtain the second matrix
33       Object[][] secondMatrix =  secondGenericMatrix.getMatrix();
34
```

```
35      // Check bounds of the two matrices
36      if ((matrix.length != secondMatrix.length) ||
37          (matrix[0].length != secondMatrix.length)) {
38        System.out.println(
39          "The matrices do not have the same size");
40        System.exit(0);
41      }
42
43      // Perform addition
44      for (int i = 0; i < result.length; i++)
45        for (int j = 0; j < result[i].length; j++)
46          result[i][j] = add(matrix[i][j], secondMatrix[i][j]);
47
48      return createGenericMatrix(result);
49    }
50
51    /** Multiply two matrices */
52    public GenericMatrix multiplyMatrix(
53      GenericMatrix secondGenericMatrix) {
54      // Obtain the second matrix
55      Object[][] secondMatrix = secondGenericMatrix.getMatrix();
56
57      // Create result matrix
58      Object[][] result =
59        new Object[matrix.length][secondMatrix[0].length];
60
61      // Check bounds
62      if (matrix[0].length != secondMatrix.length) {
63        System.out.println("Bounds error");
64        System.exit(0);
65      }
66
67      // Perform multiplication of two matrices
68      for (int i = 0; i < result.length; i++)
69        for (int j = 0; j < result[0].length; j++) {
70          result[i][j] = zero();
71
72          for (int k = 0; k < matrix[0].length; k++) {
73            result[i][j] = add(result[i][j],
74              multiply(this.matrix[i][k], secondMatrix[k][j]));
75          }
76        }
77
78      return createGenericMatrix(result);
79    }
80
81    /** Print matrices, the operator, and their operation result */
82    public static void printResult(
83      GenericMatrix m1, GenericMatrix m2, GenericMatrix m3, char op) {
84      for (int i = 0; i < (m1.getMatrix()).length; i++) {
85        for (int j = 0; j < (m1.getMatrix())[0].length; j++)
86          System.out.print(" " + (m1.getMatrix())[i][j]);
87
88        if (i == (m1.getMatrix()).length / 2)
89          System.out.print( "  " + op + "  " );
90        else
91          System.out.print( "      " );
92
93        for (int j = 0; j < (m2.getMatrix()).length; j++)
94          System.out.print(" " + (m2.getMatrix())[i][j]);
95
```

continues

425

Example 10.3 Continued

```
96            if (i == (m1.getMatrix()).length / 2)
97              System.out.print( "  =  " );
98            else
99              System.out.print( "     " );
100
101            for (int j = 0; j < (m3.getMatrix()).length; j++)
102              System.out.print(" " + (m3.getMatrix())[i][j]);
103
104            System.out.println();
105        }
106      }
107
108      /** Abstract method for adding two elements of the matrices */
109      protected abstract Object add(Object o1, Object o2);
110
111      /** Abstract method for multiplying two elements of the matrices */
112      protected abstract Object multiply(Object o1, Object o2);
113
114      /** Abstract method for defining zero for the matrix element */
115      protected abstract Object zero();
116    }
```

```
1    // IntegerMatrix.java:
2    // Declare IntegerMatrix derived from GenericMatrix
3    package chapter10;
4
5    public class IntegerMatrix extends GenericMatrix {
6      /** Construct an IntegerMatrix */
7      public IntegerMatrix(Object[][] m) {
8        super(m);
9      }
10
11      /** Implement the createGenericMatrix method */
12      public GenericMatrix createGenericMatrix(Object[][] matrix) {
13        return new IntegerMatrix(matrix);
14      }
15
16      /** Implement the add method for adding two matrix elements */
17      protected Object add(Object o1, Object o2) {
18        Integer i1 = (Integer)o1;
19        Integer i2 = (Integer)o2;
20        return new Integer(i1.intValue() + i2.intValue());
21      }
22
23      /** Implement the multiply method for multiplying two
24         matrix elements */
25      protected Object multiply(Object o1, Object o2) {
26        Integer i1 = (Integer)o1;
27        Integer i2 = (Integer)o2;
28        return new Integer(i1.intValue() * i2.intValue());
29      }
30
31      /** Implement the zero method to specify zero for Integer */
32      protected Object zero() {
33        return new Integer(0);
34      }
35    }
```

```
1    /** RationalMatrix.java:
2       Declare RationalMatrix derived from GenericMatrix */
3    package chapter10;
4
```

```
5    public class RationalMatrix extends GenericMatrix {
6      /** Construct a RationalMatrix for a given Rational array */
7      public RationalMatrix(Object[][] m1) {
8        super(m1);
9      }
10
11     /** Implement the createGenericMatrix method */
12     public GenericMatrix createGenericMatrix(Object[][] matrix) {
13       return new RationalMatrix(matrix);
14     }
15
16     /** Implement the add method for adding two rational elements */
17     protected Object add(Object o1, Object o2) {
18       Rational r1 = (Rational)o1;
19       Rational r2 = (Rational)o2;
20       return r1.add(r2);
21     }
22
23     /** Implement the multiply method for multiplying
24         two rational elements */
25     protected Object multiply(Object o1, Object o2) {
26       Rational r1 = (Rational)o1;
27       Rational r2 = (Rational)o2;
28       return r1.multiply(r2);
29     }
30
31     /** Implement the zero method to specify zero for Rational */
32     protected Object zero() {
33       return new Rational(0,1);
34     }
35   }
```

The following is a test program that uses the IntegerMatrix class. A sample run of the program is shown in Figure 10.15.

```
1    // TestIntegerMatrix.java: Test matrix operations involving
2    // integer values
3    package chapter10;
4
5    public class TestIntegerMatrix {
6      public static void main(String[] args) {
7        // Create Integer arrays m1, m2
8        Object[][] m1 = new Integer[5][5];
9        Object[][] m2 = new Integer[5][5];
10
11       // Initialize Integer arrays m1 and m2
12       for (int i = 0; i < m1.length; i++)
13         for (int j = 0; j < m1[0].length; j++) {
14           m1[i][j] = new Integer(i);
15         }
16
17       for (int i = 0; i < m2.length; i++)
18         for (int j = 0; j < m2[0].length; j++) {
19           m2[i][j] = new Integer(i + j);
20         }
21
22       // Create instances of IntegerMatrix
23       IntegerMatrix im1 = new IntegerMatrix(m1);
24       IntegerMatrix im2 = new IntegerMatrix(m2);
25
```

continues

427

Example 10.3 Continued

```
26          // Perform integer matrix addition, and multiplication
27          IntegerMatrix im3 = (IntegerMatrix)im1.addMatrix(im2);
28          IntegerMatrix im4 = (IntegerMatrix)im1.multiplyMatrix(im2);
29
30          // Display im1, im2, im3, im4
31          System.out.println("m1 + m2 is ...");
32          GenericMatrix.printResult(im1, im2, im3, '+');
33
34          System.out.println("\nm1 * m2 is ...");
35          GenericMatrix.printResult(im1, im2, im4, '*');
36        }
37      }
```

```
Command Prompt                                      _ □ ×
C:\example>java chapter10.TestIntegerMatrix
m1 + m2 is ...
 0 0 0 0 0      0 1 2 3 4      0 1 2 3 4
 1 1 1 1 1      1 2 3 4 5      2 3 4 5 6
 2 2 2 2 2  +   2 3 4 5 6  =   4 5 6 7 8
 3 3 3 3 3      3 4 5 6 7      6 7 8 9 10
 4 4 4 4 4      4 5 6 7 8      8 9 10 11 12

m1 * m2 is ...
 0 0 0 0 0      0 1 2 3 4      0 0 0 0 0
 1 1 1 1 1      1 2 3 4 5      10 15 20 25 30
 2 2 2 2 2  *   2 3 4 5 6  =   20 30 40 50 60
 3 3 3 3 3      3 4 5 6 7      30 45 60 75 90
 4 4 4 4 4      4 5 6 7 8      40 60 80 100 120


C:\example>
```

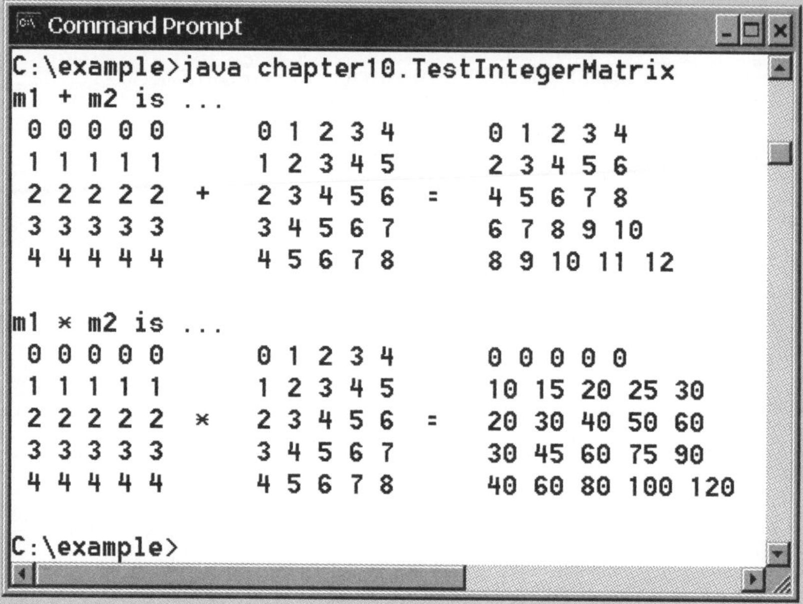

Figure 10.15 *The program creates two* Integer *matrices and performs addition and multiplication on them.*

Next is a test program that uses the RationalMatrix class. A sample run of the program is shown in Figure 10.16.

```
1       // TestRationalMatrix.java: Test matrix operations involving
2       // Rational values
3       package chapter10;
4
5       public class TestRationalMatrix {
6         public static void main(String[] args) {
7           // Declare Rational arrays m1, m2
8           Object[][] m1 = new Rational[4][4];
9           Object[][] m2 = new Rational[4][4];
10
11          // Initialize Rational arrays m1 and m2
12          for (int i = 0; i < m1.length; i++)
13            for (int j = 0; j < m1[0].length; j++) {
```

```
14            m1[i][j] = new Rational(i + 1, i + 3);
15            m2[i][j] = new Rational(i + 1, i + 3);
16          }
17
18        // Create RationalMatrix instances
19        RationalMatrix rm1 = new RationalMatrix(m1);
20        RationalMatrix rm2 = new RationalMatrix(m2);
21
22        // Perform Rational matrix addition, and multiplication
23        RationalMatrix rm3 = (RationalMatrix)rm1.addMatrix(rm2);
24        RationalMatrix rm4 = (RationalMatrix)rm1.multiplyMatrix(rm2);
25
26        // Display rm1, rm2, rm3, rm4
27        System.out.println("m1 + m2 is ...");
28        GenericMatrix.printResult(rm1, rm2, rm3, '+');
29
30        System.out.println("\nm1 * m2 is ...");
31        GenericMatrix.printResult(rm1, rm2, rm4, '*');
32      }
33    }
```

```
 Command Prompt                                             _ □ ×

C:\example>java chapter10.TestRationalMatrix
m1 + m2 is ...
 1/3 1/3 1/3 1/3      1/3 1/3 1/3 1/3      2/3 2/3 2/3 2/3
 1/2 1/2 1/2 1/2      1/2 1/2 1/2 1/2      1 1 1 1
 3/5 3/5 3/5 3/5  +   3/5 3/5 3/5 3/5  =   6/5 6/5 6/5 6/5
 2/3 2/3 2/3 2/3      2/3 2/3 2/3 2/3      4/3 4/3 4/3 4/3

m1 × m2 is ...
 1/3 1/3 1/3 1/3      1/3 1/3 1/3 1/3      7/10 7/10 7/10 7/10
 1/2 1/2 1/2 1/2      1/2 1/2 1/2 1/2      21/20 21/20 21/20 21/20
 3/5 3/5 3/5 3/5  ×   3/5 3/5 3/5 3/5  =   63/50 63/50 63/50 63/50
 2/3 2/3 2/3 2/3      2/3 2/3 2/3 2/3      7/5 7/5 7/5 7/5

C:\example>_
```

Figure 10.16 *The program creates two matrices of rational numbers and performs addition and multiplication on them.*

Review

Because the matrix element type in the GenericMatrix class is a generic object, the program doesn't know how to add or multiply two matrix elements and doesn't know what the zero value is for the element (e.g., 0 for int or 0/1 for Rational). Therefore, add, multiply, and zero are defined as abstract methods. These methods are implemented in the subclasses in which the matrix element type is specified.

The matrix element type in GenericMatrix is Object. This enables you to use an object of any class as long as you can implement the abstract add, multiply, and zero methods in subclasses.

continues

429

Example 10.3 Continued

The addMatrix and multiplyMatrix methods (Lines 25–79 in the GenericMatrix class) are concrete methods. They are ready to use as long as the add, multiply, and zero methods are implemented in the subclasses.

The createGenericMatrix method creates an instance of GenericMatrix. This method is used in the addMatrix and multiplyMatrix methods for returning instances of the GenericMatrix type. Since GenericMatrix is an abstract class, the createGenericMatrix method must be declared abstract in the GenericMatrix class.

The printResult method (Lines 81–106 in GenericMatrix) displays the matrix on the console. The toString() method is used to display the element.

The addMatrix and multiplyMatrix methods check the bounds of the matrices before performing operations. If the two matrices have incompatible bounds, the program terminates.

IntegerMatrix and RationalMatrix are concrete subclasses of GenericMatrix for integer matrix arithmetic. These classes extend the GenericMatrix class and implement the add, multiply, and zero methods.

Casting the object from type Object to type Integer in the IntegerMatrix class (Lines 18–19, 26–27) is necessary because the program has to use the intValue method for integer addition and multiplication, and it is not available in Object. For the same reason, casting from type Object to type Rational is needed in the RationalMatrix class (Lines 18–19, 26–27).

The TestIntegerMatrix program creates and initializes two matrices: m1 and m2. The statement (Lines 23–24)

```
IntegerMatrix im1 = new IntegerMatrix(m1);
IntegerMatrix im2 = new IntegerMatrix(m2);
```

in TestIntegerMatrix creates im1 as an instance of IntegerMatrix for matrix m1, so you can use im1.addMatrix(im2) and im1.multiplyMatrix(im2) to perform matrix addition and multiplication for im1 and im2. The variables rm1 and rm2 were created for the same reason in TestRationalMatrix.

10.9   Designing Classes for Linked Lists (Optional)

Arrays are useful for storing and managing a set of elements of the same type. Since the length of an array is fixed once the array is created, however, you need to know the length before you create the array. If you don't know the length of the array in advance, you have to estimate it when creating the array. If the estimate is larger than the actual length, valuable memory space may be wasted; if the estimate is smaller than the actual length, your program could run into trouble. Obviously, it would be unwise to use an array to store an unspecified number of elements. You can use a linked list to store a collection of elements. A linked list can grow or shrink dynamically as needed. This section demonstrates designing classes for a generic linked list.

A linked list consists of nodes, as shown in Figure 10.17. Each node contains an element, and each node is linked to its next neighbor. Thus a node can be defined as a class, as follows:

```
public class Node {
  Object element;
  Node next;

  public Node(Object o) {
    element = o;
  }
}
```

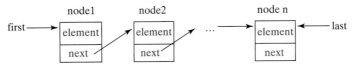

Figure 10.17   *A linked list consists of any number of nodes chained together.*

The variable `first` refers to the first node in the list, and the variable `last` refers to the last node in the list. If the list is empty, both are `null`. For example, you can create three nodes to store three circle objects (radius 1, 2, and 3) in a list:

```
Node first;
Node last;
```
← see Figure 10.18(A)

```
// Create a node to store the first circle object
first = new Node(new Circle(1));
last = first;
```
← see Figure 10.18(B)

```
// Create a node to store the second circle object
last.next = new Node(new Circle(2));
last = last.next;
```
← see Figure 10.18(C)

```
// Create a node to store the third circle object
last.next = new Node(new Circle(3));
last = last.next;
```
← see Figure 10.18(D)

The process of creating a new linked list and adding three nodes is shown in Figure 10.18.

You can create a linked list to store a collection of objects, add objects to the list, remove objects from the list, search an object, or sort objects in the list. To make it easy to use and reusable, create a class named `GenericLinkedList` to model all the linked lists, as shown in Figure 10.19.

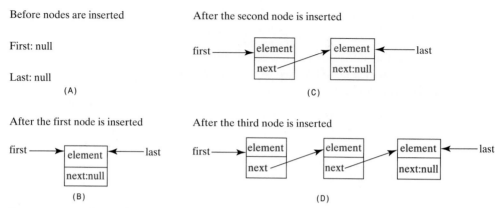

Figure 10.18   *Three nodes are added to a new linked list.*

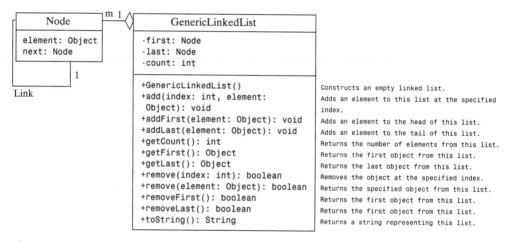

Figure 10.19   *The* GenericLinkedList *class encapsulates a generic linked list.*

The class source code is given as follows:

```
1      // GenericLinkedList.java
2      package chapter10;
3
4      public class GenericLinkedList {
5        private Node first, last;
6        private int count = 0; // The number of elements in the list
7
8        public GenericLinkedList() {
9        }
10
11       /** Return the first element in the list */
12       public Object getFirst() {
13         if (count == 0) return null;
14         else return first.element;
15       }
16
17       /** Return the last element in the list */
18       public Object getLast() {
19         if (count == 0) return null;
20         else return last.element;
```

```
21        }
22
23        /** Add an element to the beginning of the list */
24        public void addFirst(Object element) {
25          Node newNode = new Node(element);
26          newNode.next = first;
27          first = newNode;
28          count++;
29
30          if (last == null)
31            last = first;
32        }
33
34        /** Add an element to the end of the list */
35        public void addLast(Object element) {
36          if (last == null) {
37            first = last = new Node(element);
38          }
39          else {
40            last.next = new Node(element);
41            last = last.next;
42          }
43
44          count++;
45        }
46
47        /** Add an element at the specified index.
48         * The index of the first element is 0.
49         */
50        public void add(int index, Object element) {
51          if (index == 0) addFirst(element);
52          else if (index >= count) addLast(element);
53          else {
54            Node current = first;
55            for (int i = 1; i < index; i++)
56              current = current.next;
57            Node temp = current.next;
58            current.next = new Node(element);
59            (current.next).next = temp;
60            count++;
61          }
62        }
63
64        /** Remove the first node */
65        public boolean removeFirst() {
66          if (count == 0) return false;
67          else {
68            first = first.next;
69            count--;
70            return true;
71          }
72        }
73
74        /** Remove the last node */
75        public boolean removeLast() {
76          if (count == 0) return false;
77          else {
78            Node current = first;
79
80            for (int i = 0; i < count - 2; i++) {
81              current = current.next;
82            }
83
84            last = current;
85            last.next = null;
```

```
86              count--;
87              return true;
88            }
89          }
90
91          /** Remove the first node that contains the specified element
92           * Return true if the element is removed
93           * Return false if no element is removed
94           */
95          public boolean remove(Object element) {
96            Node previous = first;
97            Node current;
98
99            if (first != null) {
100             if (element.equals(first.element)) {
101               first = first.next;
102               count--;
103               return true;
104             }
105             else {
106               current = first.next;
107             }
108           }
109           else
110             return false;
111
112           for (int i = 0; i < count - 1; i++) {
113             if (element.equals(current.element)) {
114               previous.next = current.next; // Remove the current element
115               count--;
116               return true;
117             }
118             else {
119               previous = current;
120               current = current.next;
121             }
122           }
123
124           return false;
125         }
126
127         /** Remove the node at the specified index.
128          * The index of the first element is 0.
129          * Return true if the element is removed
130          * Return false if no element is removed
131          */
132         public boolean remove(int index) {
133           if ((index < 0) || (index >= count)) return false;
134           else if (index == 0) return removeFirst();
135           else if (index == count - 1) return removeLast();
136           else {
137             Node current = first;
138
139             for (int i = 1; i < index; i++) {
140               current = current.next;
141             }
142
143             current.next = current.next.next;
144             count--;
145             return true;
146           }
147         }
148
149         /** Return the number of elements in the list */
150         public int getCount() {
```

```
151        return count;
152      }
153
154      /** Override toString() to return elements in the list */
155      public String toString() {
156        StringBuffer result = new StringBuffer("[");
157
158        Node current = first;
159        for (int i = 0; i < count; i++) {
160          result.append(current.element);
161          current = current.next;
162          if (current != null)
163            result.append(", "); // Seperate two elements with a comma
164          else
165            result.append("]"); // Insert the closing ] in the string
166        }
167
168        return result.toString();
169      }
170    }
```

The variable count (Line 6) tracks the number of elements in the list. When a new element is added to the list, count is incremented by 1, and when an element is removed from the list, count is decremented by 1. The variables first and last (Line 5) refer to the first and last nodes in the list, respectively. The getFirst() and getLast() methods (Lines 11–21) return the first and last elements in the list, respectively.

The addFirst(Object) method (Line 23–32) adds an element to the beginning of the list. After the insertion, first should refer to this new element node. The addLast(Object) method (Lines 34–45) adds an element to the end of the list. After the insertion, last should refer to this new element node. The add(Object element, int index) method (Lines 47–62) adds an element to the list at the specified index. The method first locates where to insert the new element. As shown in Figure 10.20, the new element is to be inserted between the nodes current and temp. The

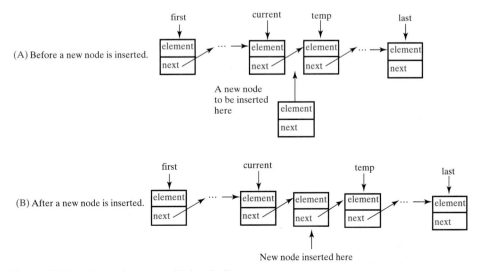

Figure 10.20 *A new element is added to the list.*

435

method then assigns the new node to `current.next` and assigns `temp` to the new node's `next`.

The `removeFirst()` method (Lines 64–72) removes the first element in the list by pointing `first` to the second element. The `removeLast()` method (Lines 74–89) removes the last element from the list. Afterwards, `last` should refer to the former second-last element. The `remove(Object element)` method (Lines 91–125) finds the element in the list and then removes it. The method locates the current node for the current element and the node formerly before the current element, as shown in

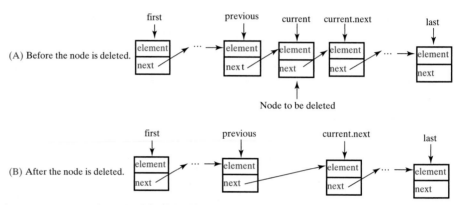

Figure 10.21   *An element is deleted from the list.*

Example 10.4 Using Linked Lists

Problem

Write a program that creates a linked list using `GenericLinkedList`. It then uses the `add` method to add strings to the list and the `remove` method to remove strings from the list.

Solution

The following code gives the solution to the problem. A sample run of the program is shown in Figure 10.22.

```
1    // TestLinkedList.java: Test GenericLinkedList class
2    package chapter10;
3
4    public class TestLinkedList {
5      public static void main(String[] args) {
6        // Create a linked list
7        GenericLinkedList list = new GenericLinkedList();
8
9        // Add elements to the list
10       list.addFirst("Tom"); // Add it to the beginning of the list
11       list.addFirst("John"); // Add it to the beginning of the list
12       list.addLast("George"); // Add it to the end of the list
13       list.addLast("Michael"); // Add it to the end of the list
14       list.add(2, "Michelle"); // Add it to the list at index 2
15       list.add(5, "Samantha"); // Add it to the list at index 5
16       list.add(0, "Daniel"); // Same as list.addFirst("Daniel")
17
```

```
18          // Print the list
19          System.out.println("Strings are added to the list");
20          System.out.println(list);
21
22          // Remove elements from the list
23          list.remove("Daniel"); // Same as list.remove(0) in this case
24          list.remove(2); // Remove the element at index 2
25          list.removeLast(); // Remove the last element
26
27          // Print the list
28          System.out.println("The contents of the list after deletions");
29          System.out.println(list);
30      }
31   }
```

```
Command Prompt                                          _ □ ×
C:\example>java chapter10.TestLinkedList
Strings are added to the list
[Daniel, John, Tom, Michelle, George, Michael, Samantha]
The contents of the list after deletions
[John, Tom, George, Michael]

C:\example>
```

Figure 10.22   *The program uses a linked list to store and process strings.*

Review

The GenericLinkedList class is a typical example of object-oriented software development. The GenericLinkedList class contains a dynamic data structure for storing elements. The data structures are hidden from the user. The class provides public methods to enable the client to add or remove elements. The linked list can hold any objects.

The data structure in GenericLinkedList is one-directional, enabling one-way traversal of the list. You can modify the data structure to bi-directional traversal. See Exercise 10.4.

 NOTE

A class for linked lists is already provided in Java in java.util.LiskedList. The purpose of this section is to demonstrate how to design generic classes using a linked list as example. The java.util.LinkedList class will be introduced in the Java Collections Framework in Chapter 17, "Java Data Structures."

10.10   Framework-Based Programming Using Java API

The Java API (*Application Program Interface*) consists of numerous classes and interfaces grouped into more than a dozen of packages. You have used classes and interfaces in the `java.lang`, `javax.swing`, and `java.util` packages.

- `java.lang` contains core Java classes (e.g., `System`, `Math`, `Object`, `String`, `StringBuffer`, `Number`, `Character`, `Boolean`, `Byte`, `Short`, `Integer`, `Long`, `Float`, `Double`, `Comparable`, and `Cloneable`). This package is implicitly imported to every Java program.

- `javax.swing` contains the lightweight graphical user interface components for developing Swing GUI programs.

- `java.util` contains many utilities, such as `StringTokenizer`, `Date`, `Calendar`, and `GregorianCalendar`.

These are just a few of the classes and interfaces you have learned. To create comprehensive projects, you have to use more classes and interfaces in the Java API. The classes and interfaces in the Java API establish a framework for programmers to develop applications using Java. For example, the classes and interfaces in the Java GUI API establish a framework for developing GUI programs. You have to use these classes and interfaces and follow their conventions and rules to create applications. This is referred to as *framework-based programming*.

Once you understand the concept of Java and object-oriented programming, the most important lesson from now on is learning how to use the API to develop useful programs. The most effective way to achieve this is to imitate good examples. The book provides many carefully designed examples to demonstrate the concept of the framework-based programming using the Java API. You will learn the Java GUI programming framework in Chapters 11, 12, 13, and 14, the Java exception handling framework in Chapter 15, the Java IO framework in Chapter 16, the Java collections framework in Chapter 17, and the Java multithreading framework in Chapter 18.

Chapter Summary

- Developing a project involves *requirements specification, system analysis, system design, implementation, testing, deployment*, and *maintenance*.

- The relationships among classes can be classified into three types: *association, aggregation*, and *inheritance*.

- *Association* is a general binary relationship that describes an activity between two classes.

- *Aggregation* is a special form of association that represents an ownership relationship between two classes. An object may be owned by several other aggregated objects. If an object is exclusively owned by an aggregated object, the relationship between the object and its aggregated object is referred to as *composition*.

■ *Inheritance* models the is-a relationship between two classes. A strong is-a relationship describes a direct inheritance relationship between two classes. A weak is-a relationship describes that a class has certain properties. A strong is-a relationship can be represented using class inheritance. A weak is-a relationship can be represented using interfaces.

■ The `Rational` class extends `java.lang.Number` and implements `java.lang.Comparable`. A rational object represents a rational number.

■ A class should describe a single entity or a set of similar operations. A single entity with too many responsibilities can be broken into several classes to separate responsibilities. The `String` class, `StringBuffer` class, and `StringTokenizer` class all deal with strings, for example, but have different responsibilities.

■ Classes are usually designed for use by many different customers. In order to be useful in a wide range of applications, a class should provide a variety of ways for customization through properties and methods.

■ Provide a public default constructor and override the methods `equals` and `toString` defined in the `Object` class whenever possible. Override the `hashCode` method whenever the `equals` method is overridden.

■ A class should use the `private` modifier to hide its data from direct access by clients. Provide a *get* method only if you want the field to be readable, and provide a *set* method only if you want the field to be updateable. A class should also hide methods not intended for client use.

■ A property that is shared by all the instances of a class should be declared as a static property.

■ In general, the difference between inheritance and composition is the difference between an is-a relationship and a has-a relationship.

■ Both interfaces and abstract classes can be used to generalize common features. How do you decide whether to use an interface or a class? In general, a *strong is-a relationship* that clearly describes a parent-child relationship should be modeled using classes.

■ Interfaces are more flexible than abstract classes, because a subclass can extend only one superclass but implement any number of interfaces. However, interfaces cannot contain concrete methods.

■ Sequence diagrams describe interactions among objects by depicting the time-ordering of method invocations. A sequence diagram consists of class roles, lifelines, activation, and method invocations. *Class role* represents the roles the object plays. The objects at the top of the diagram represent class roles. *Lifeline* represents the existence of an object over a period of time. A vertical dotted line extending from the object is used to denote a lifeline. *Activation* represents the time during which an object is performing an operation. Thin rectangles placed on lifelines are used to denote activations. *Method invocation* represents communication between objects. Horizontal arrows labeled with method calls are used to denote method invocations.

- Statechart diagrams describe the flow of control of an object. A statechart diagram contains states and transitions. *State* represents a situation during the life of an object in which it satisfies some condition, performs some action, or waits for some event to occur. *Transition* represents the relationship between two states, indicating that an object will perform some action to transfer from one state to the other.

Review Questions

10.1 What are the types of relationships among classes? Describe the graphical notations for modeling the relationships among classes.

10.2 What relationship is appropriate for the following classes? Draw the relationships using UML diagrams.

- Company and Employee

- Course and Faculty

- Student and Person

- House and Window

- Account and Savings Account

10.3 What is wrong in the following code?

```
Number r = new Rational();
System.out.println(r);
System.out.println(r.doubleValue());
System.out.println(r.add(new Rational()));
System.out.println((Rational)r.add(new Rational()));
System.out.println(((Rational)r).add(new Rational()));
```

10.4 What is wrong in the following code?

```
Number r = new Number();
System.out.println(r);
```

10.5 Is the following code correct?

```
Comparable r = new Rational();
System.out.println(r);
```

10.6 Is the following code correct?

```
Comparable r = new Rational();
System.out.println(r.compareTo(new Rational()));
```

Programming Exercises

10.1 (Using the `Rational` class) Write a program that will compute the following summation series using the `Rational` class.

```
1/1 + 1/2 + 1/3 +...+ 1/n
1/1 + 1/2 + 1/2² +...+ 1/2ⁿ
```

10.2 (Demonstrating the benefits of encapsulation) Rewrite the `Rational` class in Example 10.2, "The Rational Class," using a new internal representation for numerator and denominator. Declare an array of two integers as follows:

```
private long[] r = new long[2];
```

Use `r[0]` to represent the numerator and `r[1]` to represent the denominator. The signatures of the methods in the `Rational` class are not changed, so a client application that uses the previous `Rational` class can continue to use this new `Rational` class without being recompiled.

10.3 (Creating a rational number calculator) Write a program similar to the one in Example 7.5, "Using Command-Line Parameters." Instead of using integers, use rationals, as shown in Figure 10.23. You will need to use the `StringTokenizer` class, introduced in Chapter 7, "Strings," to retrieve the numerator string and denominator string, and convert strings into integers using the `Integer.parseInt` method.

Figure 10.23 *The program takes three parameters (an operator and two rational operands) from the command line and displays the expression and the result of the arithmetic operation.*

10.4 (Creating a two-way linked list) The `GenericLinkedList` class used in Example 10.4 is a one-way directional linked list that enables one-way traversal of the list. Modify the `Node` class to add a new field name `previous` to refer to the previous node in the list, as follows:

```
public class Node {
  Object element;
  Node next;
  Node previous;

  public Node(Object o) {
    element = o;
  }
}
```

Simplify the implementation of the add(Object element, int index) method and the remove(int index) and remove(Object element) to take advantage of the bi-directional linked list.

Add a new method in the class to sort the elements in the list, provided that all the elements are instances of the Comparable interface.

10.5 (The Person and Student classes) Create the classes as shown in Figure 10.24. Implement the compareTo method in the Person class to compare persons in alphabetical order of their last name, first name, and middle-name initial. Implement the compareTo method to compare students in alphabetical order of their major, last name, first name, and middle-name initial.

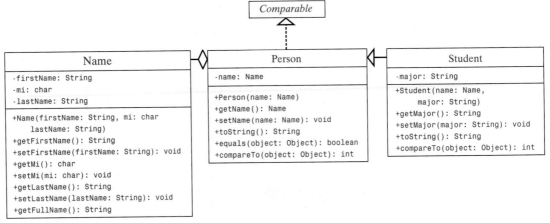

Figure 10.24 *A person has a name, a student is a person, and students are comparable.*

Write a test program with the following three methods:

```
/** Sort an array of comparable objects   */
public static void sort(Object[] list)

/** Return the max object in an array of comparable objects */
public static Object max(Object[] list)
```

main method: Test the *sort* and *max* methods using an array of four students, an array of four strings, an array of one hundred random rationals, and an array of one hundred random integers.

10.6 (The Queue class) A queue is a data structure that stores and retrieves data in a first-in, first-out fashion. It has many applications. For example, a checkout line in a supermarket is a queue. The customers enter the checkout line at the end and the cashier services the customer at the beginning of the line. Use the GenericLinkedList class to implement the Queue class, as shown in Figure 10.25. The enqueue method appends an object to the queue, the dequeue

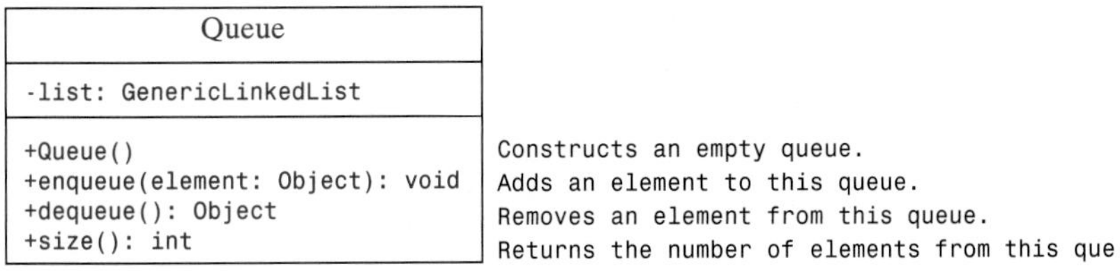

Queue
-list: GenericLinkedList
+Queue() +enqueue(element: Object): void +dequeue(): Object +size(): int

Constructs an empty queue.
Adds an element to this queue.
Removes an element from this queue.
Returns the number of elements from this que

Figure 10.25   *The* Queue *class uses the* GenericLinkedList *class to hold objects.*

method removes the first object from the queue and returns the removed object, and the size method returns the number of elements in the queue.

10.7 (The Stack class) Implement StackOfObjects in Exercise 8.4 using the GenericLinkedList class.

GUI Programming

Part I, "Fundamentals of Programming," introduced basic programming concepts that are supported in all programming languages. Part II, "Object-Oriented Programming," introduced object-oriented programming concepts, principles, and practices that are common in the object-oriented programming languages. Java is not simply a programming language. It is also a development and deployment platform with an extensive set of classes and interfaces in the API. You have to use the classes and interfaces in the API and follow their conventions and rules to develop your own projects. The design of the API for Java GUI programming is an excellent example of how the object-oriented principle is applied. In the chapters that follow, you will learn the framework of Java GUI API and use the GUI components to develop user-friendly interfaces for applications and applets.

CHAPTER 11 GETTING STARTED WITH GUI PROGRAMMING

CHAPTER 12 EVENT-DRIVEN PROGRAMMING

CHAPTER 13 CREATING USER INTERFACES

CHAPTER 14 APPLETS

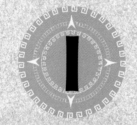

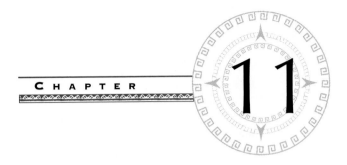
GETTING STARTED WITH GUI PROGRAMMING

Objectives

- To describe the Java GUI API hierarchy.

- To create user interfaces using frames, panels, and simple UI components.

- To understand the role of layout managers.

- To use the FlowLayout, GridLayout, and BorderLayout managers to layout components in a container.

- To paint graphics using the paintComponent method.

- To specify colors and fonts using the Color, Font, and FontMetrics classes.

- To draw strings, lines, rectangles, ovals, arcs, and polygons using the drawing methods in the Graphics class.

- To develop a reusable component MessagePanel to display a message on a panel.

- To develop a reusable component StillClock to emulate an analog clock.

447

11.1   Introduction

Until now, you have only used dialog boxes and the command window for input and output. You used JOptionPane.showInputDialog to obtain input, and JOptionPane.showMessageDialog and System.out.println to display results. These approaches have limitations and are inconvenient. For example, to read ten numbers, you have to open ten input dialog boxes. Starting with this chapter, you will learn Java GUI programming. You will create custom graphical user interfaces (GUI, pronounced *goo-ee*) to obtain input and display output in the same user interface.

When Java was introduced, the GUI components were bundled in a library known as the Abstract Windows Toolkit (AWT). For every platform on which Java runs, the AWT components are automatically mapped to the platform-specific components through their respective agents, known as *peers*. AWT is fine for developing simple graphical user interfaces, but not for developing comprehensive GUI projects. Besides, AWT is prone to platform-specific bugs because its peer-based approach relies heavily on the underlying platform. With the release of Java 2, the AWT user-interface components were replaced by a more robust, versatile, and flexible library known as *Swing components*. Swing components are painted directly on canvases using Java code, except for components that are subclasses of java.awt.Window or java.awt.Panel, which must be drawn using native GUI on a specific platform. Swing components are less dependent on the target platform and use less of the native GUI resource. For this reason, Swing components that don't rely on native GUI are referred to as *lightweight components,* and AWT components are referred to as *heavyweight components*. Although AWT components are still supported in Java 2, I recommend that you learn to program using Swing components, because the AWT user-interface components will eventually fade away.

Java provides a rich set of classes to help you build graphical user interfaces. You can use various GUI-building classes—frames, panels, labels, buttons, text fields, text areas, combo boxes, check boxes, radio buttons, menus, scroll bars, scroll panes, and tabbed panes—to construct user interfaces. This chapter introduces the basics of Java GUI programming. Specifically, it discusses GUI components and their relationships, containers and layout managers, colors, fonts, and drawing geometric figures, such as lines, rectangles, ovals, arcs, polygons, and polylines.

 NOTE

The Swing components do not replace all the classes in AWT, only the AWT user-interface components (Button, TextField, TextArea, etc.). The AWT helper classes (Graphics, Color, Font, FontMetrics, and LayoutManager) remain unchanged. In addition, the Swing components use the AWT event model.

11.2   The Java GUI API

The design of the Java API for GUI programming is an excellent example of the use of classes, inheritance, and interfaces. The API contains the essential classes listed below. Their hierarchical relationships are shown in Figures 11.1 and 11.2.

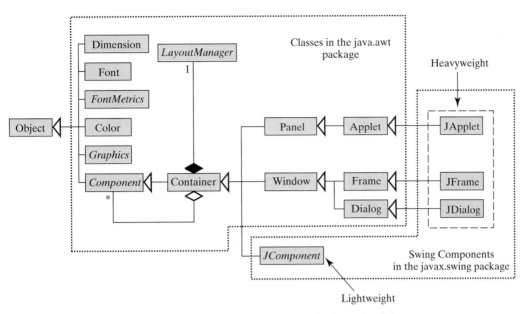

Figure 11.1 *Java GUI programming utilizes the classes shown in this hierarchical diagram.*

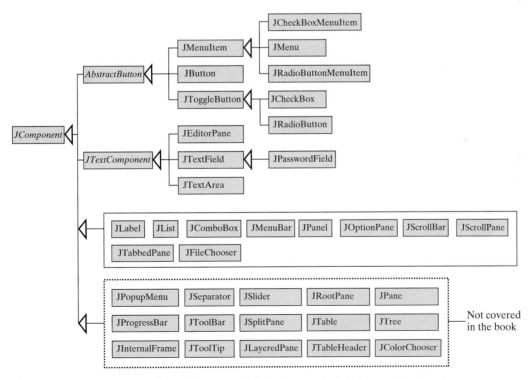

Figure 11.2 JComponent *and its subclasses are the basic elements for building graphical user interfaces.*

The GUI classes can be classified into three groups: *container classes*, *helper classes*, and *component classes*, The container classes, such as `JFrame`, `JPanel`, and `JApplet`, are used to contain other components. The helper classes, such as `Graphics`, `Color`, `Font`, `FontMetrics`, and `Dimension`, are used by components and containers to draw and place objects. The UI component classes, such as `JButton`, `JTextField`, `JTextArea`, `JComboBox`, `JList`, `JRadioButton`, and `JMenu`, are subclasses of `JComponent`.

11.2.1   Container Classes

`Window`, `Panel`, `Applet`, `Frame`, and `Dialog` are the container classes for AWT components. To work with Swing components, use `Component`, `Container`, `JFrame`, `JDialog`, `JApplet`, and `JDialog`.

- **Container** is used to group components. A layout manager is used to position and place components in a container in the desired location and style. Frames, panels, and applets are examples of containers.

- **JFrame** is a window not contained inside another window. It is the container that holds other Swing user-interface components in Java graphical applications.

- **JDialog** is a popup window or message box generally used as a temporary window to receive additional information from the user or to provide notification that an event has occurred.

- **JApplet** is a subclass of `Applet`. You must extend `JApplet` to create a Swing-based Java applet.

- **JPanel** is an invisible container that holds user-interface components. Panels can be nested. You can place panels inside a container including a panel. `JPanel` can also be used as a canvas to draw graphics.

11.2.2   GUI Helper Classes

The helper classes, such as `Graphics`, `Color`, `Font`, `FontMetrics`, and `Dimension`, are not subclasses of `Component`. They are used to describe the properties of GUI components such as graphics context, colors, fonts, and dimension.

- **Graphics** is an abstract class that provides a graphical context for drawing strings, lines, and simple shapes.

- **Color** deals with the colors of GUI components. For example, you can specify background or foreground colors in components like `JFrame` and `JPanel`, or you can specify colors of lines, shapes, and strings in drawings.

- **Font** specifies fonts for the text and drawings on GUI components. For example, you can specify the font type (e.g., SansSerif), style (e.g., bold), and size (e.g., 24 points) for the text on a button.

- **FontMetrics** is an abstract class used to get the properties of the fonts.

- **Dimension** encapsulates the width and height of a component (in integer precision) in a single object.

11.2.3   Swing GUI Components

Component is a superclass of all user-interface classes, and JComponent is a superclass of all the lightweight Swing components, Since JComponent is an abstract class, you cannot use new JComponent() to create an instance of JComponent. However, you can use the constructors of concrete subclasses of JComponent to create JComponent instances. The following are the examples to create buttons, labels, text fields, check boxes, radio buttons, and combo boxes.

```
// Create a button with text OK
JButton jbtOK = new JButton("OK");

// Create a label with text "Enter your name: "
JLabel jlblName = new JLabel("Enter your name: ");

// Create a text field
JTextField jtfName = new JTextField("Type Name Here");

// Create a check box with text bold
JCheckBox jchkBold = new JCheckBox("Bold");

// Create a radio button with text red
JRadioButton jrbRed = new JRadioButton("Red");

// Create a combo box with choices red, green, and blue
JComboBox jcboColor = new JComboBox(new String[]{"Red",
  "Green", "Blue"});
```

In order to display GUI components, as shown in Figure 11.3, you have to place them in a frame or an applet. This will be introduced in the next section.

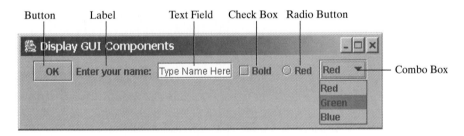

Figure 11.3   *The GUI components are placed in a frame or an applet.*

◈ **NOTE**

Chapter 13, "Creating User Interfaces," discusses in detail how to use Swing GUI components to create user interfaces. Swing is a comprehensive solution to developing graphical user interfaces. There are more than 250 classes in Swing, some of which are illustrated in Figure 11.2. Since the discussion in this book is only an introduction to Java GUI programming using Swing, the Swing components listed in the dotted rectangle are not covered in this book.

NOTE

The `JFrame`, `JApplet`, `JDialog`, and `JComponent` classes and their subclasses are grouped in the `javax.swing` package. All the other classes in Figure 11.1 are grouped in the `java.awt` package. Swing GUI components are named with a prefixed *J*. For example, the Swing version of `Button` is called `JButton` to distinguish it from its AWT counterpart.

 TIP

Do not mix Swing user-interface components like `JButton` with AWT user-interface components like `Button`. For example, do not place `JButton` in `java.awt.Panel`, and similarly do not place Button in `javax.swing.JPanel`. Mixing them may cause problems. This book uses Swing user interfaces exclusively.

11.3   Frames

To create a user interface, you need to create either a frame or an applet to hold the user-interface components. Figure 11.4 provides examples of possible user-interface layouts in a frame and an applet.

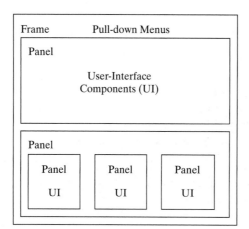 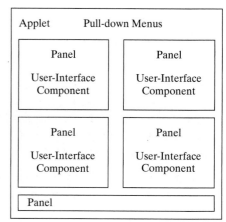

Figure 11.4   *Frames and applets can both contain menus, panels, and user-interface components. Panels are used to group user-interface components. Panels can contain other panels.*

Creating Java applets will be introduced in Chapter 14, "Applets." This section introduces the procedure for creating frames.

11.3.1   Creating a Frame

The following program creates a frame:

```
1    // MyFrame.java: Display a frame
2    package chapter11;
3
```

```
 4      import javax.swing.*;
 5
 6      public class MyFrame {
 7        public static void main(String[] args) {
 8          JFrame frame = new JFrame("Test Frame");
 9          frame.setSize(400, 300);
10          frame.setVisible(true);
11          frame.setDefaultCloseOperation(JFrame.EXIT_ON_CLOSE);
12        }
13      }
```

Because JFrame is in the javax.swing package, the statement import javax.swing.* (Line 4) makes available all the classes from the javax.swing package, including JFrame, so that they can be used in the MyFrame class.

The following two constructors are used to create a JFrame object.

```
public JFrame()
```

Constructs an untitled JFrame object.

```
public JFrame(String title)
```

Constructs a JFrame object with a specified title. The title appears in the title bar of the frame.

The frame is not displayed *until* the frame.setVisible(true) method is applied. frame.setSize(400, 300) specifies that the frame is 400 pixels wide and 300 pixels high. If the setSize method is not used, the frame will be sized to display just the title bar. Since the setSize and setVisible methods are both defined in the Component class, they are inherited by the JFrame class. Later you will see that these methods are also useful in many other subclasses of Component.

When you run the MyFrame program, the following window will be displayed on-screen (see Figure 11.5).

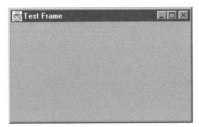

Figure 11.5   *The program creates and displays a frame with the title* Test Frame.

frame.setDefaultCloseOperation(JFrame.EXIT_ON_CLOSE) (Line 11) tells the program to terminate when the frame is closed. If this statement is not used, the program does not terminate when the frame is closed. In that case, you have to stop the program by pressing Ctrl + C at the DOS prompt window in Windows or use the kill command to stop the process in Unix.

11.3.2   Centering a Frame

By default, a frame is displayed in the upper-left corner of the screen. The coordinates at the upper-left corner of the screen are (0, 0). The *x* coordinate increases rightward, and the *y* coordinate increases downward. To display a frame at a specified location, use the setLocation(x, y) method in the JFrame class. This method places the upper-left corner of the frame at location (x, y) on the screen.

To center a frame on the screen, you need to know the width and height of the screen and the frame in order to determine the frame's upper-left coordinates. The screen's width and height can be obtained using the java.awt.Toolkit class:

```
Dimension screenSize = Toolkit.getDefaultToolkit().getScreenSize();
int screenWidth = screenSize.width;
int screenHeight = screenSize.height;
```

Therefore, as shown in Figure 11.6, the upper-left x and y coordinates of the centered frame frame are:

```
// Locate the upper-left corner (x, y) of the centered frame
int x = (screenWidth - frame.getWidth()) / 2;
int y = (screenHeight - frame.getHeight()) / 2;
```

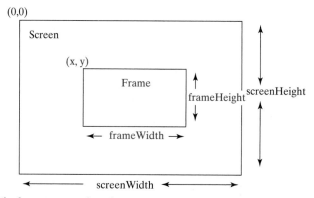

Figure 11.6   *The frame is centered on the screen.*

The java.awt.Dimension class encapsulates the width and height of a component (in integer precision) in a single object. The methods getWidth() and getHeight() are defined in the Component class. You can apply these methods to get the width and height of any component.

To display a centered frame, the program can be modified as follows:

```
1    // CenterFrame.java: Display a frame
2    package chapter11;
3
4    import javax.swing.*;
5    import java.awt.*;
6    public class CenterFrame {
7      public static void main(String[] args) {
8        JFrame frame = new JFrame("Centered Frame");
9        frame.setSize(400, 300);
10
11       // New since JDK 1.3 to exit the program upon closing
```

```
12        frame.setDefaultCloseOperation(JFrame.EXIT_ON_CLOSE);
13
14        // Get the dimension of the screen
15        Dimension screenSize =
16          Toolkit.getDefaultToolkit().getScreenSize();
17        int screenWidth = screenSize.width;
18        int screenHeight = screenSize.height;
19
20        // Locate the upper-left corner (x, y) of the centered frame
21        int x = (screenWidth - frame.getWidth()) / 2;
22        int y = (screenHeight - frame.getHeight()) / 2;
23
24        // Set the location of the frame
25        frame.setLocation(x, y);
26        frame.setVisible(true);
27      }
28    }
```

11.3.3   Adding Components to a Frame

The frame shown in Figure 11.5 is empty. Using the add method, you can add components into the frame's content pane, as follows:

```
1     // MyFrameWithComponents.java: Add components into a frame
2     package chapter11;
3
4     import javax.swing.*;
5
6     public class MyFrameWithComponents {
7       public static void main(String[] args) {
8         JFrame frame = new JFrame("Adding Components into the Frame");
9
10        // Add a button into the frame
11        java.awt.Container container = frame.getContentPane();
12        JButton jbtOK = new JButton("OK");
13        container.add(jbtOK);
14
15        frame.setSize(400, 300);
16        frame.setVisible(true);
17        frame.setDefaultCloseOperation(JFrame.EXIT_ON_CLOSE);
18      }
19    }
```

The getContentPane method (Line 11) in the JFrame class returns the content pane of the frame, which is an instance of java.awt.Container. The content pane holds the frame's components. An object of JButton was created using new JButton("OK"), and this object was added to the content pane of the frame (Line 13).

You may wonder how the content pane (a Container object) is created. The getContentPane method does not produce it. The content pane is created when a JFrame object is created. The getContentPane method simply returns a reference to the content pane, so you can use it to reference the content pane.

The add(Component comp) method defined in the Container class adds an instance of Component to the container. Since JButton is a subclass of Component, an instance of JButton is also an instance of Component. To remove a component from a container, use the remove method. The following statement removes the button from the container:

```
container.remove(jbtOK);
```

When you run the program MyFrameWithComponents, the following window will be displayed in Figure 11.7. The button is always centered in the frame and occupies the entire frame no matter how you resize it. This is because components are put in the frame by the content pane's layout manager, and the default layout manager for the content pane places the button in the center. In the next section, you will use several different layout managers to place components in other locations as desired.

Figure 11.7   *An OK button is added to the frame.*

11.4   Layout Managers

In many other window systems, the user-interface components are arranged by using hard-coded pixel measurements. For example, put a button at location (10, 10) in the window. Using hard-coded pixel measurements, the user interface might look fine on one system but be unusable on another. Java's layout managers provide a level of abstraction that automatically maps your user interface on all window systems.

The Java GUI components are placed in containers, where they are arranged by the container's layout manager. In the preceding program, you did not specify where to place the OK button in the frame, but Java knows where to place it because the layout manager works behind the scenes to place components in the correct locations. A layout manager is created using a layout manager class. Every layout manager class implements the LayoutManager interface.

Layout managers are set in containers using the setLayout(LayoutManager layout-Manager) method. For example, you can use the following statements to create an instance of XLayout and set it in a container:

```
LayoutManager layoutManager = new XLayout();
container.setLayout(layoutManager);
```

The five basic layout managers are FlowLayout, GridLayout, BorderLayout, CardLayout, and GridBagLayout. The following sections introduce the FlowLayout, GridLayout, and BorderLayout managers. CardLayout and GridBagLayout are introduced in Bonus Supplement G, "CardLayout, GridBagLayout, and Null Layout."

11.4.1 FlowLayout

FlowLayout is the simplest layout manager. The components are arranged in the container from left to right in the order in which they were added. When one row is filled, a new row is started. You can specify the way the components are aligned by using one of three constants: FlowLayout.RIGHT, FlowLayout.CENTER, or FlowLayout.LEFT. You can also specify the gap between components in pixels. FlowLayout has three constructors:

■ public FlowLayout(int align, int hGap, int vGap)

Constructs a new FlowLayout with the specified alignment, horizontal gap, and vertical gap. The gaps are the distances in pixels between components.

■ public FlowLayout(int alignment)

Constructs a new FlowLayout with a specified alignment and a default gap of 5 pixels horizontally and vertically.

■ public FlowLayout()

Constructs a new FlowLayout with a default center alignment and a default gap of 5 pixels horizontally and vertically.

Example 11.1 Testing the FlowLayout Manager

Problem

Write a program that adds ten buttons labeled Component 1, ..., and Component 10 into the content pane of a frame with a FlowLayout manager, as shown in Figure 11.8.

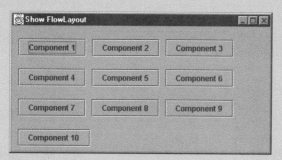

Figure 11.8 *The components are added with the* FlowLayout *manager to fill in the rows in the container one after another.*

Solution

Create a subclass of JFrame, set the layout manager of the content pane to a FlowLayout, and add ten buttons into the content pane using a loop.

continues

457

Example 11.1 Continued

```
1    // ShowFlowLayout.java: Demonstrate using FlowLayout
2    package chapter11;
3
4    import javax.swing.JButton;
5    import javax.swing.JFrame;
6    import java.awt.Container;
7    import java.awt.FlowLayout;
8
9    public class ShowFlowLayout extends JFrame {
10     /** Default constructor */
11     public ShowFlowLayout() {
12       // Get the content pane of the frame
13       Container container = getContentPane();
14
15       // Set FlowLayout, aligned left with horizontal gap 10
16       // and vertical gap 20 between components
17       container.setLayout(new FlowLayout(FlowLayout.LEFT, 10, 20));
18
19       // Add buttons to the frame
20       for (int i = 1; i <= 10; i++)
21         container.add(new JButton("Component " + i));
22     }
23
24     /** Main method */
25     public static void main(String[] args) {
26       ShowFlowLayout frame = new ShowFlowLayout();
27       frame.setTitle("Show FlowLayout");
28       frame.setDefaultCloseOperation(JFrame.EXIT_ON_CLOSE);
29       frame.setSize(200, 200);
30       frame.setVisible(true);
31     }
32   }
```

Review

This example creates a program using a style different from the programs in the preceding section, where frames were created using the JFrame class. This example creates a class named ShowFlowLayout that extends the JFrame class. The main method in this program creates an instance of ShowFlowLayout (Line 26). The constructor of ShowFlowLayout constructs and places the components in the frame. This is the preferred style of creating GUI applications for two reasons: (1) creating a GUI application means creating a frame, so it is natural to define a frame to extend JFrame; (2) the new class can be reused if desirable. Using one style consistently makes programs easy to read. From now on, all the GUI main classes will extend the JFrame class. The constructor of the main class constructs the user interface. The main method creates an instance of the main class and then displays the frame.

In this example, the FlowLayout manager is used to place components in a frame. If you resize the frame, the components are automatically rearranged to fit in it.

If you replace the setLayout statement (Line 17) with setLayout(new FlowLayout(FlowLayout.RIGHT, 0, 0)), all the rows of buttons will be right-aligned with no gaps.

An anonymous `FlowLayout` object was created in the statement (Line 17):

```
container.setLayout(new FlowLayout(FlowLayout.LEFT, 10, 20));
```

This statement is equivalent to the following code:

```
FlowLayout layout = new FlowLayout(FlowLayout.LEFT, 10, 20);
container.setLayout(layout);
```

This code creates an explicit reference to the object `layout` of the `FlowLayout` class. The explicit reference is not necessary, because the object is not directly referenced in the `ShowFlowLayout` class.

The `setTitle` method (Line 27) is defined in the `java.awt.Frame` class. Since `JFrame` is a subclass of `Frame`, you can use it to set a title for an object of `JFrame`.

CAUTION

Do not forget to put the `new` operator before a layout manager class when setting a layout style; for example, `setLayout(new FlowLayout())`.

NOTE

The constructor `ShowFlowLayout()` does not explicitly invoke the constructor `JFrame()`, but the constructor `JFrame()` is invoked implicitly. See the second Note box on page 339.

11.4.2   GridLayout

The `GridLayout` manager arranges components in a grid (matrix) formation with the number of rows and columns defined by the constructor. The components are placed in the grid from left to right, starting with the first row, then the second, and so on, in the order in which they are added. The `GridLayout` manager has three constructors:

■ `public GridLayout(int rows, int columns, int hGap, int vGap)`

Constructs a new `GridLayout` with the specified number of rows and columns, along with specified horizontal and vertical gaps between components in the container.

■ `public GridLayout(int rows, int columns)`

Constructs a new `GridLayout` with the specified number of rows and columns. The horizontal and vertical gaps are zero.

■ `public GridLayout()`

Constructs a new `GridLayout` with one column in a single row.

You can specify the number of rows and columns in the grid. The basic rule is as follows:

- The number of rows or the number of columns can be zero, but not both. If one is zero and the other is nonzero, the nonzero dimension is fixed, while the zero dimension is determined dynamically by the layout manager. For example, if you specify zero rows and three columns for a grid that has ten components, GridLayout creates three fixed columns of four rows, with the last row containing one component. If you specify three rows and zero columns for a grid that has ten components, GridLayout creates three fixed rows of four columns, with the last row containing two components.

- If both the number of rows and the number of columns are nonzero, the number of rows is the dominating parameter; that is, the number of rows is fixed, and the layout manager dynamically calculates the number of columns. For example, if you specify three rows and three columns for a grid that has ten components, GridLayout creates three fixed rows of four columns, with the last row containing two components.

Example 11.2 Testing the GridLayout Manager

Problem

Write a program that adds ten buttons labeled Component 1, ..., and Component 10 into the content pane of a frame with a GridLayout manager, as shown in Figure 11.9.

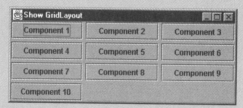

Figure 11.9   *The* GridLayout *manager divides the container into grids, then the components are added to fill in the cells row by row.*

Solution

Create a subclass of JFrame, set the layout manager of the content pane to a GridLayout with four rows and three columns, and add ten buttons into the content pane using a loop.

```
1    // ShowGridLayout.java: Demonstrate using GridLayout
2    package chapter11;
3
4    import javax.swing.JButton;
5    import javax.swing.JFrame;
6    import java.awt.GridLayout;
7    import java.awt.Container;
8
9    public class ShowGridLayout extends JFrame {
10     /** Default constructor */
11     public ShowGridLayout() {
```

```
12          // Get the content pane of the frame
13          Container container = getContentPane();
14
15          // Set GridLayout, 4 rows, 3 columns, and gaps 5 between
16          // components horizontally and vertically
17          container.setLayout(new GridLayout(4, 3, 5, 5));
18
19          // Add buttons to the frame
20          for (int i = 1; i <= 10; i++)
21            container.add(new JButton("Component " + i));
22        }
23
24        /** Main method */
25        public static void main(String[] args) {
26          ShowGridLayout frame = new ShowGridLayout();
27          frame.setTitle("Show GridLayout");
28          frame.setDefaultCloseOperation(JFrame.EXIT_ON_CLOSE);
29          frame.setSize(200, 200);
30          frame.setVisible(true);
31        }
32      }
```

Review

If you resize the frame, the layout of the buttons remains unchanged (i.e., the number of rows and columns does not change, and the gaps don't change either).

All components are given equal size in the container of `GridLayout`.

Replacing the `setLayout` statement (Line 17) with `setLayout(new GridLayout(3, 10))` would yield three rows and *four* columns, with the last row containing two components. The columns parameter is ignored because the rows parameter is nonzero. The actual number of columns is calculated by the layout manager.

 NOTE

In `FlowLayout` and `GridLayout`, the order in which the components are added to the container is important. It determines the location of the components in the container.

11.4.3   BorderLayout

The `BorderLayout` manager divides the window into five areas: East, South, West, North, and Center. Components are added to a `BorderLayout` by using `add (Component, index)`, where index is a constant `BorderLayout.EAST`, `Border Layout.SOUTH`, `BorderLayout.WEST`, `BorderLayout.NORTH`, or `BorderLayout.CENTER`. You can use one of the following two constructors to create a new `BorderLayout`:

■   `public BorderLayout(int hGap, int vGap)`

Constructs a new `BorderLayout` with the specified horizontal and vertical gaps between the components.

■   `public BorderLayout()`

Constructs a new `BorderLayout` without horizontal or vertical gaps.

The components are laid out according to their preferred sizes and where they are placed in the container. The North and South components can stretch horizontally; the East and West components can stretch vertically; the Center component can stretch both horizontally and vertically to fill any empty space.

Example 11.3 Testing the `BorderLayout` Manager

Problem

Write a program that adds five buttons labeled `East`, `South`, `West`, `North`, and `Center` into the content pane of a frame with a `BorderLayout` manager, as shown in Figure 11.10.

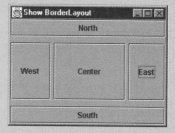

Figure 11.10   `BorderLayout` *divides the container into five areas, each of which can hold a component.*

Solution

Create a subclass of `JFrame`, set the layout manager of the content pane to a `BorderLayout`, and add five buttons into the content pane.

```
1    // ShowBorderLayout.java: Demonstrate using BorderLayout
2    package chapter11;
3
4    import javax.swing.JButton;
5    import javax.swing.JFrame;
6    import java.awt.Container;
7    import java.awt.BorderLayout;
8
9    public class ShowBorderLayout extends JFrame {
10     /** Default constructor */
11     public ShowBorderLayout() {
12       // Get the content pane of the frame
13       Container container = getContentPane();
14
15       // Set BorderLayout with horizontal gap 5 and vertical gap 10
16       container.setLayout(new BorderLayout(5, 10));
17
18       // Add buttons to the frame
19       container.add(new JButton("East"), BorderLayout.EAST);
20       container.add(new JButton("South"), BorderLayout.SOUTH);
21       container.add(new JButton("West"), BorderLayout.WEST);
```

```
22          container.add(new JButton("North"), BorderLayout.NORTH);
23          container.add(new JButton("Center"), BorderLayout.CENTER);
24        }
25
26        /** Main method */
27        public static void main(String[] args) {
28          ShowBorderLayout frame = new ShowBorderLayout();
29          frame.setTitle("Show BorderLayout");
30          frame.setDefaultCloseOperation(JFrame.EXIT_ON_CLOSE);
31          frame.setSize(300, 200);
32          frame.setVisible(true);
33        }
34      }
```

Review

The buttons are added to the frame (Lines 19–23). Note that the add method for BorderLayout is different from the one for FlowLayout and GridLayout. With BorderLayout you specify where to put the components.

It is unnecessary to place components to occupy all the areas. If you remove the East button from the program and rerun it, you will see that the center stretches rightward to occupy the East area.

◈ **NOTE**

For convenience, BorderLayout interprets the absence of an index specification as BorderLayout.CENTER. For example, add(component) is the same as add(Component, BorderLayout.CENTER). If you add two components into a container of the BorderLayout, as follows:

```
container.add(component1);
container.add(component2);
```

only the last component is displayed.

11.4.4   Properties of Layout Managers (Optional)

Layout managers have properties that can be changed dynamically. FlowLayout has alignment, hGap, and vGap properties. You can use the setAlignment, setHGap, and setVGap methods to specify the alignment, and the horizontal and vertical gaps. GridLayout has the rows, columns, hGap, and vGap properties. You can use the setRows, setColumns, setHGap, and setVGap methods to specify the number of rows, the number of columns, and the horizontal and vertical gaps. BorderLayout has the hGap and vGap properties. You can use the setHGap and setVGap methods to specify the horizontal and vertical gaps.

In the preceding sections, an anonymous layout manager is used because the properties of a layout manager do not change once it is created. If you have to change the properties of a layout manager dynamically, the layout manager must be explicitly referenced by a variable. You can then change the properties of the layout manager through the variable. For example, the following code creates a layout manager and sets its properties:

```
// Create a layout manager
FlowLayout flowLayout = new FlowLayout();

// Set layout properties
flowLayout.setAlignment(FlowLayout.RIGHT);
flowLayout.setHGap(10);
flowLayout.setVGap(20);
```

11.4.5   The *validate* and *doLayout* Methods (Optional)

A container can have only one layout manager at a time. You can change its layout manager by using the setLayout (aNewLayout) method and use the validate() method to force the container to again lay out the components in the container using the new layout manager.

If you use the same layout manager but change its properties, you need to use the doLayout() method to force the container to lay out the components using the new properties of the layout manager.

11.5   Using Panels as Containers

Suppose that you want to place ten buttons and a text field on a frame. The buttons are placed in grid formation, but the text field is placed on a separate row. It is difficult to achieve the desired look by placing all the components in a single container. With Java GUI programming, you can divide a window into panels. Panels act as smaller containers to group user-interface components. You add the buttons in one panel, and then add the panel into the frame.

The Swing version of panel is JPanel. To add a button to panel p, for instance, you can use:

```
JPanel p = new JPanel();
p.add(new JButton("ButtonName"));
```

By default, JPanel uses FlowLayout. Panels can be placed inside a frame or inside another panel. The following statement places panel p into frame f:

```
f.getContentPane().add(p);
```

NOTE
To add a component to JFrame, you actually add it to the content pane of JFrame. To add a component to a panel, you add it directly to the panel using the **add** method.

Example 11.4 Testing Panels

Problem

Write a program that uses panels to organize components. The program creates a user interface for a microwave oven, as shown in Figure 11.11.

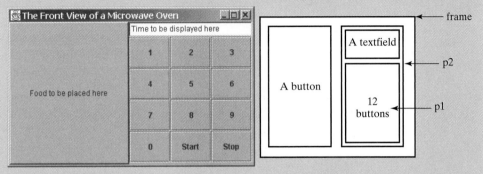

Figure 11.11   *The program uses panels to organize components.*

Solution

The program is given as follows:

```
1    // TestPanels.java: Use panels to group components
2    package chapter11;
3
4    import java.awt.*;
5    import javax.swing.*;
6
7    public class TestPanels extends JFrame {
8      /** Default constructor */
9      public TestPanels() {
10        // Get the content pane of the frame
11        Container container = getContentPane();
12
13        // Set BorderLayout for the frame
14        container.setLayout(new BorderLayout());
15
16        // Create panel p1 for the buttons and set GridLayout
17        JPanel p1 = new JPanel();
18        p1.setLayout(new GridLayout(4, 3));
19
20        // Add buttons to the panel
21        for (int i = 1; i <= 9; i++) {
22          p1.add(new JButton("" + i));
23        }
24
25        p1.add(new JButton("" + 0));
26        p1.add(new JButton("Start"));
27        p1.add(new JButton("Stop"));
28
29        // Create panel p2 to hold a text field and p1
30        JPanel p2 = new JPanel();
31        p2.setLayout(new BorderLayout());
32        p2.add(new JTextField("Time to be displayed here"),
33          BorderLayout.NORTH);
```

continues

465

Example 11.4 Continued

```
34          p2.add(p1, BorderLayout.CENTER);
35
36          // Add p2 and a button to the frame
37          container.add(p2, BorderLayout.EAST);
38          container.add(new JButton("Food to be placed here"),
39            BorderLayout.CENTER);
40        }
41
42        /** Main method */
43        public static void main(String[] args) {
44          TestPanels frame = new TestPanels();
45          frame.setTitle("The Front View of a Microwave Oven");
46          frame.setDefaultCloseOperation(JFrame.EXIT_ON_CLOSE);
47          frame.setSize(400, 250);
48          frame.setVisible(true);
49        }
50      }
```

Review

To achieve the desired layout, the program uses panel p1 of GridLayout to group the number buttons, the **Stop** button, and the **Start** button, and uses panel p2 of BorderLayout to hold a text field in the north and p1 in the center. The button representing the food is placed in the center of the frame, and p2 is placed in the east of the frame.

The statement (Lines 32–33)

```
p2.add(new JTextField("Time to be displayed here"),
  BorderLayout.NORTH);
```

creates an instance of JTextField and adds it to p2.

Text field is a GUI component that can be used for user input as well as to display values. Text fields will be introduced in Chapter 13, "Creating User Interfaces."

11.6   Drawing Graphics in Panels

Panels are invisible and are used as small containers that group components to achieve a desired layout. Another important use of JPanel is for drawing.

To draw in a JPanel, you create a new class that extends JPanel and overrides the paintComponent method to tell the panel how to draw things. Although you can draw things directly in a frame or an applet using the paint method, I recommend that you use JPanel to draw strings and shapes and to show images; this way your drawing will not interfere with other components.

The paintComponent method is defined in JComponent, and its signature is as follows:

```
protected void paintComponent(Graphics g)
```

The Graphics object g is created automatically by the JVM for every visible GUI component. This object controls how information is drawn. You can use various drawing methods defined in the Graphics class to draw strings and geometric figures. For example, you can draw a string using the following method in the Graphics class:

```
drawString(string, x, y);
```

The program given below draws a message "Welcome to Java" on the panel, as shown in Figure 11.12.

Figure 11.12 *The message is drawn on a panel, and the panel is placed inside the frame.*

```
// DrawMessage.java: Display a message on a JPanel
package chapter11;

import javax.swing.*;
import java.awt.*;

public class DrawMessage extends JPanel {
  /** Main method */
  public static void main(String[] args) {
    JFrame frame = new JFrame("DrawMessage");
    frame.getContentPane().add(new DrawMessage());
    frame.setDefaultCloseOperation(JFrame.EXIT_ON_CLOSE);
    frame.setSize(300, 200);
    frame.setVisible(true);
  }

  /** Paint the message */
  protected void paintComponent(Graphics g) {
    super.paintComponent(g);

    g.drawString("Welcome to Java!", 40, 40);
  }
}
```

All the drawing methods have arguments that specify the locations of the subjects to be drawn. All measurements in Java are made in pixels. Each component has its own coordinate system with the origin (0, 0) at the upper-left corner of the component. The *x* coordinate increases to the right, and the *y* coordinate increases downward. Note that the Java coordinate system is different from the traditional coordinate system, as shown in Figure 11.13.

◈ NOTE

The Graphics class is an abstract class for displaying figures and images on the screen on different platforms. The Graphics class is implemented on the native platform in the JVM. When you use the paintComponent method to draw things on a graphics context g, this g is an instance of a concrete subclass of the abstract Graphics class for the specific platform. The Graphics class encapsulates the platform details and enables you to draw things uniformly without concerning specific platforms.

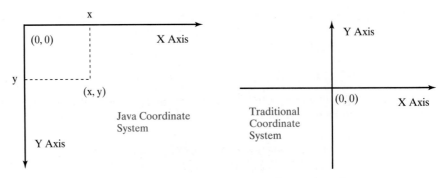

Figure 11.13 *The Java graphics coordinate system is measured in pixels, with* (0, 0) *at its upper-left corner.*

 NOTE

Whenever a component is displayed, a `Graphics` object is created for the component. The Swing components use the `paintComponent` method to draw things. The `paintComponent` method is automatically invoked to paint the graphics context when the component is first displayed or whenever the component needs to be redisplayed. Invoking `super.paintComponent(g)` is necessary to ensure that the viewing area is cleared before a new drawing is displayed. The user can request the component to be redisplayed by invoking the `repaint()` method defined in the `Component` class. Invoking `repaint()` causes `paintComponent` to be invoked by the JVM. The user should never invoke `paintComponent` directly. For this reason, the protected visibility is sufficient for `paintComponent`.

 NOTE

To draw things, normally you create a subclass of `JPanel` and override its `paintComponent` method to tell the system how to draw. In fact, you can draw things on any GUI component. See Exercise 11.16 for a custom button class that displays a figure instead of a text in the button.

You can draw things using appropriate colors and fonts. The next sections introduce the `Color` class, the `Font` class, the `FontMetrics` class, and drawing methods in the `Graphics` class.

11.7 The *Color* Class

You can set colors for GUI components by using the `java.awt.Color` class. Colors are made of red, green, and blue components, each of which is represented by a byte value that describes its intensity, ranging from 0 (darkest shade) to 255 (lightest shade). This is known as the *RGB model*.

The syntax to create a `Color` object is

```
Color color = new Color(r, g, b);
```

in which r, g, and b specify a color by its red, green, and blue components. For example:

```
Color color = new Color(128, 100, 100);
```

You can use the setBackground(Color c) and setForeground(Color c) methods defined in the Component class to set a component's background and foreground colors. Here is an example of setting the background of a panel using a color:

```
JPanel myPanel = new JPanel();
myPanel.setBackground(color);
```

Alternatively, you can use one of the thirteen standard colors (black, blue, cyan, darkGray, gray, green, lightGray, magenta, orange, pink, red, white, yellow) defined as constants in java.awt.Color. The following code, for instance, sets the background color of a panel to yellow:

```
JPanel myPanel = new JPanel();
myPanel.setBackground(Color.yellow);
```

 NOTE

The standard color names are constants, but they are named as variables with lowercase for the first word and uppercase for the first letters of subsequent words. Thus the color names violate the Java naming convention. Since JDK 1.4, you can also use the new constants: BLACK, BLUE, CYAN, DARK_GRAY, GRAY, GREEN, LIGHT_GRAY, MAGENTA, ORANGE, PINK, RED, WHITE, and YELLOW.

11.8 The *Font* and *FontMetrics* Classes

You can set fonts for the components or subjects you draw, and use font metrics to measure font size. Fonts and font metrics are encapsulated in the classes Font and FontMetrics.

Whatever font is current will be used in the subsequent drawing. To set a font, you need to create a Font object from the Font class. The syntax is:

```
Font myFont = new Font(name, style, size);
```

You can choose a font name from SansSerif, Serif, Monospaced, Dialog, or DialogInput, and choose a style from Font.PLAIN, Font.BOLD, and Font.ITALIC. The styles can be combined, as in the following code:

```
Font myFont = new Font("SansSerif", Font.BOLD, 16);
Font myFont = new Font("Serif", Font.BOLD + Font.ITALIC, 12);
```

If your system supports other fonts, such as "Times New Roman," you can use it to create a font object. To find the fonts available on your system, you need to create an instance of java.awt.GraphicsEnvironment using its static method getLocalGraphicsEnvironment(). GraphicsEnvironment is an abstract class that describes the graphics environment on a particular system. You can use its getAllFonts() method to obtain all the available fonts on the system, and its getAvailableFontFamilyNames() method to obtain the names of all the available fonts. For example, the following statements print all the available font names in the system:

```
GraphicsEnvironment e =
  GraphicsEnvironment.getLocalGraphicsEnvironment();
String[] fontnames = e.getAvailableFontFamilyNames();

for (int i = 0; i < fontnames.length; i++)
  System.out.println(fontnames[i]);
```

FontMetrics can be used to compute the exact length and width of a string, which is helpful for measuring the size of a string in order to display it in the right position. For example, you can center strings in the viewing area with the help of the FontMetrics class. A FontMetrics is measured by the following attributes (see Figure 11.14):

Figure 11.14   *The* FontMetrics *class can be used to determine the font properties of characters.*

- **Leading,** pronounced *ledding,* is the amount of space between lines of text.

- **Ascent** is the height of a character, from the baseline to the top.

- **Descent** is the distance from the baseline to the bottom of a descending character, such as *j, y,* and *g.*

- **Height** is the sum of leading, ascent, and descent.

FontMetrics is an abstract class. To get a FontMetrics object for a specific font, use the following getFontMetrics methods defined in the Graphics class:

- `public FontMetrics getFontMetrics(Font f)`

  Returns the font metrics of the specified font.

- `public FontMetrics getFontMetrics()`

  Returns the font metrics of the current font.

You can use the following instance methods in the FontMetrics class to obtain the attributes of a font and the width of a string when it is drawn using the font.

```
public int getAscent()
public int getDescent()
public int getLeading()
public int getHeight()
public int stringWidth(String str)
```

Example 11.5 Creating a Message Panel Class

Problem

This example creates a useful class that displays a message in a panel. The class enables the user to set the location of the message, center the message, and move the message with the specified interval. Use this class to display a message "Welcome to Java" centered in the frame, as shown in Figure 11.15.

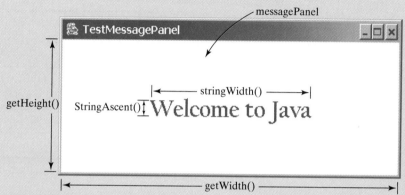

Figure 11.15 *The program uses the* FontMetrics *class to measure the string width and height, and displays it at the center of the frame.*

Solution

Here are the steps for the program:

1. Create a panel named MessagePanel to display the message. MessagePanel extends JPanel to display a message in a specified location or centered. The properties and methods in MessagePanel are shown in Figure 11.16.

2. Create a frame named TestMessagePanel that extends JFrame. TestMessagePanel creates an instance of MessagePanel and places it in the center of the frame. The relationship between TestMessagePanel and MessagePanel is shown in Figure 11.16.

```
1   // MessagePanel.java: Display a message on a JPanel
2   package chapter11;
3
4   import java.awt.Font;
5   import java.awt.FontMetrics;
6   import java.awt.Dimension;
7   import java.awt.Graphics;
8   import javax.swing.JPanel;
9
10  public class MessagePanel extends JPanel {
11    /** The message to be displayed */
12    private String message = "Welcome to Java";
13
14    /** The x coordinate where the message is displayed */
15    private int xCoordinate = 20;
16
17    /** The y coordinate where the message is displayed */
18    private int yCoordinate = 20;
19
```

continues

471

Example 11.5 Continued

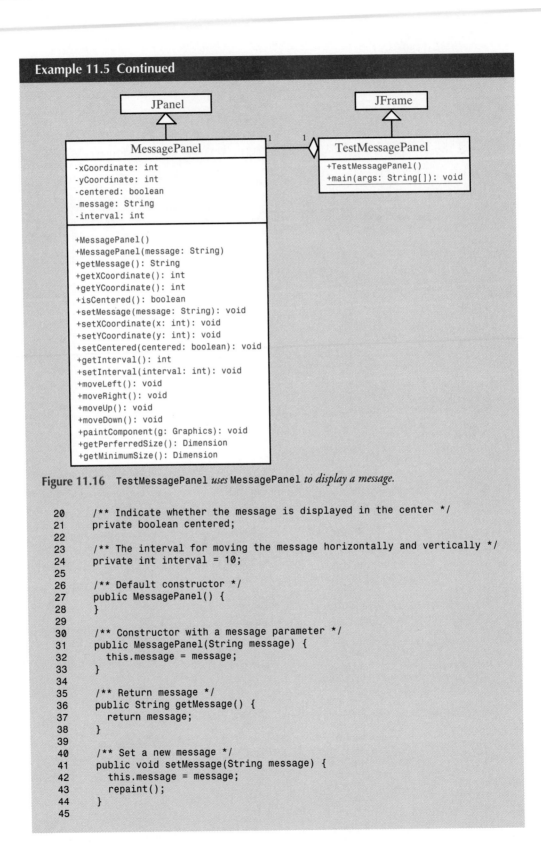

Figure 11.16   TestMessagePanel *uses* MessagePanel *to display a message.*

```
20      /** Indicate whether the message is displayed in the center */
21      private boolean centered;
22
23      /** The interval for moving the message horizontally and vertically */
24      private int interval = 10;
25
26      /** Default constructor */
27      public MessagePanel() {
28      }
29
30      /** Constructor with a message parameter */
31      public MessagePanel(String message) {
32        this.message = message;
33      }
34
35      /** Return message */
36      public String getMessage() {
37        return message;
38      }
39
40      /** Set a new message */
41      public void setMessage(String message) {
42        this.message = message;
43        repaint();
44      }
45
```

```
46      /** Return xCoordinator */
47      public int getXCoordinate() {
48        return xCoordinate;
49      }
50
51      /** Set a new xCoordinator */
52      public void setXCoordinate(int x) {
53        this.xCoordinate = x;
54        repaint();
55      }
56
57      /** Return yCoordinator */
58      public int getYCoordinate() {
59        return yCoordinate;
60      }
61
62      /** Set a new yCoordinator */
63      public void setYCoordinate(int y) {
64        this.yCoordinate = y;
65        repaint();
66      }
67
68      /** Return centered */
69      public boolean isCentered() {
70        return centered;
71      }
72
73      /** Set a new centered */
74      public void setCentered(boolean centered) {
75        this.centered = centered;
76        repaint();
77      }
78
79      /** Return interval */
80      public int getInterval() {
81        return interval;
82      }
83
84      /** Set a new interval */
85      public void setInterval(int interval) {
86        this.interval = interval;
87        repaint();
88      }
89
90      /** Paint the message */
91      protected void paintComponent(Graphics g) {
92        super.paintComponent(g);
93
94        if (centered) {
95          // Get font metrics for the current font
96          FontMetrics fm = g.getFontMetrics();
97
98          // Find the center location to display
99          int stringWidth = fm.stringWidth(message);
100         int stringAscent = fm.getAscent();
101         // Get the position of the leftmost character in the baseline
102         xCoordinate = getWidth() / 2 - stringWidth / 2;
103         yCoordinate = getHeight() / 2 + stringAscent / 2;
104       }
105
106       g.drawString(message, xCoordinate, yCoordinate);
107     }
108
```

continues

Example 11.5 Continued

```
109      /** Move the message left */
110      public void moveLeft() {
111        xCoordinate -= interval;
112        repaint();
113      }
114
115      /** Move the message right */
116     public void moveRight() {
117        xCoordinate += interval;
118        repaint();
119      }
120
121      /** Move the message up */
122      public void moveUp() {
123        yCoordinate -= interval;
124        repaint();
125      }
126
127      /** Move the message down */
128      public void moveDown() {
129        yCoordinate -= interval;
130        repaint();
131      }
132
133      /** Override get method for preferredSize */
134      public Dimension getPreferredSize() {
135        return new Dimension(200, 30);
136      }
137
138      /** Override get method for minimumSize */
139      public Dimension getMinimumSize() {
140        return new Dimension(200, 30);
141      }
142    }
```

```
1    // TestMessagePanel.java: Draw a message at the center of a panel
2    package chapter11;
3
4    import java.awt.Font;
5    import java.awt.FontMetrics;
6    import java.awt.Graphics;
7    import java.awt.Color;
8    import javax.swing.*;
9
10   public class TestMessagePanel extends JFrame {
11     /** Default constructor */
12     public TestMessagePanel() {
13       MessagePanel messagePanel = new MessagePanel("Welcome to Java");
14
15       // Set background color and font in messagePanel
16       messagePanel.setBackground(Color.white);
17       messagePanel.setFont(new Font("Californian FB", Font.BOLD, 30));
18
19       // Center the message
20       messagePanel.setCentered(true);
21
22       getContentPane().add(messagePanel);
23     }
24
25     /** Main method */
26     public static void main(String[] args) {
27       TestMessagePanel frame = new TestMessagePanel();
```

```
28       frame.setDefaultCloseOperation(JFrame.EXIT_ON_CLOSE);
29       frame.setSize(300, 200);
30       frame.setTitle("TestMessagePanel");
31       frame.setVisible(true);
32     }
33   }
```

Review

TestMessagePanel creates an instance of MessagePanel to display a message at the center of the panel. The setFont method (Line 17) sets a new font for the message panel. This method is available for all subclasses of Component. The new font is created using new Font("Californian FB", Font.BOLD, 30). It is used to display the message in the panel.

The MessagePanel class has the properties message, xCoordinate, yCoordinate, and centered. xCoordinate and yCoordinate specify where the message is displayed if centered is false. If centered is true, the message is displayed at the center of the panel.

The methods getWidth() and getHeight() (Lines 102–103), defined in the Component class, return the component's width and height, respectively.

Since the centered property is set to true in TestMessagePanel, the message is displayed in the center of the panel. Resizing the frame results in the message always being displayed in the center of the panel.

yCoordinate is the height of the baseline for the first character of the string to be displayed. When centered is true, yCoordinate should be getHeight() / 2 + h / 2, where h is the ascent of the string.

The getPreferredSize() method (Lines 134–136), defined in Component, is overridden in MessagePanel to specify the preferred size for the layout manager to consider when laying out a MessagePanel object.

The getMinimumSize() method (Lines 139–141), defined in Component, is overridden in MessagePanel to specify the minimum size for the layout manager to consider when laying out a MessagePanel object.

The drawString method draws on the panel (Line 106). The drawString(s, x, y) method draws a string s whose left end of the baseline starts at (x, y).

There are many ways to write Java programs. You can rewrite this example using one class. See Exercise 11.17.

The repaint method is defined in the Component class. Invoking repaint causes the paintComponent method to be called. The repaint method is invoked to refresh the viewing area. Typically, you call it if you have new things to display.

⚠ CAUTION

The paintComponent method should never be invoked directly. It is invoked either by the JVM whenever the viewing area changes or by the repaint method. You should override the paintComponent method to tell the system how to paint the viewing area, but never override the repaint method.

---

continues

Example 11.5 Continued

 NOTE

The `repaint` method lodges a request to update the viewing area and returns immediately. Its effect is asynchronous, and if several requests are outstanding, it is likely that only the last `paintComponent` will be done.

 CAUTION

The `MessagePanel` class uses the properties `xCoordinate` and `yCoordinate` to specify the position of the message displayed on the panel. Do not use the property names `x` and `y`, because they are already defined in the `Component` class to specify the position of the component in the parent's coordinate system.

 NOTE

The `Component` class has the `setBackground`, `setForeground`, and `setFont` methods. These methods are for setting colors and fonts for the entire component. Suppose you want to draw several messages in a panel with different colors and fonts; you have to use the `setColor` and `setFont` methods in the `Graphics` class to set the color and font for the current drawing.

 NOTE

One of the key features of Java programming is the reuse of classes. Throughout the book, you will develop reusable classes and later reuse them. `MessagePanel` is an example of this. It can be reused whenever you need to display a message on a panel. To make your class reusable in a wide range of applications, you should provide a variety of ways to use it. `MessagePanel` provides many properties and methods that will be used in several examples in the book.

11.9 Drawing Geometric Figures

This section introduces the methods in the `Graphics` class for drawing lines, rectangles, ovals, arcs, polygons, and polylines.

11.9.1 Drawing Lines

You can use the method shown below to draw a straight line:

```
drawLine(x1, y1, x2, y2);
```

The parameters x1, y1, x2, and y2 represent the starting point (x1, y1) and the ending point (x2, y2) of the line, as shown in Figure 11.17.

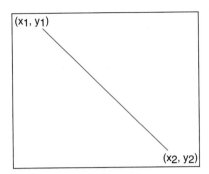

Figure 11.17 *The* `drawLine` *method draws a line between two specified points.*

11.9.2 Drawing Rectangles

Java provides six methods for drawing rectangles in outline or filled with color. You can draw plain rectangles, rounded rectangles, or three-dimensional rectangles.

To draw a plain rectangle, use the following code:

```
drawRect(x, y, w, h);
```

To draw a rectangle filled with color, use:

```
fillRect(x, y, w, h);
```

The parameters x and y represent the upper-left corner of the rectangle, and w and h are its width and height (see Figure 11.18).

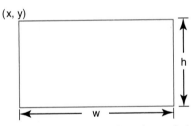

Figure 11.18 *The* `drawRect` *method draws a rectangle with specified upper-left corner* (x, y), *width, and height.*

To draw a rounded rectangle, use the following method:

```
drawRoundRect(x, y, w, h, aw, ah);
```

To draw a rounded rectangle filled with color, use this method:

```
fillRoundRect(x, y, w, h, aw, ah);
```

Parameters x, y, w, and h are the same as in the `drawRect` method, parameter aw is the horizontal diameter of the arcs at the corner, and ah is the vertical diameter of the arcs at the corner (see Figure 11.19). In other words, aw and ah are the width and the height of the oval that produces a quarter-circle at each corner.

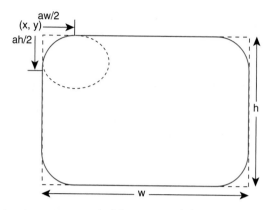

Figure 11.19 *The* drawRoundRect *method draws a rounded rectangle.*

To draw a 3D rectangle, use

```
draw3DRect(x, y, w, h, raised);
```

in which x, y, w, and h are the same as in the drawRect method. The last parameter, a Boolean value, indicates whether the rectangle is raised above the surface or etched into the surface.

The example given below demonstrates these methods. The output is shown in Figure 11.20.

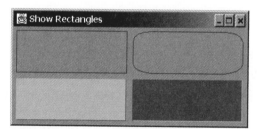

Figure 11.20 *The program draws a rectangle, a rounded rectangle, a raised 3D rectangle, and a plain 3D rectangle.*

```java
// TestRect.java: Demonstrate drawing rectangles
package chapter11;

import java.awt.Graphics;
import java.awt.Color;
import javax.swing.JPanel;
import javax.swing.JFrame;

public class TestRect extends JFrame {
  /** Default constructor */
  public TestRect() {
    setTitle("Show Rectangles");
    getContentPane().add(new RectPanel());
  }
```

```java
  /** Main method */
  public static void main(String[] args) {
    TestRect frame = new TestRect();
    frame.setDefaultCloseOperation(JFrame.EXIT_ON_CLOSE);
    frame.setSize(300, 250);
    frame.setVisible(true);
  }
}

class RectPanel extends JPanel {
  protected void paintComponent(Graphics g) {
    super.paintComponent(g);

    // Set new color
    g.setColor(Color.red);

    // Draw a rectangle
    g.drawRect(5, 5, getWidth() / 2 - 10, getHeight() / 2 - 10);

    // Draw a rounded rectangle
    g.drawRoundRect(getWidth() / 2 + 5, 5,
      getWidth() / 2 - 10, getHeight() / 2 - 10, 60, 30);

    // Change the color to cyan
    g.setColor(Color.cyan);

    // Draw a 3D rectangle
    g.fill3DRect(5, getHeight() / 2 + 5, getWidth() / 2 - 10,
      getHeight() / 2 - 10, true);

    // Draw a raised 3D rectangle
    g.fill3DRect(getWidth() / 2 + 5, getHeight() / 2 + 5,
      getWidth() / 2 - 10, getHeight() / 2 - 10, false);
  }
}
```

11.9.3   Drawing Ovals

Depending on whether you wish to draw an oval in outline or filled solid, you can use either the drawOval method or the fillOval method. Since an oval in Java is drawn based on its bounding rectangle, give the parameters as if you were drawing a rectangle.

Here is the method for drawing an oval:

```java
drawOval(x, y, w, h);
```

To draw a filled oval, use the following method:

```java
fillOval(x, y, w, h);
```

Parameters x and y indicate the top-left corner of the bounding rectangle, and w and h indicate the width and height, respectively, of the bounding rectangle, as shown in Figure 11.21.

The following is an example of how to draw ovals, with the output in Figure 11.22.

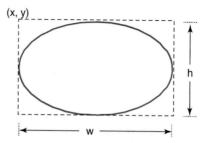

Figure 11.21   *The* drawOval *method draws an oval based on its bounding rectangle.*

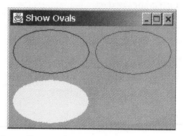

Figure 11.22   *The program draws four ovals.*

```java
// TestOvals.java: Demonstrate drawing ovals
package chapter11;

import javax.swing.JFrame;
import javax.swing.JPanel;
import java.awt.Color;
import java.awt.Graphics;

public class TestOvals extends JFrame {
  /** Default constructor */
  public TestOvals() {
    setTitle("Show Ovals");
    getContentPane().add(new OvalsPanel());
  }

  /** Main method */
  public static void main(String[] args) {
    TestOvals frame = new TestOvals();
    frame.setDefaultCloseOperation(JFrame.EXIT_ON_CLOSE);
    frame.setSize(250, 250);
    frame.setVisible(true);
  }
}

// The class for drawing the ovals on a panel
class OvalsPanel extends JPanel {
  protected void paintComponent(Graphics g) {
    super.paintComponent(g);

    g.drawOval(5, 5, getWidth() / 2 - 10, getHeight() / 2 - 10);
    g.setColor(Color.red);
    g.drawOval(getWidth() / 2 + 5, 5, getWidth() / 2 - 10,
      getHeight() / 2 - 10);
    g.setColor(Color.yellow);
    g.fillOval(5, getHeight() / 2 + 5, getWidth() / 2 - 10,
      getHeight() / 2 - 10);
    g.setColor(Color.orange);
```

```
        g.fillOval(getWidth() / 2 + 5, getHeight() / 2 + 5,
            getWidth() / 2 - 10, getHeight() / 2 - 10);
    }
}
```

11.9.4   Drawing Arcs

An arc is conceived as part of an oval. Like an oval, an arc is drawn based on its bounding rectangle. The methods to draw or fill an arc are as follows:

```
drawArc(x, y, w, h, startAngle, arcAngle);
fillArc(x, y, w, h, startAngle, arcAngle);
```

Parameters x, y, w, and h are the same as in the drawOval method; parameter startAngle is the starting angle; arcAngle is the spanning angle (i.e., the angle covered by the arc). Angles are measured in degrees and follow the usual mathematical conventions (i.e., 0 degrees is in the easterly direction, and positive angles indicate counterclockwise rotation from the easterly direction; see Figure 11.23).

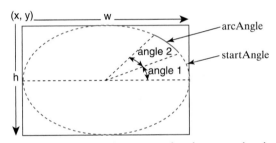

Figure 11.23   *The* drawArc *method draws an arc based on an oval with specified angles.*

Shown below is an example of how to draw arcs; the output is shown in Figure 11.24.

 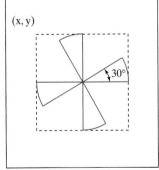

Figure 11.24   *The program draws four filled arcs.*

```
// TestArcs.java: Demonstrate drawing arcs
package chapter11;

import javax.swing.JFrame;
import javax.swing.JPanel;
import java.awt.Color;
import java.awt.Graphics;
```

```java
public class TestArcs extends JFrame {
  /** Default constructor */
  public TestArcs() {
    setTitle("Show Arcs");
    getContentPane().add(new ArcsPanel());
  }

  /** Main method */
  public static void main(String[] args) {
    TestArcs frame = new TestArcs();
    frame.setDefaultCloseOperation(JFrame.EXIT_ON_CLOSE);
    frame.setSize(250, 300);
    frame.setVisible(true);
  }
}

// The class for drawing arcs on a panel
class ArcsPanel extends JPanel {
  // Draw four blazes of a fan
  protected void paintComponent(Graphics g) {
    super.paintComponent(g);

    int xCenter = getWidth() / 2;
    int yCenter = getHeight() / 2;
    int radius =
      (int)(Math.min(getWidth(), getHeight()) * 0.4);

    int x = xCenter - radius;
    int y = yCenter - radius;

    g.fillArc(x, y, 2 * radius, 2 * radius, 0, 30);
    g.fillArc(x, y, 2 * radius, 2 * radius, 90, 30);
    g.fillArc(x, y, 2 * radius, 2 * radius, 180, 30);
    g.fillArc(x, y, 2 * radius, 2 * radius, 270, 30);
  }
}
```

11.9.5   The *Polygon* class and Drawing Polygons and Polylines

The Polygon class encapsulates a description of a closed, two-dimensional region within a coordinate space. This region is bounded by an arbitrary number of line segments, each of which is one side (or edge) of the polygon. Internally, a polygon comprises a list of (x, y) coordinate pairs in which each pair defines a vertex of the polygon, and two successive pairs are the endpoints of a line that is a side of the polygon. The first and final pairs of (x, y) points are joined by a line segment that closes the polygon.

The following two constructors are used to create a Polygon object.

■   public Polygon()

Constructs an empty polygon.

■   Polygon(int[] xpoints, int[] ypoints, int npoints)

Constructs and initializes a Polygon with specified points. Parameters xpoints and ypoints are arrays representing x-coordinates and y-coordinates, and npoints indicates the number of points.

To append a point to the polygon, use the addPoint(int x, int y) method. The Polygon class has the public data fields xpoints, ypoints, and npoints, which represent the array of x-coordinates and y-coordinates, and the total number of points.

Here is an example of creating a polygon and adding points into it:

```
Polygon polygon = new Polygon();
polygon.addPoint(40, 20);
polygon.addPoint(70, 40);
polygon.addPoint(60, 80);
polygon.addPoint(45, 45);
polygon.addPoint(20, 60);
```

To draw or fill a polygon, use one of the following methods:

```
drawPolygon(Polygon polygon);

fillPolygon(Polygon polygon);

drawPolygon(int[] xpoints, int[] ypoints, int npoints);

fillPolygon(int[] xpoints, int[] ypoints, int npoints);
```

For example:

```
int x[] = {40, 70, 60, 45, 20};
int y[] = {20, 40, 80, 45, 60};
g.drawPolygon(x, y, x.length);
```

The drawing method opens the polygon by drawing lines between point (x[i], y[i]) and point (x[i+1], y[i+1]) for i = 0, . . ., x.length-1; it closes the polygon by drawing a line between the first and last points (see Figure 11.25).

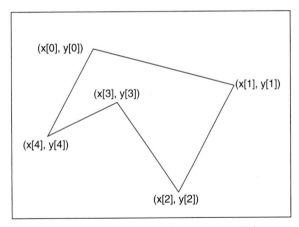

Figure 11.25 *The drawPolygon method draws a polygon with specified points.*

Next is an example of how to draw a hexagon, with the output shown in Figure 11.26.

483

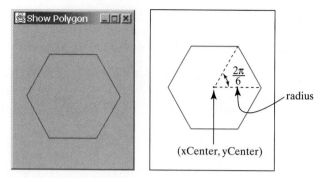

Figure 11.26   *The program uses the* drawPolygon *method to draw a polygon.*

```java
// TestPolygon.java: Demonstrate drawing polygons
package chapter11;

import javax.swing.JFrame;
import javax.swing.JPanel;
import java.awt.Graphics;
import java.awt.Polygon;

public class TestPolygon extends JFrame {
  /** Default constructor */
  public TestPolygon() {
    setTitle("Show Polygon");
    getContentPane().add(new PolygonsPanel());
  }

  /** Main method */
  public static void main(String[] args) {
    TestPolygon frame = new TestPolygon();
    frame.setDefaultCloseOperation(JFrame.EXIT_ON_CLOSE);
    frame.setSize(200, 250);
    frame.setVisible(true);
  }
}

// Draw a polygon in the panel
class PolygonsPanel extends JPanel {
  protected void paintComponent(Graphics g) {
    super.paintComponent(g);

    int xCenter = getWidth() / 2;
    int yCenter = getHeight() / 2;
    int radius =
      (int)(Math.min(getWidth(), getHeight()) * 0.4);

    // Create a Polygon object
    Polygon polygon = new Polygon();

    // Add points to the polygon
    polygon.addPoint(xCenter + radius, yCenter);
    polygon.addPoint((int)(xCenter + radius *
      Math.cos(2 * Math.PI / 6)), (int)(yCenter - radius *
      Math.sin(2 * Math.PI / 6)));
    polygon.addPoint((int)(xCenter + radius *
      Math.cos(2 * 2 * Math.PI / 6)), (int)(yCenter - radius *
      Math.sin(2 * 2 * Math.PI / 6)));
    polygon.addPoint((int)(xCenter + radius *
      Math.cos(3 * 2 * Math.PI / 6)), (int)(yCenter - radius *
```

```
        Math.sin(3 * 2 * Math.PI / 6)));
      polygon.addPoint((int)(xCenter + radius *
        Math.cos(4 * 2 * Math.PI / 6)), (int)(yCenter - radius *
        Math.sin(4 * 2 * Math.PI / 6)));
      polygon.addPoint((int)(xCenter + radius *
        Math.cos(5 * 2 * Math.PI / 6)), (int)(yCenter - radius *
        Math.sin(5 * 2 * Math.PI / 6)));

      // Draw the polygon
      g.drawPolygon(polygon);
    }
  }
```

To draw a polyline, use the `drawPolyline(int[] x, int[] y, int nPoints)` method, which draws a sequence of connected lines defined by arrays of x and y coordinates. For example, the following code draws the polyline shown in Figure 11.27.

```
int x[] = {40, 70, 60, 45, 20};
int y[] = {20, 40, 80, 45, 60};
g.drawPolygon(x, y, x.length);
```

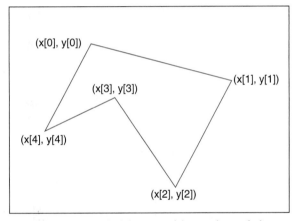

Figure 11.27   *The `drawPolyline` method draws a polyline with specified points.*

11.10   Case Studies

This case study presents an example that uses several drawing methods and trigonometric methods to draw a clock showing the current time in a frame. To draw a clock, you need to draw a circle and three hands for second, minute, and hour. To draw a hand, you need to specify the two ends of the line. As shown in Figure 11.28, one end is the center of the clock at (`xCenter`, `yCenter`); the other end, at (`xEnd`, `yEnd`), is determined by the following formula:

```
xEnd = xCenter + handLength × sin(θ)
yEnd = yCenter - handLength × cos(θ)
```

Angle θ is in radians. Let `second`, `minute`, and `hour` denote the current second, minute, and hour.

Since there are sixty seconds in one minute, the angle for the second hand is

```
second × (2π/60)
```

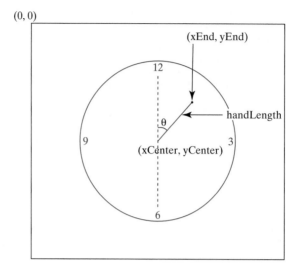

(0, 0)

Figure 11.28   *The end point of a clock hand can be determined given the spanning angle, the hand length, and the center point.*

The position of the minute hand is determined by the minute and second. The exact minute value combined with seconds is `minute + second/60`. For example, if the time is 3 minutes and 30 seconds, the total minutes are 3.5. Since there are sixty minutes in one hour, the angle for the minute hand is

```
(minute + second/60) × (2π/60)
```

Since one circle is divided into twelve hours, the angle for the hour hand is

```
(hour + minute/60 + second/(60 × 60))) × (2π/12)
```

For simplicity, you can omit the seconds in computing the angles of the minute hand and the hour hand, since they are very small and can be neglected. Therefore, the end points for the second hand, minute hand, and hour hand can be computed as:

```
xSecond = xCenter + secondHandLength × sin(second × (2π/60))
ySecond = yCenter - secondHandLength × cos(second × (2π/60))
xMinute = xCenter + minuteHandLength × sin(minute × (2π/60))
yMinute = yCenter - minuteHandLength × cos(minute × (2π/60))
xHour = xCenter + hourHandLength × sin((hour + minute/60) × (2π/60)))
yHour = yCenter - hourHandLength × cos((hour + minute/60) × (2π/60)))
```

Example 11.6 Drawing a Clock

Problem

Write a program that displays the current time, as shown in Figure 11.29.

Solution

The current hour, minute, and second can be obtained using the `Gregorian-Calendar` class, which was introduced in Section 9.3, "The `Calendar` and `GregorianCalendar` Classes."

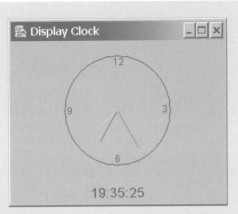

Figure 11.29   *The program displays a clock that shows the current time.*

The program declares a panel named StillClock to display the clock with the current hour, minute, and second. The hour, minute, and second are defined as the data fields in StillClock. The paintComponent method draws the clock.

The program creates a frame named DisplayClock that extends JFrame, creates a StillClock to display time in a clock, and creates a MessagePanel to display time numerically. The StillClock object is placed in the center of the frame, and the MessagePanel object is placed in the south of the frame.

```
1    // StillClock.java: Display a clock in JPanel
2    package chapter11;
3
4    import java.awt.*;
5    import javax.swing.*;
6    import java.util.*;
7
8    public class StillClock extends JPanel {
9      private int hour;
10     private int minute;
11     private int second;
12
13     /** Construct a default clock with the current time*/
14     public StillClock() {
15       setCurrentTime();
16     }
17
18     /** Construct a clock */
19     public StillClock(int hour, int minute, int second) {
20       this.hour = hour;
21       this.minute = minute;
22       this.second = second;
23     }
24
25     /** Return hour */
26     public int getHour() {
27       return hour;
28     }
29
30     /** Set a new hour */
```

continues

Example 11.6 Continued

```
31        public void setHour(int hour) {
32          this.hour = hour;
33          repaint();
34        }
35
36        /** Return minute */
37        public int getMinute() {
38          return minute;
39        }
40
41        /** Set a new minute */
42        public void setMinute(int minute) {
43          this.minute = minute;
44          repaint();
45        }
46
47        /** Return second */
48        public int getSecond() {
49          return second;
50        }
51
52        /** Set a new second */
53        public void setSecond(int second) {
54          this.second = second;
55          repaint();
56        }
57
58        /** Draw the clock */
59        protected void paintComponent(Graphics g) {
60          super.paintComponent(g);
61
62          // Initialize clock parameters
63          int clockRadius =
64            (int)(Math.min(getWidth(), getHeight()) * 0.8 * 0.5);
65          int xCenter = getWidth() / 2;
66          int yCenter = getHeight() / 2;
67
68          // Draw circle
69          g.setColor(Color.black);
70          g.drawOval(xCenter - clockRadius, yCenter - clockRadius,
71            2 * clockRadius, 2 * clockRadius);
72          g.drawString("12", xCenter - 5, yCenter - clockRadius + 12);
73          g.drawString("9", xCenter - clockRadius + 3, yCenter + 5);
74          g.drawString("3", xCenter + clockRadius - 10, yCenter + 3);
75          g.drawString("6", xCenter - 3, yCenter + clockRadius - 3);
76
77          // Draw second hand
78          int sLength = (int)(clockRadius * 0.8);
79          int xSecond = (int)(xCenter + sLength *
80            Math.sin(second * (2 * Math.PI / 60)));
81          int ySecond = (int)(yCenter - sLength *
82            Math.cos(second * (2 * Math.PI / 60)));
83          g.setColor(Color.red);
84          g.drawLine(xCenter, yCenter, xSecond, ySecond);
85
86          // Draw minute hand
87          int mLength = (int)(clockRadius * 0.65);
88          int xMinute = (int)(xCenter + mLength *
89            Math.sin(minute * (2 * Math.PI / 60)));
90          int yMinute = (int)(yCenter - mLength *
91            Math.cos(minute * (2 * Math.PI / 60)));
92          g.setColor(Color.blue);
```

```
 93          g.drawLine(xCenter, yCenter, xMinute, yMinute);
 94
 95          // Draw hour hand
 96          int hLength = (int)(clockRadius * 0.5);
 97          int xHour = (int)(xCenter + hLength *
 98            Math.sin((hour % 12 + minute / 60.0) * (2 * Math.PI / 12)));
 99          int yHour = (int)(yCenter - hLength *
100            Math.cos((hour % 12 + minute / 60.0) * (2 * Math.PI / 12)));
101          g.setColor(Color.green);
102          g.drawLine(xCenter, yCenter, xHour, yHour);
103        }
104
105      public void setCurrentTime() {
106          // Construct a calendar for the current date and time
107          Calendar calendar = new GregorianCalendar();
108
109          // Set current hour, minute and second
110          this.hour = calendar.get(Calendar.HOUR_OF_DAY);
111          this.minute = calendar.get(Calendar.MINUTE);
112          this.second = calendar.get(Calendar.SECOND);
113        }
114    }
```

```
 1    // DisplayClock.java: Display a clock in a panel
 2    package chapter11;
 3
 4    import java.awt.*;
 5    import javax.swing.*;
 6    import java.util.*;
 7
 8    public class DisplayClock extends JFrame {
 9      public DisplayClock() {
10        // Create an analog clock for the current time
11        StillClock clock = new StillClock();
12
13        // Display hour, minute, and hour in the message panel
14        MessagePanel messagePanel = new MessagePanel(clock.getHour() +
15          ":" + clock.getMinute() + ":" + clock.getSecond());
16        messagePanel.setCentered(true);
17        messagePanel.setForeground(Color.blue);
18        messagePanel.setFont(new Font("Courie", Font.BOLD, 16));
19
20        // Add the clock and message panel to the frame
21        getContentPane().add(clock);
22        getContentPane().add(messagePanel, BorderLayout.SOUTH);
23      }
24
25      public static void main(String[] args) {
26        DisplayClock frame = new DisplayClock();
27        frame.setTitle("Display Clock");
28        frame.setDefaultCloseOperation(JFrame.EXIT_ON_CLOSE);
29        frame.setSize(300, 350);
30        frame.setVisible(true);
31      }
32    }
```

continues

Example 11.6 Continued

Review

StillClock is a subclass of JPanel, which is responsible for drawing the clock in a panel. The setCurrentTime method (Lines 105–113) creates a default GregorianCalendar for the current date and time. The get method extracts hour, minute, and second and stores them in StillClock. The default constructor of StillClock creates a clock to show the current time.

The program enables the clock size to adjust as the frame resizes. Every time you resize the frame, the paintComponent method is automatically invoked to paint the new frame. The paintComponent method displays the clock in proportion to the panel width (getWidth()) and height (getHeight()) (Lines 62–66 in StillClock).

The constructor of the DisplayClock creates an instance of StillClock to display the current time (Line 11). The numeric time (consisting of hour, minute, and second) is displayed below the clock in a MessagePanel object (Lines 13–18).

 NOTE

Like the MessagePanel class, the StillClock class is another example of developing reusable classes. StillClock will be used throughout the book. StillClock provides many properties and methods to enable it to be used in a wide range of applications.

Chapter Summary

- The java.awt.Component class is the root class for all GUI components.

- The javax.swing.JComponent class is the root class for all Swing GUI components, such as JButton, JLabel, JTextField, and JPanel.

- The java.awt.Container class is the root class for all container classes. The container classes (e.g., JFrame, JPanel, JApplet) are used to contain other components.

- Each container uses a layout manager to position and place components in a container in the desired location.

- In a container with FlowLayout, the components are arranged in the container from left to right in the order in which they were added. When one row is filled, a new row is started.

- The GridLayout manager arranges components in a grid (matrix) formation with the number of rows and columns defined by the constructor. The components are placed in the grid from left to right, starting with the first row, then the second, and so on, in the order in which they are added.

■ The BorderLayout manager divides the window into five areas: East, South, West, North, and Center. Components are added to a BorderLayout by using add(Component, index), where index is a constant BorderLayout.EAST, BorderLayout.SOUTH, BorderLayout.WEST, BorderLayout.NORTH, or Border-Layout.CENTER.

■ Panels are invisible and are used as small containers that group components to achieve a desired layout. Another important use of JPanel is for drawing. To draw in a JPanel, you create a new class that extends JPanel and overrides the paintComponent method to tell the panel how to draw things.

■ To add components to a JFrame, you need to add them into the JFrame's content pane. You can directly add components into a JPanel. By default, the content pane's layout is BorderLayout, and the JPanel's layout is FlowLayout.

■ The paintComponent method is defined in JComponent, and its signature is protected void paintComponent(Graphics g). The Graphics object g is created automatically by the JVM for every visible GUI component. This object controls how information is drawn. You can use various drawing methods defined in the Graphics class to draw figures.

■ The Graphics class is an abstract class for displaying figures and images on the screen on different platforms. The Graphics class is implemented on the native platform in the JVM. When you use the paintComponent method to draw things on a graphics context g, this g is an instance of a concrete subclass of the abstract Graphics class for the specific platform. The Graphics class encapsulates the platform details and enables you to draw things uniformly without concern for specific platforms.

■ Invoking super.paintComponent(g) is necessary to ensure that the viewing area is cleared before a new drawing is displayed. The user can request the component to be redisplayed by invoking the repaint() method defined in the Component class. Invoking repaint() causes paintComponent to be invoked by the JVM. The user should never invoke paintComponent directly. For this reason, the protected visibility is sufficient for paintComponent.

■ Each component has its own coordinate system with the origin (0, 0) at the upper-left corner of the window. The x coordinate increases to the right, and the y coordinate increases downward.

■ You can set colors for GUI components by using the java.awt.Color class. Colors are made of red, green, and blue components, each of which is represented by a byte value that describes its intensity, ranging from 0 (darkest shade) to 255 (lightest shade). This is known as the *RGB model*.

■ The syntax to create a Color object is Color color = new Color(r, g, b), in which r, g, and b specify a color by its red, green, and blue components. Alternatively, you can use one of the thirteen standard colors (black, blue, cyan, darkGray, gray, green, lightGray, magenta, orange, pink, red, white, yellow) defined as constants in java.awt.Color.

■ You can use the setBackground(Color c) and setForeground(Color c) methods defined in the Component class to set a component's background and foreground colors.

■ You can set fonts for the components or subjects you draw, and use font metrics to measure font size. Fonts and font metrics are encapsulated in the classes Font and FontMetrics.

■ To set a font, you need to create a Font object from the Font class. The syntax is Font myFont = new Font(name, style, size).

■ FontMetrics can be used to compute the exact length and width of a string, which is helpful for measuring the size of a string in order to display it in the right position.

■ A FontMetrics is measured by the attributes: leading, ascent, descent, and height. Leading is the amount of space between lines of text. Ascent is the height of a character, from the baseline to the top. Descent is the distance from the baseline to the bottom of a descending character, such as *j*, *y*, and *g*. Height is the sum of leading, ascent, and descent.

■ The Component class has the setBackground, setForeground, and setFont methods. These methods are for setting colors and fonts for the entire component. Suppose you want to draw several messages in a panel with different colors and fonts; you have to use the setColor and setFont methods in the Graphics class to set the color and font for the current drawing.

■ The method to draw a string is drawString(string, x, y). To draw a line, use drawLine(x1, y1, x2, y2). To draw a plain rectangle, use drawRect(x, y, w, h). To draw a filled rectangle, use fillRect(x, y, w, h). To draw a rounded rectangle, use drawRoundRect(x, y, w, h, aw, ah). To draw a 3D rectangle, use draw3DRect(x, y, w, h, raised). To draw an oval, use drawOval(x, y, w, h). To draw a filled oval, use fillOval(x, y, w, h). To draw an arc, use drawArc(x, y, w, h, startAngle, arcAngle). To draw a filled arc, use fillArc(x, y, w, h, startAngle, arcAngle). To draw a polygon, use drawPpolygon(Polygon polygon) or drawPolygon(int[] xpoints, int[] ypoints, int npoints). To draw a filled polygon, use fillPolygon(Polygon polygon) or fillPolygon(int[] xpoints, int[] ypoints, int npoints).

Review Questions

11.1 Describe the Java GUI class hierarchy.

11.2 Describe the methods in Component, JFrame, JComponent, and JPanel.

11.3 Explain the difference between AWT UI components, such as java.awt.Button, and Swing components, such as javax.swing.JButton.

11.4 How do you create a frame? How do you set the size for a frame? How do you get the size of a frame? How do you add components to a frame? What would happen if the statements `frame.setSize(400, 300)` and `frame.setVisible` `(true)` were swapped in the `MyFrameWithComponents` class in Section 11.3.3, "Adding Components to a Frame"?

11.5 Determine whether the following statements are true or false:

- You can add a button to a frame.

- You can add a frame to a panel.

- You can add a panel to a frame.

- You can add any number of components to a panel, a frame, or an applet.

- You can derive a class from `JPanel`, `JFrame`, or `JApplet`.

11.6 Why do you need to use the layout managers? What is the default layout manager for the content pane of a frame? What is the default layout manager for a `JPanel`?

11.7 Can you use the `setTitle` method in a panel? What is the purpose of using a panel?

11.8 Describe `FlowLayout`. How do you create a `FlowLayout` manager? How do you add a component to a `FlowLayout` container? Is there a limit to the number of components that can be added to a `FlowLayout` container?

11.9 Describe `GridLayout`. How do you create a `GridLayout` manager? How do you add a component to a `GridLayout` container? Is there a limit to the number of components that can be added to a `GridLayout` container?

11.10 Describe `BorderLayout`. How do you create a `BorderLayout` manager? How do you add a component to a `BorderLayout` container? Can you add multiple components in the same section?

11.11 Suppose that you want to draw a new message below an existing message. Should the `x, y` coordinate increase or decrease?

11.12 How do you set colors and fonts in a graphics context? How do you find the current color and font style?

11.13 Describe the methods for drawing lines, rectangles, ovals, arcs, and polygons.

11.14 Write a statement to draw the following shapes:

- Draw a thick line from (10, 10) to (70, 30). You can draw several lines next to each other to create the effect of one thick line.

- Draw a rectangle of width 100 and height 50 with the upper-left corner at (10, 10).

- Draw a rounded rectangle with width 100, height 200, corner horizontal diameter 40, and corner vertical diameter 20.

- Draw a circle with radius 30.

■ Draw an oval with width 50 and height 100.

■ Draw the upper half of a circle with radius 50.

■ Draw a polygon connecting the following points: (20, 40), (30, 50), (40, 90), (90, 10), (10, 30).

■ Draw a 3D cube like the one in Figure 11.30.

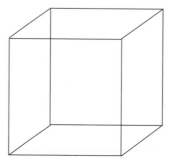

Figure 11.30   *Use the* drawLine *method to draw a 3D cube.*

11.15 Describe the paintComponent method. Where is it defined? How is it invoked? Can you use the paintComponent method to draw things directly on a frame?

11.16 The following program is supposed to display a message on the panel, but nothing is displayed. There are problems in Lines 2 and 14. Identify them.

```
1   public class TestDrawMessage extends javax.swing.JFrame {
2     public void TestDrawMessage() {
3       getContentPane().add(new DrawMessage());
4     }
5
6     public static void main(String[] args) {
7       javax.swing.JFrame frame = new TestDrawMessage();
8       frame.setSize(100, 200);
9       frame.setVisible(true);
10    }
11  }
12
13  class DrawMessage extends javax.swing.JPanel {
14    protected void PaintComponent(java.awt.Graphics g) {
15      super.paintComponent(g);
16      g.drawString("Welcome to Java", 20, 20);
17    }
18  }
```

Programming Exercises

11.1 (Using the FlowLayout manager) Write a program that meets the following requirements (see Figure 11.30):

■ Create a frame and set its content pane's layout to FlowLayout.

■ Create two panels and add the panels to the frame.

■ Each panel contains three buttons. The panel uses FlowLayout.

Figure 11.31 *The first three buttons are placed in one panel, and the remaining three buttons are placed in another panel.*

11.2 (Using the BorderLayout manager) Rewrite the preceding program to create the same user interface. Instead of using FlowLayout for the frame's content pane, use BorderLayout. Place one panel in the south of the content pane, and the other panel in the center of the content pane.

11.3 (Using the GridLayout manager) Rewrite the preceding program to create the same user interface. Instead of using FlowLayout for the panels, use a GridLayout of two rows and three columns.

11.4 (Creating a subclass of JPanel to group buttons) Rewrite the preceding program to create the same user interface. Instead of creating buttons and panels separately, define a class that extends the JPanel class. Place three buttons in your panel class, and create two panels from the user-defined panel class.

11.5 (Displaying four messages using MessagePanel) Write a program that uses the MessagePanel class in Example 11.5, "Creating a Message Panel Class," to display four message panels in a frame of the GridLayout of two rows and two columns, as shown in Figure 11.32.

Figure 11.32 *The program displays four message panels.*

11.6 (Displaying a multiplication table) Write a program that displays a multiplication table in a panel using the drawing methods, as shown in Figure 11.33.

11.7 (Displaying numbers in a triangle pattern) Write a program that displays numbers, as shown in Figure 11.34. The number of lines in the display changes to fit the window as the window resizes.

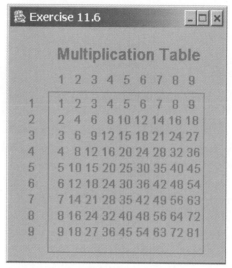

Figure 11.33 *The program displays a multiplication table.*

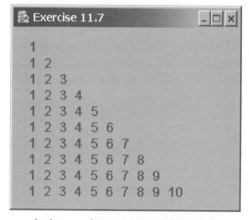

Figure 11.34 *The program displays numbers in a triangle formation.*

11.8 (Plotting the square function) Write a program that draws a diagram for the function $f(x) = x^2$ (see Figure 11.35).

✎ HINT

Add points to a polygon p using the following loop:

```
double scaleFactor = 0.1;

for (int x = -100; x <= 100; x++) {
  p.addPoint(x + 200, 200 - (int)(scaleFactor * x * x));
}
```

Connect the points using g.drawPolyline(p.xpoints, p.ypoints, p.npoints) for a Graphics object g. p.xpoints returns an array of *x* coordinates, p.ypoints returns an array of *y* coordinates, and p.npoints returns the number of points in Polygon object p.

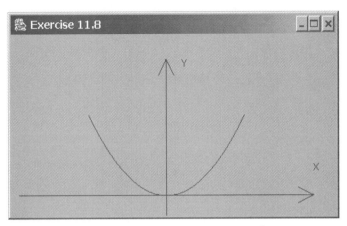

Figure 11.35 *The program draws a diagram for function $f(x) = x^2$.*

11.9 (Plotting the sine function) Write a program that draws a diagram for the sine function, as shown in Figure 11.36.

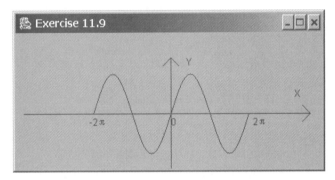

Figure 11.36 *The program draws a diagram for function $f(x) = \sin(x)$.*

⊗ **HINT**

The Unicode for π is \u03c0. To display -2π, use `g.drawString("-2\u03c0", x, y)`. For a trigonometric function like `sin(x)`, x is in radians. Use the following loop to add the points to a polygon p:

```
for (int x = -100; x <= 100; x++) {
  p.addPoint(x + 200,
    100 - (int)(50 * Math.sin((x / 100.0) * 2 * Math.PI)));
}
```

-2π is at (100, 100), the center of the axes is at (200, 100), and 2π is at (300, 100). Use the `drawPolyline` method in the `Graphics` class to connect the points.

11.10 (Plotting functions using generic methods) Write a generic class that draws the diagram for a function. The class is defined as follows:

```
public abstract class AbstractDrawFunction extends JPanel {
  /** Polygon to hold the points */
  private Polygon p = new Polygon();

  /** Default constructor */
  protected AbstractDrawFunction () {
    drawFunction();
  }

  /** Return the y coordinate */
  abstract double f(double x);

  /** Obtain points for x coordinates 100, 101, ..., 300 */
  public void drawFunction() {
    for (int x = -100; x <= 100; x++) {
      p.addPoint(x + 200, 200 - (int)f(x));
    }
  }

  /** Implement paintComponent to draw axes, labels, and
    *connecting points */
  protected void paintComponent(Graphics g) {
    // To be completed by you
  }
}
```

Test the class with the following functions:

```
f(x) = x²;
f(x) = sin(x);
f(x) = cos(x);
f(x) = tan(x);
f(x) = cos(x) + 5sin(x);
f(x) = cos(x) + 5sin(x);
f(x) = log(x) + x²;
```

For each function, create a class that extends the AbstractDrawFunction class and implements the f method. Figure 11.37 displays the drawings for the sine function and the cosine function.

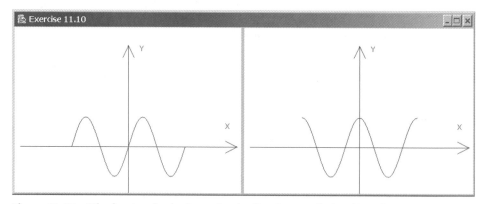

Figure 11.37 *The drawings for the sine and cosine functions are displayed in a frame.*

11.11 (Drawing an octagon) Write a program that draws an octagon, as shown in Figure 11.38.

498

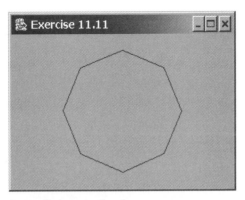

Figure 11.38 *The drawing methods are used to draw an octagon.*

11.12 (Drawing a detailed clock) Modify Example 11.6, "Drawing a Clock," to draw the clock with more details on the hours and minutes, as shown in Figure 11.39.

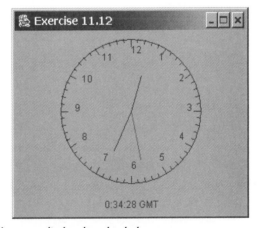

Figure 11.39 *All the hours are displayed on the clock.*

11.13 (Creating four fans) Write a program that places four fans in a frame of GridLayout with two rows and two columns, as shown in Figure 11.40.

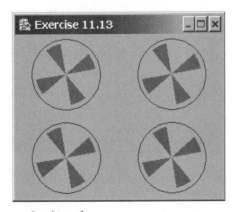

Figure 11.40 *Four fans are placed in a frame.*

11.14 (Displaying a pie chart) Write a program that uses a pie chart to display the percentages of the overall grade represented by projects, quizzes, midterm exams, and the final exam, as shown in Figure 11.41. Suppose that projects take 20 percent and are displayed in red, quizzes take 20 percent and are displayed in blue, midterm exams take 30 percent and are displayed in green, and the final exam takes 40 percent and is displayed in orange.

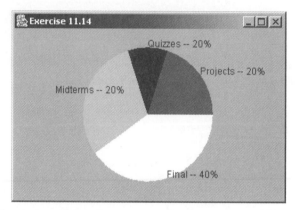

Figure 11.41   *The pie chart displays the percentages of projects, quizzes, midterm exams, and final exam in the overall grade.*

11.15 (Creating four panels of various shapes) Write a program that creates four panels using the classes RectPanel, OvalsPanel, ArcsPanel, and PolygonsPanel presented in Section 11.9, "Drawing Geometric Figures," and places the panels in the content pane of the frame using a GridLayout, as shown in Figure 11.42.

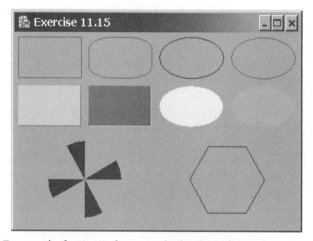

Figure 11.42   *Four panels of geometric figures are displayed in a frame of GridLayout.*

11.16 (Creating a custom button class) Develop a custom button class named OvalButton that extends JButton and displays the button text inside an oval. Figure 11.43 shows two buttons created using the OvalButton class. Here is the outline of the OvalButton class:

```
public class OvalButton extends JButton {
  public OvalButton() {
  }

  public OvalButton(String text) {
    super(text);
  }

  protected void paintComponent(Graphics g) {
    // Draw an oval
  }

  /** Override get method for preferredSize */
  public Dimension getPreferredSize() {
    return new Dimension(100, 50);
  }

  /** Override get method for minimumSize */
  public Dimension getMinimumSize() {
    return new Dimension(100, 50);
  }

  /** Main method */
  public static void main(String[] args) {
    // Create a frame and add two OvalButtons to
    // the frame
  }
}
```

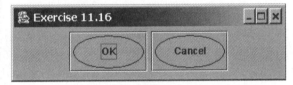

Figure 11.43   *Two objects of OvalButton are created.*

11.17 (Revising Example 11.5, "Creating a Message Panel Class") Rewrite Example 11.5 to test MessagePanel from a main method inside MessagePanel, as follows:

■ Add a main method in the MessagePanel class. The main method creates a JFrame instance.

■ Create and add a MessagePanel instance to the JFrame object.

11.18 (Creating a reusable pie chart component) In Exercise 11.14, you wrote a program that displays data in a pie chart. The program is difficult to reuse. In this exercise you will write a reusable component named PieChart to display a pie chart for *any* set of data. Suppose the data are stored in an array of double elements named data, and the names for the data are stored in an array of strings named dataName. For example, the enrollment data 200, 40, 50, 100, 40 stored in the array data are for "CS," "Math," "Chem," "Biol," "Phys" in the array dataName. The outline of this component is as follows:

```java
public class PieChart extends JPanel {
  /** Sample data, and data names */
  private double[] dataValue = {200, 140, 100, 60, 40};
  private String[] dataName = {"CS", "Math", "Chem", "Biol",
    "Phys"};

  /** Display the pie chart */
  protected void paintComponent(Graphics g) {
    // Write your code here
  }

  /** Set data */
  public void setData(String[] dataName , double[] dataValue) {
    this.dataName = dataName;
    this.dataValue = dataValue;
    repaint();
  }
}
```

HINT

Each pie represents a percentage of the total data. Color the pie using the colors from an array named colors, which is Color.red, Color.yellow, Color.green, Color.blue, Color.cyan, Color.magenta, Color.orange, Color.pink, Color.darkGray. Use colors[i % colors.length] for the *i*th pie. Use black color to display the data names. Figure 11.44 shows three pie charts created using this component.

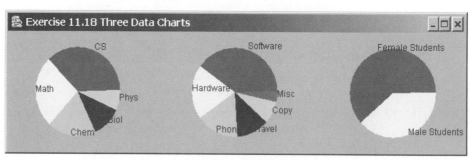

Figure 11.44   *Three pie charts are placed in a frame of GridLayout.*

11.19 (Creating a reusable bar chart component) Similar to Exercise 11.18, create a new chart component named BarChart to display bar charts, as shown in Figure 11.45. Can you combine the PieChart and BarChart components into one component named Chart? Add a property named chartType to determine which type of chart is displayed.

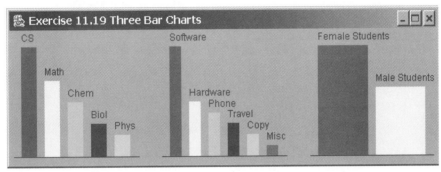

Figure 11.45 *Three bar charts are placed in a frame of* GridLayout.

EVENT-DRIVEN PROGRAMMING

Objectives

- To explain the concept of event-driven programming.
- To declare listener classes and write the code to handle events.
- To register listener objects in the source object.
- To describe event classes, event listener interfaces, and event registration methods.
- To understand how an event is handled.
- To write programs to deal with various types of events.

12.1   Introduction

All non-GUI programs execute in a procedural order. Java GUI programming is event-driven. In event-driven programming, code is executed when an event occurs—a button click, perhaps, or a mouse movement. This chapter introduces the concepts and techniques for Java event-driven programming.

12.2   Event and Event Source

When you run Java GUI programs, the program interacts with the user and the events drive its execution. An *event* can be defined as a signal to the program that something has happened. The event is triggered either by external user actions, such as mouse movements, button clicks, and keystrokes, or by the operating system, such as a timer. The program can choose to respond to or ignore the event.

The component on which an event is generated is called the *source object*. For example, a button is the source object for a button-clicking action event. An event is an instance of an event class. The root class of the event classes is `java.util.EventObject`. The hierarchical relationships of the event classes used in this book are shown in Figure 12.1.

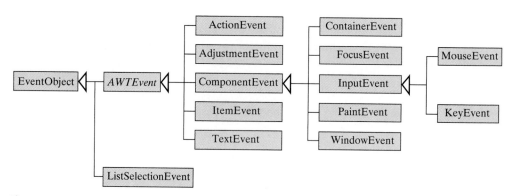

Figure 12.1   *An event is an object of the* `EventObject` *class.*

An event object contains whatever properties are pertinent to the event. You can identify the source object of the event using the `getSource()` instance method in the `EventObject` class. The subclasses of `EventObject` deal with special types of events, such as button actions, window events, component events, mouse movements, and keystrokes. Table 12.1 lists external user actions, source objects, and event types generated.

◈ NOTE

If a component can generate an event, any subclass of the component can generate the same type of event. For example, every GUI component can generate `MouseEvent`, `KeyEvent`, `FocusEvent`, and `ComponentEvent`, since `Component` is the superclass of all GUI components.

TABLE 12.1   User Action, Source Object, and Event Type

User Action	Source Object	Event Type Generated
Click a button	JButton	ActionEvent
Press return on a text field	JTextField	ActionEvent
Select a new item	JComboBox	ItemEvent, ActionEvent
Select item(s)	JList	ListSelectionEvent
Click a check box	JCheckBox	ItemEvent, ActionEvent
Click a radio button	JRadioButton	ItemEvent, ActionEvent
Select a menu item	JMenuItem	ActionEvent
Move the scroll bar	JScrollBar	AdjustmentEvent
Window opened, closed, iconified, deiconified, or closing	Window	WindowEvent
Component added or removed from the container	Container	ContainerEvent
Component moved, resized, hidden, or shown	Component	ComponentEvent
Component gained or lost focus	Component	FocusEvent
Key released or pressed	Component	KeyEvent
Mouse pressed, released, clicked, entered, or exited	Component	MouseEvent
Mouse moved or dragged	Component	MouseEvent

NOTE

All the event classes in Figure 12.1 are included in the `java.awt.event` package except `ListSelectionEvent`, which is in the `javax.swing.event` package. The AWT events were originally designed for AWT components, but many Swing components fire them.

12.3   Listeners, Registrations, and Handling Events

Java uses a delegation-based model for event handling: an external user action on a source object triggers an event, and an object interested in the event receives the event. The latter object is called a *listener*. Two things are needed for an object to be a listener for an event on a source object:

■ The listener object's class must implement the corresponding event-listener interface. Java provides a listener interface for every type of GUI event. In general, the listener interface is named *X*Listener for *X*Event, except for MouseMotionListener. For example, the corresponding listener interface for ActionEvent is ActionListener; each listener for ActionEvent should implement the ActionListener interface. Table 12.2 lists event types, the corresponding listener interfaces, and the

TABLE 12.2   **Events, Event Listeners, and Listener Methods**

Event Class	Listener Interface	Listener Methods (Handlers)
ActionEvent	ActionListener	actionPerformed(ActionEvent e)
ItemEvent	ItemListener	itemStateChanged(ItemEvent e)
WindowEvent	WindowListener	windowClosing(WindowEvent e)
		windowOpened(WindowEvent e)
		windowIconified(WindowEvent e)
		windowDeiconified(WindowEvent e)
		windowClosed(WindowEvent e)
		windowActivated(WindowEvent e)
		windowDeactivated(WindowEvent e)
ContainerEvent	ContainerListener	componentAdded(ContainerEvent e)
		componentRemoved(ContainerEvent e)
ComponentEvent	ComponentListener	componentMoved(ComponentEvent e)
		componentHidden(ComponentEvent e)
		componentResized(ComponentEvent e)
		componentShown(ComponentEvent e)
FocusEvent	FocusListener	focusGained(FocusEvent e)
		focusLost(FocusEvent e)
TextEvent	TextListener	textValueChanged(TextEvent e)
KeyEvent	KeyListener	keyPressed(KeyEvent e)
		keyReleased(KeyEvent e)
		keyTyped(KeyEvent e)
MouseEvent	MouseListener	mousePressed(MouseEvent e)
		mouseReleased(MouseEvent e)
		mouseEntered(MouseEvent e)
		mouseExited(MouseEvent e)
		mouseClicked(MouseEvent e)
	MouseMotionListener	mouseDragged(MouseEvent e)
		mouseMoved(MouseEvent e)
AdjustmentEvent	AdjustmentListener	adjustmentValueChanged(AdjustmentEvent e)

methods defined in the listener interfaces. The listener interface contains the method(s), known as the *handler(s)*, which process the events.

■ The listener object must be registered by the source object. Registration methods are dependent on the event type. For ActionEvent, the method is addActionListener. In general, the method is named addXListener for XEvent. A source object may fire several types of events. For each event, the source object maintains a list of listeners and notifies all the registered listeners by invoking the *handler* on the listener object to respond to the event, as shown in Figure 12.2.

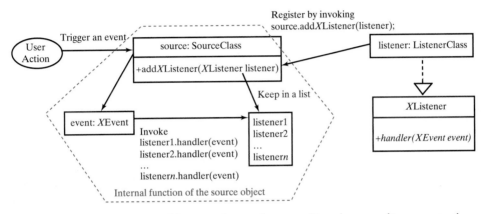

Figure 12.2 *An event is triggered by user actions on the source object; the source object generates the event object and invokes the handler of the listener object to process the event.*

For example, if an object is interested in listening to an action event on a JButton source object, its defining class must implement the ActionListener interface and the actionPerformed method. The listener object must also register with the JButton object. The registration is done by invoking the addActionListener method in the JButton object, as follows:

```
ListenerClass listener = new ListenerClass();
JButton jbt = new JButton("OK");
jbt.addActionListener(listener);
```

When you click the button, the JButton object generates an ActionEvent and passes it to invoke the actionPerformed method to handle the event.

The event object contains information pertinent to the event type. You can get useful data values from the event object for processing the event. For example, you can use e.getSource() to obtain the source object in order to determine whether it is a button, a check box, a radio button, or a menu item.

Three examples of the use of event handling are given below. The first is for ActionEvent, the second for WindowEvent, and the third involves multiple listeners for a source.

Example 12.1 Handling Simple Action Events

Problem

Write a program that displays two buttons, OK and Cancel, in the window. A message is displayed on the console to indicate which button is clicked, as shown in Figure 12.3.

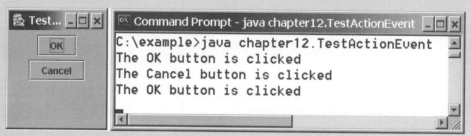

Figure 12.3 *The program responds to the button action events.*

Solution

Here are the steps in the program:

1. Create a listener class named `ButtonListener` for handling `ActionEvent` on the buttons. This class implements the `ActionListener` interface.

2. Create a test program named `TestActionEvent` that extends `JFrame`. Add two buttons to the frame, and create a listener object from `ButtonListener`. Register the listener with the buttons.

```
1   // TestActionEvent.java: Test ActionEvent
2   package chapter12;
3
4   import javax.swing.*;
5   import java.awt.*;
6   import java.awt.event.*;
7
8   public class TestActionEvent extends JFrame {
9     // Create two buttons
10    private JButton jbtOk = new JButton("OK");
11    private JButton jbtCancel = new JButton("Cancel");
12
13    /** Default constructor */
14    public TestActionEvent() {
15      // Set the window title
16      setTitle("TestActionEvent");
17
18      // Set FlowLayout manager to arrange the components
19      // inside the frame
20      getContentPane().setLayout(new FlowLayout());
21
22      // Add buttons to the frame
23      getContentPane().add(jbtOk);
24      getContentPane().add(jbtCancel);
25
26      // Create a listener object
27      ButtonListener btListener = new ButtonListener();
28
```

```
29        // Register listeners
30        jbtOk.addActionListener(btListener);
31        jbtCancel.addActionListener(btListener);
32    }
33
34    /** Main method */
35    public static void main(String[] args) {
36      TestActionEvent frame = new TestActionEvent();
37      frame.setDefaultCloseOperation(JFrame.EXIT_ON_CLOSE);
38      frame.setSize(100, 80);
39      frame.setVisible(true);
40    }
41  }
42
43  class ButtonListener implements ActionListener {
44    /** This method will be invoked when a button is clicked */
45    public void actionPerformed(ActionEvent e) {
46      if (e.getActionCommand().equals("OK")) {
47        System.out.println("The OK button is clicked");
48      }
49      else if (e.getActionCommand().equals("Cancel")) {
50        System.out.println("The Cancel button is clicked");
51      }
52    }
53  }
```

Review

The button objects jbtOk and jbtCancel are the source of ActionEvent. The ButtonListener class defines the listeners for the buttons, and its instance btListener is registered with the buttons (Lines 30–31).

Clicking a button causes the actionPerformed method in btListener to be invoked. The e.getActionCommand() method returns the action command from the button. By default, a button's action command is the text of the button. You can use the action command to determine which button has been clicked. You can also use the e.getSource() method to return the reference of the source object and determine which button was clicked, as follows:

```
if (e.getSource() == jbtOk) {
  System.out.println("The OK button is clicked");
}
else if (e.getSource() == jbtCancel) {
  System.out.println("The Cancel button is clicked");
}
```

The TestActionEvent class itself can be a listener class if you rewrite the program as follows:

```
// TestActionEvent.java: Test ActionEvent
package chapter12;

import javax.swing.*;
import java.awt.*;
import java.awt.event.*;

public class TestActionEvent extends JFrame
  implements ActionListener {
```

continues

Example 12.1 Continued

```
                // Create two buttons
                private JButton jbtOk = new JButton("OK");
                private JButton jbtCancel = new JButton("Cancel");

                /** Default constructor */
                public TestActionEvent() {
                  // Set the window title
                  setTitle("TestActionEvent");

                  // Set FlowLayout manager to arrange the components
                  // inside the frame
                  getContentPane().setLayout(new FlowLayout());

                  // Add buttons to the frame
                  getContentPane().add(jbtOk);
                  getContentPane().add(jbtCancel);

                  // Register listeners
                  jbtOk.addActionListener(this);
                  jbtCancel.addActionListener(this);
                }

                /** Main method */
                public static void main(String[] args) {
                  TestActionEvent frame = new TestActionEvent();
                  frame.setDefaultCloseOperation(JFrame.EXIT_ON_CLOSE);
                  frame.setSize(100, 80);
                  frame.setVisible(true);
                }

                /** This method will be invoked when a button is clicked */
                public void actionPerformed(ActionEvent e) {
                  if (e.getSource() == jbtOk) {
                    System.out.println("The OK button is clicked");
                  }
                  else if (e.getSource() == jbtCancel) {
                    System.out.println("The Cancel button is clicked");
                  }
                }
              }
```

The statements

```
    jbtOk.addActionListener(this);
    jbtCancel.addActionListener(this);
```

register this (referring to TestActionEvent) to listen to ActionEvent on jbtOk and jbtCancel.

CAUTION

Missing listener registration is a common mistake in event handling. If the source object doesn't notify the listener, the listener cannot act on the event.

NOTE

If a listener is registered with a source twice, the handler of the listener will be invoked twice when an event occurs.

JBUILDER TIP

To debug event-driven programs in JBuilder, you can insert a breakpoint at a statement in a handling method that you want to trace. For example, to trace the `actionPerformed` handler, insert a breakpoint at the first line in this method. When a button is clicked, the `actionPerformed` handler is invoked, and the program pauses at the breakpoint so that you can debug the handler.

Example 12.2 Handling Window Events

Problem

Write a program that demonstrates handling window events.

Solution

Any subclass of the `Window` class can generate the following window events: window opened, closing, closed, activated, deactivated, iconified, and deiconified. This program creates a frame, listens to the window events, and displays a message to indicate the occurring event. Figure 12.4 shows a sample run of the program.

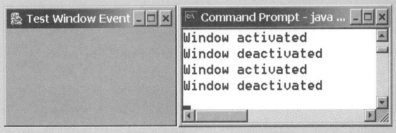

Figure 12.4 *The window events are displayed on the console when you run the program from a DOS prompt.*

```
1    // TestWindowEvent.java: Create a frame to test window events
2    package chapter12;
3
4    import java.awt.*;
5    import java.awt.event.*;
6    import javax.swing.JFrame;
7
8    public class TestWindowEvent extends JFrame
9      implements WindowListener {
10     // Main method
11     public static void main(String[] args) {
12       TestWindowEvent frame = new TestWindowEvent();
13       frame.setDefaultCloseOperation(JFrame.EXIT_ON_CLOSE);
14       frame.setTitle("Test Window Event");
15       frame.setSize(100, 80);
16       frame.setVisible(true);
17     }
18
```

continues

Example 12.2 Continued

```
19        /** Default constructor */
20        public TestWindowEvent() {
21          addWindowListener(this);   // Register listener
22        }
23
24        /**
25         * Handler for window deiconified event
26         * Invoked when a window is changed from a minimized
27         * to a normal state.
28         */
29        public void windowDeiconified(WindowEvent event) {
30          System.out.println("Window deiconified");
31        }
32
33        /**
34         * Handler for window iconified event
35         * Invoked when a window is changed from a normal to a
36         * minimized state. For many platforms, a minimized window
37         * is displayed as the icon specified in the window's
38         * iconImage property.
39         */
40        public void windowIconified(WindowEvent event) {
41          System.out.println("Window iconified");
42        }
43
44        /**
45         * Handler for window activated event
46         * Invoked when the window is set to be the user's
47         * active window, which means the window (or one of its
48         * subcomponents) will receive keyboard events.
49         */
50        public void windowActivated(WindowEvent event) {
51          System.out.println("Window activated");
52        }
53
54        /**
55         * Handler for window deactivated event
56         * Invoked when a window is no longer the user's active
57         * window, which means that keyboard events will no longer
58         * be delivered to the window or its subcomponents.
59         */
60        public void windowDeactivated(WindowEvent event) {
61          System.out.println("Window deactivated");
62        }
63
64        /**
65         * Handler for window opened event
66         * Invoked the first time a window is made visible.
67         */
68        public void windowOpened(WindowEvent event) {
69          System.out.println("Window opened");
70        }
71
72        /**
73         * Handler for window closing event
74         * Invoked when the user attempts to close the window
75         * from the window's system menu.  If the program does not
76         * explicitly hide or dispose the window while processing
77         * this event, the window close operation will be cancelled.
78         */
```

```
79        public void windowClosing(WindowEvent event) {
80          System.out.println("Window closing");
81        }
82
83        /**
84         * Handler for window closed event
85         * Invoked when a window has been closed as the result
86         * of calling dispose on the window.
87         */
88        public void windowClosed(WindowEvent event) {
89          System.out.println("Window closed");
90        }
91      }
```

Review

The WindowEvent can be generated by the Window class or any subclass of Window. Since JFrame is a subclass of Window, it can generate WindowEvent.

TestWindowEvent extends JFrame and implements WindowListener. The WindowListener interface defines several abstract methods (windowActivated, window Closed, windowClosing, windowDeactivated, windowDeiconified, windowIconified, windowOpened) for handling window events when the window is activated, closed, closing, deactivated, deiconified, iconified, or opened.

When a window event, such as activation, occurs, the windowActivated method is triggered. Implement the windowActivated method with a concrete response if you want the event to be processed.

Because the methods in the WindowListener interface are abstract, you must implement all of them even if your program does not care about some of the events.

For an object to receive event notification, it must register as an event listener. addWindowListener(this) (Line 21) registers the object of TestWindowEvent as a window-event listener so that it can receive notification about the window event. TestWindowEvent is both a listener and a source object.

 NOTE

As demonstrated in this example, a source object and a listener object may be the same.

Example 12.3 Multiple Listeners for a Single Source

Problem

Write a program that modifies Example 12.1, "Handling Simple Action Events," to add a new listener for the OK and Cancel buttons. This example creates a new listener class as an additional listener for the action events on the buttons. When a button is clicked, both listeners respond to the action event.

continues

Example 12.3 Continued

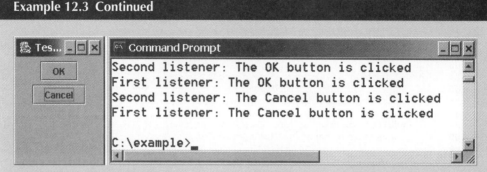

Figure 12.5 *Both listeners respond to the button action events.*

Solution

The following code gives the solution to the problem. Figure 12.5 shows a sample run of the program.

```
1    // TestMultipleListener.java: Test multiple listeners
2    package chapter12;
3
4    import javax.swing.*;
5    import java.awt.*;
6    import java.awt.event.*;
7
8    public class TestMultipleListener extends JFrame
9      implements ActionListener {
10     // Create two buttons
11     private JButton jbtOk = new JButton("OK");
12     private JButton jbtCancel = new JButton("Cancel");
13
14     /** Default constructor */
15     public TestMultipleListener() {
16       // Set the window title
17       setTitle("TestMultipleListener");
18
19       // Set FlowLayout manager to arrange the components
20       // inside the frame
21       getContentPane().setLayout(new FlowLayout());
22
23       // Add buttons to the frame
24       getContentPane().add(jbtOk);
25       getContentPane().add(jbtCancel);
26
27       // Register the frame as listeners
28       jbtOk.addActionListener(this);
29       jbtCancel.addActionListener(this);
30
31       // Register a second listener for buttons
32       SecondListener secondListener = new SecondListener();
33       jbtOk.addActionListener(secondListener);
34       jbtCancel.addActionListener(secondListener);
35     }
36
37     /** Main method */
38     public static void main(String[] args) {
39       TestMultipleListener frame = new TestMultipleListener();
40       frame.setDefaultCloseOperation(JFrame.EXIT_ON_CLOSE);
41       frame.setSize(100, 80);
```

```
42        frame.setVisible(true);
43      }
44
45      /** This method will be invoked when a button is clicked */
46      public void actionPerformed(ActionEvent e) {
47        System.out.print("First listener: ");
48
49        if (e.getSource() == jbtOk) {
50          System.out.println("The OK button is clicked");
51        }
52        else if (e.getSource() == jbtCancel) {
53          System.out.println("The Cancel button is clicked");
54        }
55      }
56    }
57
58    /** The class for the second listener */
59    class SecondListener implements ActionListener {
60      /** Handle ActionEvent */
61      public void actionPerformed(ActionEvent e) {
62        System.out.print("Second listener: ");
63
64        // A button has an actionCommand property, which is same as the
65        // text of the button by default.
66        if (e.getActionCommand().equals("OK")) {
67          System.out.println("The OK button is clicked");
68        }
69        else if (e.getActionCommand().equals("Cancel")) {
70          System.out.println("The Cancel button is clicked");
71        }
72      }
73    }
```

Review

Each source object in the preceding two examples has a single listener. Each button in this example has two listeners: one is an instance of TestMultiple Listener, and the other is an instance of SecondListener.

When a button is clicked, both listeners are notified and their respective actionPerformed methods are invoked. Using this method can detect which button is clicked. If you want to use the getSource method to detect which button is clicked, see Exercise 12.2.

The source object maintains a list of all its listeners. When a listener is registered with the source object, it is added at the top of the list. When an event occurs, the source object notifies the listener objects on the list by invoking each listener's handler. In this case, the handler is the actionPerformed method.

What would happen if you replaced the highlighted code (Lines 32–34) in the example with the following code?

```
// Register a second listener for buttons
jbtOk.addActionListener(new SecondListener());
jbtCancel.addActionListener(new SecondListener());
```

Two instances of SecondListener would be created. The program would run just as before the change, but the change is obviously not good.

12.4   Mouse Events

A mouse event is generated whenever a mouse is clicked, released, moved, or dragged on a component. The mouse event object captures the event, such as the number of clicks associated with it or the location (x and y coordinates) of the mouse. Java provides two listener interfaces, `MouseListener` and `MouseMotionListener`, to handle mouse events. Implement the `MouseListener` interface to listen for such actions as pressing, releasing, entering, exiting, or clicking the mouse, and implement the `MouseMotionListener` interface to listen for such actions as dragging or moving the mouse.

The `MouseListener` interface has the following handlers:

- The `mouseEntered(MouseEvent e)` and `mouseExit(MouseEvent e)` handlers are invoked when a mouse enters a component or exits the component.

- The `mousePressed(MouseEvent e)` and `mouseReleased(MouseEvent e)` handlers are invoked when a mouse is pressed or released.

- The `mouseClicked(MouseEvent e)` handler is invoked when a mouse is pressed and then released.

- The `mouseMoved(MouseEvent e)` handler is invoked when the mouse is moved without a button being pressed.

- The `mouseDragged(MouseEvent e)` handler is invoked when the mouse is moved with a button pressed.

The `Point` class is often used for handling mouse events. The `Point` class encapsulates a point in a plane. The class contains two instance variables, x and y, for coordinates. To create a point object, use the following constructor:

```
Point(int x, int y)
```

This constructs a `Point` object with the specified x and y coordinates.

You can use the `move(int x, int y)` method to move the point to the specified x and y coordinates. You can use the following methods from a `MouseEvent` object when a mouse event occurs:

- `public int getClickCount()`

  Returns the number of mouse clicks associated with the event.

- `public Point getPoint()`

  Returns the x and y coordinates of the mouse on the source component.

- `public int getX()`

  Returns the x coordinate of the mouse on the source component.

- `public int getY()`

  Returns the y coordinate of the mouse on the source component.

Since the MouseEvent class inherits InputEvent, you can use the methods defined in the InputEvent class on a MouseEvent object. The following methods in InputEvent are often useful for handling mouse events:

■ public long getWhen()

Returns a time stamp indicating when the event occurred.

■ public boolean isAltDown()

Returns whether the Alt key is down on the event.

■ public boolean isControlDown()

Returns whether the Control key is down on the event.

■ public boolean isMetaDown()

Returns true if the right mouse button is pressed.

■ public boolean isShiftDown()

Returns whether the Shift key is down on the event.

Example 12.4 Moving a Message on a Panel Using a Mouse

Problem

Write a program that displays a message in a panel. You can use the mouse to move the message. The message moves as the mouse drags and is always displayed at the mouse point. A sample run of the program is shown in Figure 12.6.

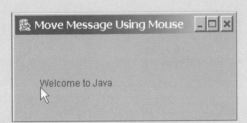

Figure 12.6 *You can move the message by dragging the mouse.*

Solution

The following code gives the solution to the problem.

```
1    // MoveMessageDemo.java: Move the message in a panel using mouse
2    package chapter12;
3
4    import java.awt.*;
5    import java.awt.event.*;
6    import javax.swing.*;
7    import chapter11.MessagePanel;
8
```

continues

Example 12.4   Continued

```
 9    public class MoveMessageDemo extends JFrame {
10      /** Default constructor */
11      public MoveMessageDemo() {
12        // Create a MoveMessagePanel instance for drawing a message
13        MoveMessagePanel p = new MoveMessagePanel("Welcome to Java");
14
15        // Place the message panel in the frame
16        getContentPane().setLayout(new BorderLayout());
17        getContentPane().add(p);
18      }
19
20      /** Main method */
21      public static void main(String[] args) {
22        MoveMessageDemo frame = new MoveMessageDemo();
23        frame.setTitle("Move Message Using Mouse");
24        frame.setDefaultCloseOperation(JFrame.EXIT_ON_CLOSE);
25        frame.setSize(100, 80);
26        frame.setVisible(true);
27      }
28    }
29
30    // MoveMessagePanel draws a message
31    class MoveMessagePanel extends MessagePanel
32      implements MouseMotionListener {
33      /** Construct a panel to draw string s */
34      public MoveMessagePanel(String s) {
35        super(s); // What if this line is omitted?
36        this.addMouseMotionListener(this);
37      }
38
39      /** Handle mouse moved event */
40      public void mouseMoved(MouseEvent e) {
41      }
42
43      /** Handle mouse dragged event */
44      public void mouseDragged(MouseEvent e) {
45        // Get the new location and repaint the screen
46        setXCoordinate(e.getX());
47        setYCoordinate(e.getY());
48      }
49    }
```

Review

The class MoveMessagePanel extends MessagePanel and implements MouseMotion-Listener. The MessagePanel class was presented in Example 11.5, "Creating a MessagePanel Class," to display a message in a panel. The MoveMessagePanel class inherits all the features from MessagePanel. Additionally, it handles redisplaying the message when the mouse is dragged.

The MouseMotionListener interface contains two handlers, mouseMoved and mouseDragged, for handling mouse-motion events. When you move the mouse with the button pressed, the mouseDragged method is invoked to repaint the viewing area and display the message at the mouse point. When you move the mouse without pressing the button, the mouseMoved method is invoked.

Because the methods in the MouseMotionListener interface are abstract, you must implement all of them even if your program does not care about some of the events. In MoveMessagePanel, the mouseMoved and mouseDragged event handlers are both implemented, although only the mouseDragged handler is needed.

For an object to receive event notification, it must register as an event listener. addMouseMotionListener(this) (Line 36) registers the object of MoveMessage Panel as a mouse-motion event listener so that the object can receive notification about the mouse-motion event. MoveMessagePanel is both a listener and a source object.

The mouseDragged method is invoked when you move the mouse with a button pressed. This method obtains the mouse location using getX and getY methods (Lines 46–47) in the MouseEvent class. This becomes the new location for the message, which is set using the MessagePanel's setXCoordinate and setYCoordinate methods.

Example 12.5 Scribbling with a Mouse

Problem

Write a program that uses a mouse for scribbling. It can be used to draw things on a panel by dragging with the left mouse button pressed. The drawing can be erased by dragging with the right button pressed. A sample run of the program is shown in Figure 12.7.

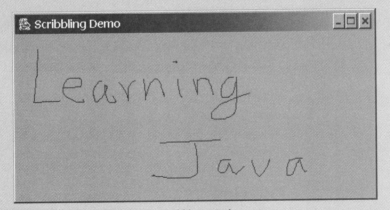

Figure 12.7   *The program enables you to scribble using the mouse.*

Solution

The following code gives the solution to the problem.

continues

Example 12.5 Continued

```
1     // ScribbleDemo.java: Scribble using mouse
2     package chapter12;
3
4     import java.awt.*;
5     import javax.swing.*;
6     import java.awt.event.*;
7
8     public class ScribbleDemo extends JFrame {
9       /** Default constructor */
10      public ScribbleDemo() {
11        // Create a PaintPanel and add it to the content pane
12        getContentPane().add(new ScribblePanel(), BorderLayout.CENTER);
13      }
14
15      /** Main method */
16      public static void main(String[] args) {
17        ScribbleDemo frame = new ScribbleDemo();
18        frame.setTitle("Scribbling Demo");
19        frame.setDefaultCloseOperation(JFrame.EXIT_ON_CLOSE);
20        frame.setSize(300, 300);
21        frame.setVisible(true);
22      }
23    }
24
25    // ScribblePanel for scribbling using the mouse
26    class ScribblePanel extends JPanel
27      implements MouseListener, MouseMotionListener {
28      final int CIRCLESIZE = 20; // Circle diameter used for erasing
29      private Point lineStart = new Point(0, 0); // Line start point
30      private Graphics g; // Create a Graphics object for drawing
31
32      public ScribblePanel() {
33        // Register listener for the mouse event
34        addMouseListener(this);
35        addMouseMotionListener(this);
36      }
37
38      public void mouseClicked(MouseEvent e) {
39      }
40
41      public void mouseEntered(MouseEvent e) {
42      }
43
44      public void mouseExited(MouseEvent e) {
45      }
46
47      public void mouseReleased(MouseEvent e) {
48      }
49
50      public void mousePressed(MouseEvent e) {
51        lineStart.move(e.getX(), e.getY());
52      }
53
54      public void mouseDragged(MouseEvent e) {
55        g = getGraphics(); // Get graphics context
56
57        if (e.isMetaDown()) { // Detect right button pressed
58          // Erase the drawing using an oval
59          g.setColor(getBackground());
60          g.fillOval(e.getX() - (CIRCLESIZE / 2),
61            e.getY() - (CIRCLESIZE / 2), CIRCLESIZE, CIRCLESIZE);
62        }
```

```
63            else {
64              g.setColor(Color.black);
65              g.drawLine(lineStart.x, lineStart.y,
66                e.getX(), e.getY());
67            }
68
69            lineStart.move(e.getX(), e.getY());
70
71            // Dispose this graphics context
72            g.dispose();
73          }
74
75          public void mouseMoved(MouseEvent e) {
76          }
77        }
```

Review

The program creates a `ScribblePanel` instance to capture mouse movements on the panel. Lines are created or erased by dragging the mouse with the left or right button pressed.

When a button is pressed, the `mousePressed` handler is invoked. This handler sets the `lineStart` to the current mouse point as the starting point. Drawing begins when the mouse is dragged with the left button pressed. In this case, the `mouseDragged` handler sets the foreground color to black, and draws a line along the path of the mouse movement.

When the mouse is dragged with the right button pressed, erasing occurs. In this case, the `mouseDragged` handler sets the foreground color to the background color and draws an oval filled with the background color at the mouse pointer to erase the area covered by the oval.

The program does not use the `paintComponent(Graphics g)` method. Instead, it uses `getGraphics()` to obtain a `Graphics` instance and draws on this.

Because the `mousePressed` handler is defined in the `MouseListener` interface, and the `mouseDragged` handler is defined in the `MouseMotionListener` interface, the program implements both interfaces (Line 27).

The `dispose` method (Line 72) disposes of this graphics context and releases any system resources it is using. Although the finalization process of the Java runtime system automatically disposes of the object after it is no longer in use, I recommend that you manually free the associated resources by calling this method rather than rely on a finalization process that may take a long time to run to completion. In this program, a large number of `Graphics` objects can be created within a short time. The program would run fine if these objects were not disposed of manually, but they would consume a lot of memory.

12.5 Keyboard Events

Keyboard events enable the use of the keys to control and perform actions or get input from the keyboard.

The keyboard event object describes the nature of the event (namely, that a key is pressed, released, or typed) and the value of the key. The following handlers from the `KeyListener` interface are used to process keyboard events:

- `public void keyPressed(KeyEvent e)`

  Called when a key is pressed.

- `public void keyReleased(KeyEvent e)`

  Called when a key is released.

- `public void keyTyped(KeyEvent e)`

  Called when a key is pressed and then released.

The keys captured in an event are integers representing Unicode character values, which include alphanumeric characters, function keys, the Tab key, the Enter key, and so on. Every keyboard event has an associated key character or key code that is returned by the `getKeyChar()` or `getKeyCode()` method in `KeyEvent`.

Java defines many constants for keys, including function keys in the `KeyEvent` class. Table 12.3 shows the most common ones.

TABLE 12.3   **Key Constants**

Constant	Description
VK_HOME	The Home key
VK_End	The End key
VK_PGUP	The Page Up key
VK_PGDN	The Page Down key
VK_UP	The up-arrow key
VK_DOWN	The down-arrow key
VK_LEFT	The left-arrow key
VK_RIGHT	The right-arrow key
VK_ESCAPE	The Esc key
VK_TAB	The Tab key
VK_CONTROL	The Control key
VK_SHIFT	The Shift key
VK_BACK_SPACE	The Backspace key
VK_CAPS_LOCK	The Caps Lock key
VK_NUM_LOCK	The Num Lock key
VK_ENTER	The Enter key
VK_F1 to VK_F12	The function keys from F1 to F12
VK_0 to VK_9	The number keys from 0 to 9
VK_A to VK_Z	The letter keys from A to Z

Example 12.6 Handling Key Events

Problem

Write a program that displays a user-input character. The user can move the character up, down, left, and right, using the arrow keys VK_UP, VK_DOWN, VK_LEFT, and VK_RIGHT. Figure 12.8 contains a sample run of the program.

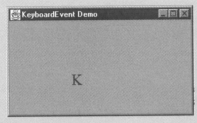

Figure 12.8 *The program responds to keyboard events by displaying a character and moving it up, down, left, or right.*

Solution

The following code gives the solution to the problem.

```
1    // KeyboardEventDemo.java: Receive key input
2    package chapter12;
3
4    import java.awt.*;
5    import java.awt.event.*;
6    import javax.swing.*;
7
8    public class KeyboardEventDemo extends JFrame {
9      private KeyboardPanel keyboardPanel = new KeyboardPanel();
10
11     /** Initialize UI */
12     public KeyboardEventDemo() {
13       // Add the keyboard panel to accept and display user input
14       getContentPane().add(keyboardPanel);
15
16       // Set focus
17       keyboardPanel.setFocusable(true);
18     }
19
20     /** Main method */
21     public static void main(String[] args) {
22       KeyboardEventDemo frame = new KeyboardEventDemo();
23       frame.setTitle("KeyboardEvent Demo");
24       frame.setDefaultCloseOperation(JFrame.EXIT_ON_CLOSE);
25       frame.setSize(300, 300);
26       frame.setVisible(true);
27     }
28   }
29
30   // KeyboardPanel for receiving key input
31   class KeyboardPanel extends JPanel implements KeyListener {
32     private int x = 100;
33     private int y = 100;
34     private char keyChar = 'A'; // Default key
35
```

continues

525

Example 12.6 Continued

```
36        public KeyboardPanel() {
37          addKeyListener(this); // Register listener
38        }
39
40        public void keyReleased(KeyEvent e) {
41        }
42
43        public void keyTyped(KeyEvent e) {
44        }
45
46        public void keyPressed(KeyEvent e) {
47          switch (e.getKeyCode()) {
48            case KeyEvent.VK_DOWN: y += 10; break;
49            case KeyEvent.VK_UP: y -= 10; break;
50            case KeyEvent.VK_LEFT: x -= 10; break;
51            case KeyEvent.VK_RIGHT: x += 10; break;
52            default: keyChar = e.getKeyChar();
53          }
54
55          repaint();
56        }
57
58        /** Draw the character */
59        protected void paintComponent(Graphics g) {
60          super.paintComponent(g);
61
62          g.setFont(new Font("TimesRoman", Font.PLAIN, 24));
63          g.drawString(String.valueOf(keyChar), x, y);
64        }
65      }
```

Review

When a nonarrow key is pressed, the key is displayed. When an arrow key is pressed, the character moves in the direction indicated by the arrow key.

Because the program gets input from the keyboard, it listens for KeyEvent and implements KeyListener to handle key input.

When a key is pressed, the keyPressed handler is invoked. The program uses e.getKeyCode() to obtain the int value for the key and e.getKeyChar() to get the character for the key. In fact, (int)e.getKeyChar() is the same as e.getKeyCode().

Only a focused component can receive KeyEvent. To set a component focusable, set its isFocusable property to true (Line 17). This new property was introduced in JDK 1.4.

Chapter Summary

- An event object contains whatever properties are pertinent to the event.

- The root class of the event classes is `java.util.EventObject`. The subclasses of `EventObject` deal with special types of events, such as button actions, window events, component events, mouse movements, and keystrokes.

- The component on which an event is generated is called the *source object*. You can identify the source object of an event using the `getSource()` instance method in the `EventObject` class.

- If a component can generate an event, any subclass of the component can generate the same type of event.

- The listener object's class must implement the corresponding event-listener interface. Java provides a listener interface for every type of GUI event. In general, the listener interface is named `XListener` for `XEvent`, except for `MouseMotionListener`. For example, the corresponding listener interface for `ActionEvent` is `ActionListener`; each listener for `ActionEvent` should implement the `ActionListener` interface. The listener interface contains the method(s), known as the *handler(s)*, which process the events.

- The listener object must be registered by the source object. Registration methods are dependent on the event type. For `ActionEvent`, the method is `addActionListener`. In general, the method is named `addXListener` for `XEvent`.

- A source object may fire several types of events. For each event, the source object maintains a list of listeners and notifies all the registered listeners by invoking the *handler* on the listener object to respond to the event.

- A mouse event is generated whenever a mouse is clicked, released, moved, or dragged on a component. The mouse event object captures the event, such as the number of clicks associated with it or the location (x and y coordinates) of the mouse.

- Java provides two listener interfaces, `MouseListener` and `MouseMotionListener`, to handle mouse events. Implement the `MouseListener` interface to listen for such actions as pressing, releasing, entering, exiting, or clicking the mouse, and implement the `MouseMotionListener` interface to listen for such actions as dragging or moving the mouse.

- The `Point` class is often used for handling mouse events. The `Point` class encapsulates a point on a plane. The class contains two instance variables, x and y, for coordinates.

- The keyboard event object describes the nature of the event (namely, that a key is pressed, released, or typed) and the value of the key.

■ The keys captured in an event are integers representing Unicode character values, which include alphanumeric characters, function keys, the Tab key, the Enter key, and so on. Every keyboard event has an associated key character or key code that is returned by the getKeyChar() or getKeyCode() method in KeyEvent.

■ Java defines many constants for keys, including function keys in the KeyEvent class. For example, the number keys from 0 to 9 are VK_0 to VK_9. The letter keys from A to Z are VK_A to VK_Z, and the up-arrow key is VK_UP.

Review Questions

12.1 Can a button generate a WindowEvent? Can a button generate a MouseEvent? Can a button generate an ActionEvent?

12.2 Explain how to register a listener object and how to implement a listener interface.

12.3 What information is contained in an AWTEvent object and the objects of its subclasses? Find the variables, constants, and methods defined in these event classes.

12.4 How do you override a method defined in the listener interface? Do you need to override all the methods defined in the listener interface?

12.5 What is the event type for a mouse movement? What is the event type for getting key input?

12.6 What is the listener interface for mouse pressed, released, clicked, entered, and exited? What is the listener interface for mouse moved and dragged?

12.7 What method is used to process a key event?

12.8 What methods are used in responding to a mouse-motion event?

12.9 What is wrong in the following code?

```
1   import java.awt.*;
2   import java.swing.*;
3
4   public class Test extends JFrame implements ActionListener {
5     public Test() {
6       JButton jbtOK = new JButton("OK");
7       getContentPane().add(jbtOK);
8     }
9
10    public void actionPerform(ActionEvent e) {
11      if (e.getSource() == jbtOK)
12        System.out.println("OK button is clicked");
13    }
14  }
```

Programming Exercises

12.1 (Displaying which button is clicked) Add the code into Exercise 11.1 to display a message on the console indicating which button has been clicked.

12.2 (Revising Example 12.3 "Multiple Listeners for a Single Source") Rewrite Example 12.3 as follows:

- Create a method in `TestMultipleListener`:

```
public void processButtons(ActionEvent e) {
  if (e.getSource() == jbtOk) {
    System.out.println("The OK button is clicked");
  }
  else if (e.getSource() == jbtCancel) {
    System.out.println("The Cancel button is clicked");
  }
}
```

- Invoke `processButtons(e)` from the `actionPerformed(e)` method in `TestMultipleListener`.

- Modify `SecondListener` to invoke `processButtons(e)` defined in `TestMultipleListener` from the `actionPerformed` method in `SecondListener`. For the `actionPerformed` method in the `SecondListener` class to invoke the `processButtons(e)` method in the `TestMultipleListener` class, you may pass a reference of a `TestMultipleListener` object to `SecondListener` through the constructor of `SecondListener`.

12.3 (Displaying the mouse position) Write a program that displays the mouse position when the mouse is pressed (see Figure 12.9).

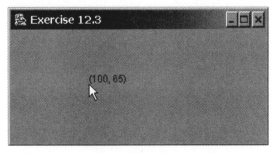

Figure 12.9 *When you click the mouse, the pixel coordinates are shown.*

12.4 (Drawing lines using the arrow keys) Write a program that draws line segments using the arrow keys. The line starts from the center of the frame and draws toward east, north, west, or south when the right-arrow key, up-arrow key, left-arrow key, or down-arrow key is clicked, as shown in Figure 12.10.

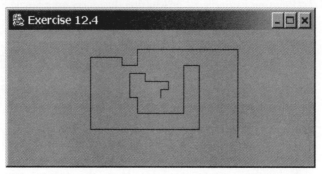

Figure 12.10 *You use the arrow keys to draw the line.*

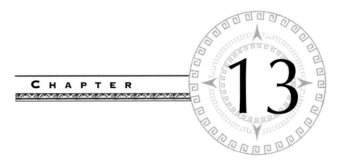

CREATING USER INTERFACES

Objectives

- ◉ To create graphical user interfaces with various user-interface components: JButton, JLabel, JTextField, JTextArea, JComboBox, JList, JCheckBox, JRadioButton, JMenuBar, JMenu, JMenuItem, JCheckBoxMenuItem, JRadioButtonMenuItem, JScrollBar, JScrollPane, and JTabbedPane.

- ◉ To show images with the ImageIcon class.

- ◉ To use borders to visually group user-interface components.

- ◉ To interact with the user using the JOptionPane dialog boxes.

- ◉ To display multiple windows in an application.

- ◉ To implement the listener interface for the listeners of various types of events.

13.1   Introduction

A graphical user interface (GUI) makes a system user-friendly and easy to use. Creating a GUI requires creativity and knowledge of how GUI components work. Since the GUI components in Java are very flexible and versatile, you can create a wide assortment of useful user interfaces.

Many Java IDEs provide tools for visually designing and programming Java classes. This enables you to rapidly assemble the elements of a user interface (UI) for a Java application or applet with minimum coding. Tools, however, cannot do everything. You have to modify the programs they produce. Consequently, before you begin to use the visual tools, it is imperative that you understand the basic concepts of Java GUI programming. Students should finish Chapter 14, "Applets," before attempting to use JBuilder's visual tools. Bonus Supplement L, "Rapid Java Application Development Using JBuilder," provides an introduction to JBuilder's UI designer.

This chapter concentrates on creating user interfaces. In particular, it discusses the various GUI components that make up a user interface and how to make them work.

13.2   The *Component* and *JComponent* Classes

Once you understand the basics of Java GUI programming, such as containers, layout managers, and event handling, you will be able to learn new components and explore their properties. The `Component` class is the root for all UI components and containers. Here is a list of frequently used properties in `Component`:

- **`font`** is the font used to display text on the component.

- **`background`** is the background color of the component.

- **`foreground`** is the foreground color of the component.

- **`height`** is the current height of the component.

- **`width`** is the current width of the component.

- **`locale`** is the locale of the component. This topic will be introduced in Bonus Chapter 20, "Internationalization."

- **`preferredSize`** specifies the ideal size at which the component looks best. This property may or may not be considered by the layout manager, depending on its rules. For example, a component uses its preferred size in a container with a `FlowLayout` manager, but its preferred size may be ignored if it is placed in a container with a `GridLayout` manager.

- **`minimumSize`** specifies the minimum size for the component to be useful. For most Swing components, `minimumSize` is the same as `preferredSize`. Layout managers generally respect `minimumSize` more than `preferredSize`.

- **`maximumSize`** specifies the maximum size the component needs so that the layout manager won't waste space by giving it to a component that does not need it. For instance, `BorderLayout` could limit the center component's size to its maximum size, and then either give the space to border components or limit the size of the outer window when resized.

All but a few Swing components, such as JFrame, JApplet, and JDialog, are subclasses of JComponent. Many of the properties of the Swing components are defined in the JComponent class. Here is a list of frequently used properties in JComponent:

- **toolTipText** specifies the text displayed when the mouse points on the component without clicking. This text is generally used to give the user a tip about the component's function.

- **doubleBuffered** specifies whether the component is painted using double-buffering. This is a technique for reducing flickering. In AWT programming, you have to manually implement this technique in the program. With Swing, this capability is automatically supported if the doubleBuffered property is set to true. By default, it is true.

- **border** specifies a border of the component. The border types and styles will be introduced in Section 13.11, "Borders."

All the properties in the Swing components are associated with accessor methods. You can retrieve them using get methods and modify them using set methods.

◈ NOTE

Throughout this book, the prefixes jbt, jlbl, jtf, jta, jcbo, jlst, jchk, jrb, jmi, jchkmi, and jrbmi are used to name objects of JButton, JLabel, JTextField, JTextArea, JComboBox, JList, JCheckBox, JRadioButton, JMenuItem, JCheckBoxMenuItem, and JRadioButtonMenuItem.

13.3   Buttons

A *button* is a component that triggers an action event when clicked. The Swing version of a button is named JButton. Its default constructor creates an empty button. In addition, JButton has the following constructors:

- public JButton(String text)

  Creates a button labeled with the specified text.

- public JButton(Icon icon)

  Creates a button with the specified icon.

- public JButton(Icon icon)

  Creates a button with the specified text and icon.

An icon is a fixed-size picture; typically it is small and used to decorate components. An icon can be obtained from an image file by using the ImageIcon class, such as:

```
Icon icon = new ImageIcon("photo.gif");
```

javax.swing.ImageIcon is a subclass of javax.swing.Icon.

NOTE

Java currently supports three image formats: GIF (Graphics Interchange Format), JPEG (Joint Photographic Experts Group), and PNG (Portable Network Graphics). The image file names for these types end with .gif, .jpg, and .png respectively. If you have a bitmap file or image files in other formats, you can use image-processing utilities to convert them into GIF, JPEG, or PNG format for use in Java.

 NOTE

File names are not case-sensitive on Windows, but are case-sensitive on Unix. To enable your programs to run on all platforms, I recommend that you name all the image files consistently.

Since `JButton` is a subclass of `JComponent`, all the properties in `JComponent` can be used in `JButton`. Additionally, `JButton` has the following useful properties:

- **text** is the label on the button. For example, to set the label "OK" on the button jbt, you can use `jbt.setText("OK")`.

- **icon** is the image icon on the button. For example, to set the icon on jbt using the image file smiley.gif, you can use `jbt.setIcon(new ImageIcon("smiley.gif"))`.

- **mnemonic** specifies a shortcut key. You can select the button by pressing the ALT key and the mnemonic key at the same time. For example, to set the mnemonic key O on jbt, you can use `jbt.setMnemonic('O')`.

- **horizontalAlignment** is one of the three values (`SwingConstants.LEFT`, `SwingConstants.CENTER`, and `SwingConstants.RIGHT`) that specify how the icon and text are placed horizontally on a button. The default horizontal alignment is `SwingConstants.CENTER`.

 NOTE

`SwingConstants` is an interface that contains the constants used by Swing components. All Swing GUI components implement `SwingConstants`. Therefore, you can reference the constants through `SwingConstants` or a GUI component. For example, `SwingConstants.CENTER` is the same as `JButton.CENTER`.

- **verticalAlignment** is one of the three values (`SwingConstants.TOP`, `SwingConstants.CENTER`, and `SwingConstants.BOTTOM`) that specify how the icon and text are placed vertically on a button. The default vertical alignment is `SwingConstants.CENTER`.

- **horizontalTextPosition** is one of the three values (`SwingConstants.LEFT`, `SwingConstants.CENTER`, and `SwingConstants.RIGHT`) that specify the horizontal position of the text relative to the icon. The default horizontal text position is `SwingConstants.RIGHT`.

■ **verticalTextPosition** is one of the three values (SwingConstants.TOP, SwingConstants.CENTER, and SwingConstants.BOTTOM) that specify the vertical position of the text relative to the icon. The default vertical text position is SwingConstants.CENTER.

◈ **NOTE**

The Container class is the superclass for many GUI component classes, such as JButton. In theory, you could use the setLayout method to set the layout in a button and add components into a button, because all the public methods in the Container class are inherited into JButton, but for practical reasons they should not be used in JButton.

Buttons can generate many types of events, but often you need to respond to an ActionEvent. In order to make a button responsive to an ActionEvent, you must implement the actionPerformed method in the ActionListener interface. The following code is an example of how to handle a button event. The code prints out "Button clicked" on the console when the button is clicked.

```
public void actionPerformed(ActionEvent e) {
  // Make sure the event source is a button.
  if (e.getSource() instanceof JButton)
    System.out.println("Button clicked!");
}
```

Example 13.1 Using Buttons

Problem

Write a program that displays a message on a panel and uses two buttons, <= and =>, to move the message on the panel to the left or right. The layout of the UI and the output of the program are shown in Figure 13.1.

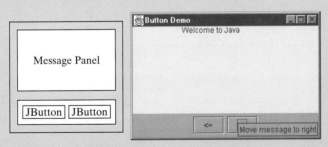

Figure 13.1 *Clicking the <= and => buttons causes the message on the panel to move to the left and right, respectively.*

Solution

Here are the major steps in the program:

continues

Example 13.1 Continued

1. Create the user interface.

Create a MessagePanel object to display the message. The MessagePanel class was created in Example 11.5, "Creating a Message Panel Class." Place it in the center of the frame. Create two buttons, <= and =>, on a panel. Place the panel in the south of the frame.

2. Process the event.

Implement the actionPerformed handler to move the message left or right according to whether the left or right button was clicked.

```java
1   // ButtonDemo.java: Use buttons to move message in a panel
2   package chapter13;
3
4   import java.awt.*;
5   import java.awt.event.ActionListener;
6   import java.awt.event.ActionEvent;
7   import javax.swing.*;
8   import chapter11.MessagePanel;
9
10  public class ButtonDemo extends JFrame implements ActionListener {
11    // Create a panel for displaying message
12    private MessagePanel messagePanel
13      = new MessagePanel("Welcome to Java");
14
15    // Declare two buttons to move the message left and right
16    private JButton jbtLeft, jbtRight;
17
18    /** Main method */
19    public static void main(String[] args) {
20      ButtonDemo frame = new ButtonDemo();
21      frame.setDefaultCloseOperation(JFrame.EXIT_ON_CLOSE);
22      frame.setSize(200, 200);
23      frame.setVisible(true);
24    }
25
26    /** Default constructor */
27    public ButtonDemo() {
28      setTitle("Button Demo");
29
30      // Set the background color of messagePanel
31      messagePanel.setBackground(Color.yellow);
32
33      // Create Panel jpButtons to hold two Buttons "<=" and "right =>"
34      JPanel jpButtons = new JPanel();
35      jpButtons.setLayout(new FlowLayout());
36      jpButtons.add(jbtLeft = new JButton());
37      jpButtons.add(jbtRight = new JButton());
38
39      // Set button text
40      jbtLeft.setText("<=");
41      jbtRight.setText("=>");
42
43      // Set keyboard mnemonics
44      jbtLeft.setMnemonic('L');
45      jbtRight.setMnemonic('R');
46
48      // Set icons
49      //jbtLeft.setIcon(new ImageIcon("image/left.gif"));
```

```
50          //jbtRight.setIcon(new ImageIcon("image/right.gif"));
51
52          // Set toolTipText on the "<=" and "=>" buttons
53          jbtLeft.setToolTipText("Move message to left");
54          jbtRight.setToolTipText("Move message to right");
55
56          // Place panels in the frame
57          getContentPane().setLayout(new BorderLayout());
58          getContentPane().add(messagePanel, BorderLayout.CENTER);
59          getContentPane().add(jpButtons, BorderLayout.SOUTH);
60
61          // Register listeners with the buttons
62          jbtLeft.addActionListener(this);
63          jbtRight.addActionListener(this);
64      }
65
66      /** Handle button events */
67      public void actionPerformed(ActionEvent e) {
68        if (e.getSource() == jbtLeft) {
69          messagePanel.moveLeft();
70        }
71        else if (e.getSource() == jbtRight) {
72          messagePanel.moveRight();
73        }
74      }
75    }
```

Review

Each button has a tool-tip text (Lines 53–54), which appears when the mouse is set on the button without clicking, as shown in Figure 13.1.

You can set an icon image on the button by using the setIcon method. If you replace the setText method with the setIcon method (Lines 49–50), as follows:

```
jbtLeft.setIcon(new ImageIcon("image/left.gif"));
jbtRight.setIcon(new ImageIcon("image/right.gif"));
```

the texts are replaced by the icons, as shown in Figure 13.2. "image/left.gif" is located in "c:\example\image\left.gif." Note that the back slash is the Windows file path notation. In Java, the forward slash should be used.

Figure 13.2   *You can set an icon on a* JButton.

You can set icons and labels on a button at the same time, if you wish. By default, the labels and icons are centered horizontally and vertically.

The button can also be accessed by using the keyboard mnemonics. Pressing ALT + L is equivalent to clicking the <= button, since you set the mnemonic

continues

Example 13.1 Continued

property to 'L' in the left button (Line 44). If you change the left button text to "Left" and the right button to "Right," the L and R in the captions of these buttons will be underlined, as shown in Figure 13.3.

Figure 13.3   *The buttons can be accessed by using the keyboard mnemonics.*

13.4   Labels

A *label* is a display area for a short text, an image, or both. It is often used to label other components (usually text fields). The default constructor of JLabel creates an empty label. Other constructors for JLabel are as follows:

- ■ public JLabel(String text, int horizontalAlignment)

  Creates a label with the specified string and horizontal alignment (SwingConstants.LEFT, SwingConstants.RIGHT, or SwingConstants.CENTER).

- ■ public JLabel(String text)

  Creates a label with a specified text.

- ■ public JLabel(Icon icon)

  Creates a label with an icon.

- ■ public JLabel(Icon icon, int horizontalAlignment)

  Creates a label with the specified image and horizontal alignment.

- ■ public JLabel(String text, Icon icon, int horizontalAlignment)

  Creates a label with the specified text, image, and horizontal alignment.

For example, the following statement creates a label with the string "Interest Rate":

```
JLabel myLabel = new JLabel("Interest Rate");
```

The following statement creates a label with the specified image in the file "image/map.gif":

```
JLabel mapLabel = new JLabel(new ImageIcon("image/map.gif"));
```

JLabel inherits all the properties from JComponent and has many properties used in JButton, such as text, icon, horizontalAlignment, and verticalAlignment.

Example 13.2 Using Labels

Problem

Write a program that uses a label as an area for displaying images. There are nine images in image files named flag1.gif, flag2.gif, ..., flag9.gif stored in the **image** directory under **c:\example**. You can use two buttons, Prior and Next, to browse the images, as shown in Figure 13.4.

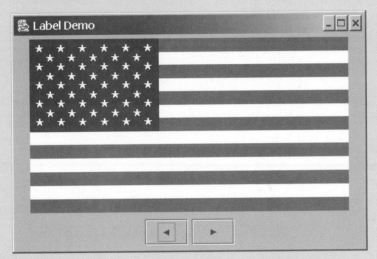

Figure 13.4 *You can use the label to display images.*

Solution

Here are the major steps in the program:

1. Create the user interface.

    Create a JLabel object to display image icons, and place the label in the center of the frame. Create two buttons, Prior and Next, on a panel. Place the panel in the south of the frame.

2. Process the event.

    Implement the actionPerformed handler to set the appropriate image icon in the label according to whether the Prior or Next button was clicked.

```
1    // LabelDemo.java: Use label to display images
2    package chapter13;
3
4    import java.awt.*;
5    import java.awt.event.*;
6    import javax.swing.*;
7
8    public class LabelDemo extends JFrame implements ActionListener {
9      final int NUMBER_OF_IMAGES = 9;
10
11      // Declare an ImageIcon array. There are total 9 images
12      private ImageIcon[] imageIcons = new ImageIcon[NUMBER_OF_IMAGES];
13
```

continues

Example 13.2 Continued

```
14      // The current image index
15      private int currentIndex = 0;
16
17      // Buttons for browsing images
18      private JButton jbtPrior, jbtNext;
19
20      // Label for displaying images
21      private JLabel jlblImageViewer = new JLabel();
22
23      /** Main Method */
24      public static void main(String[] args) {
25        LabelDemo frame = new LabelDemo();
26        frame.setDefaultCloseOperation(JFrame.EXIT_ON_CLOSE);
27        frame.setSize(500, 500);
28        frame.setVisible(true);
29      }
30
31      /** Default Constructor */
32      public LabelDemo() {
33        setTitle("Label Demo");
34
35        // Load images into imageIcon array
36        for (int i = 1; i <= NUMBER_OF_IMAGES; i++) {
37          imageIcons[i - 1] = new ImageIcon("image/flag" + i + ".gif");
38        }
39
40        // Show the first image
41        jlblImageViewer.setIcon(imageIcons[currentIndex]);
42
43        // Set center alignment
44        jlblImageViewer.setHorizontalAlignment(SwingConstants.CENTER);
45        jlblImageViewer.setVerticalAlignment(SwingConstants.CENTER);
46
47        // Panel jpButtons to hold two buttons for browsing images
48        JPanel jpButtons = new JPanel();
49        jpButtons.add(jbtPrior = new JButton());
50        jbtPrior.setIcon(new ImageIcon("image/left.gif"));
51        jpButtons.add(jbtNext = new JButton());
52        jbtNext.setIcon(new ImageIcon("image/right.gif"));
53
54        // Add jpButton and the label to the frame
55        getContentPane().add(jlblImageViewer, BorderLayout.CENTER);
56        getContentPane().add(jpButtons, BorderLayout.SOUTH);
57
58        // Register listeners
59        jbtPrior.addActionListener(this);
60        jbtNext.addActionListener(this);
61      }
62
63      /** Handle ActionEvent from buttons */
64      public void actionPerformed(ActionEvent e) {
65        if (e.getSource() == jbtPrior) {
66          // Make sure index is nonnegative
67          if (currentIndex == 0) currentIndex = NUMBER_OF_IMAGES;
68          currentIndex = (currentIndex - 1) % NUMBER_OF_IMAGES;
69          jlblImageViewer.setIcon(imageIcons[currentIndex]);
70        }
```

```
71              else if (e.getSource() == jbtNext) {
72                currentIndex = (currentIndex + 1) % NUMBER_OF_IMAGES;
73                jlblImageViewer.setIcon(imageIcons[currentIndex]);
74              }
75          }
76      }
```

Review

The images are stored in files flag1.gif, flag2.gif, ..., and flag9.gif under the \example\image directory, and are loaded to an array of ImageIcon in a for loop (Lines 36–38).

The variable currentIndex (Line 15) tracks which image icon is displayed in the label. When the Prior button or the Next button is clicked, the currentIndex is decremented or incremented by 1.

By default, the icon is centered vertically but left-aligned horizontally. The following statement (Line 44) ensures that the image is displayed in the center of the viewing area.

```
jlblImageViewer.setHorizontalAlignment(SwingConstants.CENTER);
```

13.5   Text Fields

A *text field* can be used to enter or display a string. The default constructor of JTextField creates an empty text field. Other constructors of JTextField are:

■ public JTextField(int columns)

Creates an empty text field with the specified number of columns.

■ public JTextField(String text)

Creates a text field initialized with the specified text.

■ public JTextField(String text, int columns)

Creates a text field initialized with the specified text and the number of columns.

In addition to such properties as text and horizontalAlignment, JTextField has the following properties:

■ **editable** is a boolean property indicating whether the text field can be edited by the user. The default value is true. I recommend that you always set editable false if you don't want the user to edit the text field.

■ **columns** specifies the number of columns in the text field.

JTextField can generate ActionEvent among many other events. Pressing Enter in a text field triggers the ActionEvent.

Here is an example of how to react to an `ActionEvent` on a text field.

```
public void actionPerformed(ActionEvent e) {
  // Make sure it is a text field
  if (e.getSource() instanceof JTextField)
    // Process the event
    ...
}
```

Example 13.3 Using Text Fields

Problem

Write a program that converts Celsius and Fahrenheit temperatures, as shown in Figure 13.5. If you enter a value in the Celsius-degree text field and press the Enter key, the Fahrenheit temperature is displayed in the Fahrenheit text field. Likewise, if you enter a value in the Fahrenheit-degree text field, and press the Enter key, the corresponding Celsius degree is displayed in the Celsius text field.

Figure 13.5   *The program converts Celsius to Fahrenheit, and vice versa.*

Solution

Here are the major steps in the program:

1. Create the user interface.

   Create a panel of `GridLayout` with two rows to hold two labels, and create another panel of `GridLayout` with two rows to hold two text fields. Add the first panel to the west and the second panel to the center of the frame's content pane.

2. Process the event.

   Implement the `actionPerformed` handler to detect which text field has been entered. If the Celsius-degree text field is entered, retrieve the number from the text field, compute its corresponding Fahrenheit value, and display the result in the Fahrenheit-degree text. If the Fahrenheit-degree text field is entered, it can be processed in the same way.

```
1    // TextFieldDemo.java: Add two numbers in the text fields
2    package chapter13;
3
4    import java.awt.*;
5    import java.awt.event.*;
6    import javax.swing.*;
7
```

```
8    public class TextFieldDemo extends JFrame
9      implements ActionListener {
10     private JTextField jtfCelsius = new JTextField(10);
11     private JTextField jtfFahrenheit = new JTextField(10);
12
13     /** Main method */
14     public static void main(String[] args) {
15       TextFieldDemo frame = new TextFieldDemo();
16       frame.pack();
17       frame.setTitle("TextFieldDemo");
18       frame.setDefaultCloseOperation(JFrame.EXIT_ON_CLOSE);
19       frame.setVisible(true);
20     }
21
22     public TextFieldDemo() {
23       // Panel p1 to hold labels
24       JPanel p1 = new JPanel();
25       p1.setLayout(new GridLayout(2, 1));
26       p1.add(new JLabel("Celsius"));
27       p1.add(new JLabel("Fahrenheit"));
28
29       // Panel p2 to hold text fields
30       JPanel p2 = new JPanel();
31       p2.setLayout(new GridLayout(2, 1));
32       p2.add(jtfCelsius);
33       p2.add(jtfFahrenheit);
34
35       // Add p1 and p3 to the frame
36       getContentPane().add(p1, BorderLayout.WEST);
37       getContentPane().add(p2, BorderLayout.CENTER);
38
39       // Set horizontal alignment to RIGHT for text fields
40       jtfCelsius.setHorizontalAlignment(JTextField.RIGHT);
41       jtfFahrenheit.setHorizontalAlignment(JTextField.RIGHT);
42
43       // Register listener
44       jtfCelsius.addActionListener(this);
45       jtfFahrenheit.addActionListener(this);
46     }
47
48     /** Handle ActionEvent */
49     public void actionPerformed(ActionEvent e) {
50       if (e.getSource() == jtfCelsius) {
51         double celsius =
52           Double.parseDouble(jtfCelsius.getText().trim());
53         double fahrenheit = (9.0 / 5.0) * celsius + 32;
54         jtfFahrenheit.setText(new Double(fahrenheit).toString());
55         jtfFahrenheit.requestFocusInWindow();
56       }
57       else {
58         double fahrenheit =
59           Double.parseDouble(jtfFahrenheit.getText().trim());
60         double celsius = (5.0 / 9.0) * (fahrenheit - 32);
61         jtfCelsius.setText(new Double(celsius).toString());
62         jtfCelsius.requestFocusInWindow();
63       }
64     }
65   }
```

continues

543

Example 13.3 Continued

Review

Instead of using the `setSize` method to set the size for the frame, the program uses the `pack()` method (Line 16), which automatically sizes up the frame according to the size of the components placed in it.

The program uses two panels, `p1` and `p2`, to contain the components. Panel `p1` is for the labels (Lines 24–27), and `p2` is for the text fields (Lines 30–33).

The `jtfCelsius.getText()` method (Line 52) returns the text in the text field `jtfCelsius`, and `jtfFahrenheit.setText(s)` (Line 54) sets the specified string into the text field `jtfFahrenheit`.

The `trim()` method (Lines 52, 59) is useful for removing blank space from both ends of a string. If you run the program without applying `trim()` to the string, a runtime exception may occur when the string is converted to an integer.

Pressing Enter in a text field triggers an `ActionEvent`. The `actionPerformed` handler (Lines 49–64) checks which text field is the source of the event to process the event accordingly.

The `requestFocusInWindow()` method (Lines 55, 62) defined in the `Component` class requests the component to receive input focus. Thus, `jtfCelsius.request FocusInWindow()` (Line 62) requests the input focus on `jtfCelsius`. So you will see the cursor on `jtfCelsius` after you enter a value in the Fahrenheit text field and press the Enter key.

13.6   Text Areas

If you want to let the user enter multiple lines of text, you have to create several instances of `JTextField`. A better alternative is to use `JTextArea`, which enables the user to enter multiple lines of text.

The default constructor of `JTextArea` creates an empty text area. Other constructors of `JTextArea` are listed below:

■ `public JTextArea(int rows, int columns)`

Creates a text area with the specified number of rows and columns.

■ `public JTextArea(String text, int rows, int columns)`

Creates a text area with the specified text and the number of rows and columns specified.

In addition to `text`, `editable`, and `columns`, `JTextArea` has the following properties:

■ `lineWrap` is a `boolean` property indicating whether the line in the text area is automatically wrapped.

- **wrapStyleWord** is a `boolean` property indicating whether the line is wrapped on words or characters. The default value is `false`, which indicates that the line is wrapped on characters.

- **rows** specifies the number of lines in the text area.

- **lineCount** specifies the number of lines in the text.

- **tabSize** specifies the number of spaces inserted when the Tab key is pressed.

You can use the following methods to insert, append, and replace text:

- `public void insert(String s, int pos)`

  Inserts string s in the specified position in the text area.

- `public void append(String s)`

  Appends string s to the end of the text.

- `public void replaceRange(String s, int start, int end)`

  Replaces partial texts in the range from position `start` to position `end` with string s.

`JTextArea` does not handle scrolling, but you can create a `JScrollPane` object to hold an instance of `JTextArea` and let `JScrollPane` handle scrolling for `JTextArea`, as follows:

```
// Create a scroll pane to hold text area
JScrollPane scrollPane = new JScrollPane(jta = new JTextArea());
getContentPane().add(scrollPane, BorderLayout.CENTER);
```

`JScrollPane` will be discussed further in Section 13.16, "Scroll Panes."

Example 13.4 Using Text Areas

Problem

Write a program that displays an image in a label, a title in a label, and a text in a text area. A sample run of the program is shown in Figure 13.6.

Figure 13.6   *The program displays an image in a label, a title in a label, and a text in the text area.*

continues

545

Example 13.4 Continued

Solution

Here are the major steps in the program:

1. Create a class named `DescriptionPanel` that extends `JPanel`. This class contains a text area inside a scroll pane, a label for displaying an image icon, and a label for displaying a title. This class is used in this example and will also be used in later examples.

2. Create a class named `TextAreaDemo` that extends `JFrame`. Create an instance of `DescriptionPanel` and add it to the center of the frame. The relationship between `DescriptionPanel` and `TextAreaDemo` is shown in Figure 13.7.

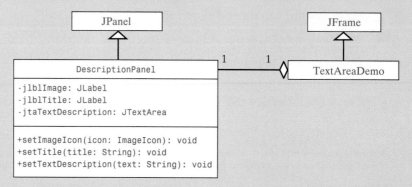

Figure 13.7 `TextAreaDemo` *uses* `DescriptionPanel` *to display an image, title, and text description of a national flag.*

```
1     // TextAreaDemo.java: Display an image in a label, the title for
2     // the image in a label, and the description of the image in a
3     // text area
4     package chapter13;
5
6     import java.awt.*;
7     import javax.swing.*;
8
9     public class TextAreaDemo extends JFrame {
10      // Declare and create a description panel
11      private DescriptionPanel descriptionPanel = new DescriptionPanel();
12
13      /** Main method */
14      public static void main(String[] args) {
15        TextAreaDemo frame = new TextAreaDemo();
16        frame.pack();
17        frame.setDefaultCloseOperation(JFrame.EXIT_ON_CLOSE);
18        frame.setTitle("Text Area Demo");
19        frame.setVisible(true);
20      }
21
22      /** Default constructor */
23      public TextAreaDemo() {
24        // Set title, text and image in the description panel
25        descriptionPanel.setTitle("Canada");
```

```
26        String description = "The Maple Leaf flag \n\n" +
27          "The Canadian National Flag was adopted by the Canadian " +
28          "Parliament on October 22, 1964 and was proclaimed into law " +
29          "by Her Majesty Queen Elizabeth II (the Queen of Canada) on " +
30          "February 15, 1965. The Canadian Flag (colloquially known " +
31          "as The Maple Leaf Flag) is a red flag of the proportions " +
32          "two by length and one by width, containing in its center a " +
33          "white square, with a single red stylized eleven-point " +
34          "mapleleaf centered in the white square.";
35        descriptionPanel.setTextDescription(description);
36        descriptionPanel.setImageIcon(new ImageIcon("image/ca.gif"));
37
38        // Add the description panel to the frame
39        getContentPane().setLayout(new BorderLayout());
40        getContentPane().add(descriptionPanel, BorderLayout.CENTER);
41      }
42    }
43
44  // Define a panel for displaying image and text
45  class DescriptionPanel extends JPanel {
46    /** Label for displaying an image icon */
47    private JLabel jlblImage = new JLabel();
48
49    /** Label for displaying a title */
50    private JLabel jlblTitle = new JLabel();
51
52    /** Text area for displaying text */
53    private JTextArea jtaTextDescription;
54
55    /** Default constructor */
56    public DescriptionPanel() {
57      // Group image label and title label in a panel
58      JPanel panel = new JPanel();
59      panel.setLayout(new BorderLayout());
60      panel.add(jlblImage, BorderLayout.CENTER);
61      panel.add(jlblTitle, BorderLayout.SOUTH);
62
63      // Create a scroll pane to hold text area
64      JScrollPane scrollPane = new JScrollPane
65        (jtaTextDescription = new JTextArea());
66
67      // Center the title on the label
68      jlblTitle.setHorizontalAlignment(JLabel.CENTER);
69
70      // Set the font for the title and text
71      jlblTitle.setFont(new Font("SansSerif", Font.BOLD, 16));
72      jtaTextDescription.setFont(new Font("Serif", Font.PLAIN, 14));
73
74      // Set lineWrap and wrapStyleWord true for text area
75      jtaTextDescription.setLineWrap(true);
76      jtaTextDescription.setWrapStyleWord(true);
77
78      // Set preferred size for the scroll pane
79      scrollPane.setPreferredSize(new Dimension(200, 100));
80
81      // Set BorderLayout for the whole panel, add panel and scrollpane
82      setLayout(new BorderLayout(5, 5));
83      add(scrollPane, BorderLayout.CENTER);
84      add(panel, BorderLayout.WEST);
85    }
86
```

continues

547

Example 13.4 Continued

```
87          /** Set the title */
88          public void setTitle(String title) {
89            jlblTitle.setText(title);
90          }
91
92          /** Set the image icon */
93          public void setImageIcon(ImageIcon icon) {
94            jlblImage.setIcon(icon);
95            Dimension dimension = new Dimension(icon.getIconWidth(),
96              icon.getIconHeight());
97            jlblImage.setPreferredSize(dimension);
98          }
99
100         /** Set the text description */
101         public void setTextDescription(String text) {
102           jtaTextDescription.setText(text);
103         }
104       }
```

Review

TextAreaDemo creates an instance of DescriptionPanel (Line 11), and sets the title (Line 25), image (Line 36), and text in the description panel (Line 35). DescriptionPanel is a subclass of JPanel. DescriptionPanel contains a label for displaying the image icon, a label for displaying the title, and a text area for displaying a description of the image.

It is not necessary to create a separate class for DescriptionPanel in this example. Nevertheless, this class was created for reuse in the next example, where you will use it to display a description panel for various images.

The text area is inside a JScrollPane, which provides scrolling functions for the text area. Scrollbars automatically appear if there is more text than the physical size of the text area, and disappear if the text is deleted and the remaining text does not exceed the text area size.

The lineWrap property is set to true (Line 75) so that the line is automatically wrapped when the text cannot fit in one line. The wrapStyleWord property is set to true (Line 76) so that the line is wrapped on words rather than characters.

The text area is editable. It supports editing functions, such as cut, paste, and copy.

The preferredSize property in jlblImage is set to the size of the image icon (Line 79). The getIconWidth() and getIconHeight() methods (Lines 95–96) obtain the width and height of the icon. The preferredSize property (Line 79) in scrollPane is set to 200 in width and 100 in height. The BorderLayout manager respects the preferred size of the components.

13.7   Combo Boxes

A *combo box*, also known as *choice* or *drop-down list*, contains a list of items from which the user can choose. It is useful in limiting a user's range of choices and avoids the cumbersome validation of data input.

To create a JComboBox, use its default constructor, or use the following constructor to create a combo box with a set of strings:

```
public JComboBox(Object[] stringItems)
```

where stringItems is an array of String.

The following properties are often useful:

■ **selectedIndex** is an int value indicating the index of the selected item in the combo box.

■ **selectedItem** holds a selected item whose type is Object.

The following methods are useful for operating a JComboBox object:

■ public void addItem(Object item)

Adds the item of any object into the combo box.

■ public Object getItemAt(int index)

Gets an item from the combo box at the specified index.

■ public void removeItem(Object anObject)

Removes the specified item from the item list.

■ public void removeAllItems()

Removes all the items from the item list.

Here is an example of how to create a combo box and add items to the object:

```
JComboBox jcb = new JComboBox();
jcb.addItem("Item 1");
jcb.addItem("Item 2");
jcb.addItem("Item 3");
```

This creates a JComboBox with three items in the combo box.

To get data from a JComboBox menu, you can use getSelectedItem() to return the currently selected item, or e.getItem() method to get the item from the itemStateChanged(ItemEvent e) handler.

JComboBox can generate ActionEvent and ItemEvent, among many other events. Whenever a new item is selected, JComboBox generates ItemEvent twice, once for de-selecting the previously selected item, and the other for selecting the currently selected item. JComboBox generates an ActionEvent after generating ItemEvent. To respond to an ItemEvent, you need to implement the itemStateChanged(ItemEvent e) handler for processing a choice. Here is an example of how to get data from the itemStateChanged(ItemEvent e) handler:

```
public void itemStateChanged(ItemEvent e) {
  // Make sure the source is a combo box
  if (e.getSource() instanceof JComboBox)
    String s = (String)e.getItem();
}
```

Example 13.5 Using Combo Boxes

Problem

Write a program that lets users view an image and a description of a country's flag by selecting the country from a combo box. Figure 13.8 shows a sample run of the program.

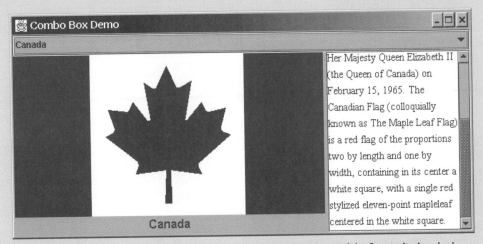

Figure 13.8 *A country's info, including a flag image and a description of the flag, is displayed when the country is selected in the combo box.*

Solution

Here are the major steps in the program:

1. Create the user interface.

   Create a combo box with country names as its selection values. Create a DescriptionPanel object. The DescriptionPanel class was introduced in the preceding example. Place the combo box in the north of the frame and the description panel in the center of the frame.

2. Process the event.

   Implement the itemStateChanged handler to set the flag title, image, and text in the description panel for the selected country name.

```
1   // ComboBoxDemo.java: Use a combo box to select a country and
2   // display the selected country's flag information
3   package chapter13;
4
```

```
 5    import java.awt.*;
 6    import java.awt.event.*;
 7    import javax.swing.*;
 8
 9    public class ComboBoxDemo extends JFrame implements ItemListener {
10      // Declare an array of Strings for flag titles
11      private String[] flagTitle = {"Canada", "China", "Denmark",
12        "France", "Germany", "India", "Norway", "United Kingdom",
13        "United States of America"};
14
15      // Declare an ImageIcon array for the national flags of 9 countries
16      private ImageIcon[] flagImage = {
17        new ImageIcon("image/ca.gif"),
18        new ImageIcon("image/china.gif"),
19        new ImageIcon("image/denmark.gif"),
20        new ImageIcon("image/fr.gif"),
21        new ImageIcon("image/germany.gif"),
22        new ImageIcon("image/india.gif"),
23        new ImageIcon("image/norway.gif"),
24        new ImageIcon("image/uk.gif"),
25        new ImageIcon("image/us.gif")
26      };
27
28      // Declare an array of strings for flag descriptions
29      private String[] flagDescription = new String[9];
30
31      // Declare and create a description panel
32      private DescriptionPanel descriptionPanel = new DescriptionPanel();
33
34      // The combo list for selecting countries
35      private JComboBox jcbo;
36
37      /** Main Method */
38      public static void main(String[] args) {
39        ComboBoxDemo frame = new ComboBoxDemo();
40        frame.pack();
41        frame.setTitle("Combo Box Demo");
42        frame.setDefaultCloseOperation(JFrame.EXIT_ON_CLOSE);
43        frame.setVisible(true);
44      }
45
46      /** Default Constructor */
47      public ComboBoxDemo() {
48        // Set text description
49        flagDescription[0] = "The Maple Leaf flag \n\n" +
50          "The Canadian National Flag was adopted by the Canadian " +
51          "Parliament on October 22, 1964 and was proclaimed into law " +
52          "by Her Majesty Queen Elizabeth II (the Queen of Canada) on " +
53          "February 15, 1965. The Canadian Flag (colloquially known " +
54          "as The Maple Leaf Flag) is a red flag of the proportions " +
55          "two by length and one by width, containing in its center a " +
56          "white square, with a single red stylized eleven-point " +
57          "mapleleaf centered in the white square.";
58        flagDescription[1] = "Description for China ... ";
59        flagDescription[2] = "Description for Denmark ... ";
60        flagDescription[3] = "Description for France ... ";
61        flagDescription[4] = "Description for Germany ... ";
62        flagDescription[5] = "Description for India ... ";
63        flagDescription[6] = "Description for Norway ... ";
64        flagDescription[7] = "Description for UK ... ";
65        flagDescription[8] = "Description for US ... ";
66
```

continues

551

Example 13.5 Continued

```
67            // Create items into the combo box
68            jcbo = new JComboBox(flagTitle);
69
70            // Set the first country (Canada) for display
71            setDisplay(0);
72
73            // Add combo box and description panel to the list
74            getContentPane().add(jcbo, BorderLayout.NORTH);
75            getContentPane().add(descriptionPanel, BorderLayout.CENTER);
76
77            // Register listener
78            jcbo.addItemListener(this);
79        }
80
81        /** Handle item selection */
82        public void itemStateChanged(ItemEvent e) {
83          setDisplay(jcbo.getSelectedIndex());
84        }
85
86        /** Set display information on the description panel */
87        public void setDisplay(int index) {
88          descriptionPanel.setTitle(flagTitle[index]);
89          descriptionPanel.setImageIcon(flagImage[index]);
90          descriptionPanel.setTextDescription(flagDescription[index]);
91        }
92    }
```

Review

The frame listens to `ItemEvent` from the `JComboBox` item, so it implements `ItemListener` (Lines 82–84). Instead of using the `ItemEvent`, you can rewrite the program to use `ActionEvent` for handling combo box item selection.

The program stores the flag information in three arrays: `flagTitle`, `flagImage`, and `flagDescription` (Lines 11–29). The array `flagTitle` contains the names of nine countries, the array `flagImage` contains images of the nine countries' flags, and the array `flagDescription` contains descriptions of the flags.

The program creates an instance of `DescriptionPanel` (Line 32), which was presented in Example 13.4, "Using Text Areas." The program creates a combo box with initial values from `flagTitle` (Line 68). When the user selects an item in the combo box, the `ItemStateChanged` handler is executed, which finds the selected index and sets its corresponding flag title, flag image, and flag description on the panel.

13.8   Lists

A *list* is a component that basically performs the same function as a combo box but enables the user to choose a single value or multiple values. The Swing `JList` is very versatile. Its advanced features are beyond the scope of this book. This section demonstrates selecting string items from a list.

To create a list with a set of strings, use the following constructor:

```
public JList(Object[] stringItems)
```

where `stringItems` is an array of `String`.

The following properties are often useful:

- **selectedIndex** is an `int` value indicating the index of the selected item in the list.

- **selectedIndices** is an array of `int` values representing the indices of the selected items in the list.

- **selectedValue** is the first selected value in the list.

- **selectedValues** is an array of objects representing selected values in the list.

- **selectionMode** is one of the three values (SINGLE_SELECTION, SINGLE_INTERVAL_SELECTION, MULTIPLE_INTERVAL_SELECTION) that indicate whether a single item, single-interval item, or multiple-interval item can be selected. Single selection allows only one item to be selected. Single-interval selection allows multiple selections, but the selected items must be contiguous. Multiple-interval selection allows selections of multiple contiguous items with no restrictions. The default value is MULTIPLE_INTERVAL_SELECTION.

- **visibleRowCount** is the preferred number of rows in the list that can be displayed without a scroll bar. The default value is 8.

Lists do not scroll automatically. To make a list scrollable, create a scroll pane and add the list to it. Text areas are made scrollable in the same way.

`JList` generates `javax.swing.event.ListSelectionEvent` to notify the listeners of the selections. The listener must implement the `valueChanged` handler to process the event. Here is an example of how to get a selected item from the `valueChanged` (`ListSelectionEvent e`) handler:

```
public void valueChanged(ListSelectionEvent e) {
  String selectedItem = (String)jlst.getSelectedValue();
}
```

Example 13.6 Using Lists

Problem

Write a program that lets users select countries in a list and display the flags of the selected countries in the labels. Figure 13.9 shows a sample run of the program.

continues

Example 13.6 Continued

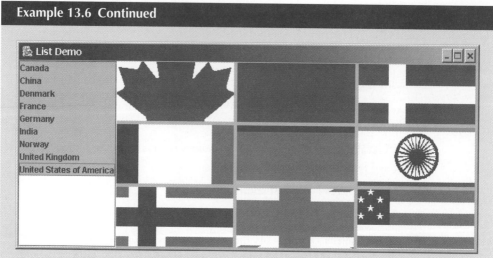

Figure 13.9   *When the countries in the list are selected, corresponding images of their flags are displayed in the labels.*

Solution

Here are the major steps in the program:

1. Create the user interface.

   Create a list with nine country names as selection values, and place the list inside a scroll pane. Place the scroll pane in the west of the frame. Create nine labels to be used to display the countries' flag images. Place the labels in the panel, and place the panel in the center of the frame.

2. Process the event.

   Implement the `valueChanged` method to set the selected countries' flag images in the labels.

```
1    // ListDemo.java: Use list to select a country and display the
2    // selected country's flag
3    package chapter13;
4
5    import java.awt.*;
6    import java.awt.event.*;
7    import javax.swing.*;
8    import javax.swing.event.*;
9
10   public class ListDemo extends JFrame
11     implements ListSelectionListener {
12     final int NUMBER_OF_FLAGS = 9;
13
14     // Declare an array of Strings for flag titles
15     private String[] flagTitle = {"Canada", "China", "Denmark",
16       "France", "Germany", "India", "Norway", "United Kingdom",
17       "United States of America"};
18
19     // The list for selecting countries
20     private JList jlst = new JList(flagTitle);
21
```

```
22        // Declare an ImageIcon array for the national flags of 9 countries
23        private ImageIcon[] imageIcons = {
24          new ImageIcon("image/ca.gif"),
25          new ImageIcon("image/china.gif"),
26          new ImageIcon("image/denmark.gif"),
27          new ImageIcon("image/fr.gif"),
28          new ImageIcon("image/germany.gif"),
29          new ImageIcon("image/india.gif"),
30          new ImageIcon("image/norway.gif"),
31          new ImageIcon("image/uk.gif"),
32          new ImageIcon("image/us.gif")
33        };
34
35        // Arrays of labels for displaying images
36        private JLabel[] jlblImageViewer = new JLabel[NUMBER_OF_FLAGS];
37
38        /** Main Method */
39        public static void main(String[] args) {
40          ListDemo frame = new ListDemo();
41          frame.setSize(650, 500);
42          frame.setTitle("List Demo");
43          frame.setDefaultCloseOperation(JFrame.EXIT_ON_CLOSE);
44          frame.setVisible(true);
45        }
46
47        /** Default Constructor */
48        public ListDemo() {
49          // Create a panel to hold nine labels
50          JPanel p = new JPanel();
51          p.setLayout(new GridLayout(3, 3, 5, 5));
52
53          for (int i = 0; i < NUMBER_OF_FLAGS; i++) {
54            p.add(jlblImageViewer[i] = new JLabel());
55            jlblImageViewer[i].setHorizontalAlignment
56              (SwingConstants.CENTER);
57          }
58
59          // Add p and the list to the frame
60          getContentPane().add(p, BorderLayout.CENTER);
61          getContentPane().add(new JScrollPane(jlst), BorderLayout.WEST);
62
63          // Register listeners
64          jlst.addListSelectionListener(this);
65        }
66
67        /** Handle list selection */
68        public void valueChanged(ListSelectionEvent e) {
69          // Get selected indices
70          int[] indices = jlst.getSelectedIndices();
71
72          int i;
73          // Set icons in the labels
74          for (i = 0; i < indices.length; i++) {
75            jlblImageViewer[i].setIcon(imageIcons[indices[i]]);
76          }
77
78          // Remove icons from the rest of the labels
79          for ( ; i < NUMBER_OF_FLAGS; i++) {
80            jlblImageViewer[i].setIcon(null);
81          }
82        }
83      }
```

continues

555

Example 13.6 Continued

Review

The frame listens to `ListSelectionEvent` for handling the selection of country names in the list, so it implements `ListSelectionListener` (Line 11). `ListSelectionEvent` and `ListSelectionListener` are defined in the `javax.swing.event` package, so this package is imported in the program.

The program creates an array of nine labels for displaying flag images for nine countries. The program loads the images of the nine countries into an image array (Lines 23–33) and creates a list of the nine countries in the same order as in the image array (Line 15–17). Thus the index 0 of the image array corresponds to the first country in the list.

The list is placed in a scroll pane (Line 61) so that it can be scrolled when the number of items in the list extends beyond the viewing area.

By default, the selection mode of the list is multiple-interval, which allows the user to select multiple items from different blocks in the list. When the user selects countries in the list, the `valueChanged` handler (Lines 67–82) is executed, which gets the indices of the selected item and sets their corresponding image icons in the label to display the flags.

13.9   Check Boxes

A *check box* is a component that enables the user to toggle a choice on or off, like a light switch.

To create a check box, use the following constructors:

- `public JCheckBox()`

  Creates an unselected empty check box.

- `public JCheckBox(String text)`

  Creates an unselected check box with the specified text.

- `public JCheckBox(String text, boolean selected)`

  Creates a check box with a text and specifies whether the check box is initially selected.

- `public JCheckBox(Icon icon)`

  Creates an unselected check box with an icon.

- `public JCheckBox(Icon icon, boolean selected)`

  Creates a check box with an icon and specifies whether the check box is initially selected.

■ `public JCheckBox(String text, Icon icon)`

Creates an unselected check box with an icon and a text.

■ `public JCheckBox (String text, Icon icon, boolean selected)`

Creates a check box with an icon and a text, and specifies whether the check box is initially selected.

In addition to text, icon, mnemonic, verticalAlignment, horizontalAlignment, horizontalTextPosition, and verticalTextPosition, JCheckBox has the following property:

selected specifies whether the check box is selected.

JCheckBox can generate ActionEvent and ItemEvent, among many other events. The following code shows you how to implement the itemStateChanged handler to determine whether a box is checked or unchecked in response to an ItemEvent:

```
public void itemStateChanged(ItemEvent e) {
  // Make sure the source is a JCheckBox
  if (e.getSource() instanceof JCheckBox)
    if (jchk1.isSelected())
      // Process the selection for jchk1;
    if (jchk2.isSelected())
      // Process the selection for jchk2;
}
```

Example 13.7 Using Check Boxes

Problem

Write a program that can dynamically change the font of a message to be displayed on a panel. The message can be displayed in bold and italic at the same time, or can be displayed in the center of the panel. You can select the font name or font size from combo boxes, as shown in Figure 13.10.

Figure 13.10   *The program uses three* JCheckBox *components to let the user choose the font style for the message displayed and specify whether the message is centered, and uses combo boxes for selecting font names and font sizes.*

continues

Example 13.7 Continued

Solution

Here are the major steps in the program:

1. Create the user interface.

   Create a panel to hold font name and size combo boxes, and place the panel in the north of the frame. Create a MessagePanel object, and place it in the center of the frame. Create a panel to hold three check boxes for Centered, Bold, and Italic, and place the panel in the south of the frame.

2. Process the event.

   Implement the itemStateChanged method to set appropriate font, size, and style for the message in the MessagePanel based on the item selections from the combo boxes and check boxes.

```
1    // CheckBoxDemo.java: Use check boxes to select one or more choices
2    package chapter13;
3
4    import java.awt.BorderLayout;
5    import java.awt.FlowLayout;
6    import java.awt.Color;
7    import java.awt.Font;
8    import java.awt.GraphicsEnvironment;
9    import java.awt.event.*;
10   import chapter11.MessagePanel;
11   import javax.swing.*;
12
13   public class CheckBoxDemo extends JFrame implements ItemListener {
14     // Declare check boxes
15     private JCheckBox jchkCentered, jchkBold, jchkItalic;
16
17     // Declare a combo box to hold font names
18     private JComboBox jcboFontName = new JComboBox();
19
20     // Declare a combo box to hold font sizes
21     private JComboBox jcboFontSize = new JComboBox();
22
23     // Font name
24     private String fontName = "SansSerif";
25
26     // Font style
27     private int fontStyle = Font.PLAIN;
28
29     // Font Size
30     private int fontSize = 12;
31
32     // Declare a panel for displaying message
33     private MessagePanel messagePanel
34       = new MessagePanel("Welcome to Java!");
35
36     /** Main method */
37     public static void main(String[] args) {
38       CheckBoxDemo frame = new CheckBoxDemo();
39       frame.setDefaultCloseOperation(JFrame.EXIT_ON_CLOSE);
40       frame.pack();
41       frame.setVisible(true);
42     }
43
```

```
44      /** Default constructor */
45      public CheckBoxDemo() {
46        setTitle("Check Box Demo");
47
48        // Set the background color of messagePanel
49        messagePanel.setBackground(Color.yellow);
50
51        // Find all available font names
52        GraphicsEnvironment e =
53          GraphicsEnvironment.getLocalGraphicsEnvironment();
54        String[] fontnames = e.getAvailableFontFamilyNames();
55        for (int i = 0; i < fontnames.length; i++)
56          jcboFontName.addItem(fontnames[i]);
57        jcboFontName.setSelectedItem("" + fontName);
58
59        // Add font sizes into jcboFontSize
60        for (int i = 1; i <= 100; i++)
61          jcboFontSize.addItem("" + i);
62        jcboFontSize.setSelectedItem("" + fontSize);
63
64        // Hold font name label and combo box
65        JPanel p1 = new JPanel();
66        p1.setLayout(new BorderLayout());
67        p1.add(new JLabel("Font Name"), BorderLayout.WEST);
68        p1.add(jcboFontName, BorderLayout.CENTER);
69
70        // Hold font size label and combo box
71        JPanel p2 = new JPanel();
72        p2.setLayout(new BorderLayout());
73        p2.add(new JLabel("Font Size"), BorderLayout.WEST);
74        p2.add(jcboFontSize, BorderLayout.CENTER);
75
76        // Add p1 and p2 into p3
77        JPanel p3 = new JPanel();
78        p3.setLayout(new BorderLayout());
79        p3.add(p1, BorderLayout.CENTER);
80        p3.add(p2, BorderLayout.EAST);
81
82        // Put three check boxes in panel p
83        JPanel p = new JPanel();
84        p.add(jchkCentered = new JCheckBox("Centered"));
85        p.add(jchkBold = new JCheckBox("Bold"));
86        p.add(jchkItalic = new JCheckBox("Italic"));
87
88        // Set keyboard mnemonics
89        jchkCentered.setMnemonic('C');
90        jchkBold.setMnemonic('B');
91        jchkItalic.setMnemonic('I');
92
93        // Place messagePanel, p3, and p in the frame
94        getContentPane().setLayout(new BorderLayout());
95        getContentPane().add(messagePanel, BorderLayout.CENTER);
96        getContentPane().add(p3, BorderLayout.NORTH);
97        getContentPane().add(p, BorderLayout.SOUTH);
98
99        // Register listeners on jcboFontName and jcboFontSize
100       jcboFontName.addItemListener(this);
101       jcboFontSize.addItemListener(this);
102
103       // Register listeners on jchkCentered, jchkBold, and jchkItalic
104       jchkCentered.addItemListener(this);
```

continues

Example 13.7 Continued

```
105            jchkBold.addItemListener(this);
106            jchkItalic.addItemListener(this);
107        }
108
109        /** Handle check box selection */
110        public void itemStateChanged(ItemEvent e) {
111            if (e.getSource() == jcboFontName) {
112                fontName = (String)(jcboFontName.getSelectedItem());
113
114                // Set font for the message
115                messagePanel.setFont(new Font(fontName, fontStyle, fontSize));
116            }
117            else if (e.getSource() == jcboFontSize) {
118                fontSize = Integer.parseInt(
119                    (String)(jcboFontSize.getSelectedItem()));
120
121                // Set font for the message
122                messagePanel.setFont(new Font(fontName, fontStyle, fontSize));
123            }
124            else if ((e.getSource() == jchkBold) ||
125                (e.getSource() == jchkItalic)) {
126                fontStyle = Font.PLAIN;
127
128                // Determine a font style
129                if (jchkBold.isSelected())
130                    fontStyle = fontStyle + Font.BOLD;
131                if (jchkItalic.isSelected())
132                    fontStyle = fontStyle + Font.ITALIC;
133
134                // Set font for the message
135                messagePanel.setFont(new Font(fontName, fontStyle, fontSize));
136            }
137            else if (e.getSource() == jchkCentered) {
138                if (jchkCentered.isSelected())
139                    messagePanel.setCentered(true);
140                else
141                    messagePanel.setCentered(false);
142            }
143        }
144    }
```

Review

The program displays the message using the MessagePanel class. The user can choose a font name, style, and size for the font in MessagePanel. The font name and size are selected in the combo boxes. The font styles (Font.BOLD and Font.ITALIC) are specified in the check boxes. If no font style is selected, the font style is Font.PLAIN. You can also specify whether a message is centered in the Centered check box.

The combo boxes and check boxes can all fire ItemEvent. When the itemStateChanged handler is invoked (Line 110), it checks the source of the event and processes the event accordingly. For an event from the font name combo box, the handler stores the selected font name to fontName (Line 112). For an event from the font size combo box, the handler stores the selected font size to fontSize (Lines 118–119). For an event from a check box, the handler determines the state of each check box and combines all selected fonts (Lines 126–132). The font styles are the int constants Font.BOLD and Font.ITALIC, and the default font style is Font.PLAIN. Font styles are combined by adding together the selected integers representing the fonts. When the Centered check box is checked or unchecked, the centered property of the MessagePanel class is set to true or false (Lines 138–141).

The keyboard mnemonics 'C', 'B', and 'I' are set on the check boxes "Centered," "Bold," and "Italic," respectively (Lines 89–91). You can use a mouse gesture or a shortcut key to select a check box.

The setFont method (Line 135) defined in the Component class is inherited in the MessagePanel class. This method automatically invokes the repaint method. Invoking setFont in messagePanel automatically repaints the message.

13.10   Radio Buttons

Radio buttons, also known as *option buttons*, enable you to choose a single item from a group of choices. In appearance radio buttons resemble check boxes, but check boxes display a square that is either checked or blank, whereas radio buttons display a circle that is either filled (if selected) or blank (if not selected).

The constructors of JRadioButton, shown directly below, are similar to the constructors of JCheckBox.

- ■ public JRadioButton()

  Creates an unselected empty radio button.

- ■ public JRadioButton(String text)

  Creates an unselected radio button with the specified text.

- ■ public JRadioButton(String text, boolean selected)

  Creates a radio button with a text and specifies whether the radio button is initially selected.

- ■ public JRadioButton(Icon icon)

  Creates an unselected radio button with an icon.

- ■ public JRadioButton(Icon icon, boolean selected)

  Creates a radio button with an icon and specifies whether the radio button is initially selected.

- ■ public JRadioButton(String text, Icon icon)

  Creates an unselected radio button with an icon and a text.

- ■ public JRadioButton(String text, Icon icon, boolean selected)

  Creates a radio button with an icon and a text, and specifies whether the radio button is initially selected.

Here is how to create a radio button with a text and an icon:

```
JRadioButton jrb = new JRadioButton(
  "My Radio Button", new ImageIcon("imagefile.gif"));
```

Radio buttons are added to a container just like buttons. To group radio buttons, you need to create an instance of java.swing.ButtonGroup and use the add method to add them to it, as follows:

```
ButtonGroup btg = new ButtonGroup();
btg.add(jrb1);
btg.add(jrb2);
```

This code creates a radio button group for radio buttons jrb1 and jrb2 so that jrb1 and jrb2 are selected mutually exclusively. Without grouping, jrb1 and jrb2 would be independent.

◈ **NOTE**

ButtonGroup is not a subclass of java.awt.Component. So a ButtonGroup object cannot be added to a container.

JRadioButton has such properties as text, icon, mnemonic, verticalAlignment, horizontalAlignment, selected, horizontalTextPosition, and verticalText Position.

JRadioButton can generate ActionEvent and ItemEvent among many other events. The following code shows you how to implement the itemStateChanged handler to determine whether a box is checked or unchecked in response to an ItemEvent:

```
public void itemStateChanged(ItemEvent e) {
  // Make sure the source is a JRadioButton
  if (e.getSource() instanceof JRadioButton)
    if (jrb1.isSelected())
      // Process the selection for jrb1
    else if (jrb2.isSelected())
      // Process the selection for jrb2
}
```

Example 13.8 Using Radio Buttons

Problem

Write a program that simulates a traffic light. The program lets the user select one of three lights: red, yellow, or green. When a radio button is selected, the corresponding light is turned on, and only one light can be on at a time. No light is on when the program starts. Figure 13.11 contains the output of a sample run of the program.

Solution

Here are the major steps in the program:

1. Define a subclass of JPanel named Light to draw three traffic lights (Red, Green, and Yellow). Create a Light object and place it in the center of the frame. Create three radio buttons for Red, Green, and Yellow, place them in a panel, and place the panel in the south of the frame.

Figure 13.11 *The radio buttons are grouped to let you select only one color in the group to control a traffic light.*

2. Create a `ButtonGroup` object and use it to group three radio buttons.

3. Implement the `itemStateChanged` method to check which radio button is selected, and set the corresponding light in the `Light` object.

```
1   // RadioButtonDemo.java: Use radio buttons to select a choice
2   package chapter13;
3
4   import java.awt.*;
5   import java.awt.event.*;
6   import javax.swing.*;
7
8   public class RadioButtonDemo extends JFrame
9     implements ItemListener {
10    // Declare radio buttons
11    private JRadioButton jrbRed, jrbYellow, jrbGreen;
12
13    // Create a radio button group
14    private ButtonGroup btg = new ButtonGroup();
15
16    // Create a traffic light display panel
17    private Light light = new Light();
18
19    /** Main method */
20    public static void main(String[] args) {
21      RadioButtonDemo frame = new RadioButtonDemo();
22      frame.setDefaultCloseOperation(JFrame.EXIT_ON_CLOSE);
23      frame.setSize(250, 170);
24      frame.setVisible(true);
25    }
26
27    /** Default constructor */
28    public RadioButtonDemo() {
29      setTitle("RadioButton Demo");
30
31      // Add traffic light panel to panel p1
32      JPanel p1 = new JPanel();
33      p1.setLayout(new FlowLayout(FlowLayout.CENTER));
34      p1.add(light);
35
36      // Put the radio button in Panel p2
37      JPanel p2 = new JPanel();
38      p2.setLayout(new FlowLayout());
39      p2.add(jrbRed = new JRadioButton("Red"));
40      p2.add(jrbYellow = new JRadioButton("Yellow"));
41      p2.add(jrbGreen = new JRadioButton("Green"));
42
```

continues

563

Example 13.8 Continued

```
43              // Set keyboard mnemonics
44              jrbRed.setMnemonic('R');
45              jrbYellow.setMnemonic('Y');
46              jrbGreen.setMnemonic('G');
47
48              // Group radio buttons
49              btg.add(jrbRed);
50              btg.add(jrbYellow);
51              btg.add(jrbGreen);
52
53              // Place p1 and p2 in the frame
54              getContentPane().setLayout(new BorderLayout());
55              getContentPane().add(p1, BorderLayout.CENTER);
56              getContentPane().add(p2, BorderLayout.SOUTH);
57
58              // Register listeners for check boxes
59              jrbRed.addItemListener(this);
60              jrbYellow.addItemListener(this);
61              jrbGreen.addItemListener(this);
62
63              // Set initial light green
64              jrbGreen.setSelected(true);
65              light.turnOnGreen();
66            }
67
68            /** Handle checkbox events */
69            public void itemStateChanged(ItemEvent e) {
70              if (jrbRed.isSelected())
71                light.turnOnRed(); // Set red light
72              if (jrbYellow.isSelected())
73                light.turnOnYellow(); // Set yellow light
74              if (jrbGreen.isSelected())
75                light.turnOnGreen(); // Set green light
76            }
77          }
78
79          // Three traffic lights shown in a panel
80          class Light extends JPanel {
81            private boolean red;
82            private boolean yellow;
83            private boolean green;
84
85            /** Default constructor */
86            public Light() {
87            }
88
89            /** Set red light on */
90            public void turnOnRed() {
91              red = true;
92              yellow = false;
93              green = false;
94              repaint();
95            }
96
97            /** Set yellow light on */
98            public void turnOnYellow() {
99              red = false;
100             yellow = true;
101             green = false;
102             repaint();
103           }
104
```

```
105     /** Set green light on */
106     public void turnOnGreen() {
107       red = false;
108       yellow = false;
109       green = true;
110       repaint();
111     }
112
113     /** Display lights */
114     protected void paintComponent(Graphics g) {
115       super.paintComponent(g);
116
117       if (red) {
118         g.setColor(Color.red);
119         g.fillOval(10, 10, 20, 20);
120         g.setColor(Color.black);
121         g.drawOval(10, 35, 20, 20);
122         g.drawOval(10, 60, 20, 20);
123         g.drawRect(5, 5, 30, 80);
124       }
125       else if (yellow) {
126         g.setColor(Color.yellow);
127         g.fillOval(10, 35, 20, 20);
128         g.setColor(Color.black);
129         g.drawRect(5, 5, 30, 80);
130         g.drawOval(10, 10, 20, 20);
131         g.drawOval(10, 60, 20, 20);
132       }
133       else if (green) {
134         g.setColor(Color.green);
135         g.fillOval(10, 60, 20, 20);
136         g.setColor(Color.black);
137         g.drawRect(5, 5, 30, 80);
138         g.drawOval(10, 10, 20, 20);
139         g.drawOval(10, 35, 20, 20);
140       }
141       else {
142         g.setColor(Color.black);
143         g.drawRect(5, 5, 30, 80);
144         g.drawOval(10, 10, 20, 20);
145         g.drawOval(10, 35, 20, 20);
146         g.drawOval(10, 60, 20, 20);
147       }
148     }
149
150     /** Set preferred size */
151     public Dimension getPreferredSize() {
152       return new Dimension(40, 90);
153     }
154   }
```

Review

The lights are displayed on a panel. The program groups the radio buttons in a panel and places it below the traffic light panel. BorderLayout is used to arrange these components.

The Light class, a subclass of JPanel, contains the methods turnOnRed(), turnOnYellow(), and turnOnGreen() to control the lights. For example, use light.turnOnRed() to turn on the red light, where light is an instance of Light.

continues

565

Example 13.8 Continued

The program creates a `ButtonGroup` `btg` and puts three `JRadioButton` instances (`jrbRed`, `jrbYellow`, and `jrbGreen`) in the group (Lines 49–51). When the user checks a button in the group, the handler, `itemStateChanged(ItemEvent e)`, determines which radio button is selected, using the `isSelected()` method, and turns on the corresponding light (Lines 70–76).

The `getPreferredSize()` method is overridden to set the preferred size to 40 by 90 (Lines 151–153). This is just the right size for displaying the traffic lights.

13.11   Borders

Borders are an interesting and useful feature. You can set a border on any object of the `JComponent` class, but often it is useful to set a titled border on a `JPanel` that groups a set of related user-interface components.

There are several basic types of borders to choose from. The titled border is the most useful. To create a titled border, use the following statement:

```
Border titledBorder = new TitledBorder("A Title");
```

`Border` is the interface for all types of borders. `TitledBorder` is an implementation of `Border` with a title. You can create a border as desired by using the following properties:

- **title** specifies the title of the border.

- **titleColor** specifies the color of the title.

- **titleFont** specifies the font of the title.

- **titleJustification** specifies `Border.LEFT`, `Border.CENTER`, or `Border.RIGHT` for left, center, or right title justification.

- **titlePosition** is one of the six values (`Border.ABOVE_TOP`, `Border.TOP`, `Border.BELOW_TOP`, `Border.ABOVE_BOTTOM`, `Border.BOTTOM`, `Border.BELOW_BOTTOM`) that specify the title position above the border line, on the border line, or below the border line.

- **border** is a property in `TitleBorder` for building composite borders. You can have borders inside borders.

The other types of borders can be created by using the following classes:

- **BevelBorder** is a 3D-look border that can be lowered or raised. To construct a `BevelBorder`, use the following constructor, which creates a `BevelBorder` with the specified `bevelType` (`BevelBorder.LOWERED` or `BevelBorder.RAISED`):

  ```
  public BevelBorder(int bevelType)
  ```

- **EtchedBorder** is an etched border that can be etched-in or etched-out. You can use its default constructor to construct an EtchedBorder with a lowered border. EtchedBorder has a property etchType with the value LOWERED or RAISED.

- **LineBorder** is a line border of arbitrary thickness and a single color. To create a LineBorder, use the following constructor:

  ```
  public LineBorder(Color c, int thickness)
  ```

- **MatteBorder** is a matte-like border padded with the icon images. To create a MatteBorder, use the following constructor:

  ```
  public MatteBorder(Icon tileIcon)
  ```

- **EmptyBorder** is a border with border space but no drawings. To create an EmptyBorder, use the following constructor:

  ```
  public EmptyBorder(int top, int left, int bottom, int right)
  ```

 NOTE

All the border classes and interfaces are grouped in the package javax.swing.border.

Swing also provides the javax.swing.BorderFactory class, which contains static methods for creating borders. Some of the static methods are:

```
public static TitledBorder createTitledBorder(String title)

public static Border createLoweredBevelBorder()

public static Border createRaisedBevelBorder()

public static Border createLineBorder(Color color)

public static Border createLineBorder(Color color, int thickness)

public static Border createEtchedBorder()

public static Border createEtchedBorder(
  Color highlight, Color shadow)

public static Border createEmptyBorder()

public static Border createEmptyBorder(
  int top, int left, int bottom, int right)

public static MatteBorder createMatteBorder(
  int top, int left, int bottom, int right, Color color)

public static MatteBorder createMatteBorder(
  int top, int left, int bottom, int right, Icon tileIcon)

public static Border createCompoundBorder(
  Border outsideBorder, Border insideBorder)
```

For example, to create an etched border, use the following statement:

```
Border border = BorderFactory.createEtchedBorder();
```

567

◈ **NOTE**

Borders and icons can be shared. Thus you can create a border or icon and use it to set the `border` or `icon` property for any GUI component. For example, the following statements set a border b for two panels p1 and p2:

```
p1.setBorder(b);
p2.setBorder(b);
```

Example 13.9 Using Borders

Problem

Write a program that creates and displays various types of borders. You can select a border with a title or without a title. For a border without a title, you can choose a border style from Lowered Bevel, Raised Bevel, Etched, Line, Matte, or Empty. For a border with a title, you can specify the title position and justification. You can also embed another border into a titled border. Figure 13.12 displays a sample run of the program.

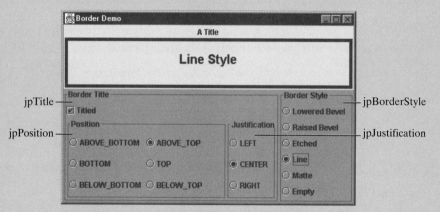

Figure 13.12   *The program demonstrates various types of borders.*

Solution

Here are the major steps in the program:

1. Create the user interface.

   a. Create a `MessagePanel` object and place it in the center of the frame.

   b. Create a panel named `jpPositon` to group the radio buttons for selecting the border title position. Set the border of this panel in the titled border with the title "Position."

   c. Create a panel named `jpJustification` to group the radio buttons for selecting the border title justification. Set the border of this panel in the titled border with the title "Justification."

    d. Create a panel named `jpTitleOptions` to hold the `jpPosition` panel and the `jpJustification` panel.

    e. Create a panel named `jpTitle` to hold a check box named "Titled" and the `jpTitleOptions` panel.

    f. Create a panel named `jpBorderStyle` to group the radio buttons for selecting border styles.

    g. Create a panel named `jpAllChoices` to hold the panels `jpTitle` and `jpBorderStyle`. Place `jpAllChoices` in the south of the frame.

2. Process the event.

    Implement the `actionPerformed` handler to set the border for the message panel according to the events from the check box, and all the radio buttons.

```
1   // BorderDemo.java: Use borders for JComponent components
2   import java.awt.*;
3   import java.awt.event.ActionListener;
4   import java.awt.event.ActionEvent;
5   import javax.swing.*;
6   import javax.swing.border.*;
7
8   public class BorderDemo extends JFrame implements ActionListener {
9     // Declare a panel for displaying message
10    private MessagePanel messagePanel;
11
12    // A check box for selecting a border with or without a title
13    private JCheckBox jchkTitled;
14
15    // Radio buttons for border styles
16    private JRadioButton jrbLoweredBevel, jrbRaisedBevel,
17      jrbEtched, jrbLine, jrbMatte, jrbEmpty;
18
19    // Radio buttons for titled border options
20    private JRadioButton jrbAboveBottom, jrbBottom,
21      jrbBelowBottom, jrbAboveTop, jrbTop, jrbBelowTop,
22      jrbLeft, jrbCenter, jrbRight;
23
24    // TitledBorder for the message panel
25    private TitledBorder messagePanelBorder;
26
27    /** Main method */
28    public static void main(String[] args) {
29      BorderDemo frame = new BorderDemo();
30      frame.setDefaultCloseOperation(JFrame.EXIT_ON_CLOSE);
31      frame.pack();
32      frame.setVisible(true);
33    }
34
35    /** Constructor */
36    public BorderDemo() {
37      setTitle("Border Demo");
38
39      // Create a MessagePanel instance and set colors
40      messagePanel = new MessagePanel("Display the border type");
41      messagePanel.setCentered(true);
```

continues

Example 13.9 Continued

```
42          messagePanel.setBackground(Color.yellow);
43          messagePanel.setBorder(messagePanelBorder);
44
45          // Place title position radio buttons
46          JPanel jpPosition = new JPanel();
47          jpPosition.setLayout(new GridLayout(3, 2));
48          jpPosition.add(
49            jrbAboveBottom = new JRadioButton("ABOVE_BOTTOM"));
50          jpPosition.add(jrbAboveTop = new JRadioButton("ABOVE_TOP"));
51          jpPosition.add(jrbBottom = new JRadioButton("BOTTOM"));
52          jpPosition.add(jrbTop = new JRadioButton("TOP"));
53          jpPosition.add(
54            jrbBelowBottom = new JRadioButton("BELOW_BOTTOM"));
55          jpPosition.add(jrbBelowTop = new JRadioButton("BELOW_TOP"));
56          jpPosition.setBorder(new TitledBorder("Position"));
57
58          // Place title justification radio buttons
59          JPanel jpJustification = new JPanel();
60          jpJustification.setLayout(new GridLayout(3,1));
61          jpJustification.add(jrbLeft = new JRadioButton("LEFT"));
62          jpJustification.add(jrbCenter = new JRadioButton("CENTER"));
63          jpJustification.add(jrbRight = new JRadioButton("RIGHT"));
64          jpJustification.setBorder(new TitledBorder("Justification"));
65
66          // Create panel jpTitleOptions to hold jpPosition and
67          // jpJustification
68          JPanel jpTitleOptions = new JPanel();
69          jpTitleOptions.setLayout(new BorderLayout());
70          jpTitleOptions.add(jpPosition, BorderLayout.CENTER);
71          jpTitleOptions.add(jpJustification, BorderLayout.EAST);
72
73          // Create Panel jpTitle to hold a check box and title position
74          // radio buttons, and title justification radio buttons
75          JPanel jpTitle = new JPanel();
76          jpTitle.setBorder(new TitledBorder("Border Title"));
77          jpTitle.setLayout(new BorderLayout());
78          jpTitle.add(jchkTitled = new JCheckBox("Titled"),
79            BorderLayout.NORTH);
80          jpTitle.add(jpTitleOptions, BorderLayout.CENTER);
81
82          // Group radio buttons for title position
83          ButtonGroup btgTitlePosition = new ButtonGroup();
84          btgTitlePosition.add(jrbAboveBottom);
85          btgTitlePosition.add(jrbBottom);
86          btgTitlePosition.add(jrbBelowBottom);
87          btgTitlePosition.add(jrbAboveTop);
88          btgTitlePosition.add(jrbTop);
89          btgTitlePosition.add(jrbBelowTop);
90
91          // Group radio buttons for title justification
92          ButtonGroup btgTitleJustification = new ButtonGroup();
93          btgTitleJustification.add(jrbLeft);
94          btgTitleJustification.add(jrbCenter);
95          btgTitleJustification.add(jrbRight);
96
97          // Create Panel jpBorderStyle to hold border style radio buttons
98          JPanel jpBorderStyle = new JPanel();
99          jpBorderStyle.setBorder(new TitledBorder("Border Style"));
100         jpBorderStyle.setLayout(new GridLayout(6, 1));
```

```
101        jpBorderStyle.add(jrbLoweredBevel =
102          new JRadioButton("Lowered Bevel"));
103        jpBorderStyle.add(jrbRaisedBevel =
104          new JRadioButton("Raised Bevel"));
105        jpBorderStyle.add(jrbEtched = new JRadioButton("Etched"));
106        jpBorderStyle.add(jrbLine = new JRadioButton("Line"));
107        jpBorderStyle.add(jrbMatte = new JRadioButton("Matte"));
108        jpBorderStyle.add(jrbEmpty = new JRadioButton("Empty"));
109
110        // Group radio buttons for border styles
111        ButtonGroup btgBorderStyle = new ButtonGroup();
112        btgBorderStyle.add(jrbLoweredBevel);
113        btgBorderStyle.add(jrbRaisedBevel);
114        btgBorderStyle.add(jrbEtched);
115        btgBorderStyle.add(jrbLine);
116        btgBorderStyle.add(jrbMatte);
117        btgBorderStyle.add(jrbEmpty);
118
119        // Create Panel jpAllChoices to place jpTitle and jpBorderStyle
120        JPanel jpAllChoices = new JPanel();
121        jpAllChoices.setLayout(new BorderLayout());
123        jpAllChoices.add(jpTitle, BorderLayout.CENTER);
124        jpAllChoices.add(jpBorderStyle, BorderLayout.EAST);
125
126        // Place panels in the frame
127        getContentPane().setLayout(new BorderLayout());
128        getContentPane().add(messagePanel, BorderLayout.CENTER);
129        getContentPane().add(jpAllChoices, BorderLayout.SOUTH);
130
131        // Register listeners
132        jchkTitled.addActionListener(this);
133        jrbAboveBottom.addActionListener(this);
134        jrbBottom.addActionListener(this);
135        jrbBelowBottom.addActionListener(this);
136        jrbAboveTop.addActionListener(this);
137        jrbTop.addActionListener(this);
138        jrbBelowTop.addActionListener(this);
139        jrbLeft.addActionListener(this);
140        jrbCenter.addActionListener(this);
141        jrbRight.addActionListener(this);
142        jrbLoweredBevel.addActionListener(this);
143        jrbRaisedBevel.addActionListener(this);
144        jrbLine.addActionListener(this);
145        jrbEtched.addActionListener(this);
146        jrbMatte.addActionListener(this);
147        jrbEmpty.addActionListener(this);
148      }
149
150      /** Handle ActionEvents on check box and radio buttons */
151      public void actionPerformed(ActionEvent e) {
152        // Get border style
153        Border border = new EmptyBorder(2, 2, 2, 2);
154
155        if (jrbLoweredBevel.isSelected()) {
156          border = new BevelBorder(BevelBorder.LOWERED);
157          messagePanel.setMessage("Lowered Bevel Style");
158        }
159        else if (jrbRaisedBevel.isSelected()) {
160          border = new BevelBorder(BevelBorder.RAISED);
161          messagePanel.setMessage("Raised Bevel Style");
162        }
```

continues

571

Example 13.9 Continued

```
163          else if (jrbEtched.isSelected()) {
164            border = new EtchedBorder();
165            messagePanel.setMessage("Etched Style");
166          }
167          else if (jrbLine.isSelected()) {
168            border = new LineBorder(Color.black, 5);
169            messagePanel.setMessage("Line Style");
170          }
171          else if (jrbMatte.isSelected()) {
172            border = new MatteBorder(20, 20, 20, 20,
173              new ImageIcon("image/swirl.gif"));
174            messagePanel.setMessage("Matte Style");
175          }
176          else if (jrbEmpty.isSelected()) {
177            border = new EmptyBorder(2, 2, 2, 2);
178            messagePanel.setMessage("Empty Style");
179          }
180
181          if (jchkTitled.isSelected()) {
182            // Get the title position and justification
183            int titlePosition = TitledBorder.DEFAULT_POSITION;
184            int titleJustification = TitledBorder.DEFAULT_JUSTIFICATION;
185
186            if (jrbAboveBottom.isSelected())
187              titlePosition = TitledBorder.ABOVE_BOTTOM;
188            else if (jrbBottom.isSelected())
189              titlePosition = TitledBorder.BOTTOM;
190            else if (jrbBelowBottom.isSelected())
191              titlePosition = TitledBorder.BELOW_BOTTOM;
192            else if (jrbAboveTop.isSelected())
193              titlePosition = TitledBorder.ABOVE_TOP;
194            else if (jrbTop.isSelected())
195              titlePosition = TitledBorder.TOP;
196            else if (jrbBelowTop.isSelected())
197              titlePosition = TitledBorder.BELOW_TOP;
198
199            if (jrbLeft.isSelected())
200              titleJustification = TitledBorder.LEFT;
201            else if (jrbCenter.isSelected())
202              titleJustification = TitledBorder.CENTER;
203            else if (jrbRight.isSelected())
204              titleJustification = TitledBorder.RIGHT;
205
206            messagePanelBorder = new TitledBorder("A Title");
207            messagePanelBorder.setBorder(border);
208            messagePanelBorder.setTitlePosition(titlePosition);
209            messagePanelBorder.setTitleJustification(titleJustification);
210            messagePanel.setBorder(messagePanelBorder);
211          }
212          else {
213            messagePanel.setBorder(border);
214          }
215        }
216    }
```

Review

This example uses many panels to group UI components to achieve the desired look. Figure 13.12 illustrates the relationship of the panels. The Border Title panel groups all the options for setting title properties. The position options are grouped in the Position panel. The justification options are grouped in the Justification panel. The Border Style panel groups the radio buttons for choosing Lowered Bevel, Raised Bevel, Etched, Line, Matte, and Empty borders.

The `MessagePanel` displays the selected border with or without a title, depending on the selection of the title check box. The `MessagePanel` also displays a message indicating which type of border is being used, depending on the selection of the radio button in the Border Style panel.

The `TitledBorder` can be mixed with other borders. To do so, simply create an instance of `TitledBorder`, and use the `setBorder` method to embed a new border in `TitledBorder`.

The `MatteBorder` can be used to display icons on the border, as shown in Figure 13.13.

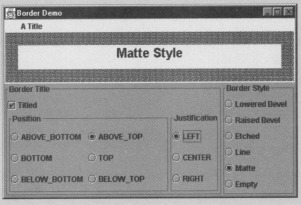

Figure 13.13   `MatteBorder` *can display icons on the border.*

13.12   *JOptionPane* Dialogs

You have used `JOptionPane` to create input and output dialog boxes. This section provides a comprehensive introduction to `JOptionPane` and other dialog boxes. A *dialog box* is normally used as a temporary window to receive additional information from the user or to provide notification that some event has occurred. Java provides the `JOptionPane` class, which can be used to create standard dialogs. You can also build custom dialogs by extending the `JDialog` class.

The `JOptionPane` class can be used to create four kinds of standard dialogs:

■ **Message dialog** shows a message and waits for the user to click OK.

■ **Confirmation dialog** shows a question and asks for confirmation, such as OK or Cancel.

■ **Input dialog** shows a question and gets the user's input from a text field, combo box, or list.

■ **Option dialog** shows a question and gets the user's answer from a set of options.

These dialogs are created using the static methods show*Xxx*Dialog and generally appear as shown in Figure 13.14.

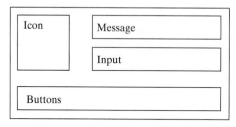

Figure 13.14   *A* JOptionPane *dialog can display an icon, a message, an input, and option buttons.*

For example, you can use the following method to create a message dialog box, as shown in Figure 13.15:

```
JOptionPane.showMessageDialog(null, "SSN not found",
  "For Your Information", JOptionPane.INFORMATION_MESSAGE);
```

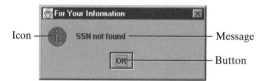

Figure 13.15   *The message dialog displays a message and waits for the user to click OK.*

13.12.1   Message Dialogs

A *message dialog* box displays a message that alerts the user and waits for the user to click the OK button to close the dialog. The methods for creating message dialogs are:

```
public static void showMessageDialog(Component parentComponent,
                                     Object message)
public static void showMessageDialog(Component parentComponent,
                                     Object message,
                                     String title,
                                     int messageType)
public static void showMessageDialog(Component parentComponent,
                                     Object message,
                                     String title,
                                     int messageType,
                                     Icon icon)
```

The parentComponent can be any component or null. The message is an object, but often a string is used. These two parameters must always be specified. The title is a string displayed in the title bar of the dialog with the default value "Message."

574

The messageType is one of the following constants:

```
JOptionPane.ERROR_MESSAGE
JOptionPane.INFORMATION_MESSAGE
JOptionPane.PLAIN_MESSAGE
JOptionPane.WARNING_MESSAGE
JOptionPane.QUESTION_MESSAGE
```

By default, messageType is JOptionPane.INFORMATION_MESSAGE. Each type has an associated icon except the PLAIN_MESSAGE type, as shown in Figure 13.16. You can also supply your own icon in the icon parameter.

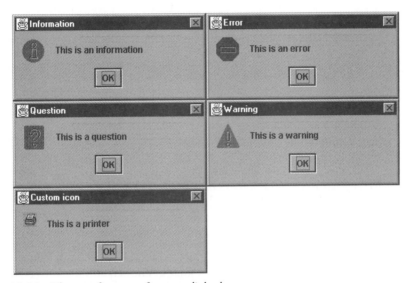

Figure 13.16 *There are five types of message dialog boxes.*

The message parameter is an object. If it is a GUI component, the component is displayed. If it is a non-GUI component, the string representation of the object is displayed. For example, the following statement displays a clock in a message dialog, as shown in Figure 13.17.

Figure 13.17 *A clock is displayed in a message dialog.*

575

```
        JOptionPane.showMessageDialog(null, new stillClock),
          "Current Time", JOptionPane.PLAIN_MESSAGE);
```

13.12.2   Confirmation Dialogs

A message dialog box displays a message and waits for the user to click the OK button to dismiss the dialog. The message dialog does not return any value. A *confirmation dialog* asks a question and requires the user to respond with an appropriate button. The confirmation dialog returns a value that corresponds to a selected button.

The methods for creating confirmation dialogs are:

```
public static int showConfirmDialog(Component parentComponent,
                                    Object message)
public static int showConfirmDialog(Component parentComponent,
                                    Object message,
                                    String title,
                                    int optionType)
public static int showConfirmDialog(Component parentComponent,
                                    Object message,
                                    String title,
                                    int optionType,
                                    int messageType)
public static int showConfirmDialog(Component parentComponent,
                                    Object message,
                                    String title,
                                    int optionType,
                                    int messageType,
                                    Icon icon)
```

The parameters parentComponent, message, title, icon, and messageType are the same as in the showMessageDialog method. The default value for title is "Select an Option" and for messageType is QUESTION_MESSAGE. The optionType determines which buttons are displayed in the dialog. The possible values are:

```
JOptionPane.YES_NO_OPTION
JOptionPane.YES_NO_CANCEL_OPTION
JOptionPane.OK_CANCEL_OPTION
```

Figure 13.18 shows the confirmation dialogs with these options.

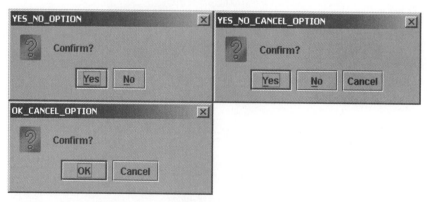

Figure 13.18   *The confirmation dialog displays a question and three types of option buttons, and requires responses from the user.*

The `showConfirmDialog` method returns one of the following `int` values corresponding to the selected option:

```
JOptionPane.YES_OPTION
JOptionPane.NO_OPTION
JOptionPane.CANCEL_OPTION
JOptionPane.OK_OPTION
JOptionPane.CLOSED_OPTION
```

These options correspond to the button that was activated, except for the `CLOSED_OPTION`, which implies that the dialog box is closed without buttons activated.

13.12.3 Input Dialogs

An *input dialog* box is used to receive input from the user. The input can be entered from a text field or selected from a combo box or a list. Selectable values can be specified in an array, and one of them can be designated as the initial selected value. If no selectable value is specified when an input dialog is created, a text field is used for entering input. If fewer than twenty selection values are specified, a combo box is displayed in the input dialog. If twenty or more selection values are specified, a list is used in the input dialog.

The methods for creating input dialogs are shown below:

```
public static String showInputDialog(Object message)
public static String showInputDialog(Component parentComponent,
                                     Object message)
public static String showInputDialog(Component parentComponent,
                                     Object message,
                                     String title,
                                     int messageType)
public static Object showInputDialog(Component parentComponent,
                                     Object message,
                                     int messageType,
                                     Icon icon,
                                     Object[] selectionValues,
                                     Object initialSelectionValue)
```

The first three methods listed above use text field for input, as shown in Figure 13.19. The last method listed above specifies an array of `Object` type as selection values in addition to an object specified as an initial selection. The first three methods return a `String` that is entered from the text field in the input dialog. The last method returns an `Object` selected from a combo box or a list. The input dialog dis-

Figure 13.19 *When creating an input dialog without specifying selection values, the input dialog displays a text field for data entry.*

plays a combo box if there are fewer than twenty selection values, as shown in Figure 13.20; it displays a list if there are twenty or more selection values, as shown in Figure 13.21.

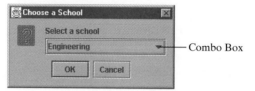

Figure 13.20   *When creating an input dialog with selection values, the input dialog displays a combo box if there are fewer than twenty selection values.*

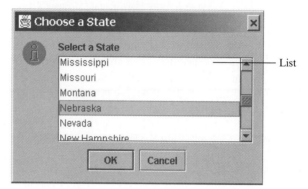

Figure 13.21   *When creating an input dialog with selection values, the input dialog displays a list if there are twenty or more selection values.*

 NOTE

The `showInputDialog` method does not have the `optionType` parameter. The buttons for input dialog are not configurable. The OK and Cancel buttons are always used.

13.12.4   Option Dialogs

An *option dialog* allows you to create custom buttons. You can create an option dialog using the following method:

```
public static int showOptionDialog(Component parentComponent,
                                    Object message,
                                    String title,
                                    int optionType,
                                    int messageType,
                                    Icon icon,
                                    Object[] options,
                                    Object intialValue)
```

The buttons are specified using the `options` parameter. The `intialValue` parameter allows you to specify a button to receive initial focus. The `showOptionDialog` method returns an `int` value indicating the button that was activated. For example, here is the code that creates an option dialog, as shown in Figure 13.22:

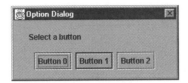

Figure 13.22 *The option dialog displays the custom buttons.*

```
int value =
  JOptionPane.showOptionDialog(null, "Select a button",
    "Option Dialog", JOptionPane.DEFAULT_OPTION,
    JOptionPane.PLAIN_MESSAGE, null,
    new Object[]{"Button 0", "Button 1", "Button 2"}, "Button 1");
```

Example 13.10 Creating JOptionPane Dialogs

Problem

Write a program that demonstrates the use of JOptionPane dialogs. The program prompts the user to select the annual interest rate from a list in an input dialog, the number of years from a combo box in an input dialog, and the loan amount from an input dialog, and displays the loan payment schedule in a text area inside a JScrollPane in a message dialog, as shown in Figure 13.23.

Solution

Here are the major steps in the program:

1. Display an input dialog box to let the user select an annual interest rate from a list.

2. Display an input dialog box to let the user select the number of years from a combo box.

3. Display an input dialog box to let the user enter the loan amount.

4. Compute the monthly payment, total payment, and loan payment schedule, and display the result in a text area in a message dialog box.

```
1   // JOptionPaneDemo.java: Using stadard dialogs
2   package chapter13;
3
4   import javax.swing.*;
5   import chapter6.Loan;
6
7   public class JOptionPaneDemo {
8     public static void main(String args[]) {
9       // Create an array for annual interest rates
10      Object[] rateList = new Object[25];
11      int i = 0;
12      for (double rate = 5; rate <= 8; rate += 1.0 / 8)
13        rateList[i++] = new Double(rate);
14
15      // Prompt the user to select an annual interest rate
16      Object annualInterstRateObject = JOptionPane.showInputDialog(
17        null, "Select annual interest rate:", "JOptionPane Demo",
18        JOptionPane.QUESTION_MESSAGE, null, rateList, null);
```

continues

579

Example 13.10 Continued

```
19          double annualInterestRate =
20            ((Double)annualInterstRateObject).doubleValue();
21
22          // Create an array for number of years
23          Object[] yearList = {new Integer(7), new Integer(15),
24            new Integer(30)};
25
26          // Prompt the user to enter number of years
27          Object numOfYearsObject = JOptionPane.showInputDialog(null,
28            "Select number of years:", "JOptionPane Demo",
29            JOptionPane.QUESTION_MESSAGE, null, yearList, null);
30          int numOfYears = ((Integer)numOfYearsObject).intValue();
31
32          // Prompt the user to enter loan amount
33          String loanAmountString = JOptionPane.showInputDialog(null,
34            "Enter loan amount,\nfor example, 150000 for $150000",
35            "JOptionPane Demo", JOptionPane.QUESTION_MESSAGE);
36          double loanAmount = Double.parseDouble(loanAmountString);
37
38          // Obtain monthly payment and total payment
39          Loan loan = new Loan(
40            annualInterestRate, numOfYears, loanAmount);
41          double monthlyPayment = loan.monthlyPayment();
42          double totalPayment = loan.totalPayment();
43
44          // Prepare output string
45          String output = "Interest Rate: " + annualInterestRate + "%" +
46            " Number of Years: " + numOfYears + " Loan Amount: $"
47            + loanAmount;
48          output += "\nMonthly Payment: " + "$" +
49            (int)(monthlyPayment * 100) / 100.0;
50          output += "\nTotal Payment: $" +
51            (int)(monthlyPayment * 12 * numOfYears * 100) / 100.0 + "\n";
52
53          // Obtain monthly interest rate
54          double monthlyInterestRate = annualInterestRate / 1200;
55
56          double balance = loanAmount;
57          double interest;
58          double principal;
59
60          // Display the header
61          output += "\nPayment#\tInterest\tPrincipal\tBalance\n";
62
63          for (i = 1; i <= numOfYears * 12; i++) {
64            interest = (int)(monthlyInterestRate * balance * 100) / 100.0;
65            principal = (int)((monthlyPayment - interest) * 100) / 100.0;
66            balance = (int)((balance - principal) * 100) / 100.0;
67            output += i + "\t" + interest + "\t" + principal + "\t" +
68              balance + "\n";
69          }
70
71          // Display monthly payment and total payment
72          JOptionPane.showMessageDialog(null,
73            new JScrollPane(new JTextArea(output)),
74            "JOptionPane Demo", JOptionPane.INFORMATION_MESSAGE, null);
75
76          System.exit(0);
77        }
78      }
```

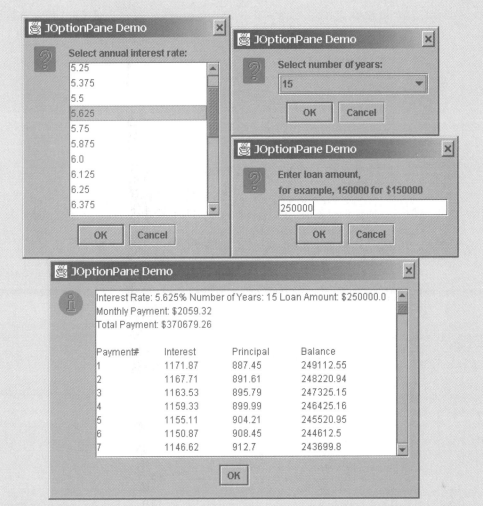

Figure 13.23 *The input dialogs can contain a list or a combo box for selecting input, and the message dialogs can contain GUI objects like* JScrollPane.

Review

The JOptionPane dialog boxes are *modal*, which means that no other window can be accessed until a dialog box is dismissed.

Earlier you used the input dialog box to enter input from a text field. This example shows that input dialog boxes can also contain a list (Lines 16–18) or a combo box (Lines 27–29) to list input options. The elements of the list are objects. The return value from these input dialog boxes is of the Object type. To obtain a double value or a int value, you have to cast the return object into Double or Integer, then use the doubleValue or intValue method to get the double or *int* value (see Lines 19–20 and 30).

continues

Example 13.10 Continued

You have already used the message dialog box to display a string. This example shows that the message dialog box can also contain GUI objects. The output string is contained in a text area, the text area is inside a scroll pane, and the scroll pane is placed in the message dialog box (Lines 72–74).

13.13 Menus

Menus make selection easier and are widely used in window applications. Java provides five classes that implement menus: JMenuBar, JMenu, JMenuItem, JCheckBoxMenuItem, and JRadioButtonMenuItem.

JMenuBar is a top-level menu component used to hold the menus. A menu consists of *menu items* that the user can select (or toggle on or off). A menu item can be an instance of JMenuItem, JCheckBoxMenuItem, or JRadioButtonMenuItem.

13.13.1 Creating Menus

The sequence of implementing menus in Java is as follows:

1. Create a menu bar and associate it with a frame by using the setJMenuBar method.

```
JFrame frame = new JFrame();
frame.setSize(300, 200);
frame.setVisible(true);
JMenuBar jmb = new JMenuBar();
frame.setJMenuBar(jmb);  // Attach a menu bar to a frame
```

This code creates a frame and a menu bar, and sets the menu bar in the frame.

2. Create menus and associate them with the menu bar.

You can use the following constructor to create a menu:

```
public JMenu(String label)
```

Here is an example of creating menus:

```
JMenu fileMenu = new JMenu("File");
JMenu helpMenu = new JMenu("Help");
```

This creates two menus labeled File and Help, as shown in Figure 13.24. The menus will not be seen until they are added to an instance of JMenuBar, as follows:

```
jmb.add(fileMenu);
jmb.add(helpMenu);
```

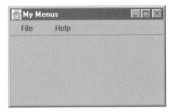

Figure 13.24   *The menu bar appears below the title bar on the frame.*

3. Create menu items and add them to the menus.

```
fileMenu.add(new JMenuItem("New"));
fileMenu.add(new JMenuItem("Open"));
fileMenu.addSeparator();
fileMenu.add(new JMenuItem("Print"));
fileMenu.addSeparator();
fileMenu.add(new JMenuItem("Exit"));
```

This code adds the menu items New, Open, a separator bar, Print, another separator bar, and Exit, in this order, to the File menu, as shown in Figure 13.25.

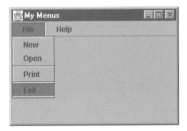

Figure 13.25   *Clicking a menu on the menu bar reveals the items under the menu.*

The addSeparator() method adds a separator bar in the menu.

3.1. Creating submenu items.

You can also embed menus inside menus so that the embedded menus become submenus. Here is an example:

```
JMenu softwareHelpSubMenu = new JMenu("Software");
JMenu hardwareHelpSubMenu = new JMenu("Hardware");
helpMenu.add(softwareHelpSubMenu);
helpMenu.add(hardwareHelpSubMenu);
softwareHelpSubMenu.add(new JMenuItem("Unix"));
softwareHelpSubMenu.add(new JMenuItem("NT"));
softwareHelpSubMenu.add(new JMenuItem("Win95"));
```

This code adds two submenus, softwareHelpSubMenu and hardware-HelpSubMenu, in helpMenu. The menu items Unix, NT, and Win95 are added to softwareHelpSubMenu (see Figure 13.26).

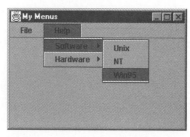

Figure 13.26   *Clicking a menu item reveals the submenu items under the menu item.*

3.2. Creating check box menu items.

You can also add a JCheckBoxMenuItem to a JMenu. JCheckBoxMenuItem is a subclass of JMenuItem that adds a Boolean state to the JMenuItem, and displays a check when its state is true. You can click a menu item to turn it on and off. For example, the following statement adds the check box menu item Check it (see Figure 13.27).

```
helpMenu.add(new JCheckBoxMenuItem("Check it"));
```

Figure 13.27   *A check box menu item lets you check or uncheck a menu item just like a check box.*

3.3. Creating radio button menu items.

You can also add radio buttons to a menu, using the JRadioButton MenuItem class. This is often useful when you have a group of mutually exclusive choices in the menu. For example, the following statements add a submenu named Color and a set of radio buttons for choosing a color (see Figure 13.28):

```
JMenu colorHelpSubMenu = new JMenu("Color");
helpMenu.add(colorHelpSubMenu);

JRadioButtonMenuItem jrbmiBlue, jrbmiYellow, jrbmiRed;
colorHelpSubMenu.add(jrbmiBlue =
  new JRadioButtonMenuItem("Blue"));
colorHelpSubMenu.add(jrbmiYellow =
  new JRadioButtonMenuItem("Yellow"));
colorHelpSubMenu.add(jrbmiRed =
  new JRadioButtonMenuItem("Red"));

ButtonGroup btg = new ButtonGroup();
btg.add(jrbmiBlue);
btg.add(jrbmiYellow);
btg.add(jrbmiRed);
```

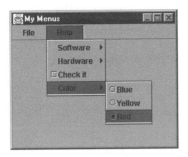

Figure 13.28 *You can use* JRadioButtonMenuItem *to choose among mutually exclusive menu choices.*

4. The menu items generate ActionEvent. Your program must implement the ActionListener and the actionPerformed handler to respond to the menu selection. The following is an example:

```
public void actionPerformed(ActionEvent e) {
  String actionCommand = e.getActionCommand();

  // Make sure the source is JMenuItem
  if (e.getSource() instanceof JMenuItem)
    if ("New".equals(actionCommand))
      respondToNew();
}
```

This code executes the method respondToNew() when the menu item labeled New is selected.

13.13.2 Image Icons, Keyboard Mnemonics, and Keyboard Accelerators

The menu components JMenu, JMenuItem, JCheckBoxMenuItem, and JRadioButton-MenuItem have the icon and mnemonic properties. For example, using the following code, you can set icons for the New and Open menu items, and set keyboard mnemonics for File, Help, New, and Open:

```
JMenuItem jmiNew, jmiOpen;
fileMenu.add(jmiNew = new JMenuItem("New"));
fileMenu.add(jmiOpen = new JMenuItem("Open"));
jmiNew.setIcon(new ImageIcon("image/new.gif"));
jmiOpen.setIcon(new ImageIcon("image/open.gif"));
helpMenu.setMnemonic('H');
fileMenu.setMnemonic('F');
jmiNew.setMnemonic('N');
jmiOpen.setMnemonic('O');
```

The new icons and mnemonics are shown in Figure 13.29. You can also use JMenuItem constructors like the ones that follow to construct and set an icon or mnemonic in one statement.

```
public JMenuItem(String label, Icon icon);
public JMenuItem(String label, int mnemonic);
```

By default, the text is at the right of the icon. Use setHorizontalTextPosition (SwingConstants.LEFT) to set the text to the left of the icon.

Figure 13.29 *You can set image icons, keyboard mnemonics, and keyboard accelerators in menus.*

To select a menu, press the ALT key and the mnemonic key. For example, press ALT + F to select the File menu, and then press ALT + O to select the Open menu item. Keyboard mnemonics can be useful, but only lets you select menu items from the currently open menu. Key accelerators, however, let you select a menu item directly by pressing the CTRL and accelerator keys. For example, by using the following code, you can attach the accelerator key CTRL + O to the Open menu item:

```
jmiOpen.setAccelerator(KeyStroke.getKeyStroke
    (KeyEvent.VK_O, ActionEvent.CTRL_MASK));
```

The `setAccelerator` method takes a `KeyStroke` object. The static method `getKeyStroke` in the `KeyStroke` class creates an instance of the keystroke. `VK_O` is a constant representing the O key, and `CTRL_MASK` is a constant indicating that the CTRL key is associated with the keystroke.

Example 13.11 Using Menus

Problem

Write a program that creates a user interface to perform arithmetic. The interface contains labels and text fields for Number 1, Number 2, and Result. The Result text field displays the result of the arithmetic operation between Number 1 and Number 2. Figure 13.30 contains a sample run of the program.

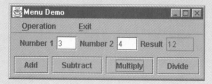

Figure 13.30 *Arithmetic operations can be performed by clicking buttons or by choosing menu items from the Operation menu.*

Solution

Here are the major steps in the program:

1. Create a menu bar and set it in the frame. Create the menus Operation and Exit, and add them to the menu bar. Add the menu items Add, Subtract,

Multiply, and Divide under the Operation menu, and add the menu item Close under the Exit menu.

2. Create a panel to hold labels and text fields, and place the panel in the center of the frame.

3. Create a panel to hold the four buttons labeled Add, Subtract, Multiply, and Divide. Place the panel in the south of the frame.

4. Implement the `actionPerformed` handler to process the events from the menu items and the buttons.

```java
1    // MenuDemo.java: Use menus to move message in a panel
2    package chapter13;
3
4    import java.awt.*;
5    import java.awt.event.*;
6    import javax.swing.*;
7
8    public class MenuDemo extends JFrame implements ActionListener {
9      // Text fields for Number 1, Number 2, and Result
10     private JTextField jtfNum1, jtfNum2, jtfResult;
11
12     // Buttons "Add", "Subtract", "Multiply" and "Divide"
13     private JButton jbtAdd, jbtSub, jbtMul, jbtDiv;
14
15     // Menu items "Add", "Subtract", "Multiply","Divide" and "Close"
16     private JMenuItem jmiAdd, jmiSub, jmiMul, jmiDiv, jmiClose;
17
18     /** Main method */
19     public static void main(String[] args) {
20       MenuDemo frame = new MenuDemo();
21       frame.setDefaultCloseOperation(JFrame.EXIT_ON_CLOSE);
22       frame.pack();
23       frame.setVisible(true);
24     }
25
26     /** Default constructor */
27     public MenuDemo() {
28       setTitle("Menu Demo");
29
30       // Create menu bar
31       JMenuBar jmb = new JMenuBar();
32
33       // Set menu bar to the frame
34       setJMenuBar(jmb);
35
36       // Add menu "Operation" to menu bar
37       JMenu operationMenu = new JMenu("Operation");
38       operationMenu.setMnemonic('O');
39       jmb.add(operationMenu);
40
41       // Add menu "Exit" in menu bar
42       JMenu exitMenu = new JMenu("Exit");
43       exitMenu.setMnemonic('E');
44       jmb.add(exitMenu);
45
```

continues

587

Example 13.11 Continued

```
46        // Add menu items with mnemonics to menu "Operation"
47        operationMenu.add(jmiAdd= new JMenuItem("Add", 'A'));
48        operationMenu.add(jmiSub = new JMenuItem("Subtract", 'S'));
49        operationMenu.add(jmiMul = new JMenuItem("Multiply", 'M'));
50        operationMenu.add(jmiDiv = new JMenuItem("Divide", 'D'));
51        exitMenu.add(jmiClose = new JMenuItem("Close", 'C'));
52
53        // Set keyboard accelerators
54        jmiAdd.setAccelerator(
55          KeyStroke.getKeyStroke(KeyEvent.VK_A, ActionEvent.CTRL_MASK));
56        jmiSub.setAccelerator(
57          KeyStroke.getKeyStroke(KeyEvent.VK_S, ActionEvent.CTRL_MASK));
58        jmiMul.setAccelerator(
59          KeyStroke.getKeyStroke(KeyEvent.VK_M, ActionEvent.CTRL_MASK));
60        jmiDiv.setAccelerator(
61          KeyStroke.getKeyStroke(KeyEvent.VK_D, ActionEvent.CTRL_MASK));
62
63        // Panel p1 to hold text fields and labels
64        JPanel p1 = new JPanel();
65        p1.setLayout(new FlowLayout());
66        p1.add(new JLabel("Number 1"));
67        p1.add(jtfNum1 = new JTextField(3));
68        p1.add(new JLabel("Number 2"));
69        p1.add(jtfNum2 = new JTextField(3));
70        p1.add(new JLabel("Result"));
71        p1.add(jtfResult = new JTextField(4));
72        jtfResult.setEditable(false);
73
74        // Panel p2 to hold buttons
75        JPanel p2 = new JPanel();
76        p2.setLayout(new FlowLayout());
77        p2.add(jbtAdd = new JButton("Add"));
78        p2.add(jbtSub = new JButton("Subtract"));
79        p2.add(jbtMul = new JButton("Multiply"));
80        p2.add(jbtDiv = new JButton("Divide"));
81
82        // Add panels to the frame
83        getContentPane().setLayout(new BorderLayout());
84        getContentPane().add(p1, BorderLayout.CENTER);
85        getContentPane().add(p2, BorderLayout.SOUTH);
86
87        // Register listeners
88        jbtAdd.addActionListener(this);
89        jbtSub.addActionListener(this);
90        jbtMul.addActionListener(this);
91        jbtDiv.addActionListener(this);
92        jmiAdd.addActionListener(this);
93        jmiSub.addActionListener(this);
94        jmiMul.addActionListener(this);
95        jmiDiv.addActionListener(this);
96        jmiClose.addActionListener(this);
97      }
98
100     /** Handle ActionEvent from buttons and menu items */
101     public void actionPerformed(ActionEvent e) {
102       String actionCommand = e.getActionCommand();
103
104       // Handle button events
105       if (e.getSource() instanceof JButton) {
106         if ("Add".equals(actionCommand))
107           calculate('+');
```

```
108            else if ("Subtract".equals(actionCommand))
109              calculate('-');
110            else if ("Multiply".equals(actionCommand))
111              calculate('*');
112            else if ("Divide".equals(actionCommand))
113              calculate('/');
114          }
115        else if (e.getSource() instanceof JMenuItem) {
116          // Handle menu item events
117          if ("Add".equals(actionCommand))
118            calculate('+');
119          else if ("Subtract".equals(actionCommand))
120            calculate('-');
121          else if ("Multiply".equals(actionCommand))
122            calculate('*');
123          else if ("Divide".equals(actionCommand))
124            calculate('/');
125          else if ("Close".equals(actionCommand))
126            System.exit(0);
127        }
128      }
129
130      /** Calculate and show the result in jtfResult */
131      private void calculate(char operator) {
132        // Obtain Number 1 and Number 2
133        int num1 = (Integer.parseInt(jtfNum1.getText().trim()));
134        int num2 = (Integer.parseInt(jtfNum2.getText().trim()));
135        int result = 0;
136
137        // Perform selected operation
138        switch (operator) {
139          case '+': result = num1 + num2;
140                    break;
141          case '-': result = num1 - num2;
142                    break;
143          case '*': result = num1 * num2;
144                    break;
145          case '/': result = num1 / num2;
146        }
147
148        // Set result in jtfResult
149        jtfResult.setText(String.valueOf(result));
150      }
151    }
```

Review

The program creates a menu bar, jmb, which holds two menus: operationMenu and exitMenu (Lines 31–44). The operationMenu contains four menu items for doing arithmetic: Add, Subtract, Multiply, and Divide. The exitMenu contains the menu item Close for exiting the program. The menu items in the Operation menu are created with keyboard mnemonics and accelerators.

The user enters two numbers in the number fields. When an operation is chosen from the menu, its result, involving two numbers, is displayed in the Result field. The user can also click the buttons to perform the same operation.

The private method calculate(char operator) (Lines 131–150) retrieves operands from the text fields in Number 1 and Number 2, applies the binary operator on the operands, and sets the result in the Result text field.

13.14 Creating Multiple Windows

Occasionally, you may want to create multiple windows in an application. Suppose that your application has two tasks: displaying traffic lights and doing arithmetic calculations. You can design a main frame with two buttons representing the two tasks. When the user clicks one of the buttons, the application opens a new window to perform the specified task. The new windows are called *subwindows*, and the main frame is called the *main window*.

To create a subwindow from an application, you need to create a subclass of JFrame that defines the task and tells the new window what to do. You can then create an instance of this subclass in the application and launch the new window by setting the frame instance to be visible.

Example 13.12 Creating Multiple Windows

Problem

Write a program that creates a main window with a text area in the scroll pane and a button named "Show Histogram." When the user clicks the button, a new window appears that displays a histogram to show the occurrence of the letters in the text area. Figure 13.31 contains a sample run of the program.

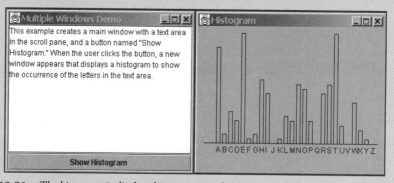

Figure 13.31 *The histogram is displayed in a separate frame.*

Solution

Here are the major steps in the program:

1. Create a main class for the frame named MultipleWindowsDemo. Add a text area inside a scroll pane, and place the scroll pane in the center of the frame. Create a button "Show Histogram" and place it in the south of the frame.

2. Create a subclass of JPanel named Histogram. The class contains a data field named count of the int[] type, which counts the occurrence of twenty-six letters. The values in *count* are displayed in the histogram.

3. Implement the `actionPerformed` handler in `MultipleWindowsDemo`, as follows:

a. Create an instance of `Histogram`. Count the letters in the text area and pass the count to the `Histogram` object.

b. Create a new frame and place the `Histogram` object in the center of frame. Display the frame.

```
1   // MultipleWindowsDemo.java: Display histogram in a separate window
2   package chapter13;
3
4   import java.awt.*;
5   import java.awt.event.*;
6   import javax.swing.*;
7
8   public class MultipleWindowsDemo extends JFrame
9     implements ActionListener {
10    private JTextArea jta;
11    private JButton jbtShowHistogram = new JButton("Show Histogram");
12    private Histogram histogram = new Histogram();
13
14    // Create a new frame to hold the histogram panel
15    private JFrame histogramFrame = new JFrame();
16
17    /** Default construct */
18    public MultipleWindowsDemo() {
19      // Store text area in a scroll pane
20      JScrollPane scrollPane = new JScrollPane(jta = new JTextArea());
21      scrollPane.setPreferredSize(new Dimension(300, 200));
22      jta.setWrapStyleWord(true);
23      jta.setLineWrap(true);
24
25      // Place scroll pane and button in the frame
26      getContentPane().add(scrollPane, BorderLayout.CENTER);
27      getContentPane().add(jbtShowHistogram, BorderLayout.SOUTH);
28
29      // Register listener
30      jbtShowHistogram.addActionListener(this);
31
32      // Create a new frame to hold the histogram panel
33      histogramFrame.getContentPane().add(histogram);
34      histogramFrame.pack();
35      histogramFrame.setTitle("Histogram");
36    }
37
38    /** Handle the button action */
39    public void actionPerformed(ActionEvent e) {
40      // Count the letters in the text area
41      int[] count = countLetters();
42
43      // Set the letter count to histogram for display
44      histogram.showHistogram(count);
45
46      // Show the frame
47      histogramFrame.setVisible(true);
48    }
49
```

continues

591

Example 13.12 Continued

```
50       /** Count the letters in the text area */
51       private int[] countLetters() {
52         // Count for 26 letters
53         int[] count = new int[26];
54
55         // Get contents from the text area
56         String text = jta.getText();
57
58         // Count occurrence of each letter (case insensitive)
59         for (int i = 0; i < text.length(); i++) {
60           char character = text.charAt(i);
61
62           if ((character <= 'A') && (character <= 'Z')) {
63             count[(int)character - 65]++; // The ASCII for 'A' is 65
64           }
65           else if ((character <= 'a') && (character <= 'z')) {
66             count[(int)character - 97]++; // The ASCII for 'a' is 97
67           }
68         }
69
70         return count; // Return the count array
71       }
72
73       /** Main method */
74       public static void main(String[] args) {
75         MultipleWindowsDemo frame = new MultipleWindowsDemo();
76         frame.setDefaultCloseOperation(JFrame.EXIT_ON_CLOSE);
77         frame.setTitle("Multiple Windows Demo");
78         frame.pack();
79         frame.setVisible(true);
80       }
81     }
```

```
1     // Histogram.java: Display a histogram in a panel to show the
2     // occurrence of the letters
3     package chapter13;
4
5     import javax.swing.*;
6     import java.awt.*;
7
8     public class Histogram extends JPanel {
9       // Count the occurrence of 26 letters
10      private int[] count;
11
12      /** Set the count and display histogram */
13      public void showHistogram(int[] count) {
14        this.count = count;
15        repaint();
16      }
17
18      /** Paint the histogram */
19      protected void paintComponent(Graphics g) {
20        if (count == null) return; // No display if count is null
21
22        super.paintComponent(g);
23
24        // Find the panel size and bar width and interval dynamically
25        int width = getWidth();
26        int height = getHeight();
27        int interval = (width - 40) / count.length;
```

```
28          int individualWidth = (int)(((width - 40) / 24) * 0.60);
29
30          // Find the maximum count. The maximum count has the highest bar
31          int maxCount = 0;
32          for (int i = 0; i < count.length; i++) {
33            if (maxCount < count[i])
34              maxCount = count[i];
35          }
36
37          // x is the start position for the first bar in the histogram
38          int x = 30;
39
40          // Draw a horizontal base line
41          g.drawLine(10, height - 45, width - 10, height - 45);
42          for (int i = 0; i < count.length; i++) {
43            // Find the bar height
44            int barHeight =
45              (int)(((double)count[i] / (double)maxCount) * (height - 55));
46
47            // Display a bar (i.e. rectangle)
48            g.drawRect(x, height - 45 - barHeight, individualWidth,
49              barHeight);
50
51            // Display a letter under the base line
52            g.drawString((char)(65 + i) + "", x, height - 30);
53
54            // Move x for displaying the next character
55            x += interval;
56          }
57        }
58
59        /** Override getPreferredSize */
60        public Dimension getPreferredSize() {
61          return new Dimension(300, 300);
62        }
63      }
```

Review

The program contains two classes: `MultipleWindowsDemo` and `Histogram`. Their relationship is shown in Figure 13.32.

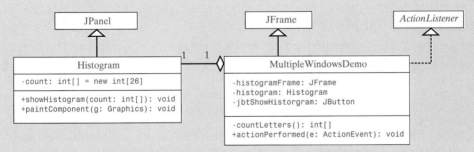

Figure 13.32 *MultipleWindowsDemo uses* Histogram *to display a histogram of the occurrence of the letters in a text area in the frame.*

continues

Example 13.12   Continued

MultipleWindowsDemo is a frame that holds a text area in a scroll pane and a button. Histogram is a subclass of JPanel that displays a histogram for the occurrence of letters in the text area.

When the user clicks the "Show Histogram" button, the handler counts the occurrences of letters in the text area. Letters are counted regardless of their case. Nonletter characters are not counted. The count is stored in an int array of twenty-six elements. The first element stores the count for letter 'a' or 'A,' and the last element in the array stores the count for letter 'z' or 'Z.' The count array is passed to the histogram for display.

The MultipleWindowsDemo class contains a main method. The main method creates an instance of MultipleWindowsDemo and displays the frame. The MultipleWindowsDemo class also contains an instance of JFrame, named histogramFrame, which holds an instance of Histogram. When the user clicks the "Show Histogram" button, histogramFrame is set to visible to display the histogram.

The height and width of the bars in the histogram are determined dynamically according to the window size of the histogram.

You cannot add an instance of JFrame to a container. For example, adding histogramFrame to the main frame would cause a runtime exception. However, you can create a frame instance and set it visible to launch a new window.

13.15   Scrollbars

A *scrollbar* is a control that enables the user to select from a range of values. Scroll bars appear in two styles, *horizontal* and *vertical*.

You can use the following constructors to create a scroll bar:

- public JScrollBar()

  Constructs a new vertical scroll bar.

- public JScrollBar(int orientation)

  Constructs a new scroll bar with the specified orientation (JScrollBar.HORIZONTAL or JScrollBar.VERTICAL).

- public JScrollbar(int orientation, int value, int visible, int minimum, int maximum)

  Constructs a new scroll bar with the specified orientation, initial value, visible bubble size, and minimum and maximum values, as shown in Figure 13.33.

JScrollBar has the following properties:

- **orientation** specifies horizontal or vertical style, with JScrollBar.HORIZONTAL (0) for horizontal and JScrollBar.VERTICAL (1) for vertical.

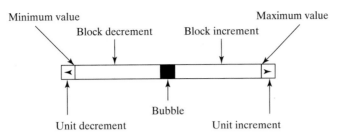

Figure 13.33 *A scroll bar represents a range of values graphically.*

- **maximum** specifies the maximum value the scroll bar represents when the bubble reaches the right end of the scroll bar for horizontal style or the bottom of the scroll bar for vertical style.

- **minimum** specifies the minimum value the scroll bar represents when the bubble reaches the left end of the scroll bar for horizontal style or the top of the scroll bar for vertical style.

- **visibleAmount** specifies the relative width of the scroll bar's bubble. The actual width appearing on the screen is determined by the maximum value and the value of visibleAmount.

- **value** represents the current value of the scroll bar. Normally, a program should change a scroll bar's value by calling the setValue method. The setValue method simultaneously and synchronously sets the minimum, maximum, visible amount, and value properties of a scroll bar, so that they are mutually consistent.

- **blockIncrement** is the value added (subtracted) when the user activates the block-increment (decrement) area of the scroll bar, as shown in Figure 13.33. The blockIncrement property, which is new in JDK 1.1, supersedes the pageIncrement property used in JDK 1.02.

- **unitIncrement** is the value added (subtracted) when the user activates the unit-increment (decrement) area of the scroll bar, as shown in Figure 13.33. The unitIncrement property, which is new in JDK 1.1, supersedes the lineIncrement property used in JDK 1.02.

◈ **NOTE**

The width of the scroll bar's track corresponds to maximum + visibleAmount. When a scroll bar is set to its maximum value, the left side of the bubble is at maximum, and the right side is at maximum + visibleAmount.

Normally, the user changes the value of the scroll bar by making a gesture with the mouse. For example, the user can drag the scroll bar's bubble up and down, or click in the scroll bar's unit-increment or block-increment areas. Keyboard gestures can also be mapped to the scroll bar. By convention, the Page Up and Page Down keys are equivalent to clicking in the scroll bar's block-increment and block-decrement areas.

When the user changes the value of the scroll bar, the scroll bar generates an instance of `AdjustmentEvent`, which is passed to every registered listener. An object that wishes to be notified of changes to the scroll bar's value should implement the `adjustmentValueChanged` method in the `AdjustmentListener` interface defined in the package `java.awt.event`.

Example 13.13 Using Scroll Bars

Problem

Write a program that uses horizontal and vertical scroll bars to control a message displayed on a panel. The horizontal scroll bar is used to move the message to the left or the right, and the vertical scroll bar to move it up and down. A sample run of the program is shown in Figure 13.34.

Figure 13.34   *The scroll bars move the message on a panel horizontally and vertically.*

Solution

Here are the major steps in the program:

1. Create the user interface.

   Create a `MessagePanel` object and place it in the center of the frame. Create a vertical scroll bar and place it in the east of the frame. Create a horizontal scroll bar and place it in the south of the frame.

2. Process the event.

   Implement the `adjustmentValueChanged` handler to move the message according to the bar movement in the scroll bars.

```
1   // ScrollBarDemo.java: Use scroll bars to move the message
2   package chapter13;
3
4   import java.awt.*;
5   import java.awt.event.*;
6   import javax.swing.*;
7   import chapter11.MessagePanel;
8
9   public class ScrollBarDemo extends JFrame
10    implements AdjustmentListener {
11    // Create horizontal and vertical scrollbars
12    private JScrollBar jscbHort =
13      new JScrollBar(JScrollBar.HORIZONTAL);
14    private JScrollBar jscbVert =
15      new JScrollBar(JScrollBar.VERTICAL);
16
```

```
17        // Create a MessagePanel
18        private MessagePanel messagePanel =
19          new MessagePanel("Welcome to Java");
20
21        /** Main method */
22        public static void main(String[] args) {
23          ScrollBarDemo frame = new ScrollBarDemo();
24          frame.setDefaultCloseOperation(JFrame.EXIT_ON_CLOSE);
25          frame.pack();
26          frame.setVisible(true);
27        }
28
29        /** Default constructor */
30        public ScrollBarDemo() {
31          setTitle("ScrollBar Demo");
32
33          // Add scrollbars and message panel to the frame
34          getContentPane().setLayout(new BorderLayout());
35          getContentPane().add(messagePanel, BorderLayout.CENTER);
36          getContentPane().add(jscbVert, BorderLayout.EAST);
37          getContentPane().add(jscbHort, BorderLayout.SOUTH);
38
39          // Register listener for the scrollbars
40          jscbHort.addAdjustmentListener(this);
41          jscbVert.addAdjustmentListener(this);
42        }
43
44        /** Handle scrollbar adjustment actions */
45        public void adjustmentValueChanged(AdjustmentEvent e) {
46          if (e.getSource() == jscbHort) {
47            // getValue() and getMaximumValue() return int, but for better
48            // precision, use double
49            double value = jscbHort.getValue();
50            double maximumValue = jscbHort.getMaximum();
51            double newX =
52              (value * messagePanel.getWidth() / maximumValue);
53            messagePanel.setXCoordinate((int)newX);
54          }
55          else if (e.getSource() == jscbVert) {
56            // getValue() and getMaximumValue() return int, but for better
57            // precision, use double
58            double value = jscbVert.getValue();
59            double maximumValue = jscbVert.getMaximum();
60            double newY =
61              (value * messagePanel.getHeight() / maximumValue);
62            messagePanel.setYCoordinate((int)newY);
63          }
64        }
65      }
```

Review

The program creates an instance of MessagePanel (messagePanel) (Line 18–19) and two scroll bars (jscbVert and jscbHort) (Lines 12–15). messagePanel is placed in the center of the frame; jscbVert and jscbHort are placed in the east and south sections of the frame (Lines 35–37), respectively.

You can specify the orientation of the scroll bar in the constructor or use the setOrientation method. By default, the property value is 100 for maximum, 0 for minimum, 10 for blockIncrement, and 10 for visibleAmount.

Example 13.13   Continued

When the user drags the bubble, or clicks the increment or decrement unit, the value of the scroll bar changes. An instance of `AdjustmentEvent` is generated and passed to the listener by invoking the `adjustmentValueChanged` handler. Since there are two scroll bars in the frame, the `e.getSource()` method is used to determine the source of the event. The vertical scroll bar moves the message up and down, and the horizontal bar moves the message to right and left.

The maximum value of the vertical scroll bar corresponds to the height of the panel, and the maximum value of the horizontal scroll bar corresponds to the width of the panel. The ratio between the current and maximum values of the horizontal scroll bar is the same as the ratio between the x value and the width of the panel. Similarly, the ratio between the current and maximum values of the vertical scroll bar is the same as the ratio between the y value and the height of the panel.

13.16   Scroll Panes

Often you need to use a scroll bar to scroll the contents of an object that does not fit completely into the viewing area. `JScrollBar` can be used for this purpose, but you have to *manually* write the code to implement scrolling with it. `JScrollPane` is a component that supports *automatic* scrolling without coding. It was used to scroll the text area in Example 13.4, "Using Text Areas." In fact, it can be used to scroll any subclass of `JComponent`.

A `JScrollPane` can be viewed as a specialized container with a view port for displaying the contained component. In addition to horizontal and vertical scroll bars, a `JScrollPane` can have a column header, a row header, and corners, as shown in Figure 13.35.

The view port is an instance of `JViewport` through which a scrollable component is displayed. When you add a component to a scroll pane, you are actually placing it in the scroll pane's view port.

To construct a `JScrollPane` instance, use the following constructors:

- `public JScrollPane()`

  Creates an empty scroll pane with a view port and no viewing component where both horizontal and vertical scroll bars appear when needed.

- `public JScrollPane(Component view)`

  Creates a scroll pane and a view port to display the contents of the specified component, where both horizontal and vertical scroll bars appear whenever the component's contents are larger than the view.

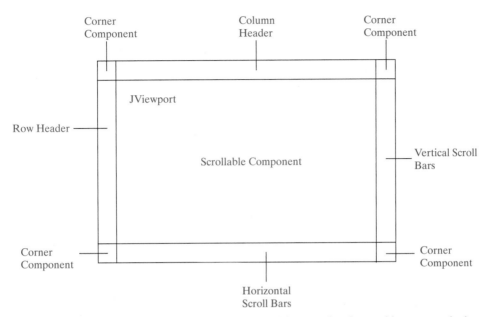

Figure 13.35 *A* JScrollPane *has a view port, optional horizontal and vertical bars, optional column and row headers, and optional corners.*

■ `public JScrollPane(Component view, int vsbPolicy, int hsbPolicy)`

Creates a scroll pane that displays the view component in a view port whose view position can be controlled with a pair of scroll bars.

■ `public JScrollPane(int vsbPolicy, int hsbPolicy)`

Creates an empty scroll pane with specified scroll bar policies.

The constructor always creates a view port regardless of whether the viewing component is specified. The `vsbPolicy` parameter can be one of the following three values:

```
JScrollPane.VERTICAL_SCROLLBAR_AS_NEEDED
JScrollPane.VERTICAL_SCROLLBAR_NEVER
JScrollPane.VERTICAL_SCROLLBAR_ALWAYS
```

The `hsbPolicy` parameter can be one of the following three values:

```
JScrollPane.HORIZONTAL_SCROLLBAR_AS_NEEDED
JScrollPane.HORIZONTAL_SCROLLBAR_NEVER
JScrollPane.HORIZONTAL_SCROLLBAR_ALWAYS
```

The following properties of JScrollPane are often useful:

■ **horizontalScrollBarPolicy** specifies when the horizontal scroll bar appears in the scroll pane. The default value is `JScrollPane.HORIZONTAL_SCROLLBAR_AS NEEDED`.

■ **verticalScrollBarPolicy** specifies when the vertical scroll bar appears in the scroll pane. The default value is `JScrollPane.VERTICAL_SCROLLBAR_AS_NEEDED`.

599

- **viewportView** specifies the component to be viewed in the view port.

- **viewportBorder** specifies a border around the view port in the scroll pane.

- **rowHeaderView** specifies the row header view component to be used in the scroll pane.

- **columnHeaderView** specifies the column header view component to be used in the scroll pane.

To set a corner component, use the following method:

```
public void setCorner(String key, Component corner)
```

The legal values for the key are:

```
JScrollPane.LOWER_LEFT_CORNER
JScrollPane.LOWER_RIGHT_CORNER
JScrollPane.UPPER_LEFT_CORNER
JScrollPane.UPPER_RIGHT_CORNER
```

Example 13.14 Using Scroll Panes

Problem

Write a program that uses a scroll pane to browse a large map. The program lets you choose a map from a combo box and display it in the scroll pane, as shown in Figure 13.36.

Figure 13.36   *The scroll pane can be used to scroll contents automatically.*

Solution

Here are the major steps in the program:

1. Create the user interface.

   Create a scroll pane and place it in the center of the frame. Set the appropriate row header, column header, and corners for the scroll pane. Create a combo box with the string values "Indiana" and "Ohio," and place it in the south of the frame. Create two labels named `lblIndianaMap` and `lblOhioMap` to display maps for Indiana and Ohio.

2. Process the events.

   Implement the `itemStateChanged` handler to set the label `lblIndianaMap` or `lblOhioMap` in the view port of the scroll pane according to whether Indiana or Ohio is selected in the combo box.

```java
// ScrollPaneDemo.java: Use scroll pane to view large maps
package chapter13;

import java.awt.*;
import java.awt.event.*;
import javax.swing.*;
import javax.swing.border.*;

public class ScrollPaneDemo extends JFrame implements ItemListener {
  // Create images in labels
  private JLabel lblIndianaMap =
    new JLabel(new ImageIcon("image/indianaMap.gif"));
  private JLabel lblOhioMap =
    new JLabel(new ImageIcon("image/ohioMap.gif"));

  // Create a scroll pane to scroll map in the labels
  private JScrollPane jspMap = new JScrollPane(lblIndianaMap);

  /** Main method */
  public static void main(String[] args) {
    ScrollPaneDemo frame = new ScrollPaneDemo();
    frame.setDefaultCloseOperation(JFrame.EXIT_ON_CLOSE);
    frame.setSize(300, 300);
    frame.setVisible(true);
  }

  /** Default constructor */
  public ScrollPaneDemo() {
    setTitle("ScrollPane Demo");

    // Create a combo box for selecting maps
    JComboBox jcboMap = new JComboBox();
    jcboMap.addItem("Indiana");
    jcboMap.addItem("Ohio");

    // Panel p to hold combo box
    JPanel p = new JPanel();
    p.setLayout(new BorderLayout());
    p.add(jcboMap);
    p.setBorder(new TitledBorder("Select a map to display"));

    // Set row header, column header and corner header
    jspMap.setColumnHeaderView(
      new JLabel(new ImageIcon("image/horizontalRuler.gif")));
    jspMap.setRowHeaderView(
      new JLabel(new ImageIcon("image/verticalRuler.gif")));
    jspMap.setCorner(JScrollPane.UPPER_LEFT_CORNER,
      new CornerPanel(JScrollPane.UPPER_LEFT_CORNER));
    jspMap.setCorner(ScrollPaneConstants.UPPER_RIGHT_CORNER,
      new CornerPanel(JScrollPane.UPPER_RIGHT_CORNER));
```

continues

Example 13.14 Continued

```
51        jspMap.setCorner(JScrollPane.LOWER_RIGHT_CORNER,
52          new CornerPanel(JScrollPane.LOWER_RIGHT_CORNER));
53        jspMap.setCorner(JScrollPane.LOWER_LEFT_CORNER,
54          new CornerPanel(JScrollPane.LOWER_LEFT_CORNER));
55
56        // Add the scroll pane and combo box panel to the frame
57        getContentPane().add(jspMap, BorderLayout.CENTER);
58        getContentPane().add(p, BorderLayout.NORTH);
59
60        // Register listener
61        jcboMap.addItemListener(this);
62      }
63
64      /** Show the selected map */
65      public void itemStateChanged(ItemEvent e) {
66        String selectedItem = (String)e.getItem();
67        if (selectedItem.equals("Indiana")) {
68          // Set a new view in the view port
69          jspMap.setViewportView(lblIndianaMap);
70        }
71        else if (selectedItem.equals("Ohio")) {
72          // Set a new view in the view port
73          jspMap.setViewportView(lblOhioMap);
74        }
75
76        // Revalidate the scroll pane
77        jspMap.revalidate();
78      }
79    }
80
81    // A panel displaying a line used for scroll pane corner
82    class CornerPanel extends JPanel implements ScrollPaneConstants {
83      // Line location
84      private String location;
85
86      /** Default constructor */
87      public CornerPanel(String location) {
88        this.location = location;
89      }
90
91      /** Draw a line depending on the location */
92      protected void paintComponent(Graphics g) {
93        super.paintComponents(g);
94
95        if (location == "UPPER_LEFT_CORNER")
96          g.drawLine(0, getHeight(), getWidth(), 0);
97        else if (location == "UPPER_RIGHT_CORNER")
98          g.drawLine(0, 0, getWidth(), getHeight());
99        else if (location == "LOWER_RIGHT_CORNER")
100          g.drawLine(0, getHeight(), getWidth(), 0);
101        else if (location == "LOWER_LEFT_CORNER")
102          g.drawLine(0, 0, getWidth(), getHeight());
103      }
104    }
```

Review

The program creates a scroll pane to view image maps. The image maps are created using the ImageIcon class and are placed in labels (Lines 11–14). To view an image, the label that contains the image is placed in the scroll pane's view port.

The scroll pane has a main view, a header view, a column view, and four corner views. Each view is a subclass of `Component`. Since `ImageIcon` is not a subclass of `Component`, it cannot be directly used as a view in the scroll pane. Instead the program places an `ImageIcon` to a label and uses the label as a view.

The `CornerPanel` (Lines 81–103) is a subclass of `JPanel`, which is used to display a line. How the line is drawn depends on the `location` of the corner. The `location` is a string, passed in as a parameter in the `CornerPanel`'s constructor. The `CornerPanel` class also implements the `ScrollPaneConstants` interface. The constants representing the location of the four corners are available in `CornerPanel`.

Whenever a new map is selected, the label for displaying the map image is set to the scroll pane's view port. The `validate()` method (Line 77) must be invoked to cause the new image to be displayed. The `validate()` method causes a container to lay out its subcomponents again after the components it contains have been added to or modified.

13.17   Tabbed Panes

`JTabbedPane` is a useful Swing component that provides a set of mutually exclusive tabs for accessing multiple components. Usually you place the panels inside a `JTabbedPane` and associate a tab with each panel. `JTabbedPane` is easy to use, since the selection of the panel is handled automatically by clicking the corresponding tab. You can switch between a group of panels by clicking a tab with a given title and/or icon.

To construct a `JTabbedPane` instance, use the following constructors:

■   `public JTabbedPane()`

   Creates an empty tabbed pane.

■   `public JTabbedPane(int tabPlacement)`

   Creates an empty `JTabbedPane` with the specified tab placement of either `SwingConstants.TOP`, `SwingConstants.BOTTOM`, `SwingConstants.LEFT`, or `Swing-Constants.RIGHT`.

You can also set the tab placement using the following method:

```
public void setTabPlacement(int tabPlacement)
```

By default, the tabs are placed at the top.

To add a component to a `JTabbedPane`, use the following add method:

```
add(Component component, Object constraints)
```

where `component` is the component to be displayed when the tab is clicked, and `constraints` can be a title for the tab.

603

Example 13.15 Using Tabbed Panes

Problem

Write a program that uses a tabbed pane with four tabs to display four types of figures: a square, a rectangle, a circle, and an oval. You click the corresponding tab to select a figure to be displayed. You can also use the radio buttons to specify the tab placement. A sample run of the program is shown in Figure 13.37.

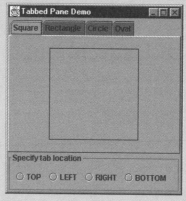

Figure 13.37 *A tabbed pane can be used to access multiple components using tabs.*

Solution

Here are the major steps in the program:

1. Create a subclass of JPanel named FigurePanel to display the figures based on the figureType property in the class.

2. Create the user interface.

   Create a JTabbedPane object and place it in the center of the frame. Create four objects of FigurePanel for square, rectangle, circle, and oval, and add them to the tabbed pane. Create a panel to hold four radio buttons for specifying tab locations. Place the panel in the south of frame.

3. Process the events.

   Implement the itemStateChanged handler to set the location of the tabs according to the selection of the radio buttons.

```
1   // TabbedPaneDemo.java: Use tabbed pane to select figures
2   package chapter13;
3
4   import java.awt.*;
5   import java.awt.event.*;
6   import javax.swing.*;
7   import javax.swing.border.TitledBorder;
8
9   public class TabbedPaneDemo extends JFrame implements ItemListener {
10    // Create a tabbed pane to hold figure panels
11    private JTabbedPane jtpFigures = new JTabbedPane();
12
```

```
13      // Radio buttons for specifying where tab is placed
14      private JRadioButton jrbTop, jrbLeft, jrbRight, jrbBottom;
15
16      /** Main method */
17      public static void main(String[] args) {
18        TabbedPaneDemo frame = new TabbedPaneDemo();
19        frame.setDefaultCloseOperation(JFrame.EXIT_ON_CLOSE);
20        frame.setSize(200, 300);
21        frame.setVisible(true);
22      }
23
24      /** Default constructor */
25      public TabbedPaneDemo() {
26        setTitle("Tabbed Pane Demo");
27
28        jtpFigures.add(new FigurePanel(FigurePanel.SQUARE), "Square");
29        jtpFigures.add(
30          new FigurePanel(FigurePanel.RECTANGLE), "Rectangle");
31        jtpFigures.add(new FigurePanel(FigurePanel.CIRCLE), "Circle");
32        jtpFigures.add(new FigurePanel(FigurePanel.OVAL), "Oval");
33
34        // Panel p to hold radio buttons for specifying tab location
35        JPanel p = new JPanel();
36        p.add(jrbTop = new JRadioButton("TOP"));
37        p.add(jrbLeft = new JRadioButton("LEFT"));
38        p.add(jrbRight = new JRadioButton("RIGHT"));
39        p.add(jrbBottom = new JRadioButton("BOTTOM"));
40        p.setBorder(new TitledBorder("Specify tab location"));
41
42        // Group radio buttons
43        ButtonGroup btg = new ButtonGroup();
44        btg.add(jrbTop);
45        btg.add(jrbLeft);
46        btg.add(jrbRight);
47        btg.add(jrbBottom);
48
49        // Select the Top radio button
50        jrbTop.setSelected(true);
51
52        // Place tabbed pane and panel p into the frame
53        this.getContentPane().add(jtpFigures, BorderLayout.CENTER);
54        this.getContentPane().add(p, BorderLayout.SOUTH);
55
56        // Register listeners
57        jrbTop.addItemListener(this);
58        jrbLeft.addItemListener(this);
59        jrbRight.addItemListener(this);
60        jrbBottom.addItemListener(this);
61      }
62
63      /** Handle radio button selection */
64      public void itemStateChanged(ItemEvent e) {
65        if (jrbTop.isSelected())
66          jtpFigures.setTabPlacement(SwingConstants.TOP);
67        else if (jrbLeft.isSelected())
68          jtpFigures.setTabPlacement(SwingConstants.LEFT);
69        else if (jrbRight.isSelected())
70          jtpFigures.setTabPlacement(SwingConstants.RIGHT);
71        else if (jrbBottom.isSelected())
72          jtpFigures.setTabPlacement(SwingConstants.BOTTOM);
73      }
74    }
75
```

continues

605

Example 13.15 Continued

```
76      // The panel for displaying a figure
77      class FigurePanel extends JPanel {
78        final static int SQUARE = 1;
79        final static int RECTANGLE = 2;
80        final static int CIRCLE = 3;
81        final static int OVAL = 4;
82        private int figureType = 1;
83
84        /** Construct a panel for a specified figure */
85        public FigurePanel(int figureType) {
86          this.figureType = figureType;
87        }
88
89        /** Return figureType */
90        public int getFigureType() {
91          return figureType;
92        }
93
94        /** Set figureType */
95        public void setFigureType(int figureType) {
96          this.figureType = figureType;
97          repaint();
98        }
99
100       /** Draw a figure on the panel */
101       protected void paintComponent(Graphics g) {
102         super.paintComponent(g);
103
104         // Get the appropriate size for the figure
105         int width = getWidth();
106         int height = getHeight();
107         int side = (int)(0.80 * Math.min(width, height));
108
109         switch (figureType) {
110           case 1:
111             g.drawRect((width - side) / 2, (height - side) / 2,
112               side, side);
113             break;
114           case 2:
115             g.drawRect((int)(0.1 * width), (int)(0.1 * height),
116               (int)(0.8 * width), (int)(0.8 * height));
117             break;
118           case 3:
119             g.drawOval((width - side) /2, (height - side) / 2,
120               side, side);
121             break;
122           case 4:
123             g.drawOval((int)(0.1 * width), (int)(0.1 * height),
124               (int)(0.8 * width), (int)(0.8 * height));
125             break;
126         }
127       }
128     }
```

Review

The program creates a tabbed pane that holds four panels, each of which displays a figure. A panel is associated with a tab. Tabs are created using the add method and are titled Square, Rectangle, Circle, and Oval (Lines 28–32).

By default, the tabs are placed at the top of the tabbed pane. You can use the radio buttons to select a different placement, as shown in Figure 13.38.

Figure 13.38 *The tabs can be placed at the top, bottom, left, or right of the tabbed pane.*

Chapter Summary

- Commonly used properties in `Component` are `font`, `background`, `foreground`, `height`, `width`, `preferredSize`, and `minimumSize`.

- Commonly used properties in `JComponent` are `toolTipText`, `doubleBuffered`, and `border`.

- `JButton` is used to activate actions. The user expects something to happen when a button is clicked. Clicking a button generates the `ActionEvent` and invokes the listener's `actionPerformed` method. Commonly used properties in `JButton` are `text`, `icon`, `mnemonic`, `horizontalAlignment`, `verticalAlignment`, `HorizontalTextPosition`, and `verticalTextPosition`.

- `JLabel` is an area for displaying texts or images, or both. Commonly used properties in `JLabel` are `text`, `icon`, `horizontalAlignment`, and `vertical Alignment`.

- `JTextField` is used to accept user input into a string. Commonly used properties in `JLabel` are `text`, `horizontalAlignment`, `editable`, and `columns`. `JTextField` can generate `ActionEvent` among many other events. Pressing Enter in a text field triggers the `ActionEvent`.

- `JTextArea` can accept multiple lines of strings. Commonly used properties in `JTextArea` are `text`, `editable`, `columns`, `lineWrap`, `wrapStyleWord`, `rows`, `lineCount`, and `tabSize`.

- A *combo box*, also known as *choice* or *drop-down list*, is a simple list of items from which the user can choose. It is useful in limiting a user's range of choices and avoids the cumbersome validation of data input. `JComboBox` can generate `ActionEvent` and `ItemEvent`, among many other events. Commonly used properties in `JComboBox` are `selectedIndex` and `selectedItem`. Commonly used methods are `addItem(Object)`, `getItemAt(index)`, `remove-Item(Object)`, and `removeAllItems()`.

■ A *list* is a component that basically performs the same function as a combo box but enables the user to choose a single value or multiple values. Commonly used properties in `JComboBox` are `selectedIndex`, `selectedIndices`, `selectedValue`, `selectedValues`, `selectionMode`, and `visibleRowCount`. `JList` generates `javax.swing.event.ListSelectionEvent` to notify the listeners of the selections. The listener must implement the `valueChanged` handler to process the event.

■ A *check box* is a component that enables the user to toggle a choice on or off, like a light switch.

■ Commonly used properties in `JComboBox` are `text`, `icon`, `mnemonic`, `verticalAlignment`, `horizontalAlignment`, `horizontalTextPosition`, `verticalTextPosition`, and `selected`. `JCheckBox` can generate `ActionEvent` and `ItemEvent`, among many other events.

■ *Radio buttons*, also known as *option buttons*, enable you to choose a single item from a group of choices.

■ `JRadioButton` is similar to `JCheckBox`, but is generally used to select a value exclusively. `JRadioButton` has such properties as `text`, `icon`, `mnemonic`, `verticalAlignment`, `horizontalAlignment`, `selected`, `horizontalTextPosition`, and `verticalTextPosition`. `JRadioButton` can generate `ActionEvent` and `ItemEvent` among many other events.

■ You can set a border on any Swing UI component.

■ There are several basic types of borders to choose from. The titled border is the most useful. To create a titled border, use `Border titledBorder = new TitledBorder("A Title")`.

■ The `JOptionPane` class can be used to create four kinds of standard dialogs: Message dialog, Confirmation dialog, Input dialog, and Option dialog.

■ Menus can be placed in a frame or an applet. A menu bar is used to hold the menus. You must use the `setJMenuBar` method to add a menu bar to the frame or applet, add menus to the menu bar, and add menu items to a menu.

■ Scroll bars are the controls for selecting from a range of values. You can create scroll bars using the `JScrollBar` class and specify horizontal or vertical scroll bars using the `setOrientation` method.

■ `JScrollPane` provides automatic scrolling, so using it is convenient in most cases.

■ JTabbedPane can be used to select multiple panels using tabs. The tabs can be placed at the top, left, right, or bottom. Since tab selection is automatically implemented in JTabbedPane, clicking a tab causes the associated panel to be displayed.

Review Questions

13.1 How do you create a button labeled "OK"? How do you change text on a button? How do you set an icon in a button?

13.2 How do you create a label named "Address"? How do you change the name on a label? How do you set an icon in a label?

13.3 How do you create a text field with ten columns and the default text "Welcome to Java"?

13.4 How do you create a text area with ten rows and twenty columns? How do you insert three lines into the text area? How do you create a scrollable text area?

13.5 How do you create a combo box, add three items to it, and retrieve a selected item?

13.6 How do you create a check box? How do you determine whether a check box is selected?

13.7 How do you create a radio button? How do you group the radio buttons together? How do you determine whether a radio button is selected?

13.8 Can you have a border for any subclass of JComponent? How do you set a titled border for a panel?

13.9 How do you create the menus File, Edit, View, Insert, Format, and Help, and add the menu items Toolbar, Format Bar, Ruler, Status Bar, and Options to the View menu? (See Figure 13.39.)

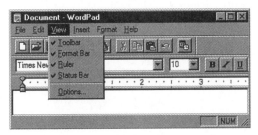

Figure 13.39 *Create a menu like this in WordPad, with menus and menu items.*

13.10 How do you create a vertical scroll bar? What event can a scroll bar generate?

13.11 How do you create a scroll pane to view an image file?

13.12 Describe how to create a simple message dialog box. Describe the message types used in the JOptionPane class.

13.13 Explain how to create and show multiple frames in an application.

13.14 What method causes the layout manager to lay out the components in a container again? When should a container be laid out again?

13.15 Suppose you want to display the same component named c in the four corners of a scroll pane named jsp. What would be wrong with using the following statements?

```
jsp.setCorner(JScrollPane.UPPER_LEFT_CORNER, c);
jsp.setCorner(JScrollPane.UPPER_RIGHT_CORNER, c);
jsp.setCorner(JScrollPane.LOWER_RIGHT_CORNER, c);
jsp.setCorner(JScrollPane.LOWER_LEFT_CORNER, c);
```

(Since each corner view is an individual component, you need to create four separate objects.)

13.16 Can you share a border or icon for GUI components?

13.17 Which of the following statements have syntax errors?

```
Component c1 = new Component();
JComponent c2 = new JComponent();
Component c3 = new JButton();
JComponent c4 = new JButton();
Container c5 = new JButton();
c5.add(c4);
Object c6 = new JButton();
c5.add(c6);
```

13.18 What happens if you add a button to a container several times, as follows?

```
JButton jbt = new JButton();
JPanel panel = new JPanel();
panel.add(jbt);
panel.add(jbt);
panel.add(jbt);
```

Programming Exercises

13.1 (Revising Example 13.1 "Using Buttons") Rewrite Example 13.1 to add a group of radio buttons to select background colors. The available colors are red, yellow, white, gray, and green (see Figure 13.40).

Figure 13.40   *The <= and => buttons move the message on the panel, and you can also set the color for the message.*

13.2 (Creating a simple calculator) Write a program to perform add, subtract, multiply, and divide operations (see Figure 13.41).

Figure 13.41 *The program does addition, subtraction, multiplication, and division on double numbers.*

13.3 (Adding new features into Example 13.1, "Using Buttons," incrementally) Improve Example 13.1 incrementally as follows (see Figure 13.42):

1. Add a text field labeled "Enter a new message" in the same panel with the buttons. Upon typing a new message in the text field and pressing the Enter key, the new message is displayed in the message panel.

2. Add a combo box labeled "Select an interval" in the same panel with the buttons. The combo box enables the user to select a new interval for moving the message. The selection values range from 5 to 100 with interval 5. The user can also type a new interval in the combo box.

3. Add three radio buttons that enable the user to select the foreground color for the message as Red, Green, and Blue. The radio buttons are grouped in a panel, and the panel is placed in the north of the frame's content pane.

4. Add three check boxes that enable the user to center the message and display it in italic or bold. Place the check boxes in the same panel with the radio buttons.

5. Add a border titled "Message Panel" on the message panel, add a border titled "South Panel" on the panel for buttons, and add a border titled "North Panel" on the panel for radio buttons and check boxes.

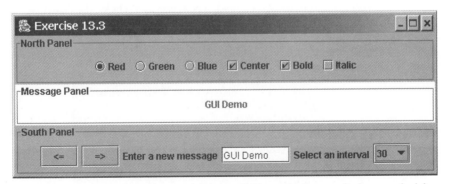

Figure 13.42 *The program uses buttons, labels, text fields, combo boxes, radio buttons, check boxes, and borders.*

13.4 (Creating a miles/kilometers converter) Write a program that converts miles and kilometers, as shown in Figure 13.43. If you enter a value in the Mile text field and press the Enter key, the corresponding kilometer is displayed in the Kilometer text field. Likewise, if you enter a value in the Kilometer text field and press the Enter key, the corresponding mile is displayed in the Mile text field.

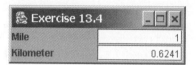

Figure 13.43   *The program converts miles to kilometers, and vice versa.*

13.5 (Selecting geometric figures) Write a program that draws various figures on a panel. The user selects a figure from a radio button. The selected figure is then displayed on the panel (see Figure 13.44).

Figure 13.44   *The program displays lines, rectangles, ovals, arcs, or polygons when you select a shape type.*

13.6 (Creating an investment value calculator) Write a program that calculates the future value of an investment at a given interest rate for a specified number of years. The formula for the calculation is as follows:

$$futureValue = investmentAmount * (1 + monthlyInterestRate)^{years*12}$$

Use text fields for interest rate, investment amount, and years. Display the future amount in a text field when the user clicks the Calculate button or chooses Calculate from the Operation menu (see Figure 13.45). Show a mes-

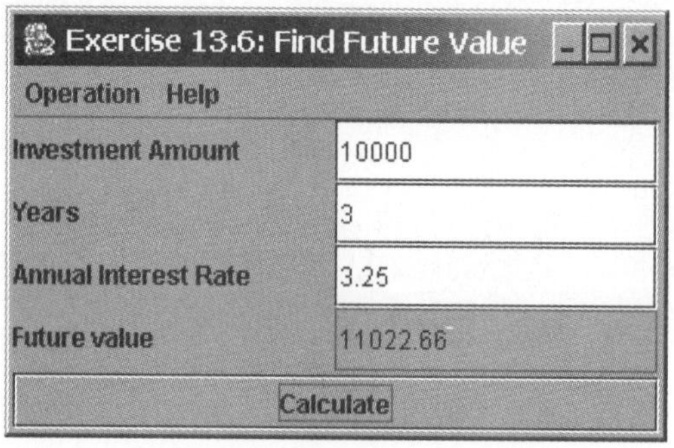

Figure 13.45   *The user enters the investment amount, years, and interest rate to compute future value.*

sage dialog box when the user clicks the About menu item from the Help menu.

13.7 (Collecting information) Write a program that lets users enter their name, department, university, city, state, and zip code, and stores the information in a text area. The state is a JComboBox item. Figure 13.46 shows a sample run of the program.

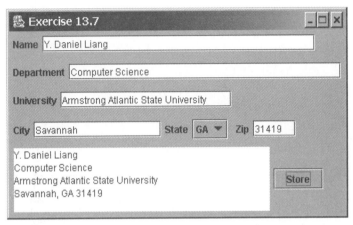

Figure 13.46 *When the Store button is clicked, the name, department, university, city, state, and zip code are displayed in the text area.*

13.8 (Creating multiple windows) Create a main window with two buttons: Simple Calculator and Traffic Lights. When the user clicks Simple Calculator, a new window appears. This new window lets the user perform add, subtract, multiply, and divide operations. When the user clicks Traffic Lights, another window appears that displays traffic lights (see Figure 13.47).

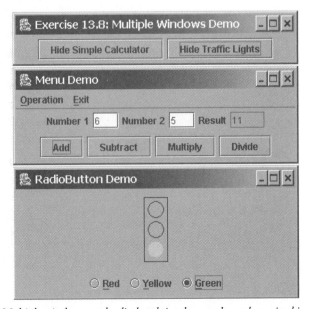

Figure 13.47 *Multiple windows can be displayed simultaneously, as shown in this exercise.*

The Simple Calculator frame named MenuDemo is given in Example 13.11, "Using Menus," and the Traffic Lights frame named RadioButtonDemo is given in Example 13.8, "Using Radio Buttons." They can be used directly in this exercise without modification.

When the user clicks the Simple Calculator button, the Calculator window appears, and the name of the button changes to Hide Calculator. When the user clicks the Hide Calculator button, the window is closed, and the name of the button changes back to Simple Calculator. Implement the function of the Traffic Lights button in the same way.

13.9 (Creating a color selector) Write a program that uses scroll bars to select the foreground color for a label, as shown in Figure 13.48. Three horizontal scroll bars are used for selecting the red, green, and blue components of the color. Use a title border on the panel that holds the scroll bars.

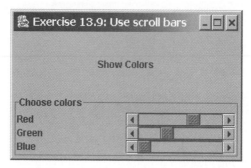

Figure 13.48   *The foreground color changes in the label as you adjust the scrollbars.*

13.10 (Computing sales amount/commission) Write a program that computes sales amount or commission, as shown in Figure 13.49. When the user types a sales amount in the Sales Amount text field and presses the Enter key, the commission is displayed in the Commission text field. Likewise, when the user types a commission, the corresponding sales amount is displayed. The commission rates are the same as in Example 3.7, "Finding the Sales Amount." The commission rates are displayed using labels.

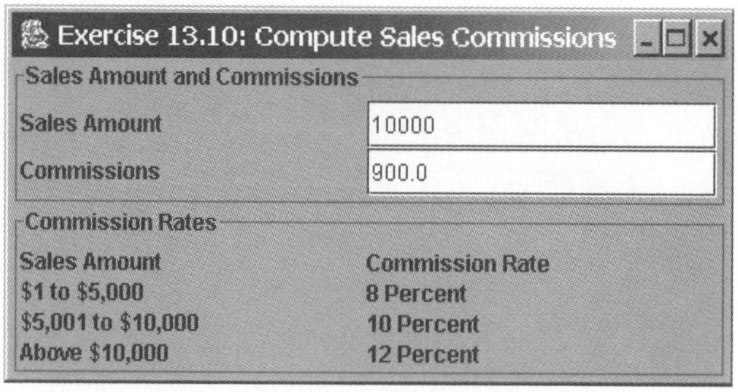

Figure 13.49   *The sales amount and the commission are synchronized. You can compute sales amount given the commission or commission given the sales amount.*

13.11 (Demonstrating JButton properties) Write a program that sets the alignment and text position properties of a button dynamically, as shown in Figure 13.50. The program places a button in the center of the frame. The button has a text "Banana," and an image icon for banana. Use combo boxes for the user to select horizontal-position alignment, vertical-position alignment, text horizontal–position alignment, and text vertical–position alignment.

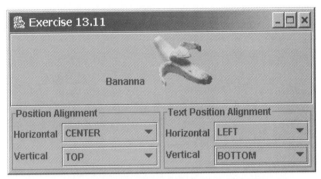

Figure 13.50 *You can set the alignment and text-position properties of a button dynamically.*

13.12 (Demonstrating JTextField properties) Write a program that sets the horizontal-alignment and column-size properties of a text field dynamically, as shown in Figure 13.51.

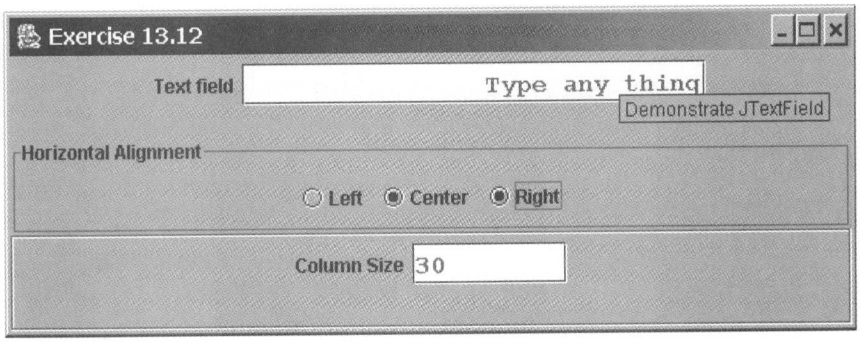

Figure 13.51 *You can set the horizontal-alignment and column-size properties of a text field dynamically.*

13.13 (Demonstrating JTextArea properties) Write a program that demonstrates the wrapping styles of the text area. The program uses a check box to indicate whether the text area is wrapped. In the case where the text area is wrapped, you need to specify whether it is wrapped by characters or by words, as shown in Figure 13.52.

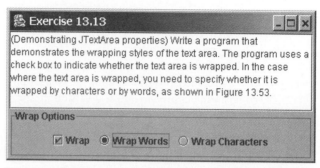

Figure 13.52   *You can set the options to wrap a text area by characters or by words dynamically.*

13.14 (Using `JComboBox` and `JList`) Write a program that demonstrates selecting items in a list. The program uses a combo box to specify a selection mode, as shown in Figure 13.53. When you select items, they are displayed in a label below the list.

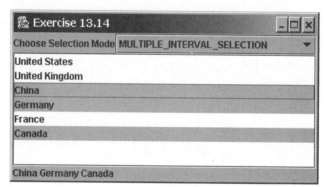

Figure 13.53   *You can choose single selection, single-interval selection, or multiple-interval selection in a list.*

13.15 (Demonstrating `FlowLayout` properties) Create a program that enables the user to set the properties of a `FlowLayout` manager dynamically, as shown in Figure 13.54. The `FlowLayout` manager is used to place fifteen components in a panel. You can set the `alignment`, `hgap`, and `vgap` properties of the `FlowLayout` dynamically. (Hint: See Sections 11.4.4, "Properties of Layout Managers" and 11.4.5, "The `validate` and `doLayout` Methods.")

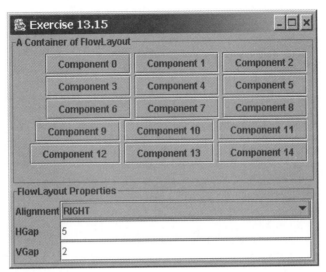

Figure 13.54 *The program enables you to set the properties of a* FlowLayout *manager dynamically.*

13.16 (Demonstrating GridLayout properties) Create a program that enables the user to set the properties of a GridLayout manager dynamically, as shown in Figure 13.55. The GridLayout manager is used to place fifteen components in a panel. You can set the rows, columns, hgap, and vhap properties of the GridLayout dynamically. (Hint: See Sections 11.4.4 "Properties of Layout Managers" and 10.4.5, "The validate and doLayout Methods.")

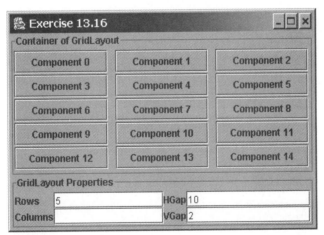

Figure 13.55 *The program enables you to set the properties of a* GridLayout *manager dynamically.*

13.17 (Using JTabbedPane) Use JTabbedPane to write a program that displays flags for the United States, United Kingdom, Germany, Canada, China, and India (see Figure 13.56).

Figure 13.56   *You can show the flag by selecting a tab in the tabbed pane.*

13.18 (Revising Example 13.12 "Creating Multiple Windows") Instead of displaying the occurrence of the letters using the Histogram component in Example 13.12, use the BarChart component in Exercise 11.19, so that the display is shown in Figure 13.57.

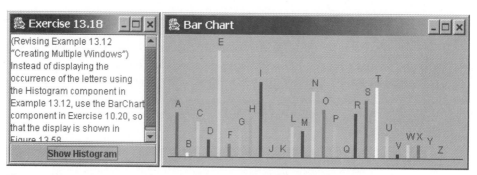

Figure 13.57   *The number of occurrences of each letter is displayed in a bar chart.*

13.19 (Comparing loans with various interest rates) Rewrite Exercise 3.14 to create a user interface, as shown in Figure 13.58. Your program should let the user enter the loan amount and loan period in number of years from a text field, and should display the monthly and total payments for each interest rate starting from 5 percent to 8 percent, with an increment of one-eighth in a text area.

Interest Rate	Monthly Payment	Total Payment
5.0	188.71	11322.74
5.125	189.28	11357.13
5.25	189.85	11391.59
5.375	190.43	11426.11
5.5	191.01	11460.69
5.625	191.58	11495.34
5.75	192.16	11530.06

Loan Amount 10000   Number of Years 5   Show Table

Figure 13.58   *The program displays a table for monthly payments and total payments on a given loan based on various interest rates.*

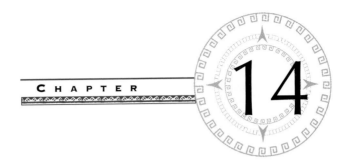

APPLETS

Objectives

- To explain how the Web browser controls and executes applets.
- To describe the init, start, stop, and destroy methods in the Applet class.
- To know how to embed applets in Web pages.
- To pass parameters to applets from HTML.
- To write a Java program that can run as both an application and an applet.
- To create applets using the JBuilder Applet wizard.

14.1   Introduction

Java's early success has been attributed to applets. Running from a Java-enabled Web browser, applets bring dynamic interaction and live animation to an otherwise static HTML page. It is safe to say that Java would be nowhere today without applets. They made Java instantly appealing, attractive, and popular during its infancy stage. Java is now used not only for applets, but also for stand-alone applications and as a programming language for developing server-side applications and for mobile devices.

In this book so far, you have only used Java applications. Everything you have learned about writing applications, however, also applies to writing applets. Applications and applets share many common programming features, although they differ slightly in some respects. For example, every application must have a `main` method, which is invoked by the Java interpreter. Java applets, on the other hand, do not need a `main` method. They run in the Web browser environment. Because applets are invoked from a Web page, Java provides special features that enable applets to run from a Web browser.

In this chapter, you will learn how to write Java applets, discover the relationship between applets and the Web browser, and explore the similarities and differences between applications and applets.

14.2   The *Applet* Class

The `Applet` class provides the essential framework that enables applets to be run by a Web browser. While every Java application has a `main` method that is executed when the application starts, applets do not have a `main` method. Instead they depend on the browser to call the methods. Every applet is made up of the following methods:

```
public class MyApplet extends java.applet.Applet {
  ...
  /** The default constructor is called by the browser when the Web
     page containing this applet is initially loaded, or reloaded
    */
  public MyApplet() {
    ...
  }

  /** Called by the browser after the applet is loaded
    */
  public void init() {
    ...
  }

  /** Called by the browser after the init() method, or
     every time the Web page is visited
    */
  public void start() {
    ...
  }

  /** Called by the browser when the page containing this
```

```
    applet becomes inactive
    */
public void stop() {
    ...
}

/** Called by the browser when the Web browser exits */
public void destroy() {
    ...
}

/** Other methods if necessary... */
}
```

When the applet is loaded, the Web browser creates an instance of the applet by invoking the applet's default constructor. The browser uses the `init`, `start`, `stop`, and `destroy` methods to control the applet. By default, these methods do nothing. To perform specific functions, they need to be modified in the user's applet so that the browser can call your code properly. Figure 14.1 (A) shows how the browser calls these methods, and Figure 14.1 (B) illustrates the flow of control of an applet using a statechart diagram.

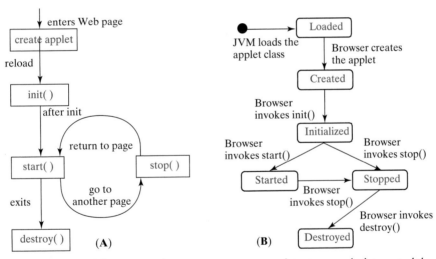

Figure 14.1   *The Web browser uses the `init`, `start`, `stop`, and `destroy` methods to control the applet.*

14.2.1   The *init* Method

The `init` method is invoked after the applet is created or recreated.

A subclass of `Applet` should override this method if the subclass has an initialization to perform. The functions usually implemented in this method include creating new threads, loading images, setting up user-interface components, and getting parameters from the `<applet>` tag in the HTML page. Chapter 18, "Multithreading," discusses threads in more detail; passing `Applet` parameters is discussed below in Section 14.7, "Passing Parameters to Applets."

14.2.2   The *start* Method

The start method is invoked after the init method. It is also called whenever the applet becomes active again after the page containing the applet is revisited. The start method is called, for example, when the user returns to the Web page containing the applet after surfing other pages.

A subclass of Applet overrides this method if it has any operation that needs to be performed whenever the Web page containing the applet is visited. An applet with animation, for example, might use the start method to resume animation.

14.2.3   The *stop* Method

The stop method is the opposite of the start method. The start method is called when the user moves back to the page that contains the applet. The stop method is invoked when the user leaves the page.

A subclass of Applet overrides this method if it has any operation that needs to be performed each time the Web page containing the applet is no longer visible. When the user leaves the page, any threads the applet has started but not completed will continue to run. You should override the stop method to suspend the running threads so that the applet does not take up system resources when it is inactive.

14.2.4   The *destroy* Method

The destroy method is invoked when the browser exits normally to inform the applet that it is no longer needed and should release any resources it has allocated. The stop method is always called before the destroy method.

A subclass of Applet overrides this method if it has any operation that needs to be performed before it is destroyed. Usually, you won't need to override this method unless you wish to release specific resources, such as threads that the applet created.

14.3   The *JApplet* Class

The Applet class is an AWT class and is not designed to work with Swing components. To use Swing components in Java applets, it is necessary to create a Java applet that extends javax.swing.JApplet, which is a subclass of java.applet.Applet. JApplet inherits all the methods from the Applet class. In addition, it provides support for laying out Swing components.

To add a component to a JApplet, you add it to the content pane of a JApplet instance, which is the same as adding a component to a JFrame instance. By default, the content pane of JApplet uses BorderLayout. Here is an example of a simple applet that uses JLabel to display a message.

```
// WelcomeApplet.java: Applet for displaying a message
package chapter14;

import javax.swing.*;

public class WelcomeApplet extends JApplet {
  /** Initialize the applet */
```

```
  public void init() {
    getContentPane().add(
      new JLabel("Welcome to Java", JLabel.CENTER));
  }
}
```

You cannot run this applet stand-alone, because it does not have a `main` method. To run this applet, you have to create an HTML file with the applet tag that references the applet. When you write Java GUI applications, you must create a frame to hold graphical components, set the frame size, and make the frame visible. Applets are run from the Web browser. The Web browser automatically places the applet inside it and makes it visible. The following section shows how to create HTML files for applets.

 NOTE

You could rewrite the `WelcomeApplet` by moving the code in the `init` method to the default constructor, as follows:

```
// WelcomeApplet.java: Applet for displaying a message
package chapter14;

import javax.swing.*;

public class WelcomeApplet extends JApplet {
  /** Construct the applet */
  public WelcomeApplet() {
    getContentPane().add(
      new JLabel("Welcome to Java", JLabel.CENTER));
  }
}
```

14.4   Creating a Java Applet Using the Applet Wizard

The following steps create template files for a new applet:

1. Choose *File*, *New* to display the object gallery. Click the Applet icon in the Web tab to open the Applet wizard.

2. JBuilder starts Applet Wizard Step 1 of 4 to configure your applet (see Figure 14.2). Edit the Package field to `chapter14` and the Class field to `WelcomeApplet`, as shown in Figure 14.2. Click *Finish*.

The Applet wizard generates two files: WelcomeApplet.html and WelcomeApplet.java. The source code for WelcomeApplet.html is shown in the content pane of the AppBrowser in Figure 14.3. The source code for welcomeApplet.java is shown in Figure 14.4.

 NOTE

The HTML file WelcomeApplet.html is stored in the project source path (i.e., c:\example), and the Java source file WelcomeApplet.java is stored in the project source path/packageName (i.e., c:\example\chapter 14). To view the code in WelcomeApplet.html, choose the *Source* tab at the bottom of the content pane.

623

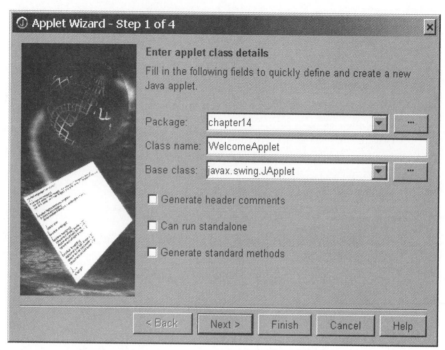

Figure 14.2 *Applet Wizard Step 1 of 4 prompts you to enter the package name, the applet class name, and other optional information.*

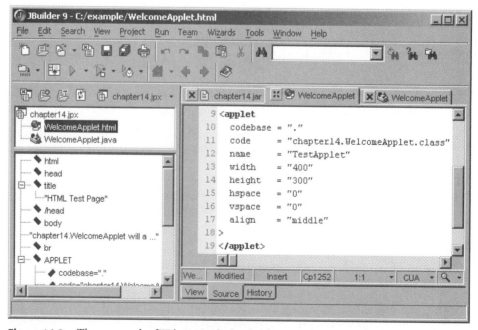

Figure 14.3 *The source code of WelcomeApplet.html is shown in the content pane.*

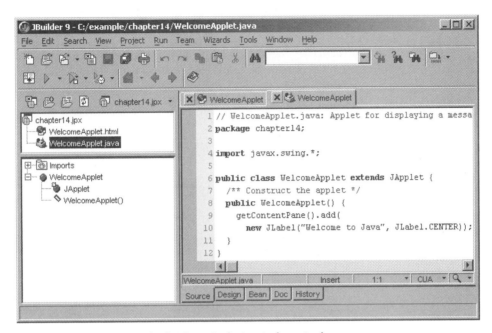

Figure 14.4 *The source code of WelcomeApplet.java is shown in the content pane.*

14.5 Viewing Applets

Assume that you have compiled the applet's source code. You have the applet's class file and the HTML file for displaying the applet. There are several ways to view the applet.

14.5.1 Viewing Applets in the Content Pane

You can view the applet in the content pane, using JBuilder's applet viewer, by selecting the applet's HTML file (e.g., WelcomeApplet.html) in the project pane and the View tab in the content pane, as shown in Figure 14.5.

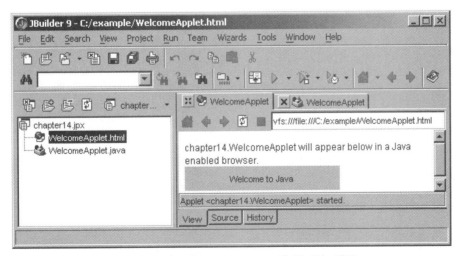

Figure 14.5 *The applet is displayed in the content pane inside JBuilder IDE.*

14.5.2   Viewing Applets Using the Applet Viewer Utility

You can also view a Java applet using the Sun applet viewer. Choose the applet's HTML file (i.e., WelcomeApplet.html) in the project pane. Right-click it to display its context menu. Click *Run* in the Context menu. The applet is displayed in the applet viewer, as shown in Figure 14.6.

Figure 14.6   *The WelcomeApplet program is running from the applet viewer.*

You can also invoke the applet viewer from the DOS prompt using the following command:

```
appletview WelcomeApplet.html
```

14.5.3   Viewing Applets from a Web Browser

Applets are eventually displayed in a Web browser. Using JBuilder's applet viewer and Sun's applet viewer, you do not need to start a Web browser. Both applet viewers function as browsers. They are convenient for testing applets before deploying them on a Web site. JBuilder's applet viewer has limited functions. For example, you cannot use menus from JBuilder's applet viewer. Sun's applet viewer fully simulates a Web browser. To display an applet from a Web browser, open the applet's HTML file (i.e., WelcomeApplet.html) Its output is shown in Figure 14.7.

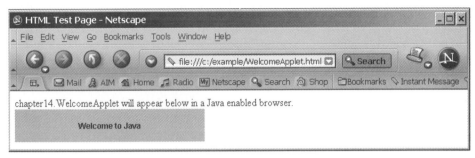

Figure 14.7 *The WelcomeApplet program is displayed in Netscape 7.*

◈ **NOTE**

You have to view the above applet using a Web browser that supports Java 2. At present, Netscape 6/7 and IE 5/6 support Java 2.

To make your applet accessible on the Web, you need to store the Welcome-Applet.class and WelcomeApplet.html on a Web server. You can view the applet from an appropriate URL. For example, I have uploaded these two files on Web server **www.cs.armstrong.edu**. As shown in Figure 14.8, you can access the applet from **www.cs.armstrong.edu/liang/introjb3e/example/WelcomeApplet.html**.

Figure 14.8 *The WelcomeApplet program is downloaded from the Web server.*

14.6   The HTML File and the *<applet>* Tag

HTML is a markup language that presents static documents on the Web. It uses tags to instruct the Web browser how to render a Web page and contains a tag called <applet> that incorporates applets into a Web page.

The following HTML file named WelcomeApplet.html invokes the **Welcome Applet.class**:

```
<html>
<head>
<title>Welcome Java Applet</title>
</head>
<body>
<applet
  code = "chapter14.WelcomeApplet.class"
  width = 350
  height = 200>
</applet>
</body>
</html>
```

A *tag* is an instruction to the Web browser. The browser interprets the tag and decides how to display or otherwise treat the subsequent contents of the HTML document. Tags are enclosed inside brackets. The first word in a tag, called the *tag name*, describes tag functions. Tags can have additional attributes, sometimes with values after an equals sign, which further define the tag's action. For example, in the preceding HTML file, <applet> is the tag name, and code, width, and height are the attributes. The width and height attributes specify the rectangular viewing area of the applet.

Most tags have a *start tag* and a corresponding *end tag*. The tag has a specific effect on the region between the start tag and the end tag. For example, <applet...>· ...</applet> tells the browser to display an applet. An end tag is always the start tag's name preceded by a slash.

An HTML document begins with the <html> tag, which declares that the document is written in HTML. Each document has two parts, a *head* and a *body*, defined by <head> and <body> tags, respectively. The head part contains the document title, using the <title> tag and other parameters the browser can use when rendering the document, and the body part contains the actual contents of the document. The header is optional. For more information, refer to Bonus Supplement F, "HTML Tutorial."

The complete syntax of the <applet> tag is as follows:

```
<applet
  [codebase=applet_url]
  code=classfilename.class
  width=applet_viewing_width_in_pixels
  height=applet_viewing_height_in_pixels
  [archive=archivefile]
  [vspace=vertical_margin]
  [hspace=horizontal_margin]
  [align=applet_alignment]
```

```
    [alt=alternative_text]
  >
  <param name=param_name1 value=param_value1>
  <param name=param_name2 value=param_value2>
  ...
  <param name=param_name3 value=param_value3>
  </applet>
```

The code, width, and height attributes are required; all the others are optional. The <param> tag is introduced in Section 14.7, "Passing Parameters to Applets." The meanings of the other attributes are explained below:

- **codebase** specifies a base where your classes are loaded. If this attribute is not used, the Web browser loads the applet from the directory in which the HTML page is located. If your applet is located in a different directory from the HTML page, you must specify the applet_url for the browser to load the applet. This attribute enables you to load the class from anywhere on the Internet. The classes used by the applet are dynamically loaded when needed.

- **archive** instructs the browser to load an archive file that contains all the class files needed to run the applet. Archiving allows the Web browser to load all the classes from a single compressed file at one time, thus reducing loading time and improving performance. To create archives, see Bonus Supplement H, "Packaging and Deploying Java Projects."

- **vspace** and **hspace** specify the size, in pixels, of the blank margin to pad around the applet vertically and horizontally.

- **align** specifies how the applet will be aligned in the browser. One of nine values is used: left, right, top, texttop, middle, absmiddle, baseline, bottom, or absbottom.

- **alt** attribute specifies the text to be displayed in case the browser cannot run Java.

◈ **NOTE**

The W3 consortium (www.w3.org) has introduced the <object> tag as a replacement for the <applet> tag. The <object> tag has more options and is more versatile than the <applet> tag. This book will continue to use the <applet> tag, however, because not all Web browsers support the <object> tag as yet.

Example 14.1 Using Applets

Problem

Write an applet that computes loan payments. The applet enables the user to enter the interest rate, the number of years, and the loan amount. Clicking the Compute Payment button displays the monthly payment and the total payment.

Solution

The applet and the HTML code containing the applet are provided in the following code. Figure 14.9 contains a sample run of the applet.

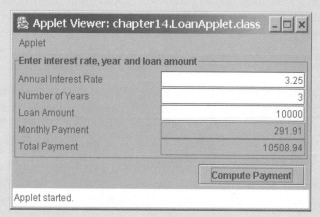

Figure 14.9   *The applet computes the monthly payment and the total payment when provided with the interest rate, number of years, and loan amount.*

```
1    // LoanApplet.java: Applet for computing loan payments
2    package chapter14;
3
4    import chapter6.Loan;
5    import java.awt.*;
6    import java.awt.event.*;
7    import javax.swing.*;
8    import javax.swing.border.TitledBorder;
9
10   public class LoanApplet extends JApplet
11     implements ActionListener {
12     // Declare and create text fields for interest rate
13     // year, loan amount, monthly payment, and total payment
14     private JTextField jtfAnnualInterestRate = new JTextField();
15     private JTextField jtfNumOfYears = new JTextField();
16     private JTextField jtfLoanAmount = new JTextField();
17     private JTextField jtfMonthlyPayment = new JTextField();
18     private JTextField jtfTotalPayment = new JTextField();
19
20     // Declare and create a Compute Payment button
21     private JButton jbtComputeLoan = new JButton("Compute Payment");
22
23     /** Initialize user interface */
24     public void init() {
25       // Set properties on the text fields
26       jtfMonthlyPayment.setEditable(false);
27       jtfTotalPayment.setEditable(false);
28
```

```
29          // Right align text fields
30          jtfAnnualInterestRate.setHorizontalAlignment(JTextField.RIGHT);
31          jtfNumOfYears.setHorizontalAlignment(JTextField.RIGHT);
32          jtfLoanAmount.setHorizontalAlignment(JTextField.RIGHT);
33          jtfMonthlyPayment.setHorizontalAlignment(JTextField.RIGHT);
34          jtfTotalPayment.setHorizontalAlignment(JTextField.RIGHT);
35
36          // Panel p1 to hold labels and text fields
37          JPanel p1 = new JPanel();
38          p1.setLayout(new GridLayout(5, 2));
39          p1.add(new Label("Annual Interest Rate"));
40          p1.add(jtfAnnualInterestRate);
41          p1.add(new Label("Number of Years"));
42          p1.add(jtfNumOfYears);
43          p1.add(new Label("Loan Amount"));
44          p1.add(jtfLoanAmount);
45          p1.add(new Label("Monthly Payment"));
46          p1.add(jtfMonthlyPayment);
47          p1.add(new Label("Total Payment"));
48          p1.add(jtfTotalPayment);
49          p1.setBorder(new
50            TitledBorder("Enter interest rate, year and loan amount"));
51
52          // Panel p2 to hold the button
53          JPanel p2 = new JPanel();
54          p2.setLayout(new FlowLayout(FlowLayout.RIGHT));
55          p2.add(jbtComputeLoan);
56
57          // Add the components to the applet
58          getContentPane().add(p1, BorderLayout.CENTER);
59          getContentPane().add(p2, BorderLayout.SOUTH);
60
61          // Register listener
62          jbtComputeLoan.addActionListener(this);
63        }
64
65        /** Handle the Compute Payment button */
66        public void actionPerformed(ActionEvent e) {
67          if (e.getSource() == jbtComputeLoan) {
68            // Get values from text fields
69            double interest = (Double.valueOf(
70              jtfAnnualInterestRate.getText())).doubleValue();
71            int year =
72              (Integer.valueOf(jtfNumOfYears.getText())).intValue();
73            double loanAmount =
74              (Double.valueOf(jtfLoanAmount.getText())).doubleValue();
75
76            // Create a loan object
77            Loan loan = new Loan(interest, year, loanAmount);
78
79            // Display monthly payment and total payment
80            jtfMonthlyPayment.setText("" +
81              (int)(loan.monthlyPayment() * 100) / 100.0);
82            jtfTotalPayment.setText("" +
83              (int)(loan.totalPayment() * 100) / 100.0);
84          }
85        }
86      }
```

```
<!--HTML code, this code is separated from the preceding Java code-->
<html>
```

continues

Example 14.1 Continued

```
<head>
<title>Loan Applet</title>
</head>
<body>
This is a loan calculator. Enter your input for interest, year, and
loan amount. Click the "Compute Payment" button, you will get the
payment information.<p>
<applet
  code = "chapter14.LoanApplet.class"
  width = 300
  height = 150
  alt="You must have a Java 2-enabled browser to view the applet">
</applet>
</body>
</html>
```

Review

You need to use the `public` modifier for the `LoanApplet`; otherwise, the Web browser cannot load it.

`LoanApplet` implements `ActionListener` because it listens for button actions.

The `init` method initializes the user interface. The program overrides this method to create user-interface components (labels, text fields, and a button), and places them in the applet.

The only event handled is the Compute Payment button. When this button is clicked, the `actionPerformed` method gets the interest rate, number of years, and loan amount from the text fields. It then creates a `Loan` object (Line 77) to obtain the monthly payment and the total payment. Finally, it displays the monthly and total payments in their respective text fields.

The `Loan` class is responsible for computing the payments. This class was introduced in Example 6.7, "the `Loan` Class."

The monthly and total payments are not displayed in currency format. To display a number as currency, see Bonus Chapter 20, "Internationalization."

14.7   Passing Parameters to Applets

In Chapter 7, "Strings," you learned how to pass parameters to Java applications from a command line. Parameters are passed to the `main` method as an array of strings. When the application starts, the `main` method can use these strings. There is no `main` method in an applet, however, and applets are not run from the command line by the Java interpreter.

How, then, can applets accept arguments? In this section, you will learn how to pass parameters to Java applets. To be passed to an applet, a parameter must be declared in the HTML file, and must be read by the applet when it is initialized. Parameters are declared using the `<param>` tag. The `<param>` tag must be embedded in the `<applet>` tag and has no end tag. The syntax for the `<param>` tag is given below:

```
<param name=parametername value=parametervalue>
```

This tag specifies a parameter and its corresponding value.

 NOTE

There is no comma separating the parameter name from the parameter value in the HTML code. The HTML parameter names are not case-sensitive.

Suppose you want to write an applet to display a message. The message is passed as a parameter. In addition, you want the message to be displayed at a specific location. The start location of the message is also passed as a parameter in two values, x coordinate and y coordinate. Assume that the applet is named DisplayMessage. The parameters and their values are listed in Table 14.1.

TABLE 14.1   **Parameter Names and Values for the DisplayMessage Applet**

Parameter Name	Parameter Value
MESSAGE	"Welcome to Java"
X	20
Y	30

The HTML source file is given as follows:

```
<html>
<head>
<title>Passing Parameters to Java Applets</title>
</head>
<body>
This applet gets a message from the HTML page and displays it.
<p>
<applet
  code = "chapter14.DisplayMessage.class"
  width = 200
  height = 50
  alt="You must have a Java 2-enabled browser to view the applet"
>
<param name = MESSAGE value = "Welcome to Java">
<param name = X value = 20>
<param name = Y value = 30>
</applet>
</body>
</html>
```

To read the parameter from the applet, use the following method defined in the Applet class:

```
public String getParameter("parametername");
```

This returns the value of the specified parameter.

Example 14.2 Passing Parameters to Java Applets

Problem

Write an applet that displays a message at a specified location. The message and the location (x, y) are obtained from the HTML source.

Solution

The program creates a Java source file named **DisplayMessage.java**, as shown below. The output of a sample run is shown in Figure 14.10.

```
1    // DisplayMessage.java: Display a message on a panel in the applet
2    package chapter14;
3
4    import javax.swing.*;
5    import chapter11.MessagePanel;
6
7    public class DisplayMessage extends JApplet {
8      /** Initialize the applet */
9      public void init() {
10       // Get parameter values from the HTML file
11       String message = getParameter("MESSAGE");
12       int x = Integer.parseInt(getParameter("X"));
13       int y = Integer.parseInt(getParameter("Y"));
14
15       // Create a message panel
16       MessagePanel messagePanel = new MessagePanel(message);
17       messagePanel.setXCoordinate(x);
18       messagePanel.setYCoordinate(y);
19
20       // Add the message panel to the applet
21       getContentPane().add(messagePanel);
22     }
23   }
```

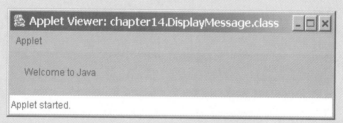

Figure 14.10   *The applet displays the message passed from the HTML page.*

Review

The program gets the parameter values from the HTML in the init method. The values are strings obtained using the getParameter method (Lines 11–13). Because x and y are int, the program uses Integer.parseInt(string) to parse a digital string into an int value.

If you change *Welcome to Java* in the HTML file to *Welcome to HTML*, and reload the HTML file in the Web browser, you should see *Welcome to HTML* displayed. Similarly, the x and y values can be changed to display the message in a desired location.

CAUTION

The `Applet`'s `getParameter` method can be invoked only after an instance of the applet is created. Therefore, this method cannot be invoked in the constructor of the applet class. You should invoke this method from the `init` method.

14.8   Enabling Applets to Run as Applications

The `JFrame` class and the `JApplet` class have a lot in common despite some differences. Since they both are subclasses of the `Container` class, all their user-interface components, layout managers, and event-handling features are the same. Applications, however, are invoked from the static *main* method by the Java interpreter, and applets are run by the Web browser. The Web browser creates an instance of the applet using the applet's default constructor and controls and executes the applet through the `init`, `start`, `stop`, and `destroy` methods.

For security reasons, the restrictions listed below are imposed on applets to prevent destructive programs from damaging the system on which the browser is running.

- Applets are not allowed to read from, or write to, the file system of the computer. Otherwise, they could damage the files and spread viruses.

- Applets are not allowed to run programs on the browser's computer. Otherwise, they might call destructive local programs and damage the local system on the user's computer.

- Applets are not allowed to establish connections between the user's computer and any other computer, except for the server where the applets are stored. This restriction prevents the applet from connecting the user's computer to another computer without the user's knowledge.

 NOTE

A new security protocol was introduced in Java 2. You can use a security policy file to grant applets access to local files.

In general, an applet can be converted to an application without loss of functionality. An application can be converted to an applet as long as it does not violate the security restrictions imposed on applets. You can implement a `main` method in an applet to enable the applet to run as an application. This feature has both theoretical and practical implications. Theoretically, it blurs the difference between applets and applications. You can write a class that is both an applet and an application. From the standpoint of practicality, it is convenient to be able to run a program in two ways.

It is not difficult to write such programs on your own. Suppose you have an applet named TestApplet. To enable it to run as an application, all you need to do is add a main method in the applet with the implementation, as follows:

```java
public static void main(String[] args) {
  // Create a frame
  JFrame frame = new JFrame (
    "Running a program as applet and frame");

  // Create an instance of TestApplet
  TestApplet applet = new TestApplet();

  // Add the applet instance to the frame
  frame.getContentPane().add(applet, BorderLayout.CENTER);

  // Invoke init and start
  applet.init();
  applet.start();

  // Display the frame
  frame.setSize(300, 300);
  frame.setVisible(true);
}
```

Since the JApplet class is a subclass of Component, it can be placed in a frame. You can invoke the init and start methods of the applet to run a JApplet object in an application.

Example 14.3 Running a Program as an Applet and as an Application

Problem

Write a program that modifies the DisplayMessage applet in Example 14.2, "Passing Parameters to Java Applets," to enable it to run both as an applet and as an application.

Solution

The program is identical to DisplayMessage except for the addition of a new main method and of a variable named isStandalone to indicate whether it is running as an applet or as an application. The following code gives the solution to the problem.

```java
1    // DisplayMessageApp.java: the applet can run as application
2    package chapter14;
3
4    import javax.swing.*;
5    import java.awt.Font;
6    import java.awt.BorderLayout;
7    import chapter11.MessagePanel;
8
9    public class DisplayMessageApp extends JApplet {
10     private String message = "A default message"; // Message to display
11     private int x = 20; // Default x coordinate
12     private int y = 20; // Default y coordinate
13
14     /** Determine if it is application */
15     private boolean isStandalone = false;
16
```

```
17      /** Initialize the applet */
18      public void init() {
19        if (!isStandalone) {
20          // Get parameter values from the HTML file
21          message = getParameter("MESSAGE");
22          x = Integer.parseInt(getParameter("X"));
23          y = Integer.parseInt(getParameter("Y"));
24        }
25
26        // Create a message panel
27        MessagePanel messagePanel = new MessagePanel(message);
28        messagePanel.setFont(new Font("SansSerif", Font.BOLD, 20));
29        messagePanel.setXCoordinate(x);
30        messagePanel.setYCoordinate(y);
31
32        // Add the message panel to the applet
33        getContentPane().add(messagePanel);
34      }
35
36      /** Main method to display a message
37          @param args[0] x coordinate
38          @param args[1] y coordinate
39          @param args[2] message
40      */
41      public static void main(String[] args) {
42        // Create a frame
43        JFrame frame = new JFrame("DisplayMessageApp");
44
45        // Create an instance of the applet
46        DisplayMessageApp applet = new DisplayMessageApp();
47
48        // It runs as an application
49        applet.isStandalone = true;
50
51        // Get parameters from the command line
52        applet.getCommandLineParameters(args);
53
54        // Add the applet instance to the frame
55        frame.getContentPane().add(applet, BorderLayout.CENTER);
56
57        // Invoke init() and start()
58        applet.init();
59        applet.start();
60
61        // Display the frame
62        frame.setSize(300, 300);
63        frame.setDefaultCloseOperation(JFrame.EXIT_ON_CLOSE);
64        frame.setVisible(true);
65      }
66
67      /** Get command line parameters */
68      private void getCommandLineParameters(String[] args) {
69        // Check usage and get x, y and message
70        if (args.length != 3) {
71          System.out.println(
72            "Usage: java DisplayMessageApp x y message");
73          System.exit(0);
74        }
```

continues

Example 14.3 Continued

```
75          else {
76            x = Integer.parseInt(args[0]);
77            y = Integer.parseInt(args[1]);
78            message = args[2];
79          }
80        }
81      }
```

Review

When you run the program as an applet, the `main` method is ignored. When you run it as an application, the `main` method is invoked. A sample run of the program as an application and as an applet is shown in Figure 14.11.

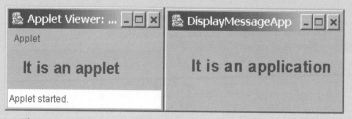

Figure 14.11   *The* `DisplayMessageApp` *class can run as an application and as an applet.*

The `main` method creates a `JFrame` object `frame` and creates a `JApplet` object `applet`, then places the applet `applet` into the frame `frame` and invokes its `init` method. The application runs just like an applet.

The `main` method sets `isStandalone` true (Line 49) so that it does not attempt to retrieve HTML parameters when the `init` method is invoked.

The `setVisible(true)` method (Line 64) is invoked after the components are added to the applet, and the applet is added to the frame to ensure that the components will be visible. Otherwise, the components are not shown when the frame starts.

14.9   Case Studies (Optional)

You have learned about objects, classes, arrays, class inheritance, GUI, event-driven programming, and applets from the many examples in this chapter and the preceding chapters. Now it is time to put what you have learned to work in developing comprehensive projects. In this section, you will develop a Java applet with which to play the popular game of TicTacToe.

Example 14.4 The TicTacToe Game

Problem

Create a program for playing TicTacToe. In a game of TicTacToe, two players take turns marking an available cell in a 3 × 3 grid with their respective tokens (either X or O). When one player has placed three tokens in a horizontal, vertical, or diagonal row on the grid, the game is over and that player has won. A draw (no winner) occurs when all the cells on the grid have been filled with tokens and neither player has achieved a win. Figures 14.12 and 14.13 are representative sample runs of the example.

Figure 14.12 *This sample shows that the X player has won.*

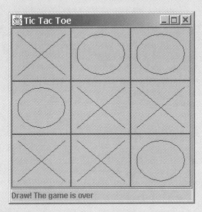

Figure 14.13 *This sample shows a draw with no winner.*

Solution

All the examples you have seen so far show simple behaviors that are easy to model with classes. The behavior of the TicTacToe game is somewhat more complex. To create classes that model the behavior, you need to study and understand the game.

continues

Example 14.4 Continued

Assume that all the cells are initially empty, and that the first player takes the X token, and the second player takes the O token. To mark a cell, the player points the mouse to the cell and clicks it. If the cell is empty, the token (X or O) is displayed. If the cell is already filled, the player's action is ignored.

From the preceding description, it is obvious that a cell is a GUI object that handles the mouse-click event and displays tokens. Such an object could be either a button or a panel. Drawing on panels is more flexible than on buttons, because the token (X or O) can be drawn on a panel in any size, but on a button it can only be displayed as a text label. Therefore, a panel should be used to model a cell.

Let `Cell` be a subclass of `JPanel`. You can declare the 3 × 3 grid to be an array new `Cell[3][3]` to model the game. How do you know the state of the cell (empty, X, or O)? You use a property named `token` of char type in the `Cell` class. The `Cell` class is responsible for drawing the token when an empty cell is clicked, so you need to write the code for listening to the `MouseEvent` and for painting the shape for tokens X and O. To determine which shape to draw, you can introduce a variable named `whoseTurn` of char type. `whoseTurn` is initially X, then changes to O, and subsequently changes between X and O whenever a new cell is occupied.

Finally, how do you know whether the game is over, whether there is a winner, and who the winner, if any, is? You can create a method named `isWon(char token)` to check whether a specified token has won and a method named `isFull()` to check whether all the cells are occupied.

Clearly, two classes emerge from the foregoing analysis. One is the `Cell` class, which handles operations for a single cell; and the other is the `TicTacToe` class, which plays the whole game and deals with all the cells. The relationship between these two classes is shown in Figure 14.14.

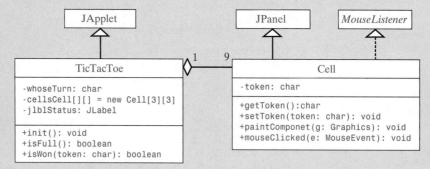

Figure 14.14 *The* `TicTacToe` *class contains nine cells.*

640

The `Cell` class has the following data field and methods:

Data field:

`char token`: This represents the token used in the cell. The initial value is ' ';

Methods:

- `public char getToken()`

  Returns the token of the cell.

- `public void setToken(char token)`

  Sets the token in the cell.

- `protected void paintComponent(Graphics g)`

  Overrides this method to display the token in the cell.

- `public void mouseClicked(MouseEvent e)`

  Implements this method in the `MouseListener` to handle a mouse click on the cell.

The `TicTacToe` class has the following data fields and methods:

Data fields:

- `char whoseTurn`: This indicates which player has the turn. The initial value is 'X', which indicates that it is player X's turn.

- `Cell[][] cells`: This represents the cells.

- `JLabel jlblStatus`: This is a label for displaying game status.

Methods:

- `public void init()`

  Overrides this method to initialize variables and create UI.

- `public boolean isFull()`

  Checks whether all the cells are filled.

- `public boolean isWon(char token)`

  Checks whether the player with the specified token wins.

The interaction between the `TicTacToe` object and a `Cell` object is shown in Figure 14.15.

continues

Example 14.4 Continued

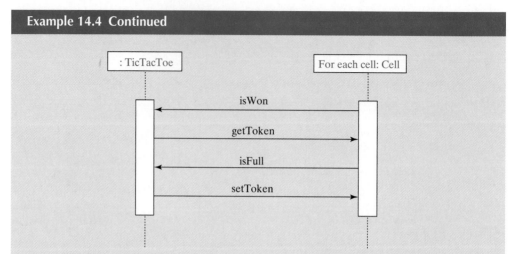

Figure 14.15 *Each* `Cell` *object communicates with the* `TicTacToe` *object to play the game.*

The program is given below:

```
1    // TicTacToe.java: Play the TicTacToe game
2    package chapter14;
3
4    import java.awt.*;
5    import java.awt.event.*;
6    import javax.swing.*;
7    import javax.swing.border.LineBorder;
8
9    public class TicTacToe extends JApplet {
10     // Indicate which player has a turn, initially it is the X player
11     private char whoseTurn = 'X';
12
13     // Create and initialize cells
14     private Cell[][] cells =  new Cell[3][3];
15
16     // Create and initialize a status label
17     private JLabel jlblStatus = new JLabel("X's turn to play");
18
19     /** Initialize UI */
20     public TicTacToe() {
21       // Panel p to hold cells
22       JPanel p = new JPanel();
23       p.setLayout(new GridLayout(3, 3, 0, 0));
24       for (int i = 0; i < 3; i++)
25         for (int j = 0; j < 3; j++)
26           p.add(cells[i][j] = new Cell());
27
28       // Set line borders on the cells panel and the status label
29       p.setBorder(new LineBorder(Color.red, 1));
30       jlblStatus.setBorder(new LineBorder(Color.yellow, 1));
31
32       // Place the panel and the label to the applet
33       this.getContentPane().add(p, BorderLayout.CENTER);
34       this.getContentPane().add(jlblStatus, BorderLayout.SOUTH);
35     }
36
```

```
37     /** This main method enables the applet to run as an application */
38     public static void main(String[] args) {
39       // Create a frame
40       JFrame frame = new JFrame("Tic Tac Toe");
41
42       // Create an instance of the applet
43       TicTacToe applet = new TicTacToe();
44
45       // Add the applet instance to the frame
46       frame.getContentPane().add(applet, BorderLayout.CENTER);
47
48       // Invoke init() and start()
49       applet.init();
50       applet.start();
51
52       // Display the frame
53       frame.setSize(300, 300);
54       frame.setDefaultCloseOperation(JFrame.EXIT_ON_CLOSE);
55       frame.setVisible(true);
56     }
57
58     /** Determine if the cells are all occupied */
59     public boolean isFull() {
60       for (int i = 0; i < 3; i++)
61         for (int j = 0; j < 3; j++)
62           if (cells[i][j].getToken() == ' ')
63             return false;
64
65       return true;
66     }
67
68     /** Determine if the player with the specified token wins */
69     public boolean isWon(char token) {
70       for (int i = 0; i < 3; i++)
71         if ((cells[i][0].getToken() == token)
72             && (cells[i][1].getToken() == token)
73             && (cells[i][2].getToken() == token)) {
74           return true;
75         }
76
77       for (int j = 0; j < 3; j++)
78         if ((cells[0][j].getToken() ==  token)
79             && (cells[1][j].getToken() == token)
80             && (cells[2][j].getToken() == token)) {
81           return true;
82         }
83
84       if ((cells[0][0].getToken() == token)
85           && (cells[1][1].getToken() == token)
86           && (cells[2][2].getToken() == token)) {
87         return true;
88       }
89
90       if ((cells[0][2].getToken() == token)
91           && (cells[1][1].getToken() == token)
92           && (cells[2][0].getToken() == token)) {
93         return true;
94       }
95
96       return false;
97     }
98
```

continues

643

Example 14.4 Continued

```
99       // An inner class for a cell
100      public class Cell extends JPanel implements MouseListener {
101        // Token used for this cell
102        private char token = ' ';
103
104        public Cell() {
105          setBorder(new LineBorder(Color.black, 1)); // Set cell's border
106          addMouseListener(this);   // Register listener
107        }
108
109        /** Return token */
110        public char getToken() {
111          return token;
112        }
113
114        /** Set a new token */
115        public void setToken(char c) {
116          token = c;
117          repaint();
118        }
119
120        /** Paint the cell */
121        protected void paintComponent(Graphics g) {
122          super.paintComponent(g);
123
124          if (token == 'X') {
125            g.drawLine(10, 10, getWidth() - 10, getHeight() - 10);
126            g.drawLine(getWidth() - 10, 10, 10, getHeight() - 10);
127          }
128          else if (token == 'O') {
129            g.drawOval(10, 10, getWidth() - 20, getHeight() - 20);
130          }
131        }
132
133        /** Handle mouse click on a cell */
134        public void mouseClicked(MouseEvent e) {
135          if (token == ' ') { // If cell is not occupied
136            if (whoseTurn == 'X') { // If it is the X player's turn
137              setToken('X');   // Set token in the cell
138              whoseTurn = 'O';   // Change the turn
139              jlblStatus.setText("O's turn");   // Display status
140              if (isWon('X'))
141                jlblStatus.setText("X won! The game is over");
142              else if (isFull())
143                jlblStatus.setText("Draw! The game is over");
144            }
145            else if (whoseTurn == 'O') { // If it is the O player's turn
146              setToken('O'); // Set token in the cell
147              whoseTurn = 'X';   // Change the turn
148              jlblStatus.setText("X's turn"); // Display status
149              if (isWon('O'))
150                jlblStatus.setText("O won! The game is over");
151              else if (isFull())
152                jlblStatus.setText("Draw! The game is over");
153            }
154          }
155        }
156
157        public void mousePressed(MouseEvent e) {
158          // TODO: implement this java.awt.event.MouseListener method;
159        }
160
```

```
161          public void mouseReleased(MouseEvent e) {
162              // TODO: implement this java.awt.event.MouseListener method;
163          }
164
165          public void mouseEntered(MouseEvent e) {
166              // TODO: implement this java.awt.event.MouseListener method;
167          }
168
169          public void mouseExited(MouseEvent e) {
170              // TODO: implement this java.awt.event.MouseListener method;
171          }
172      }
173  }
```

Review

The TicTacToe class initializes the user interface with nine cells placed in a panel of GridLayout (Lines 22–26). A label named jlblStatus is used to show the status of the game (Line 34). The variable whoseTurn (Line 11) is used to track the next type of token to be placed in a cell. The methods isFull (Line 59) and isWon (Line 69) are for checking the status of the game.

It is worth noting that the Cell class is declared as an inner class for TicTacToe. This is because the mouseClicked method in Cell references the variable whoseTurn and invokes isFull and isWon in the TicTacToe class. Since Cell is an inner class in TicTacToe, the variable and methods defined in TicTacToe can be used directly in it. This approach makes programs simple and concise. If Cell were not declared as an inner class of TicTacToe, you would have to pass an object of TicTacToe to Cell in order for the variables and methods in TicTacToe to be used in Cell. You will rewrite the program without using an inner class in Exercise 14.6.

The Cell class implements MouseListener to listen for MouseEvent. When a cell is clicked, it draws a shape determined by the variable whoseTurn, and then checks whether the game is won or all the cells are occupied.

There is a problem in this program in that the user may continue to mark the cells even after the game is over. You will fix this problem in Exercise 14.6.

 TIP

You should use an incremental approach in developing a Java project of this kind, working one step at a time. The foregoing program can be divided into five steps:

1. Lay out the user interface and display a fixed token X on a cell.

2. Enable the cell to display a fixed token X upon a mouse click.

3. Coordinate between the two players so as to display tokens X and O alternately.

4. Check whether a player wins, or whether all the cells are occupied without a winner.

5. Implement displaying a message on the label upon each move by a player.

Chapter Summary

- The Web browser controls and executes applets through the init, start, stop, and destroy methods in the Applet class. Applets always extend the Applet class and implement these methods, if applicable, so that they can be run by a Web browser.

- JApplet is a subclass of Applet. It should be used for developing Java applets with Swing components.

- The applet bytecode must be specified, using the <applet> tag in an HTML file to tell the Web browser where to find the applet. The applet can accept parameters from HTML using the <param> tag.

- When an applet is loaded, the Web browser creates an instance of the applet by invoking its default constructor.

- The init method is invoked after the applet is created or recreated.

- The start method is invoked after the init method. It is also called whenever the applet becomes active again after the page containing the applet is revisited.

- The stop method is invoked when the user leaves the page for the applet.

- The destroy method is invoked when the browser exits normally to inform the applet that it is no longer needed and should release any resources it has allocated. The stop method is always called before the destroy method.

- The procedures for writing applications and writing applets are very similar. An applet can easily be converted into an application, and vice versa. Moreover, an applet can be written with the additional capability of running as an application.

- You can pass arguments to an applet using the param attribute in the applet's tag in HTML. To retrieve the value of the parameter, invoke the getParameter(paramName) method.

- The Applet's getParameter method can be invoked only after an instance of the applet is created. Therefore, this method cannot be invoked in the constructor of the **applet** class. You should invoke this method from the init method.

Review Questions

14.1 How do you write a Web page that will contain an applet?

14.2 Describe the init(), start(), stop(), and destroy() methods in the Applet class.

14.3 Where is the getParameter method defined?

14.4 How do you add components to a JApplet?

14.5 Describe the `<applet>` HTML tag. How do you pass parameters to an applet?

14.6 What are the differences between applications and applets? How do you run an application, and how do you run an applet? Is the compilation process different for applications and applets? List some security restrictions on applets.

14.7 Can you place a frame in an applet?

14.8 Can you place an applet in a frame?

14.9 Why does the following applet have a runtime `NullPointerException` error on Line 9?

```
1   public class WelcomeApplet extends JApplet {
2     MessagePanel messagePanel;
3
4     public WelcomeApplet() {
5       MessagePanel messagePanel = new MessagePanel("Welcome to Java!");
6     }
7
8     public void init() {
9       getContentPane().add(messagePanel);
10    }
11  }
```

14.10 What is wrong if the `DisplayMessage` applet is revised as follows?

Revision 1

```
public class DisplayMessage extends JApplet {
  /** Initialize the applet */
  public DisplayMessage() {
    // Get parameter values from the HTML file
    String message = getParameter("MESSAGE");
    int x =
      Integer.parseInt(getParameter("X"));
    int y =
      Integer.parseInt(getParameter("Y"));

    // Create a message panel
    MessagePanel messagePanel =
      new MessagePanel(message);
    messagePanel.setXCoordinate(x);
    messagePanel.setYCoordinate(y);

    // Add the message panel to the applet
    getContentPane().add(messagePanel);
  }
}
```

Revision 2

```
public class DisplayMessage extends JApplet {
  private String message;
  private int x;
  private int y;

  /** Initialize the applet */
  public void init() {
    // Get parameter values from the HTML file
    message = getParameter("MESSAGE");
    x = Integer.parseInt(getParameter("X"));
    y = Integer.parseInt(getParameter("Y"));
  }

  public DisplayMessage() {
    // Create a message panel
    MessagePanel messagePanel =
      new  MessagePanel(message);
    messagePanel.setXCoordinate(x);
    messagePanel.setYCoordinate(y);

    // Add the message panel to the applet
    getContentPane().add(messagePanel);
  }
}
```

Programming Exercises

14.1 (Converting applications to applets) Convert Example 13.8, "Using Radio Buttons," into an applet.

14.2 (Passing parameters to applets) Rewrite Example 14.2, "Passing parameters to Java applets," to display a message with a standard color, font, and size. The message, x, y, color, fontname, and fontsize are parameters in the `<applet>` tag, as shown below:

```
<applet
  code = "Exercise14_2.class"
  width = 200
  height = 50>
  <param name=MESSAGE value="Welcome to Java">
  <param name=X value=40>
  <param name=Y value=50>
  <param name=COLOR value="red">
  <param name=FONTNAME value="Monospaced">
  <param name=FONTSIZE value=20>
You must have a Java-enabled browser to view the applet
</applet>
```

14.3 (Enabling applets to run stand-alone) Rewrite the `LoanApplet` in Example 14.1, "Using Applets," to enable it to run as an application as well as an applet.

14.4 (Creating multiple windows from an applet) Write an applet that contains two buttons called Simple Calculator and Loan. When you click Simple Calculator, a frame for Example 13.11, "Using Menus," appears in a new window so that you can perform arithmetic (see Chapter 13, "Creating User Interfaces"). When you click Loan Calculator, a frame for computing loan payments appears in a separate new window so that you can calculate a loan (see Figure 14.16).

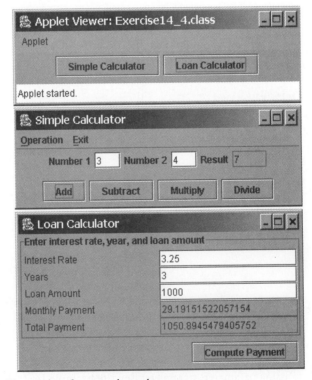

Figure 14.16   *You can show frames in the applets.*

14.5 (Creating a maze) Write an applet that will find a path in a maze, as shown in Figure 14.17. The applet should also run as an application. The maze is represented by an 8 × 8 board. The path must meet the following conditions:

- The path is between the upper-left corner cell and the lower-right corner cell in the maze.

- The applet enables the user to insert or remove a mark on a cell. A path consists of adjacent unmarked cells. Two cells are said to be adjacent if they are horizontal or vertical neighbors, but not diagonal neighbors.

- The path does not contain cells that form a square. The path in Figure 14.18, for example, does not meet this condition. (The condition makes a path easy to identify on the board.)

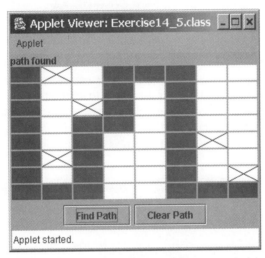

Figure 14.17 *The program finds a path from the upper-left corner to the bottom-right corner.*

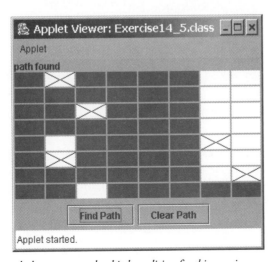

Figure 14.18 *The path does not meet the third condition for this exercise.*

14.6 (Revising Example 14.4 "The TicTacToe Game") Rewrite Example 14.4 with the following modifications:

■ Declare Cell as a stand-alone class rather than an inner class.

■ When the game is over, the user cannot click to mark empty cells.

■ Add a menu named File with a menu item New, as shown in Figure 14.19. The New menu item starts a new game.

Figure 14.19 *The New menu item starts a new game.*

14.7 (Tax calculator) Create an applet to compute tax, as shown in Figure 14.20. The applet lets the user select the tax status and enter the taxable income to compute the tax based on the 2001 federal tax rates, as shown in Exercise 6.9 on page 303. Enable it to run as an application.

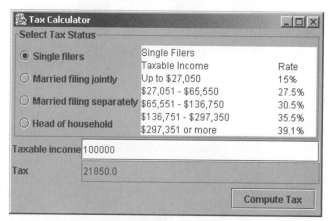

Figure 14.20 *The tax calculator computes the tax for the specified taxable income and tax status.*

14.8 (Creating a calculator) Use various panels of FlowLayout, GridLayout, and BorderLayout to lay out the following calculator and to implement addition (+), subtraction (−), division (/), square root (sqrt), and modulus (%) functions (see Figure 14.21).

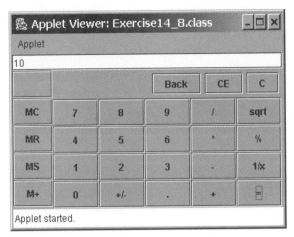

Figure 14.21   *This is a Java implementation of a popular calculator.*

14.9   (Playing TicTacToe with a computer) Example 14.4, "The TicTacToe Game," facilitates two players. Write a new game to enable a player to play with the computer. Add a File menu with two items: New Game and Exit. When you click New Game, it displays a dialog box. From this dialog box, you can decide whether to let the computer go first.

14.10   (Using `KeyboardEvent`) Write a program to get character input from the keyboard and put the characters where the mouse points.

14.11   (Creating a paint utility) Write an applet that emulates a paint utility. Your program should enable the user to choose options and, based on them, to draw shapes or get characters from the keyboard (see Figure 14.22). Enable the applet to run as an application.

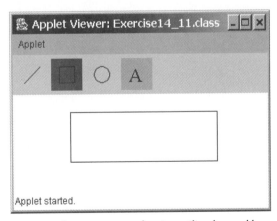

Figure 14.22   *This exercise produces a prototype drawing utility that enables you to draw lines, rectangles, ovals, and characters.*

PART IV

DEVELOPING COMPREHENSIVE PROJECTS

This part of the book is devoted to several advanced features of Java programming. The subjects treated include the use of exception handling to make programs robust and of assertions to ensure correctness, the use of input and output to manage and process large quantities of data, the use of the Java Collections Framework to support Java data structures, the use of multithreading to make programs more responsive and interactive, and the incorporation of sound and images to make programs user-friendly. You will learn how to use these features to develop comprehensive programs.

CHAPTER 15   EXCEPTIONS AND ASSERTIONS

CHAPTER 16   INPUT AND OUTPUT

CHAPTER 17   JAVA DATA STRUCTURES

CHAPTER 18   MULTITHREADING

CHAPTER 19   MULTIMEDIA

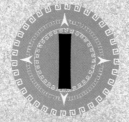

CHAPTER

EXCEPTIONS AND ASSERTIONS

Objectives

- ◉ To understand the concept of exception handling.
- ◉ To distinguish exception types: Error (fatal) vs. Exception (nonfatal), and checked versus uncheck exceptions.
- ◉ To declare exceptions in the method header.
- ◉ To throw exceptions out of a method.
- ◉ To write a try-catch block to handle exceptions.
- ◉ To explain how an exception is propagated.
- ◉ To rethrow exceptions in a try-catch block.
- ◉ To use the finally clause in a try-catch block.
- ◉ To declare custom exception classes.
- ◉ To apply assertions to help ensure program correctness.
- ◉ To know when to use exceptions and assertions.

15.1   Introduction

Programming errors are unavoidable, even for experienced programmers. In Chapter 2, "Primitive Data Types and Operations," you learned that there are three categories of errors: syntax errors, runtime errors, and logic errors. *Syntax errors* arise because the rules of the language have not been followed. They are detected by the compiler. *Runtime errors* occur while the program is running if the environment detects an operation that is impossible to carry out. *Logic errors* occur when a program doesn't perform the way it was intended to. In general, syntax errors are easy to find and easy to correct because the compiler indicates where they came from and why they occurred. You can use the debugging techniques introduced in Section 2.18, "Debugging," to find logic errors. This chapter introduces using exception handling to deal with runtime errors and using assertions to help ensure program correctness.

15.2   Exceptions and Exception Types

Runtime errors cause *exceptions*, which are events that occur during the execution of a program and disrupt the normal flow of control. A program that does not provide code to handle exceptions may terminate abnormally, causing serious problems. For example, if your program attempts to transfer money from a savings account to a checking account, but because of a runtime error is terminated *after* the money is drawn from the savings account and *before* the money is deposited in the checking account, the customer will lose money.

Java provides programmers with the capability to elegantly handle runtime errors. With this capability, referred to as *exception handling*, you can develop robust programs for mission-critical computing.

Here is an example. The following program terminates abnormally because the divisor is 0, which causes a numerical error.

```java
public class Test {
  public static void main(String[] args) {
    System.out.println(3 / 0);
    System.out.println("Welcome to Java");
  }
}
```

Java allows the programmer to catch this error when it occurs, and perform some specific actions, including choosing whether to halt the program or not. You can handle this error in the following code, using a new construct called the *try-catch block* to enable the program to catch the error and continue to execute.

```java
public class Test {
  public static void main(String[] args) {
    try {
      System.out.println(3 / 0);
    }
    catch (Exception ex) {
      System.out.println("Error: " + ex.getMessage());
    }

    System.out.println("Execution continues");
  }
}
```

Runtime errors occur for various reasons. The user may enter an invalid input, for example, or the program may attempt to open a file that doesn't exist, or the network connection may hang up, or the program may attempt to access an out-of-bounds array element. When a runtime error occurs, Java raises an exception.

Exceptions are handled differently from the events of GUI programming. (In Chapter 12, "Event-Driven Programming," you learned the events used in GUI programming.) An *event* may be ignored in GUI programming, but an *exception* cannot be ignored. In GUI programming, a listener must register with the source object. External user action on the source object generates an event, and the source object notifies the listener by invoking the handlers implemented by the listener. If no listener is registered with the source object, the event is ignored. When an exception occurs, however, the program will terminate if the exception is not caught by the program.

15.2.1   Exception Classes

A Java exception is an instance of a class derived from `Throwable`. The `Throwable` class is contained in the `java.lang` package, and subclasses of `Throwable` are contained in various packages. Errors related to GUI components are included in the `java.awt` package; numeric exceptions are included in the `java.lang` package because they are related to the `java.lang.Number` class. You can create your own exception classes by extending `Throwable` or a subclass of `Throwable`. Figure 15.1 shows some of Java's predefined exception classes.

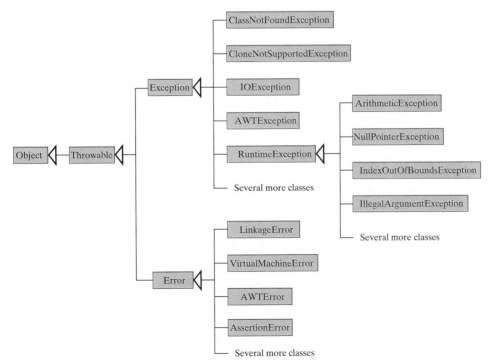

Figure 15.1   *Exceptions thrown are instances of the classes shown in this diagram, or a subclass of one of these classes.*

NOTE

The class names `Error`, `Exception`, and `RuntimeException` are somewhat confusing. All these classes are exceptions. `Exception` is just one of these classes, and all the errors discussed here occur at runtime.

The `Error` class describes internal system errors. Such errors rarely occur. If one does, there is little you can do beyond notifying the user and trying to terminate the program gracefully. Examples of subclasses of `Error` are `LinkageError`, `VirtualMachineError`, `AWTError`, and `AssertionError`. Subclasses of `LinkageError` indicate that a class has some dependency on another class, but that the latter class has changed incompatibly after the compilation of the former class. Subclasses of `VirtualMachineError` indicate that the Java Virtual Machine is broken or has run out of the resources necessary for it to continue operating. `AWTError` is caused by a fatal error in the GUI runtime system. `AssertionError` is raised if an assertion has failed.

The `Exception` class describes errors caused by your program and external circumstances. These errors can be caught and handled by your program. `Exception` has many subclasses, among them `ClassNotFoundException`, `CloneNotSupportedException`, `IOException`, `RuntimeException`, and `AWTException`.

The `ClassNotFoundException` is raised if you attempt to use a class that does not exist. It would occur, for example, if you tried to run a nonexistent class using the **java** command, or your program was composed of, say, three class files, only two of which could be found.

The `CloneNotSupportedException` is raised if you attempt to clone an object whose defining class does not implement the `Cloneable` interface. Cloning objects were introduced in Chapter 9, "Abstract Classes and Interfaces."

The `RuntimeException` class describes programming errors, such as bad casting, accessing an out-of-bounds array, and numeric errors. Examples of subclasses of `RuntimeException` are `ArithmeticException`, `NullPointerException`, `IndexOutOfBoundsException`, and `IllegalArgumentException`.

`ArithmeticException` is for integer arithmetic. Java deals with integer arithmetic differently from floating-point arithmetic. Dividing by zero or modulus by zero is invalid for integer arithmetic and throws `ArithmeticException`. Floating-point arithmetic does not throw exceptions. For floating-point arithmetic, dividing by zero overflows to infinity. See Appendix F, "Special Floating-Point Values," for a discussion of special values for floating-point arithmetic.

`NullPointerException` is thrown if you attempt to access the object through a `null` reference variable. `IndexOutOfBoundsException` is thrown if an index to an array is out of range. `IllegalArgumentException` is thrown if a method is passed an argument that is illegal or inappropriate.

The `IOException` class describes errors related to input/output operations, such as invalid input, reading past the end of a file, and opening a nonexistent file. Examples of subclasses of `IOException` are `InterruptedIOException`, `EOFException` (EOF short for End Of File), and `FileNotFoundException`.

The `AWTException` class describes exceptions in GUI components.

15.2.2   Checked and Unchecked Exceptions

`RuntimeException`, `Error`, and their subclasses are known as *unchecked exceptions*. All other exceptions are known as *checked exceptions*, meaning that the compiler forces the programmer to check and deal with them.

In most cases, unchecked exceptions reflect programming logic errors that are not recoverable. For example, a `NullPointerException` is thrown if you access an object through a reference variable before an object is assigned to it; an `IndexOutOfBounds-Exception` is thrown if you access an element in an array outside the bounds of the array. These are logic errors that should be corrected in the program. Unchecked exceptions can occur anywhere in a program. To avoid cumbersome overuse of try-catch blocks, Java does not mandate that you write code to catch unchecked exceptions.

15.3   Understanding Exception Handling

Java's exception-handling model is based on three operations: *declaring an exception, throwing an exception*, and *catching an exception*, as shown in Figure 15.2.

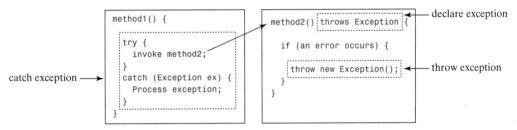

Figure 15.2   *Exception handling in Java consists of declaring exceptions, throwing exceptions, and catching and processing exceptions.*

15.3.1   Declaring Exceptions

In Java, the statement currently being executed belongs to a method. The Java interpreter invokes the `main` method for a Java application, and the Web browser invokes the applet's default constructor and then the `init` method for a Java applet. Every method must state the types of unchecked exceptions it might throw. This is known as *declaring exceptions*. Because system errors and runtime errors can happen to any code, Java does not require that you declare `Error` and `RuntimeException` (unchecked exceptions) explicitly in the method. However, all other exceptions must be explicitly declared in the method declaration if they are thrown by the method so that the caller of the method is informed of the exception.

To declare an exception in a method, use the `throws` keyword in the method declaration, as in this example:

```
public void myMethod() throws IOException
```

The `throws` keyword indicates that `myMethod` might throw an `IOException`. If the method might throw multiple exceptions, you can add a list of the exceptions, separated by commas, after `throws`:

```
public void myMethod()
    throws Exception1, Exception2, ..., ExceptionN
```

15.3.2   Throwing Exceptions

A program that detects an error can create an instance of an appropriate exception type and throw it. This is known as *throwing an exception*. Here is an example: Suppose the program detected that an argument passed to the method violates the method contract (e.g., the argument must be nonnegative, but a negative argument is passed); the program can create an instance of `IllegalArgumentException` and throw it, as follows:

```
IllegalArgumentException ex =
    new IllegalArgumentException("Wrong Argument");
throw ex;
```

Or if you prefer, you can use the following:

```
throw new IllegalArgumentException("Wrong Argument");
```

 NOTE

The keyword to declare an exception is `throws`, and the keyword to throw an exception is `throw`.

A method can always throw an unchecked exception. If a method throws a checked exception, the exception must be declared in the method declaration.

15.3.3   Catching Exceptions

You now know how to declare an exception and how to throw an exception. When an exception is thrown, it can be caught and handled in a try-catch block, as follows:

```
try {
  statements;   // Statements that may throw exceptions
}
catch (Exception1 exVar1) {
  handler for exception1;
}
catch (Exception2 exVar2) {
  handler for exception2;
}
...
catch (ExceptionN exVar3) {
  handler for exceptionN;
}
```

If no exceptions arise during the execution of the `try` clause, the `catch` clauses are skipped.

If one of the statements inside the try block throws an exception, Java skips the remaining statements in the try block and starts the process of finding the code to handle the exception. The code that handles the exception is called the *exception handler*; it is found by propagating the exception backward through a chain of method calls, starting from the current method. Each catch clause is examined in turn, from first to last, to see whether the type of the exception object is an instance of the exception class in the catch clause. If so, the exception object is assigned to the variable declared and the code in the catch clause is executed. If no handler is found, Java exits this method, passes the exception to the method that invoked the method, and continues the same process to find a handler. If no handler is found in the chain of methods being invoked, the program terminates and prints an error message on the console. The process of finding a handler is called *catching an exception*.

Suppose the main method invokes method1, method1 invokes method2, method2 invokes method3, and an exception occurs in method3, as shown in Figure 15.3. Consider the following scenario:

- If method3 cannot handle the exception, method3 is aborted and the control is returned to method2. If the exception type is Exception3, it is caught by the catch clause for handling exception ex3 in method2. statement5 is skipped, and statement6 is executed.

- If the exception type is Exception2, method2 is aborted, the control is returned to method1, and the exception is caught by the catch clause for handling exception ex2 in method1. statement3 is skipped, and statement4 is executed.

- If the exception type is Exception1, method1 is aborted, the control is returned to the *main* method, and the exception is caught by the catch clause for handling exception ex1 in the main method. statement1 is skipped, and statement2 is executed.

- If the exception type is not Exception1, Exception2, or Exception3, the exception is not caught and the program terminates. statement1 and statement2 are not executed.

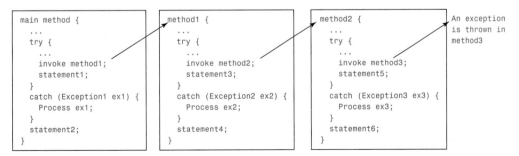

Figure 15.3 *If an exception is not caught in the current method, it is passed to its caller. The process is repeated until the exception is caught or passed to the* main *method.*

NOTE

Methods are executed on threads. If an exception occurs on a thread, the thread is terminated if the exception is not handled. However, the other threads in the application are not affected. There are several threads running to support a GUI application. A thread is launched to execute an event handler (e.g., the `actionPerformed` method for the `ActionEvent`). If an exception occurs during the execution of a GUI event handler, the thread is terminated if the exception is not handled. Interestingly, Java prints the error message on the console, but does not terminate the application. The program goes back to its user-interface-processing loop to run continuously.

An exception object contains valuable information about the exception. You may use the following instance methods in the `java.lang.Throwable` class to get information regarding the exception.

- `public String getMessage()`

  Returns the detailed message of the `Throwable` object.

- `public String toString()`

  Returns the concatenation of three strings: (1) the full name of the exception class; (2) ":" (a colon and a space); (3) the `getMessage()` method.

- `public String getLocalizedMessage()`

  Returns a localized description of the `Throwable` object. Subclasses of `Throwable` can override this method in order to produce a locale-specific message. For subclasses that do not override this method, the default implementation returns the same result as `getMessage()`. Locale-specific issues are addressed in Chapter 20, "Internationalization."

- `public void printStackTrace()`

  Prints the `Throwable` object and its trace information on the console.

NOTE

Various exception classes can be derived from a common superclass. If a `catch` clause catches exception objects of a superclass, it can catch all the exception objects of the subclasses of that superclass.

NOTE

The order in which exceptions are specified in `catch` clauses is important. A compilation error will result if a catch clause for a superclass type appears before a catch clause for a subclass type. For example, the following ordering is erroneous, since `RuntimeException` is a subclass of `Exception`:

```
try {
  ...
}
catch (Exception ex) {
  ...
}
```

```
catch (RuntimeException ex) {
  ...
}
```

The correct ordering should be:

```
try {
  ...
}
catch (RuntimeException ex) {
  ...
}
catch (Exception ex) {
  ...
}
```

 NOTE

Java forces you to deal with checked exceptions. If a method declares a checked exception (i.e., an exception other than `Error` or `RuntimeException`), you must place it in a `try` statement and handle it in order to avoid abnormal termination.

Example 15.1 Declaring, Throwing, and Catching Exceptions

Problem

This example demonstrates declaring, throwing, and catching exceptions by modifying the `setRadius` method in the `Circle` class defined in Example 6.5, "Using Instance and Static Variables and Methods." The new `setRadius` method throws an exception if the radius is negative.

Solution

Create a new `Circle` class, which is the same except that the `setRadius(double newRadius)` method throws an `IllegalArgumentException` if the argument `newRadius` is negative.

```
1   // Circle.java: setRadius throws an exception
2   package chapter15;
3
4   public class Circle {
5     /** The radius of the circle */
6     private double radius;
7
8     /** The number of the objects created */
9     private static int numOfObjects = 0;
10
11    /** Default constructor */
12    public Circle() {
13      this(1.0);
14    }
15
```

continues

Example 15.1 Continued

```
16        /** Construct a circle with a specified radius */
17        public Circle(double newRadius) {
18          setRadius(newRadius);
19          numOfObjects++;
20        }
21
22        /** Return radius */
23        public double getRadius() {
24          return radius;
25        }
26
27        /** Set a new radius */
28        public void setRadius(double newRadius)
29          throws IllegalArgumentException {
30          if (newRadius >= 0)
31            radius =  newRadius;
32          else
33            throw new IllegalArgumentException(
34              "Radius cannot be negative");
35        }
36
37        /** Return numOfObjects */
38        public static int getNumOfObjects() {
39          return numOfObjects;
40        }
41
42        /** Return the area of this circle */
43        public double findArea() {
44          return radius * radius * 3.14159;
45        }
47      }
```

A test program that uses the new Circle class is given below. Figure 15.4 shows a sample run of the test program.

```
1     // TestCircleWithException.java: Test exception handling
2     package chapter15;
3
4     public class TestCircleWithException {
5       /** Main method */
6       public static void main(String[] args) {
7         try {
8           Circle c1 = new Circle(5);
9           Circle c2 = new Circle(-5);
10          Circle c3 = new Circle(0);
11        }
12        catch (IllegalArgumentException ex) {
13          System.out.println(ex);
14        }
15
16        System.out.println("Number of objects created: " +
17          Circle.getNumOfObjects());
18      }
19    }
```

664

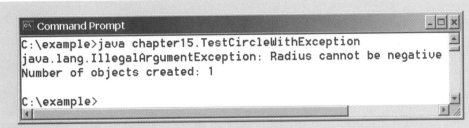

Figure 15.4   *The exception is thrown when the radius is negative.*

Review

The original `Circle` class remains intact except for the constructor `Circle(newRadius)` and the `setRadius` method. The `setRadius` method now declares an exception and throws it if the radius is negative.

The `setRadius` method declares to throw `IllegalArgumentException` in the method declaration (Lines 28–29 in Circle.java). The `Circle` class would still compile if the `throws IllegalArgumentException` clause were removed from the method declaration, since it is a subclass of `RuntimeException` and every method can throw `RuntimeException` (unchecked exception) regardless of whether it is declared in the method header.

The test program creates three `Circle` objects, c1, c2, and c3, to test how to handle exceptions. Invoking `new Circle(-5)` (Line 9 in `TestCircleWithException`) causes the `setRadius` method to be invoked, which throws an `IllegalArgumentException`, because the radius is negative. In the `catch` clause, the type of the object ex is `IllegalArgumentException`, which matches the exception object thrown by the `setRadius` method. So this exception is caught by the `catch` clause.

The exception handler simply prints a short message, `ex.toString()` (Line 13), about the exception, using `System.out.println(ex)`.

Note that the execution continues in the event of an exception. If the handlers had not caught the exception, the program would have abruptly terminated.

The test program would still compile if the `try` statement were not used, because the method throws an instance of `IllegalArgumentException`, a subclass of `RuntimeException` (unchecked exception). If a method throws an exception other than `RuntimeException` and `Error`, the method must be invoked in a `try` catch block.

Example 15.2 Exceptions in GUI Applications

Problem

Example 13.11, "Using Menus," is used here to demonstrate the effect of exceptions in GUI applications.

Solution

Run the program and enter any number in the Number 1 field and 0 in the Number 2 field; then click the Divide button (see Figure 15.5). You will see nothing in the Result field, but an error message will appear in the Output window, as shown in Figure 15.6. The GUI application continues.

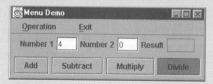

Figure 15.5 *Since the divisor is 0 in the Number 2 field, a* `RuntimeException` *is thrown when the Divide button is clicked.*

```
Command Prompt - java chapter13.MenuDemo

C:\example>java chapter13.MenuDemo
java.lang.ArithmeticException: / by zero
        at chapter13.MenuDemo.calculate(MenuDemo.java:144)
        at chapter13.MenuDemo.actionPerformed(MenuDemo.java:112)
        at javax.swing.AbstractButton.fireActionPerformed(AbstractBu
64)
        at javax.swing.AbstractButton$ForwardActionEvents.actionPerf
ctButton.java:1817)
        at javax.swing.DefaultButtonModel.fireActionPerformed(Defaul
.java:419)
        at javax.swing.DefaultButtonModel.setPressed(DefaultButtonMo
)
        at javax.swing.plaf.basic.BasicButtonListener.mouseReleased(
istener.java:245)
        at java.awt.Component.processMouseEvent(Component.java:5093)
        at java.awt.Component.processEvent(Component.java:4890)
        at java.awt.Container.processEvent(Container.java:1566)
```

Figure 15.6 *In GUI programs, if an exception is not caught, an error message appears in the console window.*

Review

An `ArithmeticException` occurred during the execution of the `actionPerformed` method. The thread on which the method is executed is terminated, but the program continues to run.

666

If you rewrite the, "calculate method," in the MenuDemo program of Example 13.11 "Using Menus," with a try-catch block to catch RuntimeException, as shown below, the program will display a message dialog box in the case of a numerical error, as shown in Figure 15.7. No errors are reported because they are handled in the program.

```java
// Calculate and show the result in jtfResult
private void calculate(char operator) {
  // Obtain Number 1 and Number 2
  int num1 = (Integer.parseInt(jtfNum1.getText().trim()));
  int num2 = (Integer.parseInt(jtfNum2.getText().trim()));
  int result = 0;

  try {
    // Perform selected operation
    switch (operator) {
      case '+': result = num1 + num2;
                break;
      case '-': result = num1 - num2;
                break;
      case '*': result = num1 * num2;
                break;
      case '/': result = num1 / num2;
    }

    // Set result in jtfResult
    jtfResult.setText(String.valueOf(result));
  }
  catch (RuntimeException ex) {
    JOptionPane.showMessageDialog(this, ex.getMessage(),
      "Operation error", JOptionPane.ERROR_MESSAGE);
  }
}
```

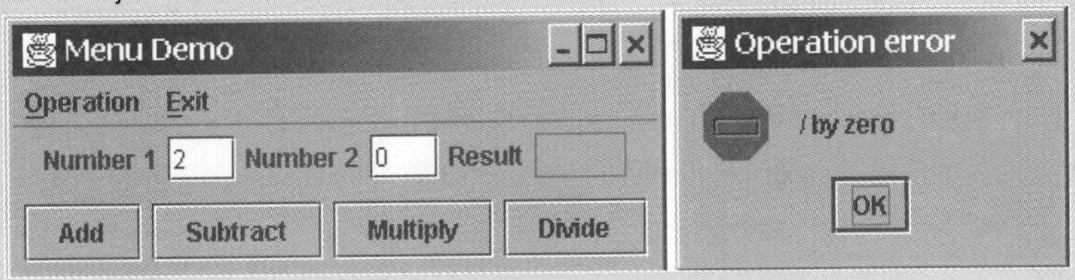

Figure 15.7 *When you click the Divide button to divide a number by 0, a numerical exception occurs. The exception is displayed in the message dialog box.*

15.4 Rethrowing Exceptions

When an exception occurs in a method, the method exits immediately if it does not catch the exception. If the method is required to perform some task before exiting, you can catch the exception in the method and then rethrow it to the real handler in a structure like the one given below:

```java
try {
  statements;
}
catch (TheException ex) {
  perform operations before exits;
  throw ex;
}
```

667

The statement `throw ex` rethrows the exception so that other handlers get a chance to process the exception `ex`.

15.5 The *finally* Clause

Occasionally, you may want some code to be executed regardless of whether an exception occurs or is caught. Java has a `finally` clause that can be used to accomplish this objective. The syntax for the `finally` clause might look like this:

```
try {
  statements;
}
catch (TheException ex) {
  handling ex;
}
finally {
  finalStatements;
}
```

The code in the `finally` block is executed under all circumstances, regardless of whether an exception occurs in the `try` block or is caught. Consider three possible cases:

■ If no exception arises in the `try` block, `finalStatements` is executed, and the next statement after the `try` statement is executed.

■ If one of the statements causes an exception in the `try` block that is caught in a `catch` clause, the other statements in the `try` block are skipped, the `catch` clause is executed, and the `finally` clause is executed. If the `catch` clause does not rethrow an exception, the next statement after the `try` statement is executed. If it does, the exception is passed to the caller of this method.

■ If one of the statements causes an exception that is not caught in any `catch` clause, the other statements in the `try` block are skipped, the `finally` clause is executed, and the exception is passed to the caller of this method.

 NOTE
The `catch` clause may be omitted when the `finally` clause is used.

15.6 When to Use Exceptions

Exception handling separates error-handling code from normal programming tasks, thus making programs easier to read and to modify. Be aware, however, that exception handling usually requires more time and resources because it requires instantiating a new exception object, rolling back the call stack, and propagating the exception through the chain of methods invoked to search for the handler.

An exception occurs in a method. If you want the exception to be processed by its caller, you should create an exception object and throw it. If you can handle the exception in the method where it occurs, there is no need to throw it.

In general, common exceptions that may occur in multiple classes in a project are candidates for exception classes. Simple errors that may occur in individual methods are best handled locally without throwing out exceptions.

When should you use a *try-catch* block in the code? Use it when you have to deal with unexpected error conditions. Do not use a *try-catch* block to deal with simple, expected situations. For example, the following code

```
try {
  System.out.println(refVar.toString());
}
catch (NullPointerException ex) {
  System.out.println("refVar is null");
}
```

is better replaced by

```
if (refVar != null)
  System.out.println(refVar.toString());
else
  System.out.println("refVar is null");
```

Which situations are exceptional and which are expected is sometimes difficult to decide. The point is not to abuse exception handling as a way to deal with a simple logic test.

15.7 Creating Custom Exception Classes (Optional)

Java provides quite a few exception classes. Use them whenever possible instead of creating your own exception classes. However, if you run into a problem that cannot be adequately described by the predefined exception classes, you can create your own exception class, derived from Exception or from a subclass of Exception, such as IOException. This section shows how to create your own exception class.

Example 15.3 Creating Your Own Exception Classes

Problem

Create a Java applet for handling account transactions. The applet displays the account ID and balance, and lets the user deposit to or withdraw from the account. For each transaction, a message is displayed to indicate the status of the transaction: successful or failed. In case of failure, the reason for the failure is reported. A sample run of the program is shown in Figure 15.8.

If a transaction amount is negative, the program raises a negative-amount exception. If the account's balance is less than the requested transaction amount, an insufficient-funds exception is raised.

continues

Example 15.3 Continued

Applet Viewer: chapter15.AccountApplet.class

Applet

Display Account Information

Account ID   1

Account Balance 33.0

Deposit or withdraw funds

Deposit   33   Deposit

Withdraw   1000   Withdraw

Transaction Processed

Applet started.

Figure 15.8   *The program lets you deposit and withdraw funds, and displays the transaction status on the label.*

The example consists of four classes: `Account`, `NegativeAmountException`, `InsufficientAmountException`, and `AccountApplet`. The `Account` class provides information and operations pertaining to the account. `NegativeAmountException` and `InsufficientAmountException` are the exception classes that deal with transactions of negative or insufficient amounts. The `AccountApplet` class utilizes all these classes to perform transactions, transferring funds among accounts. The relationships among these classes are shown in Figure 15.9.

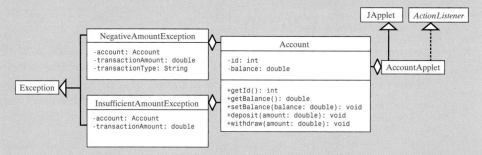

Figure 15.9   `NegativeAmountException` *and* `InsufficientAmountException` *are subclasses of* `Exception` *that contain the account information, transaction amount, and transaction type for the failed transaction.*

Solution

The code for the `Account` class follows. This class contains two data fields: `id` (for account ID) and `balance` (for current balance). The methods for `Account` are `deposit` and `withdraw`. Both methods will throw `NegativeAmountException` if the transaction amount is negative. The `withdraw` method will also throw `InsufficientFundException` if the current balance is less than the requested transaction amount.

```
1    // Account.java: The class for describing an account
2    package chapter15;
3
4    public class Account {
5      // Two data fields in an account
```

```
6      private int id;
7      private double balance;
8
9      /** Construct an account with specified id and balance */
10     public Account(int id, double balance) {
11       this.id = id;
12       this.balance = balance;
13     }
14
15     /** Return id */
16     public int getId() {
17       return id;
18     }
19
20     /** Setter method for balance */
21     public void setBalance(double balance) {
22       this.balance = balance;
23     }
24
25     /** Return balance */
26     public double getBalance() {
27       return balance;
28     }
29
30     /** Deposit an amount to this account */
31     public void deposit(double amount)
32       throws NegativeAmountException {
33       if (amount < 0)
34         throw new NegativeAmountException
35           (this, amount, "deposit");
36       balance = balance + amount;
37     }
38
39     /** Withdraw an amount from this account */
40     public void withdraw(double amount)
41       throws NegativeAmountException, InsufficientFundException {
42       if (amount < 0)
43         throw new NegativeAmountException
44           (this, amount, "withdraw");
45       if (balance < amount)
46         throw new InsufficientFundException(this, amount);
47       balance = balance - amount;
48     }
49   }
```

The NegativeAmountException exception class follows. It contains information about the attempted transaction type (deposit or withdrawal), the account, and the negative amount passed from the method.

```
1    // NegativeAmountException.java: Negative amount exception
2    package chapter15;
3
4    public class NegativeAmountException extends Exception {
5      /** Account information to be passed to the handlers */
6      private Account account;
7      private double amount;
8      private String transactionType;
9
10     /** Construct an negative amount exception */
11     public NegativeAmountException(Account account,
12                                    double amount,
13                                    String transactionType) {
```

continues

671

Example 15.3 Continued

```
14         super("Negative amount");
15         this.account = account;
16         this.amount = amount;
17         this.transactionType = transactionType;
18       }
19     }
```

The `InsufficientFundException` exception class follows. It contains information about the account and the amount passed from the method.

```
1    // InsufficientFundException.java: An exception class for describing
2    // insufficient fund exception
3    package chapter15;
4
5    public class InsufficientFundException extends Exception {
6      /** Information to be passed to the handlers */
7      private Account account;
8      private double amount;
9
10     /** Construct an insufficient exception */
11     public InsufficientFundException(Account account, double amount) {
12       super("Insufficient amount");
13       this.account = account;
14       this.amount = amount;
15     }
16
17     /** Override the "toString" method */
18     public String toString() {
19       return "Account balance is " + account.getBalance();
20     }
21   }
```

The `AccountApplet` class is given as follows:

```
1    // AccountApplet.java: Use custom exception classes
2    package chapter15;
3
4    import java.awt.*;
5    import java.awt.event.*;
6    import javax.swing.*;
7    import javax.swing.border.*;
8
9    public class AccountApplet extends JApplet
10     implements ActionListener {
11     // Declare text fields
12     private JTextField jtfID, jtfBalance, jtfDeposit, jtfWithdraw;
13
14     // Declare Deposit and Withdraw buttons
15     private JButton jbtDeposit, jbtWithdraw;
16
17     // Create an account with initial balance $1000
18     private Account account = new Account(1, 1000);
19
20     // Create a label for showing status
21     private JLabel jlblStatus = new JLabel();
22
23     /** Initialize the applet */
24     public void init() {
25       // Panel p1 to group ID and Balance labels and text fields
26       JPanel p1 = new JPanel();
27       p1.setLayout(new GridLayout(2, 2));
```

```
28          p1.add(new JLabel("Account ID"));
29          p1.add(jtfID = new JTextField(4));
30          p1.add(new JLabel("Account Balance"));
31          p1.add(jtfBalance = new JTextField(4));
32          jtfID.setEditable(false);
33          jtfBalance.setEditable(false);
34          p1.setBorder(new TitledBorder("Display Account Information"));
35
36          // Panel p2 to group deposit amount and Deposit button and
37          // withdraw amount and Withdraw button
38          JPanel p2 = new JPanel();
39          p2.setLayout(new GridLayout(2, 3));
40          p2.add(new JLabel("Deposit"));
41          p2.add(jtfDeposit = new JTextField(4));
42          p2.add(jbtDeposit = new JButton("Deposit"));
43          p2.add(new JLabel("Withdraw"));
44          p2.add(jtfWithdraw = new JTextField(4));
45          p2.add(jbtWithdraw = new JButton("Withdraw"));
46          p2.setBorder(new TitledBorder("Deposit or withdraw funds"));
47
48          // Place panels p1, p2, and label in the applet
49          this.getContentPane().add(p1, BorderLayout.WEST);
50          this.getContentPane().add(p2, BorderLayout.CENTER);
51          this.getContentPane().add(jlblStatus, BorderLayout.SOUTH);
52
53          // Refresh ID and Balance fields
54          refreshFields();
55
56          // Register listener
57          jbtDeposit.addActionListener(this);
58          jbtWithdraw.addActionListener(this);
59        }
60
61        /** Handle ActionEvent */
62        public void actionPerformed(ActionEvent e) {
63          if (e.getSource() == jbtDeposit) {
64            try {
65              double depositValue = (Double.valueOf(
66                jtfDeposit.getText().trim())).doubleValue();
67              account.deposit(depositValue);
68              refreshFields();
69              jlblStatus.setText("Transaction Processed");
70            }
71            catch (NegativeAmountException ex) {
72              jlblStatus.setText("Negative Amount");
73            }
74          }
75          else if (e.getSource() == jbtWithdraw) {
76            try {
77              double withdrawValue = (Double.valueOf(
78                jtfWithdraw.getText().trim())).doubleValue();
79              account.withdraw(withdrawValue);
80              refreshFields();
81              jlblStatus.setText("Transaction Processed");
82            }
83            catch (NegativeAmountException ex) {
84              jlblStatus.setText("Negative Amount");
85            }
86            catch (InsufficientFundException ex) {
87              jlblStatus.setText("Insufficient Funds");
88            }
89          }
90        }
91
```

continues

Example 15.3 Continued

```
92        /** Update the display for account balance */
93        public void refreshFields() {
94          jtfID.setText(String.valueOf(account.getId()));
95          jtfBalance.setText(String.valueOf(account.getBalance()));
96        }
97      }
```

Review

In the `Account` class, the `deposit` method (Line 31) throws `Negative-AmountException` (Line 34–35) if the amount to be deposited is less than 0. The `withdraw` method (Line 40) throws a `NegativeAmountException` if the amount to be withdrawn is less than 0 (Lines 43–44), and an `InsufficientFundException` if the amount to be withdrawn is less than the current balance (Line 46).

The user-defined exception class always extends `Exception` or a subclass of `Exception`. Therefore, both `NegativeAmountException` and `Insufficient-FundException` extend `Exception`. In the Java API, each exception class has at least two constructors: a default constructor and a constructor with a string parameter for a detailed message. Line 12 in `InsufficientFundException` and Line 14 in `NegativeAmountException` invoke the constructor in `Exception` using `super("Insufficient amount")` and `super("Negative amount")`.

Storing relevant information in the exception object is useful, because the handler can then retrieve the information from the exception object. For example, `NegativeAmountException` contains the account, the amount, and the transaction type.

The `AccountApplet` class creates an applet with two panels (p1 and p2) (Lines 26, 38) and a label that displays messages. Panel p1 contains account ID and balance; panel p2 contains the action buttons for depositing and withdrawing funds.

With a click of the Deposit button, the amount in the `Deposit` text field is added to the balance. With a click of the Withdraw button, the amount in the `Withdraw` text field is subtracted from the balance.

For each successful transaction, the message `Transaction Processed` is displayed. For a negative amount, the message `Negative Amount` is displayed; for insufficient funds, the message `Insufficient Funds` is displayed.

15.8 Assertions

An *assertion* is a Java statement that enables you to assert an assumption about your program. An assertion contains a Boolean expression that should be true during program execution. Assertions can be used to ensure program correctness and avoid logic errors.

15.8.1   Declaring Assertions

An *assertion* is declared using the new Java keyword assert in JDK 1.4, as follows:

assert *assertion*; or

assert *assertion* : *detailMessage*;

where *assertion* is a Boolean expression and *detailMessage* is a primitive-type or an Object value.

When an assertion statement is executed, Java evaluates the assertion. If it is false, an AssertionError will be thrown. The AssertionError class has a default constructor and seven overloaded single-argument constructors of type int, long, float, double, boolean, char, and Object. For the first assert statement with no detailed message, the default constructor of AssertionError is used. For the second assert statement with a detailed message, an appropriate AssertionError constructor is used to match the data type of the message. Since AssertionError is a subclass of Error, when an assertion becomes false, the program displays a message on the console and exits.

Here is an example of using assertions.

```
1     public class AssertionDemo {
2       public static void main(String[] args) {
3         int i; int sum = 0;
4         for (i = 0; i < 10; i++) {
5           sum += i;
6         }
7         assert i == 10;
8         assert sum > 10 && sum < 5 * 10 : "sum is " + sum;
9       }
10    }
```

The statement assert i == 10 asserts that i is 10 when the statement is executed. If i is not 10, an AssertionError is thrown. The statement assert sum > 10 && sum < 5 * 10 : "sum is " + sum asserts that sum > 10 and sum < 5 * 10. If false, an AssertionError with message "sum is " + sum is thrown.

Suppose you typed i < 100 instead of i < 10 by mistake in Line 4, the following AssertionError would be thrown:

```
Exception in thread "main" java.lang.AssertionError
        at AssertionDemo.main(AssertionDemo.java:7)
```

Suppose you typed sum += 1 instead of sum += i by mistake in Line 5, the following AssertionError would be thrown:

```
Exception in thread "main" java.lang.AssertionError: sum is 10
        at AssertionDemo.main(AssertionDemo.java:8)
```

15.8.2   Compiling Programs with Assertions

Since assert is a new Java keyword introduced in JDK 1.4, you have to compile the program using a JDK 1.4 compiler. Furthermore, you need to include the switch **-source 1.4** in the compiler command, as follows:

javac –source 1.4 AssertionDemo.java

NOTE

In JBuilder, check *Enable assert keyword* in the *Java* tab of *Build* Page in the Project properties dialog to compile and run programs with assertions enabled, as shown in Figure 15.10.

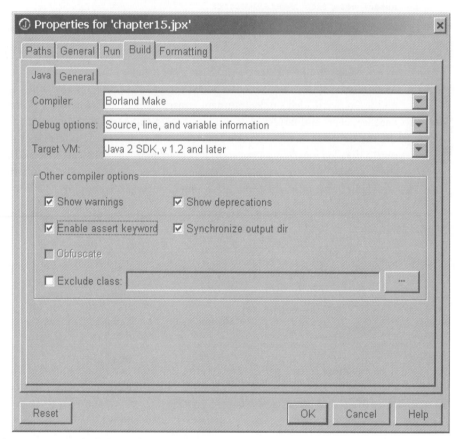

Figure 15.10   *Check the Enable assert keyword option in the project properties if your program uses assertions.*

15.8.3   Running Programs with Assertions

By default, assertions are disabled at runtime. To enable them, use the switch **-enableassertions**, or **-ea** for short, as follows:

java –ea AssertionDemo

Assertions can be selectively enabled or disabled at class level or package level. The disable switch is -**disableassertions**, or **-da** for short. For example, the following command enables assertions in package package1 and disables assertions in class Class1.

java –ea:package1 –da:Class1 AssertionDemo

15.8.4   Using Exception Handling or Assertions

Assertion should not be used to replace exception handling. Exception handling deals with unusual circumstances during program execution. Assertions are intended to ensure the correctness of the program. Exception handling addresses robustness, whereas assertion addresses correctness. Like exception handling, assertions are not used for normal tests, but for internal consistency and validity checks. Assertions are checked at runtime and can be turned on or off at startup time.

Do not use assertions for argument checking in public methods. Valid arguments that may be passed to a public method are considered to be part of the method's contract. The contract must always be obeyed whether assertions are enabled or disabled. For example, the following code should be rewritten using exception handling, as shown in Lines 28–35 in Circle.java in Example 15.1, "Declaring, Throwing, and Catching Exceptions."

```java
public void setRadius(double newRadius) {
  assert newRadius >= 0;
  radius =  newRadius;
}
```

Use assertions to reaffirm assumptions. This will increase your confidence in the program's correctness. A common use of assertions is to replace assumptions with assertions in the code. For example, the following code

```java
if (even) {
  ...
}
else { // even is false
  ...
}
```

can be replaced by

```java
if (even) {
  ...
}
else {
  assert !even;
  ...
}
```

The following code

```java
if (numOfDollars > 1) {
  ...
}
else if (numOfDollars == 1) {
  ...
}
```

can be replaced by

```
if (numOfDollars > 1) {
  ...
}
else if (numOfDollars == 1) {
  ...
}
else
  assert false : numOfDollars;
```

Another good use of assertions is to place them in a `switch` statement without a default case. For example,

```
switch (month) {
  case 1: ... ; break;
  case 2: ... ; break;
  ...
  case 12: ... ; break;
  default: assert false : "Invalid month: " + month
}
```

Chapter Summary

- When an exception occurs, Java creates an object that contains the information for the exception. You can use the information to handle the exception.

- A Java exception is an instance of a class derived from `java.lang.Throwable`. Java provides a number of predefined exception classes, such as `Error`, `Exception`, `RuntimeException`, `ClassNotFoundException`, `NullPointerException`, and `ArithmeticException`. You can also define your own exception class by extending `Exception`.

- Exceptions occur during the execution of a method. `RuntimeException` and `Error` are unchecked exceptions, and all other exceptions are checked exceptions.

- When declaring a method, you have to declare a checked exception if the method might throw that checked exception, thus telling the compiler what can go wrong.

- The keyword to declare an exception is `throws`, and the keyword to throw an exception is `throw`.

- To invoke the method that declares checked exceptions, you must enclose the method call in a `try` statement. When an exception occurs during the execution of the method, the `catch` clause catches and handles the exception.

- If an exception is not caught in the current method, it is passed to its caller. The process is repeated until the exception is caught or passed to the `main` method.

- If an exception of a subclass of `Exception` occurs in a GUI component, Java prints the error message on the console, but the program goes back to its user-interface-processing loop to run continuously. The exception is ignored.

■ Various exception classes can be derived from a common superclass. If a catch clause catches exception objects of a superclass, it can catch all the exception objects of the subclasses of that superclass.

■ The order in which the exceptions are specified in a catch clause is important. A compilation error will result if you do not specify an exception object of a class before an exception object of the superclass of that class.

■ When an exception occurs in a method, the method exits immediately if it does not catch the exception. If the method is required to perform some task before exiting, you can catch the exception in the method and then rethrow it to the real handler.

■ The code in the finally block is executed under all circumstances, regardless of whether an exception occurs in the try block or is caught.

■ Exception handling separates error-handling code from normal programming tasks, thus making programs easier to read and to modify.

■ Exception handling should not be used to replace simple tests. You should test simple exceptions whenever possible, and reserve exception handling for dealing with situations that cannot be handled with if statements.

■ An *assertion* is a Java statement that enables you to assert an assumption about your program. An assertion contains a Boolean expression that should be true during program execution. Assertions can be used to ensure program correctness.

■ Exceptions address robustness, whereas assertions address correctness. Exceptions and assertions are not meant to substitute for simple tests. Avoid using exception handling if a simple if statement is sufficient. Never use assertions to check normal conditions.

Review Questions

 NOTE

In the following questions, assume that the divide method in Rational in Example 10.2, "The Rational Class," is modified as follows:

```
public Rational divide(Rational secondRational) throws Exception {
  if (secondRational.getNumerator() == 0)
    throw new Exception("Divisor cannot be zero");

  long n = numerator * secondRational.getDenominator();
  long d = denominator * secondRational.getNumerator();
  return new Rational(n, d);
}
```

The divide method in the Rational class throws Exception if the divisor is 0.

15.1 Describe the Java Throwable class, its subclasses, and the types of exceptions.

15.2 What is the purpose of declaring exceptions? How do you declare an exception, and where? Can you declare multiple exceptions in a method declaration?

15.3 How do you throw an exception? Can you throw multiple exceptions in one throw statement?

15.4 What is the keyword `throw` used for? What is the keyword `throws` used for?

15.5 What does the Java runtime system do when an exception occurs?

15.6 How do you catch an exception?

15.7 Does the presence of a `try-catch` block impose overhead when no exception occurs?

15.8 Suppose that `statement2` causes an exception in the following `try-catch` block:

```
try {
  statement1;
  statement2;
  statement3;
}
catch (Exception1 ex1) {
}
catch (Exception2 ex2) {
}

statement4;
```

Answer the following questions:

- Will `statement3` be executed?

- If the exception is not caught, will `statement4` be executed?

- If the exception is caught in the `catch` clause, will `statement4` be executed?

- If the exception is passed to the caller, will `statement4` be executed?

15.9 Suppose that `statement2` causes an exception in the following statement:

```
try {
  statement1;
  statement2;
  statement3;
}
catch (Exception1 ex1) {
}
catch (Exception2 ex2) {
}
catch (Exception3 ex3) {
  throw ex3;
}
finally {
  statement4;
};
statement5;
```

Answer the following questions:

- Will statement5 be executed if the exception is not caught?

- If the exception is of type Exception3, will statement4 be executed, and will statement5 be executed?

15.10 What is a checked exception, and what is an unchecked exception?

15.11 What is displayed when the following program is run?

```
class Test {
  public static void main(String[] args) {
    try {
      Rational r1 = new Rational(3, 4);
      Rational r2   = new Rational(0, 1);
      Rational x = r1.divide(r2);

      int i = 0;
      int y = 2 / i;
      System.out.println("Welcome to Java");
    }
    catch (RuntimeException ex) {
      System.out.println("Integer operation error");
    }
    catch (Exception ex) {
      System.out.println("Rational operation error");
    }
  }
}
```

15.12 What is displayed when the following program is run?

```
class Test {
  public static void main(String[] args) {
    try {
      method();
      System.out.println("After the method call");
    }
    catch (RuntimeException ex) {
      System.out.println("Integer operation error");
    }
    catch (Exception e) {
      System.out.println("Rational operation error");
    }
  }

  static void method() throws Exception {
    Rational r1 = new Rational(3, 4);
    Rational r2   = new Rational(0, 1);
    Rational x = r1.divide(r2);

    int i = 0;
    int y = 2 / i;
    System.out.println("Welcome to Java");
  }
}
```

15.13 What is displayed when the following program is run?

```
class Test {
  public static void main(String[] args) {
    try {
      method();
      System.out.println("After the method call");
```

```
        }
        catch (RuntimeException ex) {
          System.out.println("Integer operation error");
        }
        catch (Exception ex) {
          System.out.println("Rational operation error");
        }
      }

      static void method() throws Exception {
        try {
          Rational r1 = new Rational(3, 4);
          Rational r2   = new Rational(0, 1);
          Rational x = r1.divide(r2);

          int i = 0;
          int y = 2 / i;
          System.out.println("Welcome to Java");
        }
        catch (RuntimeException ex) {
          System.out.println("Integer operation error");
        }
        catch (Exception ex) {
          System.out.println("Rational operation error");
        }
      }
    }
```

15.14 What is displayed when the following program is run?

```
    class Test {
      public static void main(String[] args) {
        try {
          method();
          System.out.println("After the method call");
        }
        catch (RuntimeException ex) {
          System.out.println("Integer operation error");
        }
        catch (Exception ex) {
          System.out.println("Rational operation error");
        }
      }

      static void method() throws Exception {
        try {
          Rational r1 = new Rational(3, 4);
          Rational r2   = new Rational(0, 1);
          Rational x = r1.divide(r2);

          int i = 0;
          int y = 2 / i;
          System.out.println("Welcome to Java");
        }
        catch (RuntimeException ex) {
          System.out.println("Integer operation error");
        }
        catch (Exception ex) {
          System.out.println("Rational operation error");
          throw ex;
        }
      }
    }
```

15.15 If an exception were not caught in a non-GUI application, what would happen? If an exception were not caught in a GUI application, what would happen?

15.16 What does the method printStackTrace do?

15.17 What is assertion for? How do you declare assertions? How do you compile code with assertions? How do you run programs with assertions?

Programming Exercises

15.1 (Revising Example 7.5 "Using Command-Line Parameters") Example 7.5 is a simple command-line calculator. Note that the program terminates if any operand is nonnumeric. Write a program with an exception handler that deals with nonnumeric operands; then write another program without using an exception handler to achieve the same objective. Your program should display a message that informs the user of the wrong operand type before exiting (see Figure 15.11).

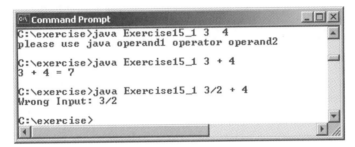

Figure 15.11 *The program performs arithmetic operations and detects input errors.*

15.2 (Revising Example 13.11 "Using Menus") Example 13.11 is a GUI calculator. Note that if Number 1 or Number 2 were a nonnumeric string, the program would report exceptions. Modify the program with an exception handler to catch ArithmeticException (e.g., divided by 0) and NumberFormatException (e.g., input is not an integer), and display the errors in a message dialog box, as shown in Figure 15.12.

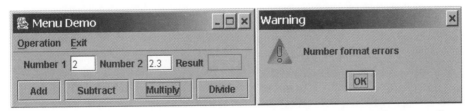

Figure 15.12 *The program displays an error message in the dialog box if the number is not well formatted.*

15.3 (Handling `ArrayIndexOutBoundsException`) Write a program that meets the following requirements:

- Create an array with one hundred randomly chosen integers.

- Create a text field to enter an array index and another text field to display the array element at the specified index (see Figure 15.13).

- Create a Show Element button to cause the array element to be displayed. If the specified index is out of bounds, display the message `Out of Bound`.

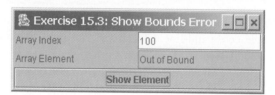

Figure 15.13   *The program displays the array element at the specified index or displays the message* `Out of Bound` *if the index is out of bounds.*

15.4 (Revising Example 6.7 "The `Loan` Class") Modify the `Loan` class in Example 6.7 to throw `IllegalArgumentException` if the loan amount, interest rate, or number of years is less than or equal to zero.

15.5 (The `IllegalTriangleException` class) Exercise 8.1 defined the `Triangle` class with three sides. In a triangle, the sum of any two sides is greater than the other side. The `Triangle` class must adhere to this rule. Create the `IllegalTriangleException` class, and modify the constructor to throw an `IllegalTriangleException` object if a triangle is created with sides that violate the rule, as follows:

```
/** Construct a triangle with the specified sides */
public Triangle(double side1, double side2, double side3)
  throws IllegalTriangleExcpetion {
  // Implement it
}
```

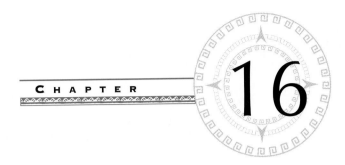

INPUT AND OUTPUT

Objectives

- ◉ To discover file properties using the `File` class.
- ◉ To understand input and output streams, and learn how to create them.
- ◉ To distinguish between byte and character streams.
- ◉ To read from or write to external files using file streams.
- ◉ To employ data streams for cross-platform data format compatibility.
- ◉ To output data of primitive types in text format using print streams.
- ◉ To display open and save file dialog boxes using `JFileChooser`.
- ◉ To input and output text on the console.
- ◉ To store and restore objects using object streams.
- ◉ To use `RandomAccessFile` for both read and write.
- ◉ To parse text files using `StreamTokenizer`. (Optional)

16.1   Introduction

Often you need to save output in a file that can be read later in the program. In this chapter, you will learn about many forms of input and output as well as how they work together. Since data are stored in files, the following section first introduces how to use the `File` class to obtain file properties and to delete and rename files.

16.2   The *File* Class

Each file is placed in a directory in the file system. The complete file name consists of the directory path and the file name. For example, `c:\example\chapter1\Welcome.java` is the complete file name for the file `Welcome.java` on the Windows operating system. Here `c:\example\chapter1` is referred to as the *directory path* for the file. The directory path and complete file name are machine-dependent. On Unix, the complete file name may be `/home/liang/example/chapter1/Welcome.java`, where `/home/liang/example/chapter1` is the directory path for the file `Welcome.java`.

The `File` class is intended to provide an abstraction that deals with most of the machine-dependent complexities of files and path names in a machine-independent fashion. The file name is a string. The `File` class is a wrapper class for the file name and its directory path.

You can create a `File` object using the following constructors:

■   `public File(String pathname)`

Creates a `File` object for the specified `pathname`. The pathname may be a directory or a file. For example, `new File("c:\\example")` creates a `File` object for the directory `c:\example`, and `new File("c:\\example\\chapter16\\test.dat")` creates a `File` object for the file `c:\\example\\chapter16\\test.dat`, both on Windows. You can use the `File` class's `isDirectory()` method to check whether the object represents a directory and the `isFile()` method to check whether the object represents a file name.

⚠ CAUTION

The directory separator for Windows is a backslash (\). The backslash is a special character and should be written as \\ (see Table 2.4 on page 60).

■   `public File(String parent, String child)`

Creates a `File` object for the `child` under the directory `parent`. `child` may be a file name or a subdirectory.

■   `public File(File parent, String child)`

Creates a `File` object for the `child` under the directory `parent`. `parent` is a `File` object. In the preceding constructor, the parent is a string.

The `File` class contains the following methods for obtaining file properties and for deleting and renaming files:

- `public boolean exists()`

Returns `true` if the file or the directory represented by the `File` object exists.

- `public boolean canRead()`

Returns `true` if the file represented by the `File` object exists and can be read.

- `public boolean canWrite()`

Returns `true` if the file represented by the `File` object exists and can be written.

- `public boolean isDirectory()`

Returns `true` if the `File` object represents a directory.

- `public boolean isFile()`

Returns `true` if the `File` object represents a file.

- `public boolean isAbsolute()`

Returns `true` if the `File` object is created using an absolute pathname. An absolute pathname is system-dependent. For example, if you create a `File` object using `new File("c:\\example\\chapter16\\test.dat")`, it is an absolute pathname. If you create a `File` object using `new File("test.dat")`, it refers to the file in the current class path directory. This path is not absolute because no system-specific path separators are used.

- `public boolean isHidden()`

Returns `true` if the file represented in the `File` object is hidden. The exact definition of *hidden* is system-dependent. On Windows, you can mark a file hidden in the File Properties dialog box. On Unix systems, a file is hidden if its name begins with a period character '.'.

- `public String getAbsolutePath()`

Returns the complete absolute file or directory name represented by the `File` object.

- `public String getCanonicalPath() throws IOException`

Returns the same as `getAbsolutePath()` except that it removes redundant names, such as "." and "..", from the pathname, resolves symbolic links (on Unix platforms), and converts drive letters to standard uppercase (on Win32 platforms).

- `public String getName()`

Returns the last name of the complete directory and file name represented by the `File` object. For example, `new File("c:\\example\\chapter16\\test.dat").getName()` returns **test.dat**.

- `public String getPath()`

Returns the complete directory and file name represented by the `File` object. For example, `new File("c:\\example\\chapter16\\test.dat").getName()` returns **c:\example\chapter16\test.dat**.

■ `public String getParent()`

Returns the complete parent directory of the current directory or the file represented by the `File` object. For example, `new File("c:\\example\\ chapter16\\test.dat").getParent()` returns **c:\example\chapter16**.

■ `public boolean delete()`

Deletes this file. The methods returns `true` if the deletion succeeds.

■ `public boolean renameTo(File dest)`

Renames this file. The method returns `true` if the operation succeeds.

The `File` class has four constants: `pathSeparator`, `pathSeparatorChar`, `separator`, and `separatorChar`. These constants are platform-dependent path separators and name separators. `separatorChar` is `'\'` on Windows and `'/'` on Unix. `separatorChar` is a char, and `separator` is a string representation of `separatorChar`. Likewise, `pathSeparator` is a string representation for `pathSeparatorChar`. `pathSeparator` is `';'` on Windows and `':'` on Unix.

◈ **NOTE**

`pathSeparator`, `pathSeparatorChar`, `separator`, and `separatorChar` are constants, but they are named as variables with lowercase for the first word and uppercase for the first letters of subsequent words. Thus these names violate the Java naming convention.

Do not use the absolute directory and file name literals in your program. If you use a literal such as `"c:\\example\\chapter16\\test.dat"`, it will work on Windows but not on other platforms. To enable the program to run correctly on different platforms, use the following string to replace `"c:\\example\\chapter16\\test.dat"`:

```
new File(".").getCanonicalPath() + "example" + File.separator
   + "chapter16" + File.separator + "test.dat";
```

Here `"."` denotes the current directory. If you run the Java program from the command line, the current directory is where the java command is issued. If you run the program from an IDE, the current directory is dependent on the IDE settings.

Example 16.1 Using the `File` Class

Problem

Write a program that demonstrates how to create files in a platform-independent way and use the methods in the `File` class to obtain their properties. Figure 16.1 shows a sample run of the program on Windows, and Figure 16.2 a sample run on Unix.

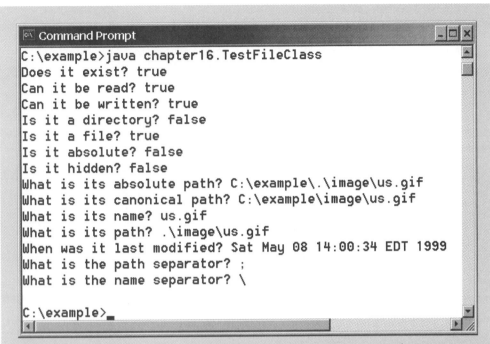

Figure 16.1 *The program creates a* File *object and displays file properties on Windows.*

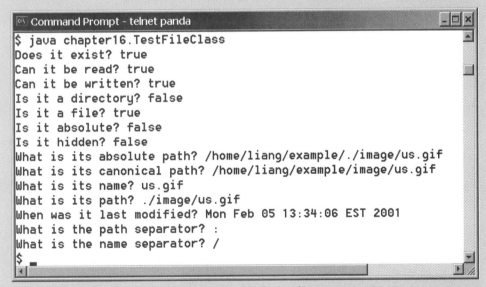

Figure 16.2 *The program creates a* File *object and displays file properties on Unix.*

Solution

The following code gives the solution to the problem.

continues

Example 16.1 Continued

```
1    // TestFileClass.java: Demonstrate the File class
2    package chapter16;
3
4    import java.io.*;
5    import java.util.*;
6
7    public class TestFileClass {
8      public static void main(String[] args) {
9        // Create a File object
10       File file = new File(".", "image" + File.separator + "us.gif");
11       System.out.println("Does it exist? " + file.exists());
12       System.out.println("Can it be read? " + file.canRead());
13       System.out.println("Can it be written? " + file.canRead());
14       System.out.println("Is it a directory? " + file.isDirectory());
15       System.out.println("Is it a file? " + file.isFile());
16       System.out.println("Is it absolute? " + file.isAbsolute());
17       System.out.println("Is it hidden? " + file.isHidden());
18       System.out.println("What is its absolute path? " +
19         file.getAbsolutePath());
20
21       try {
22         System.out.println("What is its canonical path? " +
23           file.getCanonicalPath());
24       }
25       catch (IOException ex) { }
26
27       System.out.println("What is its name? " + file.getName());
28       System.out.println("What is its path? " + file.getPath());
29       System.out.println("When was it last modified? " +
30         new Date(file.lastModified()));
31
32       System.out.println("What is the path separator? " +
33         File.pathSeparatorChar);
34       System.out.println("What is the name separator? " +
35         File.separatorChar);
36     }
37   }
```

Review

The program creates a File object for the file **us.gif**. This file is stored under the **\example\image** directory. The statement in Line 10 creates the object in a platform-independent fashion without using the platform-specific name separator and drive letter.

The getCanonicalPath() method can throw an IOException, so it is put in a try-catch block in Lines 21–25.

The lastModified() method returns the date and time when the file was last modified, measured in milliseconds since the epoch (00:00:00 GMT, January 1, 1970). The Date class is used to display it in a readable format in Lines 29–30.

 TIP

To develop platform-independent applications, it is imperative not to use absolute directory and file names.

16.3   I/O Streams

In Java, all I/O is handled in streams. A *stream* is an abstraction of the continuous one-way flow of data. Imagine a swimming pool with pipes that connect it to another pool. Let's consider the water in the first pool as the data, and the water in the second pool as your program. The flow of water through the pipes is called a *stream*. If you want input, just open the valve that lets water out of the data pool and into the program pool. If you want output, just open the valve that lets water out of the program pool and into the data pool.

It's a very simple concept, and a very efficient one. Since Java streams can be applied to any source of data, it is as easy for a programmer to input from a keyboard or output to a console as it is to input from a file or output to a file. Figure 16.3 shows the input and output streams between a program and an external file. Java streams are used liberally. There can even be input and output streams between two programs.

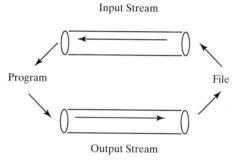

Input Stream

Program   File

Output Stream

Figure 16.3   *The program receives data through the input stream and sends data through the output stream.*

In general, all streams except random-access file streams flow in only one direction; therefore, if you want to input and output, you need two separate stream objects. In Java, streams can be *layered*; that is, connected to one another in pipeline fashion. The output of one stream may become the input of another stream.

This layering capability makes it possible to filter data along the pipeline of streams so that you can get data in the desired format. For instance, suppose you want to get integers from an external file. Use a file input stream to get raw data in binary format, then use a data input stream to extract integers from the output of the file input stream.

Streams are objects. Stream objects have methods that read and write data or do other useful things, such as flushing the stream, closing the stream, and counting the number of bytes in the stream.

16.3.1   Stream Classes

Java offers stream classes for processing all kinds of data. Figures 16.4 and 16.5 show the hierarchical relationships of these classes.

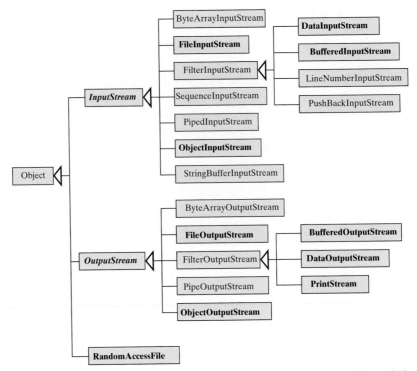

Figure 16.4 `InputStream`, `OutputStream`, `RandomAccessFile`, *and their subclasses deal with streams of bytes.*

 NOTE

As shown in Figures 16.4 and 16.5, there are many stream classes in Java. Each stream has its intended application. This chapter introduces the most frequently used streams. These stream classes appear in bold in the figures.

Stream classes can be categorized either as *byte streams* or as *character streams*. The `InputStream/OutputStream` class is the root of all byte stream classes, and the `Reader/Writer` class is the root of all character stream classes.

The `RandomAccessFile` class extends `Object` and implements the `DataInput` and `DataOutput` interfaces. It can be used to open a file that allows both reading and writing. The `StreamTokenizer` class that extends `Object` can be used for parsing text files.

16.3.2   *InputStream* and *Reader*

The abstract `InputStream` and `Reader` classes, extending `Object`, are the base classes for all of the input streams of bytes and characters, respectively. These classes and their subclasses are very similar, except that `InputStream` uses bytes for its fundamental unit of information, and `Reader` uses characters. `InputStream` and `Reader` have many common methods with identical signatures. These methods have similar

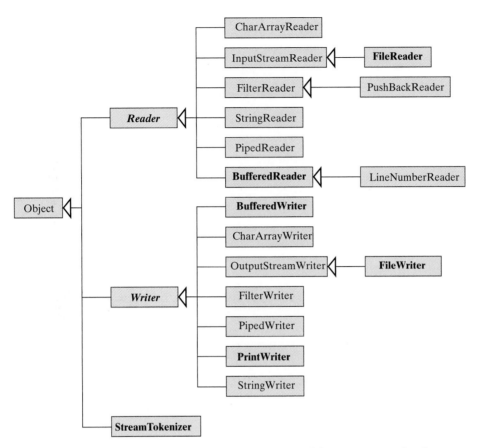

Figure 16.5 `Reader`, `Writer`, `StreamTokenizer`, *and their subclasses are concerned with streams of characters.*

functionality, but `InputStream` is designed to read bytes, and `Reader` is designed to read characters. The following methods, defined in `InputStream`, are often useful:

■ `public abstract int read() throws IOException`

Reads the next byte and returns its value. The value of the byte is returned as an `int` in the range from 0 to 255. At the end of the stream, it returns −1. This method blocks the program from executing until input data are available, the end of the stream is detected, or an exception is thrown. A concrete subclass of `InputStream` must provide an implementation of this method.

■ `public int read(byte[] b) throws IOException`

Reads up to `b.length` bytes into array `b`, returns `b.length` if the number of available bytes is more than or equal to `b.length`, returns the number of bytes read if the number of available bytes is less than `b.length`, and returns −1 at the end of the stream. This method reads all available bytes to `b` if `b` is large enough.

- `public void close() throws IOException`

  Closes the input stream.

- `public void int available() throws IOException`

  Returns the number of bytes that can be read from the input stream without blocking.

- `public long skip(long n) throws IOException`

  Skips over and discards n bytes of data from the input stream. The actual number of bytes skipped is returned.

> ◈ **NOTE**
>
> The `read()` method reads a byte from the stream. If no data are available, it blocks the thread from executing the next statement. The thread that invokes the `read()` method is suspended until the data become available.

The `Reader` class contains all of the methods listed previously except `available()`. These methods have the same functionality in `Reader` as in `InputStream`, but they are subject to character stream interpretation. For example, `read()` returns an integer in the range from 0 to 16,383, which represents a Unicode character.

16.3.3   *OutputStream and Writer*

Like `InputStream` and `Reader`, `OutputStream` and `Writer` are counterparts. They are the base classes for all the output streams of bytes and characters, respectively. The following instance methods are in both `OutputStream` and `Writer`:

- `public abstract void write(int b) throws IOException`

  Writes a byte (for `OutputStream`) or a character (for `Writer`).

- `public void write(byte[] b) throws IOException`

  Writes all the bytes in array b to the output stream (for `OutputStream`) or the characters in the array of characters (for `Writer`).

- `public void close() throws IOException`

  Closes the output stream.

- `public void flush() throws IOException`

  Flushes the output stream (i.e., sends any buffered data in the stream to their destination).

16.4   File Streams

The `File` class represents a file, but it does not provide operations for data I/O. You must use file streams to read from or write to a disk file. `FileInputStream` or `FileOutputStream` is used for byte streams, and `FileReader` or `FileWriter` for character streams. To create a file stream, use the following constructors:

694

```
public FileInputStream(String filenameString)
public FileInputStream(File file)
public FileOutputStream(String filenameString)
public FileOutputStream(File file)
public FileReader(String filenameString)
public FileReader(File file)
public FileWriter(String filenameString)
public FileWriter(File file)
```

The following statements create infile and outfile streams for the input file **in.dat** and the output file **out.dat**, respectively:

```
FileInputStream infile = new FileInputStream("in.dat");
FileOutputStream outfile = new FileOutputStream("out.dat");
```

The abstract method read(byte b) in InputStream is implemented in FileInput-Stream, and the abstract write(int b) method in the OutputStream class is implemented in FileOutputStream.

Example 16.2 Copying Files

Problem

Write a program that uses FileInputStream and FileOutputStream to copy a file, and the File class to check the properties of the file. The user needs to provide a source file and a target file as command-line arguments. The program copies the source file to the target file and displays the number of bytes in the file. A sample run of the program is shown in Figure 16.6.

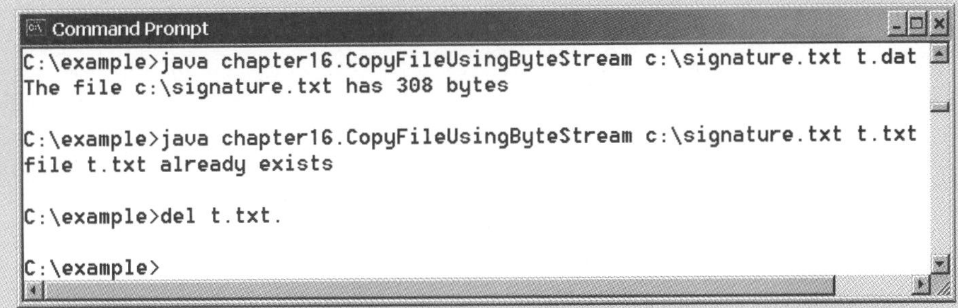

```
Command Prompt                                                   _ □ ×

C:\example>java chapter16.CopyFileUsingByteStream c:\signature.txt t.dat
The file c:\signature.txt has 308 bytes

C:\example>java chapter16.CopyFileUsingByteStream c:\signature.txt t.txt
file t.txt already exists

C:\example>del t.txt.

C:\example>
```

Figure 16.6 *The program copies a file using byte streams.*

Solution

The following code gives the solution to the problem.

```
1    // CopyFileUsingByteStream.java: Copy files
2    package chapter16;
3
4    import java.io.*;
5
6    public class CopyFileUsingByteStream {
7      /** Main method
8        @param args[0] for sourcefile
```

continues

Example 16.2 Continued

```
 9          @param args[1] for target file
10          */
11      public static void main(String[] args) {
12        // Declare input and output file streams
13        FileInputStream fis = null;
14        FileOutputStream fos = null;
15
16        // Check usage
17        if (args.length != 2) {
18          System.out.println(
19            "Usage: java CopyFileUsingByteStream fromfile tofile");
20          System.exit(0);
21        }
22
23        try {
24          // Create file input stream
25          fis = new FileInputStream(new File(args[0]));
26
27          // Create file output stream if the file does not exist
28          File file = new File(args[1]);
29          if (file.exists()) {
30            System.out.println("file " + args[1] + " already exists");
31            return;
32          }
33          else
34            fos = new FileOutputStream(args[1]);
35
36          // Display the file size
37          System.out.println("The file " + args[0] + " has "+
38            fis.available() + " bytes");
39
40          // Continuously read a byte from fis and write it to fos
41          int r;
42          while ((r = fis.read()) != -1) {
43            fos.write((byte)r);
44          }
45        }
46        catch (FileNotFoundException ex) {
47          System.out.println("File not found: " + args[0]);
48        }
49        catch (IOException ex) {
50          System.out.println(ex.getMessage());
51        }
52        finally {
53          try {
54            // Close files
55            if (fis != null) fis.close();
56            if (fos != null) fos.close();
57          }
58          catch (IOException ex) {
59            System.out.println(ex);
60          }
61        }
62      }
63    }
```

Review

The program creates the fis (Line 25) and fos (Line 34) streams for the input file args[0] and the output file args[1] (see Figure 16.7).

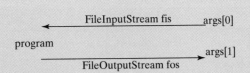

Figure 16.7 *The program uses* `FileInputStream` *to read data from the file and* `FileOutput-Stream` *to write data to the file.*

If the input file `args[0]` does not exist, `new FileInputStream(newFile(args[0]))` (Line 25) will raise the exception `FileNotFoundException`. By contrast, `new File-OutputStream(new File(args[1]))` (Line 34) will always create a file output stream, whether or not the file `args[1]` exists.

To avoid writing into an existing file, the program uses the `exists()` method (Line 29) in the `File` class to determine whether `args[1]` exists. If the file already exists, the user will be notified; if not, the file will be created.

The program continuously reads bytes from the `fis` stream and sends them to the `fos` stream until all of the bytes have been read. Recall that Java allows the assignment operator in an expression (see page 49). The expression `((r = fis.read()) != -1)` (Line 42) reads a byte from `fis.read()` and assigns it to `r` and checks if it is −1. The input value of −1 signifies the end of a file.

The program closes any open file streams in the `finally` clause (Lines 55–56). The statements in the `finally` clause are always executed, whether or not exceptions occur.

The program could be rewritten using `FileReader` and `FileWriter`. The new program would be almost exactly the same (see Exercise 16.1).

 TIP
When files are no longer needed, always close them using the `close()` method. In some cases, not closing files will cause programming errors. Files are usually closed in the `finally` clause.

16.5 Filter Streams

Filter streams are streams that filter bytes or characters for some purpose. The basic input stream provides a read method that can only be used for reading bytes or characters. If you want to read integers, doubles, or strings, you need a filter class to wrap the input stream. Using a filter class enables you to read integers, doubles, and strings instead of bytes and characters.

When you need to process primitive numeric types, use `FilterInputStream` and `FilterOutputStream` to filter bytes. When you need to process strings, use `BufferedReader` and `PushbackReader` to filter characters. `FilterInputStream` and `FilterOutputStream` are abstract classes; their subclasses (listed in Tables 16.1 and 16.2) are often used.

TABLE 16.1   FilterInputStream Subclasses

Class	Usage
DataInputStream	Handles binary formats of all the primitive data types.
BufferedInputStream	Gets data from the buffer.
LineNumberInputStream	Keeps track of how many lines are read.
PushbackInputStream	Allows single-byte lookahead. After a byte is looked at, this stream pushes it back to the stream so that the next read can read it.

TABLE 16.2   FilterOutputStream Subclasses

Class	Usage
DataOutputStream	Outputs the binary format of all the primitive types, which is useful if another program uses the output.
BufferedOutputStream	Outputs to the buffer first and then, if necessary, to the stream. Programmers can also call the flush() method to write the buffer to the stream.
PrintStream	Outputs the Unicode format of all the primitive types, which is useful if the format is output to the console.

16.6   Data Streams

The DataInputStream and DataOutputStream read and write Java primitive types in a machine-independent fashion, thereby enabling you to write a data file on one machine and read it on another machine that has a different operating system or file structure. An application uses a data output stream to write data that can later be read by a data input stream.

DataInputStream extends FilterInputStream and implements the DataInput interface. DataOutputStream extends FilterOutputStream and implements the DataOutput interface. The DataInput and DataOutput interfaces are also implemented by the RandomAccessFile class, which is discussed in Section 16.12, "Random Access Files," later in this chapter.

The following methods are defined in the DataInput interface:

```
public int readByte() throws IOException
public int readShort() throws IOException
public int readInt() throws IOException
public int readLong() throws IOException
public float readFloat() throws IOException
public double readDouble() throws IOException
public char readChar() throws IOException
public boolean readBoolean() throws IOException
public String readUTF() throws IOException
```

The following methods are defined in the DataOutput interface:

```
public void writeByte(byte b) throws IOException
public void writeShort(short s) throws IOException
public void writeInt(int i) throws IOException
public void writeLong(long l) throws IOException
public void writeFloat(float f) throws IOException
public void writeDouble(double d) throws IOException
public void writeChar(char c) throws IOException
public void writeBoolean(boolean b) throws IOException
public void writeBytes(String string) throws IOException
public void writeChars(String string) throws IOException
public void writeUTF(String string) throws IOException
```

NOTE

UTF stands for Unicode Transformation Format. The writeUTF method converts a string into a series of bytes in the UTF-8 format and writes them into a binary stream. The readUTF method reads a string that has been written using the writeUTF method. The UTF-8 format has the advantage of saving a byte for each character, since a Unicode character takes up two bytes and a UTF-8 character takes up only one byte. If your characters are regular ASCII code, using UFT-8 is more efficient.

Data streams are used as wrappers on existing input and output streams to filter data in the original stream. They are created using the following constructors:

```
public DataInputStream(InputStream instream)
public DataOutputStream(OutputStream outstream)
```

The statements given below create data streams. The first statement creates an input stream for file **in.dat**; the second statement creates an output stream for file **out.dat**.

```
DataInputStream infile =
  new DataInputStream(new FileInputStream("in.dat"));
DataOutputStream outfile =
  new DataOutputStream(new FileOutputStream("out.dat"));
```

Example 16.3 Using Data Streams

Problem

Write a program that creates ten random integers, stores them in a data file, retrieves data from the file, and then displays the integers on the console. Figure 16.8 contains a sample run of the program.

Solution

The following code gives the solution to the problem.

```
1   // TestDataStream.java: Create a file, store it in binary form, and
2   // display it on the console
3   package chapter16;
4
5   import java.io.*;
6
```

continues

Example 16.3 Continued

```
7      public class TestDataStream {
8        /** Main method */
9        public static void main(String[] args) {
10         // Declare data input and output streams
11         DataInputStream dis = null;
12         DataOutputStream dos = null;
13
14         // Construct a temp file
15         File tempFile = new File("mytemp.dat");
16
17         // Check if the temp file exists
18         if (tempFile.exists()) {
19           System.out.println("The file mytemp.dat already exists,"
20             + " delete it, rerun the program");
21           System.exit(0);
22         }
23
24         // Write data
24         try {
26           // Create data output stream for tempFile
27           dos = new DataOutputStream(new FileOutputStream(tempFile));
28           for (int i = 0; i < 10; i++)
29             dos.writeInt((int)(Math.random() * 1000));
30         }
31         catch (IOException ex) {
32           System.out.println(ex.getMessage());
33         }
34         finally {
35           try {
36             // Close files
37             if (dos != null) dos.close();
38           }
39           catch (IOException ex) {
40           }
41         }
42
43         // Read data
44         try {
45           // Create data input stream
46           dis = new DataInputStream(new FileInputStream(tempFile));
47           for (int i = 0; i < 10; i++)
48             System.out.print("  " + dis.readInt());
49         }
50         catch (FileNotFoundException ex) {
51           System.out.println("File not found");
52         }
53         catch (IOException ex) {
54           System.out.println(ex.getMessage());
55         }
56         finally {
57           try {
58             // Close files
59             if (dis != null) dis.close();
60           }
61           catch (IOException ex) {
62             System.out.println(ex);
63           }
64         }
65       }
66     }
```

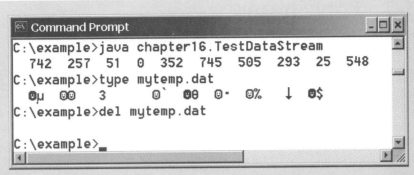

Figure 16.8 *The program creates ten random numbers and stores them in a file named* **mytemp.dat**. *It then reads the data from the file and displays them on the console.*

Review

The program creates a DataInputStream object dis wrapped on FileInputStream (Line 46) and a DataOutputStream object dos wrapped on FileOutputStream (Line 27) (see Figure 16.9).

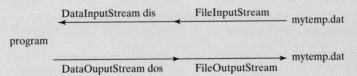

Figure 16.9 *The program uses* DataOutputStream *to write data to a file and* DataInputStream *to read the data from the file.*

The program uses a temporary file to store data. The temporary file is named **mytemp.dat**. The program first creates **mytemp.dat** if it does not exist. Then it writes ten random integers into **mytemp.dat** using the data output stream, and closes the stream.

The program creates a data input stream for **mytemp.dat**, reads integers from it, and displays it.

 NOTE

The data stored in **mytemp.dat** are in binary format, which is machine-independent and portable. If you need to transport data between different systems, use data input and output streams.

16.7   Print Streams

A data output stream outputs a binary representation of data, so you cannot view its contents as text. As shown in Figure 16.8, when you attempt to view the file **mytemp.dat** on the console, strange symbols are displayed. In Java, you can use print streams to output data into files. These files can be viewed as text.

The `PrintStream` and `PrintWriter` classes provide this functionality. You have already used `System.out.println` to display data on the console. An instance of `PrintStream`, out, is defined in the `java.lang.System` class. `PrintStream` and `PrintWriter` have similar methods, listed below:

```
public void print(Object o)
public void print(String s)
public void print(char c)
public void print(char[] cArray)
public void print(int i)
public void print(long l)
public void print(float f)
public void print(double d)
public void print(boolean b)
```

You can replace `print` with `println`. The `println` method, which prints the object, is followed by a new line. When an object is passed to `print` or `println`, the object's `toString()` method converts it to a `String` object.

 NOTE

The print methods do not throw an `IOException`. So when the `System.out.print` method is invoked, it does not need to be inside a `try-catch` block.

`PrintStream` is for byte streams, whereas `PrintWriter` is for character streams. Since printing is clearly character-related output, `PrintWriter` should be used rather than `PrintStream`. However, there is a historical reason why `System.out` and `System.err` have been used for printing to the console: `PrintStream` (in JDK 1.0) was introduced before `PrintWriter` (in JDK 1.1). So you can continue to use these two objects for output to the console.

This section gives an example using `PrintWriter`, but `PrintStream` can be used in the same way. `PrintWriter` has the following constructors:

```
public PrintWriter(Writer out)
public PrintWriter(Writer out, boolean autoFlush)
public PrintWriter(OutputStream out)
public PrintWriter(OutputStream out, boolean autoFlush)
```

Example 16.4 Using Print Streams

Problem

Write a program that creates ten random integers and stores them in a text data file. The file can be viewed on the console by using an OS command, such as type on Windows or cat on UNIX.

Solution

The following code gives the solution to the problem. Figure 16.10 contains the output of a sample run of the program.

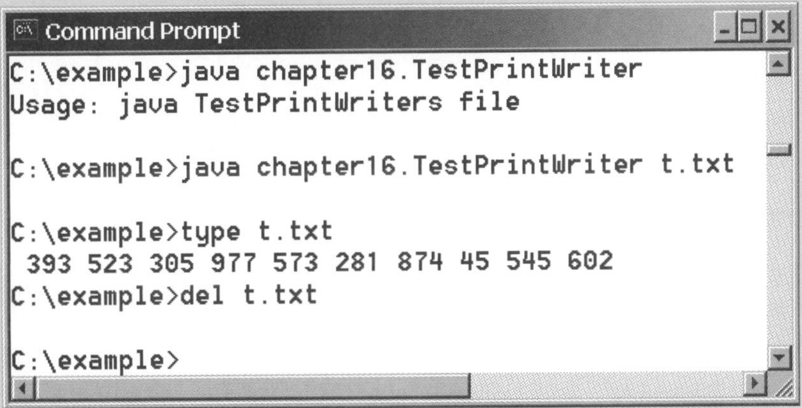

```
Command Prompt                                    _ □ x

C:\example>java chapter16.TestPrintWriter
Usage: java TestPrintWriters file

C:\example>java chapter16.TestPrintWriter t.txt

C:\example>type t.txt
 393 523 305 977 573 281 874 45 545 602
C:\example>del t.txt

C:\example>
```

Figure 16.10   *The program creates ten random numbers and stores them in a text file.*

```
1     // TestPrintWriter.java: Create a text file using PrintWriter
2     package chapter16;
3
4     import java.io.*;
5
6     public class TestPrintWriter {
7       /** Main method: args[0] is the output file */
8       public static void main(String[] args) {
9         // Declare print stream
10        PrintWriter pw = null;
11
12        // Check usage
13        if (args.length != 1) {
14          System.out.println("Usage: java TestPrintWriters file");
15          System.exit(0);
16        }
17
18        File tempFile = new File(args[0]);
19
20        if (tempFile.exists()) {
21          System.out.println("The file " + args[0] +
22            " already exists, delete it, rerun the program");
23          System.exit(0);
24        }
25
26        // Write data
27        try {
```

continues

Example 16.4 Continued

```
28              // Create data output stream for tempFile
29              pw = new PrintWriter(new FileOutputStream(tempFile), true);
30              for (int i = 0; i < 10; i++)
31                pw.print(" " + (int)(Math.random() * 1000));
32            }
33            catch (IOException ex) {
34              System.out.println(ex.getMessage());
35            }
36            finally {
37              // Close files
38              if (pw != null) pw.close();
39            }
40          }
41        }
```

Review

The program creates a print stream, pw, of `PrintWriter`, wrapped in `FileOutputStream`, for text format (Line 29) (see Figure 16.11).

Figure 16.11   *The program uses the* `PrintWriter` *stream, which is wrapped in* `FileOutputStream`, *to write data in text format.*

The program creates the file named in **args[0]** if it does not already exist, writes ten random integers into the file by using the print stream, and then closes the stream.

The output into the file is in text format. The data can be seen using the **type** command in DOS.

16.8   Buffered Streams

Java introduces buffered streams that speed input and output by reducing the number of reads and writes. Buffered streams employ a buffered array of bytes or characters that acts as a cache. In the case of input, the array reads a chunk of bytes or characters into the buffer before the individual bytes or characters are read. In the case of output, the array accumulates a block of bytes or characters before writing the entire block to the output stream.

The use of buffered streams enables you to read and write a chunk of bytes or characters at once instead of reading or writing the bytes or characters one at a time. The `BufferedInputStream`, `BufferedOutputStream`, `BufferedReader`, and `BufferedWriter` classes provide this functionality.

The following constructors are used to create a buffered stream:

```
public BufferedInputStream(InputStream in)
public BufferedInputStream(InputStream in, int bufferSize)
public BufferedOutputStream(OutputStream in)
public BufferedOutputStream(OutputStream in, int bufferSize)
public BufferedReader(Reader in)
public BufferedReader(Reader in, int bufferSize)
public BufferedWriter(Writer out)
public BufferedWriter(Writer out, int bufferSize)
```

If no buffer size is specified, the default size is 512 bytes or characters. A buffered input stream reads as many data as possible into its buffer in a single read call. By contrast, a buffered output stream calls the write method only when its buffer fills up or when the `flush()` method is called.

The buffered stream classes inherit methods from their superclasses. In addition to using the methods from their superclasses, `BufferedReader` has a `readLine()` method to read a line, and `BufferedWriter` has a `newLine()` method to write a line separator.

◈ NOTE

The `readLine()` method return a line without the line separator. The line separator string is defined by the system, and is not necessarily a single ('\n') character. To get the system line separator, use

```
static String lineSeparator = (String)java.security.
    AccessController.doPrivileged(
        new sun.security.action.GetPropertyAction("line.separator"));
```

Example 16.5 Displaying a File in a Text Area

Problem

Write a program that views a file in a text area. The user enters a file name in a text field and clicks the View button; the file is then displayed in a text area. Figure 16.12 contains the output of a sample run of the program.

Figure 16.12   *The program displays the specified file in the text area.*

continues

705

Example 16.5 Continued

Solution

The following code gives the solution to the problem.

```
1    // ViewFile.java: Read a text file and store it in a text area
2    package chapter16;
3
4    import java.awt.*;
5    import java.awt.event.*;
6    import java.io.*;
7    import javax.swing.*;
8
9    public class ViewFile extends JFrame implements ActionListener {
10     // Button to view view
11     private JButton jbtView = new JButton("View");
12
13     // Text field to receive file name
14     private JTextField jtfFilename = new JTextField(12);
15
16     // Text area to display file
17     private JTextArea jtaFile = new JTextArea();
18
19     // Obtain the system line separator
20     static String lineSeparator = (String)java.security.
21       AccessController.doPrivileged(
22       new sun.security.action.GetPropertyAction("line.separator"));
23
24     /** Main method */
25     public static void main(String[] args) {
26       ViewFile frame = new ViewFile();
27       frame.setTitle("View File");
28       frame.setSize(400, 300);
29       frame.setVisible(true);
30     }
31
32     /**  Default constructor */
33     public ViewFile() {
34       // Panel p to hold a label, a text field, and a button
35       Panel p = new Panel();
36       p.setLayout(new BorderLayout());
37       p.add(new Label("Filename"), BorderLayout.WEST);
38       p.add(jtfFilename, BorderLayout.CENTER);
39       jtfFilename.setBackground(Color.yellow);
40       jtfFilename.setForeground(Color.red);
41       p.add(jbtView, BorderLayout.EAST);
42
43       // Add jtaFile to a scroll pane
44       JScrollPane jsp = new JScrollPane(jtaFile);
45
46       // Add jsp and p to the frame
47       getContentPane().add(jsp, BorderLayout.CENTER);
48       getContentPane().add(p, BorderLayout.SOUTH);
49
50       // Register listener
51       jbtView.addActionListener(this);
52     }
53
```

```
54        /** Handle the "View" button */
55        public void actionPerformed(ActionEvent e) {
56          if (e.getSource() == jbtView)
57            showFile();
58        }
59
60        /** Display the file in the text area */
61        private void showFile() {
62          // Use a BufferedReader to read text from the file
63          BufferedReader infile = null;
64
65          // Get file name from the text field
66          String filename = jtfFilename.getText().trim();
67
68          String inLine;
69
70          try {
71            // Create a buffered stream
72            infile = new BufferedReader(new FileReader(filename));
73
74            // Read a line and append the line to the text area
75            while ((inLine = infile.readLine()) != null) {
76              jtaFile.append(inLine + lineSeparator);
77            }
78          }
79          catch (FileNotFoundException ex) {
80            System.out.println("File not found: " + filename);
81          }
82          catch (IOException ex) {
83            System.out.println(ex.getMessage());
84          }
85          finally {
86            try {
87              if (infile != null) infile.close();
88            }
89            catch (IOException ex) {
90              System.out.println(ex.getMessage());
91            }
92          }
93        }
94      }
```

Review

The user enters a file name into the File name text field. When the View button is pressed, the program gets the input file name from the text field; it then creates a data input stream. The data are read one line at a time and appended to the text area for display.

The program uses a BufferedReader stream (Line 63) to read lines from a buffer. Instead of the BufferedReader and Reader classes, BufferedInputStream and FileInputStream can also be used in this example.

You are encouraged to rewrite the program without using buffers and then compare the performance of the two programs. This will show you the improvement in performance obtained by using buffers when reading from a large file.

continues

Example 16.5 Continued

This program reads a file from the local machine, so you have to write it as a Java application. Example 21.6, "Retrieving Remote Files," in Bonus Chapter 21, "Networking," gives another program that allows reading from a file on a remote host.

> **TIP**
> Since physical input and output involving I/O devices are typically very slow compared with CPU processing speeds, you should use buffered input/output streams to improve performance.

16.9   File Dialogs

Swing provides `javax.swing.JFileChooser`, which displays a dialog box from which the user can navigate through the file system and select files to load or save, as shown in Figure 16.13.

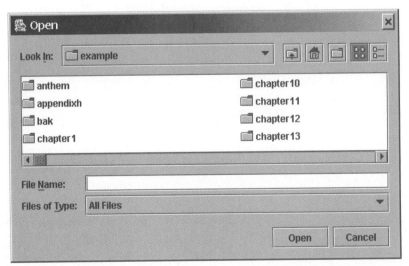

Figure 16.13 *The Swing* `JFileChooser` *shows files and directories, and enables the user to navigate through the file system visually.*

The file dialog box is modal; when displayed, it blocks the rest of the application until it is dismissed. The file dialog box can appear in two types: open and save. The *open type* is for opening a file, and the *save type* is for storing a file.

There are several ways to construct a file dialog box. The simplest is to use `JFileChooser`'s default constructor.

The JFileChooser class is a subclass of JComponent. In addition to the properties inherited from JComponent, JFileChooser has the following useful properties:

- **dialogType** specifies the type of the dialog. Use OPEN_DIALOG when you want to bring up a filechooser that the user can use to open a file. Likewise, use SAVE_DIALOG to let the user choose a file to save.

- **dialogTitle** specifies the string displayed in the title bar of the dialog box.

- **currentDirectory** specifies the current directory of the file. The type of this property is java.io.File. If you want the current directory to be used, use setCurrentDirectory(new File(".")).

- **selectedFile** specifies the selected file. You can use getSelectedFile() to return the selected file from the dialog box. The type of this property is java.io.File. If you have a default file name that you expect to use, use setSelectedFile(new File(filename)).

- **selectedFiles** specifies a list of selected files if the file chooser is set to allow multiselection. The type of this property is File[].

- **multiSelectionEnabled** specifies a boolean value indicating whether multiple files can be selected. By default, it is false.

To display the dialog box, use the following two methods:

```
public int showOpenDialog(Component parent)
public int showSaveDialog(Component parent)
```

The first method displays an "Open" dialog, and the second displays a "Save" dialog. Both methods return an int value, APPROVE_OPTION or CANCEL_OPTION, which indicates whether the OK button or the Cancel button was clicked.

Example 16.6 Using File Dialogs

Problem

Create a simple notepad using JFileChooser to open and save files. The notepad enables the user to open an existing file, edit the file, and save the note to the current file or a specified file. You can display and edit the file in a text area.

A sample run of the program is shown in Figure 16.14. When you open a file, a file dialog box with the default title "Open" appears on-screen to let you select a file for loading, as shown in Figure 16.13. When you save a file, a file dialog box with the default title "Save" appears to let you select a file for saving, as shown in Figure 16.15. The status label below the text area displays the status of the file operations.

continues

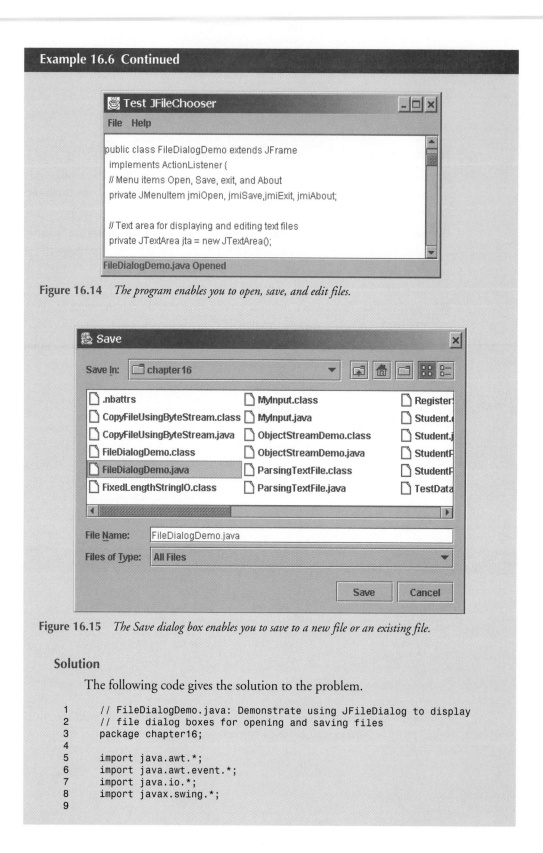

Example 16.6 Continued

Figure 16.14 *The program enables you to open, save, and edit files.*

Figure 16.15 *The Save dialog box enables you to save to a new file or an existing file.*

Solution

The following code gives the solution to the problem.

```
1   // FileDialogDemo.java: Demonstrate using JFileDialog to display
2   // file dialog boxes for opening and saving files
3   package chapter16;
4
5   import java.awt.*;
6   import java.awt.event.*;
7   import java.io.*;
8   import javax.swing.*;
9
```

```
10    public class FileDialogDemo extends JFrame
11      implements ActionListener {
12      // Menu items Open, Save, exit, and About
13      private JMenuItem jmiOpen, jmiSave,jmiExit, jmiAbout;
14
15      // Text area for displaying and editing text files
16      private JTextArea jta = new JTextArea();
17
18      // Status label for displaying operation status
19      private JLabel jlblStatus = new JLabel();
20
21      // File dialog box
22      private JFileChooser jFileChooser = new JFileChooser();
23
24      /** Main method */
25      public static void main(String[] args) {
26        FileDialogDemo frame = new FileDialogDemo();
27        frame.setSize(300, 150);
28        frame.setVisible(true);
29      }
30
31      public FileDialogDemo() {
32        setTitle("Test JFileChooser");
33
34        // Create a menu bar mb and attach to the frame
35        JMenuBar mb = new JMenuBar();
36        setJMenuBar(mb);
37
38        // Add a "File" menu in mb
39        JMenu fileMenu = new JMenu("File");
40        mb.add(fileMenu);
41
42        //add a "Help" menu in mb
43        JMenu helpMenu = new JMenu("Help");
44        mb.add(helpMenu);
45
46        // Create and add menu items to the menu
47        fileMenu.add(jmiOpen = new JMenuItem("Open"));
48        fileMenu.add(jmiSave = new JMenuItem("Save"));
49        fileMenu.addSeparator();
50        fileMenu.add(jmiExit = new JMenuItem("Exit"));
51        helpMenu.add(jmiAbout = new JMenuItem("About"));
52
53        // Set default directory to the current directory
54        jFileChooser.setCurrentDirectory(new File("."));
55
56        // Set BorderLayout for the frame
57        getContentPane().add(new JScrollPane(jta),
58          BorderLayout.CENTER);
59        getContentPane().add(jlblStatus, BorderLayout.SOUTH);
60
61        // Register listeners
62        jmiOpen.addActionListener(this);
63        jmiSave.addActionListener(this);
64        jmiAbout.addActionListener(this);
65        jmiExit.addActionListener(this);
66      }
67
68      /** Handle ActionEvent for menu items */
69      public void actionPerformed(ActionEvent e) {
70        String actionCommand = e.getActionCommand();
71
```

continues

Example 16.6 Continued

```
72          if (e.getSource() instanceof JMenuItem) {
73            if ("Open".equals(actionCommand))
74              open();
75            else if ("Save".equals(actionCommand))
76              save();
77            else if ("About".equals(actionCommand))
78              JOptionPane.showMessageDialog(this,
79                "Demonstrate Using File Dialogs",
80                "About This Demo",
81                JOptionPane.INFORMATION_MESSAGE);
82            else if ("Exit".equals(actionCommand))
83              System.exit(0);
84          }
85        }
86
87        /** Open file */
88        private void open() {
89          if (jFileChooser.showOpenDialog(this) ==
90            JFileChooser.APPROVE_OPTION) {
91            open(jFileChooser.getSelectedFile());
92          }
93        }
94
95        /** Open file with the specified File instance */
96        private void open(File file) {
97          try {
98            // Read from the specified file and store it in jta
99            BufferedInputStream in = new BufferedInputStream(
100             new FileInputStream(file));
101           byte[] b = new byte[in.available()];
102           in.read(b, 0, b.length);
103           jta.append(new String(b, 0, b.length));
104           in.close();
105
106           // Display the status of the Open file operation in jlblStatus
107           jlblStatus.setText(file.getName() + " Opened");
108         }
109         catch (IOException ex) {
110           jlblStatus.setText("Error opening " + file.getName());
111         }
112       }
113
114       /** Save file */
115       private void save() {
116         if (jFileChooser.showSaveDialog(this) ==
117           JFileChooser.APPROVE_OPTION) {
118           save(jFileChooser.getSelectedFile());
119         }
120       }
121
122       /** Save file with specified File instance */
123       private void save(File file) {
124         try {
125           // Write the text in jta to the specified file
126           BufferedOutputStream out = new BufferedOutputStream(
127             new FileOutputStream(file));
128           byte[] b = (jta.getText()).getBytes();
129           out.write(b, 0, b.length);
130           out.close();
131
```

```
132          // Display the status of the save file operation in jlblStatus
133          jlblStatus.setText(file.getName()  + " Saved ");
134        }
135      catch (IOException ex) {
136          jlblStatus.setText("Error saving " + file.getName());
137        }
138      }
139    }
```

Review

The program creates the File and Help menus. The File menu contains the menu commands Open for loading a file, Save for saving a file, and Exit for terminating the program. The Help menu contains the menu command About to display a message about the program, as shown in Figure 16.16.

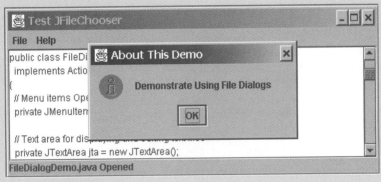

Figure 16.16 *Clicking the About menu item displays a message dialog box.*

jFileChooser, an instance of JFileChooser, is created (Line 22) for displaying the file dialog box to open and save files. The setCurrentDirectory(new File(".")) method (Line 54) is used to set the current directory to the directory where the class is stored.

The open() method (Line 74) is invoked when the user clicks the Open menu command. The showOpenDialog() method (Line 89) displays an Open dialog box, as shown in Figure 16.13. Upon receiving the selected file, the method open(file) (Line 91) is invoked to load the file to the text area, using a BufferedInputStream wrapped on a FileInputStream.

The save() method (Line 76) is invoked when the user clicks the Save menu command. The showSaveDialog() method (Line 116) displays a Save dialog box, as shown in Figure 16.15. Upon receiving the selected file, the method save(file) (Line 118) is invoked to save the contents from the text area to the file, using a BufferedOutputStream wrapped on a FileOutputStream.

16.10   Text Input and Output on the Console (Optional)

There are two types of *interactive I/O*. One involves simple input from the keyboard and simple output in a pure text form. The other involves input and output in a graphical environment. The former is referred to as *text interactive I/O*, and the latter as *graphical interactive I/O*.

Graphical interactive I/O takes an entirely different approach from text interactive I/O. In the graphical environment, input can be received from a UI component, such as a text field, text area, list, combo box, check box, or radio button. It can also be received from a keystroke or a mouse movement. Output is usually displayed in the panel, in text fields, or in text areas.

Now turn your attention to text I/O. To perform console output, you can use any of the methods for `PrintStream` in `System.out`. However, keyboard input is not directly supported in Java. In order to get input from the keyboard, you first use the following statements to read a string from the keyboard:

```
BufferedReader br
  = new BufferedReader(new InputStreamReader(System.in), 1);

// Declare and initialize the string
String string = " ";

// Get the string from the keyboard
try {
  string = br.readLine();
}
catch (IOException ex) {
  System.out.println(ex);
}
```

You then parse the string into `byte`, `short`, `int`, `long`, `float`, `double`, `char`, or `boolean`. Here is the class that contains the methods for reading primitive data type values and strings from the keyboard:

```
// MyInput.java: Contain the methods for reading primitive type
// values and string
package chapter16;

import java.io.*;

public class MyInput {
  static BufferedReader br
    = new BufferedReader(new InputStreamReader(System.in), 1);

  /** Read a string from the keyboard */
  public static String readString() {
    // Declare and initialize the string
    String string = " ";

    // Get the string from the keyboard
    try {
      string = br.readLine();
    }
    catch (IOException ex) {
```

```
      System.out.println(ex);
    }

    // Return the string obtained from the keyboard
    return string;
  }

  /** Read an int value from the keyboard */
  public static int readInt() {
    return Integer.parseInt(readString());
  }

  /** Read a double value from the keyboard */
  public static double readDouble() {
    return Double.parseDouble(readString());
  }

  /** Read a byte value from the keyboard */
  public static byte readByte() {
    return Byte.parseByte(readString());
  }

  /** Read a short value from the keyboard */
  public static short readShort() {
    return Short.parseShort(readString());
  }

  /** Read a long value from the keyboard */
  public static long readLong() {
    return Long.parseLong(readString());
  }

  /** Read a float value from the keyboard */
  public static float readFloat() {
    return Float.parseFloat(readString());
  }

  /** Read a character from the keyboard */
  public static char readChar() {
    return readString().charAt(0);
  }

  /** Read a boolean value from the keyboard */
  public static boolean readBoolean() {
    return new Boolean(readString()).booleanValue();
  }
}
```

❖ **NOTE**

Some brands of PCs running Windows 95 are prone to cause input problems if the buffer size for the `BufferedReader` stream `br` is not set to 1. Therefore, the buffer size of 1 is purposely chosen to help eliminate input problems.

❖ **NOTE**

`System.out` is a standard output object, and `System.in` is a standard input object. If you run the program from the command window, the output is displayed in the command window, and input from the keyboard is echo printed in the command window.

Below is an example that uses the methods in `MyInput`. A sample run of this program is shown in Figure 16.17.

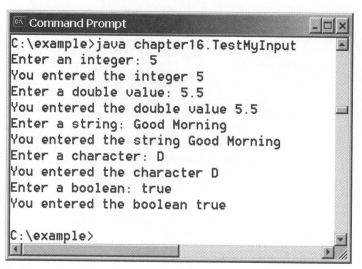

Figure 16.17 *You can enter input from a command window.*

```java
// TestMyInput.java: Demo for using MyInput
package chapter16;

public class TestMyInput {
  public static void main(String args[]) {
    // Prompt the user to enter an integer
    System.out.print("Enter an integer: ");
    int intValue = MyInput.readInt();
    System.out.println("You entered the integer " + intValue);

    // Prompt the user to enter a double value
    System.out.print("Enter a double value: ");
    double doubleValue = MyInput.readDouble();
    System.out.println("You entered the double value "
      + doubleValue);

    // Prompt the user to enter a string
    System.out.print("Enter a string: ");
    String string = MyInput.readString();
    System.out.println("You entered the string " + string);

    // Prompt the user to enter a character
    System.out.print("Enter a character: ");
    char charValue = MyInput.readChar();
    System.out.println("You entered the character " + charValue);

    // Prompt the user to enter a boolean
    System.out.print("Enter a boolean: ");
    boolean booleanValue = MyInput.readBoolean();
    System.out.println("You entered the boolean " + booleanValue);
  }
}
```

16.11 Object Streams

Thus far, this chapter has covered input and output of bytes, characters, and primitive data types. Object streams enable you to perform input and output at the object level. To enable an object to be read or written, the object's defining class has to implement the java.io.Serializable interface or the java.io.Externalizable interface. The Serializable interface is a marker interface. It has no methods, so you don't need to add additional code in your class that implements Serializable. Implementing this interface enables the Java serialization mechanism to automate the process of storing the objects and arrays. The Externalizable interface extends the Serializable interface and defines the readExternal and writeExternal methods to enable customization of object streams.

To appreciate this automation feature and understand how an object is stored, consider what you need to do in order to store an object without using this feature. Suppose you want to store an object of the MessagePanel class in Example 11.5, "Creating a Message Panel Class." To do this you need to store all the current values of the properties in a MessagePanel object. The properties defined in MessagePanel are message (String), centered (boolean), xCoordinate (int), and yCoordinate (int). Since MessagePanel is a subclass of JPanel, the property values of JPanel have to be stored as well as the properties of all the superclasses of JPanel. If a property is of an object type, storing it requires storing all the property values inside this object. As you can see, this is a very tedious process. Fortunately, you don't have to go through it manually. Java provides a built-in mechanism to automate the process of writing objects. This process is referred to as *object serialization*. In contrast, the process of reading objects is referred to as *object deserialization*.

16.11.1 The *ObjectOutputStream* and *ObjectInputStream* classes

The ObjectOutputStream class is used for storing objects, and the ObjectInput-Stream class for restoring objects. These two classes are built upon several other classes. Figure 16.18 shows the hierarchical relationship of these related classes.

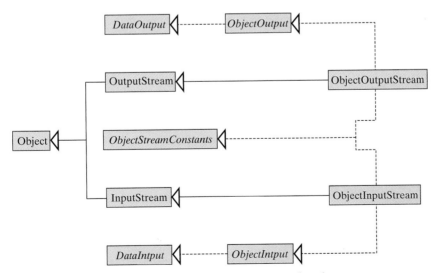

Figure 16.18 *ObjectOutputStream extends* OutputStream *and implements* ObjectOutput *and* ObjectStreamConstants. ObjectInputStream *extends* InputStream *and implements* ObjectInput *and* ObjectStreamConstants.

717

ObjectOutputStream implements ObjectOutput, which inherits DataOutput. DataOutput provides methods for writing Java primitive-data-type values and strings. ObjectOutput extends DataOutput to include output of objects and arrays. An ObjectOutputStream writes Java primitive-data-type values and objects to an OutputStream. Persistent storage can be accomplished using a file for the stream. The format of the output is platform-independent. The OutputStream can also be a network socket stream, which will be introduced in Bonus Chapter 21, "Networking."

ObjectInputStream is the inverse of ObjectOutputStream. ObjectInputStream implements ObjectInput, which inherits DataInput. DataInput provides methods for reading primitive-data-type values and strings. ObjectInput extends DataInput to include input of objects and arrays. An ObjectInputStream reads the data previously written using an ObjectOutputStream with a file stream or a network socket stream.

Only objects that implement the java.io.Serializable interface can use ObjectOutputStream and ObjectInputStream. The Serializable interface provides complete automation for serializing and deserializing an object. The Externalizable interface gives you the option of customizing how an object should be serialized and deserialized.

All user-interface classes implement Serializable, so they are serializable. The method writeObject(obj) is used to write an object to the ObjectOutputStream, and readObject() is used to read an object from the ObjectInputStream. Attempting to store an object that does not support the Serializable interface would cause a NotSerializableException.

When a serializable object is stored, the class of the object is encoded; this includes the class name and the signature of the class, the values of the object's fields and arrays, and the closure of any other objects referenced from the initial object. When a primitive-data-type value is stored, appropriate methods, such as writeInt(), writeBoolean() in the DataOutput interface, are used. Multiple objects or primitives can be written to the stream. The objects must be read back from the corresponding ObjectInputStream with the same types and in the same order as they were written. Java's safe casting should be used to get the desired type. For instance, when reading an object of the MessagePanel class, the object should be cast to MessagePanel.

Here is an example of creating an ObjectOutputStream and storing a MessagePanel object (messagePanel) and an int value to the file named **object.dat**.

```
ObjectOutputStream out = new ObjectOutputStream(
  new FileOutputStream("object.dat"));
out.writeObject(messagePanel);
out.writeInt(5);
```

The corresponding code to restore the object and the int value is shown below.

```
ObjectInputStream in = new ObjectInputStream(
  new FileInputStream("object.dat"));
MessagePanel c = (MessagePanel)in.readObject();
int x = in.readInt();
```

Example 16.7 Testing Object Streams

Problem

Write a program that manipulates MessagePanel, as shown in Figure 16.19. You will use radio buttons to set the background color, and two buttons, <= and =>, to move the message to left and right. The Store button is provided to save a MessagePanel object, and the Restore button is used to reload the saved MessagePanel object.

Figure 16.19 *You can use the Store button to save the MessagePanel object shown in the middle of the window, and the Restore button to reload the saved object later.*

Solution

The following code gives the solution to the problem.

```
1    // ObjectStreamDemo.java: Demonstrate store and restore objects
2    package chapter16;
3
4    import java.awt.*;
5    import java.awt.event.*;
6    import javax.swing.*;
7    import java.io.*;
8    import java.util.Date;
9
10   public class ObjectStreamDemo extends JFrame
11     implements ActionListener {
12     // Radio buttons for selecting a color for the message
13     JRadioButton jrbRed = new JRadioButton("Red");
14     JRadioButton jrbGreen = new JRadioButton("Green");
15     JRadioButton jrbYellow = new JRadioButton("Yellow");
16
17     // Buttons for Store, Restore, Left, and Right
18     JButton jbtStore = new JButton("Store");
19     JButton jbtRestore = new JButton("Restore");
20     JButton jbtLeft = new JButton("<=");
21     JButton jbtRight = new JButton("=>");
22
23     // Status label to display date when the object is stored
24     JLabel jlbStatusBar = new JLabel();
25
26     // Create a MessagePanel instance
27     MessagePanel messagePanel = new MessagePanel();
28
```

continues

Example 16.7 Continued

```
29        // Panel for holding radio buttons, message panel, and buttons
30        JPanel jpSerialization = new JPanel();
31
32        /** Construct the frame */
33        public ObjectStreamDemo() {
34          // Create a panel to group radio buttons
35          JPanel jpRadioButtons = new JPanel();
36          jpRadioButtons.add(jrbRed);
37          jpRadioButtons.add(jrbGreen);
38          jpRadioButtons.add(jrbYellow);
39
40          // Group radio buttons
41          ButtonGroup btg = new ButtonGroup();
42          btg.add(jrbRed);
43          btg.add(jrbGreen);
44          btg.add(jrbYellow);
45
46          // Create a panel to group buttons
47          JPanel jpButtons = new JPanel();
48          jpButtons.add(jbtStore);
49          jpButtons.add(jbtRestore);
50          jpButtons.add(jbtLeft);
51          jpButtons.add(jbtRight);
52
53          // Group jpRadioButtons, messagePanel, and jpButtons
54          jpSerialization.setLayout(new BorderLayout());
55          jpSerialization.add(jpRadioButtons, BorderLayout.NORTH);
56          jpSerialization.add(messagePanel, BorderLayout.CENTER);
57          jpSerialization.add(jpButtons, BorderLayout.SOUTH);
58
59          // Set borders
60          jpRadioButtons.setBorder(BorderFactory.createEtchedBorder());
61          jpButtons.setBorder(BorderFactory.createEtchedBorder());
62          messagePanel.setBorder(BorderFactory.createRaisedBevelBorder());
63
64          // Add jpSerialization and jlbStatusBar to the frame
65          Container container = getContentPane();
66          container.add(jlbStatusBar, BorderLayout.SOUTH);
67          container.add(jpSerialization, BorderLayout.CENTER);
68
69          // Register listeners
70          jrbRed.addActionListener(this);
71          jrbGreen.addActionListener(this);
72          jrbYellow.addActionListener(this);
73          jbtStore.addActionListener(this);
74          jbtRestore.addActionListener(this);
75          jbtLeft.addActionListener(this);
76          jbtRight.addActionListener(this);
77        }
78
79        /** Handle action events */
80        public void actionPerformed(ActionEvent e) {
81          if (e.getSource() == jrbRed)
82            messagePanel.setBackground(Color.red);
83          else if (e.getSource() == jrbGreen)
84            messagePanel.setBackground(Color.green);
85          else if (e.getSource() == jrbYellow)
86            messagePanel.setBackground(Color.yellow);
87          else if (e.getSource() == jbtStore) {
```

```
88          try {
89            ObjectOutputStream out =
90              new ObjectOutputStream(new FileOutputStream("object.dat"));
91            out.writeObject(messagePanel);
92            out.writeObject(new Date());
93            out.close();
94            jlbStatusBar.setText("The object is stored in object.dat");
95          }
96          catch (IOException ex) {
97            System.out.println(ex);
98          }
99        }
100       else if (e.getSource() == jbtRestore) {
101         try {
102           ObjectInputStream in =
103             new ObjectInputStream(new FileInputStream("object.dat"));
104           MessagePanel c = (MessagePanel)in.readObject();
105           Date d = (Date)in.readObject();
106           jpSerialization.remove(messagePanel);
107           messagePanel = c;
108           jpSerialization.add(messagePanel, BorderLayout.CENTER);
109           jpSerialization.repaint();
110           in.close();
111           jlbStatusBar.setText("The object saved at " + d.toString()
112             + " is restored");
113         }
114         catch (IOException ex1) {
115           System.out.println(ex1);
116         }
117         catch (ClassNotFoundException ex2) {
118           System.out.println(ex2);
119         }
120       }
121       else if (e.getSource() == jbtLeft)
122         left();
123       else if (e.getSource() == jbtRight)
124         right();
125     }
126
127     /** Move the message in the panel left */
128     private void left() {
129       int x = messagePanel.getXCoordinate();
130       if (x > 10) {
131         // Shift the message to the left
132         messagePanel.setXCoordinate(x - 10);
133         messagePanel.repaint();
134       }
135     }
136
137     /** Move the message in the panel right */
138     private void right() {
139       int x = messagePanel.getXCoordinate();
140       if (x < getWidth() - 20) {
141         // Shift the message to the right
142         messagePanel.setXCoordinate(x + 10);
143         messagePanel.repaint();
144       }
145     }
146
```

continues

Example 16.7 Continued

```
147        /** Main method */
148        public static void main(String[] args) {
149          ObjectStreamDemo frame = new ObjectStreamDemo();
150          frame.setTitle("Test Object Serialization");
151          frame.setDefaultCloseOperation(JFrame.EXIT_ON_CLOSE);
152          frame.pack();
153          frame.setVisible(true);
154        }
155      }
```

Review

When you click the Store button, the current state of the `messagePanel` and the current time (`new Date()`) are saved to file **object.dat** using `ObjectOutputStream` (Lines 89–90). When you click the Restore button, these objects are read back from the same file (Lines 102–103). They must be read back in the same order as they were stored. Explicit type casting must be used to ensure that the objects read are of the right type.

In the handler for the Restore button, `messagePanel` was removed from `jpSerialization` (Line 106), and then a new `messagePanel` was created and added to `jpSerialization` (Lines 107–108) This is necessary to ensure that the newly restored `messagePanel`, and not the old copy, is used in the windows.

Like many Java classes, `java.awt.Component` and `java.util.Date` implement `java.io.Serializable`, so the objects of these classes or their subclasses can be stored using object streams.

16.11.2   The *transient* Keyword

By default, all the nonstatic variables of a serialized object are written to the object stream. However, not all nonstatic variables can be serialized. For example, since the `java.awt.Thread` class does not implement `Serializable`, a `Thread` object cannot be serialized. You can use the `transient` keyword to mark a data field so that it will not be serialized. Consider the following class:

```
public class Foo {
  private int v1;
  private static double v2;
  transient Thread v3;
}
```

When an object of the `Foo` class is serialized, only variable `v1` is serialized. Variable `v2` is not serialized because it is a static variable, and variable `v3` is not serialized because it is marked `transient`. If `v3` were not marked `transient`, a `java.io.NotSerializableException` would occur.

16.12   **Random Access Files**

All of the streams you have used so far are known as *read-only* or *write-only* streams. The external files of these streams are sequential files that cannot be updated without creating a new file. It is often necessary to modify files or to insert new records into files. Java provides the RandomAccessFile class to allow a file to be read and updated at the same time.

The RandomAccessFile class extends Object and implements the DataInput and DataOutput interfaces. Because DataInputStream implements the DataInput interface, and DataOutputStream implements the DataOutput interface, many methods in RandomAccessFile are the same as those in DataInputStream and DataOutputStream. For example, readInt(), readLong(), readDouble(), readUTF(), writeInt, write-Long, writeDouble, and writeUTF can be used in data input streams or data output streams as well as in RandomAccessFile streams, since readInt(), readLong(), readDouble(), and readUTF() are defined in the DataInput interface, and writeInt, writeLong, writeDouble, and writeUTF are defined in the DataOutput interface.

Additionally, RandomAccessFile provides the following methods to deal with random access:

- public void seek(long pos) throws IOException

    Sets the offset (in bytes specified in pos) from the beginning of the RandomAccessFile to where the next read or write occurs.

- public long getFilePointer() throws IOException

    Returns the offset, in bytes, from the beginning of the file to where the next read or write occurs.

- public long length() throws IOException

    Returns the length of the file.

- public final void writeChar(int v) throws IOException

    Writes a character to the file as a two-byte Unicode, with the higher byte written first.

- public final void writeChars(String s) throws IOException

    Writes a string to the file as a sequence of characters.

When creating a RandomAccessFile, you can specify one of two modes ("r" or "rw"). Mode "r" means that the stream is read-only, and mode "rw" indicates that the stream allows both read and write. For example, the following statement creates a new stream, raf, that allows the program to read from and write to the file **test.dat**:

```
RandomAccessFile raf = new RandomAccessFile("test.dat", "rw");
```

If **test.dat** already exists, raf is created to access it; if **test.dat** does not exist, a new file named **test.dat** is created, and raf is created to access the new file. The method raf.length() returns the number of bytes in **test.dat** at any given time. If you append new data into the file, raf.length() increases.

◈ NOTE

When you use the writeChar method to write a character or the writeChars method to write characters, a character occupies two bytes.

TIP

Open the file with the `"r"` mode if the file is not intended to be modified. This prevents unintentional modification of the file.

Random access files are often used to process files of records. For convenience, fixed-length records are used in random access files so that a record can be located easily. A record consists of a fixed number of fields. A field can be a string or a primitive data type. A string in a fixed-length record has a maximum size. If a string is smaller than the maximum size, the rest of the string is padded with blanks.

Example 16.8 Using Random Access Files

Problem

Write a program that registers students and displays student information. The user interface consists of a tabbed pane with two tabs: Register Student and View Student. The Register Student tab enables you to store a student in the file, as shown in Figure 16.20. The View Student tab enables you to browse through student information, as shown in Figure 16.21.

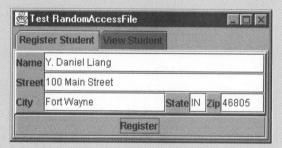

Figure 16.20 *The Register Student tab registers a student.*

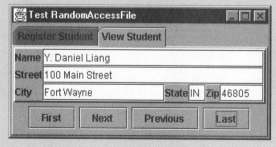

Figure 16.21 *The View Student tab displays student information.*

Solution

The following code gives the solution to the problem.

```
1    // TestRandomAccessFile.java: Store and read data
2    // using RandomAccessFile
3    package chapter16;
4
5    import java.io.*;
6    import java.awt.*;
7    import java.awt.event.*;
8    import javax.swing.*;
9    import javax.swing.border.*;
10
11   public class TestRandomAccessFile extends JFrame {
12     // Create a tabbed pane to hold two panels
13     private JTabbedPane jtpStudent = new JTabbedPane();
14
15     // Random access file for access the student.dat file
16     private RandomAccessFile raf;
17
18     /** Main method */
19     public static void main(String[] args) {
20       TestRandomAccessFile frame = new TestRandomAccessFile();
21       frame.pack();
22       frame.setTitle("Test RandomAccessFile");
23       frame.setVisible(true);
24     }
25
26     /** Default constructor */
27     public TestRandomAccessFile() {
28       // Open or create a random access file
29       try {
30         raf = new RandomAccessFile("student.dat", "rw");
31       }
32       catch(IOException ex) {
33         System.out.print("Error: " + ex);
34         System.exit(0);
35       }
36
37       // Place buttons in the tabbed pane
38       jtpStudent.add(new RegisterStudent(raf), "Register Student");
39       jtpStudent.add(new ViewStudent(raf), "View Student");
40
41       // Add the tabbed pane to the frame
42       getContentPane().add(jtpStudent);
43     }
44   }
45
46   // Register student panel
47   class RegisterStudent extends JPanel implements ActionListener {
48     // Button for registering a student
49     private JButton jbtRegister;
50
51     // Student information panel
52     private StudentPanel studentPanel;
53
54     // Random access file
55     private RandomAccessFile raf;
56
57     public RegisterStudent(RandomAccessFile raf) {
58       // Pass raf to RegisterStudent Panel
59       this.raf = raf;
60
```

continues

Example 16.8 Continued

```
61           // Add studentPanel and jbtRegister in the panel
62           setLayout(new BorderLayout());
63           add(studentPanel = new StudentPanel(),
64             BorderLayout.CENTER);
65           add(jbtRegister = new JButton("Register"),
66             BorderLayout.SOUTH);
67
68           // Register listener
69           jbtRegister.addActionListener(this);
70         }
71
72         /** Handle button actions */
73         public void actionPerformed(ActionEvent e) {
74           if (e.getSource() == jbtRegister) {
75             Student student = studentPanel.getStudent();
76
77             try {
78               raf.seek(raf.length());
79               student.writeStudent(raf);
80             }
81             catch(IOException ex) {
82               System.out.print("Error: " + ex);
83             }
84           }
85         }
86       }
87
88     // View student panel
89     class ViewStudent extends JPanel implements ActionListener {
90       // Buttons for viewing student information
91       private JButton jbtFirst, jbtNext, jbtPrevious, jbtLast;
92
93       // Random access file
94       private RandomAccessFile raf = null;
95
96       // Current student record
97       private Student student = new Student();
98
99       // Create a student panel
100      private StudentPanel studentPanel = new StudentPanel();
101
102      // File pointer in the random access file
103      private long lastPos;
104      private long currentPos;
105
106      public ViewStudent(RandomAccessFile raf) {
107        // Pass raf to ViewStudent
108        this.raf = raf;
109
110        // Panel p to hold four navigator buttons
111        JPanel p = new JPanel();
112        p.setLayout(new FlowLayout(FlowLayout.LEFT));
113        p.add(jbtFirst = new JButton("First"));
114        p.add(jbtNext = new JButton("Next"));
115        p.add(jbtPrevious = new JButton("Previous"));
116        p.add(jbtLast = new JButton("Last"));
117
118        // Add panel p and studentPanel to ViewPanel
119        setLayout(new BorderLayout());
120        add(studentPanel, BorderLayout.CENTER);
121        add(p, BorderLayout.SOUTH);
122
```

```
123          // Register listeners
124          jbtFirst.addActionListener(this);
125          jbtNext.addActionListener(this);
126          jbtPrevious.addActionListener(this);
127          jbtLast.addActionListener(this);
128        }
129
130        /** Handle navigation button actions */
131        public void actionPerformed(ActionEvent e) {
132          String actionCommand = e.getActionCommand();
133          if (e.getSource() instanceof JButton) {
134            try {
135              if ("First".equals(actionCommand)) {
136                if (raf.length() > 0)
137                  retrieve(0);
138              }
139              else if ("Next".equals(actionCommand)) {
140                currentPos = raf.getFilePointer();
141                if (currentPos < raf.length())
142                  retrieve(currentPos);
143              }
144              else if ("Previous".equals(actionCommand)) {
145                currentPos = raf.getFilePointer();
146                if (currentPos > 0)
147                  retrieve(currentPos - 2 * 2 * Student.RECORD_SIZE);
148              }
149              else if ("Last".equals(actionCommand)) {
150                lastPos = raf.length();
151                if (lastPos > 0)
152                  retrieve(lastPos - 2 * Student.RECORD_SIZE);
153              }
154            }
155            catch(IOException ex) {
156              System.out.print("Error: " + ex);
157            }
158          }
159        }
160
161        /** Retrieve a record at specified position */
162        public void retrieve(long pos) {
163          try {
164            raf.seek(pos);
165            student.readStudent(raf);
166            studentPanel.setStudent(student);
167          }
168          catch(IOException ex) {
169            System.out.print("Error: " + ex);
170          }
171        }
172      }
173
174      // This class contains static methods for reading and writing
175      // fixed length records
176      class FixedLengthStringIO {
177        // Read fixed number of characters from a DataInput stream
178        public static String readFixedLengthString(int size,
179          DataInput in) throws IOException {
180          char c[] = new char[size];
181
182          for (int i = 0; i < size; i++)
183            c[i] = in.readChar();
184
```

continues

727

Example 16.8 Continued

```
185          return new String(c);
186      }
187
188      // Write fixed number of characters (string s with padded spaces)
189      // to a DataOutput stream
190      public static void writeFixedLengthString(String s, int size,
191        DataOutput out) throws IOException {
192        char cBuffer[] = new char[size];
193        s.getChars(0, s.length(), cBuffer, 0);
194        for (int i = s.length(); i < cBuffer.length; i++)
195          cBuffer[i] = ' ';
196        String newS = new String(cBuffer);
197        out.writeChars(newS);
198      }
199  }
```

```
1    // StudentPanel.java: Panel for displaying student information
2    package chapter16;
3
4    import javax.swing.*;
5    import javax.swing.border.*;
6    import java.awt.*;
7
8    public class StudentPanel extends JPanel {
9      JTextField jtfName = new JTextField(32);
10     JTextField jtfStreet = new JTextField(32);
11     JTextField jtfCity = new JTextField(20);
12     JTextField jtfState = new JTextField(2);
13     JTextField jtfZip = new JTextField(5);
14
15     /** Construct a student panel */
16     public StudentPanel() {
17       // Set the panel with line border
18       setBorder(new BevelBorder(BevelBorder.RAISED));
19
20       // Panel p1 for holding labels Name, Street, and City
21       JPanel p1 = new JPanel();
22       p1.setLayout(new GridLayout(3, 1));
23       p1.add(new JLabel("Name"));
24       p1.add(new JLabel("Street"));
25       p1.add(new JLabel("City"));
26
27       // Panel jpState for holding state
28       JPanel jpState = new JPanel();
29       jpState.setLayout(new BorderLayout());
30       jpState.add(new JLabel("State"), BorderLayout.WEST);
31       jpState.add(jtfState, BorderLayout.CENTER);
32
33       // Panel jpZip for holding zip
34       JPanel jpZip = new JPanel();
35       jpZip.setLayout(new BorderLayout());
36       jpZip.add(new JLabel("Zip"), BorderLayout.WEST);
37       jpZip.add(jtfZip, BorderLayout.CENTER);
38
39       // Panel p2 for holding jpState and jpZip
40       JPanel p2 = new JPanel();
41       p2.setLayout(new BorderLayout());
42       p2.add(jpState, BorderLayout.WEST);
43       p2.add(jpZip, BorderLayout.CENTER);
44
```

```
45        // Panel p3 for holding jtfCity and p2
46        JPanel p3 = new JPanel();
47        p3.setLayout(new BorderLayout());
48        p3.add(jtfCity, BorderLayout.CENTER);
49        p3.add(p2, BorderLayout.EAST);
50
51        // Panel p4 for holding jtfName, jtfStreet, and p3
52        JPanel p4 = new JPanel();
53        p4.setLayout(new GridLayout(3, 1));
54        p4.add(jtfName);
55        p4.add(jtfStreet);
56        p4.add(p3);
57
58        // Place p1 and p4 into StudentPanel
59        setLayout(new BorderLayout());
60        add(p1, BorderLayout.WEST);
61        add(p4, BorderLayout.CENTER);
62      }
63
64      /** Get student information from the text fields */
65      public Student getStudent() {
66        return new Student(jtfName.getText().trim(),
67                           jtfStreet.getText().trim(),
68                           jtfCity.getText().trim(),
69                           jtfState.getText().trim(),
70                           jtfZip.getText().trim());
71      }
72
73      /** Set student information on the text fields */
74      public void setStudent(Student s) {
75        jtfName.setText(s.getName());
76        jtfStreet.setText(s.getStreet());
77        jtfCity.setText(s.getCity());
78        jtfState.setText(s.getState());
79        jtfZip.setText(s.getZip());
80      }
81    }
```

```
1    // Student.java: Student class encapsulates student information
2    package chapter16;
3
4    import java.io.*;
5
6    public class Student implements Serializable {
7      private String name;
8      private String street;
9      private String city;
10     private String state;
11     private String zip;
12
13     // Specify the size of five string fields in the record
14     final static int NAME_SIZE = 32;
15     final static int STREET_SIZE = 32;
16     final static int CITY_SIZE = 20;
17     final static int STATE_SIZE = 2;
18     final static int ZIP_SIZE = 5;
19
20     // the total size of the record in bytes, a Unicode
21     // character is 2 bytes size
22     final static int RECORD_SIZE =
23       (NAME_SIZE + STREET_SIZE + CITY_SIZE + STATE_SIZE + ZIP_SIZE);
24
```

continues

Example 16.8 Continued

```
25       /** Default constructor */
26       public Student() {
27       }
28
29       /** Construct a Student with specified name, street, city, state,
30          and zip
31          */
32       public Student(String name, String street, String city,
33         String state, String zip) {
34         this.name = name;
35         this.street = street;
36         this.city = city;
37         this.state = state;
38         this.zip = zip;
39       }
40
41       /** Return name */
42       public String getName() {
43         return name;
44       }
45
46       /** Return street */
47       public String getStreet() {
48         return street;
49       }
50
51       /** Return city */
52       public String getCity() {
53         return city;
54       }
55
56       /** Return state */
57       public String getState() {
58         return state;
59       }
60
61       /** Return zip */
62       public String getZip() {
63         return zip;
64       }
65
66       /** Write a student to a data output stream */
67       public void writeStudent(DataOutput out) throws IOException {
68         FixedLengthStringIO.writeFixedLengthString(
69           name, NAME_SIZE, out);
70         FixedLengthStringIO.writeFixedLengthString(
71           street, STREET_SIZE, out);
72         FixedLengthStringIO.writeFixedLengthString(
73           city, CITY_SIZE, out);
74         FixedLengthStringIO.writeFixedLengthString(
75           state, STATE_SIZE, out);
76         FixedLengthStringIO.writeFixedLengthString(
77           zip, ZIP_SIZE, out);
78       }
79
80       /** Read a student from data input stream */
81       public void readStudent(DataInput in) throws IOException {
82         name = FixedLengthStringIO.readFixedLengthString(
83           NAME_SIZE, in);
84         street = FixedLengthStringIO.readFixedLengthString(
85           STREET_SIZE, in);
```

```
86        city = FixedLengthStringIO.readFixedLengthString(
87          CITY_SIZE, in);
88        state = FixedLengthStringIO.readFixedLengthString(
89          STATE_SIZE, in);
90        zip = FixedLengthStringIO.readFixedLengthString(
91          ZIP_SIZE, in);
92      }
93    }
```

Review

A random file, **student.dat**, is created to store student information if the file does not yet exist. If it does exist, the file is opened. A random file object, raf, is used in both the registration and the viewing part of the program. The user can add a new student record to the file in the Register Student panel and view it immediately in the View Student panel.

Several classes are used in this example. Their relationships are shown in Figure 16.22.

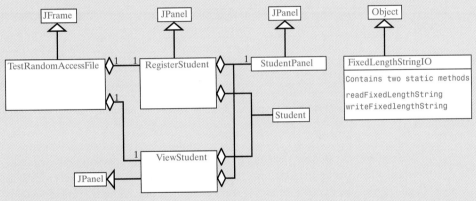

Figure 16.22 *Example 16.8 uses the* TestRandomAccessFile, RegisterStudent, ViewStudent, StudentPanel, Student, *and* FixedLengthIO *classes.*

The main class, TestRandomAccessFile, is a subclass of JFrame. It creates an instance of the RegisterStudent class and an instance of the ViewStudent class. These two instances are added to a tabbed pane with two tabs: Register Student and View Student. When the Register Student tab is clicked, the registration panel is shown. When the View Student tab is clicked, the viewing panel is shown.

The RegisterStudent class and the ViewStudent class have many things in common. They both extend the JPanel class, and they both use the StudentPanel and Student classes.

The student information panels for registering and viewing student information are identical. Therefore, the program creates one class, StudentPanel, to lay out

continues

731

Example 16.8 Continued

the labels and text fields, as shown in Figure 16.23. The StudentPanel class also provides the getStudent method for getting text fields and the setStudent method for setting text fields.

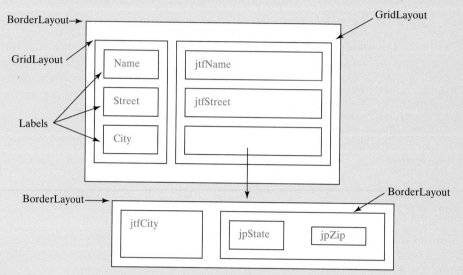

Figure 16.23 *The StudentPanel class uses several panels to group components to achieve the desired layout.*

The Student class defines the student record structure and provides methods for reading and writing a record into the file. Each field in a student record has a fixed length. The FixedLengthStringIO class defines the methods for reading and writing fixed-length strings. The Student class implements Serializable so that it can be serialized in Example 21.4, "Passing Objects in Network Programs."

The size of each field in the student record is fixed. For example, zip code is set to a maximum of five characters. If you entered a zip code of more than five characters by mistake, the ArrayIndexOutofBounds runtime error would occur when the program attempted to write the zip code into the file using the writeFixedLengthString method defined in the FixedLengthStringIO class.

16.13   Parsing Text Files (Optional)

Occasionally you need to process a text file. For example, the Java source file is a text file. The compiler reads the source file and translates it into bytecode, which is a binary file. Java provides the `StreamTokenizer` class so that you can take an input stream and parse it into words, which are known as *tokens*. The tokens are read one at a time. To construct an instance of `StreamTokenizer`, you can use `StreamTokenizer(Reader is)` on a given character input stream. The `Stream-Tokenizer` class contains the useful constants listed in Table 16.3.

TABLE 16.3   StreamTokenizer Constants

Constant	Description
TT_WORD	The token is a word.
TT_NUMBER	The token is a number.
TT_EOL	The end of the line has been read.
TT_EOF	The end of the file has been read.

The `StreamTokenizer` class also contains the useful variables listed in Table 16.4.

TABLE 16.4   StreamTokenizer Variables

Variable	Description
int ttype	Contains the current token type, which matches one of the constants listed in Table 16.3.
double nval	Contains the value of the current token if the token is a number.
String sval	Contains a string that gives the characters of the current token if the token is a word.

Typically, the `nextToken()` method is used to retrieve tokens one by one in a loop until `TT_EOF` is returned. The following method parses the next token from the input stream of a `StreamTokenizer`:

```
public int nextToken() throws IOException
```

The type of the next token is returned in the `ttype` field. If `ttype == StreamTok-enizer.TT_WORD`, the token is stored in `sval`; if `ttype == StreamTokenizer.TT_NUM-BER`, the token is stored in `nval`.

Example 16.9 Using `StreamTokenizer`

Problem

Write a program that demonstrates parsing text files. The program reads a text file containing students' exam scores. Each record in the input file consists of a student's name, two midterm exam scores, and a final exam score. The program reads the fields for each record and computes the total score. It then stores the result in a new file. The formula for computing the total score is:

```
total score = midterm1 * 0.3 + midterm2 * 0.3 + final * 0.4;
```

Each record in the output file consists of a student's name and total score.

Solution

The following code gives the solution to the problem. Figure 16.24 shows a sample run of the program.

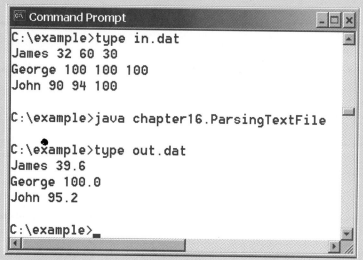

Figure 16.24   *The program uses* `StreamTokenizer` *to parse the text file into strings and numbers.*

```
1    // ParsingTextFile.java: Process text file using StreamTokenizer
2    package chapter16;
3
4    import java.io.*;
5
6    public class ParsingTextFile {
7      /** Main method */
8      public static void main(String[] args) {
9        // Declare file reader and writer streams
10       FileReader frs = null;
12       FileWriter fws = null;
13
14       // Declare streamTokenizer
15       StreamTokenizer in = null;
16
```

```
17        // Declare a print stream
18        PrintWriter out = null;
19
20        // Four input file fields: student name, midterm1,
21        // midterm2, and final exam score
22        String sname = null;
23        double midterm1 = 0;
24        double midterm2 = 0;
25        double finalScore = 0;
26
27        // Computed total score
28        double total = 0;
29
30        try {
31          // Create file input and output streams
32          frs = new FileReader("in.dat");
33          fws = new FileWriter("out.dat");
34
35          // Create a stream tokenizer wrapping file input stream
36          in = new StreamTokenizer(frs);
37          out = new PrintWriter(fws);
38
39          // Read first token
40          in.nextToken();
41
42          // Process a record
43          while (in.ttype != StreamTokenizer.TT_EOF) {
44            // Get student name
45            if (in.ttype == StreamTokenizer.TT_WORD)
46              sname = in.sval;
47            else
48              System.out.println("Bad file format");
49
50            // Get midterm1
51            if (in.nextToken() == StreamTokenizer.TT_NUMBER)
52              midterm1 = in.nval;
53            else
54              System.out.println("Bad file format");
55
56            // Get midterm2
57            if (in.nextToken() == StreamTokenizer.TT_NUMBER)
58              midterm2 = in.nval;
59            else
60              System.out.println("Bad file format");
61
62            // Get final score
63            if (in.nextToken() == StreamTokenizer.TT_NUMBER)
64              finalScore = in.nval;
65
66            total = midterm1*0.3 + midterm2*0.3 + finalScore*0.4;
67            out.println(sname + " " + total);
68
69            in.nextToken();
70          }
71        }
72        catch (FileNotFoundException ex) {
73          System.out.println("File not found: in.dat");
74        }
75        catch (IOException ex) {
76          System.out.println(ex.getMessage());
77        }
```

continues

735

Example 16.9 Continued

```
78          finally {
79            try {
80              if (frs != null) frs.close();
81              if (fws != null) fws.close();
82            }
83            catch (IOException ex) {
84              System.out.println(ex);
85            }
86          }
87        }
88      }
```

Review

Before running this program, make sure you have created the text file **in.dat**. To parse the text file **in.dat**, the program uses StreamTokenizer to wrap a File-Reader stream. The nextToken() method is used on a StreamTokenizer object to get one token at a time. The token value is stored in the nval field if the token is numeric, and in the sval field if the token is a string. The token type is stored in the ttype field.

For each record, the program reads the name and the three exam scores and then computes the total score. A FileWriter stream is used to store the name and the total score in the text file **out.dat** (see Figure 16.25).

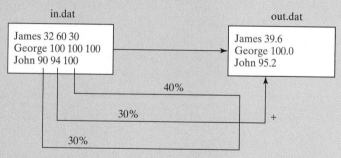

Figure 16.25   *The program reads two midterm scores and a final exam score, and then computes a total score.*

16.14   Array Streams, Piped Streams, String Streams, Pushback Streams, and Line Number Streams (Optional)

You have learned many I/O streams in this chapter. Each stream has its intended application. Streams were first used for file input/output in the C language, but Java streams are not limited to this function. There are several other stream classes that you might find useful. A brief discussion of them follows:

■ **Array streams** like `ByteArrayInputStream`, `CharArrayReader`, `ByteArray-OutputStream`, and `CharArrayWriter` are used to read and write bytes or characters from arrays.

■ **Piped streams** can be thought of as pipes that connect two processes. One process sends data out through the pipe, and the other receives data from the pipe. Piped streams are used in interprocess communication (IPC). Two processes running on separate threads can exchange data. Java provides `PipedInputStream`, `PipedOutputStream`, `PipedReader`, and `PipedWriter` to support piped streams.

■ **String streams** (`StringReader` and `StringWriter`) are exactly like character array streams, except that the source of a string stream is a string, and the destination of a string stream is a string buffer.

■ **Pushback streams** are commonly used in parsers to "push back" a single byte or character in the input stream after reading from the input stream. A pushback stream previews the input to determine what to do next. The number of bytes or characters pushed can be specified when the stream is constructed. By default, a single byte or a single character is pushed back. Java provides the `PushbackInputStream` and `PushbackReader` classes to support pushback streams.

■ **Line-number streams** allow you to track the current line number of an input stream. Java provides the `LineNumberReader` class for this purpose. This class is useful for such applications as editing and debugging. You can use the `getLineNumber()` method to get the current line number of the input, and the `getLine()` method to retrieve a line into a string.

Chapter Summary

■ The `File` class is intended to provide an abstraction that deals with most of the machine-dependent complexities of files and pathnames in a machine-independent fashion. The file name is a string. The `File` class is a wrapper class for the file name and its directory path.

■ Streams can be categorized as byte streams and character streams. The `InputStream` and `OutputStream` classes are the roots of all byte stream classes, and the `Reader` and `Writer` classes are the roots of all character stream classes.

■ The subclasses of `InputStream` and `OutputStream` are analogous to the subclasses of `Reader` and `Writer`. Many of them have similar method signatures, and you can use them in the same way.

■ File streams (`FileInputStream` and `FileOutputStream` for byte streams, `FileReader` and `FileWriter` for character streams) are used to read data from or write data to external files.

■ Data streams (`DataInputStream` and `DataOutputStream`) read or write Java primitive-data-type values in machine-independent fashion, which enables you to write a data file on one machine and read it on a machine that has a different OS or file structure.

■ Since the data output stream outputs a binary representation of data, you cannot view its content as text. The `PrintStream` and `PrintWriter` classes allow you to print streams in text format. `System.out`, `System.in`, and `System.err` are examples of `PrintStream` objects.

■ The `BufferedInputStream`, `BufferedOutputStream`, `BufferedReader`, and `BufferedWriter` classes can be used to speed input and output by reducing the number of reads and writes. Typical physical input/output involving I/O devices is very slow compared with CPU processing, so using buffered I/O can greatly improve performance.

■ The `JFileChooser` class is used to display standard file dialog boxes from which the user can navigate through the file systems and select files to open or save.

■ The `ObjectOutputStream` and `ObjectInputStream` classes are used to store and restore objects. To enable object serialization, the object's defining class must implement the `java.io.Serializable` marker interface.

■ The `RandomAccessFile` class enables you to read and write data to a file. You can open a file with the `"r"` mode to indicate that it is read-only, or with the `"rw"` mode to indicate that it is updateable. Since the `RandomAccessFile` class implements `DataInput` and `DataOutput` interfaces, many methods in `RandomAccessFile` are the same as those in `DataInputStream` and `DataOutputStream`.

■ The `StreamTokenizer` class is useful in processing text files. This class enables you to parse an input stream into tokens and read them one at a time.

Review Questions

16.1 Which streams must always be used to process external files?

16.2 What types of data are read or written by `InputStream` and `OutputStream`? Can you use `read()` or `write(byte b)` in these streams?

16.3 `InputStream` reads bytes. Why does the `read()` method return an `int` instead of a byte?

16.4 What types of data are read or written by `Reader` and `Writer`? Can you use `read()` or `write(char c)` in these streams?

16.5 What are the differences between byte streams and character streams?

16.6 What types of data are read or written by file streams? Can you use `read()` or `write(byte b)` in file streams?

16.7 How are data input and output streams used to read and write data?

16.8 What are the differences between `DataOutputStream` and `PrintStream`?

16.9 Is JFileChooser modal? What is the return type for getSelectedFile() and getSelectedDirectory()? How do you set the current directory as the default directory for a JFileChooser dialog?

16.10 What are the data types for System.in, System.out, and System.err?

16.11 What types of objects can be stored using the ObjectOutput stream? What is the method for writing an object? What is the method for reading an object? What is the return type of the method that reads an object from ObjectInput-Stream?

16.12 Can RandomAccessFile streams read a data file created by DataOutputStream?

16.13 Create a RandomAccessFile stream for the file **student.dat** to allow the updating of student information in the file. Create a DataOutputStream for the file **student.dat**. Explain the differences between these two statements.

16.14 What happens if the file **test.dat** does not exist when you attempt to compile and run the following code?

```java
import java.io.*;

class Test {
  public static void main(String[] args) {
    try {
      RandomAccessFile raf =
        new RandomAccessFile("test.dat", "r");
      int i = raf.readInt();
    }
    catch(IOException ex) {
      System.out.println("IO exception");
    }
  }
}
```

16.15 Answer the following questions regarding StreamTokenizer:

- When do you use StreamTokenizer?

- How do you read data using StreamTokenizer?

- Where is the token stored when you are using the nextToken() method?

- How do you find the data type of the token?

16.17 Can you close a StreamTokenizer?

Programming Exercises

16.1 (Revising Example 16.2 "Copying Files") Rewrite Example 16.2 using FileReader and FileWriter streams. Write another program with buffered streams to boost performance. Test the performance of these two programs (one with buffered streams and the other without buffered streams), as shown in Figure 16.26.

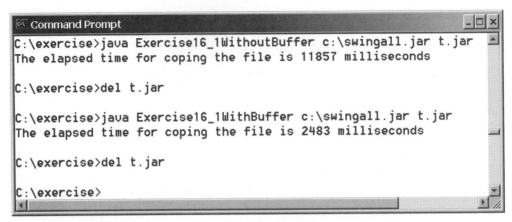

Figure 16.26 *Buffered streams can significantly boost performance.*

16.2 (Counting characters, words, and lines in a file) Write a program that will count the number of characters, including blanks, words, and lines, in a file. The file name should be passed as a command-line argument, as shown in Figure 16.27.

Figure 16.27 *The program displays the number of characters, words, and lines in the given file.*

16.3 (Processing scores in a file) Suppose that a text file **score.txt** contains an unspecified number of scores. Write a program that reads the scores from the file, displays the scores in a text area, and displays the average of the scores. Scores are separated by blanks.

 HINT

Read the scores one line at a time until all the lines are read. For each line, use `StringTokenizer` to extract the scores, and convert them into double values using the `Double.parseDouble` method.

16.4 (Revising Example 13.5 "Using Combo Boxes") Example 13.5 gives a program that lets users view a country's flag image and description by selecting the country from a combo box. The description is a string coded in the program. Rewrite the program to read the text description from a file. Suppose that the descriptions are stored in the file description0.txt, ..., and description8.txt for the nine countries Canada, China, Denmark, France, Germany, India, Norway, the United Kingdom, and the United States, in this order.

16.5 (Revising Example 16.5 "Displaying a File in a Text Area") Rewrite Example 16.5 to enable the user to view the file by opening it from a file open dialog box, as shown in Figure 16.28. A file open dialog box is displayed when the Browse button is clicked. The file is displayed in the text area, and the file name is displayed in the text field when the OK button is clicked in the file open dialog box. You can also enter the file name in the text field and press the Enter key to display the file in the text area.

Figure 16.28 *The program enables the user to view a file by selecting it from a file open dialog box.*

16.6 (Reformatting Java source code) Write a program that converts the Java source code from the next-line brace style to the end-of-line brace style. For example, the following Java source uses the next-line brace style:

```
public class Test
{
  public static void main(String[] args)
  {
    System.out.println("Welcome to Java!");
  }
}
```

Your program converts it to the end-of-line brace style, as follows:

```
public class Test {
  public static void main(String[] args) {
    System.out.println("Welcome to Java!");
  }
}
```

Your program can be invoked from the command line with the Java source code file as the argument. It converts the Java source code to a new format. For example, the following command converts the Java source code file Test.java to the end-of-line brace style.

```
java Exercise16_6 Test.java
```

16.7 (Removing a given string from a text file) Write a program that removes a specified string from a text file. Your program reads the file and generates a new file without the specified string, copies the new file to the original file, and passes the string and the file name from the command line, as follows:

```
java Exercise16_7 John StudentFile.dat
```

This command removes string John from StudentFile.dat.

16.8 (Creating a histogram for occurrence of letters) In Example 13.12, "Creating Multiple Windows," you developed a program that displays a histogram to show the occurrences of each letter in a text area. Reuse the Histogram class created in Example 13.12 to write a program that will display a histogram on a panel. The histogram should show the occurrences of each letter in a text file, as shown in Figure 16.29. Assume that the letters are not case-sensitive.

■ Place a panel that will display the histogram in the center of the frame.

■ Place a label and a text field in a panel, and put the panel in the south side of the frame. The text file will be entered from this text field.

■ Pressing the Enter key on the text field causes the program to count the occurrences of each letter and display the count in a histogram.

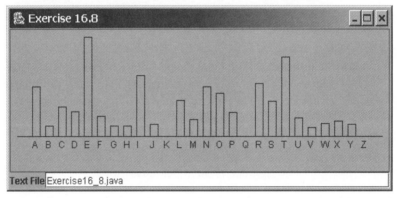

Figure 16.29 *The program displays a histogram that shows the occurrences of each letter in the file.*

16.9 (Modifying Example 16.8 "Using Random Access Files") Modify the View Student panel in Example 16.8 to add an Update button for updating the student record that is being displayed, as shown in Figure 16.30. The Tab "View Student" is now changed to "View and Update Student."

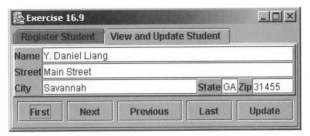

Figure 16.30   *You can browse student records and update the student record that is currently displayed.*

16.10 (Summing all the integers in a data file) Use `StreamTokenizer` to write a program that will add all of the integers in a data file. Suppose that the integers are delimited by spaces. Display the result on the console. Rewrite the program, assuming this time that the numbers are `double`.

16.11 (Revising Example 16.9 "Using `StreamTokenizer`") Rewrite Example 16.9 so that it reads a line as a string in a `BufferedReader` stream, and then use `StringTokenizer` to extract the fields.

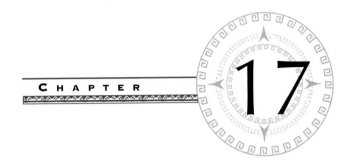

CHAPTER

17

JAVA DATA STRUCTURES

Objectives

- ◉ To explain the limitations of arrays.

- ◉ To describe the Java Collections Framework hierarchy.

- ◉ To use the Iterator interface to traverse a collection.

- ◉ To discover the Set interface, and know how and when to use HashSet, LinkedHashSet, or TreeSet to store elements.

- ◉ To explore the List interface, and know how and when to use ArrayList or LinkedList to store elements.

- ◉ To distinguish Vector and ArrayList, and know how to use Vector and Stack.

- ◉ To understand the differences between Collection and Map, and know how and when to use HashMap and LinkedHashMap to store values associated with keys.

- ◉ To use the static methods in the Collections and Arrays classes.

745

17.1   Introduction

In Chapter 5, "Arrays," you learned how to store and process elements in arrays. Arrays can be used to store a group of primitive type values or a group of objects. Once an array is created, its size cannot be altered. Arrays are a useful data structure for representing collections of elements, but they do not provide adequate support for inserting, deleting, sorting, and searching operations. The Java 2 platform introduced several new interfaces and classes that can be used to organize and manipulate data efficiently. These new interfaces and classes are known as the *Java Collections Framework*.

A *collection* is a container object that stores a group of objects, often referred to as *elements*. The Java Collections Framework supports three types of collections: *set, list*, and *map*. They are defined in the interfaces Set, List, and Map. An instance of Set stores a group of nonduplicate elements. An instance of List stores an ordered collection of elements. An instance of Map stores a group of objects, each of which is associated with a key. The relationships of the interfaces and classes in the Java Collections Framework are shown in Figures 17.1 and 17.2. These interfaces and classes provide a unified API for efficiently storing and processing a collection of objects. You will learn how to use these interfaces and classes in this chapter.

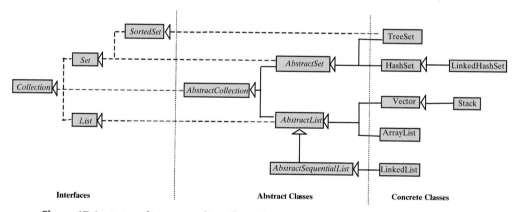

Figure 17.1   Set *and* List *are subinterfaces of* Collection.

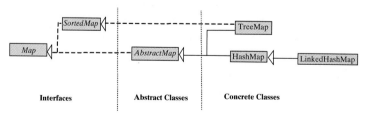

Figure 17.2   *An instance of* Map *stores a group of objects and their associated keys.*

 NOTE

All the interfaces and classes defined in the Java Collections Framework are grouped in the java.util package.

NOTE

The design of the Java Collections Framework is a good example of using interfaces, abstract classes, and concrete classes. The interfaces define the framework. The abstract classes provide partial implementation for convenience. The concrete classes implement the interfaces with concrete data structures.

 NOTE

All the concrete classes in the Java Collections Framework implement the `Cloneable` and `Serializable` interfaces. So their instances can be cloned and serialized.

17.2 The *Collection* Interface and the *AbstractCollection* Class

The `Collection` interface is the root interface for manipulating a collection of objects. Its public methods are listed in Figure 17.3. The `AbstractCollection` class is a convenience class that provides partial implementation for the `Collection` interface. It implements all the methods in `Collection` except the `size` and `iterator` methods. These are implemented in appropriate subclasses.

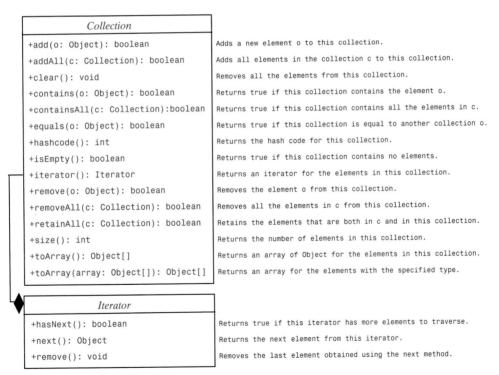

Collection	
+add(o: Object): boolean	Adds a new element o to this collection.
+addAll(c: Collection): boolean	Adds all elements in the collection c to this collection.
+clear(): void	Removes all the elements from this collection.
+contains(o: Object): boolean	Returns true if this collection contains the element o.
+containsAll(c: Collection):boolean	Returns true if this collection contains all the elements in c.
+equals(o: Object): boolean	Returns true if this collection is equal to another collection o.
+hashcode(): int	Returns the hash code for this collection.
+isEmpty(): boolean	Returns true if this collection contains no elements.
+iterator(): Iterator	Returns an iterator for the elements in this collection.
+remove(o: Object): boolean	Removes the element o from this collection.
+removeAll(c: Collection): boolean	Removes all the elements in c from this collection.
+retainAll(c: Collection): boolean	Retains the elements that are both in c and in this collection.
+size(): int	Returns the number of elements in this collection.
+toArray(): Object[]	Returns an array of Object for the elements in this collection.
+toArray(array: Object[]): Object[]	Returns an array for the elements with the specified type.

Iterator	
+hasNext(): boolean	Returns true if this iterator has more elements to traverse.
+next(): Object	Returns the next element from this iterator.
+remove(): void	Removes the last element obtained using the next method.

Figure 17.3 *The* `Collection` *interface contains the methods for manipulating the elements in a collection.*

17.2.1   The Methods in the *Collection* Interface

The `Collection` interface provides the basic operations for adding and removing elements in a collection. The `add` method adds an element to the collection. The `addAll` method adds all the elements in the specified collection to this collection. The `remove` method removes an element from the collection. The `removeAll` method removes the elements from this collection that are present in the specified collection. The `retainAll` method retains the elements in this collection that are also present in the specified collection. All these methods return `boolean`. The return value is true if the collection is changed as a result of the method execution. The `clear()` method simply removes all the elements from the collection.

 NOTE:

The methods `addAll`, `removeAll`, and `retainAll` are similar to the set union, difference, and intersection operations.

The `Collection` interface provides various query operations. The `size` method returns the number of elements in the collection. The `contains` method checks whether the collection contains the specified element. The `containsAll` method checks whether the collection contains all the elements in the specified collection. The `isEmpty` method returns true if the collection is empty.

The `Collection` interface provides two overloaded methods to convert the collection into an array. The `toArray()` method returns an array representation for the collection. The `toArray(Object[] a)` method returns an array containing all of the elements in this collection whose runtime type is that of the specified runtime type.

The `iterator` method in the `Collection` interface returns an instance of the `Iterator` interface, as shown in Figure 17.3, which can be used to traverse the collection using the `next()` method. You can also use the `hasNext()` method to check whether there are more elements in the iterator, and the `remove()` method to remove the last element returned by the iterator.

 NOTE

Some of the methods in the `Collection` interface cannot be implemented in the concrete subclass. In this case, the method would throw `java.lang.UnsupportedOperationException`, a subclass of `RuntimeException`. This is a good design that you can use in your project. Recall that `Cylinder` inherits the `findPerimeter` method from `Circle` in Chapter 9 "Abstract Classes and Interfaces," on page 371. The `findPerimeter` method has no meaning in the `Cylinder` class. Therefore, you can implement it in the `Cylinder` class, as follows:

```
public double findPerimeter() {
  throw new UnsupportedOperationException("Method not supported");
}
```

17.2.2   The *hashCode* Method and the *equals* Method

The `hashCode` method and the `equals` method are defined in the `Object` class as well as in the `Collection` interface. The contract of the two methods in the `Object` class remains the same in the `Collection` interface. A class that implements the

Collection interface does not have to implement the hashCode method and the equals method, because both methods have default implementation in the Object class. What is the benefit of defining hashCode and equals in both the Object class and the Collection interface? It is essentially for facilitating generic programming. For instance, you may have a method with a parameter of the Collection type. This parameter can use the hashCode method and the equals method, because they are in the Collection interface.

The equals(Object o) method is for checking whether an object has the same contents as another object. The hashCode method returns an int value known as the *hash code*. The hash code is used to store objects in a HashSet and a HashMap for quick lookup. Every object has a hash code. An object's reference can be stored in a hash table. The location of an object's reference in a hash table is determined by the object's hash code. The object's reference can be retrieved from a hash table through the hash code.

17.3 The *Set* Interface, the *AbstractSet* and *HashSet* Classes

The Set interface extends the Collection interface. It does not introduce new methods or constants, but it stipulates that an instance of Set contains no duplicate elements. The concrete classes that implement Set must ensure that no duplicate elements can be added to the set. That is, no two elements e1 and e2 can be in the set such that e1.equals(e2) is true.

The AbstractSet class is a convenience class that extends AbstractCollection and implements Set. The AbstractSet class provides concrete implementations for the equals method and the hashCode method. The hash code of a set is the sum of the hash codes of all the elements in the set. Since the size method and iterator method are not implemented in the AbstractSet class, AbstractSet is an abstract class.

The HashSet class is a concrete class that implements Set. You can create a HashSet using its default constructor. A HashSet can be used to store duplicate-free elements. For efficiency, objects added to a hash set need to implement the hashCode method in a manner that properly disperses the hash code. Most of the classes in the Java API implement the hashCode method. For example, the hashCode in the Integer class returns its int value. The hashCode in the String class is implemented as follows:

```
public int hashCode() {
  int h = 0;
  int off = offset;
  char val[] = value;
  int len = count;

  for (int i = 0; i < len; i++)
    h = 31 * h + val[off++];

  return h;
}
```

Example 17.1 Using HashSet and Iterator

Problem

Write a program that finds all the words used in a text. The program creates a hash set to store the words extracted from the text, and uses an iterator to traverse the elements in the set.

Solution

The following code gives the solution to the problem. The output of the program is shown in Figure 17.4.

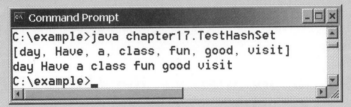

Figure 17.4 *The program adds string elements to a hash set, displays the elements using the* toString *method, and traverses the elements using an iterator.*

```
1   // TestHashSet.java: Demonstrate using HashSet and Iterator
2   package chapter17;
3
4   import java.util.*;
5
6   public class TestHashSet {
7     public static void main(String[] args) {
8       // Create a hash set
9       Set set = new HashSet();
10
11      // Text in a string
12      String text = "Have a good day. Have a good class. " +
13        "Have a good visit. Have fun!";
14
15      // Extract words from text
16      StringTokenizer st = new StringTokenizer(text, " .!?");
17      while (st.hasMoreTokens())
18        set.add(st.nextToken());
19
20      System.out.println(set);
21
22      // Obtain an iterator for the hash set
23      Iterator iterator = set.iterator();
24
25      // Display the elements in the hash set
26      while (iterator.hasNext()) {
27        System.out.print(iterator.next() + " ");
28      }
29    }
30  }
```

Review

The words are extracted using `StringTokenizer` and are added to the set (Lines 16–18). If a word like "good" is added to the set more than once, only one is stored, because a set does not allow duplicates.

As shown in Figure 17.4, the words are not stored in the order in which they are inserted into the set. There is no particular order for the elements in a hash set. To impose an order on them, you need to use the `LinkedHashSet` class, which is introduced in the next section.

17.4   The *LinkedHashSet* Class

`LinkedHashSet` was added in JDK 1.4. It extends `HashSet` with a linked list implementation that supports an ordering of the elements in the set. The elements in a `HashSet` are not ordered, but the elements in a `LinkedHashSet` can be retrieved in the order in which they were inserted into the set. A `LinkedHashSet` can be created by using its default constructor.

Example 17.2 Using `LinkedHashSet`

Problem

Rewrite the preceding example using `LinkedHashSet`.

Solution

Simply replace `HashSet` by `LinkedHashSet`. The following code gives the solution to the problem. The output of the program is shown in Figure 17.5.

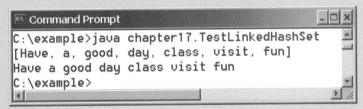

Figure 17.5   *The program adds string elements to a linked hash set, displays the elements using the `toString` method, and traverses the elements using an iterator.*

```
1     // TestLinkedHashSet.java: Demonstrate using LinkedHashSet
2     package chapter17;
3
4     import java.util.*;
5     public class TestLinkedHashSet {
6       public static void main(String[] args) {
7
8         // Create a hash set
9         Set set = new LinkedHashSet();
10
```

continues

Example 17.2 Continued

```
11          // Text in a string
12          String text = "Have a good day. Have a good class. " +
13            "Have a good visit. Have fun!";
14
15          // Extract words from text
16          StringTokenizer st = new StringTokenizer(text, " .!?");
17          while (st.hasMoreTokens())
18            set.add(st.nextToken());
19
20          System.out.println(set);
21
22          // Obtain an iterator for the hash set
23          Iterator iterator = set.iterator();
24
25          // Display the elements in the hash set
26          while (iterator.hasNext()) {
27            System.out.print(iterator.next() + " ");
28          }
29        }
30      }
```

Review

A LinkedHashSet is created in Line 9. As shown in Figure 17.5, the words are stored in the order in which they are inserted. Since LinkedHashSet is a set, no duplicate elements are stored in the set.

The LinkedHashSet maintains the order in which the elements are inserted. To impose a different order (e.g., increasing or decreasing order), you can use the TreeSet class introduced in the next section.

 TIP

If you don't need to maintain the order in which the elements are inserted, use HashSet, which is more efficient than LinkedHashSet.

17.5 The *SortedSet* Interface and the *TreeSet* Class

SortedSet is a subinterface of Set, which guarantees that the elements in the set are sorted. TreeSet is a concrete class that implements the SortedSet interface. To create a TreeSet, use its default constructor or use new TreeSet(Collection). You can add objects into a tree set as long as they can be compared with each other. There are two ways to compare objects.

■ Use the Comparable interface. Since the objects added to the set are instances of Comparable, they can be compared using the compareTo method. The Comparable interface was introduced in Chapter 9, "Abstract Classes and Interfaces." Several classes in the Java API, such as the String class and all the wrapper classes for the primitive types, implement the Comparable interface. This approach is referred to as *natural order*.

■ If the class for the elements does not implement the Comparable interface or if you don't want to use the compareTo method in the class that implements the Comparable interface, specify a comparator for the elements in the set. This approach is referred to as *order by comparator*. It will be introduced in Section 17.6, "The Comparator Interface."

Example 17.3 Using TreeSet to Sort Elements in a Set

Problem

The preceding example displays all the words used in a text. The words are displayed in no particular order. This example rewrites the preceding example to display the words in alphabetical order using the TreeSet class.

Solution

The following code gives the solution to the problem. Figure 17.6 shows a sample run of the program.

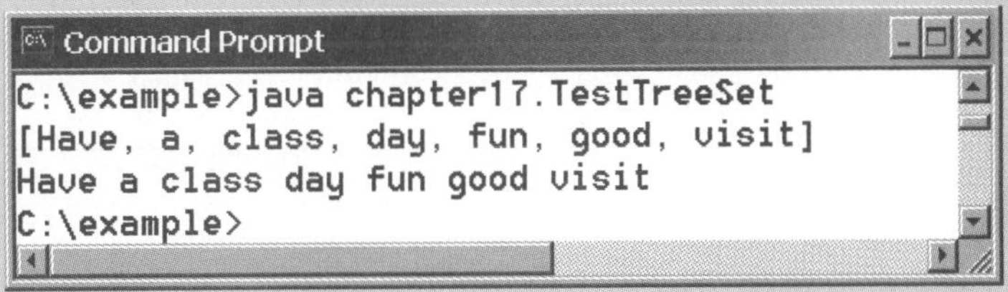

```
Command Prompt                                    _ □ ×
C:\example>java chapter17.TestTreeSet
[Have, a, class, day, fun, good, visit]
Have a class day fun good visit
C:\example>
```

Figure 17.6   *The program demonstrates the differences between hash sets and tree sets.*

```java
1    package chapter17;
2
3    import java.util.*;
4
5    public class TestTreeSet {
6      public static void main(String[] args) {
7        // Create a hash set
8        Set set = new HashSet();
9
10       // Text in a string
11       String text = "Have a good day. Have a good class. " +
12       "Have a good visit. Have fun!";
13
14       // Extract words from text
15       StringTokenizer st = new StringTokenizer(text, " .!?");
16       while (st.hasMoreTokens())
17       set.add(st.nextToken());
18
19       TreeSet treeSet = new TreeSet(set);
20       System.out.println(treeSet);
21
22       // Obtain an iterator for the hash set
23       Iterator iterator = treeSet.iterator();
24
25       // Display the elements in the hash set
26       while (iterator.hasNext()) {
27         System.out.print(iterator.next() + " ");
28       }
29     }
30   }
```

continues

Example 17.3 Continued

Review

The example creates a hash set filled with strings, and then creates a tree set for the same strings. The strings are sorted in the tree set using the `compareTo` method in the `Comparable` interface.

The elements in the set are sorted once when you create a `TreeSet` object from a `HashSet` object using `new TreeSet(hashSet)` (Line 19). You may rewrite the program to create an instance of `TreeSet` using its default constructor, and add the strings into the `TreeSet` object. Then, every time a string is added to the `TreeSet` object, the elements in it will be reordered. The approach used in the example is generally more efficient because it requires only a one-time sorting.

 NOTE

All the classes in Figure 17.1 have at least two constructors. One is the default constructor that constructs an empty collection. The other constructs instances from a collection. Thus the `TreeSet` class has the constructor `TreeSet(Collection c)` for constructing a `TreeSet` from a collection c. In this example, `new TreeSet-(hashSet)` creates an instance of `TreeSet` from the collection `hashSet`.

 TIP

If you don't need to maintain a sorted set when updating a set, you can use a hash set, because it takes less time to insert and remove elements in a hash set. When you need a set to be sorted, you can convert it into a tree set.

 CAUTION

All the elements added to the tree set must be comparable, such as all `String` objects. A runtime error will occur if you add an object that is not comparable with the existing objects in the tree set. For example, a `ClassCastingException` will occur if you add an `Integer` object to a tree set of strings.

17.6 The *Comparator* Interface

Sometimes you want to insert elements of different types into a tree set. The elements may not be instances of `Comparable` or are not comparable. You can define a comparator to compare these elements. To do so, create a class that implements the `java.util.Comparator` interface. The `Comparator` interface has two methods, `compare` and `equals`.

- `public int compare(Object element1, Object element2)`

  Returns a negative value if `element1` is less than `element2`, a positive value if `element1` is greater than `element2`, and zero if they are equal.

public boolean equals(Object element)

Returns true if the specified object is also a comparator and imposes the same ordering as this comparator.

The equals method is also defined in the Object class. Therefore, you will not get a compilation error if you don't implement the equals method in your custom comparator class. However, in some cases implementing this method may improve performance by allowing programs to determine that two distinct comparators impose the same order.

For example, you can provide the following comparator to compare two elements of the GeometricObject class, defined in Section 9.2, "Abstract Classes."

```
package chapter17;

import chapter9.GeometricObject;
import java.util.Comparator;

public class GeometricObjectComparator implements Comparator {
  public int compare(Object o1, Object o2) {
    double area1 = ((GeometricObject)o1).findArea();
    double area2 = ((GeometricObject)o2).findArea();

    if (area1 < area2)
      return -1;
    else if (area1 == area2)
      return 0;
    else
      return 1;
  }
}
```

If you create a TreeSet using its default constructor, the compareTo method is used to compare the elements in the set, assuming that the class of the elements implements the Comparable interface. To use a comparator, you have to use the constructor TreeSet(Comparator comparator) to create a sorted set that uses the compare method in the comparator to order the elements in the set.

Example 17.4 Using Comparator to Sort Elements in a Set

Problem

Write a program that demonstrates how to sort elements in a tree set using the Comparator interface. The example creates a tree set of geometric objects. The geometric objects are sorted using the compare method in the Comparator interface.

Solution

The following code gives the solution to the problem. The output of the program is shown in Figure 17.7.

continues

755

Example 17.6 Continued

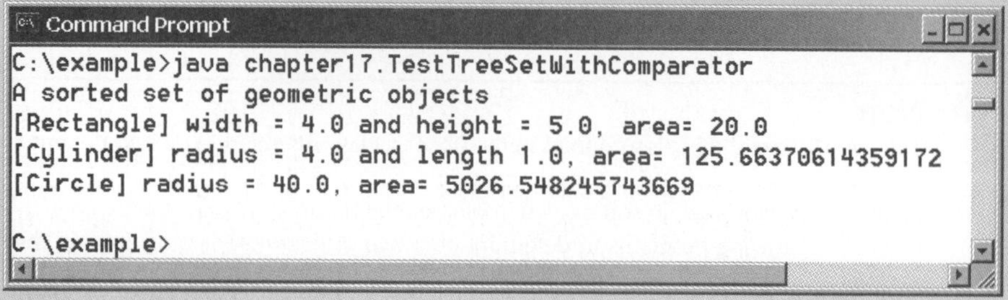

```
Command Prompt                                                    _ □ ×
C:\example>java chapter17.TestTreeSetWithComparator
A sorted set of geometric objects
[Rectangle] width = 4.0 and height = 5.0, area= 20.0
[Cylinder] radius = 4.0 and length 1.0, area= 125.66370614359172
[Circle] radius = 40.0, area= 5026.548245743669

C:\example>
```

Figure 17.7   *The program demonstrates the use of the* Comparator *interface.*

```
1      package chapter17;
2
3      import java.util.*;
4
5      import chapter9.GeometricObject;
6      import chapter9.Circle;
7      import chapter9.Rectangle;
8      import chapter9.Cylinder;
9
10     public class TestTreeSetWithComparator {
11       public static void main(String[] args) {
12         // Create a tree set for geometric objects using a comparator
13         Set geometricObjectSet =
14           new TreeSet(new GeometricObjectComparator());
15         geometricObjectSet.add(new Rectangle(4, 5));
16         geometricObjectSet.add(new Circle(40));
17         geometricObjectSet.add(new Circle(40));
18         geometricObjectSet.add(new Cylinder(4, 1));
19
20         // Obtain an iterator for the tree set of geometric objects
21         Iterator iterator = geometricObjectSet.iterator();
22
23         // Display geometric objects in the tree set
24         System.out.println("A sorted set of geometric objects");
25         while (iterator.hasNext()) {
26           GeometricObject object = (GeometricObject)iterator.next();
27           System.out.println(object + ", area= " + object.findArea());
28         }
29       }
30     }
```

Review

The Circle, Cylinder, and Rectangle classes were defined in Section 9.2, "Abstract Classes." They are all subclasses of GeometricObject.

Two circles of the same radius are added to the set in the tree set (Lines 16–17), but only one is stored, because the two circles are equal and the set does not allow duplicates.

17.7   The *List* Interface, the *AbstractList* Class, and the *AbstractSequentialList* Class

A set stores nonduplicate elements. To allow duplicate elements to be stored in a collection, you need to use a list. A list can not only store duplicate elements, but also allows the user to specify where they are stored. The user can access elements by an index. The List interface extends Collection to define an ordered collection with duplicates allowed. The List interface adds position-oriented operations, as well as a new list iterator that enables the user to traverse the list bi-directionally. The new methods in the List interface are shown in Figure 17.8.

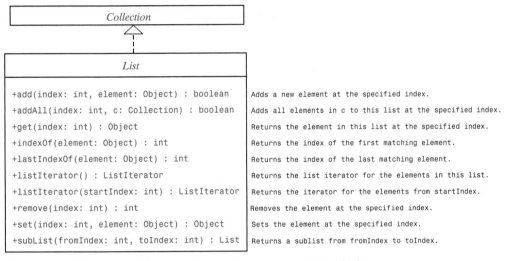

Collection	

List	
+add(index: int, element: Object) : boolean	Adds a new element at the specified index.
+addAll(index: int, c: Collection) : boolean	Adds all elements in c to this list at the specified index.
+get(index: int) : Object	Returns the element in this list at the specified index.
+indexOf(element: Object) : int	Returns the index of the first matching element.
+lastIndexOf(element: Object) : int	Returns the index of the last matching element.
+listIterator() : ListIterator	Returns the list iterator for the elements in this list.
+listIterator(startIndex: int) : ListIterator	Returns the iterator for the elements from startIndex.
+remove(index: int) : int	Removes the element at the specified index.
+set(index: int, element: Object) : Object	Sets the element at the specified index.
+subList(fromIndex: int, toIndex: int) : List	Returns a sublist from fromIndex to toIndex.

Figure 17.8 *The* List *interface stores elements in sequence, permitting duplicates.*

The add(index, element) method is used to insert an element at a specified index, and the addAll(index, collection) method to insert a collection at a specified index. The remove(index) method is used to remove an element at the specified index from the list. A new element can be set at the specified index using the set(index, element) method.

The indexOf(element) method is used to obtain the index of the first occurrence of the specified element in the list, and the lastIndexOf(element) method to obtain the index of the last occurrence of the specified element in the list. A sublist can be obtained by using the subList(fromIndex, toIndex) method.

The listIterator() or listIterator(startIndex) method returns an instance of ListIterator. The ListIterator interface extends the Iterator interface to add bi-directional traversal of the list. The methods in ListIterator are listed in Figure 17.9.

The add(element) method inserts the specified element into the list. The element is inserted immediately before the next element that would be returned by the next() method defined in the Iterator interface, if any, and after the element that would be returned by the previous() method, if any. If the list contains no elements, the

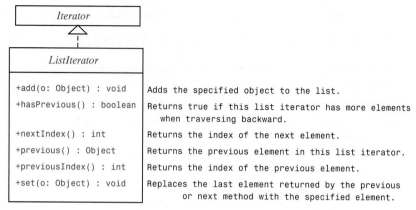

Figure 17.9   `ListIterator` *enables traversal of a list bi-directionally.*

new element becomes the sole element on the list. The `set(element)` method can be used to replace the last element returned by the `next` method or the `previous` method with the specified element.

The `hasNext()` method defined in the `Iterator` interface is used to check whether the iterator has more elements when traversed in the forward direction, and the `hasPrevious()` method to check whether the iterator has more elements when traversed in the backward direction.

The `next()` method defined in the `Iterator` interface returns the next element in the iterator, and the `previous()` method returns the previous element in the iterator. The `nextIndex()` method returns the index of the next element in the iterator, and the `previousIndex()` returns the index of the previous element in the iterator.

The `AbstractList` class provides a partial implementation for the `List` interface. The `AbstractSequentialList` class extends `AbstractList` to provide support for linked lists.

17.8   The *ArrayList* and *LinkedList* Classes

The `ArrayList` class and the `LinkedList` class are two concrete implementations of the `List` interface. `ArrayList` stores elements in an array. The array is dynamically created. If the capacity of the array is exceeded, create a new larger array and copy all the elements from the current array to the new array. `LinkedList` stores elements in a linked list. Which of the two classes you use depends on your specific needs. If you need to support random access through an index without inserting or removing elements except at the end, `ArrayList` offers the most efficient collection. If, however, your application requires the insertion or deletion of elements anywhere in the list, you should choose `LinkedList`. A list can grow or shrink dynamically. An array is fixed once it is created. If your application does not require the insertion or deletion of elements, an array is the most efficient data structure.

`ArrayList` is a resizable-array implementation of the `List` interface. In addition to implementing the `List` interface, this class provides methods for manipulating the size of the array that is used internally to store the list. Each `ArrayList` instance has a capacity. The capacity is the size of the array used to store the elements in the list. It is always at least as large as the list size. As elements are added to an `ArrayList`, its capacity grows automatically. An `ArrayList` can be constructed using its default constructor, `ArrayList` `(Collection)`, or `ArrayList(intialCapacity)`.

`LinkedList` is a linked list implementation of the `List` interface. In addition to implementing the `List` interface, this class provides the methods for retrieving, inserting, and removing elements from both ends of the list, as shown in Figure 17.10. A `LinkedList` can be constructed using its default constructor or `LinkedList(Collection)`.

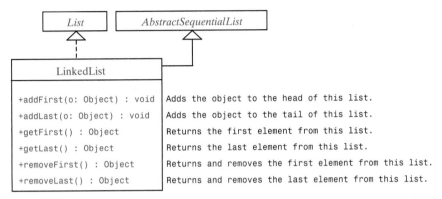

Figure 17.10 `LinkedList` *provides methods for adding and inserting elements at both ends of the list.*

Example 17.5 Using `ArrayList` and `LinkedList`

Problem

Write a program that creates an array list filled with numbers and inserts new elements into specified locations in the list. The example also creates a linked list from the array list, and inserts and removes elements from the list. Finally, the example traverses the list forward and backward.

Solution

The following code gives the solution to the problem. The output of the program is shown in Figure 17.11.

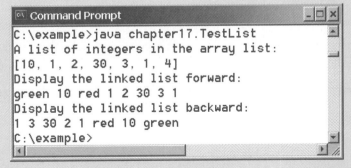

Figure 17.11   *The program uses an array list and linked lists.*

continues

Example 17.5 Continued

```
1     package chapter17;
2
3     import java.util.*;
4
5     public class TestList {
6       public static void main(String[] args) {
7         List arrayList = new ArrayList();
8         arrayList.add(new Integer(1));
9         arrayList.add(new Integer(2));
10        arrayList.add(new Integer(3));
11        arrayList.add(new Integer(1));
12        arrayList.add(new Integer(4));
13        arrayList.add(0, new Integer(10));
14        arrayList.add(3, new Integer(30));
15
16        System.out.println("A list of integers in the array list:");
17        System.out.println(arrayList);
18
19        LinkedList linkedList = new LinkedList(arrayList);
20        linkedList.add(1, "red");
21        linkedList.removeLast();
22        linkedList.addFirst("green");
23
24        System.out.println("Display the linked list forward:");
25        ListIterator listIterator = linkedList.listIterator();
26        while (listIterator.hasNext()) {
27          System.out.print(listIterator.next() + " ");
28        }
29        System.out.println();
30
31        System.out.println("Display the linked list backward:");
32        listIterator = linkedList.listIterator(linkedList.size());
33        while (listIterator.hasPrevious()) {
34          System.out.print(listIterator.previous() + " ");
35        }
36      }
37    }
```

Review

A list can hold identical elements. Integer 1 is stored twice in the list (Lines 8, 11). ArrayList and LinkedList are operated similarly. The critical difference between them pertains to internal implementation, which affects their performance. ArrayList is efficient for retrieving elements, and for inserting and removing elements from the end of the list. LinkedList is efficient for inserting and removing elements anywhere in the list.

You can use TreeSet to store sorted elements. But there is no sorted list. However, the Java Collections Framework provides static methods in the Collections class that can be used to sort a list. The Collections class is introduced in Section 17.12, "The Collections Class."

17.9   The *Vector* Class

The Java Collections Framework was introduced with Java 2. Several data structures were supported prior to Java 2. Among them were the Vector class and the Stack class. These classes were redesigned to fit into the Java Collections Framework, but all their methods are retained for compatibility. This section introduces the Vector class, and the next section introduces the Stack class.

In Java 2, Vector is the same as ArrayList, except that it contains synchronized methods for accessing and modifying the vector. None of the new collection data structures introduced so far are synchronized. If synchronization is required, you can use the synchronized versions of the collection classes. These classes are introduced in Section 17.12, "The Collections Class."

The Vector class implements the List interface. It also has the methods contained in the original Vector class defined prior to Java 2, as shown in Figure 17.12.

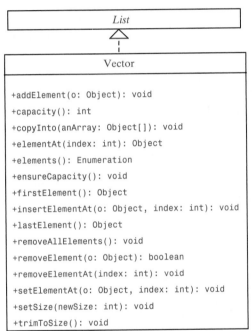

+addElement(o: Object): void	Appends the element to the end of this vector.
+capacity(): int	Returns the current capacity of this vector.
+copyInto(anArray: Object[]): void	Copies the elements in this vector to the array.
+elementAt(index: int): Object	Returns the object at the specified index.
+elements(): Enumeration	Returns an emulation of this vector.
+ensureCapacity(): void	Increases the capacity of this vector.
+firstElement(): Object	Returns the first element in this vector.
+insertElementAt(o: Object, index: int): void	Inserts o to this vector at the specified index.
+lastElement(): Object	Returns the last element in this vector.
+removeAllElements(): void	Removes all the elements in this vector.
+removeElement(o: Object): boolean	Removes the first matching element in this vector.
+removeElementAt(index: int): void	Removes the element at the specified index.
+setElementAt(o: Object, index: int): void	Sets a new element at the specified index.
+setSize(newSize: int): void	Sets a new size in this vector.
+trimToSize(): void	Trims the capacity of this vector to its size.

Figure 17.12   *The* Vector *class in Java 2 implements* List *with all its methods in the original* Vector *class retained.*

Most of the additional methods in the Vector class listed in the UML diagram in Figure 17.12 are similar to the methods in the List interface. These methods were introduced before the Java Collections Framework. For example, addElement-(Object element) is the same as the add(Object element) method, except that addElement method is synchronized. Use the ArrayList class if you don't need synchronization. It works much faster than Vector.

NOTE

The `elements()` method returns an Enumeration. The Enumeration interface was introduced prior to Java 2 and was superseded by the `Iterator` interface.

NOTE

`Vector` is widely used in Java programming because it was the Java resizable array implementation before Java 2. Many of the Swing data models use vectors.

Example 17.6 Using the `Vector` Class

Problem

Example 3.9, "Displaying Prime Numbers," determines whether a number n is prime by checking whether 2, 3, 4, 5, 6, ..., $n/2$ is a divisor. If a divisor is found, n is not prime. A more efficient approach to determine whether n is prime is to check whether any of the prime numbers less than or equal to $\sqrt{n}$ can divide n evenly. If not, n is prime. Write a program that finds all the prime numbers less than 250.

Solution

The program stores the prime numbers in a vector. Initially, the vector is empty. For n = 2, 3, 4, 5, ..., 250, the program determines whether n is prime by checking whether any prime number less than or equal to $\sqrt{n}$ in the vector is a divisor for n. If not, n is prime, so add n to the vector. The program that uses a vector is given below. Figure 17.13 shows a sample run of the program.

```
1   package chapter17;
2
3   public class FindPrimeUsingVector {
4     public static void main(String[] args) {
5       // Print 10 numbers per line
6       final int NUMBER_PER_LINE = 10;
7
8       // Count the number of primes found
9       int count = 0;
10
11      // Create a vector to store prime numbers
12      java.util.Vector vector = new java.util.Vector();
13
14      System.out.println("The prime numbers before 250 are \n");
15
16      for (int n = 2; n < 250; n++) {
17        // Test if n is prime
18        boolean isPrime = true;
19        for (int i = 0; i < vector.size(); i++) {
20          int primeNumber =
21            ((Integer)(vector.elementAt(i))).intValue();
22
23          if (primeNumber > Math.sqrt(n)) break;
24
25          if (n % primeNumber == 0) {
26            // Set isPrime to false, if the number is not prime
27            isPrime = false;
28            break; // Exit the for loop
29          }
```

```
30          }
31
34          // Print the prime number and increase the count
35          if (isPrime) {
36            count++; // Increase prime number count
37
38            // Add the prime number to the vector
39            vector.addElement(new Integer(n));
40
41            if (count % NUMBER_PER_LINE == 0) {
42              // Print the number and advance to the new line
43              System.out.println(n);
44            }
45            else
46              System.out.print(n + " ");
47          }
48        }
49      }
50    }
```

```
Command Prompt                                           _ □ X

C:\example>java chapter17.FindPrimeUsingVector
The prime numbers before 250 are

2 3 5 7 11 13 17 19 23 29
31 37 41 43 47 53 59 61 67 71
73 79 83 89 97 101 103 107 109 113
127 131 137 139 149 151 157 163 167 173
179 181 191 193 197 199 211 223 227 229
233 239 241
C:\example>
```

Figure 17.13   *The program displays all the prime numbers before 250.*

Review

The program needs to store the prime numbers and later uses them to check whether they are possible divisors for n. Since one cannot know in advance how many prime numbers are to be stored, using an array to store the prime numbers is not appropriate. So the vector is used to store the prime numbers.

Line 12 creates a vector. The size method returns the number of elements in the vector. The addElement method appends an element to the vector. Since vector elements are of the Object type, an integer is stored as an Integer object in the vector (Line 39).

TIP

The size of an array is fixed once the array is created. You should use array lists, linked lists, or vectors to store an unspecified number of elements.

CAUTION

The element type in an array can be primitive type values or objects, but the element type in the Java Collections Framework must be the Object type.

17.10   The *Stack* Class

Example 6.8, "The StackOfIntegers Class," developed a stack class for integers. The java.util.Stack class represents a last-in/first-out stack of objects. The elements are accessed only from the top of the stack. You can retrieve, insert, or remove an element from the top of the stack. Stacks are a useful data structure with many applications in computer science. The Stack class extends the Vector class and provides several methods for manipulating stacks, as shown in Figure 17.14.

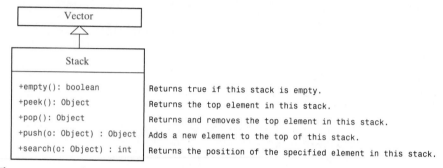

Figure 17.14   *The* Stack *class extends* Vector *to provide a last-in/first-out data structure.*

The Stack class was introduced prior to Java 2. The methods shown in Figure 17.14 were used before Java 2. The empty() method is the same as isEmpty(). The peek() method looks at the element at the top of the stack without removing it. The pop() method removes the top element from the stack and returns it. The push(Object element) method adds the specified element to the stack. The search(Object element) method checks whether the specified element is in the stack.

Example 17.7 Using the Stack Class

Problem

Write a program that reads a positive integer and displays all its distinct prime factors in decreasing order. For example, if the input integer is 6, its distinct prime factors displayed are 3, 2; if the input integer is 12, the distinct prime factors are also 3 and 2.

Solution

The program uses a stack to store all the distinct prime factors. Initially, the stack is empty. To find all the distinct prime factors for an integer *n*, use the following algorithm:

```
int factor = 2;
while (factor <= n) {
  if (n % factor == 0) {
    n = n / factor;
    if (stack is empty or factor is not in the stack)
      push factor to the stack;
  }
  else {
    factor++;
  }
}
```

To display all the prime factors in decreasing order, pop the factor from the stack and display them. Figure 17.15 shows a sample run of the program.

```
1    package chapter17;
2
3    import javax.swing.JOptionPane;
4
5    public class FindPrimeFactorUsingStack {
6      public static void main(String[] args) {
7        // Prompt the user to enter a positive integer
8        String intString = JOptionPane.showInputDialog(null,
9          "Enter a positive integer:",
10         "Example 17.7 Input", JOptionPane.QUESTION_MESSAGE);
11
12       // Convert string to int
13       int n = Integer.parseInt(intString);
14
15       // Create a stack to store prime factors
16       java.util.Stack stack = new java.util.Stack();
17
18       // Find all prime factors of the integer
19       int factor = 2;
20       while (factor <= n) {
21         if (n % factor == 0) {
22           n = n / factor;
23           if (stack.isEmpty() ||
24             ((Integer)stack.peek()).intValue() != factor)
25             stack.push(new Integer(factor));
26         }
27         else {
28           factor++;
29         }
30       }
31
32       // Prepare the output
33       String outString = "";
34       while (!stack.isEmpty()) {
35         outString += stack.pop() + " ";
36       }
37
38       // Display the output
39       JOptionPane.showMessageDialog(null, outString,
40         "Example 17.7 Output", JOptionPane.INFORMATION_MESSAGE);
41
42       System.exit(0);
43     }
44   }
```

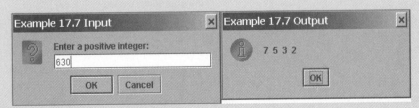

Figure 17.15   *The program receives a positive integer and displays its distinct prime factors.*

continues

Example 17.7 Continued

Review

Line 16 creates a stack to store the prime factors. The program searches for all possible factors starting with 2. If a factor is found (Line 21), push it to the stack if it is not in the stack (Lines 23–25), and remove the factor from the number (Line 22) continuously until the number does not contain this factor.

The factor to be considered is initially 2, then 3, 4, 5, 6, ... (Line 21), until the factor is greater than the number (Line 20). Ideally, you should consider only next prime numbers 3, 5, 7, 11, ..., as possible factors. But it would take more time to find these prime numbers than simply considering 2, 3, 4, 5, 6, ..., as possible factors.

The prime factors are pushed into the stack (Line 25) in increasing order. The factors are popped in decreasing order (Line 35).

17.11   The *Map* Interface, the *AbstractMap* class, the *SortedMap* interface, the *HashMap*, *LinkedHashMap*, and *TreeMap* classes

The Collection interface represents a collection of elements stored in a set or a list. The Map interface maps keys to the elements. The keys are like indexes. In List, the indexes are integers. In Map, the keys can be any objects. A map cannot contain duplicate keys. Each key can map to at most one value. The Map interface provides the methods for querying, updating, and obtaining a collection of values and a set of keys, as shown in Figure 17.16.

Map	
+clear(): void	Removes all mappings from this map.
+containsKey(key: Object): boolean	Returns true if this map contains a mapping for the specified key.
+containsValue(value: Object): boolean	Returns true if this map maps one or more keys to the specified value.
+entrySet(): Set	Returns a set consisting of the entries in this map.
+get(key: Object): Object	Returns the value for the specified key in this map.
+isEmpty(): boolean	Returns true if this map contains no mappings.
+keySet(): Set	Returns a set consisting of the keys in this map.
+put(key: Object, value: Object): Object	Puts a mapping in this map.
+putAll(m: Map): void	Adds all mappings from m to this map.
+remove(key: Object): Object	Removes the mapping for the specified key.
+size(): int	Returns the number of mappings in this map.
+values(): Collection	Returns a collection consisting of values in this map.

Figure 17.16   *The* Map *interface maps keys to values.*

The update methods include `clear`, `put`, `putAll`, and `remove`. The `clear()` method removes all mappings from the map. The `put(Object key, Object value)` method associates the specified value with the specified key in the map. If the map formerly contained a mapping for this key, the old value associated with the key is returned. The `putAll(Map m)` method adds the specified map to this map. The `remove(Object key)` method removes the map elements for the specified key from the map.

The query methods include `containsKey`, `containsValue`, `isEmpty`, and `size`. The `containsKey(Object key)` method checks whether the map contains a mapping for the specified key. The `containsValue(Object value)` method checks whether the map contains a mapping for this value. The `isEmpty()` method checks whether the map contains any mappings. The `size()` method returns the number of mappings in the map.

You can obtain a set of keys in the map using the `keySet()` method, and a collection of values in the map using the `values()` method. The `entrySet()` method returns a collection of objects that implement the `Map.Entry` interface, where `Entry` is an inner interface for the `Map` interface. Each object in the collection is a specific key-value pair in the underlying map.

The `AbstractMap` class is a convenience class that implements all the methods in the `Map` interface except the `entrySet()` method.

The `SortedMap` interface extends the `Map` interface to maintain the mapping in ascending order of keys.

The `HashMap`, `LinkedHashMap`, and `TreeMap` classes are three concrete implementations of the `Map` interface. The `HashMap` class is efficient for locating a value, inserting a mapping, and deleting a mapping.

`LinkedHashMap` was introduced in JDK 1.4. It extends `HashMap` with a linked list implementation that supports an ordering of the entries in the map. The entries in a `HashMap` are not ordered, but the entries in a `LinkedHashMap` can be retrieved in the order in which they were inserted into the map (known as the *insertion order*) or the order in which they were last accessed, from least recently accessed to most recently (*access order*). The default constructor constructs a `LinkedHashMap` with the insertion order. To construct a `LinkedHashMap` with the access order, use the `LinkedHashMap(initialCapacity, loadFactor, true)`.

The `TreeMap` class, implementing `SortedMap`, is efficient for traversing the keys in a sorted order. The keys can be sorted using the `Comparable` interface or the `Comparator` interface. If you create a `TreeMap` using its default constructor, the `compareTo` method in the `Comparable` interface is used to compare the elements in the set, assuming that the class of the elements implements the `Comparable` interface. To use a comparator, you have to use the `TreeMap(Comparator comparator)` constructor to create a sorted map that uses the `compare` method in the comparator to order the elements in the map based on the keys.

Prior to JDK 1.2, Map was supported in `java.util.Hashtable`. Hashtable was re-designed to fit into the Java Collections Framework with all its methods retained for compatibility. `Hashtable` implements the `Map` interface and is used in the same way as HashMap except that `Hashtable` is synchronized.

Example 17.8 Using HashMap, LinkedHashMap, and TreeMap

Problem

This example creates a hash map, linked hash map, and tree map that map borrowers to loans. The Loan class, introduced in Chapter 6, "Objects and Classes," was used to model loans. Recall that you can create a loan using the following constructor:

```
public Loan(double annualInterestRate, int numOfYears,
    double loanAmount)
```

The program first creates a hash map with the borrower's name as its key and the loan as its value. The program then creates a tree map from the hash map and displays the mappings in ascending order of the keys. Finally, the program creates a linked hash map, adds the same entries to the map, and displays the entries.

Solution

The following code gives the solution to the problem. The output of the program is shown in Figure 17.17.

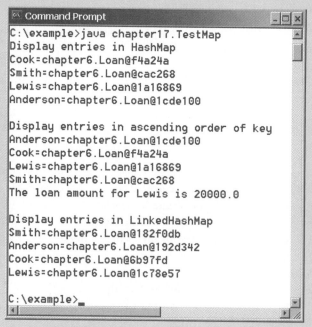

Figure 17.17   *The program demonstrates the use of* HashMap, LinkedHashMap, *and* TreeMap.

```
1    package chapter17;
2
3    import java.util.*;
4    import chapter6.Loan;
5
6    public class TestMap {
7      public static void main(String[] args) {
8        // Create a HashMap
9        Map hashMap = new HashMap();
10       hashMap.put("Smith", new Loan(7, 15, 150000));
11       hashMap.put("Anderson", new Loan(7.5, 30, 150000));
12       hashMap.put("Lewis", new Loan(7.85, 30, 20000));
13       hashMap.put("Cook", new Loan(7, 15, 100000));
14       System.out.println("Display entries in HashMap");
15       displayMapEntries(hashMap);
16
17       // Create a TreeMap from the previous HashMap
18       Map treeMap = new TreeMap(hashMap);
19       System.out.println("\nDisplay entries in ascending order of key");
20       displayMapEntries(treeMap);
21
22       // Create a LinkedHashMap
23       HashMap linkedHashMap = new LinkedHashMap(16, 0.75f, true);
24       linkedHashMap.put("Smith", new Loan(7, 15, 150000));
25       linkedHashMap.put("Anderson", new Loan(7.5, 30, 150000));
26       linkedHashMap.put("Lewis", new Loan(7.85, 30, 20000));
27       linkedHashMap.put("Cook", new Loan(7, 15, 100000));
28
29       // Display the loan amount for Gerry K Lewis
30       System.out.println("The loan amount for " + "Lewis is " +
31         ((Loan)(linkedHashMap.get("Lewis"))).getLoanAmount());
32
33       System.out.println("\nDisplay entries in LinkedHashMap");
34       displayMapEntries(linkedHashMap);
35     }
36
37     public static void displayMapEntries(Map map) {
38       // Get an entry set for the map
39       Set entrySet = map.entrySet();
40
41       // Get an iterator for the entry set
42       Iterator iterator = entrySet.iterator();
43
44       // Display mappings
45       while (iterator.hasNext()) {
46         System.out.println(iterator.next());
47       }
48     }
49   }
```

Review

As shown in Figure 17.17, the entries in the HashMap are in random order. The entries in the TreeMap are in increasing order of the keys. The entries in the LinkedHashMap are in the order of their access, from least recently accessed to most recently.

All the concrete classes that implement the Map interface have at least two constructors. One is the default constructor that constructs an empty map, and the other constructs a map from an instance of Map. So new TreeMap(hashMap) (Line 18) constructs a tree map from a hash map.

continues

769

Example 17.8 Continued

Unlike the `Collection` interface, the `Map` interface does not provide an iterator. To traverse the map, you create an entry set of the mappings using the `entrySet()` method (Line 39) in the `Map` interface. Each element in the entry set is a string that consists of the string representation of the key object and its counterpart connected by the $=$ sign. As shown in Figure 17.17, the first element in the entry set is `Cook=chapter6.Loan@f4a24a`.

 TIP

If you don't need to maintain an order in a map when updating it, use a `HashMap`, because less time is needed to insert and remove mappings in a `HashMap`. When you need to maintain the insertion order or access order in the map, use a `LinkedHashMap`. When you need the map to be sorted on keys, convert it to a tree map.

Example 17.9 Counting the Occurrences of Words in a Text

Problem

Write a program that counts the occurrences of words in a text and displays the words and their occurrences in ascending order of the number of occurrences. The program uses a hash map to store a pair consisting of a word and its count. For each word, check whether it is already a key in the map. If not, add the key and value 1 to the map. Otherwise, increase the value for the word (key) by 1 in the map. To sort the map, convert it to a tree map.

Solution

The following code gives the solution to the problem. The output of the program is shown in Figure 17.18.

```
C:\example>java chapter17.CountOccurrenceOfWords
Display words and their count in ascending order
Have=4
a=3
class=1
day=1
fun=1
good=3
visit=1

C:\example>
```

Figure 17.18   *The program finds the occurrences of each word in a text.*

```
1     package Chapter 17;
2
3     import java.util.*;
4
5     public class CountOccurrenceOfWords {
6       public static void main(String[] args) {
7         // Text in a string
8         String text = "Have a good day. Have a good class. " +
9           "Have a good visit. Have fun!";
10
11        // Create a hash map to hold words as key and count as value
12        Map hashMap = new HashMap();
13
14        StringTokenizer st = new StringTokenizer(text, " .!?");
15        while (st.hasMoreTokens()) {
16          String key = st.nextToken();
17
18          if (hashMap.get(key) != null) {
19            int value = ((Integer)hashMap.get(key)).intValue();
20            value++;
21            hashMap.put(key, new Integer(value));
22          }
23          else {
24          hashMap.put(key, new Integer(1));
25        }
26      }
27
28        // Create a tree map from the hash map
29        Map treeMap = new TreeMap(hashMap);
30
31        // Get an entry set for the tree map
32        Set entrySet = treeMap.entrySet();
33
34        // Get an iterator for the entry set
35        Iterator iterator = entrySet.iterator();
36
37        // Display mappings
38        System.out.println("Display words and their count in " +
39          "ascending order of the words");
40        while (iterator.hasNext()) {
41          System.out.println(iterator.next());
42        }
43      }
44    }
```

Review

The pairs of words and their occurrence counts are stored in the map. The words serve as the keys. Since all elements must be stored as objects in the map, the count is wrapped in an Integer object.

The program extracts a word from a text and checks whether it is already stored as a key in the map. If not, a new pair consisting of the word and a count (new Integer(1)) is stored to the map. Otherwise, the count for the word is incremented by 1.

The program first stores the pairs to a hash map, then creates a tree map from the hash map. It then creates an entry set and displays all the entries in the set. Each entry consists of a word and its count connected by the = sign in ascending order of words. To display them in ascending order of the occurrence counts, see Exercise 17.9.

17.12   The *Collections* Class

The Collections class contains static methods for operating on collections and maps, creating synchronized collection classes, and creating read-only collection classes, as shown in Figure 17.19.

Collections
+binarySearch(list: List, key: Object): int	Searches the key in the sorted list using binary search.
+binarySearch(list: List, key: Object, c: Comparator): int	Searches the key in the sorted list using binary search with the comparator.
+copy(src: List, des: List): void	Copies from the source list to the destination list.
+enumeration(c: final Collection): Enumeration	Returns the enumeration for the specified collection.
+fill(list: List, o: Object): void	Fills the list with the object.
+max(c: Collection): Object	Returns the max object in the collection.
+max(c: Collection, c: Comparator): Object	Returns the max object using the comparator.
+min(c: Collection): Object	Returns the min object in the collection.
+min(c: Collection, c: Comparator): Object	Returns the min object using the comparator.
+nCopies(n: int, o: Object): List	Returns a list consisting of n copies of the object.
+reverse(list: List): void	Reverses the specified list.
+reverseOrder(): Comparator	Returns a comparator with the reverse ordering.
+shuffle(list: List): void	Shuffles the specified list randomly.
+shuffle(list: List, rnd: Random): void	Shuffles the specified list with a random object.
+singleton(o: Object): Set	Returns a singleton set containing the specified object.
+singletonList(o: Object): List	Returns a singleton list containing the specified object.
+singletonMap(key: Object, value: Object): Map	Returns a singleton map with the key and value pair.
+sort(list: List): void	Sorts the specified list.
+sort(list: List, c: Comparator): void	Sorts the specified list with the comparator.
+synchronizedCollection(c: Collection): Collection	Returns a synchronized collection.
+synchronizedList(list: List): List	Returns a synchronized list from the specified list.
+synchronizedMap(m: Map): Map	Returns a synchronized map from the specified map.
+synchronizedSet(s: Set): Set	Returns a synchronized set from the specified set.
+synchronizedSortedMap(s: SortedMap): SortedMap	Returns a synchronized sorted map from the specified sorted map.
+synchronizedSortedSet(s: SortedSet): SortedSet	Returns a synchronized sorted set.
+unmodifiableCollection(c: Collection): Collection	Returns an unmodified collection.
+unmodifiableList(list: List): List	Returns an unmodified list.
+unmodifiableMap(m: Map): Map	Returns an unmodified map.
+unmodifiableSet(s: Set): Set	Returns an unmodified set.
+unmodifiableSortedMap(s: SortedMap): SortedMap	Returns an unmodified sorted map.
+unmodifiableSortedSet(s: SortedSet): SortedSet	Returns an unmodified sorted set.

Figure 17.19   *The* Collections *class contains static methods for supporting the Java Collections Framework.*

Most of the methods in the Collections class deal with lists. The sort methods can be used to sort a list using the Comparable interface or the Comparator interface. The binarySearch methods can be used to find an element in a presorted list. In order to use the binarySearch(list, key) method, the list must first be sorted through the Comparable interface. To use the binarySearch(list, key, comparator) method, the list must first be sorted through the Comparator interface. The binarySearch method returns the index of the search key if it is contained in the list. Otherwise, it returns – (insertion point) −1. The insertion point is the point at which the key would be inserted into the list.

Use the copy(src, des) method to copy a source list to a destination list. Use the fill(list, object) method to fill a list with a specified object. Use the nCopy(n, object) method to create a list with *n* number of a specified object.

The min and max methods are generic for all collections. You can use them to find the minimum and maximum elements in a collection.

The Collections class defines three constants: one for an empty set, one for an empty list, and one for an empty map (EMPTY_SET, EMPTY_LIST, and EMPTY_MAP). The class also provides the singleton(Object o) method for creating an immutable set containing only a single item, the singletonList(Object o) method for creating an immutable list containing only a single item, and the singletonMap(Object key, Object value) method for creating an immutable map containing only a single mapping.

The methods in the Collection and Map interfaces are not thread-safe, i.e., the contents may be corrupted if they are processed concurrently by multiple threads. The Collections class provides six static methods for wrapping a collection into a synchronized version: synchronizedCollection(Collection c), synchronizedList(List list), synchronizedMap(Map m), synchronizedSet(Set set), synchronizedSortedMap(SortedMap m), and synchronizedSortedSet(SortedSet s). The synchronized collections can be safely accessed and modified by multiple threads concurrently.

The Collections class also provides six static methods for creating read-only collections: unmodifiableCollection(Collection c), unmodifiableList(List list), unmodifiableMap(Map m), unmodifiableSet(Set set), unmodifiableSortedMap (SortedMap m), and unmodifiableSortedSet(SortedSet s). The read-only collections prevent the data in the collections from being modified, and, as well, offer better performance for read-only operations.

Example 17.10 Using the Collections Class

Problem

Write a program that demonstrates the use of the methods in the Collections class. The example creates a list, sorts it, and searches for an element. The example wraps the list into a synchronized and read-only list.

Solution

The following code gives the solution to the problem. The output of the program is shown in Figure 17.20.

continues

Example 17.10 continued

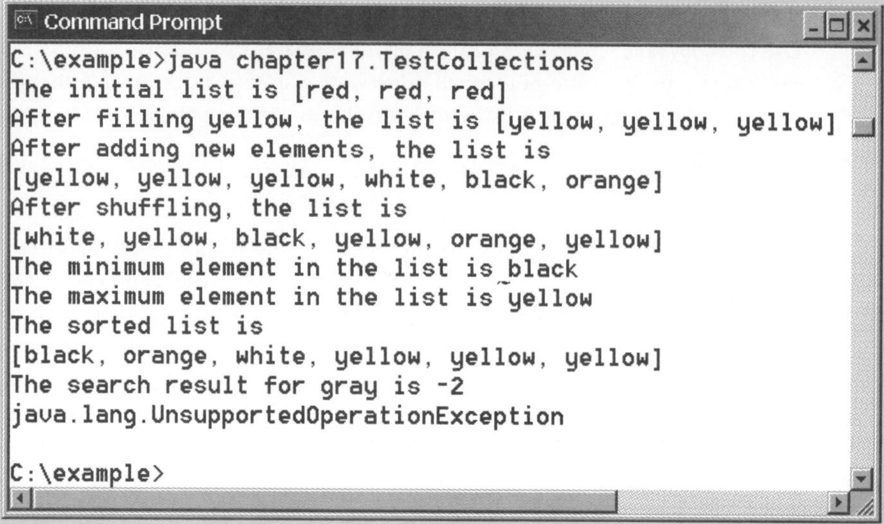

```
Command Prompt                                                    _ □ ×
C:\example>java chapter17.TestCollections
The initial list is [red, red, red]
After filling yellow, the list is [yellow, yellow, yellow]
After adding new elements, the list is
[yellow, yellow, yellow, white, black, orange]
After shuffling, the list is
[white, yellow, black, yellow, orange, yellow]
The minimum element in the list is black
The maximum element in the list is yellow
The sorted list is
[black, orange, white, yellow, yellow, yellow]
The search result for gray is -2
java.lang.UnsupportedOperationException

C:\example>
```

Figure 17.20   *The program demonstrates the use of* Collections.

```java
1      package chapter17;
2
3      import java.util.*;
4
5      public class TestCollections {
6        public static void main(String[] args) {
7          // Create a list of three strings
8          List list = Collections.nCopies(3, "red");
9
10         // Create an array list
11         ArrayList arrayList = new ArrayList(list);
12         System.out.println("The initial list is " + arrayList);
13         list = null; // Release list
14
15         // Fill in "yellow" to the list
16         Collections.fill(arrayList, "yellow");
17         System.out.println("After filling yellow, the list is " +
18           arrayList);
19
20         // Add three new elements to the list
21         arrayList.add("white");
22         arrayList.add("black");
23         arrayList.add("orange");
24         System.out.println("After adding new elements, the list is\n"
25           + arrayList);
26
27         // Shuffle the list
28         Collections.shuffle(arrayList);
29         System.out.println("After shuffling, the list is\n"
30           + arrayList);
31
32         // Find the minimum and maximum elements in the list
33         System.out.println("The minimum element in the list is "
34           + Collections.min(arrayList));
```

```
35          System.out.println("The maximum element in the list is "
36            + Collections.max(arrayList));
37
38          // Sort the list
39          Collections.sort(arrayList);
40          System.out.println("The sorted list is\n" + arrayList);
41
42          // Find an element in the list
43          System.out.println("The search result for gray is " +
44            Collections.binarySearch(arrayList, "gray"));
45
46          // Create a synchronized list
47          List syncList = Collections.synchronizedList(arrayList);
48
49          // Create a synchronized read-only list
50          List unmodifiableList = Collections.unmodifiableList(syncList);
51          arrayList = null; // Release arrayList
52          syncList = null; // Release syncList
53
54          try {
55            unmodifiableList.add("black");
56          }
57          catch (Exception ex) {
58            System.out.println(ex);
59          }
60        }
61      }
```

Review

The program first creates a list filled with the same elements three times using nCopies(3, "red") (Line 8). This list is an instance of List, but it is not an array list or a linked list. The program creates an array list from the list.

The program uses Collections.fill(arrayList, "yellow") (Line 16) to replace each element in the list with "yellow".

After adding three new elements into arrayList, Collections.shuffle(array-List) (Line 28) rearranges them in arrayList.

The program uses Collections.min(arrayList) (Line 34) to find the minimum element in arrayList, and Collections.max(arrayList) (Line 36) to find the maximum element in arrayList.

Collections.sort(arrayList) (Line 39) is invoked to sort arrayList. Collections.binarySearch(arrayList, "gray") (Line 44) is invoked to find "gray" in arrayList. This method returns -2 because $-$(insertion point) $-1 = -2$.

The program finally uses Collections.synchronizedList(arrayList) (Line 47) to create a synchronized list for arrayList, and then creates a synchronized read-only list by wrapping the synchronized list using the unmodifiableList. As shown in Figure 17.20, an UnsupportedOperationException is thrown when the program attempts to add a new element to the read-only list.

17.13   The *Arrays* Class

The Arrays class contains various static methods for sorting and searching arrays, comparing arrays, and filling array elements. It also contains a method for converting an array to a list. Figure 17.21 shows the methods in Arrays.

Arrays
+asList(a: Object[]): List
Overloaded binarySearch method for byte, char, short, int, long, float, double, and Object.
+binarySearch(a: xType[], key: xType): int
Overloaded equals method for boolean, byte, char, short, int, long, float, double, and Object.
+equals(a: xType[], a2: xType[]): boolean
Overloaded fill method for boolean char, byte, short, int, long, float, double, and Object.
+fill(a: xType[], val: xType): void
+fill(a: xType[], fromIndex: int, toIndex: xType, val: xType): void
Overloaded sort method for char, byte, short, int, long, float, double, and Object.
+sort(a: xType[]): void
+sort(a: xType[], fromIndex: int, toIndex: int): void

Returns a list from an array of objects

Overloaded binary search method to search a key in the array of byte, char, short, int, long, float, double, and Object

Overloaded equals method that returns true if a is equal to a2 for a and a2 of the boolean, byte, char, short, int, long, float, and Object type

Overloaded fill method to fill in the specified value into the array of the boolean, byte, char, short, int, long, float, and Object type

Overloaded sort method to sort the specified array of the char, byte, short, int, long, float, double, and Object type

Figure 17.21   *The* Arrays *class contains static methods for arrays.*

An array must be sorted before the binarySearch method is used. The fill method can be used to fill part of the array or the whole array with the same value. The sort method can be used to sort part of the array or the whole array. fill(a, fromIndex, toIndex, val) fills val into a[fromIndex], ..., a[toIndex − 1] and sort(a, fromIndex, toIndex, val) sorts a[fromIndex], ..., a[toIndex − 1].

Example 17.11 Using the Arrays Class

Problem

Write a program that demonstrates how to use the methods in the Arrays class. The example creates an array of int values, fills part of the array with 50, sorts it, searches for an element, and compares the array with another one.

Solution

The following code gives the solution to the problem. The output of the program is shown in Figure 17.22.

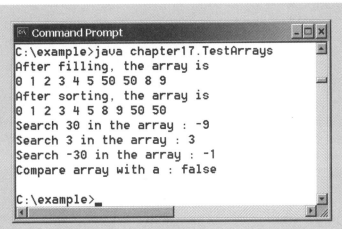

```
C:\example>java chapter17.TestArrays
After filling, the array is
0 1 2 3 4 5 50 50 8 9
After sorting, the array is
0 1 2 3 4 5 8 9 50 50
Search 30 in the array : -9
Search 3 in the array : 3
Search -30 in the array : -1
Compare array with a : false

C:\example>
```

Figure 17.22   *The program demonstrates the use of* Arrays.

```java
1    package chapter17;
2
3    import java.util.*;
4
5    public class TestArrays {
6      public static void main(String[] args) {
7        // Create an array of 10 int values
8        int[] array = {0, 1, 2, 3, 4, 5, 6, 7, 8, 9};
9
10       // Fill array from index 6 to index 7 with 50
11       Arrays.fill(array, 6, 8, 50);
12       System.out.println("After filling, the array is");
13       for (int i = 0; i < 10; i++) {
14         System.out.print(array[i] + " ");
15       }
16       System.out.println();
17
18       // Sort the array
19       Arrays.sort(array);
20       System.out.println("After sorting, the array is");
21       for (int i = 0; i < 10; i++) {
22         System.out.print(array[i] + " ");
23       }
24       System.out.println();
25
26       // Search for 30 in the array
27       System.out.println("Search 30 in the array : " +
28         Arrays.binarySearch(array, 30));
29
30       // Search for 3 in the array
31       System.out.println("Search 3 in the array : " +
32         Arrays.binarySearch(array, 3));
33
34       // Search for -30 in the array
35       System.out.println("Search -30 in the array : " +
36         Arrays.binarySearch(array, -30));
37
38       // Test if two arrays are the same
39       int[] a = new int[10];
40       System.out.println("Compare array with a : " +
41         Arrays.equals(array, a));
42     }
42   }
```

continues

Example 17.11 Continued

Review

The program first creates an array of ten `int` values (Line 8), then fills 50 in the array at index 6 and 7 (Line 11). The `sort` method is used to sort the entire array.

The program uses the `binarySearch` method to search for 30, 3, and −30 in the array (Lines 28, 32, 36). The return value is −9 for searching 30, because 30 is not in the list and the insertion point for 30 is at 8. The return value is 3 for searching 3, because 3 is in the list and its index is 3. The return value is −1 for searching −30, because −30 is not in the list and the insertion point for −30 is at 0.

The program also uses the `equals` method (Line 41) to compare two arrays.

Chapter Summary

- A *collection* is an object that contains objects, which are referred to as *elements*. The Java Collections Framework supports three types of collections: *set*, *list*, and *map*. They are defined in the interfaces `Set`, `List`, and `Map`. A set stores a group of nonduplicate elements. A list stores an ordered collection of elements. A map stores a group of objects, each of which is associated with a key.

- The `Collection` interface is the root for the `Set` and `List` interfaces. It provides the basic operations for adding and removing elements in a collection, and for querying the elements in a collection.

- The `iterator()` method in the `Collection` interface returns an instance of the `Iterator` interface, which can be used to traverse the collection using the `next()` method in `Iterator`. You can also use the `hasNext()` method to check whether there are more elements in the iterator, and the `remove()` method to remove the last element returned by the iterator.

- The `Set` interface extends the `Collection` interface. It does not introduce new methods or constants, but it stipulates that an instance of `Set` contains no duplicate elements. The concrete classes that implement `Set` must ensure that no duplicate elements can be added to the set. That is, no two elements e1 and e2 can be in the set such that `e1.equals(e2)` is true.

- The `HashSet` class is a concrete class that implements `Set`. To create a `HashSet`, use its default constructor or use `new HashSet(Collection)`.

- `LinkedHashSet` extends `HashSet` with a linked list implementation that supports an ordering of the elements in the set. A `LinkedHashSet` can be created by using its default constructor.

- The elements in a `HashSet` are not ordered, but the elements in a `LinkedHashSet` can be retrieved in the order in which they were inserted into the set.

■ SortedSet is a subinterface of Set, which guarantees that the elements in the set are sorted. TreeSet is a concrete class that implements the SortedSet interface. To create a TreeSet, use its default constructor or use new TreeSet(Collection).

■ There are two ways to compare objects. If the class for the elements implements the Comparable interface, you can compare them using the compareTo method. If the class does not implement the Comparable interface or if you don't want to use the compareTo method in the class that implements the Comparable interface, specify a comparator for the elements in the set using the Comparator interface.

■ A set stores nonduplicate elements. To allow duplicate elements to be stored in a collection, you need to use a list. A list can not only store duplicate elements, but also allows the user to specify where they are stored. The user can access elements by an index.

■ The List interface extends Collection to define an ordered collection with duplicates allowed. The List interface adds position-oriented operations, as well as a new list iterator that enables the user to traverse the list bi-directionally.

■ ArrayList is a resizable-array implementation of the List interface. In addition to implementing the List interface, this class provides methods for manipulating the size of the array that is used internally to store the list. Each ArrayList instance has a capacity. The capacity is the size of the array used to store the elements in the list. It is always at least as large as the list size. As elements are added to an ArrayList, its capacity grows automatically. An ArrayList can be constructed using its default constructor, ArrayList (Collection), or ArrayList(intialCapacity).

■ LinkedList is a linked list implementation of the List interface. In addition to implementing the List interface, this class provides the methods for retrieving, inserting, and removing elements from both ends of the list. A LinkedList can be constructed using its default constructor or LinkedList (Collection).

■ The Vector class implements the List interface. In Java 2, Vector is the same as ArrayList, except that it contains synchronized methods for accessing and modifying the vector.

■ The Stack class extends the Vector class and provides several methods for manipulating the stack.

■ The Collection interface represents a collection of elements stored in a set or a list. The Map interface maps keys to the elements. The keys are like indexes. In List, the indexes are integers. In Map, the keys can be any objects. A map cannot contain duplicate keys. Each key can map to at most one value. The Map interface provides the methods for querying, updating, and obtaining a collection of values and a set of keys.

■ The AbstractMap class is a convenience class that implements all the methods in the Map interface except the entrySet() method.

■ The SortedMap interface extends the Map interface to maintain the mapping in ascending order of keys.

■ The HashMap, LinkedHashMap, and TreeMap classes are three concrete implementations of the Map interface. The HashMap class is efficient for locating a value, inserting a mapping, and deleting a mapping.

■ LinkedHashMap extends HashMap with a linked list implementation that supports ordering of the entries in the map. The entries in a HashMap are not ordered, but the entries in a LinkedHashMap can be retrieved in the order in which they were inserted into the map (known as the *insertion order*), or in the order in which they were last accessed, from least recently accessed to most recently (*access order*).

■ The TreeMap class, implementing SortedMap, is efficient for traversing the keys in a sorted order. The keys can be sorted using the Comparable interface or the Comparator interface.

■ The Collections class provides static methods for operating on collections and maps, creating synchronized collection classes, and creating read-only collection classes.

■ The Arrays class contains static methods for sorting and searching arrays, comparing arrays, and filling array elements.

Review Questions

17.1 Describe the Java Collections Framework. What is a convenience class?

17.2 The hashCode method and the equals method are defined in the Object class. Why are they also redefined in the Collection interface?

17.3 Find the default implementation for the equals method and the hashCode method in the Object class from the source code of Object.java.

17.4 How do you create an instance of Set? How do you insert a new element in a set? How do you remove an element from a set? How do you find the size of a set? How do you traverse the elements in a set?

17.5 What are the differences among HashSet, LinkedHastSet, and TreeSet? How do you sort the elements in a set using the compareTo method in the Comparable interface? How do you sort the elements in a set using the Comparator interface? What would happen if you added an element that cannot be compared with the existing elements in a tree set?

17.6 How do you add and remove elements from a list? How do you traverse a list in both directions?

17.7 What are the differences between ArrayList and LinkedList?

17.8 How do you create an instance of Vector? How do you add or insert a new element into a vector? How do you remove an element from a vector? How do you find the size of a vector?

17.9 How do you create an instance of Stack? How do you add a new element into a stack? How do you remove an element from a stack? How do you find the size of a stack?

17.10 How do you create an instance of Map? How do you add a pair consisting of an element and a key into a map? How do you remove an entry from a map? How do you find the size of a map? How do you traverse entries in a map?

17.11 Describe the static methods in the Collections class and the Arrays class.

17.12 Which method can you use to sort the elements in an ArrayList or a LinkedList? Which method can you use to sort an array of strings?

17.13 Does Example 17.1, "Using HashSet and Iterator," compile and run if Line 7 (Set set = new HashSet()) is replaced by one of the following statements?

```
Collection set = new LinkedHashSet();
Collection set = new TreeSet();
Collection set = new ArrayList();
Collection set = new LinkedList();
Collection set = new Vector();
Collection set = new Stack();
```

Programming Exercises

17.1 (Performing set operations on hash sets) Create two hash sets {"George", "Jim", "John", "Blake", "Kevin", "Michael"} and {"George", "Katie", "Kevin", "Michelle", "Ryan"}, and find their union, difference, and intersection.

17.2 (Performing set operations on array lists) Create two array lists {"George", "Jim", "John", "Blake", "Kevin", "Michael"} and {"George", "Katie", "Kevin", "Michelle", "Ryan"} and find their union, difference, and intersection.

17.3 (The Queue class) Implement the Queue class in Exercise 10.6 using the ArrayList class.

17.4 (Revising Example 17.9, "Counting the Occurrences of Words in a Text") Rewrite Example 17.9 to read the text from a text file. The text file is passed as a command-line argument.

17.5 (Using the static methods in the Arrays class) Write a program that reads in ten double numbers and uses the sort method in the Arrays class to sort them.

17.6 (Storing numbers in a linked list) Write a program that lets the user enter numbers from a graphical user interface and display them in a text area, as shown in Figure 17.23. Use a linked list to store the numbers. Do not store duplicate numbers. Add the buttons Sort, Shuffle, and Reverse to sort, shuffle, and reverse the list.

Figure 17.23 *The program stores numbers in a list.*

17.7 (Counting the occurrences of numbers entered) Write a program that reads an unspecified number of integers and finds the one that has the most occurrences. Your input ends when the input is 0. For example, if you entered 2 3 40 3 5 4 −3 3 3 2 0, the number 3 occurred most often. Please enter one number at a time. If not one but several numbers have the most occurrences, all of them should be reported. For example, since 9 and 3 appear twice in the list 9 30 3 9 3 2 4, both should be reported.

17.8 (Counting the keywords in Java source code) Write a program that reads a Java source code file and reports the number of keywords in the file. Pass the Java file name from the command line.

⊗ HINT

Create a set to store all the Java keywords.

17.9 (Revising Example 17.9 "Counting the Occurrences of Words in a Text") Rewrite Example 17.9 to display the words in ascending order of occurrence counts.

⊗ HINT

Create a class named WordOccurrence that implements the Comparable interface. The class contains two fields, word and count. The compareTo method compares the count. For each pair in the hash set in Example 17.9, create an instance of WordOccurrence and store it in an array list. Sort the array list using Collections.sort method. What would be wrong if you stored the instances of WordOccurrence in a tree set?

17.10 (Implementing a new Stack class) Stack inherits Vector in the Java API. The advantage of this design is that you can use Stack wherever you use Vector in the program. The disadvantage is that it inherits the unnecessary methods from the Vector class. Implement a Stack class that contains a vector that stores data rather than inherits Vector.

18

MULTITHREADING

Objectives

- To understand the concept of multithreading and apply it to develop animation.
- To develop thread classes by extending the Thread class.
- To develop thread classes by implementing the Runnable interface in cases of multiple inheritance.
- To describe the life cycle of thread states and set thread priorities.
- To know how to control threads: starting, stopping, suspending, and resuming threads.
- To synchronize threads to avoid resource conflicts.
- To use the Timer class to simplify the control of Java animations.

18.1   Introduction

One of the important features of Java is its built-in support for multithreading. *Multithreading* is the capability of running multiple tasks concurrently within a program. In many programming languages, you have to invoke system-dependent procedures and functions to implement multithreading. This chapter introduces the concepts of threads and how to develop multithreading programs in Java.

18.2   Thread Concepts

A *thread* is the flow of execution, from beginning to end, of a task in a program. With Java, you can launch multiple threads from a program concurrently. These threads can be executed simultaneously in multiprocessor systems, as shown in Figure 18.1.

Figure 18.1   *Here, multiple threads are running on multiple CPUs.*

In single-processor systems, as shown in Figure 18.2, the multiple threads share CPU time, and the operating system is responsible for scheduling and allocating resources to them. This arrangement is practical because most of the time the CPU is idle. It does nothing, for example, while waiting for the user to enter data.

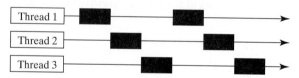

Figure 18.2   *Here, multiple threads share a single CPU.*

Multithreading can make your program more responsive and interactive, as well as enhance performance. For example, a good word processor lets you print or save a file while you are typing. In some cases, multithreaded programs run faster than single-threaded programs even on single-processor systems. Java provides exceptionally good support for creating and running threads and for locking resources to prevent conflicts.

When your program executes as an application, the Java interpreter starts a thread for the main method. When your program executes as an applet, the Web browser starts a thread to run the applet. You can create additional threads to run concurrent tasks in the program. Each new thread is an object of a class that implements the Runnable interface or extends a class that implements the Runnable interface. This new object is referred to as a *runnable object*.

You can create threads either by extending the Thread class or by implementing the Runnable interface. Both Thread and Runnable are defined in the java.lang package. Thread actually implements Runnable. In the following sections, you will learn how to use the Thread class and the Runnable interface to write multithreaded programs.

18.3 Creating Threads by Extending the *Thread* Class

The Thread class contains the constructors for creating threads, as well as many useful methods for controlling threads. To create and run a thread, first define a class that extends the Thread class. Your thread class must override the run() method, which tells the system how the thread will be executed when it runs. You can then create an object running on the thread.

Figure 18.3 illustrates the key elements of a thread class that extends the Thread class, and shows how to use it to create a thread in a class. The thread is a runnable object created from the CustomThread class. The start method tells the system that the thread is ready to run.

```
// Custom thread class
public class CustomThread extends Thread {
  ...
  public CustomThread(...) {
    ...
  }

  // Override the run method in Thread
  public void run() {
    // Tell system how to run custom thread
    ...
  }

  ...
}
```

```
// Client class
public class Client {
  ...
  public void someMethod() {
    ...
    // Create a thread
    CustomThread thread1 = new CustomThread(...);

    // Start a thread
    thread1.start();
    ...

    // Create another thread
    CustomThread thread2 = new CustomThread(...);

    // Start a thread
    thread2.start();
  }
  ...
}
```

Figure 18.3 *Define a thread class by extending the* Thread *class.*

Example 18.1 Using the Thread Class to Create and Launch Threads

Problem

Write a program that creates and runs three threads:

- The first thread prints the letter *a* one hundred times.
- The second thread prints the letter *b* one hundred times.
- The third thread prints the integers 1 through 100.

continues

Example 18.1 Continued

Solution

The program has three independent threads. To run them concurrently, it needs to create a runnable object for each thread. Because the first two threads have similar functionality, they can be defined in one thread class.

The program is given here, and its output is shown in Figure 18.4.

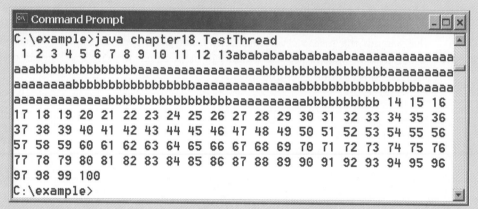

```
C:\example>java chapter18.TestThread
 1 2 3 4 5 6 7 8 9 10 11 12 13abababababababababaaaaaaaaaaaaaa
aaabbbbbbbbbbbbbbbaaaaaaaaaaaaaaaaaabbbbbbbbbbbbbbbbbbaaaaaaaaa
aaaaaaaabbbbbbbbbbbbbbbbbaaaaaaaaaaaaaaaabbbbbbbbbbbbbbbbbbaaaa
aaaaaaaaaaaaabbbbbbbbbbbbbbbbbbaaaaaaaaaaaabbbbbbbbbb 14 15 16
17 18 19 20 21 22 23 24 25 26 27 28 29 30 31 32 33 34 35 36
37 38 39 40 41 42 43 44 45 46 47 48 49 50 51 52 53 54 55 56
57 58 59 60 61 62 63 64 65 66 67 68 69 70 71 72 73 74 75 76
77 78 79 80 81 82 83 84 85 86 87 88 89 90 91 92 93 94 95 96
97 98 99 100
C:\example>
```

Figure 18.4   *Threads* printA, printB, *and* print100 *are executed simultaneously to display the letter a one hundred times, the letter b one hundred times, and the numbers from 1 to 100.*

```
1     // TestThread.java: Define threads using the Thread class
2     package chapter18;
3
4     public class TestThread {
5       /** Main method */
6       public static void main(String[] args) {
7         // Create threads
8         PrintChar printA = new PrintChar('a', 100);
9         PrintChar printB = new PrintChar('b', 100);
10        PrintNum  print100 = new PrintNum(100);
11
12        // Start threads
13        print100.start();
14        printA.start();
15        printB.start();
16      }
17    }
18
19    // The thread class for printing a specified character
20    // in specified times
21    class PrintChar extends Thread {
22      private char charToPrint;  // The character to print
23      private int times;  // The times to repeat
24
25      /** Construct a thread with specified character and number of
26        times to print the character
27        */
```

```
28        public PrintChar(char c, int t) {
29          charToPrint = c;
30          times = t;
31        }
32
33        /** Override the run() method to tell the system
34          what the thread will do
35          */
36        public void run() {
37          for (int i = 0; i < times; i++)
38            System.out.print(charToPrint);
39        }
40      }
41
42      // The thread class for printing number from 1 to n for a given n
43      class PrintNum extends Thread {
44        private int lastNum;
45
46        /** Construct a thread for print 1, 2, ... i */
47        public PrintNum(int n) {
48          lastNum = n;
49        }
50
51        /** Tell the thread how to run */
52        public void run() {
53          for (int i = 1; i <= lastNum; i++)
54            System.out.print(" " + i);
55        }
56      }
```

Review

If you run this program on a multiple-CPU system, all three threads will execute simultaneously. If you run the program on a single-CPU system, the three threads will share the CPU and take turns printing letters and numbers on the console. This is known as *time-sharing*.

The program creates thread classes by extending the Thread class. The PrintChar class (Lines 19–40), derived from the Thread class, overrides the run() method (Lines 36–39) with the print-character action. This class provides a framework for printing any single character a given number of times. The runnable objects printA and printB are instances of the user-defined thread class PrintChar.

The PrintNum class (Lines 42–56) overrides the run() method (Lines 52–55) with the print-number action. This class provides a framework for printing numbers from *1* to *n*, for any integer *n*.

In the client program, the program creates a thread, printA, for printing the letter *a*, and a thread, printB, for printing the letter *b*. Both are objects of the PrintChar class. The print100 thread object is created from the PrintNum class.

The start() method (Lines 13–15) is invoked to start a thread that causes the run() method to execute. When the run() method completes, the threads terminate.

continues

Example 18.1 Continued

◈ **JBUILDER NOTE**

You can trace the threads in the debugger. As shown in Figure 18.5, there are four active threads. Thread-0 is to run the main method. Thread-1 is to run printA, Thread-2 is to run printB, and Thread-3 is to run print100.

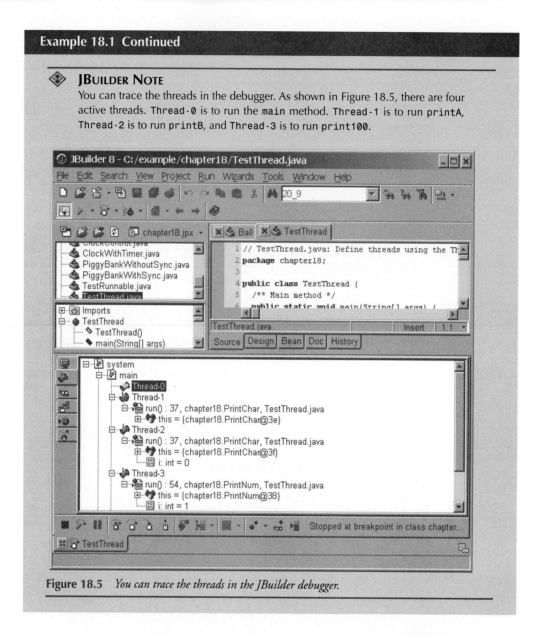

Figure 18.5   *You can trace the threads in the JBuilder debugger.*

18.4   Creating Threads by Implementing the *Runnable* Interface

In the preceding section, you created and ran a thread by declaring a user thread class that extends the Thread class. This approach works well if the user thread class inherits only from the Thread class, but not if it inherits multiple classes, as in the case of an applet. To inherit multiple classes, you have to implement interfaces. Java provides the Runnable interface as an alternative to the Thread class.

CHAPTER 18 MULTITHREADING

The `Runnable` interface is rather simple. All it contains is the `run` method. You need to implement this method to tell the system how your thread is going to run. Figure 18.6 illustrates the key elements of a thread class that implements the `Runnable` interface, and how to use it to create a thread in a class.

```
// Custom thread class
public class CustomThread
  implements Runnable { ..............
  ...
  public CustomThread(...) {
    ...
  }

// Implement the run method in Runnable
  public void run() {
    // Tell system how to run custom thread
    ...
  }

  ...
}
```

```
// Client class
public class Client {
  ...
  public void someMethod() {
    ...
    // Create an instance of CustomThread
    CustomThread customThread
      = new CustomThread(...);

    // Create a thread
    Thread thread = new Thread(customThread);

    // Start a thread
    thread.start();
    ...
  }
  ...
}
```

Figure 18.6 *Define a thread class by implementing the* `Runnable` *interface.*

To start a new thread with the `Runnable` interface, you must first create an instance of the class that implements the `Runnable` interface, then use the `Thread` class constructor to construct a thread.

The following example demonstrates how to create threads using the `Runnable` interface.

Example 18.2 Using the `Runnable` Interface to Create and Launch Threads

Problem

Modify Example 18.1, "Using the `Thread` Class to Create and Launch Threads," to create and run the same threads using the `Runnable` interface.

Solution

The following code gives the solution to the problem.

```
1   // TestRunnable.java: Define threads using the Runnable interface
2   package chapter18;
3
4   public class TestRunnable {
5     /** Main method */
6     public static void main(String[] args) {
7       new TestRunnable();
8     }
9
```

continues

Example 18.2 Continued

```
10       /** Default constructor */
11       public TestRunnable() {
12         // Create threads
13         Thread printA = new Thread(new PrintChar('a', 100));
14         Thread printB = new Thread(new PrintChar('b', 100));
15         Thread print100 = new Thread(new PrintNum(100));
16
17         // Start threads
18         print100.start();
19         printA.start();
20         printB.start();
21       }
22
23       // The thread class for printing a specified character
24       // in specified times
25       class PrintChar implements Runnable {
26         private char charToPrint;  // The character to print
27         private int times;  // The times to repeat
28
29         /** Construct a thread with specified character and number of
30            times to print the character
31            */
32         public PrintChar(char c, int t) {
33           charToPrint = c;
34           times = t;
35         }
36
37         /** Override the run() method to tell the system
38            what the thread will do
39            */
40         public void run() {
41           for (int i = 0; i <times; i++)
42             System.out.print(charToPrint);
43         }
44       }
45
46       // The thread class for printing number from 1 to n for a given n
47       class PrintNum implements Runnable {
48         private int lastNum;
49
50         /** Construct a thread for print 1, 2, ... i */
51         public PrintNum(int n) {
52           lastNum = n;
53         }
54
55         /** Tell the thread how to run */
56         public void run() {
57           for (int i = 1; i <= lastNum; i++)
58             System.out.print(" " + i);
59         }
60       }
61     }
```

Review

The program creates thread classes by implementing the Runnable interface.

This example performs the same task as in Example 18.1. The classes PrintChar and PrintNum are the same as in Example 18.1 except that they implement the Runnable interface rather than extend the Thread class.

The `PrintChar` and `PrintNum` classes are implemented as inner classes to avoid naming conflicts with the `PrintChar` and `PrintNum` classes in Example 18.1. Threads `printA`, `printB`, and `print100` are created in the constructor instead of directly in the main method. This is because the `main` method is static and the inner classes `PrintChar` and `PrintNum` are nonstatic; you cannot reference nonstatic members of a class in a static method.

An instance of the class that extends the `Thread` class is a thread, which can be started using the `start()` method in the `Thread` class. But an instance of the class that implements the `Runnable` interface is not yet a thread. You have to wrap it, using the `Thread` class, to construct a thread for the instance, such as

```
Thread printA = new Thread(new PrintChar('a', 100));
```

18.5   Thread Controls and Communications

The `Thread` class contains the following methods for controlling threads:

- `public void run()`

  Invoked by the Java runtime system to execute the thread. You must override this method and provide the code you want your thread to execute in your thread class. This method is never directly invoked by the runnable object in a program, although it is an instance method of a runnable object.

- `public void start()`

  Starts the thread that causes the `run()` method to be invoked. This method is called by the runnable object in the client class.

- `public void stop()`

  Stops the thread. As of Java 2, this method is *deprecated* (or *outdated*) because it is known to be inherently unsafe. You should assign `null` to a `Thread` variable to indicate that it is stopped rather than use the `stop()` method.

- `public void suspend()`

  Suspends the thread. As of Java 2, this method is deprecated because it is known to be deadlock-prone. You should write the code to use the `wait()` method along with a `boolean` variable to indicate whether a thread is suspended rather than use the deprecated `suspend()` method. The code will be introduced in Section 18.9, "Controlling Animation Using Threads."

- `public void resume()`

  Resumes the thread. As of Java 2, this method, along with the `suspend()` method, is deprecated because it is deadlock-prone. You should write the code to use the `notify()` method along with a `boolean` variable to indicate whether a thread is resumed rather than use the deprecated `resume()` method.

■ `public static void sleep(long millis) throws InterruptedException`

Puts the runnable object to sleep for a specified time in milliseconds. Note that the `sleep` method is a static method.

■ `public static void yield(long millis)`

Causes the currently executing thread object to temporarily pause and allow other threads to execute.

■ `public void interrupt()`

Interrupts a running thread.

■ `public static boolean isInterrupted()`

Tests whether the current thread has been interrupted.

■ `public boolean isAlive()`

Tests whether the thread is currently running.

■ `public void setPriority(int p)`

Sets priority p (ranging from 1 to 10) for this thread.

◆ **NOTE**

With the release of Java 2, some methods in the previous version have been deprecated and replaced by new methods. The deprecated methods are still supported for compatibility reasons, but Sun recommends against using them.

The `wait()`, `notify()`, and `notifyAll()` methods in the `Object` class are often used to facilitate communications among threads.

■ `public final void wait() throws InterruptedException`

Forces the thread to wait until the `notify` or `notifyAll` method is called for the object to which `wait` is called.

■ `public final void notify()`

Awakens one of the threads that are waiting on this object. Which one is notified depends on the system implementation.

■ `public final void notifyAll()`

Awakens all the threads that are waiting on this object.

18.6 Thread States

Threads can be in one of five states: new, ready, running, blocked, or finished (see Figure 18.7).

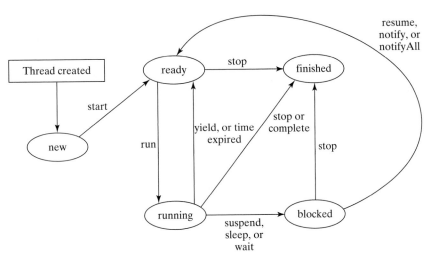

Figure 18.7   *A thread can be in one of five states: new, ready, running, blocked, or finished.*

When a thread is newly created, it enters the *new state*. After a thread is started by calling its start() method, it enters the *ready state*. A ready thread is runnable but may not be running yet. The operating system has to allocate CPU time to it.

When a ready thread begins executing, it enters the *running state*. A running thread may enter the ready state if its given CPU time expires or its yield() method is called.

A thread can enter the *blocked state* (i.e., become inactive) for several reasons. It may have invoked the sleep(), wait(), or suspend() method, or some other thread may have invoked its sleep() or suspend() method. It may be waiting for an I/O operation to finish. A blocked thread may be reactivated when the action inactivating it is reversed. For example, if a thread has been put to sleep and the sleep time has expired, the thread is reactivated and enters the ready state.

Finally, a thread is *finished* if it completes the execution of its run() method or if its stop() method is invoked.

The isAlive() method is used to find out the state of a thread. It returns true if a thread is in the ready, inactive, or running state; it returns false if a thread is new and has not started or if it is finished.

Java assigns every thread a priority. By default, a thread inherits the priority of the thread that spawned it. You can increase or decrease the priority of any thread by using the setPriority method, and you can get the thread's priority by using the getPriority method. Priorities are numbers ranging from 1 to 10. The Thread class has the int constants MIN_PRIORITY, NORM_PRIORITY, and MAX_PRIORITY, representing 1, 5, and 10, respectively. The priority of the main thread is Thread.NORM_PRIORITY.

 TIP

The priority numbers may be changed in a future version of Java. To minimize the impact of any changes, use the constants in the Thread class to specify thread priorities.

The Java runtime system always picks the currently runnable thread with the highest priority. If several runnable threads have equally high priorities, the CPU is allocated to all of them in round-robin fashion. A lower-priority thread can run only when no higher-priority threads are running.

18.7   Thread Groups

A *thread group* is a set of threads. Some programs contain quite a few threads with similar functionality. For convenience, you can group them together and perform operations on the entire group. For example, you can suspend or resume all of the threads in a group at the same time.

Listed below are the guidelines for using thread groups:

1. Use the `ThreadGroup` constructor to construct a thread group:

    ```
    ThreadGroup g = new ThreadGroup("thread group");
    ```

    This creates a thread group g named "thread group". The name is a string and must be unique.

2. Using the `Thread` constructor, place a thread in a thread group:

    ```
    Thread t = new Thread(g, new ThreadClass(), "This thread");
    ```

    This statement creates a thread and places it in the thread group g. You can add a thread group under another thread group to form a tree in which every thread group except the initial one has a parent.

3. To find out how many threads in a group are currently running, use the `activeCount()` method. The following statement displays the active number of threads in group g.

    ```
    System.out.println("The number of runnable threads in the group "
        + g.activeCount());
    ```

4. Each thread belongs to a thread group. By default, a newly created thread becomes a member of the current thread group that spawned it. To find which group a thread belongs to, use the `getThreadGroup()` method.

 NOTE

You have to start each thread individually. There is no `start()` method in `ThreadGroup`.

In the next section, you will see an example that uses the `ThreadGroup` class.

18.8   Synchronization

A shared resource may be corrupted if it is accessed simultaneously by multiple threads. The following example demonstrates the problem.

Example 18.3 Showing Resource Conflict

Problem

Write a program that demonstrates the problem of resource conflict. Suppose that you create and launch one hundred threads, each of which adds a penny to a piggy bank. Assume that the piggy bank is initially empty. You create a class named `PiggyBank` to model the piggy bank, a class named `AddAPennyThread` to add a penny to the piggy bank, and a main class that creates and launches threads. The relationships of these classes are shown in Figure 18.8.

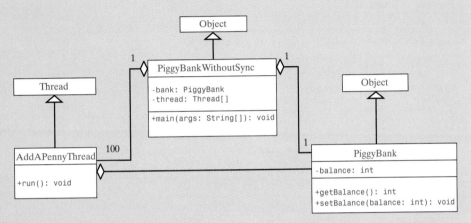

Figure 18.8 `PiggyBankWithoutSync` *contains an instance of* `PiggyBank`, *and one hundred threads of* `AddAPennyThread`.

Solution

The program is given as follows. The output of the program is shown in Figure 18.9.

```
1   // PiggyBankWithoutSync.java: Demonstrate resource conflict
2   package chapter18;
3
4   public class PiggyBankWithoutSync {
5     private PiggyBank bank = new PiggyBank();
6     private Thread[] thread = new Thread[100];
7
8     public static void main(String[] args) {
9       PiggyBankWithoutSync test = new PiggyBankWithoutSync();
10      System.out.println("What is balance ? " +
11        test.bank.getBalance());
12    }
13
14    public PiggyBankWithoutSync() {
15      ThreadGroup g = new ThreadGroup("group");
16      boolean done = false;
17
18      // Create and launch 100 threads
19      for (int i = 0; i <100; i++) {
20        thread[i] = new Thread(g, new AddAPennyThread(), "t");
21        thread[i].start();
22      }
23
```

continues

795

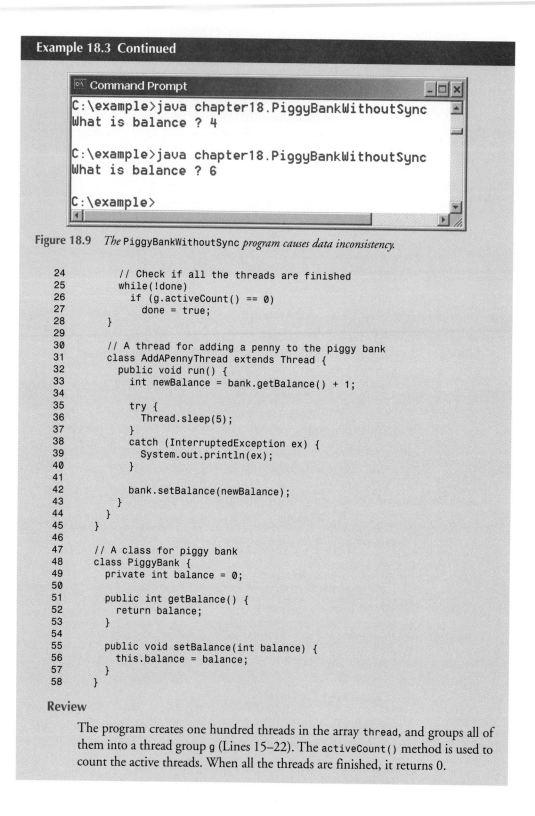

Example 18.3 Continued

```
C:\example>java chapter18.PiggyBankWithoutSync
What is balance ? 4

C:\example>java chapter18.PiggyBankWithoutSync
What is balance ? 6

C:\example>
```

Figure 18.9   *The* `PiggyBankWithoutSync` *program causes data inconsistency.*

```
24            // Check if all the threads are finished
25            while(!done)
26              if (g.activeCount() == 0)
27                done = true;
28          }
29
30          // A thread for adding a penny to the piggy bank
31          class AddAPennyThread extends Thread {
32            public void run() {
33              int newBalance = bank.getBalance() + 1;
34
35              try {
36                Thread.sleep(5);
37              }
38              catch (InterruptedException ex) {
39                System.out.println(ex);
40              }
41
42              bank.setBalance(newBalance);
43            }
44          }
45        }
46
47        // A class for piggy bank
48        class PiggyBank {
49          private int balance = 0;
50
51          public int getBalance() {
52            return balance;
53          }
54
55          public void setBalance(int balance) {
56            this.balance = balance;
57          }
58        }
```

Review

The program creates one hundred threads in the array `thread`, and groups all of them into a thread group `g` (Lines 15–22). The `activeCount()` method is used to count the active threads. When all the threads are finished, it returns 0.

The balance of the piggy bank is initially 0 (Line 49). When all the threads are finished, the balance should be 100, but the output is unpredictable. As can be seen in Figure 18.9, the answers are wrong in the sample run. This demonstrates the data-corruption problem that occurs when all the threads have access to the same data source simultaneously.

Interestingly, it is not easy to replicate the problem. The sleep method (Line 36) is deliberately added to magnify the data-corruption problem and make it easy to see. If you run the program several times but still do not see the problem, increase the sleep time. This will dramatically increase the chances for resource contention.

What, then, caused the error in Example 18.3? Here is a possible scenario, as shown in Figure 18.10.

balance	thread[i]	thread[j]
0	newBalance = bank.getBalance() + 1;	
0		newBalance = bank.getBalance() + 1;
1	bank.setBalance(newBalance);	
1		bank.setBalance(newBalance);

Figure 18.10 thread[i] *and* thread[j] *both add 1 to the same balance.*

In Step 1, thread[i], for some i, gets the balances from the bank. In Step 2, thread[j], for some j, gets the same balances from the bank. In Step 3, thread[i] writes a new balance to the bank. In Step 4, thread[j] writes a new balance to the bank.

The effect of this scenario is that thread thread[i] did nothing, because in Step 4 thread thread[j] overrides thread[i]'s result. Obviously, the problem is that thread[i] and thread[j] are accessing a common resource in a way that causes conflict.

18.8.1 The Keyword *synchronized*

To avoid resource conflicts, Java uses the keyword synchronized to synchronize method invocation so that only one thread can access a method at a time. To correct the data-corruption problem in Example 18.3, rewrite the program as follows:

```
1    // PiggyBankWithSync.java: Demonstrate avoiding resource conflict
2    package chapter18;
3
4    public class PiggyBankWithSync {
5      private PiggyBank bank = new PiggyBank();
6      private Thread[] thread = new Thread[100];
7
8      public static void main(String[] args) {
9        PiggyBankWithSync test = new PiggyBankWithSync();
```

```
10              System.out.println("What is balance ? " +
11                 test.bank.getBalance());
12          }
13
14        public PiggyBankWithSync() {
15           ThreadGroup g1 = new ThreadGroup("group");
16           boolean done = false;
17
18           for (int i = 0; i <100; i++) {
19              thread[i] = new Thread(g1, new AddAPennyThread(), "t");
20              thread[i].start();
21           }
22
23           while(!done)
24              if (g1.activeCount() == 0)
25                 done = true;
26        }
27
28        // Synchronize: add a penny one at a time
29        private static synchronized void addAPenny(PiggyBank bank) {
30           int newBalance = bank.getBalance() + 1;
31
32           try {
33              Thread.sleep(5);
34           }
35           catch (InterruptedException ex) {
36              System.out.println(ex);
37           }
38
39           bank.setBalance(newBalance);
40        }
41
42        // A thread for adding a penny to the piggy bank
43        class AddAPennyThread extends Thread {
44           public void run() {
45              addAPenny(bank);
46           }
47        }
48     }
```

With the keywords static and synchronized for the method addAPenny, the preceding scenario cannot happen. If thread thread[j] starts to enter the method, and thread thread[i] is already in the method, thread thread[j] is blocked until thread thread[i] finishes the method.

A synchronized method acquires a lock before it executes. In the case of an instance method, the lock is on the object for which the method was invoked. In the case of a static (class) method, the lock is on the class. If one thread invokes a synchronized instance method (respectively, static method) on an object, the lock of that object (respectively, class) is acquired first, then the method is executed, and finally the lock is released. Another thread invoking the same method of that object (respectively, class) is blocked until the lock is released.

You can rewrite the program to add a synchronized instance method named addAPenny in the PiggyBank class. In this case, the lock would be on a single PiggyBank object, which is sufficient to ensure that only one thread can execute the addAPenny method at any given time. See Exercise 18.11.

18.8.2 Synchronized Statements

Invoking a synchronized instance method of an object acquires a lock on the object, and invoking a synchronized static method of a class acquires a lock on the class. A synchronized statement can be used to acquire a lock on any object, not just *this* object, when executing a block of the code in a method. This block is referred to as a *synchronized block*. The general form of a synchronized statement is as follows:

```
synchronized (expr) {
  statements;
}
```

The expression `expr` must evaluate to an object reference. If the object is already locked by another thread, the thread is blocked until the lock is released. When a lock is obtained on the object, the statements in the synchronized block are executed, and then the lock is released.

Synchronized statements enable you to synchronize part of the code in a method instead of the entire method. This increases concurrency. Synchronized statements enable you to acquire a lock on any object so that you can synchronize the access to an object instead of to a method. See Exercise 18.12.

NOTE

Any synchronized instance method can be converted into a synchronized statement. Suppose that the following is a synchronized instance method:

```
public synchronized void xMethod() {
  // method body
}
```

This method is equivalent to

```
public void xMethod() {
  synchronized (this) {
    // method body
  }
}
```

18.9 Controlling Animation Using Threads

In Example 11.6, "Drawing a Clock," you drew a clock to show the current time. The clock does not tick after it is displayed. What can you do to make the clock display a new current time every second? The key to making the clock tick is to repaint it every second with a new current time. You can use a thread to control how to repaint the clock.

Example 18.4 Displaying a Running Clock in an Applet

Problem

Write an applet that displays a runnable clock. Use two buttons to suspend and resume the clock, as shown in Figure 18.11.

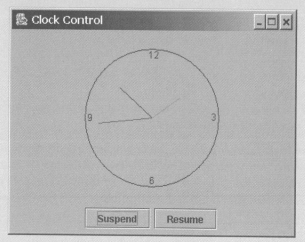

Figure 18.11 *You can click the Suspend button to suspend the clock and the Resume button to resume the clock.*

Solution

Here are the major steps to complete this example:

1. Create a subclass of StillClock named Clock to enable the clock to run.

2. Create a subclass of JPanel named ClockControl to contain the clock with two control buttons *Suspend* and *Resume*.

3. Create an applet named ClockApplet to contain an instance of ClockControl and enable the applet to run stand-alone.

The relationship among these classes is shown in Figure 18.12.

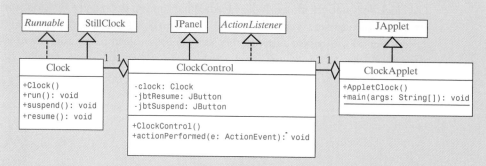

Figure 18.12 ClockApplet *contains* ClockControl, *and* ClockControl *contains* Clock.

```
1    package chapter18;
2
3    public class Clock extends chapter11.StillClock implements Runnable {
4      private boolean suspended;
5
6      public Clock() {
7        new Thread(this).start();
8      }
9
10     public void run() {
11       while (true) {
12         setCurrentTime();
13         repaint();
14
15         try {
16           Thread.sleep(1000);
17           waitForNotificationToResume();
18         }
19         catch(InterruptedException ex) {
20         }
21       }
22     }
23
24     public synchronized void suspend() {
25       suspended = true;
26     }
27
28     public synchronized void resume() {
29       if (suspended) {
30         suspended = false;
31         notifyAll();
32       }
33     }
34
35     private synchronized void waitForNotificationToResume()
36       throws InterruptedException {
37       while (suspended)
38         wait();
39     }
40   }
```

```
1    package chapter18;
2
3    import javax.swing.*;
4    import java.awt.event.*;
5    import java.awt.BorderLayout;
6
7    public class ClockControl extends JPanel implements ActionListener {
8      private Clock clock = new Clock();
9      private JButton jbtSuspend = new JButton("Suspend");
10     private JButton jbtResume = new JButton("Resume");
11
12     public ClockControl() {
13       // Group buttons in a panel
14       JPanel panel = new JPanel();
15       panel.add(jbtSuspend);
16       panel.add(jbtResume);
17
```

continues

Example 18.4 Continued

```
18        // Add clock and buttons to the panel
19        setLayout(new BorderLayout());
20        add(clock, BorderLayout.CENTER);
21        add(panel, BorderLayout.SOUTH);
22
23        // Register listeners
24        jbtSuspend.addActionListener(this);
25        jbtResume.addActionListener(this);
26      }
27
28      public void actionPerformed(ActionEvent e) {
29        if (e.getSource() == jbtSuspend)
30          clock.suspend();
31        else if (e.getSource() == jbtResume)
32          clock.resume();
33      }
34    }
```

```
1   // ClockApplet.java: Display a running clock on the applet
2   package chapter18;
3
4   import javax.swing.*;
5   import java.awt.*;
6
7   public class ClockApplet extends JApplet {
8     public ClockApplet() {
9       getContentPane().add(new ClockControl());
10    }
11
12    public static void main(String[] args) {
13      ClockApplet applet = new ClockApplet();
14      JFrame frame = new JFrame();
15      frame.setDefaultCloseOperation(JFrame.EXIT_ON_CLOSE);
16      frame.setTitle("Clock Control");
17      frame.getContentPane().add(applet, BorderLayout.CENTER);
18      frame.setSize(400, 320);
19      frame.setVisible(true);
20    }
21  }
```

Review

The `Clock` class extends `StillClock` to display the clock and implements the `Runnable` interface to enable the clock to run. Since the `suspend` and `resume` methods in the `Thread` class are deprecated, you must create new methods for resuming and suspending threads. The variable `suspended` is declared as a data member of the class (Line 4), which indicates the state of the thread. The keyword `synchronized` ensures that the `resume()` and `suspend()` methods are synchronized to avoid race conditions that could result in an inconsistent value for the variable `suspended`.

Line 7 creates and starts the thread. The `run` method (Lines 10–22) is implemented to set a new time and repaint the clock every one second continuously. In the `while` loop body, the thread is blocked if `suspended` is true. The `waitForNotificationToResume()` (Line 17) method causes the thread to suspend and wait for notification by the `notifyAll()` method (Line 31) invoked from the `resume()` method.

The ClockControl class extends JPanel to display the clock and two control buttons and implements the ActionListener to handle action events from the buttons. When the Suspend button is clicked, the clock's suspend method is invoked to suspend the clock. When the Resume button is clicked, the clock's resume method is invoked to resume the clock.

The ClockApplet class simply places an instance of ClockControl in the applet's content pane. The *main* method is provided in the applet so that you can also run it stand-alone.

NOTE

The wait(), notify(), and notifyAll() methods are used for thread communications. These methods must be called in a synchronized method or a synchronized block. Otherwise, an IllegalMonitorStateException would occur.

NOTE

When wait() is invoked, it pauses the thread and simultaneously releases the lock on the object. When the thread is restarted after being notified, the lock is automatically reacquired.

18.10 Controlling Animation Using the *Timer* Class

The preceding example creates a thread to run a while loop that repaints the clock in a panel every one second. Java animations frequently repaint panels at a predefined rate. For this reason, Java provides the javax.swing.Timer class, which can be used to control repainting a panel at a predefined rate. Using the Timer class dramatically simplifies the program. A Timer object serves as the source of an ActionEvent. It fires an ActionEvent at a fixed rate. The listeners for the event are registered with the Timer object. When you create a Timer object, you have to specify the delay and a listener using the following constructor:

```
public Timer(int delay, ActionListener listener)
```

where delay specifies the number of milliseconds between two action events. You can add additional listeners using the addActionListener method, and adjust the delay using the setDelay method. To start the timer, use the start method. To stop the timer, use the stop method. In the action listener class, you can implement the actionPerformed handler by invoking the repaint method to repaint the panel. This actionPerformed method is invoked at a rate determined by the delay.

Using the Timer class, the preceding Clock class can be modified as follows:

```
package chapter18;

import java.awt.event.*;
import javax.swing.Timer;
```

```
public class ClockWithTimer extends chapter11.StillClock
  implements ActionListener {
  // Create a timer with delay 1000 ms
  protected Timer timer = new Timer(1000, this);

  public void suspend() {
    timer.stop(); // Suspend clock
  }

  public void resume() {
    timer.start(); // Resume clock
  }

  /** Handle the action event */
  public void actionPerformed(ActionEvent e) {
    // Set new time and repaint the clock to display current time
    setCurrentTime();
    repaint();
  }
}
```

NOTE

Using a thread to control animations and using a timer to control animations are two entirely different approaches. The thread approach places the animation control on a separate thread so that it does not interfere with the drawing. The timer approach uses the action event to control the drawing. If your drawings are painted at a fixed rate, use the timer approach, because it can greatly simplify programming.

Example 18.5 Displaying a Bouncing Ball

Problem

Write an applet that displays a ball bouncing in a panel. Use two buttons to suspend and resume the movement, and use a scroll bar to control the bouncing speed, as shown in Figure 18.13.

Figure 18.13 *The ball's movement is controlled by the Suspend and Resume buttons and the scroll bar.*

Solution

Here are the major steps to complete this example:

1. Create a subclass of JPanel named Ball to display a ball bouncing.

2. Create a subclass of JPanel named BallControl to contain the ball with a scroll bar and two control buttons *Suspend* and *Resume*.

3. Create an applet named BounceBallApplet to contain an instance of BallControl and enable the applet to run standalone.

The relationship among these classes is shown in Figure 18.14.

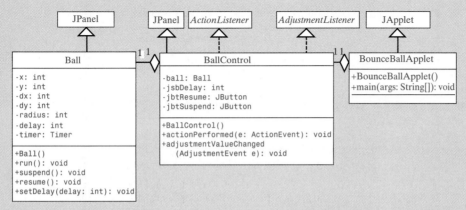

Figure 18.14 BounceBallApplet *contains* BallControl, *and* BallControl *contains* Ball.

```
1    package chapter18;
2
3    import java.awt.event.*;
4    import javax.swing.Timer;
5    import java.awt.*;
6    import javax.swing.*;
7
8    public class Ball extends JPanel implements ActionListener {
9      private int delay = 10;
10
11     // Create a timer with delay 1000 ms
12     protected Timer timer = new Timer(delay, this);
13
14     private int x = 0; private int y = 0; // Current ball position
15     private int radius = 15; // Ball radius
16     private int dx = 2; // Increment on ball's x-coordinate
17     private int dy = 2; // Increment on ball's y-coordinate
18
19     public Ball() {
20       timer.start();
21     }
22
23     /** Handle the action event */
24     public void actionPerformed(ActionEvent e) {
25       repaint();
26     }
27
```

continues

Example 18.5 Continued

```
28        public void paintComponent(Graphics g) {
29          super.paintComponent(g);
30
31          g.setColor(Color.red);
32
33          // Check boundaries
34          if (x < radius) dx = Math.abs(dx);
35          if (x > getWidth() - radius) dx = -Math.abs(dx);
36          if (y < radius) dy = Math.abs(dy);
37          if (y > getHeight() - radius) dy = -Math.abs(dy);
38
39          // Adjust ball position
40          x += dx;
41          y += dy;
42          g.fillOval(x - radius, y - radius, radius * 2, radius * 2);
43        }
44
45        public void suspend() {
46          timer.stop(); // Suspend clock
47        }
48
49        public void resume() {
50          timer.start(); // Resume clock
51        }
52
53        public void setDelay(int delay) {
54          this.delay = delay;
55          timer.setDelay(delay);
56        }
57      }
```

```
1       package chapter18;
2
3       import javax.swing.*;
4       import java.awt.event.*;
5       import java.awt.BorderLayout;
6
7       public class BallControl extends JPanel
8         implements ActionListener, AdjustmentListener {
9         private Ball ball = new Ball();
10        private JButton jbtSuspend = new JButton("Suspend");
11        private JButton jbtResume = new JButton("Resume");
12        private JScrollBar jsbDelay = new JScrollBar();
13
14        public BallControl() {
15          // Group buttons in a panel
16          JPanel panel = new JPanel();
17          panel.add(jbtSuspend);
18          panel.add(jbtResume);
19
20          // Add ball and buttons to the panel
21          ball.setBorder(BorderFactory.createEtchedBorder());
22          jsbDelay.setOrientation(JScrollBar.HORIZONTAL);
23          ball.setDelay(jsbDelay.getMaximum());
24          setLayout(new BorderLayout());
25          add(jsbDelay, BorderLayout.NORTH);
26          add(ball, BorderLayout.CENTER);
27          add(panel, BorderLayout.SOUTH);
28
29          // Register listeners
30          jbtSuspend.addActionListener(this);
31          jbtResume.addActionListener(this);
```

```
32        jsbDelay.addAdjustmentListener(this);
33      }
34
35      public void actionPerformed(ActionEvent e) {
36        if (e.getSource() == jbtSuspend)
37          ball.suspend();
38        else if (e.getSource() == jbtResume)
39          ball.resume();
40      }
41
42      public void adjustmentValueChanged(AdjustmentEvent e) {
43        ball.setDelay(jsbDelay.getMaximum() - e.getValue());
44      }
45    }
```

```
1     package chapter18;
2
3     import java.awt.*;
4     import java.awt.event.*;
5     import java.applet.*;
6     import javax.swing.*;
7
8     public class BounceBallApplet extends JApplet {
9       public BounceBallApplet() {
10        getContentPane().add(new BallControl());
11      }
12
13      public static void main(String[] args) {
14        BounceBallApplet applet = new BounceBallApplet();
15        JFrame frame = new JFrame();
16        frame.setDefaultCloseOperation(JFrame.EXIT_ON_CLOSE);
17        frame.setTitle("Bouncing Ball Control");
18        frame.getContentPane().add(applet, BorderLayout.CENTER);
19        frame.setSize(400, 320);
20        frame.setVisible(true);
21      }
22    }
```

Review

The `Ball` class extends `JPanel` to display a bouncing ball. A `Timer` object is created to enable the ball to be displayed continuously at a fixed rate. The center of the ball is at (x, y), which changes to (x + dx, y + dy) on the next display. The suspend and resume methods (Lines 45–51) can be used to stop and start the timer.

The `BallControl` class extends `JPanel` to display the clock with a scroll bar and two control buttons, implements the `ActionListener` to handle action events from the buttons, and implements the `AdjustmentListener` to handle value change events from the scroll bar. When the Suspend button is clicked, the ball's suspend method is invoked to suspend the ball movement. When the Resume button is clicked, the ball's resume method is invoked to resume the ball movement. The bouncing speed can be changed using the scroll bar.

The `BounceBallApplet` class simply places an instance of `BallControl` in the applet's content pane. The *main* method is provided in the applet so that you can also run it stand-alone.

Chapter Summary

■ You can derive your thread class from the Thread class and create a thread instance to run a task on a separate thread. If your class needs to inherit multiple classes, implement the Runnable interface to run multiple tasks in the program simultaneously.

■ After a thread object is created, use the start method to start a thread, and the sleep method to put a thread to sleep so that other threads get a chance to run. Since the stop, suspend, and resume methods are deprecated in Java 2, you need to implement these methods to stop, suspend, and resume a thread.

■ A thread object never directly invokes the run method. The Java runtime system invokes the run method when it is time to execute the thread. Your class must override the run method to tell the system what the thread will do when it runs.

■ A thread can be in one of five states: new, ready, running, blocked, or finished. When a thread is newly created, it enters the *new state*. After a thread is started by calling its start() method, it enters the *ready state*. A ready thread is runnable but may not be running yet. The operating system has to allocate CPU time to it.

■ When a ready thread begins executing, it enters the *running state*. A running thread may reenter the ready state if its given CPU time expires or its yield() method is called.

■ A thread can enter the *blocked state* (i.e., become inactive) for several reasons. It may have invoked the sleep(), wait(), or suspend() method, or some other thread may have invoked its sleep() or suspend() method. It may be waiting for an I/O operation to finish. A blocked thread may be reactivated when the action inactivating it is reversed. For example, if a thread has been put to sleep and the sleep time has expired, the thread is reactivated and enters the ready state.

■ A thread is *finished* if it completes the execution of its run() method or if its stop() method is invoked.

■ Threads can be assigned priorities. The Java runtime system always executes the ready thread with the highest priority. You can use a thread group to put relevant threads together for group control.

■ To prevent threads from corrupting a shared resource, put the keyword synchronized into the method that may cause corruption.

■ A synchronized method acquires a lock before it executes. In the case of an instance method, the lock is on the object for which the method was invoked. In the case of a static (class) method, the lock is on the class. If one thread invokes a synchronized instance method (respectively, static method) on an object, the lock of that object (respectively, class) is acquired first, then the method is executed, and finally the lock is released. Another thread invoking the same method of that object (respectively, class) is blocked until the lock is released.

808

■ You can use either the thread approach or the timer approach to control Java animations. Using a thread to control animations and using a timer to control animations are two entirely different approaches. The thread approach places the animation control on a separate thread so that it does not interfere with the drawing. The timer approach uses the action event to control the drawing. If your drawings are painted at a fixed rate, use the timer approach, because it can greatly simplify programming.

Review Questions

18.1 Why do you need multithreading capability in applications? How can multiple threads run simultaneously in a single-processor system?

18.2 What are two ways to create threads? When do you use the `Thread` class, and when do you use the `Runnable` interface? What are the differences between the `Thread` class and the `Runnable` interface?

18.3 How do you create a thread and launch a thread object? Which of the following methods are instance methods? Which of them are deprecated in Java 2?

```
run, start, stop, suspend, resume, sleep, isInterrupted
```

18.4 Will the program behave differently if `Thread.sleep(1000)` is replaced by `thread.sleep(1000)` in Example 18.4, "Displaying a Running Clock in an Applet"?

18.5 Explain the life cycle of a thread object.

18.6 How do you set a priority for a thread? What is the default priority?

18.7 Describe a thread group. How do you create a thread group? Can you control an individual thread in a thread group (suspend, resume, stop, etc.)?

18.8 Give some examples of possible resource corruption when running multiple threads. How do you synchronize conflict threads?

18.9 Why does the following class have a runtime error?

```java
class Test extends Thread {
  public static void main(String[] args) {
    Test t = new Test();
    t.start();
    t.start();
  }

  public void run() {
    System.out.println("test");
  }
}
```

18.10 Why does the following class have a syntax error?

```java
import javax.swing.*;

class Test extends JApplet implements Runnable {
  public void init() throws InterruptedException {
    Thread thread = new Thread(this);
```

```
            thread.sleep(1000);
        }

        public synchronized void run() {
        }
    }
```

18.11 How do you override the methods `init`, `start`, `stop`, and `destroy` in the `Applet` class to work well with the threads in the applets?

18.12 How do you use the `Timer` class to control Java animations?

Programming Exercises

18.1 (Displaying a flashing label) Write an applet that displays a flashing label. Enable it to run stand-alone.

✪ HINT

To make the label flash, you need to repaint the panel alternately with the label and without the label (blank screen) at a fixed rate. Use a `boolean` variable to control the alternation.

18.2 (Displaying a moving label) Write an applet that displays a moving label. The label continuously moves from right to left in the applet's viewing area. Whenever the label disappears at the far left of the viewing area, it reappears again on the right-hand side. The label freezes when the mouse is pressed, and moves again when the button is released. Enable it to run as an application.

✪ HINT

Redraw the label with a new x coordinate at a fixed rate.

18.3 (Revising Example 18.1 "Using the `Thread` Class to Create and Launch Threads") Rewrite Example 18.1 to display the output in a text area, as shown in Figure 18.15.

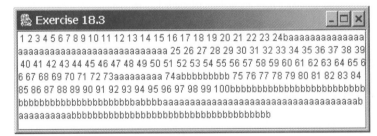

Figure 18.15   *The output from three threads is displayed in a text area.*

18.4 (Synchronizing threads) Write a program that launches one hundred threads. Each thread adds 1 to a variable sum that initially is zero. You need to pass sum by reference to each thread. In order to pass it by reference, define an `Integer`

810

wrapper object to hold sum. Run the program with and without synchronization to see its effect.

18.5 (Revising Example 18.3 "Showing Resource Conflict") Modify Example 18.3 as follows:

■ Create two panels with the titles "Synchronized Threads" and "Unsynchronized Threads," as shown in Figure 18.16. The Synchronized Threads panel displays a piggy bank balance after a penny has been added one hundred times using synchronized threads. The Unsynchronized Threads panel displays a piggy bank balance after a penny has been added one hundred times using unsynchronized threads.

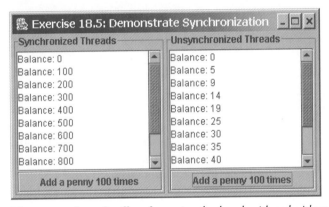

Figure 18.16 *The program shows the effect of executing the threads with and without synchronization.*

■ Since the two panels are very similar, you can create a class to model them uniformly, as shown in Figure 18.17. Use a variable named mode to indicate whether synchronized threads or unsynchronized threads are used in the panel. Invoke the method addAPennyWithSync or addAPennyWithout-Sync, depending on the mode.

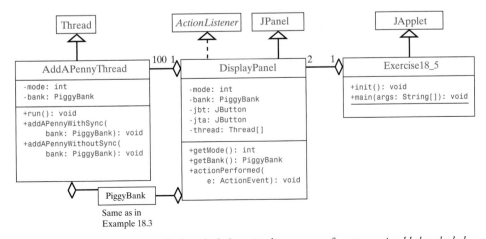

Figure 18.17 DisplayPanel *displays the balance in the text area after a penny is added to the balance one hundred times.*

18.6 (Simulating a stock ticker) Write a Java applet that displays a stock index ticker (see Figure 18.18). The stock index information is passed from the <param> tag in the HTML file. Each index has four parameters: Index Name (e.g., S&P 500), Current Time (e.g., 15:54), the index from the previous day (e.g., 919.01), and Change (e.g., 4.54). Enable the applet to run stand-alone.

Figure 18.18   *The program displays a stock index ticker.*

Use at least five indexes, such as Dow Jones, S&P 500, NASDAQ, NIKKEI, and Gold & Silver Index. Display positive changes in green, and negative changes in red. The indexes move from right to left in the applet's viewing area. The applet freezes the ticker when the mouse button is pressed; it moves again when the mouse button is released.

18.7 (Showing a running fan) Write a Java applet that simulates a running fan, as shown in Figure 18.19. The buttons Start, Stop, and Reverse control the fan. The scrollbar controls the fan's speed. Create a class named Fan, a subclass of

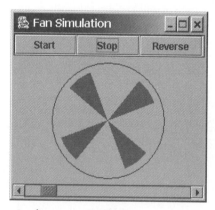

Figure 18.19   *The program simulates a running fan.*

JPanel, to display the fan. This class also contains the methods to suspend and resume the fan, set its speed, and reverse its direction. Create a class named FanControl that contains a fan, and three buttons and a scroll bar to control the fan. Create a Java applet that contains an instance of FanControl. Enable the applet to run stand-alone. The relationships of these classes are shown in Figure 18.20.

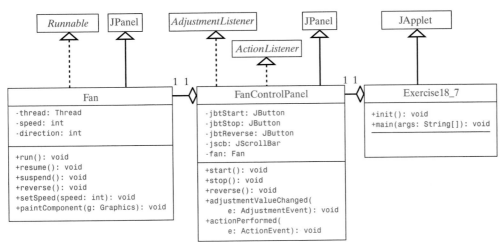

Figure 18.20 *The* `FanControl` *class contains a fan, three buttons, and a scroll bar to control the fan; and the* `Fan` *class displays a running fan.*

18.8 (Controlling a group of fans) Write a Java applet that displays three fans in a group, with control buttons to start and stop all of them, as shown in Figure 18.21. Use the `FanControl` to control and display a single fan. Enable the applet to run stand-alone.

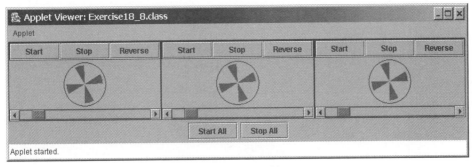

Figure 18.21 *The program runs and controls a group of fans.*

18.9 (Creating an elevator simulator) Write an applet that simulates an elevator going up and down (see Figure 18.22). The buttons on the left indicate the floor where the passenger is now located. The passenger must click a button on the left to request that the elevator come to his or her floor. On entering the elevator, the passenger clicks a button on the right to request that it go to the specified floor. Enable the applet to run stand-alone.

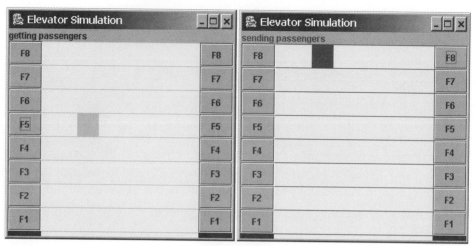

Figure 18.22   *The program simulates elevator operations.*

18.10 (Controlling a group of clocks) Write a Java applet that displays three clocks in a group, with control buttons to start and stop all of them, as shown in Figure 18.23. Use the `ClockControl` to control and display a single clock. Enable the applet to run stand-alone.

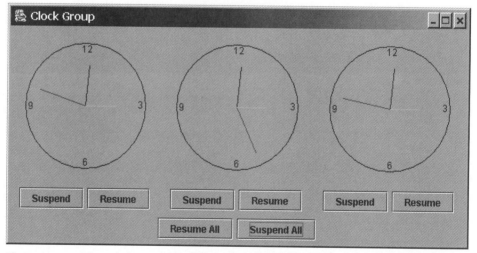

Figure 18.23   *Three clocks run independently with individual control and group control.*

18.11 (The `PiggyBank` class) Add the following method in the `PiggyBank` class:

```
public synchronized void addAPenny() {
  int newBalance = getBalance() + 1;

  try {
    Thread.sleep(5);
  }
  catch (InterruptedException ex) {
    System.out.println(ex);
  }

  setBalance(newBalance);
}
```

814

Modify Example 18.3, "Showing Resource Conflict," to create one hundred threads, each of which runs this method to add a penny to the piggy bank.

Test your program by removing the keyword `synchronized` from the method. You will see that the balance is corrupted.

18.12 (Using synchronized statements) Modify Example 18.3, "Showing Resource Conflict," using a synchronized statement to synchronize access to the `PiggyBank` object.

18.13 (Demonstrating `ConcurrentModificationException`) The iterator is *fail-fast*. This means that if you are using an iterator to traverse a collection while the underlying collection is being modified by another thread, then the iterator fails immediately by throwing `java.util.ConcurrentModificationException`. Since this exception is a subclass of `RuntimeException`, you don't have to place the methods of `Iterator` in a try-catch block. Create a program with two threads concurrently accessing and modifying a set. The first thread creates a hash set filled with numbers, and adds a new number to the set every second. The second thread obtains an iterator for the set and traverses the set back and forth through the iterator every second. You will receive a `ConcurrentModificationException`, because, while the set in the second thread is being traversed, the underlying set is being modified in the first thread.

18.14 (Using synchronized sets) Correct the problem in the preceding exercise using synchronization so that the second thread does not throw `ConcurrentModificationException`. You will have to use the `Collections.synchronizedSet(set)` method to obtain a synchronized set and acquire a lock on the returned set when traversing it. It is, however, imperative for a thread to acquire a lock on the synchronized list, set, or map when traversing it through an iterator, as shown in the following code:

```
Set hashSet = Collections.synchronizedSet(new HashSet());

synchronized (hashSet) { // Must synchronize it
  Iterator iterator = hashSet.iterator();

  while (iterator.hasNext()) {
    System.out.println(iterator.next());
  }
}
```

Failure to do so may result in nondeterministic behavior, such as `ConcurrentModificationException`.

MULTIMEDIA

Objectives

- ◉ To develop multimedia applications with audio and images.
- ◉ To get audio files and play sound in Java applets.
- ◉ To get image files and display images in Java applets.
- ◉ To display images and play audio in Java applications.
- ◉ To use `MediaTracker` to ensure that images are completely loaded before they are displayed.

19.1   Introduction

Welcome to the fascinating world of *multimedia*. You have seen computer animation used every day in TV and movies. When surfing the Web, you have seen sites with text, images, sounds, animation, and movie clips. These are examples of multimedia at work.

Multimedia is a broad term that encompasses making, storing, retrieving, transferring, and presenting various types of information, such as text, graphics, pictures, videos, and sound. Multimedia involves a complex weave of communications, electronics, and computer technologies. It is beyond the scope of this book to cover multimedia in great detail. This chapter concentrates on the presentation of multimedia in Java.

Whereas most programming languages have no built-in multimedia capabilities, Java was designed with multimedia in mind. It provides extensive built-in support that makes it easy to develop powerful multimedia applications. Java's multimedia capabilities include animation that uses drawings, audio, and images.

You have already used animation with drawings in the examples that simulated a clock, and you used the icons in the Swing components. In this chapter, you will learn how to develop Java programs with audio and images.

19.2   Playing Audio

Audio is stored in files. There are several formats of audio files. Prior to Java 2, sound files in the AU format used on the UNIX operating system were the only ones Java was able to play. With Java 2, you can play sound files in the WAV, AIFF, MIDI, AU, and RMF formats, with better sound quality.

To play an audio file in an applet, you use the following `play` method in the `Applet` class:

```
public void play(URL url, String filename);
```

This method downloads the audio file from the `url` and plays the audio in the file. Nothing happens if the audio file cannot be found.

The URL (Universal Resource Locator) describes the location of a resource on the Internet. Java provides a class that is used to manipulate URLs: `java.net.URL`. Java's security mechanism restricts all files read via a browser to the directory where the HTML file is stored or to the subdirectory of that location. You can use `getCodeBase()` to get the URL of the applet (.class file), or `getDocumentBase()` to get the URL of the HTML file that contains the applet. These two methods, `getCodeBase()` and `getDocumentBase()`, are defined in the `Applet` class:

```
play(getCodeBase(), "soundfile.au");
play(getDocumentBase(), "soundfile.au");
```

The former method plays the sound file soundfile.au, which is located in the code base directory specified by the `codebase` attribute in the `<applet>` tag. The latter method plays the sound file soundfile.au, which is located in the HTML file's directory.

The statement `play(url, filename)` downloads the audio file every time you play the audio. If you want to play the audio many times, you can create an *audio clip object* for the file. The audio clip is created once and can be played repeatedly without reloading the file. To create an audio clip, use either of the following methods:

```
public AudioClip getAudioClip(URL url);
public AudioClip getAudioClip(URL url, String name);
```

In order to specify a sound file, the former requires an absolute URL address; the latter lets you use a relative URL with the file name. Using the absolute URL address will be introduced in Bonus Chapter 21, "Networking." The relative URL is obtained by using `getCodeBase()` or `getDocumentBase()`. For example, the following statement creates an audio clip for the file soundfile.au that is stored in the same directory as the applet that contains the statement.

```
AudioClip ac = getAudioClip(getCodeBase(), "soundfile.au");
```

To manipulate a sound for an audio clip, use the following instance methods of `java.applet.AudioClip`:

■ `public void play()`

Plays the clip once. The clip is restarted from the beginning every time the method is called.

■ `public void loop()`

Plays the clip repeatedly.

■ `public void stop()`

Stops playing the clip.

Example 19.1 Incorporating Sound in Applets

Problem

Example 18.4, "Displaying a Running Clock in an Applet," displays a running clock. Rewrite the program so that it plays sound files that announce the time at one-minute intervals. For example, if the current time is 6:30:00, the applet announces, "The time is six-thirty A.M." If the current time is 20:20:00, the applet announces, "The time is eight-twenty P.M." Also add a label to display the digit time, as shown in Figure 19.1.

continues

Example 19.1 Continued

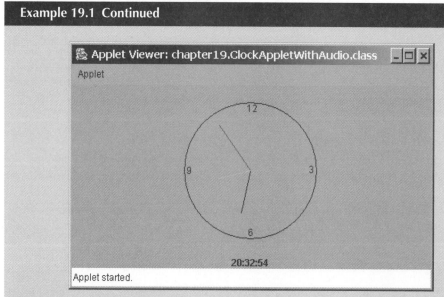

Figure 19.1   *Given the image file name, the applet displays an image.*

Solution

Create an applet named ClockAppletWithAudio that contains an instance of StillClock to display an analog clock, and an instance of JLabel to display the digit time. The StillClock class was given in Example 11.6, "Drawing a Clock." Override the init method to load the audio files. Use a Timer object to set and display the current time continuously at a fixed rate. When the second is zero, announce the current time.

```
1    // ClockAppletWithAudio.java: Display a running clock on the applet
2    // with audio
3    package chapter19;
4
5    import java.applet.*;
6    import javax.swing.*;
7    import java.awt.event.*;
8    import java.awt.*;
9    import chapter11.StillClock;
10
11   public class ClockAppletWithAudio extends JApplet
12     implements ActionListener {
13     // Declare audio files
14     protected AudioClip[] hourAudio = new AudioClip[12];
15     protected AudioClip minuteAudio;
16     protected AudioClip amAudio;
17     protected AudioClip pmAudio;
18
19     // Create a clock
20     private StillClock clock = new StillClock();
21
22     // Create a timer
23     private Timer timer = new Timer(1000, this);
24
```

```
25        // Create a label to display time
26        private JLabel jlblDigitTime = new JLabel("", JLabel.CENTER);
27
28        /** Initialize the applet */
29        public void init() {
30          // Create audio clips for pronouncing hours
31          for (int i = 0; i < 12; i++)
32            hourAudio[i] = getAudioClip(getCodeBase(),
33              "timeaudio/hour" + i + ".au");
34
35          // Create audio clips for pronouncing am and pm
36          amAudio = getAudioClip(getCodeBase(), "timeaudio/am.au");
37          pmAudio = getAudioClip(getCodeBase(), "timeaudio/pm.au");
38
39          // Add clock and time label to the content pane of the applet
40          getContentPane().add(clock, BorderLayout.CENTER);
41          getContentPane().add(jlblDigitTime, BorderLayout.SOUTH);
42        }
43
44        /** Override the applet's start method */
45        public void start() {
46          timer.start(); // Resume clock
47        }
48
49        /** Override the applet's stop method */
50        public void stop() {
51          timer.stop(); // Suspend clock
52        }
53
54        public void actionPerformed(ActionEvent e) {
55            clock.setCurrentTime();
56            clock.repaint();
57            jlblDigitTime.setText(clock.getHour() + ":" + clock.getMinute()
58              + ":" + clock.getSecond());
59            if (clock.getSecond() == 0)
60              announceTime(clock.getMinute(), clock.getHour());
61        }
62
63        /** Announce the current time at every minute */
64        public void announceTime(int m, int h) {
65          // Announce hour
66          hourAudio[h % 12].play();
67
68          // Load the minute file
69          minuteAudio = getAudioClip(getCodeBase(),
70            "timeaudio/minute" + m + ".au");
71
72          // Time delay to allow hourAudio play to finish
73          try {
74            Thread.sleep(1500);
75          }
76          catch(InterruptedException ex) {
77          }
78
79          // Announce minute
80          minuteAudio.play();
81
82          // Time delay to allow minuteAudio play to finish
83          try {
84            Thread.sleep(1500);
85          }
```

continues

Example 19.1 Continued

```
86          catch(InterruptedException ex) {
87          }
88
89          // Announce am or pm
90          if (h < 12)
91            amAudio.play();
92          else
93            pmAudio.play();
94        }
95      }
```

Review

The hourAudio is an array of twelve audio clips that are used to announce the twelve hours of the day (Line 14); the minuteAudio is an audio clip that is used to announce the minute in an hour (Line 15). The amAudio announces A.M. (Line 16); the pmAudio announces P.M. (Line 17).

The init() method creates audio clips for announcing time (Lines 31–37) and places a clock and a label in the applet (Lines 40–41).

All of the audio files are stored in the directory timeaudio, a subdirectory of the applet's directory. The twelve audio clips that are used to announce the hours are stored in the files **hour0.au**, **hour1.au**, and so on, to **hour11.au**. They are loaded using the following loop (Lines 31–33):

```
for (int i = 0; i < 12; i++)
  hourAudio[i] = getAudioClip(getCodeBase(),
    "timeaudio/hour" + i + ".au");
```

Similarly, the amAudio clip is stored in the file **am.au**, and the pmAudio clip is stored in the file **pm.au**; they are loaded along with the hour clips in the init() method (Lines 36–37).

The program created an array of twelve audio clips to announce each of the twelve hours, but did not create sixty audio clips to announce each of the minutes. Instead, it created and loaded the minute audio clip (Lines 69–70) when needed in the announceTime method. The audio files are very large. Loading all sixty audio clips at once may cause an OutOfMemoryError exception.

In the announceTime method (Lines 64–94), the sleep() method (Lines 74, 84) is purposely invoked to ensure that one clip finishes before the next clip starts, so that the clips do not interfere with each other.

An ActionEvent is fired by the timer at every one second. In the actionPerformed method (Lines 54–61), the clock is repainted with the new current time and the digit time is displayed in the label.

The applet's start and stop methods (Lines 44–52) are overridden to ensure that the timer is started or stopped when the applet is restarted or stopped.

19.3   Running Audio on a Separate Thread

If you ran the preceding program, you noticed that the second hand did not display at the first, second, and third seconds of the minute. This is because `sleep(1500)` was invoked twice in the `announceTime()` method, which takes three seconds to announce the time at the beginning of each minute. Thus, the `actionPerformed` method is delayed for three seconds during the first three seconds of each minute. As a result of this delay, the time is not updated and the clock was not repainted for these three seconds. To avoid the conflict, you should announce the time on a separate thread. This problem is fixed in the following program.

Example 19.2 Announcing the Time on a Separate Thread

Problem

To avoid a conflict between the timer and announcing the time, write a program that runs these tasks on separate threads.

Solution

The solution is to announce time on a separate thread, as follows:

```
1   // ClockAppletWithAudioOnSeparateThread.java: Display a
2   // running clock on the applet with audio on a separate thread
3   package chapter19;
4
5   import java.applet.*;
6
7   public class ClockAppletWithAudioOnSeparateThread
8      extends ClockAppletWithAudio {
9      // Declare a thread for announcing time
10     AnnounceTime announceTime;
11
12     /** Override this method defined in ClockAppletWithAudio
13        to announce the current time at every minute */
14     public void announceTime(int m, int h) {
15        // Load the minute file
16        minuteAudio = getAudioClip(getCodeBase(),
17          "timeaudio/minute" + m + ".au");
18
19        // Announce current time
20        if (h < 12)
21          announceTime = new AnnounceTime(hourAudio[h % 12],
22            minuteAudio, amAudio);
23        else
24          announceTime = new AnnounceTime(hourAudio[h % 12],
25            minuteAudio, pmAudio);
26
27        announceTime.start();
28     }
29   }
30
31   // Define a thread class for announcing time
32   class AnnounceTime extends Thread {
33     private AudioClip hourAudio, minuteAudio, amPM;
34
```

continues

Example 19.2 Continued

```
35        /** Get Audio clips */
36        public AnnounceTime(AudioClip hourAudio,
37                            AudioClip minuteAudio,
38                            AudioClip amPM) {
39          this.hourAudio = hourAudio;
40          this.minuteAudio = minuteAudio;
41          this.amPM = amPM;
42        }
43
44        public void run() {
45          // Announce hour
46          hourAudio.play();
47
48          // Time delay to allow hourAudio play to finish
49          // before playing the clip
50          try {
51            Thread.sleep(1500);
52          }
53          catch(InterruptedException ex) {
54          }
55
56          // Announce minute
57          minuteAudio.play();
58
59          // Time delay to allow minuteAudio play to finish
60          try {
61            Thread.sleep(1500);
62          }
63          catch(InterruptedException ex) {
64          }
65
66          // Announce am or pm
67          amPM.play();
68        }
69      }
```

Review

The program extends ClockAppletWithAudio (Line 8) with the capability to announce time without delaying the actionPerformed method. The program defines a new thread class, AnnounceTime (Lines 32–68), which is derived from the Thread class. This new class plays audio.

To create an instance of the AnnounceTime class, you need to pass the three audio clips used to announce the hour, the minute, and A.M. or P.M (Lines 21–22, 24–25).

When running this program, you will discover that the audio does not interfere with the clock animation because an instance of AnnounceTime starts on a separate thread to announce the current time. This thread is independent of the thread on which the actionPerformed method runs.

An object of AnnounceTime is created every minute to announce the current time. The program can be improved to run more efficiently by creating one such object in advance and passing hour audio, minute audio, and AM/PM audio to the object when it is time to announce the current time. See Exercise 19.12.

19.4   Displaying Images

In Example 13.2, "Using Labels," and Example 13.14, "Using Scroll Panes," you used the ImageIcon class to create an icon from an image file and the setIcon method to place the image in a UI component, such as a label. These examples are only applicable to Java applications and are not suitable for Java applets, because the image files are directly accessed from the local file system.

To display an image in Java applets, you need to load the image from an Internet source, using the getImage method in the Applet class. This method returns a java.awt.Image object. Two versions of the getImage method are shown below:

- `public Image getImage(URL url)`

  Loads the image from the specified URL.

- `public Image getImage(URL url, String filename)`

  Loads the image file from the specified file at the given URL.

⬥ **NOTE**

When the getImage method is invoked, it launches a separate thread to load the image, which enables the program to continue while the image is being retrieved.

Once you have an Image instance for the image file, you can create an ImageIcon using the following method:

```
ImageIcon imageIcon = new ImageIcon(image);
```

You can now convert Examples 13.2 and 13.14 to Java applets and use the getImage method to load the image files. Using a label as an area for displaying images is simple and convenient, but you don't have much control over how the image is displayed. A more flexible way to display images is to use the drawImage method of the Graphics class on a panel.

Here are four versions of the drawImage method:

- `drawImage(Image img, int x, int y, Color bgcolor, ImageObserver observer)`

  Draws the image in a specified location. The image's top-left corner is at (x, y) in the graphics context's coordinate space. Transparent pixels in the image are drawn in the specified color bgcolor. The observer is the object on which the image is displayed. The image is cut off if it is larger than the area it is being drawn on.

- `drawImage(Image img, int x, int y, ImageObserver observer)`

  This is the same as the preceding method except that it does not specify a background color.

■ drawImage(Image img, int x, int y, int width, int height, ImageObserver observer)

Draws a scaled version of the image that can fill all of the available space in the specified rectangle.

■ drawImage(Image img, int x, int y, int width, int height, Color bgcolor, ImageObserver observer)

This is the same as the preceding method except that it provides a solid background color behind the image being drawn.

ImageObserver is an asynchronous update interface that receives notifications of image information as the image is constructed. The Component class implements ImageObserver. Therefore, every GUI component is an instance of ImageObserver. To draw images using the drawImage method in a Swing component, such as JPanel, override the paintComponent method to tell the component how to display the image in the panel.

Example 19.3 Displaying Images in an Applet

Problem

Write a program that displays an image in an applet. The image is stored in a file located in the same directory as the applet. The user enters the file name in a text field and displays the image on a panel. Figure 19.2 shows a sample run of the program.

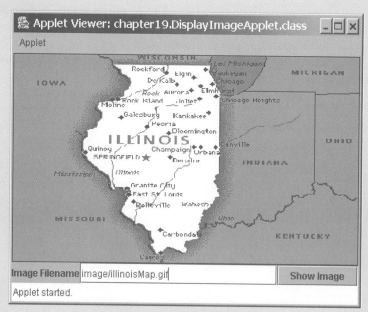

Figure 19.2   *Given the image file name, the applet displays an image.*

Solution

The following code gives the solution to the problem.

```
1   // DisplayImageApplet.java: Display an image on a panel in the applet
2   package chapter19;
3
4   import java.awt.*;
5   import java.awt.event.*;
6   import javax.swing.*;
7   import javax.swing.border.LineBorder;
8
9   public class DisplayImageApplet extends JApplet
10    implements ActionListener {
11    // The panel for displaying the image  private
12    private ImagePanel imagePanel = new ImagePanel();
13
14    // The text field for entering the name of the image file
15    private JTextField jtfFilename = new JTextField(20);
16
17    // The button for displaying the image
18    private JButton jbtShow = new JButton("Show Image");
19
20    /** Initialize the applet */
21    public void init() {
22      // Panel p1 to hold a text field and a button
23      JPanel p1 = new JPanel();
24      p1.setLayout(new BorderLayout());
25      p1.add(new JLabel("Image Filename"), BorderLayout.WEST);
26      p1.add(jtfFilename, BorderLayout.CENTER);
27      p1.add(jbtShow, BorderLayout.EAST);
28
29      // Place an ImagePanel object and p1 in the applet
30      getContentPane().add(imagePanel, BorderLayout.CENTER);
31      getContentPane().add(p1, BorderLayout.SOUTH);
32
33      // Set line border on the image panel
34      imagePanel.setBorder(new LineBorder(Color.black, 1));
35
36      // Register listener
37      jbtShow.addActionListener(this);
38      jtfFilename.addActionListener(this);
39    }
40
41    /** Handle the ActionEvent */
42    public void actionPerformed(ActionEvent e) {
43      if ((e.getSource() instanceof JButton) ||
44        (e.getSource() instanceof JTextField))
45        displayImage();
46    }
47
48    /** Display image on the panel */
49    private void displayImage() {
50      // Retrieve image
51      Image image = getImage(getCodeBase(),
52        jtfFilename.getText().trim());
53
54      // Show image in the panel
55      imagePanel.showImage(image);
56    }
57  }
58
```

continues

827

Example 19.3 Continued

```
59      // Define the panel for showing an image
60      class ImagePanel extends JPanel {
61        // Image instance
62        private Image image = null;
63
64        /** Default constructor */
65        public ImagePanel() {
66        }
67
68        /** Set image and show it */
69        public void showImage(Image image) {
70          this.image = image;
71          repaint();
72        }
73
74        /** Draw image on the panel */
75        public void paintComponent(Graphics g) {
76          super.paintComponent(g);
77
78          if (image != null)
79            g.drawImage(image, 0, 0, getWidth(), getHeight(), this);
80        }
81      }
```

Review

The image is loaded by using the `getImage` method (Lines 51–52) from the file in the same directory as the applet. The `showImage` method defined in `ImagePanel` sets the image so that it can be drawn in the `paintComponent` method.

The statement `g.drawImage(image, 0, 0, getWidth(), getHeight(), this)` (Line 79) displays the image in the `Graphics` context g on the `ImagePanel` object. To display the image, you enter the file name in the text field, then press the Enter key or click the Show Image button. The file name you enter must be located in the same directory as the applet or in one of its subdirectories.

19.5   Loading Image and Audio Files in Java Applications

The `getImage` method used in Example 19.3, "Displaying Images in an Applet," is defined in the `Applet` class, and thus is only available with the applet. The audio files in Example 19.1, "Incorporating Sound in Applets," are loaded through the URL specified by the `getCodeBase()` method, and thus this method of retrieving audio files cannot be used with Java applications.

To write code that can be used to load resource files for both applications and applets, use the `java.lang.Class` class. Whenever the Java Virtual Machine loads a class or an interface, it creates an instance of a special class named `Class`. The `Class` class provides access to useful information about the class, such as the data fields and methods. It also contains the `getResource(filename)` method, which can be used to obtain the URL of a given file name in the same directory with the class or in its subdirectory. As discussed in Section 8.10.3, "The `getClass` Method," you can obtain the class for the object at runtime. Thus, you can use the following code to get the URL of an image or audio file:

```
Class thisClass = this.getClass();
URL url = thisClass.getResource(filename);
```

To get an audio clip, use a new static method `newAudioClip()` in the `java.applet.Applet` class in Java 2:

```
AudioClip audioClip = Applet.newAudioClip(url);
```

You might attempt to use the `getImage` method to obtain an `Image` object:

```
Image image = getImage(url);
```

This method would work fine for Java applets, but not for Java applications. To get an `Image` object from the URL in a Java application, construct an `ImageIcon` object using the new `ImageIcon(url)`, and obtain an image using the `getImage()` method in the `ImageIcon` class, as follows:

```
// Obtain an image icon
ImageIcon imageIcon = new ImageIcon(url);

// Get the image from the image icon
Image image = imageIcon.getImage();
```

Example 19.4 Using Image and Audio in Applications and in Applets

Problem

Write a program that uses the `Class` class to obtain the URLs of the image and the audio resource, which are located in the program's class directory. The program enables you to select a country from a combo box and then displays the country's flag. You can play the selected country's national anthem by clicking the Play Anthem button, as shown in Figure 19.3.

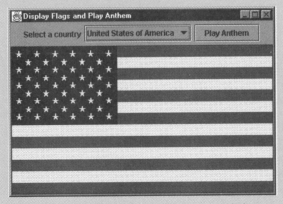

Figure 19.3   *The program displays the flag of the selected country and plays its national anthem.*

continues

Example 19.4 Continued

Solution

The following code gives the solution to the problem.

```java
1    // ResourceLocatorDemo.java: Demonstrate using resource locator to
2    // load image files and audio files to applets and applications
3    package chapter19;
4
5    import java.awt.*;
6    import java.awt.image.*;
7    import java.awt.event.*;
8    import javax.swing.*;
9    import javax.swing.border.*;
10   import java.net.URL;
11   import java.applet.*;
12
13   public class ResourceLocatorDemo extends JApplet
14     implements ActionListener, ItemListener {
15     // Image panel for displaying an image
16     private ImagePanel imagePanel = new ImagePanel();
17
18     // Combo box for selecting a country
19     private JComboBox jcboCountry = new JComboBox();
20
21     // Button to play an audio
22     private JButton jbtPlayAnthem = new JButton("Play Anthem");
23
24     // Selected country
25     private String country = "United States of America";
26
27     /** Initialize the applet */
28     public void init() {
29       // Panel p to hold a label combo box and a button for play audio
30       JPanel p = new JPanel();
31       p.add(new JLabel("Select a country"));
32       p.add(jcboCountry);
33       p.add(jbtPlayAnthem);
34
35       // Initialize the combo box
36       jcboCountry.addItem("United States of America");
37       jcboCountry.addItem("United Kingdom");
38       jcboCountry.addItem("Denmark");
39       jcboCountry.addItem("Norway");
40       jcboCountry.addItem("China");
41       jcboCountry.addItem("India");
42       jcboCountry.addItem("Germany");
43
44       // By default, the US flag is displayed
45       imagePanel.showImage(createImage("us.gif"));
46       imagePanel.setPreferredSize(new Dimension(300, 300));
47
48       // Place p and an image panel in the applet
49       getContentPane().add(p, BorderLayout.NORTH);
50       getContentPane().add(imagePanel, BorderLayout.CENTER);
51       imagePanel.setBorder(new LineBorder(Color.black, 1));
52
53       // Register listener
54       jbtPlayAnthem.addActionListener(this);
55       jcboCountry.addItemListener(this);
56     }
57
```

```
58      /** Handle ActionEvent */
59      public void actionPerformed(ActionEvent e) {
60        // Get the file name
61        String filename = null;
62
63        // The .mid audio files are stored in the anthem folder
64        if (country.equals("United States of America"))
65          filename = "us.mid";
66        else if (country.equals("United Kingdom"))
67          filename = "uk.mid";
68        else if (country.equals("Denmark"))
69          filename = "denmark.mid";
70        else if (country.equals("Norway"))
71          filename = "norway.mid";
72        else if (country.equals("China"))
73          filename = "china.mid";
74        else if (country.equals("India"))
75          filename = "india.mid";
76        else if (country.equals("Germany"))
77          filename = "germany.mid";
78
79        // Create an audio clip and play it
80        createAudioClip(filename).play();
81      }
82
83      /** Handle ItemEvent */
84      public void itemStateChanged(ItemEvent e) {
85        // Get selected country
86        country = (String)jcboCountry.getSelectedItem();
87
88        // Get the file name
89        String filename = null;
90
91        // The .gif files are stored in the image folder
92        if (country.equals("United States of America"))
93          filename = "us.gif";
94        else if (country.equals("United Kingdom"))
95          filename = "uk.gif";
96        else if (country.equals("Denmark"))
97          filename = "denmark.gif";
98        else if (country.equals("Norway"))
99          filename = "norway.gif";
100       else if (country.equals("China"))
101         filename = "china.gif";
102       else if (country.equals("India"))
103         filename = "india.gif";
104       else if (country.equals("Germany"))
105         filename = "germany.gif";
106
107       // Load image from the file and show it on the panel
108       imagePanel.showImage(createImage(filename));
109     }
110
111     /** Create an audio from the specified file */
112     public AudioClip createAudioClip(String filename) {
113       // Get the URL for the file name
114       URL url = this.getClass().getResource("anthem/" + filename);
115
116       // Return the audio clip
117       return Applet.newAudioClip(url);
118     }
119
```

continues

831

Example 19.4 Continued

```
120        /** Create an image from the specified file */
121        public Image createImage(String filename) {
122          // Get the URL for the file name
123          URL url = this.getClass().getResource("image/" + filename);
124
125          // Obtain an image icon
126          ImageIcon imageIcon = new ImageIcon(url);
127
128          // Return the image
129          return imageIcon.getImage();
130        }
131
132        /** Main method */
133        public static void main(String[] args) {
134          // Create a frame
135          JFrame frame = new JFrame("Display Flags and Play Anthem");
136
137          // Create an instance of the applet
138          ResourceLocatorDemo applet = new ResourceLocatorDemo();
139
140          // Add the applet instance to the frame
141          frame.getContentPane().add(applet, BorderLayout.CENTER);
142
143          // Invoke init() and start()
144          applet.init();
145          applet.start();
146
147          // Display the frame
148          frame.pack();
149          frame.setVisible(true);
150        }
151      }
```

Review

The program can run as an applet or an application. Obtaining the URL using the `Class` class works not only for stand-alone applications, but also for Java applets.

The `createAudioClip(filename)` method (Lines 112–118) obtains the URL instance for the file name and creates an `AudioClip` for the URL using the `newAudioClip` static method, which is a new method introduced in Java 2 to support playing audio in applications.

The `createImage(filename)` method (Lines 121–130) obtains the URL instance for the file name, creates an image icon for the URL, and obtains an `Image` object, using the `getImage` method in the `ImageIcon` class.

The program is not efficient if the user repeatedly chooses the same country and plays the same anthem, because a new `Image` instance is created for every newly selected country, and a new `AudioClip` instance is created every time an audio is played. To improve efficiency, load the image and audio files once and store them in the memory using an array.

There is an annoying problem in the program. If you play a new anthem before the preceding anthem is finished, the two audio clips play concurrently. To fix it, stop the first audio clip before playing the new one. See Exercise 19.11.

19.6   Displaying a Sequence of Images

In the preceding section, you learned how to display a single image. Now you will learn how to display a sequence of images that simulates a movie. As in the clock example in Chapter 18, "Multithreading," you can use the thread approach or the timer approach to control the animation. Since the timer approach makes programs shorter and simpler, this example uses a timer to trigger repainting of the viewing area with different images.

Example 19.5 Using Image Animation

Problem

Write a program that displays a sequence of images in order to create a movie. The images are files stored in the **image** directory that are named **L1.gif**, **L2.gif**, and so on, to **L52.gif**. When you run the program, you will see a phrase entitled "Learning Java" rotate, as shown in Figure 19.4.

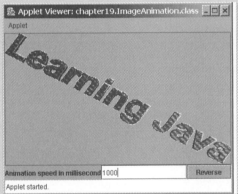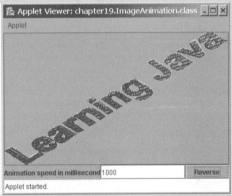

Figure 19.4   *The applet displays a sequence of images.*

Solution

The following code gives the solution to the problem.

```
1    // ImageAnimation.java: Display a sequence of images
2    package chapter19;
3
4    import java.awt.*;
5    import java.awt.event.*;
6    import javax.swing.*;
7    import javax.swing.border.*;
8
9    public class ImageAnimation extends JApplet
10     implements ActionListener {
11     // Total number of images
12     public final static int NUM_OF_IMAGES = 52;
13     private Image imageToDisplay;
14     protected Image imageArray[]; // Hold images
```

continues

Example 19.5 Continued

```
15      protected int currentImageIndex = 0, // Current image subscript
16                     sleepTime = 100; // Milliseconds to sleep
17      protected int direction = 1; // Image rotating direction
18
19      // Image display panel
20      protected PlayImage imagePanel = new PlayImage();
21
22      // Text field for receiving speed
23      protected JTextField jtfSpeed = new JTextField(5);
24
25      // Button for reversing direction
26      JButton jbtReverse = new JButton("Reverse");
27
28      /** Initialize the applet */
29      public void init() {
30        // Load the image, the image files are named
31        // L1 - L52 in image directory
32        imageArray = new Image[NUM_OF_IMAGES];
33        for (int i = 0; i < imageArray.length; i++ ) {
34          imageArray[i] = getImage(getCodeBase(),
35            "image/L" + (i + 1) + ".gif" );
36        }
37
38        // Panel p to hold animation control
39        JPanel p = new JPanel();
40        p.setLayout(new BorderLayout());
41        p.add(new JLabel("Animation speed in millisecond"),
42          BorderLayout.WEST);
43        p.add(jtfSpeed, BorderLayout.CENTER);
44        p.add(jbtReverse, BorderLayout.EAST);
45
46        // Add the image panel and p to the applet
47        getContentPane().add(imagePanel, BorderLayout.CENTER);
48        getContentPane().add(p, BorderLayout.SOUTH);
49
50        // Register listener
51        jtfSpeed.addActionListener(this);
52        jbtReverse.addActionListener(this);
53      }
54
55      /** Handle ActionEvent */
56      public void actionPerformed(ActionEvent e) {
57        if (e.getSource() == jtfSpeed) {
58          sleepTime = Integer.parseInt(jtfSpeed.getText());
59          imagePanel.setSpeed(sleepTime);
60        }
61        else if (e.getSource() == jbtReverse) {
62          direction = -direction;
63        }
64      }
65
66      /** Override the start method in the Applet class */
67      public void start() {
68        imagePanel.start();
69      }
70
71      /** Override the stop method in the Applet class */
72      public void stop() {
73        imagePanel.stop();
74      }
75
```

```
76        protected class PlayImage extends JPanel
77          implements ActionListener {
78          protected Timer timer;
79
80          /** Constructor */
81          public PlayImage() {
82            // Start with the first image
83            currentImageIndex = 0;
84
85            // Set line border on the panel
86            setBorder(new LineBorder(Color.red, 1));
87
88            // Create a timer with delay 1000 ms and listener Clock
89            timer = new Timer(1000, this);
90
91            // Start the timer
92            timer.start();
93          }
94
95          public void setSpeed(int sleepTime) {
96            timer.setDelay(sleepTime);
97          }
99
100         public void start() {
101           timer.start();
102         }
103
104         public void stop() {
105           timer.stop();
106         }
107
108         // Choose a new image to display
109         public void actionPerformed(ActionEvent e) {
110           imageToDisplay =
111             imageArray[currentImageIndex % NUM_OF_IMAGES];
112
113           // Make sure currentImageIndex is nonnegative
114           if (currentImageIndex == 0) currentImageIndex = NUM_OF_IMAGES;
115           currentImageIndex = currentImageIndex + direction;
116           repaint();
117         }
118
119         /** Display an image */
120         public void paintComponent(Graphics g) {
121           super.paintComponent(g);
122
123           if (imageToDisplay != null) {
124             g.drawImage(imageToDisplay, 0, 0, getWidth(),
125               getHeight(), this);
126           }
127         }
128       }
129     }
```

Review

Fifty-two image files are located in the **image** directory, which is a subdirectory of the code base directory. The images in these files are loaded to `imageArray` (Lines 32–35) and then painted continuously on the applet at a fixed rate using a timer.

continues

835

Example 19.5 Continued

The image is drawn to occupy the entire applet viewing area in a rectangle. It is scaled to fill in the area.

The `timer` is created and started in the `PlayImage` class's constructor (Lines 88–92). `PlayImage` is an inner class in `ImageAnimation`. `PlayImage` controls the display of the images. An instance of `PlayImage`, `imagePanel`, is created in Line 20 and placed into the applet in Line 47.

You can adjust `sleepTime` to control animation speed by entering a value in milliseconds and pressing the Enter key for the change to take place.

The display sequence can be reversed by clicking the Reverse button.

You can add a simple function to suspend a `timer` when the mouse is pressed. You can resume a suspended `timer` when the mouse is released (see Exercise 19.4).

◈ NOTE

The `JComponent` class has a property named `doubleBuffered`. By default, this property is set to `true`. Double buffering is a technique for reducing animation flickering. It creates a graphics context off-screen and does all the drawings in the off-screen context. When the drawing is complete, it displays the whole context on the real screen. Thus, there is no flickering within an image because all the drawings are displayed at the same time. To see the effect of double buffering, set the `doubleBuffered` property to false. You will be stunned by the difference.

19.7   Using MediaTracker

One problem you may face if you run the preceding example is that images are only partially displayed while being loaded. This occurs because the image has not yet been loaded completely. The problem is particularly annoying when you are downloading an image over a slow modem.

To resolve the problem, Java provides the `MediaTracker` class to track the status of a number of media objects. Media objects include audio clips as well as images, though currently only images are supported.

You can use `MediaTracker` to determine whether an image has been completely loaded. To use it, you must first create an instance of `MediaTracker` for a specific graphics component. The following is an example of creating a `MediaTracker`:

```
MediaTracker imageTracker = new MediaTracker(this);
```

To enable `imageTracker` (in order to determine whether the image has been loaded), use the `addImage` method to register the image with `imageTracker`. The following statement registers `anImage` of the `Image` type with `imageTracker`:

```
imageTracker.addImage(anImage, id);
```

The second argument, id, is an integer ID that controls the priority order in which the images are fetched. Images with a lower ID number are loaded in preference to those with a higher ID number. The ID can be used to query imageTracker about the status of the registered image. To query, use the checkID method. For example, the following method returns true if the image with the id is completely loaded:

```
checkID(id)
```

Otherwise, it returns false.

You can use the waitForID(id) method to force the program to wait until the image registered with the id is completely loaded, or you can use the waitForAll() method to wait for all of the registered images to be loaded completely. The methods shown below blocks the program until the image is completely loaded.

```
waitForID(int id) throws InterruptedException
waitForAll() throws InterruptedException
```

 TIP

To track multiple images as a group, register them with a media tracker using the same ID.

Example 19.6 Using MediaTracker

Problem

This example uses MediaTracker to improve upon the preceding example. With MediaTracker, the user of the program can ensure that all of the images are fully loaded before they are displayed.

Solution

The following code gives the solution to the problem.

```
1   // ImageAnimationUsingMediaTracker.java: Monitor loading images
2   // using MediaTracker
3   package chapter19;
4
5   import java.awt.*;
6   import javax.swing.*;
7
8   public class ImageAnimationUsingMediaTracker
9     extends ImageAnimation {
10    private MediaTracker imageTracker = new MediaTracker(this);
11
12    /** Initialize the applet */
13    public void init() {
14      // Load the image, the image files are named
15      // L1 - L52 in image directory
16      imageArray = new Image[NUM_OF_IMAGES];
17      for (int i = 0; i < imageArray.length; i++) {
18        imageArray[i] = getImage(getCodeBase(),
19          "image/L" + (i + 1) + ".gif" );
20
```

continues

Example 19.6 Continued

```
21          // Register images with the imageTracker
22          imageTracker.addImage(imageArray[i], i);
23        }
24
25        // Wait for all the images to be completely loaded
26        try {
27          imageTracker.waitForAll();
28        }
29        catch (InterruptedException ex) {
30          System.out.println(ex);
31        }
32
33        // Dispose of imageTracker since it is no longer needed
34        imageTracker = null;
35
36        // Panel p to hold animation control
37        JPanel p = new JPanel();
38        p.setLayout(new BorderLayout());
39        p.add(new JLabel("Animation speed in millisecond"),
40          BorderLayout.WEST);
41        p.add(jtfSpeed, BorderLayout.CENTER);
42        p.add(jbtReverse, BorderLayout.EAST);
43
44        // Add the image panel and p to the applet
45        getContentPane().add(new PlayImage(), BorderLayout.CENTER);
46        getContentPane().add(p, BorderLayout.SOUTH);
47
48        // Register listener
49        jtfSpeed.addActionListener(this);
50        jbtReverse.addActionListener(this);
51      }
52    }
```

Review

The `ImageAnimationUsingMediaTracker` class extends `ImageAnimation`, which was created in Example 19.5, "Using Image Animation." The `ImageAnimationUsingMediaTracker` uses `MediaTracker` to monitor loading images.

The program creates an instance of `MediaTracker`, `imageTracker`, and registers images with `imageTracker` in order to track image loading (Line 22). The program uses `imageTracker` to ensure that all the images are completely loaded before they are displayed.

The `waitForAll()` method (Line 27) forces the program to wait for all the images to be loaded before displaying any of them. Because the program needs to load fifty-two images, using `waitForAll()` results in a long delay before images are displayed. You should display something while the image is being loaded in order to keep the user attentive and/or informed. A simple approach is to use the `showStatus()` method in the `Applet` class to display some information on the Web browser's status bar. Here is a possibility:

```
showStatus("Please wait while loading images");
```

Put this statement before the `try-catch` block for `waitForAll()` in the program.

The `imageTracker` object is no longer needed after the images are loaded. The statement `imageTracker = null` (Line 34) notifies the garbage collector of the Java runtime system to reclaim the memory space previously occupied by the `imageTracker` object.

You can rewrite this example to enable it to run as an application (see Exercise 19.4).

Chapter Summary

- To play an audio file in an applet, use the method `play(URL url, String filename)` in the `Applet` class. This method downloads the audio file from the url and plays the audio in the file. Nothing happens if the audio file cannot be found.

- Use `getCodeBase()` to get the URL of the applet (.class file), or `getDocumentBase()` to get the URL of the HTML file that contains the applet. These two methods, `getCodeBase()` and `getDocumentBase()`, are defined in the `Applet` class.

- The statement `play(url, filename)` downloads the audio file every time you play the audio. If you want to play the audio many times, create an *audio clip object* for the file. The audio clip is created once and can be played repeatedly without reloading the file. To create an instance of `AudioClip`, use `getAudioClip(URL url)` or `getAudioClip(URL url, String name)`.

- To manipulate a sound for an audio clip, use the following instance methods of `java.applet.AudioClip`: `play()`, `loop()`, and `stop()`.

- To display an image in Java applets, you need to load the image from an Internet source, using the `getImage` method in the `Applet` class. This method returns a `java.awt.Image` object. Two versions of the `getImage` method are `getImage(URL url)` and `getImage(URL url, String filename)`.

- Once you have an `Image` instance for the image file, you can create an `ImageIcon` using `new ImageIcon(image)`.

- You can draw image on a graphic context using the `drawImage` method of the `Graphics` class.

- To write code that can be used to load resource files for both applications and applets, use the `java.lang.Class` class. The `getResource(filename)` method can be used to get the URL of the image or audio file.

- To get an audio clip from a Java application, use the static `newAudioClip()` method in the `java.applet.Applet`.

■ The MediaTracker class is used to determine whether one image or all of the images are completely loaded. The MediaTracker obtains this information in order to ensure that the images will be fully displayed.

Review Questions

19.1 What types of audio files are used in Java?

19.2 How do you get an audio file? How do you play, repeatedly play, and stop an audio clip?

19.3 The getAudioClip method is defined in the Applet class. If you want to use audio in Java applications, what options do you have?

19.4 What is the difference between getDocumentBase and getCodeBase?

19.5 What is the difference between the getImage method in the Applet class and the getImage method in the ImageIcon class?

19.6 How do you get the URL of an image or audio file for both Java applications and Java applets?

19.7 Describe the drawImage method in the Graphics class.

19.8 Can you create image icons and use the setIcon method to set an icon in a JLabel instance in Java applets?

19.9 Explain the differences between displaying images in a JLabel instance and in a JPanel instance.

19.10 How do you get an audio clip in Java applications?

19.11 Why do you use MediaTracker? How do you add images to a media tracker? How do you know that an image or all of the images are completely loaded? Can you assign images the same ID in order to register them with a media tracker?

Programming Exercises

19.1 (Playing, looping, and stopping a sound clip) Write an applet that meets the following requirements:

■ Get an audio file from the URL of the HTML base code.

■ Place three buttons labeled Play, Loop, and Stop, as shown in Figure 19.5.

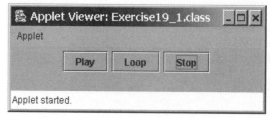

Figure 19.5 *Click Play to play an audio clip once, click Loop to play an audio repeatedly, and click Stop to terminate playing.*

■ If you click the Play button, the audio file is played once. If you click the Loop button, the audio file keeps playing repeatedly. If you click the Stop button, the playing stops.

■ The applet can run as an application.

19.2 (Repainting partial area) Sometimes, when you repaint the entire viewing area of a panel, only a tiny portion of the viewing area is changed. You can improve the performance by only repainting the affected area, but do not invoke `super.paintComponent(g)` when repainting the panel, because this will cause the entire viewing area to be cleared. Use this approach to write an applet to display the temperatures of each hour during the last twenty-four hours in a histogram. Suppose that the temperatures between 50 and 90 degrees Fahrenheit are obtained randomly and are updated every hour. The temperature of the current hour needs to be redisplayed, while the others remain unchanged. Use a unique color to highlight the temperature for the current hour (see Figure 19.6).

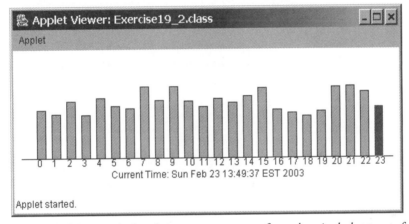

Figure 19.6 *The histogram displays the average temperature of every hour in the last twenty-four hours.*

19.3 (Adding sound into the elevator simulator) Modify the elevator program in Exercise 18.9 to add sound to the program. When the elevator stops on a floor, announce which floor it is on.

19.4 (Revising Example 19.6 "Using `MediaTracker`") Rewrite Example 19.6 to add the following new functions:

■ The animation is suspended when the mouse is pressed and resumed when the mouse is released. To implement this feature, add the code in the `PlayImage` inner class of the `ImageAnimation` class to handle the mouse event for `mousePressed` and `mouseReleased` actions.

■ Sound is incorporated into the applet so that it is played while images are displayed.

■ Enable the applet to run stand-alone.

19.5 (Creating an alarm clock) Write an applet that will display a digital clock with a large display panel that shows hour, minute, and second. This clock should allow the user to set an alarm. Figure 19.7 shows an example of such a clock. To turn on the alarm, check the Alarm check box. To specify the alarm time, click the "Set alarm" button to display a new frame, as shown in Figure 19.8. You can set the alarm time in the frame. Enable the applet to run stand-alone.

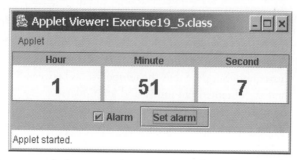

Figure 19.7   *The program displays current hour, minute, and second, and enables you to set an alarm.*

Figure 19.8   *You can set the alarm time by specifying hour, minute, and second.*

19.6 (Creating an image animator) Create animation using the applet (see Figure 19.9) to meet the following requirements:

■ Allow the user to specify the animation speed. The user can enter the speed in a text field.

■ Get the number of frames and the image file name prefix from the user. For example, if the user enters **n** for the number of frames and **L** for the image prefix, then the files are **L1**, **L2**, and so on, to **L***n*. Assume that the images are stored in the **image** directory, a subdirectory of the applet's directory.

■ Allow the user to specify an audio file name. The audio file is stored in the same directory as the applet. The sound is played while the animation runs.

■ Enable the applet to run stand-alone.

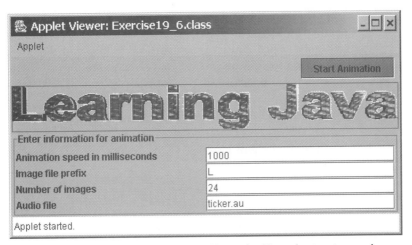

Figure 19.9   *This applet lets the user select image files, audio file, and animation speed.*

19.7 (Enlarging and shrinking an image) Write an applet that will display a sequence of images from a single image file in different sizes. Initially, the viewing area for this image has a width of 300 and a height of 300. Your program should continuously shrink the viewing area by 1 in width and 1 in height until it reaches a width of 50 and a height of 50. At that point, the viewing area should continuously enlarge by 1 in width and 1 in height until it reaches a width of 300 and a height of 300. The viewing area should shrink and enlarge (alternately) to create animation for the single image. Enable the applet to run stand-alone.

19.8 (Showing national flags) Write an applet that introduces national flags, one after the other, by presenting each one's photo, name, and description (see Figure 19.10) along with audio that reads the description.

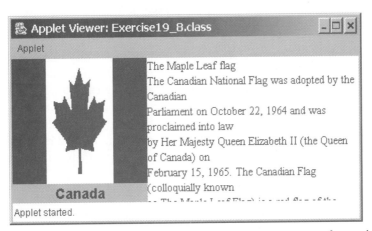

Figure 19.10   *This applet shows each country's flag, name, and description, one after another, and reads the description that is currently shown.*

Suppose your applet displays the flags of eight countries. Assume that the audio files, named **a0.au**, **a1.au**, and so on, up to **a7.au**, are stored in a subdirectory named **audio** in the applet's directory, and the photo image files, named **photo0.gif**, **photo1.gif**, and so on, up to **photo7.gif**, are stored in a subdirectory named **photo** in the applet's directory. The length of each audio is less than 10 seconds. Assume that the name and description of each country's flag are passed from the HTML using the parameters name0, name1, ..., name7, and description0, description1, ..., and description7. Pass the number of the countries as an HTML parameter using numOfCountries. Here is an example:

```
<param name="numOfCountries" value=8>
<param name="name0" value="Canada">
<param name="description0" value=
"The Maple Leaf flag
The Canadian National Flag was adopted by the Canadian
Parliament on October 22, 1964 and was proclaimed into law
by Her Majesty Queen Elizabeth II (the Queen of Canada) on
February 15, 1965. The Canadian Flag (colloquially known
as The Maple Leaf Flag) is a red flag of the proportions
two by length and one by width, containing in its center a
white square, with a single red stylized eleven-point
mapleleaf centered in the white square.">
```

HINT

Use the DescriptionPanel class to display the image, name, and the text. The DescriptionPanel class was introduced in Example 13.4, "Using Text Area."

19.9 (Revising Example 19.4 "Using Image and Audio in Applications and in Applets") Rewrite Example 19.4 to use the resource bundle to retrieve image and audio files.

HINT

When a new country is selected, set an appropriate locale for it. Have your program look for the flag and audio file from the resource file for the locale.

19.10 (Scaling images) Rewrite Exercise 19.8 to display an image to fit in a panel of fixed size. In Exercise 19.8, you used the DescriptionPanel class to display an image icon in a label. The image icon is not scalable. If the label dimension is smaller than the image icon, you will see only part of the image. In this exercise, use the ImagePanel class, introduced in Example 19.3, "Displaying Images in an Applet," to display an image in a panel. You can modify the DescriptionPanel class to use ImagePanel to replace the label for displaying images.

19.11 (Improving Example 19.4 "Using Image and Audio in Applications and in Applets") In Example 19.4, if you play a new audio before the preceding audio has played to its completion, the new audio overlaps the preceding audio. Rewrite Example 19.4 to avoid this.

 HINT

Use the `stop` method to terminate the audio clip.

19.12 (Revising Example 19.2 "Announcing the Time on a Separate Thread") In Example 19.2, an object of `AnnounceTime` is created every minute to announce the current time. Rewrite the program by creating one such object in advance and passing hour audio, minute audio, and AM/PM audio to the object when it is time to announce the current time.

APPENDIXES

The appendixes cover a mixed bag of topics. Appendix A lists Java keywords. Appendix B gives tables of ASCII characters and their associated codes in decimal and in hex. Appendix C shows the operator precedence. Appendix D summarizes Java modifiers and their usage. Appendix E lists UML Graphical Notations for describing classes and their relationships. Appendix F covers special floating-point values. Finally, Appendix G provides a glossary of key terms used in the text.

APPENDIX A   JAVA KEYWORDS

APPENDIX B   THE ASCII CHARACTER SET

APPENDIX C   OPERATOR PRECEDENCE CHART

APPENDIX D   JAVA MODIFIERS

APPENDIX E   UML GRAPHICAL NOTATIONS

APPENDIX F   SPECIAL FLOATING-POINT VALUES

APPENDIX G   GLOSSARY

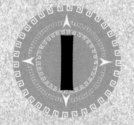

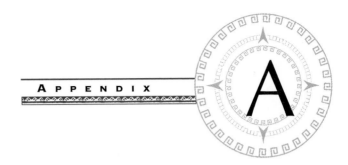

APPENDIX A

JAVA KEYWORDS

The following forty-nine keywords are reserved for use by the Java language:

abstract	double	interface	switch
assert	else	long	synchronized
boolean	extends	native	this
break	for	new	throw
byte	final	package	throws
case	finally	private	transient
catch	float	protected	try
char	goto	public	void
class	if	return	volatile
const	implements	short	while
continue	import	static	
default	instanceof	strictfp*	
do	int	super	

The keywords goto and const are C++ keywords reserved, but not currently used, in Java. This enables Java compilers to identify them and to produce better error messages if they appear in Java programs.

The literal values true, false, and null are not keywords, just like literal value 100. However, you cannot use them as identifiers, just as you cannot use 100 as an identifier.

---

*The strictfp keyword is a modifier for method or class to use strict floating-point calculations. Floating-point arithmetic can be executed in one of two modes: *strict* or *nonstrict*. The strict mode guarantees that the evaluation result is the same on all Java Virtual Machine implementations. The nonstrict mode allows intermediate results from calculations to be stored in an extended format different from the standard IEEE floating-point number format. The extended format is machine-dependent and enables code to be executed faster. However, when you execute the code using the nonstrict mode on different JVMs, you may not always get precisely the same results. By default, the nonstrict mode is used for floating-point calculations. To use the strict mode in a method or a class, add the strictfp keyword in the method or the class declaration. Strict floating-point may give you slightly better precision than nonstrict floating-point, but the distinction will only affect some applications. Strictness is not inherited; that is, the presence of strictfp on a class or interface declaration does not cause extended classes or interfaces to be strict.

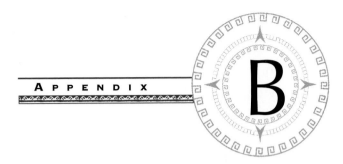

A P P E N D I X

THE ASCII CHARACTER SET

Tables B.1 and B.2 show ASCII characters and their respective decimal and hexadecimal codes. The decimal or hexadecimal code of a character is a combination of its row index and column index. For example, in Table B.1, the letter A is at row 6 and column 5, so its decimal equivalent is 65; in Table B.2, letter A is at row 4 and column 1, so its hexadecimal equivalent is 41.

TABLE B.1   ASCII Character Set in the Decimal Index

	0	1	2	3	4	5	6	7	8	9
0	nul	soh	stx	etx	eot	enq	ack	bel	bs	ht
1	nl	vt	ff	cr	so	si	dle	dc1	dc2	dc3
2	dc4	nak	syn	etb	can	em	sub	esc	fs	gs
3	rs	us	sp	!	"	#	$	%	&	'
4	(	)	*	+	,	-	.	/	0	1
5	2	3	4	5	6	7	8	9	:	;
6	<	=	>	?	@	A	B	C	D	E
7	F	G	H	I	J	K	L	M	N	O
8	P	Q	R	S	T	U	V	W	X	Y
9	Z	[	\	]	<	_	`	a	b	c
10	d	e	f	g	h	i	j	k	l	m
11	n	o	p	q	r	s	t	u	v	w
12	x	y	z	{	|	}	~	del		

TABLE B.2   ASCII Character Set in the Hexadecimal Index

	0	1	2	3	4	5	6	7	8	9	A	B	C	D	E	F
0	nul	soh	stx	etx	eot	enq	ack	bel	bs	ht	nl	vt	ff	cr	so	si
1	dle	dc1	dc2	dc3	dc4	nak	syn	etb	can	em	sub	esc	fs	gs	rs	us
2	sp	!	"	#	$	%	&	'	(	)	*	+	,	-	.	/
3	0	1	2	3	4	5	6	7	8	9	:	;	<	=	>	?
4	@	A	B	C	D	E	F	G	H	I	J	K	L	M	N	O
5	P	Q	R	S	T	U	V	W	X	Y	Z	[	\	]	^	_
6	`	a	b	c	d	e	f	g	h	i	j	k	l	m	n	o
7	p	q	r	s	t	u	v	w	x	y	z	{	|	}	~	del

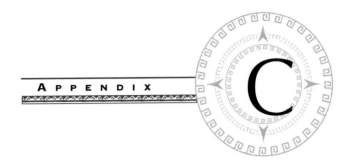

OPERATOR
PRECEDENCE CHART

The operators are shown in decreasing order of precedence from top to bottom. Operators in the same group have the same precedence, and their associativity is shown in the table.

Operator	Name	Associativity
()	Parentheses	Left to right
()	Function call	Left to right
[]	Array subscript	Left to right
.	Object member access	Left to right
++	Postincrement	Right to left
--	Postdecrement	Right to left
++	Preincrement	Right to left
--	Predecrement	Right to left
+	Unary plus	Right to left
-	Unary minus	Right to left
!	Unary logical negation	Right to left
(type)	Unary casting	Right to left
new	Creating object	Right to left
*	Multiplication	Left to right
/	Division	Left to right
%	Remainder	Left to right
+	Addition	Left to right
-	Subtraction	Left to right
<<	Left shift	Left to right
>>	Right shift with sign extension	Left to right
>>>	Right shift with zero extension	Left to right
<	Less than	Left to right
<=	Less than or equal to	Left to right
>	Greater than	Left to right
>=	Greater than or equal to	Left to right
instanceof	Checking object type	Left to right
==	Equal comparison	Left to right
!=	Not equal	Left to right
&	(Unconditional AND)	Left to right
^	(Exclusive OR)	Left to right
¦	(Unconditional OR)	Left to right

Operator	Name	Associativity
&&	Conditional AND	Left to right
¦¦	Conditional OR	Left to right
?:	Ternary condition	Right to left
=	Assignment	Right to left
+=	Addition assignment	Right to left
-=	Subtraction assignment	Right to left
*=	Multiplication assignment	Right to left
/=	Division assignment	Right to left
%=	Remainder assignment	Right to left

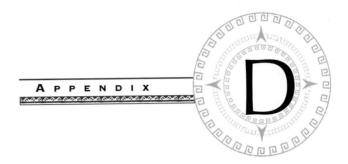

JAVA MODIFIERS

Modifiers are used on classes and class members (methods and data), but the `final` modifier can also be used on local variables in a method. A modifier that can be applied to a class is called a *class modifier*. A modifier that can be applied to a method is called a *method modifier*. A modifier that can be applied to a data field is called a *data modifier*. The following table gives a summary of the Java modifiers.

Modifier	class	method	data	Explanation
(default)	√	√	√	A class, method, or data field is visible in this package.
public	√	√	√	A class, method, or data field is visible to all the programs in any package.
private		√	√	A method or data field is only visible in this class.
protected		√	√	A method or data field is visible in this package and in subclasses of this class in any package.
static		√	√	Defines a class method or a class data field.
final	√	√	√	A final class cannot be extended. A final method cannot be modified in a subclass. A final data field is a constant.
abstract	√	√		An abstract class must be extended. An abstract method must be implemented in a concrete subclass.
native		√		A native method indicates that the method is implemented using a language other than Java.
synchronized		√		Only one thread at a time can execute this method.
strictfp	√	√		Use strict floating-point calculations to guarantee that the evaluation result is the same on all JVMs.

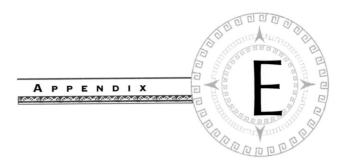

UML GRAPHICAL NOTATIONS

This appendix summarizes the UML notations used in this book.

Classes and Objects

A class is described using a rectangle box with three sections.

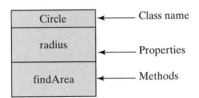

The top section gives the class name, the middle section describes the fields, and the bottom section describes the methods. The middle and bottom sections are optional, but the top section is required.

An object is described using a rectangle box with two sections.

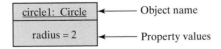

The top section is required. It gives the object's name and its defining class. The second section is optional; it indicates the object's field values.

The Modifiers *public*, *private*, *protected*, and *static*

The symbols +, −, and # are used to denote, respectively, public, private, and protected modifiers in the UML. The static fields and methods are underlined.

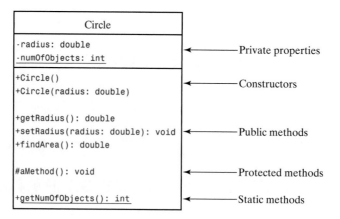

Class Relationships

The relationships of the classes are association, aggregation, and inheritance.

An *association* is illustrated using a solid line between the two classes with an optional label that describes their relationship.

Each class involved in an association may specify a multiplicity. A multiplicity is a number or an interval that specifies the number of objects of the class that are involved in the relationship. The character * means that the number of objects is unlimited, and an interval `1..u` means that the number of objects should be between 1 and u, inclusive.

A filled diamond is attached to the composed class to denote the composition relationship, and a hollow diamond is attached to the aggregated class to denote the *aggregation* relationship, as shown below.

Inheritance models the is-a relationship between two classes, as shown below. An open triangle pointing to the superclass is used to denote the inheritance relationship between the two classes involved.

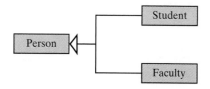

Abstract Classes and Interfaces

Abstract class names, interface names, and abstract methods are italicized. Dashed lines are used to link to the interface, as shown below:

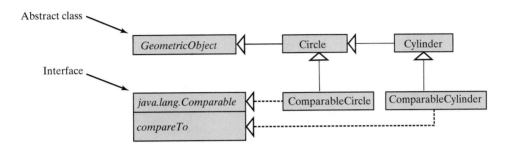

Sequence Diagrams

Sequence diagrams describe interactions among objects by depicting the time ordering of method invocations. The sequence diagram shown below consists of the following elements:

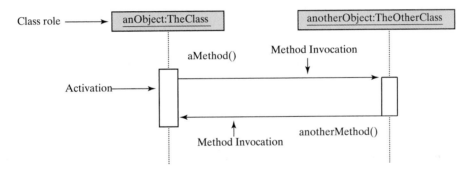

- Class role represents the role an object plays. The objects at the top of the diagram represent class roles.

- Lifeline represents the existence of an object over a period of time. A vertical dashed line extending from the object is used to denote a lifeline.

- Activation represents the time during which an object is performing an operation. Thin rectangles placed on lifelines are used to denote activations.

- Method invocation represents communications between objects. Horizontal arrows labeled with method calls are used to denote method invocations.

Statechart Diagrams

Statechart diagrams describe the flow of control of an object. The statechart diagram shown below contains the following elements:

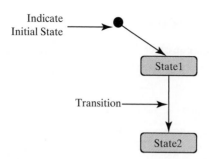

■ State represents a situation during the life of an object in which it satisfies some condition, performs some action, or waits for some event to occur. Every state has a name. Rectangles with rounded corners are used to represent states. The small filled circle is used to denote the initial state.

■ Transition represents the relationship between two states, indicating that an object will perform some action to transfer from one state to the other. A solid arrow with appropriate method invocation is used to denote a transition.

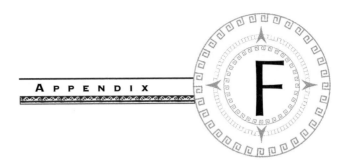

SPECIAL FLOATING-POINT VALUES

Dividing an integer by zero is invalid and throws `ArithmeticException`, but dividing a floating-point value by zero does not cause an exception. Floating-point arithmetic can overflow to infinity if the result of the operation is too large for a `double` or a `float`, or underflow to zero if the result is too small for a double or a `float`. Java provides the special floating-point values `POSITIVE_INFINITY`, `NEGATIVE_INFINITY`, and `NaN` (Not a Number) to denote these results. These values are defined as special constants in the `Float` class and the `Double` class.

If a positive floating-point number is divided by zero, the result is `POSITIVE_INFINITY`. If a negative floating-point number is divided by zero, the result is `NEGATIVE_INFINITY`. If a floating-point zero is divided by zero, the result is `NaN`, which means that the result is undefined mathematically. The string representation of these three values are Infinity, -Infinity, and NaN. For example,

```
System.out.print(1.0 / 0); // Print Infinity
System.out.print(-1.0 / 0); // Print -Infinity
System.out.print(0.0 / 0); // Print NaN
```

These special values can also be used as operands in computations. For example, a number divided by `POSITIVE_INFINITY` yields a positive zero. Table F.1 summarizes various combinations of the /, *, %, +, and - operators.

TABLE F.1 Special Floating-Point Values

x	y	x/y	$x\overset{*}{\vphantom{x}}y$	$x\%y$	$x + y$	$x - y$
Finite	±0.0	± ∞	±0.0	NaN	Finite	Finite
Finite	± ∞	±0.0	± ∞	x	±∞	∞
±0.0	±0.0	NaN	± ∞	NaN	±0.0	±0.0
± ∞	Finite	± ∞	± ∞	NaN	± ∞	± ∞
± ∞	± ∞	NaN	± ∞	NaN	± ∞	∞
±0.0	± ∞	±0.0	NaN	±0.0	± ∞	±0.0
NaN	Any	NaN	NaN	NaN	NaN	NaN
Any	NaN	NaN	NaN	NaN	NaN	NaN

◆ **NOTE**

If one of the operands is NaN, the result is NaN.

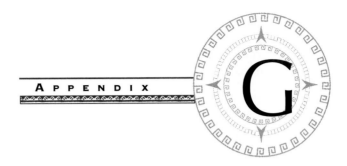

GLOSSARY

This glossary lists and defines the key terms used in the book.

.class file   The output of the Java compiler. A .class file contains the byte code for a class.

.java file   The source code of a Java program. It may contain one or more Java classes and interfaces. A .java file can be created using a text editor or a Java IDE such as Sun ONE Studio and JBuilder.

.html or .htm file   The source code of an HTML file. It contains HTML tags and text. It is the input for a Web browset. A Web browser displays the contents of an .html or .htm file.

abstract class   When you are designing classes, a superclass should contain common features that are shared by subclasses. Sometimes the superclass is so abstract that it cannot have any specific instances. These classes are called abstract classes and are declared using the abstract modifier. Abstract classes are like regular classes with data and methods, but you cannot create instances of abstract classes using the new operator.

abstraction   A technique in software development that hides detailed implementation. Java supports method abstraction and class abstraction. Method abstraction is defined as separating the use of a method from its implementation. The client can use a method without knowing how it is implemented. If you decide to change the implementation, the client program will not be affected. Similarly, class abstraction hides the implementation of the class from the client.

abstract method   A method signature without implementation. Its implementation is provided by its subclasses. An abstract method is denoted with an abstract modifier and must be contained in an abstract class. In a nonabstract subclass extended from an abstract class, all abstract methods must be implemented, even if they are not used in the subclass.

Abstract Window Toolkit (AWT)   The set of components for developing simple graphics applications that was in use before the introduction of Swing components. The AWT user interface components have now been replaced by the Swing components, but other AWT classes such as helper classes, and event-handling classes are still used.

accessor method   The get and set methods for retrieving and setting private fields in an object.

actual parameter   The value passed to a method when it is invoked. Actual parameters should match formal parameters in type, order, and number.

algorithm   Describes how a problem is solved in terms of the actions to be executed, and specifies the order in which these actions should be executed. Algorithms can help the programmer plan a program before writing it in a programming language.

aggregation   A special form of association that represents an ownership relationship between two classes.

ambiguous invocation   There are two or more possible methods to match an invocation of a method, neither is more specific than the other(s). Therefore, the invocation is ambiguous.

applet   A special kind of Java program that can run directly from a Web browser or an applet viewer. Various security restrictions are imposed on applets. For example, they cannot perform input/output operations on a user's system and therefore cannot read or write files or transmit computer viruses.

application   A stand-alone program, such as any program written using a high-level language. Applications can be executed from any computer with a Java interpreter. Applications are not subject to the security restrictions imposed on Java applets. An application class must contain a main method.

API (Application Program Interface)   A set of classes and interfaces that can be used to develop Java programs.

argument   Same as actual parameter.

array   A container object that stores an indexed sequence of the same types of data. Typically, the individual elements are referenced by an index value. The index is an int value starting with 0 for the first element, 1 for the second, and so on.

assignment statement   A simple statement that assigns a value to a variable using an assignment operator (=).

assignment operator (=)   Assigns a value to a variable.

association   A general binary relationship that describes an activity between two classes.

backslash (\)   A character that precedes another character to denote the following character has a special meaning. For example, '\t' denotes a tab character. The backslash character is also used to denote a Unicode character like '\u00FF'.

binary search   An efficient method to search a key in an array. Binary search first compares the key with the element in the middle of the array and reduces the search range by half. For binary search to work, the array must be presorted.

bit   A binary digit 0 or 1.

block   A sequence of statements enclosed in braces ({}).

boolean   A primitive data type for Boolean values (true or false).

boolean expression   An expression that evaluates to a Boolean value.

byte   A unit of storage. Each byte consists of 8 bits. The size of hard disk and memory is measured in bytes. A megabyte is roughly a million bytes.

byte type   Primitive data type that represents an integer in a byte. The range of a byte value is from -2^7 (-128) to $2^7 - 1$ (127).

bytecode   The result of compiling Java source code. Bytecode is machine-independent and can run on any machine that has a Java runtime environment.

call-by-value   Same as pass-by-value.

casting   The process of converting a primitive data type value into another primitive type or converting an object of one object type into another object type. For example, `(int) 3.5` converts 3.5 into an int value, and `(Cylinder)c` converts an object c into the `Cylinder` type. For the object casting to be successful, the object to be cast must be instance of the target class.

char type   A primitive data type that represents a Unicode character.

child class   Same as subclass.

class   An encapsulated collection of data and methods that operate on data. A class may be instantiated to create an object that is an instance of the class.

class hierarchy   A collection of classes organized in terms of superclass and subclass relationships.

class method   A method that can be invoked without creating an instance of the class. To define class methods, put the modifier `static` in the method declaration.

class variable   A data member declared using the `static` modifier. A class variable is shared by all instances of that class. Class variables are used to communicate between different objects of the same class and to handle global states among these objects.

class's contract   Refers to the collection of methods and fields that are accessible from outside a class, together with the description of how these members are expected to behave.

comment   Comments document what a program is and how it is constructed. They are not programming statements and are ignored by the compiler. In Java, comments are preceded by two slashes (//) in a line or enclosed between /* and */ in multiple lines. The javadoc comments are enclosed between /** and */.

compiler   A software program that translates Java source code into bytecode.

composition   A form of relationship that represents exclusive ownership of the class by the aggregated class.

constant   A variable declared `final` in Java. Since a class constant is usually shared by all objects of the same class, a class constant is often declared `static`. A local constant is a constant declared inside a method.

constructor   A special method for initializing objects when creating objects using the `new` operator. The constructor has exactly the same name as its defining class. Constructors can be overloaded, making it easier to construct objects with different initial data values.

data type   Data type is used to define variables. Java supports primitive data types and object data types.

debugger   A program that facilitates debugging. It enables the program to be executed one statement at a time and enables the contents of the variable to be examined during execution.

debugging   The process of finding and fixing errors in a program.

declaration   Defines variables, methods, and classes in a program.

decrement operator (--)   Subtracts one from a numeric variable or a char variable.

default constructor   A constructor that has no parameters. A default constructor is required for a JavaBeans component.

definition   Alternative term for a declaration.

deserialization   The process of restoring an object that was previously serialized.

design   To plan how a program can be structured and implemented by coding.

double buffering   A technique to reduce flickering in image animation in Java.

double type   A primitive data type to represent double precision floating-point numbers with 14 to 15 significant digits of accuracy.

dot operator (.)   An operator used to access members of an object. If the member is static, it can be accessed through the class name using the dot operator.

dynamic binding   An object of a subclass can be used by any code designed to work with an object of its superclass. For example, if a method expects a parameter of the `GeometricObject` type, you can invoke it with a `Circle` object. A `Circle` object can be used as both a `Circle` object and a `GeometricObject` object. This feature is known as Polymorphism (a Greek word meaning "many forms"). A method may be defined in a superclass, but is overridden in a subclass. Which implementation of the method is used on a particular call will be determined dynamically by the JVM at runtime. This capability is known as dynamic binding.

encapsulation   Combining of methods and data into a single data structure. In Java, this is known as a class.

event   A signal to the program that something has happened. Events are generated by external user actions, such as mouse movements, mouse button clicks, and keystrokes, or by the operating system, such as a timer. The program can choose to respond to an event or to ignore it.

event adapter A class used to filter event methods and only handle specified ones.

event delegation In Java event-driven programming, events are assigned to the listener object for processing. This is referred to as event delegation.

event-driven programming Java GUI programming is event-driven. In event-driven programming, codes are executed upon the activation of events, such as clicking a button or moving the mouse.

event handler A method in the listener's object that is designed to do some specified processing when a particular event occurs.

event listener The object that receives and handles the event.

event listener interface An interface implemented by the listener class to handle the specified events.

event registration To become a listener, an object must be registered as a listener by the source object. The source object maintains a list of listeners and notifies all the registered listeners when an event occurs.

event source The object that generates the event.

exception An unexpected event indicating that a program has failed in some way. Exceptions are represented by exception objects in Java. Exceptions can be handled in a `try·catch block`.

expression represents a computation involving values, variables, and operators, which evaluates to a value.

`final` A modifier for classes, data, methods, and local variables. A final class cannot be extended, a final data or local variable is a constant, and a final method cannot be overridden in a subclass.

float type A primitive data type to represent single precision floating-point numbers with 6 to 7 significant digits of accuracy. The double type is used to represent double precisions with 14 to 15 significant digits of accuracy.

floating-point number A decimal number with an optional fractional part.

formal parameter The parameters defined in the method signature.

garbage collection A JVM feature that automatically detects and reclaims the space occupied by unreferenced objects.

get method For retrieving private data in a class.

graphical user interface (GUI) An interface to a program that is implemented using AWT or Swing components, such as frames, buttons, labels, text fields, and so on.

HTML (Hypertext Markup Language)   A script language to design Web pages for creating and sharing multimedia-enabled, integrated electronic documents over the Internet.

increment operator (++)   Adds one to a numeric variable or a char variable.

identifier   A name of a variable, method, class, interface, or package.

identation   The use of tabs and spaces to indent the source code to make it easy to read and understand.

index   An integer value used to specify the position of an element in the array.

infinite loop   A loop that runs indefinitely due to a bug in the loop.

information hiding   A software engineering concept for hiding and protecting an object's internal features and structure.

inheritance   In object-oriented programming, the use of the `extends` keyword to derive new classes from existing classes.

initialization block   A block of statements that appears in the class declaration, not inside a method. A nonstatic initialization block is executed as if it were placed at the beginning of every constructor in the class. A static initialization block is executed when the class is loaded.

inner class   A class embedded in another class. Inner classes enable you to define small auxiliary objects and pass units of behavior, thus making programs simple and concise.

instance   An object of a class.

instance method   A nonstatic method in a class. Instance methods belong to instances and can only be invoked by them.

instance variable   A nonstatic data member of a class. An instance variable belongs to an instance of the class.

instantiation   The process of creating an object of a class.

int type   A primitive data type to represent an integer in the range from -2^{31} (-2147483648) to $2^{31} - 1$ (2147483647).

Integrated Development Environment (IDE)   Software that helps programmers write code efficiently. IDE tools integrate editing, compiling, building, debugging, and online help in one graphical user interface.

interface   An interface is treated like a special class in Java. Each interface is compiled into a separate bytecode file, just like a regular class. You cannot create an instance for an interface. The structure of a Java interface is similar to that of an abstract class in that it can have data and methods. The data, however, must be constants, and the methods can have only declarations without implementation. Single inheritance is the Java restriction wherein a class can inherit from a single superclass. This restriction is eased by the use of an interface.

interpreter   Software for interpreting and running Java bytecode.

iteration   One time execution of the loop body.

Java Virtual Machine (JVM)   A machine that runs Java bytecode. It is called virtual because it is usually implemented in software rather than in hardware.

java   The command to run a Java program from the command line.

javac   The command to compile a Java program from the command line.

Java Development Toolkit (JDK)   Defines the Java API and contains a set of command-line utilities, such as javac (compiler) and java (interpreter). With Java 2, Sun renamed JDK 1.2 to Java 2 SDK v 1.2. SDK stands for Software Development Toolkit.

Just-in-Time compiler   Capable of compiling each bytecode once, and then reinvoking the compiled code repeatedly when the bytecode is executed.

keyword   A reserved word defined as part of Java language. (See Appendix A, "Java Keywords," for a full list of keywords.)

linear search   A method to search an element in an array. Linear search compares the key with the element in the array sequentially.

literal   A constant value that appears directly in the program. A literal may be numeric, character, boolean, or null for object type.

local variable   A variable defined inside a method.

logic error   An error that causes the program to produce incorrect results.

main class   A class that contains a main method.

marker interface   An empty interface that is used to signify that all the classes implementing the interface share certain properties.

method   A collection of statements grouped together to perform an operation. See class method; instance method.

method overloading   Method overloading means that you can define methods with the same name in a class as long as there is enough difference in their parameter profiles.

method overriding   Method overriding means that you can modify a method in a subclass that was originally defined in a superclass.

method signature   The combination of the name of a method and the list of its parameter types.

modal dialog box   A dialog box that prevents the user from using other windows before it is dismissed.

modifier   A Java keyword that specifies the properties of data, methods, and classes and how they can be used. Examples of modifiers are `public`, `private`, and `static`.

multidimensional array An array with more than one dimension.

multithreading The capability of a program to perform several tasks simultaneously within a program.

mutator A set method that changes the value of an instance variable.

narrowing (of types) Casting a variable of a type with a larger range to a variable of a type with a smaller range.

null A literal of an object variable that does not reference any concrete object.

object Same as instance.

object-oriented programming (OOP) An approach to programming that involves organizing objects and their behavior into classes of reusable components.

operand evaluation order Defines the order in which individual operands are evaluated.

operating system Software that manages computer resources and provides services to programs.

operator Operations for primitive data type values and on objects. Examples of operators are +, -, *, /, %, <, <=, ==, !=, >, >=, &&, &, ¦¦, ¦, !, and ^.

operator associativity Defines the order in which operators will be evaluated in an expression if the operators have the same precedence order.

operator precedence Defines the order in which operators will be evaluated in an expression.

overloading Making more than one method or constructor the same name with different signatures in the same class.

override Implement the method in a subclass that is declared in a superclass.

package A collection of classes.

parameter Refers to a value passed to a method.

parameter profile Refers to the type of the parameters, the order of parameters, and the number of parameters.

parent class Same as superclass.

pass-by-value A term used when a copy of an argument is passed as a method parameter. For a parameter of a primitive type, the actual value is passed; for a parameter of a reference type, the reference for the object is passed.

polymorphism See dynamic binding.

primitive data type The primitive data types are byte, short, int, long, float, double, boolean, and char.

private A modifier for members of a class. A private member can only be referenced inside the class.

protected   A modifier for members of a class. A protected member of a class can be used in the class in which it is declared or any subclass derived from that class.

public   A modifier for classes, data, and methods that can be accessed by all programs.

ragged array   A multidimensional array with different length in the subarrays.

recursive method   A method that invokes itself, directly or indirectly.

reference type   A data type that is a class or an interface.

reference   A value that references an object.

reserved word   Same as keyword.

runtime error   An error that causes the program to terminate abnormally.

return type   The data type for the return value in a method.

return value   A value returned from a method using the return statement.

sentinel value   A special input value that signifies the end of the input.

sequence diagram   A UML diagram that describes interactions among objects by depicting the time-ordering of method invocations.

serialization   The process of writing an object to a stream.

set method   For updating private data in a class.

short type   A primitive data type that represents an integer in the range from -2^{15} (-32768) to $2^{15} - 1$ (32767).

short-circuit evaluation   Evaluation that stops when the result of the expression has been determined, even if not all the operands are evaluated. The evaluation involving && or ¦¦ are examples of short-circuit evaluation.

socket   The facilitation of communication between a server and a client.

source code   A program written in a programming language such as Java.

source file   A file that stores the source code.

statechart   A UML diagram that describes the flow of control of an object.

statement   A unit of code that represents an action or a sequence of actions.

static method   Same as class method.

static variable   Same as class variable.

stub   A simple, but not a complete version of the method. The use of stubs enables you to test invoking the method from a caller.

stream   The continuous one-way flow of data between a sender and a receiver.

subclass   A class that inherits from or extends a superclass.

superclass A class inherited from a subclass.

Swing component The Swing GUI components are painted directly on canvases using Java code except for components that are subclasses of java.awt.Window or java.awt.Panel, which must be drawn using native GUI on a specific platform. Swing components are less dependent on the target platform and use less resource of the native GUI. Swing components are more flexible and versatile than their AWT counterparts.

syntax error An error in the program that violates syntax rules of the language.

tag An HTML instruction that tells a Web browser how to display a document. Tags are enclosed in brackets, such as `<html>`, `<i>`, `<b>`, and `</html>`.

this Refers to the object itself.

thread A flow of execution of a task, with a beginning and an end, in a program.

throw Causes an exception.

throws A keyword used to declare a method that may throw an exception.

type Specifies a range of values.

Unicode A code system for international characters managed by the Unicode Consortium. Java supports Unicode.

Unified Modeling Language (UML) A graphical notation for describing classes and their relationships.

Universal Resource Locator (URL) A mechanism that uniquely identifies resources on the Internet.

widening (of types) Casting a variable of a type with a smaller range to a variable of a type with a larger range.

wrapper class A class that provides an object representation for primitive data type values. Java provides wrapper classes `Byte`, `Short`, `Integer`, `Long`, `Float`, `Double`, `Character`, and `Boolean` for primitive data types `byte`, `short`, `int`, `long`, `float`, `double`, `char`, and `boolean`.

INDEX

Symbols

+ (addition), 856
+= (addition assignment), 54, 857
&& (and), 62
[ ] (array subscript), 856
= (assignment), 857
=, +=, -=, *=, /=, %= (assignment operator), 65
\\ (backslash escape sequence), 60
\b (backspace), 60
+,- (binary addition and subtraction), 65
\r (carriage return), 60
<, <=, >, >= (comparison), 65
&& (conditional AND), 65, 857
|| (conditional OR), 65, 857
/ (division), 856
/= (division assignment), 54
* (double quote escape sequence), 60
== (equal to), 61, 856
==, ! = (equality), 65
^ (exclusive or), 62–63, 65, 856
\f (form feed), 60
() (function call), 856
> = (greater than), 61, 856
<< (left shift), 856
< (less than), 61, 856
<= (less than or equal to), 61, 856
\n (linefeed), 60
*, /, % (multiplication, division, and remainder), 65
* (multiplication), 856
*= (multiplication assignment), 54, 857
! (not), 62, 65
!= (not equal to), 61, 856
. (object member access), 856
|| (or), 62
() (parentheses), 856
  using to force an evaluation order, 65
-- (postdecrement), 856
++ (postincrement), 856
-- (predecrement), 856
++ (preincrement), 856
% (remainder), 856
%= (remainder assignment), 54, 857
>> (right shift with sign extension), 856
>>> (right shift with zero extension), 856
_ (single quote escape sequence), 60

- (subtraction), 856
-= (subtraction assignment), 54, 857
\t (tab), 60
?: (ternary condition), 857
! (unary logical negation), 856
- (unary minus), 65, 856
+ (unary plus), 65, 856
& (unconditional AND), 63, 65, 856
| (unconditional OR), 63, 65, 856
++var operator, 55, 65
--var operator, 55, 65
var-- operator, 55, 65
var++ operator, 55, 65

A

abs method, 170
Abstract classes, 368–375, 392, 420–421
  Calendar class, 375–376
  compared to regular classes, 369
  GeometricObject class, 368–375
    Circle class, 370
    Cylinder class, 371, 373
    findArea method, 369, 372, 373
    findPerimeter method, 369, 372, 373
    Rectangle class, 370–371
    toString() method, 372
  GregorianCalendar class, 375–376
  interfaces vs., 381–382
  methods, 392
  UML graphical notation, 863
abstract modifier, 16, 860
Abstract Windows Toolkit (AWT), 448
AbstractCollection class, 747–749
Abstraction:
  classes, 283
  methods, 175
AbstractList class, 757–758
AbstractMap class, 767, 780
AbstractSequentialList class, 757–758
AbstractSet class, 749–751
Access order, 780
Accessibility modifiers, 353
Accessors, 264–269
ActionEvent, 507–508, 662

ActionListener interface, 508, 509, 527
actionPerfomed(ActionEvent), 508, 662
actionPerformed method, 509, 511, 535
Activation, sequence diagrams, 422, 863
Ada, 5–6, 254
Add Watch command, 87–89
addActionListener method, 509, 527
add(Component) method, Container class, 455
add(element) method, List interface, 757–758
add(index, element) method, List interface, 757
AdjustmentEvent, 507–508
AdjustmentListener interface, 508
adjustmentValueChanged (AdjustmentEvent), 508
Aggregation, 403–404, 438, 862
  UML graphical notation, 862
AIFF format, 818
Algorithms, 42
align attribute, 629
alt attribute, 629
Animation, controlling using threads, 799–803
AppBrowser, 19
<applet> tag, 628–632, 818
Applet class, 620–622
  destroy method, 622, 635
  init method, 621, 635
  methods, 620–621
  start method, 622, 635
  stop method, 622, 635
Applets, 7, 10, 14, 451, 619–651
  Applet class, 620–622
  case studies, 638–645
  creating using the Applet Wizard, 623–625
  enabling to run as applications, 635–638
  HTML file and the <applet> tag, 628–632
  incorporating sound in (Example 19.1), 819–822
  JApplet class, 622–623

Applets, *(cont.)*
  passing parameters to, 632–635
    example (14.2), 634–635
  using (Example 14.1), 630–632
  viewing, 625–627
    in the content pane, 625
    using the applet viewer utility, 626
    from a Web browser, 626–627
Application program interface (API), Java, 12–13
Applications, 14
`archive` attribute, 629
Arcs, drawing, 481–482
Arithmetic expressions, 53–54
`ArithmeticException` class, 658, 666
Array initializer, Java, 208
Array of reference variables, 280
Array streams, 737
`ArrayList` class, 758–760, 779
  using (Example 17.5), 759–760
Arrays, 430
  array variables, declaring, 206–207
  computing deviations using (Example 5.5), 221–223
  conversion between strings and, 313
  copying (Example 5.3), 214–217
  creating, 206–207
  defined, 206
  initializing/processing, 208–214
  multidimensional, 226–233, *See also* Multidimensional arrays
  passing as arguments (Example 5.4), 219–221
  passing to methods, 217–225
  searching, 237–243
  sorting, 234–237
    example (5.10), 235–237
    example (9.4), 234–237
  testing (Example 5.1), 209–212
`Arrays` class, 776–778, 780
  `fill` method, 776
  methods, 776
  using (Example 17.11), 776–778
Ascent, 470
ASCII (American Standard Code for Information Interchange), 59
ASCII character set, 851–853
  in decimal index, 852
  in hexadecimal index, 853

ASCII code, 57–58
`AssertionError`, 658, 675
Assertions, 674–678, 679
  compiling programs with, 675–676
  declaring, 675
  defined, 674
  running programs with, 676–677
Assignment operator, 49
Assignment statements (assignment expressions), 49–50
Association, 401–403, 438
  parameter order, 157
Associativity, 64–65
AU format, 818
Audio:
  announcing the time on a separate thread (Example 19.2), 823–824
  playing, 818–822
  running on a separate thread, 823–824
  using in applications/applets (Example 19.4), 829–832
Audio clip object, 819
Audio files, loading in Java applications, 828–832
Audio tab, *Autofeedback enabled option*, 33–34
Auto popup MemberInsight/Auto popup ParameterInsight, 30
`available()` method, `InputStream` class, 694
`AWTError`, 658
`AWTException` class, 658, 659

B

\b (backspace character escape sequence), 60
`background` property, `Component` class, 532
Base class, 359
BASIC (Beginner All-purpose Symbolic Instructional Code), 5, 254
`BevelBorder` class, 566
Binary operators, 52
Binary search, testing (Example 5.12), 241–243
Blocked state, threads, 793, 808
`blockIncrement` property, `JScrollBar` class, 595
Blocks, 17

<body> tag, 628
`Boolean` class, 315, 386
`boolean` data type, 61–64, 67
  comparison operators, 61
Boolean operators, 62
  truth tables for, 62–63
  unconditional vs. conditional, 63–64
Boolean variables, 61–62
`border` property:
  `Border` interface, 566
  `JComponent` class, 533
`BorderFactory` class, 567
`BorderLayout` manager, 461–463, 491, 532–533
  testing (Example 11.3), 462–463
Borders, 566–573, 608
  `BevelBorder` class, 566
  `border` property, 566
  classes, 566–567
  `EmptyBorder` class, 567
  `EtchedBorder` class, 567
  `LineBorder` class, 567
  `MatteBorder` class, 567
  properties, 566
  `title` property, 566
  `titleColor` property, 566
  `TitledBorder`, 566
  `titleFont` property, 566
  `titlePosition` property, 566
  types of, 566
  using (Example 13.9), 568–573
Borrowing loans (Example 10.1), 405–412
`break` statement, 130–131
  demonstrating (Example 3.5), 130–131
Buffered streams, 704–708
  `BufferedInputStream`, 698, 704–705
  `BufferedOutputStream`, 698, 704–705
  `BufferedReader`, 704–705, 708
  `BufferedWriter`, 704–705, 738
  displaying a file in a text area (Example 16.5), 705–708
`BufferedInputStream` class, 698, 704–705
`BufferedOutputStream` class, 698, 704–705
`BufferedReader`, 704–705, 708

BufferedWriter, 704–705, 738
ButtonGroup, 562
Buttons, 533–538
  defined, 533
  JButton class:
    constructors, 533
    properties, 534
  using (Example 13.1), 535–538
Byte class, 315, 380
byte data type, 52, 67
ByteArrayInputStream class, 737
ByteArrayOutputStream class, 737
Bytecode, 6–7, 28

C

C language, 5–6, 254
C++ language, 5–6, 8
Calendar class, 375–376
Calendars, displaying (Example 4.7), 176–182
canRead() method, File class, 687
canWrite() method, File class, 687
capacity() method, StringBuffer class, 320
Case studies:
  applets, 638–645
  classes, 283–291
  control statements, 134–140
  GUI programming, 485–490
  methods, 175–182
  object-oriented modeling, 423–430
  simple programs, 70–76
Casting, 57, 346–350
  downcasting, 347
  explicit, 347
  implicit, 346
  upcasting, 347
Catching exceptions, 660–665
Chapter dependency chart, xvi
char data type, 57, 67
  casting between numeric types and, 60–61
Character class, 315–318, 330, 386
Character data type and operations, 57
  ASCII code, 57–58
  escape sequences for special characters, 58–59
  Unicode, 57–58
CharArrayReader class, 737

CharArrayWriter class, 737
charAt() method, StringBuffer class, 321
charAt(index) method, 308
charAt(index) method, StringBuffer class, 321
Check boxes, 556–561, 608
  defined, 556
  JCheckBox class, 556–557
  using (Example 13.7), 557–561
Checked exceptions, 659
Child class, 336, 359
Choice lists, *See* Combo boxes
Circle, computing the area of (Example 2.1), 44–45
Class abstraction, 283
Class block, 17
Class class, 828
Class design guidelines, 419–421
  abstract classes, 420–421
  composition, 420
  inheritance, 420
  interfaces, 420–421
  private modifier, 419–420
  protected modifier, 419–420
  public modifier, 419–420
  static modifier, 420
Class encapsulation, 283
Class inheritance, 336, 359
Class methods, 272–273
Class modifier, 859
Class role, sequence diagrams, 421, 439–440, 863
Class tracing view, 86
Classes, 17, 255
  case studies, 283–291
  contract, 283
  inner, 291–292
  from the Java Library, using (Example 6.2), 262–263
  Loan class (Example 6.7), 284–287
  StackOfIntegers class (Example 6.8), 287–291
  this keyword, 279–280
  variables, scope of, 278–279
ClassNotFoundException, 658
Clients, 264–265
clone method, 356
Cloneable interface, 382–386, 392
CloneNotSupportedException, 658

close() method:
  InputStream class/Reader class, 694
  OutputStream class/Writer class, 694
COBOL (COmmon Business Oriented Language), 5, 254
code attribute, 628–629
Code, reuse of, 4
codebase attribute, 629
Code-completion assistance, 30
Coding, 42
Collection interface, 747–749, 778, 779
  equals method, 748–749
  hashCode method, 748–749
  methods, 748
Collections, 746
  defined, 778
Collections class, 772–775, 780
  binarySearch methods, 772–773
  constants, 773
  methods, 773
  sort methods, 772
  using (Example 17.10), 773–775
Color class, 450, 468–469
columnHeaderView property, JScrollPane class, 600
columns property, JTextField class, 541
Combo boxes, 549–552, 607–608
  JComboBox class, 549–550
  using (Example 13.5), 550–552
Command-line arguments, strings, 326–329
Command-line parameters, using (Example 7.5), 327–329
Comments, 15–16, 77
  styles, 77
Companion Web site, xviii
Comparable interface, 377–381, 392, 404, 421, 779
Comparator interface, 754–756, 779
  using to sort elements in a set (Example 17.4), 755–756
compare() method, Comparator interface, 754
compareTo method, 330, 377, 779
Comparisons, strings, 310–311
Compilation errors, 80–81

Compile time, 351, 360
Compiler, 27–28, 32, 66
Component class, 492, 506–507, 532–533, 826
  background property, 532
  font property, 532
  foreground property, 532
  height property, 532
  locale property, 532
  maximumSize property, 532–533
  minimumSize property, 532
  preferredSize property, 532
  properties, 532–533, 607
  width property, 532
componentAdded(ContainerEvent), 508
ComponentEvent, 506–507, 508
componentHidden(ComponentEvent), 508
ComponentListener interface, 508
componentMoved(ComponentEvent), 508
componentRemoved(ContainerEvent), 508
componentResized(ComponentEvent), 508
componentShown(ComponentEvent), 508
Composition, 420
ComputeArea program, 50–51
ComputeLoan application, 89–90
Computer languages, rules of usage, 12
Computing taxes, 112–115
  with methods (Example 4.4), 165–166
  using arrays (Example 5.8), 230–232
Concatenation, strings, 309
Conditional AND operator, 63
Conditional OR operator, 63
Confirmation dialogs, 573, 576–577
Console view, 86
Constants, 50–51
Constructor chaining, 359
Constructors, 255–257
Container class, 450, 507
Container classes, 450
ContainerEvent, 508
ContainerListener interface, 508
Containers, using panels as, 464–466
Content pane, JBuilder, 21–22

Contents tab, JBuilder Help, 93
continue statement, 130–132
  demonstrating (Example 3.6), 131–132
Control statements, 105–152
  breaking with labels, 133
  case studies, 134–140
  debugging loops, 141
  loop statements, 117–133
  nested loops, 127–128
  selection statements, 106–117
  statement labels, 133
Conversions, strings, 311–312
Copying arrays, 214–217
Counting each letter in a string (Example 7.2), 317–318
countTokens() method, StringTokenizer class, 324
Current execution point, 86
Custom exception classes, creating (Example 15.3), 669–674

D

Data field encapsulation, 265
Data fields (properties), 254
Data modifier, 859
Data streams, 698–701, 737
  DataInputStream, 698–699, 737
  DataInput methods, 698
  DataOutput methods, 699
  DataOutputStream, 698–699, 737
  using (Example 16.3), 699–701
DataInputStream, 698–699, 737
DataOutputStream class, 698–699, 737
Debugging, 83
  in JBuilder, 84–91
  loops, 141
Declared type of reference variable, 351, 360
Declaring assertions, 675
Declaring exceptions, 659–660, 663–665
Default constructor, 255
delete() method, File class, 688
Delphi, 5
Deployment, 401, 438
Derived class, 336, 359
Descent, 470
Descriptive identifiers, 48

destroy() method, Applet class, 622
Dialog boxes, 573
  entering input from (Example 2.2), 68–69
dialogTitle property, JFileChooser class, 709
dialogType property, JFileChooser class, 709
Dimension class, 450
Directory path, 686
-disenableassertions (-da) switch, 676
DisplayMessage applet, parameter names/values for, 633
Distributed computing, 6
Division by zero, and runtime errors, 81
Documentation, 76
doLayout() method, 464
Double class, 67, 315, 386
double data type, 52
double reserved word, 43
doubleBuffered proerpty, JComponent class, 836
doubleBuffered property, JComponent class, 533
do-while loop, 121–123
drawArc method, 481
drawImage methods, 825–826
drawOval method, 479–480
drawRect method, 477–478
drawString method, 467, 492
Drop-down lists, See Combo boxes
Dynamic binding, 346, 360

E

editable property, JTextField class, 541
Editor Options dialog, 30
e.getSource() method, 509, 511
Elements, 746, 778
EmptyBorder class, 567
-enableassertions (-ea) switch, 676
Encapsulation, 168
End tag, 628
End-of-line style, 79
equals() method, 310
  Collection interface, 748–749
  Comparator interface, 754
  Object class, 343–344

equalsIgnoreCase method, String class, 311
Error class, 658
Escape sequences for special characters, 58–59
EtchedBorder class, 567
Evaluate/Modify command, 89–90
Event handling, 507–517
Event-driven programming, 505–530
  event handling, 507–517
  events/event source, 506–507
  keyboard events, 523–526
  listeners, 507–517
  mouse events, 518–523
  registrations, 507–517
  source object, 506–507, 527
EventObject class, 506
Events, 657
Exception class, 658, 662, 669
Exception handler, 661
Exception handling, 656, 668, 679
  using, 677–678
Exceptions, 656–684
  ArithmeticException class, 658
  assertions, 674–678
    compiling programs with, 675–676
    declaring, 675
    defined, 674
    running programs with, 676–677
    using, 677–678
  AWTException class, 659
  catching, 660–663
    example (15.1), 663–665
  checked/unchecked, 659
  ClassNotFoundException, 658
  CloneNotSupportedException, 658
  custom exception classes, creating (Example 15.3), 669–674
  declaring, 659–660
    example (15.1), 663–665
  defined, 656
  Error class, 658
  Exception class, 658
  exception classes, 657–659
  exception handler, 661
  exception handling, 656, 668, 679
    using, 677–678

finally clause, 668, 679
  in GUI applications (Example 15.2), 666–667
  IOException class, 658–659
  NullPointerException class, 658
  rethrowing, 667–668
  RuntimeException class, 658
  Throwable class, 657
    methods, 662
  throwing, 660
    example (15.1), 663–665
  try-catch block, 656
  when to use, 668–669
exists() method, File class, 687
Explicit, casting, 347
Exponent methods, 169
Expressions, 49
Extended class, 336
Extracting strings, 309–310

F
\f (formfeed escape sequence), 60
Factorials:
  computing, 182–186
    example (4.8), 183–186
Fibonacci, Leonardo, 187
Fibonacci numbers:
  computing, 186–189
    example (4.9), 187–189
File class, 686–690, 737
  canRead() method, 687
  canWrite() method, 687
  constants, 688
  constructors, 686
  delete() method, 688
  exists() method, 687
  getAbsolutePath() method, 687
  getBoolean() method, 688
  getCanonicalPath() method, 687
  getName() method, 687
  getParent() method, 688
  getPath() method, 687
  isAbsolute() method, 687
  isDirectory() method, 687
  isFile() method, 687
  isHidden() method, 687
  methods, 686–688
  renameTo(File dest) method, 688

using, 688–690
  using (Example 16.1), 688–690
File dialogs, 708–713
  constructing, 708–709
  defined, 708
  JFileChooser class, 708–709, 738
    dialogTitle property, 709
    dialogType property, 709
    multiSelectionEnabled property, 709
    selectedFile property, 709
    selectedFiles property, 709
  using (Example 16.6), 709–713
File streams, 694–697
  copying files (Example 16.2), 695–697
  FileInputStream class, 694–695, 698, 737
  FileOutputStream class, 694–695, 698, 737
FileInputStream class, 694–695, 698, 737
  subclasses, 698
FileOutputStream class, 694–695, 698, 737
  subclasses, 698
FileReader, 694–695, 737
FileWriter, 694–695, 737
fillOval method, 479
fillRect method, 477
final modifier, 16, 336, 860
  classes/methods/variables, 354
finalize method, 354–355
finally clause, 668, 679
Find tab, JBuilder Help, 93
findVolume method, 347
Finished state, threads, 793
Float class, 315, 386
float data type, 52, 67
Floating-point literals, 53
FlowLayout manager, 457–459, 490
  testing (Example 11.1), 457–459
flush() method, OutputStream class/Writer class, 694
FocusEvent, 506–507
focusGained (FocusEvent), 508
FocusListener interface, 508
focusLost (FocusEvent), 508

Font class, 450, 492

`font` property, `Component` class, 532

`FontMetrics` class, 450, 492

for loops, 123–127
using (Example 3.3), 126–127

`foreground` property, `Component` class, 532

Forte, 83

FORTRAN (FORmula TRANslation), 5

Frames, 451, 452–456
adding components to, 455–456
centering, 454–455
creating, 452–453

Framework-based programming using Java API, 438

G

Generic classes, matrix operations, designing (Example 10.3), 346

Generic programming, 346

`GenericLinkedList` class, 431–437

`GenericMatrix` class, 423–430

Geometric figures:
drawing, 476–485
arcs, 481–482
lines, 476–477
ovals, 479–481
polygons/polylines, 482–485
rectangles, 477–479

`GeometricObject` class, 368–375
`Circle` class, 370
`Cylinder` class, 371, 373
`findArea` method, 369, 372, 373
`findPerimeter` method, 369, 372, 373
`Rectangle` class, 370–371
`toString()` method, 372
using (Example 9.1), 373–375

`getAbsolutePath()` method, `File` class, 687

`getAllFonts()` method, `GraphicsEnvironment` class, 469

`getAvailableFontFamilyNames()` method, `GraphicsEnvironment` class, 469

`getBoolean()` method, `File` class, 688

`getCanonicalPath()` method, `File` class, 687

`getClass` method, 356

`getClickCount()` method, 518

`getCodeBase()` method, 818, 819, 828, 839

`getContentPane` method, `JFrame` class, 455

`getDocumentBase()` method, 818, 839

`getFilePointer()` method, `RandomAccessFile` class, 723

`getFontMetrics()` methods, 470

`getImage` method, `Applet` class, 825, 828

`getKeyChar()` method, 524

`getKeyCode()` method, 524

`getLocalGraphicsEnvironment()` method, `GraphicsEnvironment` class, 469

`getLocalizedMessage()` method, `Throwable` class, 662

`getMessage()` method, `Throwable` class, 662

`getName()` method, `File` class, 687

`getParent()` method, `File` class, 688

`getPath()` method, `File` class, 687

`getPoint()` method, 518

`getResource()` method, 828

`getWhen()` method, `InputEvent`, 518

`getX()` method, 518

`getY()` method, 518

Glossary, 867–876

Gosling, James, 4, 37

Grades, assigning (Example 5.2), 212–214

Graphical interactive I/O, 714

Graphical notations, UML:
abstract classes, 863
aggregation, 862
inheritance, 862
interfaces, 863
sequence diagrams, 863
statechart diagrams, 863–864

Graphical user interface (GUI), 9, 532, *See also* GUI programming

applications, exceptions in (Example 15.2), 666–667

classes, classification of, 450
helper classes, 450

`Graphics` class, 450, 467, 491

Graphics, drawing in panels, 466–468

`GraphicsEnvironment` class, 469

`GregorianCalendar` class, 375–376

`GridLayout` manager, 459–461, 490
testing (Example 12.2), 460–461

GUI programming:
basics of, 447–503
case studies, 485–490
`Color` class, 468–469
event-driven programming, 505–530
Font class, 469–476
`FontMetrics` class, 469–476
frames, 452–456
adding components to, 455–456
centering, 454–455
creating, 452–453
geometric figures, drawing, 476–485
Java GUI API, 448–452
container classes, 450
GUI helper classes, 450
Swing GUI components, 451–452
layout managers, 456–464
`BorderLayout`, 461–463
defined, 456
`doLayout` method, 464
`FlowLayout`, 457–459
`GridLayout`, 459–461
properties of, 463–464
`validate` method, 464
panels:
drawing graphics in, 466–468
using as containers, 464–466
`Polygon` class, 482–485

H

Handlers, 509

Handtracing, 83

`hashCode` method, `Collection` interface, 748–749

`hashCode()` method, `Object` class, 344

HashMap class, 767–770, 780
using (Example 17.8), 768–770
HashSet class, 749–751, 778
using (Example 17.1), 750–751
hasMoreTokens() method,
StringTokenizer class, 324
hasNext() method, List interface,
758
hasPrevious() method, List
interface, 758
<head> tag, 628
Heavyweight components, 448
Height, 470
height attribute, 628–629
height property, Component class,
532
Hiding fields and static methods,
351–352
Horizontal scrollbars, 594
horizontalAlignment property,
JButton class, 534
horizontalScrollBarPolicy
property, JScrollPane class,
599
horizontalTextPosition
property, JButton class, 534
hspace attribute, 629
Hypertext Markup Language
(HTML), 10

I

icon property, JButton class, 534
Identifiers, 46–48
descriptive, 48
naming conventions, 48
IEEE 754 standard, 51
if ... else statements, 108–109
IllegalArgumentException, 658,
660, 665
Image animation, using (Example
19.5), 833–836
Image files, loading in Java applications, 828–832
ImageIcon class, 539–541, 825
ImageObserver interface, 826
Images:
displaying, 825–828
in an applet (Example 19.3),
826–828
using in applications/applets (Example 19.4),
829–832

Implementation, 401, 438
Implicit casting, 346
Increment and decrement operators,
54–55
Index tab, JBuilder Help, 93
indexOf() method, List interface,
757
indexOf() methods, 312
IndexOutOfBoundsException,
658, 659
Information hiding, 168
Inheritance, 359, 404, 420, 438, 439,
862
defined, 336
demonstrating (Example 8.1),
336–338
and the power of classes, 405
strong is-a relationship, 404, 420
UML graphical notation, 862
weak is-a relationship, 404, 421
init method, Applet class, 621
Initialization blocks, 356–359
static, 357–359
Inner classes, 291–292
Input dialogs, 66–69, 574, 577–578
converting strings to number',
67
Input errors, 81
Input/output, 685–743
array streams, 737
buffered streams, 704–708
BufferedInputStream,
704–705
BufferedOutputStream,
704–705
BufferedReader, 704–705,
708
BufferedWriter, 704–705,
738
displaying a file in a text area
(Example 16.5), 705–708
data streams, 698–701
DataInputStream, 698–699
DataInput methods, 698
DataOutput methods, 699
DataOutputStream, 698–699
using (Example 16.3), 699–701
File class, 686–690
constants, 688
constructors, 686
methods, 686–688
using, 688–690

file dialogs, 708–713
constructing, 708–709
defined, 708
JFileChooser class, 708–709,
738
using (Example 16.6), 709–713
file streams, 694–697
copying files (Example 16.5),
695–697
FileInputStream class,
694–695, 698
FileOutputStream class,
694–695, 698
Input/output (cont.)
I/O streams, 691–694
InputStream class, 692–694
OutputStream class, 694
Reader class, 692–694
stream classes, 691–692
Writer class, 694
line-number streams, 737
object streams, 716–722
defined, 716–717
ObjectInputStream class,
717–718, 738
ObjectOutputStream class,
717–718, 738
testing (Example 16.7), 719–722
transient keyword, 722
piped streams, 737
print streams, 702–704
PrintStream class, 702
PrintWriter class, 702
using (Example 16.4), 703–704
pushback streams, 737
random access files, 722–732
processing of records, 724
RandomAccessFile class, 723,
738
using (Example 16.8), 724–732
string streams, 737
text files, parsing, 733–736
text input/output on the console,
714–716
InputStream class, 692–694,
737
methods, 693–694
Insertion order, 780
Instance, 256
Instance methods, 324
instanceOf operator, 346–347,
360, 856

Instantiation, 256
Instnace variable, 272
int data type, 52
Integer class, 67, 315, 386
IntegerMatrix subclass,
    GenericMatrix class,
    423–430
Integrated development environment
    (IDE), 13
Interactive I/O, 714
Interfaces, 5, 376–386, 392,
    420–421, 439
    abstract classes vs., 381–382
    Cloneable interface, 382–386
    distinguishing from classes, 376
    marker, 382
    Max class, 377–381
    UML graphical notation, 863
    using (Example 9.2), 378–381
Internet, defined, 10
Interpreter, 6–7
interrupt() method, Thread
    class, 792
I/O streams, 691–694
    InputStream class, 692–694
    OutputStream class, 694
    Reader class, 692–694
    stream classes, 691–692
    Writer class, 694
IOException class, 658–659
isAbsolute() method, File class,
    687
isAlive() method, Thread class,
    792
isAltDown() method,
    InputEvent, 518
isControlDown() method,
    InputEvent, 518
isDigit(char ch) method, 316
isDirectory() method, File
    class, 687
isFile() method, File class, 687
isHidden() method, File class,
    687
Is-kind-of relationship, 421
isLetter(char ch) method, 316
isLetterOrDigit(char ch)
    method, 316
isLowerCase(char ch) method,
    316
isMetaDown() method,
    InputEvent, 518

isShiftDown() method,
    InputEvent, 518
isUpperCase(char ch) method,
    316
ItemEvent, 507–508
ItemListener interface, 508
itemStateChanged(ItemEvent),
    508
Iteration, recursion vs., 193
iterator() method, Collection
    interface, 778

J
JApplet class, 450, 533, 622–623
Java, See also Java data structures; Java
    programs
    as architecture-neutral language, 8
    array initializer, 208
    case sensitivity of, 16
    characteristics of, 5–9
    distributed computing i, 6
    as dynamic language, 9
    history of, 4
    as Internet programming language,
        7
    interpreter, 6–7
    keywords, 849
    language specification, 12–13
    modifiers, 859–866
    and memory allocation/garbage
        collection, 5
    multithreading, 9
    object-oriented programming, 5–6
    performance of, 8–9
    portability of, 8
    power of, 4
    robustness of, 7
    runtime exception-handling fea-
        ture, 7
    security of, 7–8
    simple program, 14–15
    simplicity of, 5
    source programs, 31
    versatility of, 11
Java 2 Enterprise Edition (J2EE),
    13
Java 2 Micro Edition (J2ME), 13
Java 2 Standard Edition (J2SE),
    13
    versions of, 13
Java API (Application Program Inter-
    face), 438

Java Collections Framework, 746,
    761, 772
java command, 658
Java data structures, 745–782
    AbstractCollection class,
        747–749
    AbstractList class, 757–758
    AbstractSequentialList class,
        757–758
    AbstractSet class, 749–751
    ArrayList class, 758–760, 779
    Arrays class, using (Example
        17.11), 776–778
    Collection interface, 747–749
        equals method, 748–749
        hashCode method, 748–749
        methods, 748
    collections, 746
        defined, 778
    Collections class, 772–775
    Comparator interface, 754–756,
        779
        using to sort elements in a set
            (Example 17.4), 755–756
    elements, 746, 778
    HashSet class, 749–751, 778
    LinkedHashSet class, 751–752,
        778
    LinkedList class, 758–760, 779
    List interface, 746, 757–758
    Map interface, 746, 766–771
        AbstractMap class, 767, 780
        clear() method, 767
        containsKey (Object key)
            method, 767
        containsValue (Object
            value) method, 767
        HashMap class, 767–770, 780
        isEmpty() method, 767
        keyset() method, 767
        LinkedHashMap class,
            767–770, 780
        putAll(Map m) method, 767
        put(Object Key, Object
            value) method, 767
        query methods, 767
        remove(Object key) method,
            767
        size() method, 767
        TreeMap class, 767–770, 780
        update methods, 767
    Set interface, 746, 749–751

SortedMap interface, 767, 780
SortedSet interface, 752–754
Stack class, 764–766
TreeSet class, 752–754
    using to sort elements in a set
        (Example 17.3), 753–754
Vector class, 761–763, 779
Java Development Toolkit (JDK 1.4),
    13
    command-line debugger (jdb), 83
Java GUI API, 448–452
    container classes, 450
    GUI helper classes, 450
    Swing GUI components, 451–452
Java HotSpot Performance Engine,
    9
Java programs:
    anatomy of, 15–17
    blocks, 17
    classes, 17
    comments, 15–16
    compiling, 32–33
    creating, 28–31
    executing, 34–35
    main method, 17
    methods, 17
    modifiers, 16
    packages, 16
    reserved words (keywords), 16
    running from the command line,
        89–90
    statements, 16
Java servlets, 13
Java Virtual Machine, 346
java.applet.Applet, 839
java.applet.AudioClip, 839
    loop() method, 819, 839
    play() method, 819, 839
    stop() method, 819, 839
java.awt, 657
java.awt.Dimension class, 454
java.awt.event , 507
java.awt.GraphicsEnvironment,
    469
java.awt.Image, 825
java.awt.Panel, 448
java.awt.Toolkit class, 454
java.awt.Window, 448
javadoc comments, 16
java.io.Serializable interface,
    718
java.lang, 657

java.lang.Cloneable interface,
    382–386, 392
java.lang.Comparable interface,
    377–381, 392, 404, 421
java.lang.Number class, 657
java.lang.Object class, 359
java.lang.String class, 306
java.net.URL, 818
JavaServer Pages, 13
java.swing.ButtonGroup, 562
java.util.Calendar, 375
java.util.Date, 375
java.util.EventObject, 506,
    527
java.util.GregorianCalendar,
    375
javax.swing.BorderFactory
    class, 567
javax.swing.event.ListSelecti
    onEvent, 553
JBuilder, 83
    AppBrowser, 19
    Auto feedback enabled
        option, 33
    backup files, 25
    bytecode, 33
    code-completion assistance, 30
    content pane, 21–22
    creating projects incorrectly, 25
    creating a project, 23–26
    debugging in, 84–91
        controlling program execution,
            86–87
        examining/modifying data val-
            ues, 87–91
        starting the debugger, 84–86
    documentation, 92
    getting started with, 18–23
    indentation, 78
    installing, 18
    Java programs:
        compiling, 32–33
        creating, 28–31
        executing, 34–35
    Java source programs:
        case sensitivity of, 31
    main menu, 19
    multiple files, selecting, 21
    online help, 92–95, See also
        JBuilder Help
        accessing from the Help menu,
            92–93

project pane, 20–21
    Run command, 34
    running programs, 34
    source code file, 31
    status bar, 20
    structure pane, 23
JBuilder (cont.)
    toolbar, 19
    user interface, 19
JBuilder 9, versions of, 13–14
JBuilder Developer, 14
JBuilder Enterprise, 14
JBuilder Help:
    accessing from the Help menu,
        92–93
    navigation pane, 92–93
    obtaining help on Java keywords
        and classes, 93–95
    tabs, 93
JBuilder Personal, 13
JButton class, 507, 509, 538, 607
    constructors, 533
    horizontalAlignment property,
        534
    horizontalTextPosition
        property, 534
    icon property, 534
    mnemonic property, 534
    text property, 534
    verticalAlignment property,
        534
    verticalTextPosition
        property, 535
JCheckBox class, 507, 556–557
    constructors, 556
    events, 557
    properties, 557
    selected property, 557
JCheckBoxMenuItem class, 582,
    584, 585
JComboBox class, 507, 549–550
    constructors, 549
    events, 549–550
    properties, 549
JComboBox menu, getting items
    from, 549
JComponent class, 449, 451,
    532–533
    doubleBuffered property, 836
    properties, 533, 607
jdb (command-line debugger), 83
JDialog class, 450, 533

JFileChooser class, 708–709, 738
  dialogTitle property, 709
  dialogType property, 709
  multiSelectionEnabled
    property, 709
  selectedFile property, 709
  selectedFiles property, 709
JFrame class, 450, 453, 464, 533
  getContentPane method, 455
JLabel class, 538–539, 607
  constructors, 538
  properties, 538–539
JList class, 507, 552–553
  constructors, 553
  properties, 553
JMenu class, 582, 585
JMenuItem class, 507, 582, 584, 585
JOptionPane class, 36, 573–582
  confirmation dialogs, 573
  input dialogs, 574
  message dialogs, 573
  option dialogs, 574
JOptionPane dialogs, 608
  confirmation dialogs, 576–577
  creating (Example 13.10), 579–582
  input dialogs, 577–578
  message dialogs, 574–576
  option dialogs, 578–579
JPanel class, 464, 491
JRadioButton class, 507, 608
JRadioButtonMenuItem class, 582,
  584, 585
JScrollBar class, 507, 598
  blockIncrement property, 595
  constructors, 594
  maximum property, 595
  minimum property, 595
  orientation property, 594
  properties, 594–595
  unitIncrement property, 595
  value property, 595
  visibleAmount property, 595
JScrollPane class, 598–600
  columnHeaderView property,
    600
  constructors, 598–599
  horizontalScrollBarPolicy
    property, 599
  properties, 599–600
  rowHeaderView property, 600
  verticalScrollBarPolicy
    property, 599

  viewportBorder property, 600
  viewportView property, 600
JScrollPane class, 545
JTabbedPane class, 603, 609
  constructors, 603
JTextArea class, 544–545, 607
  constructors, 544
  lineCount property, 545
  lineWrap property, 544
  properties, 544–545
  rows property, 545
  tabSize property, 545
  wrapStyleWord property, 545
JTextField class, 507, 541–542,
  607
  constructors, 541
  events, 541–542
  properties, 541
Just-in-time compilation, 9

K
Key events, handling (Example 12.6),
  525–526
Keyboard events, 523–526, 527
  defined, 523
  key constants, 524
KeyEvent, 506–507, 508
KeyListener interface, 508, 524
keyPressed(KeyEvent), 508, 524
keyReleased(KeyEvent), 508, 524
keyTyped(KeyEvent), 508, 524
Keywords, 16

L
Labels, 538–541
  defined, 538
  JLabel class, 538–539
    constructors, 538
    properties, 538–539
  using (Example 13.2), 539–541
lastIndexOf() method, List
  interface, 757
lastIndexOf() methods, 312–313
Layout managers, 456–464, 490
  BorderLayout, 461–463, 490
  defined, 456
  doLayout method, 464
  FlowLayout, 457–459, 490
  GridLayout, 459–461, 490
  properties of, 463–464
  validate method, 464
Leading, 470

Left-associative, 64
length() method:
  RandomAccessFile class, 723
  StringBuffer class, 320
Lifeline, sequence diagrams, 421, 863
Lightweight components, 448
Linear search, testing (Example 5.11),
  237–239
LineBorder class, 567
lineCount property, JTextArea
  class, 545
Line-number streams, 737
LineNumberInputStream class,
  698
LineNumberReader class, 737
Lines, drawing, 476–477
lineWrap property, JTextArea
  class, 544
LinkageError, 658
Linked lists:
  designing classes for, 430–437
  nodes, 431
  using (Example 10.4), 436–437
LinkedHashMap class, 767–770, 780
  using (Example 17.8), 768–770
LinkedHashSet class, 778
  using (Example 17.2), 751–752
LinkedList class, 758–760, 779
List interface, 746, 757–758, 779
  add(element) method, 757–758
  add(index, element) method,
    757
  hasNext() method, 758
  hasPrevious() method, 758
  indexOf() method, 757
  lastIndexOf() method, 757
  listIterator() method, 757
  next() method, 758
  nextIndex() method, 758
  previousIndex() method, 758
  set(element) method, 758
Listeners, 507–517
  defined, 507
  object class, 508
  registration, 509
ListIterator interface, 757
listIterator() method, List
  interface, 757
Lists, 552–556, 608
  defined, 552
  JList class, 552–553
  using (Example 13.6), 553–556

ListSelectionEvent, 507
Loaded class view, 86
Loan class, 284–287
Loan payments, computing (Example 2.3), 70–72
Local variables:
    defined, 167
    scope of, 167–168
locale property, Component class, 532
Logic errors, 82, 656
Long class, 315, 386
long type, 52, 67
loop() method,
        java.applet.AudioClip, 819, 839
Loop statements, 55, 117–133
    break statement, 130–131
    continue statement, 130–133
    do-while loop, 121–123
    for loop, 123–127
    loop-continuation-condition, 117, 119, 124
    which to use, 129–130
    while loop, 118–121
Loops, defined, 117

M
Main menu, JBuilder, 19
main method, 17, 326
Maintenance, 401, 438
Map interface, 746, 766–771
    AbstractMap class, 767, 780
    clear() method, 767
    containsKey (Object key) method, 767
    containsValue (Object value) method, 767
    HashMap class, 767–770, 780
    isEmpty() method, 767
    keySet() method, 767
    LinkedHashMap class, 767–770, 780
    putAll(Map m) method, 767
    put(Object Key, Object value) method, 767
    query methods, 767
    remove(Object key) method, 767
    size() method, 767
    TreeMap class, 767–770, 780
    update methods, 767

Marker interface, 382
Math class, 168–171, 266
    exponent methods, 169
    min, max, abs, and random methods, 170
    rounding methods, 169–170
    trigonometric methods, 169
MatteBorder class, 567
Max class, 377–381
max method, 162, 170
    overloading (Example 4.3), 162–165
    testing (Example 4.1), 156–159
maximum property, JScrollBar class, 595
maximumSize property, Component class, 532–533
Mean, computing (Example 4.5), 171–173
MediaTracker class, 836–839
    using (Example 19.6), 836–839
Menus, 608
    addSeparator() method, 583
    creating, 582–585
    creating checkbox menu items, 584
    creating menu items, 583
    creating radio button menu items, 584–585
    creating submenu items, 583–584
    defined, 582
    events, 585
    image icons, 585–586
    JMenuBar class, 582
    keyboard accelerators, 585–586
    keyboard mnemonics, 585–586
    setJMenuBar method, 582
    using (Example 13.11), 586–589
Message dialog boxes:
    displaying text in, 35–37
    using (Example 1.2), 35–37
Message dialogs, 573, 574–576
Message Panel class, creating (Example 11.5), 471–476
Method abstraction, 168, 175
Method invocation, 155–159
    sequence diagrams, 422, 863
Method modifier, 859
Methods, 17, 153–203
    abstraction, 168, 175
    block, 17
    body, 155
    calling (invoking), 155–159

sequence diagrams, 422, 863
case studies, 175–182
creating, 154–155
header, 154
Math class, 168–171
overloading, 162–166
overriding, 341–343
parameter list, 155
passing arrays to, 217–225
passing objects to, 270–272
passing parameters, 157–162
recursion, 182–193
scope of local variables, 167–168
structure, 154
values returned by, 155
Microsoft Visual J++, 13
MIDI format, 818
min method, 170
minimum property, JScrollBar class, 595
minimumSize property, Component class, 532
mnemonic property, JButton class, 534
Modifiers, 16
Mouse events, 518–523
Mouse, scribbling with (Example 12.5), 521–523
mouseClicked(MouseEvent), 508, 518
mouseDragged(MouseEvent), 508, 518
mouseEntered(MouseEvent), 508, 518
MouseEvent class, 506–507, 508, 518–519
mouseExited(MouseEvent), 508, 518
MouseListener interface, 508, 527
    handlers, 518, 527
MouseMotionListener interface, 508, 527
mouseMoved(MouseEvent), 508, 518
mousePressed(MouseEvent), 508, 518
mouseReleased(MouseEvent), 508, 518
Multidimensional arrays, 226–233
    creating, 226–227
    declaring variables of, 226–227

Multidimensional arrays, (*cont.*)
obtaining the lengths of, 227
ragged arrays, 227–228
Multimedia, 817–845
audio:
announcing the time on a separate thread (Example 19.2),
823–824
playing, 818–822
running on a separate thread,
823–824
loading image/audio files in Java
applications, 828–832
`MediaTracker` class, 836–839
using (Example 19.6), 837–839
sequence of images, displaying,
833–836
sound, incorporating in applets
(Example 19.1), 819–822
Multiple windows, creating (Example
13.12), 590–594
Multiple-choice test, grading (Example 5.7), 228–230
Multiplication table, displaying (Example 3.4), 127–128
Multiplicity, 403
`multiSelectionEnabled` property,
`JFileChooser` class,
709
Multithreading, 9, 783–815, *See also*
Threads
defined, 784
images, displaying, 825–828
`Runnable` interface, creating
threads by implementing,
788–791
synchronization, 794–799
showing resource conflict (Example 18.3), 795–797
`synchronized` keyword,
797–798
synchronized statements,
799
`Thread` class, creating threads by
extending, 785–788
threads:
concepts, 784–785
controlling animation using,
799–803
controls/communications,
791–792
defined, 784

groups, 794
states, 792–793
`Timer` class, controlling animation
using, 803–807
Mutators, 265–269

N
\n (linefeed escape sequence), 60
Naming conventions, 77
identifiers, 48
Narrowing a type, 57
`native` modifier, 860
Natural order, 752
Nested blocks, 17
Nested classes, 291–292
Nested `if` statements, 109–111
Nested loops, 127–128
`new` (creating object), 856
New state, threads, 793, 808
`next()` method, `List` interface,
758
`nextIndex()` method, `List`
interface, 758
Next-line style, 79
`nextToken()` method,
`StringTokenizer` class, 324
Non-alphanumeric characters, ignoring when checking palin-
dromes (Example 7.3),
321–323
`notify()` method, `Object` class,
792
`notifyAll()` method, `Object`
class, 792
`NullPointerException` class,
658
Numeric data types, 51–52
Numeric literals, 53
Numeric operators, 52
Numeric type conversions, 56–58
Numeric wrapper class:
constants, 387–388
constructors, 387

O
Oak, 4
`Object` class, 336, 343–345, 359
`equals()` method, 343–344
`hashCode()` method, 344
`toString()` method, 344–345
Object streams, 716–722
defined, 716–717

`ObjectInputStream` class,
717–718, 738
`ObjectOutputStream` class,
717–718, 738
testing (Example 16.7), 719–722
`transient` keyword, 722
Object-oriented modeling, 399–443,
See also Objects
analyzing relationships among objects, 401–404
aggregation, 403–404
association, 401–403
inheritance, 404
case studies, 423–430
class design guidelines, 419–421
class development, 404–412
framework-based programming
using Java API, 438
linked lists, designing classes for,
430–437
modeling dynamic behavior,
421–423
sequence diagrams, 421–422
statechart diagrams, 422–423
`Rational` class, 413–418
software development process,
400–401
Object-oriented programming
(OOP), 4
Objects:
accessing data/methods,
258–263
accessing via reference variables,
257–264
analyzing relationships among:
aggregation, 403–404
association, 401–403
inheritance, 404
array of, 280–282
behavior of, 254
constructing, using constructors,
255–257
data fields (properties), 254
default constructor, 255
defined, 254
defining classes for, 254–255
passing to methods, 270–272
processing primitive data type values as objects, 386–391
Online help, *See also* JBuilder Help
JBuilder, 92–95
Operand evaluation order, 65–66

Operator precedence:
  and associativity, 64–65
  chart, 65, 855–857
Option buttons, *See* Radio buttons
Option dialogs, 574, 578–579
Order by comparator, 753
orientation property,
    JScrollBar class, 594
OutputPath\PackageName, 33
OutputStream class, 694, 737
Ovals, drawing, 479–481
Overloading methods, 162–166
Overriding methods, 341–343

P
Package-access, 265
Package-private, 265
Packages, 16
  creating, 25
paintComponent method, 466,
    468, 491, 826
Palindromes, checking (Example 7.1),
    314–315
  non-alphanumeric characters, ig-
    noring (Example 7.3),
    321–323
Panels:
  drawing graphics in, 466–468
  testing (Example 11.4), 465–466
  using as containers, 464–466
Parameter order association, 157
Parent class, 359
parseInt method, 67
Parsing strings into numbers, meth-
    ods, 388–389
Pascal, 5, 254
Pass by value, 218
  testing (Example 4.2), 160–163
Passing objects:
  as arguments (Example 6.4),
    270–272
  to methods, 270–272
Passing parameters, 157–162
  to applets, 632–635
  pass by value, 160–163, 218
  passing arrays to methods,
    217–225
Peers, 448
Piped streams, 737
PipedInputStream class, 737
PipedOutputStream class,
    737

PipedReader class, 737
PipedWriter class, 737
play() method,
    java.applet.AudioClip,
    819, 839
Point class, 518, 527
Polygons/polylines, drawing,
    482–485
Polymorphism, 345, 360
  demonstrating (Example 8.3),
    348–350
Postdecrement operator, 54
Postincrement operator, 54
Predecrement operator, 54
preferredSize property,
    Component class, 532
Preincrement operator, 54
previousIndex() method, List
    interface, 758
Prime numbers, displaying (Example
    3.9), 138–139
primitive data type values, processing
    as objects, 386–391
Primitive data types, 42
Print streams, 702–704, 738
  PrintStream class, 702, 738
  PrintWriter class, 702, 738
  constructors, 702
  using (Example 16.4), 703–704
printStackTrace() method,
    Throwable class, 662
PrintStream class, 698, 702,
    738
PrintWriter class, 702, 738
  constructors, 702
private modifier, 16, 265, 353,
    419–420, 860
Procedural programming languages,
    6
Programming errors, 80–82
  input errors, 81
  logic errors, 82
  runtime errors, 81–82
  syntax errors (compilation errors),
    80–81
Programming style, 76–80
  block styles, 79
  code style examples, 79–80
  comments/comment styles, 77
  indentation, 77–78
  naming conventions, 77
  spacing, 77–78

Project pane, JBuilder, 20–21
Properties, 254
protected modifier, 16, 265, 336,
    419–420, 860
  data and methods, 352–353
public modifier, 16, 265, 353,
    419–420, 860
Pushback streams, 737
PushbackInputStream class, 698
PushbackReader class, 737
PushInputStream class, 737
Pyramid of numbers, displaying (Ex-
    ample 3.8), 119–121

R
\r (carriage return character escape se-
    quence), 60
Radio buttons, 561–566, 608
  constructors, 561
  defined, 561
  events, 562
  properties, 562
  using (Example 13.8), 562–566
Ragged arrays, 227–228
Random access files, 722–732
  processing of records, 724
  RandomAccessFile class, 723,
    738
  using (Example 16.8), 724–732
random method, 170
Rational class, 413–418
  data fields (properties), 414
  example (10.2), 413–418
  methods, 414
rational.com/uml, 256
RationalMatrix subclass,
    GenericMatrix class,
    423–430
read() method, InputStream
    class, 693
read(byte[] b) method,
    InputStream class, 693
Reader class, 692–694
Read-only streams, 722
Ready state, threads, 793, 808
Rectangles, drawing, 477–479
Recursion, 182–193
  computing factorials, 182–186
  computing Fibonacci numbers,
    186–189
  defined, 182
  iteration vs., 193

Recursion, *(cont.)*
  Towers of Hanoi problem,
    189–193
Reference type, 257
Reference variables:
  accessing an object's data and
    methods, 258–263
  accessing objects via, 257–264
  differences between variables of
    primitive types and reference
    types, 263–264
`regionMatches` method, `String`
    class, 311
Registrations, 507–517
`renameTo(File dest)` method,
    `File` class, 688
`repaint()` method, 468
  `String` class, 311–312
Requirements specification, 400,
    438
Reserved words (keywords), 16
`resume()` method, `Thread` class,
    791
Rethrowing exceptions, 667–668
`returnValueType`, 155
RGB model, 468
Right-associative, 64
RMF format, 818
Rounding methods, 169–170
`rowHeaderView` property,
    `JScrollPane` class, 600
`rows` property, `JTextArea` class,
    545
Run menu, 86
`run()` method, `Thread` class,
    791
`Runnable` interface:
  creating threads by implementing,
    788–791
  using to create and launch threads
    (Example 18.2), 789–791
Runnable object, 784
Running state, threads, 793, 808
Runtime errors, 81–82, 656
  as exceptions, 656
`RuntimeException` class, 658, 659,
    662, 663, 665, 667

S

Sales amount, finding (Example 3.7),
    134–138
`s.charAt(index)` method, 308

Scientific notation, and floating-point
    literals, 53
Scope of local variables, 167–168
Scroll panes, 598–603
  `JScrollPane` class, 598–600
  using (Example 13.14), 600–603
Scrollbars, 594–598
  constructors, 594
  defined, 594
  `JScrollBar` class:
    constructors, 594
    properties, 594–595
  using (Example 13.13), 596–598
Searching arrays, 237–243
  binary search approach, 239–243
  linear search approach, 237–239
`seek(long pos)` method,
    `RandomAccessFile` class,
    723
`selected` property, `JCheckBox`
    class, 557
`selectedFile` property,
    `JFileChooser` class, 709
`selectedFiles` property,
    `JFileChooser` class,
    709
`selectedIndex` property:
  `JComboBox` class, 549
  `JList` class, 553
`selectedIndices` property, `JList`
    class, 553
`selectedItem` property,
    `JComboBox` class, 549
`selectedValues` property, `JList`
    class, 553
Selection statements, 106–117
  `if ... else` statements,
    108–109
  nested `if` statements, 109–111
  simple `if` statements, 106–108
  `switch` statements, 115–116
`selectionMode` property, `JList`
    class, 553
Self-Test Web site, 11
Sequence diagrams, 439–440
  UML graphical notation, 863
`Set` interface, 746, 749–751, 778
`setAlignment` method,
    `FlowLayout` manager, 463
`setBackground (Color c)`
    method, and `Color` class,
    469, 492

`setColumns` method, `GridLayout`
    manager, 463
`set(element)` method, `List`
    interface, 758
`setForeground (Color c)`
    method, and `Color` class,
    469, 492
`setHGap` method:
  `BorderLayout` manager, 463
  `FlowLayout` manager, 463
  `GridLayout` manager, 463
`setLayout` method, 456, 464,
    535
`setLength(newLength)` method,
    `StringBuffer` class, 320
`setLength(newLength)` method,
    `StringBuffer` class, 320
`setPriority(int)` method,
    `Thread` class, 792
`setRows` method, `GridLayout`
    manager, 463
Setter, 266
`setVGap` method:
  `BorderLayout` manager, 463
  `FlowLayout` manager, 463
  `GridLayout` manager, 463
`Short` class, 315, 380
`short` data type, 52, 67
Short-circuit AND operator, 63
Short-circuit OR operator, 63
Shortcut operators, 54–56
`showInputDialog` method,
    `JOptionPane` class, 66–67,
    168
`showMessageDialog` method,
    35–37
Simple application (Example 1.1),
    14–15
Simple `if` statements, 106–108
Simple programs:
  arithmetic expressions, 53–54
  assignment statements (assignment
    expressions), 49–50
  case studies, 70–76
  constants, 50–51
  identifiers, 46–48
  numeric data types, 51–52
  numeric literals, 53
  numeric operators, 52
  shortcut operators, 54–56
  variables, 48–49
  writing, 42–45

skip(long n) method,
    InputStream class, 694
sleep(long) method, Thread
    class, 792, 808
Software development process,
    400–401
    deployment, 401, 438
    implementation, 401, 438
    maintenance, 401, 438
    requirements specification, 400,
        438
    system analysis, 400–401, 438
    system design, 401, 438
    testing, 401, 438
SortedMap interface, 767
SortedSet interface, 752–754, 779
Sorting arrays, 234–237
Source object, 506–507, 527
SourcePath\PackageName, 31
Special floating-point values,
    865–866
Stack, 156
Stack class, 764–766, 779
    using (Example 17.7), 764–766
Stack view, 86
StackOfIntegers class (Example
    6.8), 287–291
Standard output objects, 17
start() method:
    Applet class, 622
    Thread class, 791, 808
Start tag, 628
State, statechart diagrams, 423
Statechart diagrams, UML graphical
    notation, 863–864
Statements, 16
Static initialization blocks, 357–359
Static inner class, 292
Static methods, 36, 272–273
static modifier, 16, 420, 860
Static valueOf methods, 388
Static variables, 272–277
Status bar, JBuilder, 20
stop() method:
    java.applet.AudioClip, 819,
        839
    Thread class, 791
stop method, Applet class, 622
Stream classes, 691–692
StreamTokenizer class, 733–736,
    738
    constants, 733

using (Example 16.9), 734–736
variables, 733
strictfp keyword, 849, 860
String class, 419
    equalsIgnoreCase method, 311
    regionMatches method, 311
    replace() method, 311–312
    toLowerCase method, 311–312
    toUpperCase method, 311–312
String streams, 737
StringBuffer class, 318–323, 330,
    419
    capacity() method, 320
    charAt() method, 321
    charAt(index) method, 321
    constructing a string buffer,
        318–319
    constructors, 318–319
    length() method, 320
    modifying strings in the buffer,
        319–320
    setLength(newLength) method,
        320
    setLength(newLength) method,
        320
    toString() method, 320
Strings, 305–334
    Character class, 315–318
    command-line arguments,
        326–329
        passing arguments to Java pro-
            grams, 326
        processing command-line para-
            meters, 326–329
    comparisons, 310–311
    concatenation, 309
    constructing, 306–308
    conversion between arrays and, 313
    conversions, 311–312
    converting characters and numeric
        values to, 313
Strings (cont.)
    converting to numbers, 67
    counting each letter in (Example
        7.2), 317–318
    extracting, 309–310
    finding a character/substring in,
        312–313
    length() method, 308
    String class, 306
    string length, and retrieving indi-
        vidual characters, 308–309

StringBuffer class, 318–323
StringTokenizer class,
    323–325
substring() method, 309–310
StringTokenizer class, 323–325,
    330, 419
    constructors, 324
    countTokens() method, 324
    hasMoreTokens() method, 324
    instance methods, 324
    nextToken() method, 324
    testing (Example 7.4), 324–325
Strong is-a relationship, 404, 420,
    439
Structure pane, JBuilder, 23
Student CD-ROM, xviii
Subclasses, 336–338, 359, 392
substring() method, 309–310
Sun ONE Studio, 27
super keyword, 338–340
    calling superclass constructors,
        338–340
    calling superclass methods,
        340
Superclasses, 336–338, 359
super.paintComponent(g), 468,
    491
suspend() method, Thread class,
    791
Swing components, 448
Swing GUI components, 451–452
switch statements, 115–116
Synchronization, 794–799
    showing resource conflict (Example
        18.3), 795–797
    synchronized keyword, 797–798
    synchronized statements, 799
    synchronized modifier, 860
Syntax errors, 656
Syntax errors (compilation errors),
    80–81
System analysis, 400–401, 438
System class, 36
System design, 401, 438
System.out.print, 168
System.out.println, 16–17

T
\t (tab escape sequence), 60
Tabbed panes, 603–607
    JTabbedPane class, 603
    using (Example 13.15), 604–607

tabSize property, JTextArea class, 545

Testing, 401, 438

Testing panels (Example 11.4), 465–466

Text areas, 544–548
  JTextArea class, 544–545, 607
  using (Example 13.4), 545–548

Text fields, 541–544
  JTextField class, 541–542, 607
  using (Example 13.3), 542–544

Text files, parsing, 733–736

Text input/output on the console, 714–716

Text interactive I/O, 714

text property, JButton class, 534

TextEvent, 508

TextListener interface, 508

textValueChanged(TextEvent), 508

this keyword, 279–280

Thread class:
  creating threads by extending, 785–788
  interrupt() method, 792
  isAlive() method, 792
  MAX_PRIORITY, 793
  MIN_PRIORITY, 793
  NORM_PRIORITY, 793
  resume() method, 791
  run() method, 791
  setPriority(int) method, 792
  sleep(long) method, 792, 808
  start() method, 791, 808
  stop() method, 791
  suspend() method, 791
  using to create and launch threads (Example 18.1), 785–788
  yield() method, 792

Threads, See also Multithreading
  blocked state, 793, 808
  concepts, 784–785
  controlling animation using, 799–803
  controls/communications, 791–792
  defined, 784
  finished state, 793
  groups, 794
  new state, 793, 808

ready state, 793, 808

running state, 793, 808

states, 792–793

Throwable class, 657
  methods, 662

Throwing exceptions, 660, 663–665

TicTacToe Game (Example 14.4), 638–645

Timer class:
  controlling animation using, 803–807
  Bouncing Ball (Example 18.5), 804–807

Time-sharing, 787

title property, Border interface, 566

<title> tag, 628

titleColor property, Border interface, 566

Titled borders, 566, 608

titleFont property, Border interface, 566

titlePosition property, Border interface, 566

toCharArray method, 313

toLowerCase method, String class, 311–312, 316

Toolbar, JBuilder, 19

toolTipText property, JComponent class, 533

toString() method:
  Object class, 344–345
  StringBuffer class, 320

toUpperCase method, String class, 311–312, 316

transient keyword, 722

Transition, statechart diagrams, 423

TreeMap class, 767–770, 780
  using (Example 17.8), 768–770

TreeSet class, 752–754
  using to sort elements in a set (Example 17.3), 753–754

Trigonometric methods, 169

try-catch block, 656, 660, 669

TT_WORD, 733

Type casting, 57

(type) (unary casting), 856

U

UML, See Unified Modeling Language (UML)

Unary operators, 52

Unchecked exceptions, 659

Unconditional AND operator, 63

Unconditional OR operator, 63

Unicode, 57–58

Unified Modeling Language (UML), 400, 403
  graphical notations, 861–866
    abstract classes, 863
    aggregation, 862
    class relationships, 862
    classes/objects, 861
    inheritance, 862
    interfaces, 863
    private modifier, 861–862
    protected modifier, 861–862
    public modifier, 861–862
    sequence diagrams, 863
    statechart diagrams, 863–864
    static modifier, 861–862

unitIncrement property, JScrollBar class, 595

URL (Universal Resource Locator), 818

User interfaces:
  borders, 566–573, 608
    BevelBorder class, 566
    border property, 566
    classes, 566–567
    EmptyBorder class, 567
    EtchedBorder class, 567
    LineBorder class, 567
    MatteBorder class, 567
    properties, 566
    title property, 566
    titleColor property, 566
    TitledBorder, 566
    titleFont property, 566
    titlePosition property, 566
    types of, 566
    using (Example 13.9), 568–573
  buttons, 533–538
    defined, 533
    JButton class, 533–534
    using (Example 13.1), 535–538
  checkboxes, 556–561, 608
    defined, 556
    JCheckBox class, 556–557
    using (Example 13.7), 557–561

combo boxes, 549–552, 607–608
  JComboBox class, 549–550
Component class, 532–533
creating, 531–618
JComponent class, 532–533
JOptionPane dialogs, 573–582
labels, 538–541
  defined, 538
  JLabel class, 538–539
  using (Example 13.2), 539–541
lists, 552–556
  defined, 552
  JList class, 552–553
  using (Example 13.6), 553–556
menus, 582–589, 608
  addSeparator() method, 583
  creating, 582–585
  creating checkbox menu items, 584
  creating menu items, 583
  creating radio button menu items, 584–585
  creating submenu items, 583–584
  defined, 582
  events, 585
  image icons, 585–586
  JMenuBar class, 582
  keyboard accelerators, 585–586
  keyboard mnemonics, 585–586
  setJMenuBar method, 582
  using, 586–589
multiple windows, creating (Example 13.12), 590–594
radio buttons, 561–566, 608
  constructors, 561
  defined, 561
  events, 562
  properties, 562
  using (Example 13.8), 562–566
scroll panes, 598–603
  JScrollPane class, 598–600
  using (Example 13.14), 600–603
scrollbars, 594–598
  constructors, 594
  defined, 594
  JScrollBar properties, 594–595
  using (Example 13.13), 596–598
tabbed panes, 603–607

JTabbedPane class, 603, 609
  using (Example 13.15), 604–607
text areas, 544–548
  JTextArea class, 544–545, 607
text fields, 541–544
  JTextField class, 541–542

V
validate method, 464
value property, JScrollBar class, 595
valueOf method, 313
--var operator, 55
var-- operator, 55
var++ and var- (postincrement and postdecrement), 65
var++ operator, 55
Variables, 43, 48–49
  declaring/initializing in one step, 50
  names, 49
  scope of, 278–279
  variable declaration, 48
Vector class, 761–763, 779
  using (Example 17.6), 762–763
Vertical scrollbars, 594
verticalAlignment property, JButton class, 534
verticalScrollBarPolicy property, JScrollPane class, 599
verticalTextPosition property, JButton class, 535
viewportBorder property, JScrollPane class, 600
viewportView property, JScrollPane class, 600
VirtualMachineError, 658
Visibility modifiers, 264–269, 353
visibleAmount property, JScrollBar class, 595
visibleRowCount property, JList class, 553
Visual Basic, 5–6
Visual Cafe, 83
Visual J++, 83
VK_0 to VK_9, 524
VK_A to VK_Z, 524
VK_BACK_SPACE, 524
VK_CAPS_LOCK, 524

VK_CONTROL, 524
VK_DOWN, 524
VK_End, 524
VK_ENTER, 524
VK_ESCAPE, 524
VK_F1 to VK_F12, 524
VK_HOME, 524
VK_LEFT, 524
VK_NUM_LOCK, 524
VK_PGDN, 524
VK_PGUP, 524
VK_RIGHT, 524
VK_SHIFT, 524
VK_TAB, 524
VK_UP, 524
vspace attribute, 629

W
wait() method, Object class, 792
WAV format, 818
Weak is-a relationship, 404, 421
Web browsers, 10
WebGain Visual Cafe, 13
WelcomeApplet.html, 628
Welcome.class, 28
  running, 34–35
Welcome.java, 27
  compiling, 32–33
while loops, 118–121
  using (Example 3.2), 119–121
Widening a type, 57
width attribute, 628–629
width property, Component class, 532
Window class, 507
windowActivated(WindowEvent), 508
windowClosed(WindowEvent e), 508
windowClosing(WindowEvent e), 508
windowDeactivated(WindowEvent e), 508
windowDeiconified(WindowEvent e), 508
WindowEvent, 508
windowIconified(WindowEvent e), 508
WindowListener interface, 508
windowOpened(WindowEvent e), 508

World Wide Web, 10
Wrapper classes, 386–389, 392
  conversion methods, 388
  defined, 386
  numeric wrapper class constants, 387–388
  numeric wrapper class constructors, 387
  parsing strings into numbers, methods for, 388–389
  static `valueOf` methods, 388

`wrapStyleWord` property, `JTextArea` class, 545
`write(byte[] b)` method, `OutputStream` class/`Writer` class, 694
`writeChar(int v)` method, `RandomAccessFile` class, 723
`writeChars(String s)` method, `RandomAccessFile` class, 723

`write(int b)` method, `OutputStream` class/`Writer` class, 694
Write-only streams, 722
`Writer` class, 694

Y
`yield()` method, `Thread` class, 792

SINGLE PC LICENSE AGREEMENT AND LIMITED WARRANTY

READ THIS LICENSE CAREFULLY BEFORE INSTALLING THIS SOFTWARE. BY INSTALLING THIS SOFTWARE, YOU ARE AGREEING TO THE TERMS AND CONDITIONS OF THIS LICENSE. IF YOU DO NOT AGREE, DO NOT INSTALL THIS SOFTWARE. PROMPTLY RETURN THIS PACKAGE AND THE SOFTWARE AND ALL ACCOMPANYING ITEMS TO THE PLACE YOU OBTAINED THEM. *THESE TERMS APPLY TO ALL LICENSED SOFTWARE ON THE CD-ROM EXCEPT THAT THE TERMS FOR USE OF ANY SHAREWARE OR FREEWARE ON THE CD-ROM ARE AS SET FORTH IN THE ELECTRONIC LICENSE LOCATED ON THE CD-ROM:*

1. GRANT OF LICENSE and OWNERSHIP: The contents of this CD-ROM ("Software") are licensed, not sold, to you by Pearson Education, Inc. publishing as Pearson Prentice Hall ("We" or the "Company") and in consideration of your adoption of the accompanying Company textbooks and/or other materials, and your agreement to these terms. We reserve any rights not granted to you. You own only the disc(s) but we and/or our licensors own the Software itself. This license allows you to use and display your copy of the Software on a single computer (i.e., with a single CPU) at a single location for <u>academic</u> use only, so long as you comply with the terms of this Agreement. You may make one copy for back up, or transfer your copy to another CPU, provided that the Software is usable on only one computer.

2. RESTRICTIONS: You may <u>not</u> transfer or distribute the Software or documentation to anyone else. Except for backup, you may <u>not</u> copy the documentation or the Software. You may <u>not</u> network the Software or otherwise use it on more than one computer or computer terminal at the same time. You may <u>not</u> reverse engineer, disassemble, decompile, modify, adapt, translate, or create derivative works based on the Software or the Documentation. You may be held legally responsible for any copying or copyright infringement that is caused by your failure to abide by the terms of these restrictions.

3. TERMINATION: This license is effective until terminated. This license will terminate automatically without notice from the Company if you fail to comply with any provisions or limitations of this license. Upon termination, you shall destroy the Documentation and all copies of the Software. All provisions of this Agreement as to limitation and disclaimer of warranties, limitation of liability, remedies or damages, and our ownership rights shall survive termination.

4. LIMITED WARRANTY AND DISCLAIMER OF WARRANTY: Company warrants that for a period of 60 days from the date you purchase this SOFTWARE (or purchase or adopt the accompanying textbook), the Software, when properly installed and used in accordance with the Documentation, will operate in substantial conformity with the description of the Software set forth in the Documentation, and that for a period of 30 days the disc(s) on which the Software is delivered shall be free from defects in materials and workmanship under normal use. The Company does <u>not</u> warrant that the Software will meet your requirements or that the operation of the Software will be uninterrupted or error-free. Your only remedy and the Company's only obligation under these limited warranties is, at the Company's option, return of the disc for a refund of any amounts paid for it by you or replacement of the disc. THIS LIMITED WARRANTY IS THE ONLY WARRANTY PROVIDED BY THE COMPANY AND ITS LICENSORS, AND THE COMPANY AND ITS LICENSORS DISCLAIM ALL OTHER

WARRANTIES, EXPRESS OR IMPLIED, INCLUDING WITHOUT LIMITATION, THE IMPLIED WARRANTIES OF MERCHANTABILITY AND FITNESS FOR A PARTICULAR PURPOSE. THE COMPANY DOES NOT WARRANT, GUARANTEE OR MAKE ANY REPRESENTATION REGARDING THE ACCURACY, RELIABILITY, CURRENTNESS, USE, OR RESULTS OF USE, OF THE SOFTWARE.

5. LIMITATION OF REMEDIES AND DAMAGES: IN NO EVENT, SHALL THE COMPANY OR ITS EMPLOYEES, AGENTS, LICENSORS, OR CONTRACTORS BE LIABLE FOR ANY INCIDENTAL, INDIRECT, SPECIAL, OR CONSEQUENTIAL DAMAGES ARISING OUT OF OR IN CONNECTION WITH THIS LICENSE OR THE SOFTWARE, INCLUDING FOR LOSS OF USE, LOSS OF DATA, LOSS OF INCOME OR PROFIT, OR OTHER LOSSES, SUSTAINED AS A RESULT OF INJURY TO ANY PERSON, OR LOSS OF OR DAMAGE TO PROPERTY, OR CLAIMS OF THIRD PARTIES, EVEN IF THE COMPANY OR AN AUTHORIZED REPRESENTATIVE OF THE COMPANY HAS BEEN ADVISED OF THE POSSIBILITY OF SUCH DAMAGES. IN NO EVENT SHALL THE LIABILITY OF THE COMPANY FOR DAMAGES WITH RESPECT TO THE SOFTWARE EXCEED THE AMOUNTS ACTUALLY PAID BY YOU, IF ANY, FOR THE SOFTWARE OR THE ACCOMPANYING TEXTBOOK. BECAUSE SOME JURISDICTIONS DO NOT ALLOW THE LIMITATION OF LIABILITY IN CERTAIN CIRCUMSTANCES, THE ABOVE LIMITATIONS MAY NOT ALWAYS APPLY TO YOU.

6. GENERAL: THIS AGREEMENT SHALL BE CONSTRUED IN ACCORDANCE WITH THE LAWS OF THE UNITED STATES OF AMERICA AND THE STATE OF NEW YORK, APPLICABLE TO CONTRACTS MADE IN NEW YORK, AND SHALL BENEFIT THE COMPANY, ITS AFFILIATES AND ASSIGNEES. THIS AGREEMENT IS THE COMPLETE AND EXCLUSIVE STATEMENT OF THE AGREEMENT BETWEEN YOU AND THE COMPANY AND SUPERSEDES ALL PROPOSALS OR PRIOR AGREEMENTS, ORAL, OR WRITTEN, AND ANY OTHER COMMUNICATIONS BETWEEN YOU AND THE COMPANY OR ANY REPRESENTATIVE OF THE COMPANY RELATING TO THE SUBJECT MATTER OF THIS AGREEMENT. If you are a U.S. Government user, this Software is licensed with "restricted rights" as set forth in subparagraphs (a)-(d) of the Commercial Computer-Restricted Rights clause at FAR 52.227-19 or in subparagraphs (c)(1)(ii) of the Rights in Technical Data and Computer Software clause at DFARS 252.227-7013, and similar clauses, as applicable.

Should you have any questions concerning this agreement or if you wish to contact the Company for any reason, please contact in writing:

ESM Media Development
Higher Education Division
Pearson Education
One Lake Street
Upper Saddle River, NJ 07458